Why You Need This New Edition

Juvenile Delinquency, Eighth Edition
Thompson/Bynum

This Eighth Edition of *Juvenile Delinquency: A Sociological Approach* reflects the most substantial revisions since the first edition appeared in 1989. Changes in society in the United States as well as globally have significantly impacted youths and their social experiences. Consequently, as social values have been challenged, concepts of deviance and conformity have been reconstructed, as have social expectations for children, adolescents, and adults.

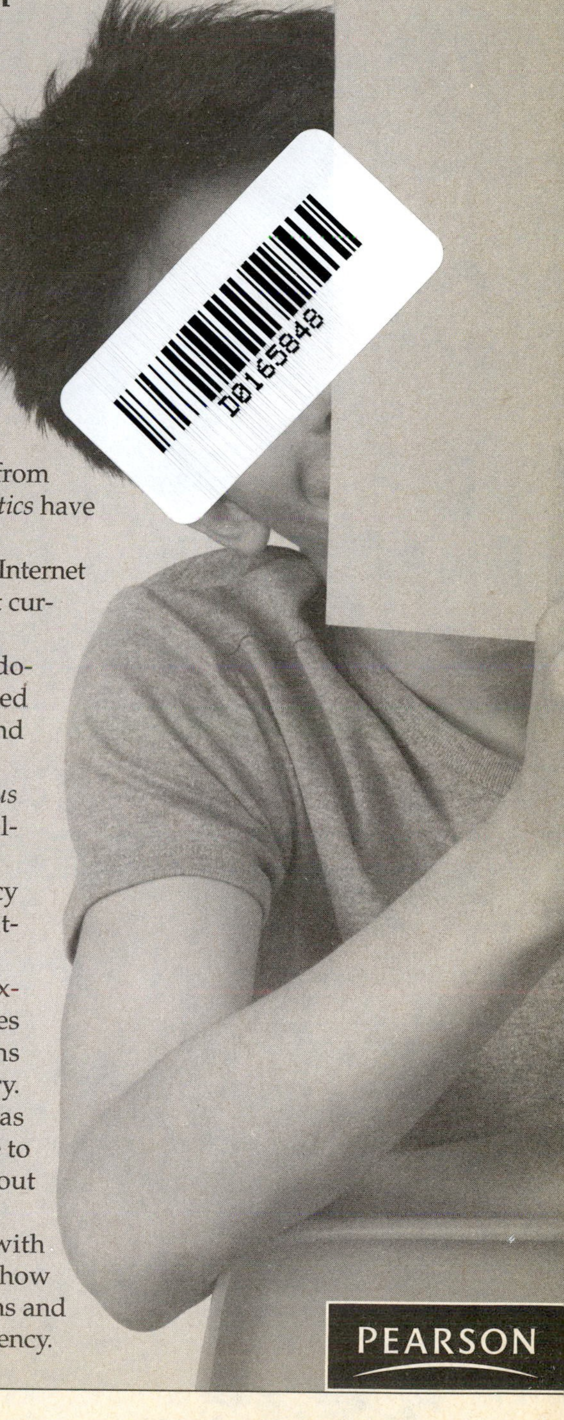

1. All data on delinquents and delinquency derived from FBI *Uniform Crime Reports* and *Juvenile Court Statistics* have been updated.
2. Important Department of Justice and other relevant Internet websites, from which students may derive the most current crime and delinquency data, are included.
3. Increased emphasis on the changing concept of adolescence and the resultant marginality experienced by American youths is introduced in Chapter 1 and reflected throughout the entire book.
4. Every chapter now includes a *Cross-Cultural Focus* box, reflecting the increased importance of globalization in the world.
5. Biological and psychological theories of delinquency are streamlined into a concise, yet thorough, treatment of those perspectives.
6. Chapter 8 has been significantly revised and expanded to cover contemporary integrative theories of juvenile delinquency, including contributions from rational choice, deterrence, and feminist theory.
7. An expanded section on female delinquency has been added to Chapter 8, and the authors continue to integrate research on female delinquency throughout all the chapters.
8. Part V, Applied Theory: Strategies for Dealing with Juvenile Delinquency, contains a greater focus on how abstract theories can be applied to concrete situations and programs to help correct, treat, and prevent delinquency.

PEARSON

EIGHTH EDITION

JUVENILE DELINQUENCY

A SOCIOLOGICAL APPROACH

William E. Thompson
Texas A&M University–Commerce

Jack E. Bynum
Professor Emeritus of Sociology
Oklahoma State University

Allyn & Bacon
Boston Columbus Indianapolis New York San Francisco Upper Saddle River
Amsterdam Cape Town Dubai London Madrid Milan Munich Paris Montreal Toronto
Delhi Mexico City Sao Paolo Sydney Hong Kong Seoul Singapore Taipei Tokyo

Publisher: Karen Hanson
Editorial Assistant: Courtney Shea
Executive Marketing Manager: Kelly May
Production Assistant: Maggie Brobeck
Editorial Production Service: GGS Higher Education Resources, A division of PreMedia Global
Manufacturing Buyer: Fran Russello
Electronic Composition: GGS Higher Education Resources, A division of PreMedia Global
Manager, Visual Research: Beth Brenzel
Photo Researcher: Martha Shethar
Manager, Rights and Permissions: Zina Arabia
Image Permission Coordinator: Debbie Hewitson
Manager, Cover Visual Research & Permissions: Karen Sanatar
Cover image credit: Ingram Publishing/Alamy
Creative Director: Jayne Conte
Cover Designer: Margaret Kenselaar

Credits: 3, David McNew/Getty Images; 25, Imageworks; 49, Craig Line/AP Wide World Photos; 86, 119, 167, 188, 258, Getty Images; 145, 430, PhotoEdit; 211 AP Images; 234, David Young-Wolff/PhotoEdit; 288, Corbis; 323, Lou Dematteis/The Image Works; 348, John Neubauer/PhotoEdit; 374, Robin Nelson/PhotoEdit; 405, Bebeto Matthews/AP Wide World Photos

Library of Congress Cataloging-in-Publication Data

Bynum, Jack E.
Juvenile delinquency : a sociological approach / Jack E. Bynum, William E. Thompson.— 8th ed.
p. cm.
Includes index.
1. Juvenile delinquency—United States. I. Thompson, William E. (William Edwin), 1950- II. Title.
HV9104.B9 2009
364.360973—dc22

2009008666

10 9 8 7 6 5 4 3 2 1 RRD-VA 13 12 11 10 09

Allyn & Bacon is an imprint of

www.pearsonhighered.com

ISBN-10: 0-205-66571-3
ISBN-13: 978-0-205-66571-6

Dedication

To the memory of our parents—Jack and Frances Bynum and Edwin and Flora Thompson—who through their precepts and examples helped us become the authors of this book and not the subjects

BRIEF CONTENTS

CONTENTS

FIGURES

TABLES

PREFACE

As we launch the Eighth Edition of this book, juvenile delinquency is one of the most complex, interesting, and challenging phenomena in the United States. The media bombard us with accounts of juvenile misbehavior and crime that range from truancy to first-degree murder. Consequently, youths who violate the law receive considerable attention from law enforcement officials, social agencies, criminologists, and social and behavioral scientists.

This book is guided by the basic premise that juvenile delinquency is inherently social in nature. It is a social concept, part and product of the society in which it occurs. Thus, any meaningful discussion of delinquency must be expressed in a sociological framework that views it in relation to the normative processes and societal responses that define it. More specifically, this book approaches delinquency as it relates to and emerges from the youth's family, neighborhood, school, peer group, social class, and overall cultural and social environment.

Rather than aligning this analysis to any particular theoretical perspective, we use an eclectic sociological approach that integrates elements from a wide spectrum of causal theories. Thus, we present delinquency in its broadest sociological context. This approach should give the reader a growing awareness of and sensitivity to the social nature of human behavior, whether it be socially adjudged as conforming or nonconforming, normative or deviant, acceptable or unacceptable, good or bad, or some paradoxical mixture of these seemingly antithetical evaluations.

This sociological work has been enhanced by the inclusion of some important contributions of social workers, criminologists, social and behavioral scientists, and other specialists who have sought to understand, explain, control, and prevent juvenile delinquency. The reader will note that each section of the book is carefully grounded in knowledge and research and unified by the sociological theme that delinquency must be viewed within its social context.

The book is organized in a format that guides the reader through an unfolding sequence of interrelated dimensions of the study of juvenile delinquency: conformity, causes, social context, and social control. Each part begins with a brief introduction that includes basic sociological concepts and ideas related to the topical theme of that section. For example, Part I, Conformity, Deviance, and Juvenile Delinquency, defines juvenile delinquency and then incorporates a brief introduction to sociology and the sociological perspective. The normative system of society and the concepts of conformity and deviance are introduced and explained. In Part II, Causes of Juvenile Delinquency, students are first introduced to the nature of scientific theory and the theory-building process. Then, they are presented with specific theories that attempt to explain the causes of delinquency. Part III, Juvenile Delinquency in a Social Context, begins by looking at the nature of social groups and their impact upon individuals. It then proceeds to explore the influence of family, schools, youth subcultures, and gangs on juvenile behavior. The social control of juvenile behavior is presented in the last two sections of the text. Part IV, Applied Theory and Social Control: The Juvenile Justice System, includes detailed coverage of those arenas of social confrontation encountered by recalcitrant youth: police contacts, juvenile courts, and community correctional agencies. Part V, Applied Theory: Strategies for Dealing with Juvenile Delinquency, begins with a systematic evaluation of the major classic and contemporary programs developed for the prevention and treatment of delinquency in the United States. Part V concludes the book with a challenging call for applying sociological theories to develop innovative revisions in the social and legal status of young people and in our approach to the problem of juvenile delinquency.

Each of the five parts is divided into topically related chapters. Again, as in earlier editions of this book, each chapter begins with a list of *Reading Objectives* for that particular unit of content. These objectives alert the readers in advance to the specific learning expectations for that chapter so that they may identify, extrapolate, and integrate major concepts while proceeding through the chapter. The learning objectives are reemphasized at the end of the chapter through the use of *Questions and Topics for Study and Discussion*, which are designed to help prepare students for examinations and to stimulate class discussion. These teaching and learning aids are reinforced by a comprehensive glossary at the end of the book that includes definitions of key terms and concepts.

We continue our use of three types of innovative and instructive boxes: *Concept Application, Cross-Cultural Focus,* and *Controversial Issue.* Each chapter contains at least two of these boxes, which have proven to be popular with students. The *Concept Application* boxes apply abstract theoretical concepts to concrete situations facing young people today. *Cross-Cultural Focus* boxes incorporate an international and multicultural dimension providing examples of delinquency in other societies, cultures, and subcultures. *Controversial Issue* boxes address some of the critical juvenile delinquency questions facing society.

NEW TO THIS EDITION

This Eighth Edition of *Juvenile Delinquency: A Sociological Approach* reflects the most substantial revisions and changes since the first edition appeared in 1989. A lot of changes have occurred around the world and in the United States that have had significant impact—both positive and negative—on youths and their social experiences. Consequently, important social values have been challenged and concepts of deviance and conformity have changed, as have social expectations for children, adolescents, and adults. While striving to preserve the sociological integrity and traditional strengths and insights of the first seven editions of this work, several important changes and additions are included in this Eighth Edition to bring it more up-to-date and to reflect the latest research and theoretical and applied strategies related to juvenile delinquency. For example, all data on delinquents and delinquency derived from FBI *Uniform Crime Reports* and *Juvenile Court Statistics* have been updated. Moreover, we have inserted important Department of Justice and other relevant Internet websites where students may derive the most currently available crime and delinquency data, as opposed to merely relying on tables and figures that, because of delays in reporting and publication, are necessarily out-of-date. Where tables and figures are used to illustrate and identify important trends and patterns, students are guided to corresponding Web sites where the most up-to-date data can be found.

Increased emphasis on the changing concept of adolescence and the resultant marginality experienced by American youths is introduced in Chapter 1, and reflected throughout the book. Because of the importance of globalization, every chapter now includes a *Cross-Cultural Focus* box. In order to streamline our discussion of biological and psychological theories of delinquency, Chapters 4 and 5 from previous editions have been combined into one more concise, yet thorough treatment of those perspectives with increased emphasis on contemporary research and the medical model of delinquency. Chapter 8 has been significantly revised and expanded to cover contemporary integrative theories of juvenile delinquency including contributions from rational choice, deterrence, and feminist theory. Also an expanded section on female delinquency has been added to Chapter 8, and we continue to integrate research on female delinquency throughout all the chapters. Additionally, every chapter has undergone revision of numerous references and incorporation of new substantive content. Our objective has been to focus and integrate the most important contributions of classical theorists with contemporary etiology and treatment initiatives. Part V has been re-titled "Applied Theory: Strategies for Dealing with Juvenile Delinquency" with increased focus on how abstract theories can be applied to concrete situations and programs to help correct, treat, and prevent delinquency.

The Eighth Edition retains the popular and useful pedagogical aids of beginning each chapter with a set of *Reading Objectives* and ending each chapter with *Concept Integration: Questions and Topics for Study and Discussion*. Additionally, in this edition, every carefully chosen box, figure, table, and even photographs are accompanied by critical-thinking questions that ask students to analyze them in reference to the theories, concepts, and data presented in that chapter. Moreover, Pearson supplies a host of online pedagogical aids and ancillaries to supplement and enhance material presented in the text.

While the authors assume final responsibility for the book, as with any other work of this magnitude, many people made significant contributions for which we are indebted. We appreciate the help, support, and encouragement from many friends and colleagues during our exciting journey through the eight editions of this book.

Special thanks are extended to those who, through the years, have reviewed the entire manuscript and made helpful and constructive suggestions for revisions: John A. Arthur, University of Minnesota–Duluth; Pierette R. Ayotte, Thomas College; Roger C. Barnes, University of the Incarnate Word; Steven R. Cureton, University of North Carolina–Greensboro; Craig J. Forsyth, University of Louisiana at Lafayette; Kathleen Heide, University of South Florida; Hua-Lun Huang, University of Louisiana at Lafayette; Lisa A. Kort-Butler, University of Nebraska–Lincoln; Megan Kurlycheck, University of South Carolina; Mark Mantyh, University of Wisconsin–Milwaukee; Stephanie Amedco Marquez, Arizona State University; Wilson R. Palacios, University of South Florida; Jerome Rosonke, Northern State University; Raghu Singh, Texas A&M University–Commerce; Susan E. Webb, Coastal Carolina University; and Professor Craig C. White, Fairmont State College.

We are also indebted to the editors, staff, and production affiliates of Pearson for their help and technical assistance with this Eighth Edition, especially Karen Hanson and Courtney Shea. Finally, our most heartfelt thanks and love go to our families for their unwavering love, support, and encouragement.

W.E.T.
J.E.B.

Part I

CONFORMITY, DEVIANCE, AND JUVENILE DELINQUENCY

INTRODUCTION: The Sociological Perspective and Focus on Juvenile Delinquency

There are several reasons why most readers will identify with the subject of this book. For one thing, the book is about young people—in many cases, not much younger than most of the college students who will be reading the book. Moreover, you may experience a powerful empathy for American youths in general as we explore and explain the frustrations and marginality of being adolescent—a situation and status shared by nearly every youth who grows up in the United States.

Additionally, as the thoughtful reader gains insight into the deviant and disruptive behavior of juvenile offenders, personal youthful escapades may be recalled that, if discovered or reported, might have resulted in a confrontation with society and adjudication as a juvenile delinquent. The reader will probably be surprised to learn that most illegal acts attributed to young people do not apply to adults and violate the law only if the offender happens to be a minor.

Part One sets the stage and furnishes direction to our unfolding study of juvenile delinquency. The sociological approach to defining, understanding, and measuring this form of deviant behavior views it as part and product of the social context in which it occurs. Chapter 1 identifies and analyzes various approaches to defining juvenile delinquency. For example, the legal definition emphasizes a specific age as the dividing line between juvenile delinquency and adult crime. A different approach utilizes the role definition, which discounts the occasional youthful misbehavior and focuses instead on the individual who sustains a consistent pattern of delinquent conduct. Yet a third image of the delinquent and the nonconforming behavior is supplied by the societal response definition, which concentrates on the perceptual exchanges between the actor (the alleged delinquent) and the audience (society) that judges the behavior in question and can impute a delinquent identity. In actual practice, and in Chapter 1, all three of these definitions are combined to give us a complete and operational description of what constitutes "juvenile delinquency" in American society.

Chapter 2 focuses on society, rules of conduct, conformity, and deviance and places juvenile delinquency in an overall social context. Thus, the sociological perspective supplies an appropriate foundation and an ongoing framework for the consideration of juvenile delinquency as a significant social problem in American society.

Chapter 3 explains the various sources of juvenile crime statistics and a catalog of the kinds and incidences of juvenile offenses. The longitudinal national trends in juvenile delinquency are set forth, and some of the weaknesses of data on delinquency are discussed. Chapter 3 concludes with a composite profile of those demographic traits that most nearly characterize the "typical" juvenile delinquent. The reader is cautioned, however, that while such profiles may be helpful in summarizing and pointing out statistical trends in arrests and court referrals, they can also unfairly stereotype groups identified by the composite profile unless we are acutely aware of certain weaknesses in official crime and delinquency statistics.

As you read Part One and embark upon your study of juvenile delinquency, we encourage you to approach the subject and this book with an open mind. While common sense can and should play an important role in the attempt to understand any social issue, much of what passes for common sense about juvenile delinquency may, in fact, be nothing more than "common nonsense." The astute student involved in sociological inquiry will attempt to avoid some of the common misconceptions and pitfalls related to the study of delinquency by developing critical thinking skills and laying aside personal feelings about the subject.

Chapter 1

Juvenile Delinquency

The Act, the Actor, and the Audience

READING OBJECTIVES

Reading this chapter will help you achieve the following objectives:

1. Comprehend the legal and social importance of carefully and accurately defined terms such as *juvenile* and *adult*.
2. Understand the difference between criminal behavior and juvenile delinquency.
3. Understand the difference between criminal offenders and juvenile delinquents.
4. Conceptualize and compare the legal definition, role definition, and societal response definition of juvenile delinquency.
5. Understand social status and social role and explain how these concepts can be used to describe a youth's commitment to a delinquent career.
6. See how the identification of an individual or a behavior as delinquent is possible only in a social context, involving the interplay between the actor, a norm, an act, and an audience perception of the act.

INTRODUCTION

In this opening chapter, we emphasize the sociological nature of juvenile delinquency and how society defines delinquency by looking at the social dynamics of the act, the actor, and the audience. The terms **act**, **actor**, and **audience** conjure up images of the theater, but can be used as analogs to help us understand much of our behavior in everyday life.

Ever since the comedies and tragedies of life were adapted for the stage by early Greek actors, the theater has held fascinating appeal for performers and spectators alike. One reason for the powerful appeal of the stage, the actors, and the roles they play is that humans are naturally imitative. We can readily identify with many parts and plots that reflect our own real or imaginary lives, in the past, present, or future. William Shakespeare (1623), the 17th-century dramatist, was alluding to this trait in human nature when he generalized in Act II of *As You Like It* that all the world is a stage and we are the actors in the drama of life.

Sociologist Erving Goffman (1971) appropriated elements of the theater to analyze social life as a carefully orchestrated drama. Similarly, Thompson and Hickey (2008) observed that deviance involves a complex interplay between a social norm, an actor, an act, and an audience, and, in today's world, the media that define the act as nonconforming. This dramaturgical analogy offers an excellent sociological framework within which to define and commence our study of juvenile delinquency. More specifically to this chapter, these theatrical metaphors help us identify, state, and differentiate the major definitions of juvenile delinquency prevalent among sociologists and criminologists.

WHAT IS JUVENILE DELINQUENCY?

In order for any communication to be successful, there must be common language or shared mutual understanding of key words, terms, and concepts. This applies to mass media communication, public stage performances, classroom learning environments occupied by teachers and students, and even to an informal dialogue between two friends.

The principle of effective communication is especially important in the academic and scientific communities, where the specialized and precise terminology of various disciplines is used liberally to describe complex phenomena. Therefore, it is customary to begin a discussion or discourse with carefully structured definitions in order to promote clarity and comprehension.

To begin our study of juvenile delinquency, two basic questions must be answered: first, who is a juvenile? and second, what is delinquency? While the two terms *juvenile* and *delinquency* are used frequently by Americans, they are relatively new concepts that do not necessarily connote the same meanings to all who use them.

Who Is a Juvenile? The Creation of Adolescence

In 16th- and 17th-century American society, essentially two life stages existed: childhood and adulthood. In traditional agrarian America, the normative expectations for children and for adults were clearly differentiated and well defined. Very young children were considered helpless and totally dependent upon other family members for survival. However, as soon as a child was physically capable of helping around the house or in the fields, some routine chores were assigned. Children were expected to obey their parents, and the old adage "Children shall be seen but not heard" was widely practiced. Early American colonists, reflecting the sober child-rearing practices of their European and religious backgrounds, were strict disciplinarians. For example, the laws of 1660 even made lying by children and failure to observe the Sabbath punishable offenses. Normative conformity and "godliness" were almost synonymous; and parents, supported by the clergy, considered punishment and correction of children as a family responsibility.

While no American laws explicitly defined "childhood," the practice of exempting young children from legal responsibility for their deviant behavior was widely followed. British common law exempted children under the age of 7 from the criminal courts because they lacked **mens rea**, or *criminal intent*, required for criminal conviction. Since much of American criminal law is based upon British common law, the same practice was traditional in the United States. Children over the age of 7 were considered old enough to know right from wrong and to understand the consequences of their actions, and they were considered responsible for their law-violating behavior.

However, a child over the age of 7 was not viewed as an adult. Adulthood was not reached until after the onset of puberty, when expectations of work, marriage, and other "adult" activities were assumed. An adult was perceived as a man or a woman who was physically developed and had reached mature size and strength.

The Industrial Revolution came to the United States in the 19th century with the mechanization of factory production, rapid urbanization, and mass migration of rural people into large cities—all with historic and often traumatic implications for children. Children, especially those of immigrants and the poor, came to be seen as cheap factory workers until the cruelty of child labor was made public. Near the end of the 19th century, child labor laws were legislated to protect youths from such exploitation:

> The awareness of childhood as a distinct period of life is, then, a historical creation. Once this awareness developed, the nature of childhood and what should be done about it became a matter of ideological controversy, and it has remained so down to our time. At some periods and among

During the colonial period it was customary to publicly punish common criminals and disobedient children. Should there be a modern-day equivalent?

Illustration by Marilyn Thompson

> some groups, the child has been regarded as basically tender and innocent. In opposition to this has been the notion that the child is wild and needs to be tamed. These two images continue to have their respective adherents. (Elkin and Handel, 1978:62)

Rapid social changes associated with the American experience continued to have an impact on attitudes and values related to young people. No longer able to assume meaningful responsibilities as members of farm families, urban youths were required to undergo a much longer period of dependence and extended preparation before entering adulthood and the world of work:

> The ensuing social reform movement transformed the image of the child from one of cheap factory labor to one of apprentice to factory work. Instead of being sent to the factory, children were sent to school to prepare them to work in factories. School bells, like factory whistles, signaled the beginning and the end of the school day. And children, like their parents, carried lunch pails to be opened at the noon whistle. (Elkind, 1991:136)

During the 20th century, the special social status of children was even more clearly defined, and the parameters around their place and participation in U.S. society were delimited. The values of extended dependency and formal education, and the absence of fulfilling roles evolved into social realities. What developed in American society was the emergence of a new life stage to identify the period in life in which a young person was no longer considered a child, but was not yet fully considered an adult. The concept of **adolescence** was socially created to describe *that period of life between childhood and adulthood* (White, 1992; Arnett, 2007).

The creation of adolescence produced a legal dilemma in terms of dealing with youths who violated the law. In response to society's desire to hold children over the age of 7 legally accountable for their behavior, but not as fully accountable as adults, new laws were enacted to deal with the special problem of law violation by youths. The term *juvenile* began to be used when states passed laws establishing the legal age for adulthood. **Juvenile** referred to *any person under the **legal age of majority**—the chronological age at which a person is no longer considered a minor and commences adulthood (age 18 in most states)*. Hence, the term encompasses a broader age range than adolescence, which is generally considered to begin with the onset of puberty. However, most juvenile law violation that comes to the attention of juvenile courts occurs during the period of adolescence. Consequently, in relation to delinquency, the terms *juvenile* and *adolescent* are virtually interchangeable, with *juvenile* denoting a legal concept and *adolescent* a sociocultural one. The emergence of the social concept of adolescence along with the legal concept of juvenile created a new social problem for the United States: *juvenile delinquency*—which continues as a major challenge today.

What Is Delinquency?

We may begin to answer this question by examining newspaper headlines gathered from several states:

"Teen gang war erupts in central city"
"High school vandalized and burned by students"
"Home invasion by teenagers leaves elderly couple injured"
"Six-year old boy shoots first-grade classmate"
"Police battle professional shoplifting ring of juveniles"

Many people at first glance might assume that these news reports reflect typical cases of juvenile delinquency. However, consignment to a juvenile court is seldom that simple. The short, attention-grabbing headlines do not supply enough information upon which to base any final conclusions. We know nothing about such important matters as guilt, motives, extenuating circumstances, or the age at which people become legally responsible for their behavior as adults in each state. Moreover, there is nothing typical about these publicized events. Most juvenile behavior conforms to the normative standards of the larger society, and conforming behavior is seldom considered newsworthy. Furthermore, most juvenile delinquency is less sensational, is treated routinely, and receives little public notice. To begin this inquiry into the nature of juvenile delinquency, an operational definition is in order.

There are hundreds of definitions of juvenile delinquency already in existence. The majority of the definitions contain only minor differences, that is, they use different words to describe the same idea. Many definitions of juvenile delinquency vary only in emphasis or approach, according to the academic background, specialty, or interest of their originators. The sociological perspective and the dramaturgical analysis cited earlier suggest a summary of all these definitions into three categories:

1. ***The legal definition.*** Here the emphasis is almost entirely on *the act,* the norm-violating behavior that is legally classified as juvenile delinquency.
2. ***The role definition.*** In this case, the focus is primarily on *the actor,* the juvenile whose role performance is identified as delinquent.
3. ***The societal response definition.*** This approach concentrates more on *the audience,* the members of the social group or society that reacts to the actor and the act and determines whether or not delinquency has been committed and if the offender is a juvenile delinquent.

These definitional categories or approaches are not mutually exclusive. They cannot be completely separated or isolated from one another. Some overlap is inevitable and even desirable. They differ mainly in emphasis. Therefore, they are best understood as three vital dimensions of juvenile delinquency, and all must be considered together in order to formulate a complete definition of this complex social phenomenon. The thorough student of juvenile delinquency utilizes all three of these definitional approaches in determining whether the headlined incidents cited earlier, or any other events, represent genuine cases of juvenile delinquency.

The Legal Definition

The oldest and most familiar description of criminal misconduct by a juvenile is the legal definition based upon formally codified laws, which specify offenses, sanctions, and age parameters. Until the late 19th century, less serious deviance on the part of youths was considered to be a family matter. On the other hand, extreme or persistent cases of youthful nonconformity or obstinacy became a matter for community discipline. Public rebuke, whippings, and even capital punishment were administered to children (Reid, 2008).

As the United States developed, major changes in social values and social organization took place. As the population grew and the power of the state was extended, the authority of the family and religious institutions was reduced. For example, stronger feelings emerged and prevailed that the prevention of juvenile crime and the treatment of offenders were community as well as familial responsibilities. The outcome was that more and more troublesome children and youths were subjected to confinement and community-based programs of correction (Schlossman, 1977). Finally, during the last quarter of the 19th century, as the concept of adolescence emerged, the nation experienced a growing humanitarian desire to deal differently with the delinquent juvenile than with the criminal adult. Further modification in juvenile corrections soon followed.

The historical development of a formal juvenile justice system in the United States began in 1899. The Illinois state legislature passed a revolutionary bill regarding "juvenile delinquency" and authorized the establishment of the first juvenile court in Cook County (Chicago). From that beginning, similar legislation was successfully enacted in all the other states, creating special legal procedures apart from the older criminal court system for dealing with children and youths accused of violating a state law or municipal ordinance (Mennel, 1982). The historical development of the juvenile court and subsequent developments in juvenile justice are more thoroughly discussed in Chapter 14, Juvenile Courts.

Included within the various laws establishing juvenile courts is a formal, *legal definition* of juvenile delinquency. In general, **juvenile delinquency** is legally defined as *any act that, if committed by an adult, would be a crime.* Such forbidden activities are reflected in the codified criminal statutes of federal, state, and local governments. Both juvenile and adult violators may expect serious sanctions or penalties.

Each state legislature has also designated a specific age as the dividing line between juvenile and criminal offenders. This arbitrary boundary between childhood and adulthood reaffirms the historical position that most individuals below the "age of majority" or "adulthood" are presumed to lack the maturity necessary for full legal responsibility. Therefore, their cases are normally processed through the juvenile court where penalties are usually less severe than in the adult criminal court. The legal concept of *mens rea* still prevails in United States jurisprudence and typically sets the minimum age for delinquency at 7 years, when it is assumed that the child is old enough to consciously demonstrate criminal intent (Willing, 2000). The upper chronological boundary line is demarcated by the laws of most states, which declare people to be adults on their eighteenth birthday, and juvenile court jurisdiction ends. In recent years, some states have lowered this maximum age for juvenile court jurisdiction to 17 or 16, and in some cases as low as 15 under extenuating circumstances (Cox, et al., 2008). Persons older than the maximum age under juvenile court jurisdiction in their state are considered to be adults and their cases are adjudicated in the criminal court. There are important exceptions to these rules, however, which apply to juveniles remanded to the criminal court to face trial as adults for particularly serious crimes (see Chapter 14).

Most Americans are more or less familiar with the legal definition of juvenile delinquency, especially the chronological demarcation between juvenile delinquency and adult crime. This may be traced to the cultural importance many people place on the attainment of the legal age of 18, when citizens can vote, enlist in a branch of the military, marry without parental consent (in some states), and do many other things that are forbidden before adult status is achieved. The legal definition is also in harmony with the traditional view held by laypersons regarding criminals and delinquents. According to Don Gibbons (1976:1), the person on the street tends to divide the world into "the good guys" and "the bad guys." "The common view is that delinquents, criminals, and other deviants are alien persons among us." It follows that the arbitrary and apparently explicit codification of illegal behavior, and recommended procedures for dealing with it, are supported by the majority of people.

The establishment of a legal definition of juvenile delinquency that differentiated youthful offenders from adult criminals generally has been viewed as a commendable development and step forward in the jurisprudence of this country. It reinforced the normative system of society and offered a humane measure of differential treatment for children and youth who ran afoul of the law. A major strength of the legal definition is its practicality and utility for law enforcement officers, who often must make procedural decisions in the field based upon the age of suspects.

STATUS OFFENSES Many other youthful activities, while not criminal in the usual sense, may also come to the attention of law enforcement agencies if they appear to conflict with the best interests of a given community or the youth in question. Such acts as school truancy, running away from home, or the consumption of alcoholic beverages are not illegal when done by adults but are prohibited for juveniles. Thus, because the community forbids such behavior by minors, these acts are *illegal due only to the age status of the juvenile offenders* and are appropriately referred to as **status offenses**.

What has emerged is a two-dimensional legal definition of delinquency. This definition includes criminal acts by juveniles along with the acknowledgment of the juvenile court's ability to adjudicate children as delinquent if they have committed an act that, while not generally illegal, is considered inappropriate for juveniles. Consequently, the **legal definition** of delinquency has become *any act that would be a crime if committed by an adult, or any act that the juvenile court may deem inappropriate and for which a juvenile can be adjudicated delinquent.* (Chapter 3 contains a more detailed discussion of status offenses.)

Why might teenage girls find smoking appealing? Should this be considered juvenile delinquency?

PROBLEMS WITH THE LEGAL DEFINITION A recurring complaint about this approach to classifying juvenile misbehavior is that the "explicit" guidelines are often vague. The legal definitions of delinquency used by the various states adequately extend the adult criminal code forbidding such acts as murder and rape to children and youths. However, annual statistical summaries reveal that the largest proportion of juvenile offenses are status offenses and are often included under such imprecise, catchall phrases in the legal definitions as "ungovernable behavior" and "incorrigible." Rather than defining delinquent conduct with any uniform and objective consistency, these broad descriptions permit much more subjective interpretation by local police and juvenile authorities than is found in adult criminal cases.

As an example of how such wide latitude in interpretation of juvenile laws can lead to capricious adjudication, we note that children can be referred to juvenile courts for "knowingly associating with vicious and immoral persons." In such cases, someone in authority must resolve these ponderous issues: Who is an "immoral person"? What are the criteria for immorality? Exactly what is meant by "associating" with such persons? Can guilt by association be imputed to a child? Does "associating with vicious and immoral persons" make one an accomplice to crime? Does "association" mean any contact or is association a matter of degree? It is little wonder that there are great inconsistencies and variabilities in the adjudication of delinquency from state to state, court to court, time to time, and case to case. The problem is compounded when the lack of uniformity in age parameters, vague definitions of delinquency, and subjective dispositions lead to questionable credibility of national delinquency statistics. How can the incidence of various forms of youthful crime be compiled and compared adequately in the absence of a fairly uniform legal definition?

For decades, criminologists, sociologists, and law enforcement authorities have argued that the measurement of the volume, character, and trends of juvenile delinquency would be improved if the legal definitions were clarified, consistent, and reduced in scope. Since 1970, about half of the state legislatures in the United States have passed laws modifying the social identity and treatment of status offenders. Such changes have been encouraged by the Juvenile Justice and Delinquency Act of 1974, which would withhold federal funds for delinquency prevention from states that "place in detention or correctional facilities children who are charged with offenses that would not be criminal if committed by adults" (Diegmueller, 1987:15).

In 1976, the National Advisory Committee on Criminal Justice Standards and Goals urged that the long list of vague and often capricious status offenses be delimited to five specific categories:

1. School truancy
2. Repeated disregard for or misuse of lawful parental authority
3. Repeated running away from home
4. Repeated use of intoxicating beverages
5. Delinquent acts committed by a juvenile younger than 10 years of age (Weis, 1980:9)

A new nomenclature evolved in some states to define status offenders with less stigmatization and more appropriateness to the nature of their offenses. For example, New York passed a "Person in Need of Supervision" (PINS) law, which itself was later declared discriminatory by a New York Court of Appeals. Other states adopted one or more of the following descriptive titles for status offenders and youths who were neglected, abused, or otherwise dependent upon the state: "Juvenile in Need of Supervision" (JINS), "Minor in Need of Supervision" (MINS), "Child in Need of Supervision" (CHINS), and "Children in Need of Assistance" (CHINA). Texas shifts the focus from the youth to the act with the phrase "Conduct in Need of Supervision" (CINS). A few states, prompted by a 1973 recommendation from the International Association of Chiefs of Police, have even sought to replace the acrimonious term "juvenile delinquent" with the less damaging designation of "unruly child" (Kobetz and Bosarge, 1973:37).

While these efforts to refine the definition and improve the treatment of status offenders are promising, they fall short of effective nationwide reforms. The systemic injustices to juveniles in the United States and errors in delinquency data are chronic and continuous. (A more detailed discussion of status offense reforms is presented in Chapter 17 of this book.)

Another problem encountered with the legal definitions of juvenile delinquency is the common practice among young and chronic criminals in big cities to use the juvenile court age limitation as a shelter to avoid criminal prosecution. A magazine report described how society's program for lenient and rehabilitative treatment of juvenile offenders has been misused in some places:

> When he (sic) is caught, the courts usually spew him out again. If he is under a certain age, 16 to 18 depending on the state, he is almost always taken to juvenile court, where he is treated as if he were still the child he is supposed to be. Even if he has murdered somebody, he may be put away for only a few months. . . . Small wonder that hardened juveniles laugh, scratch, yawn, mug and even fall asleep while their crimes are revealed in court. A New York teenager explained in a WCBS radio interview how he started at the age of 12 to rob old women: "I was young, and I knew I wasn't gonna get no big time. So, you know, what's to worry? If you're doin' wrong, do it while you're young, because you won't do that much time." (*Time,* 1977:19)

The Role Definition

The legal definition, if used as the sole criterion for determining delinquent behavior and juvenile status, would make it difficult for law enforcement officers to consider any relevant variables other than age and the specific offense brought to their attention. The **role definition** of juvenile delinquency, by focusing on the actor rather than on the act, functions as an important corollary to the legal definition. This definitional approach expands the inquiry from "What is juvenile delinquency?" to include the question: "Who are the juvenile delinquents?"

The role definition partially repudiates the strictly legal definition by rejecting the notion that the casual or occasional experimenter with such behavior as truancy, vandalism, fighting, and running away is a true juvenile delinquent. According to the **role definition**, the juvenile delinquent is *the individual who sustains a pattern of delinquency over a long period of time, and whose life and identity are organized around a pattern of deviant behavior.*

With this definition in mind, the ordinarily conforming and law-abiding boys who, on Halloween night, disregarded laws concerning the drinking of alcoholic beverages by minors, disturbing the peace, malicious mischief, assault, and the curfew were not considered juvenile delinquents even though they violated those norms (see the **Concept Application** at the end of Chapter 2). In fact, the entire community seemed to anticipate and aid the annual Halloween "riot," which functioned as a "release valve," permitting bored and restrained teenagers to "blow off some steam." The role definition insists that the actor's behavior reflect a commitment to a delinquent role and lifestyle before the actor can be realistically identified as a juvenile delinquent.

Two fundamental sociological concepts are inherent in this description of the delinquent: **social status** and social role. **Status** is defined as *the prestige position of a person in relation to other persons in the social group or society.* Any social group or society of people who are together for any length of time will develop a status hierarchy or system of social rankings. Those at the top of the social stratification system have more wealth, power, prestige, and authority than those at the bottom. Most of us learn where we and others stand on the "ladder of social status" in our social group and community.

There are two ways by which we may acquire social status in our society. **Ascribed status** is *a status position or level of prestige assigned (usually at birth) to an individual on the basis of certain social criteria such as race, sex, and parents' social status.* For example, Queen Elizabeth II of England was fortunate enough to have been born to parents who were members of the royal family, and they passed this high-status position on to the present queen. If there had been a male heir to the throne, however, her ascribed status as a female would have made her the King's sister instead of the ruling monarch. Ascribed status is also the category of status often imputed to those at the bottom of the stratification system who, because of the poor and lowly circumstances of their birth, may be relegated to an inferior status as residents of slums, ghettos, and migrant labor camps.

The second way to acquire social status is through the exercise of individual ability and effort or by undertaking certain status-changing experiences in life such as attending college. This is called **achieved status**, and in our society is *usually based upon educational level and occupation.* Sociologists have found that Americans have a well-defined hierarchy of occupations, each with a designated level of prestige or status attached. As each person enters the workforce, there is general consensus regarding the appropriate level of the individual's social status based upon occupation, together with concomitant levels of formal education and income. Thus, the unemployed—especially men of working age—have low social status.

The juvenile or adolescent status in our society is a rather precarious one. Neither adult nor child, the adolescent has a *marginal* social status. He or she is often torn between the normative expectations and responsibilities associated with adulthood, and the freedom from accountability afforded children. The marginality experienced by young people is extremely important from a sociological perspective, and will be further explored throughout this book as a major contributing factor to the problem of juvenile delinquency.

Social role is defined as *the behavioral performance expected of a person who holds a certain status in the social group or society.* A role assignment goes with every status and thus

BOX 1.1

CONTROVERSIAL ISSUE: "Child or Adult?"

The following anecdote is an experience of one of the authors while he was an assistant principal at a public high school, and illustrates one of the important concepts discussed in this chapter.

Juvenile is a status in our society—a social position somewhere between "child" and "adult." Like any social status, it is accompanied by a set of role expectations. While the normative role expectations for adults and for children are fairly clear-cut, those for juveniles are much more ambiguous. Told by parents, "You're a young adult now, why don't you act like it?" only to be denied responsibilities and freedom with the phrase "You're too young," juveniles find themselves in a societal "double bind" where they are simultaneously "too old" and "too young" for a realistic and viable role.

I recall an encounter with a ninth-grade student. He had been sent to my office for "acting childishly" in class. He had no doubt been involved in behavior that was disruptive, and the teacher had become exasperated and sent him to the office. In my typical assistant-principal-disciplinary tone, I asked, "What seems to be the problem?" With a confused look, the student replied, "I don't know what the teacher expects out of me . . . in fact . . . I don't know what anybody expects out of me!"

Without any coaxing on my part, the student described the predicament he had experienced in the classroom. He pointed out that since the first day of school, all the teachers had emphasized that he was in high school now; that he was a young adult and would be treated as such; and that he was expected to act like one. He said that even though one particular teacher constantly reminded her students that they were adults, she often treated them like small children. He cited some of the classroom rules that he considered petty and humiliating, including not being allowed to chew gum and having to ask permission to go to the bathroom. "Does that sound like the way to treat adults?" he asked. Before I could answer, he related a brief story about his parents demanding that he "act his age" and show more responsibility and maturity. Yet, when he wanted to stay home one weekend when his parents planned to be out of town, they flatly refused, reminding him that "he was only fourteen," and that if he insisted on staying home, they would have to hire a *babysitter*.

I tried to interrupt to respond (I probably would have offered some type of defense for both the teacher and his parents), but before I could speak, he recited some examples of contradictory expectations he had experienced:

> After passing a required examination, he was legally licensed to operate a motorcycle, and was expected to obey all traffic laws like an adult—but he could not legally drive a car. . . . If he went to see a movie rated G he was considered an adult and was required to pay adult admission; but if he tried to see an X or NC-17-rated movie, he was told that it was for adults only, and he was a child.

These examples reflect some of the inconsistent, confusing, and contradictory normative expectations faced by adolescents in our society. Between the ages of 12 and 18, the majority of American youths find themselves in a social "no man's land." They are no longer children and childish behavior is not tolerated, yet they are not adults and many adult behaviors are strictly prohibited.

Compare and contrast children, adolescents, and adults with regard to legal and social rights and responsibilities. Have you experienced similar circumstances where you were expected to behave as an adult while still being treated like a child? What problems did you experience? What could be done to help reduce some of the problems associated with the ambiguity of the status of adolescence?

What mixed messages are sent to a 15-year-old girl who is given full responsibility for babysitting a 3-year-old child, but is considered too young and irresponsible to legally drive a car?

© Corbis RF

becomes an important part of the normative system that organizes society and controls the behavior of its members. Over time, certain statuses and their associated roles become infused with honored tradition, and little deviation is tolerated. For example, in our society, men are expected to be "masculine"—traditionally viewed as being competitive and aggressive—and to refrain from weeping. Women are still often expected to be "feminine"—stereotypically viewed as being nonassertive—and eager for fulfillment as wives and mothers. Soldiers are expected to be brave and not cowardly. Ministers are expected to be devout and less susceptible to the temptations of "the world, the flesh, and the devil." The role expectations for juveniles are much less clear than they are for adult men and women. However, as was indicated in the legal definition of delinquency, certain behaviors by adults that are tolerated violate the normative expectations for youth (e.g., drinking alcoholic beverages, smoking, and engaging in sexual activity). Consequently, society's perception of the juvenile status and its concomitant role expectations are major influences in the process of defining juvenile delinquency.

Like status, some roles are imputed to members of society and can be difficult to change. Generally, people can perform only the roles that are approved and assigned by social consensus. However, occasionally roles can be successfully manipulated or modified. For example, the feminist movement has made substantial gains in weakening the traditional and stereotyped role of women in the United States by promoting contemporary and alternative roles.

Some roles are considered "off limits" to all the members of society. Theoretically, at least, the criminal and delinquent roles are not legal or legitimate alternatives. This is

Bill DeOre/The Dallas Morning News

What does this cartoon tell us about marginality and possible delinquency?

the heart of the role definition of juvenile delinquency. A persistent and consistent pattern of delinquent behavior may be perceived by the larger society as a valid indicator of the desired and intended role and lifestyle of the youth in question. Although some role behavior is the result of unconscious socialization and the internalization of social expectations, at other times we consciously and purposely act out roles that afford a dramatized presentation of self-identity (Goffman, 1971).

Attempts have been made to integrate the legal definition with the role definition of juvenile delinquency. The legal definition, with its emphasis on the norm and the act of violation, theoretically merges very well with the role definition stressing the actor's patterned delinquent performance. However, the combined product is, in some instances at least, difficult to operationalize:

> For example, New Mexico rests its definition of delinquency on the word "habitual": A delinquent child is one who, by habitually refusing to obey the reasonable and lawful commands of his parents or other persons of lawful authority, is deemed to be habitually uncontrolled, habitually disobedient, or habitually wayward; or who habitually is a truant from home or school; or who habitually so deports himself as to injure or endanger the morals, health, or welfare of himself or others. (Cavan, 1961:243)

A problem with such laws is that there is no clear definition of what is meant by terms such as *incorrigible, habitual,* or *indecent conduct.* As Cavan (1961:243) asked, "How often may a child perform an act before it is considered habitual?" Paradoxically, the search for a committed and consistent pattern of delinquency can sometimes frustrate the effort toward consistent judicial treatment of American youth.

Another criticism of the role definition is that it overlooks the fact that a deviant role seldom occupies all of a person's time, energy, and behavior. Nearly everyone, even a child, has several different roles and is usually able to easily and quickly move from one to another. A juvenile delinquent may alternately be student, part-time employee, brother, son, and gang member, depending upon the circumstances and with whom he is interacting. He spends his time eating, sleeping, working, playing, stealing cars, and doing many other diversified activities. Only one of his roles and a very small portion of his time involve illegal behavior. David Matza (1964) contended that juvenile delinquents are very much like everyone else; that only intermittently are the social bonds tying them to the mass of conforming society loosened enough to permit an occasional deviation. This is a serious contradiction in the role definition, which describes the delinquent as an actor whose life and identity are wholly organized around deviant behavior.

The Societal Response Definition

The emphasis on a social norm, an individual actor, or a norm-violating act, either alone or in combination, does not equate with an adequate or complete definition of juvenile delinquency. While these factors are all relevant and vital to a conceptualization of the process and condition of delinquency, something is still lacking.

According to the **societal response definition**, *in order for an act and/or an actor to be defined as deviant or delinquent, an audience must perceive and judge the behavior in question.* The **audience** is *the social group or society to which the actor belongs or aspires to belong.* It is not possible or necessary for all the members of the social group to view and evaluate the conforming or nonconforming quality of a person's behavior. In the case of juvenile delinquency, significant and representative members of the social group—parents, teachers, neighbors, police officers, or others—may perform the audience function by having knowledge of or witnessing the act and making the societal conclusion and response. It is even possible for the juveniles committing law-violating behavior to identify their actions as delinquent and, in a sense, to act as their own social audience. The social consequences of delinquency are not experienced, however, unless the deviant perception is shared by authoritative and influential others who can affect one's life.

The major sociological concept of *society* includes the notion of an "audience," that is, the social group that formulates the rules or norms, and thereby oversees and judges the subsequent behavior of all the members of the group. In this sense, "social groups create deviance by making the rules whose infraction constitutes deviance . . ." (Becker, 1963:9). In other words, without society there would be no norms; without norms there would be no deviant behavior; without deviant behavior there would be no system of sanctions. "Just as crime is a creation of the criminal law, so juvenile delinquency is a creation of the statutes establishing the juvenile courts" (Cohen and Short, 1971:91). Over time, the process of becoming delinquent develops sequentially from a socially derived norm, to the violation of that norm by an actor, to social definition and adjudication by an audience. A youth is finally and officially defined as a juvenile delinquent when that status is conferred upon the youth by a court. This process is discussed in Chapter 14.

We may extend the dramaturgical analogy a bit further by perceiving society as being more involved than a passive audience of spectators. Society's active audience

How does this police officer's response to a problem between students determine whether the act is "school misconduct" or "juvenile delinquency?"

role is similar to that of the theater audience that scrutinizes each actor's performance. The audience communicates to the actors its estimation of the quality of the performance with appropriate sanctions—applause, hisses, or other expressions of judgment. Societal response to behavior—the official judgment regarding normative expectations and the actor's conforming or deviant act—is the last and determining dimension to be incorporated into a more complete *sociolegal* definition of juvenile delinquency.

PROBLEMS WITH THE SOCIETAL RESPONSE DEFINITION This definition reflects the labeling approach to juvenile delinquency. The labeling perspective views delinquency as a social "label" placed on juveniles and their actions when those viewing the acts (or who are later apprised of them) judge them to be deviant. The labeling perspective is more thoroughly explained in Chapter 7, Sociological Explanations of Juvenile Delinquency.

Society is an association designed to improve the personal and collective welfare and survival chances of all of its members. A society is endowed with remarkable endurance and usually outlives its individual members. Over time, social norms, values, attitudes, and viewpoints are also manipulated, changed, discarded, or replaced, in harmony with the changing pragmatic needs of the social group. So, while a society may prevail for a long time, the cultural components are not always as permanent and invariable. This adaptability and flexibility have greatly aided the survival of society. For example, every major world religion traces the norm "Thou shalt not kill" to both social and divine origins. Modern nations have institutionalized that canon, and compliance is required of their citizens. The norm is widely and thoroughly internalized so that people are shocked and indignant by the disregard for human life manifested in some criminal activities. However, when society perceives it as necessary, that norm can be modified or reduced in importance or relevancy. Medals and public honors are bestowed on military men for their prowess in killing the national enemy. One of the most successful and popular dramatic plots involves one of the "good guys" gunning down the "bad guys" in "winning the West." The point is that an **a priori** definition of the situation (based on prior reasoning and conclusion) can intervene between the definitive norm and its applications which influences the social judgment of a given act.

The societal response definition of juvenile delinquency, while incorporating some elements of other definitional approaches, is not without its problems. The sociolegal focus on the audience, comprised of direct and indirect witnesses, becomes the key variable in determining the delinquent or nondelinquent status of an act or actor. But witnesses do not always agree on what they are seeing. As an example, consider the case of a teenage girl who is caught shoplifting in a department store. Her parents may view this as a single isolated act, incompatible with their daughter's usual behavior. If the police are called, the responding officer may see the shoplifting activity as theft and feel obliged to arrest the youth. The perception and reaction of the store manager are also influenced by personal background and circumstances. If continually victimized by widespread shoplifting on the part of high school students, the store manager may decide to "make an example" of the girl and prosecute her. On the other hand, if her parents are affluent or prominent in the community, the store manager may regard the incident as trivial rather than risk alienating the family and their friends. Audience evaluation of the act and the actor may be further diversified if the youth belongs to a peer group in her school or neighborhood that values such daring and nonconforming escapades and rewards her with higher status within the group. The conflict and varying dominance of these segments of the perceiving and reacting audience often result in differential treatment of many young offenders. This persistent definitional inconsistency is underscored in the discussion of juvenile delinquency statistics presented in Chapter 3.

AN INTEGRATED DEFINITION OF DELINQUENCY

The conceptual definition of juvenile delinquency utilized throughout this book combines aspects of all three of the major definitional categories. It includes criminal acts committed by juveniles and the status offenses deemed to be inappropriate behavior for youths. It includes the fulfillment of the delinquent role and also takes into account the complex social processes involved in the societal assessment and response to delinquency. Consequently, when we use the term **juvenile delinquency,** we are referring to *illegal conduct by a juvenile that reflects a persistent delinquent role and results in society regarding the offender as seriously deviant.* This integrated definition, however, while operational for present consideration, suggests a variety of problems, such as lack of uniformity in laws, and lack of consistency in what is considered appropriate and inappropriate behavior in society. Resolutions to these problems in defining juvenile delinquency are suggested in Chapter 17 as we rethink the delinquency problem.

BOX 1.2

Cross-Cultural Focus: The Cultural and Legal Definitions of "Child" and "Juvenile Offender" in Other Nations

In the United States, juvenile delinquency is legally defined as any act which, if committed by an adult, would be a crime. For example, many states define delinquency as the behavior of children between specific ages (usually between the ages of 7 and 18) that violates state or local criminal statutes (Willing, 2000). With these definitions as a reference point, many interesting comparisons and contrasts can be made with prevailing cultural and legal definitions in a cross section of other nations.

Australia

Sweeping changes were introduced through the Juvenile Court Courts Act of 1971 and the Community Welfare Act of 1972 for dealing with juveniles in trouble in South Australia. The significant features of the legislation included the following (Nichols, 1980:155, 156, 157):

1. Juvenile Aid Panels were established as an alternative to court proceedings for most 10- to 16-year-old offenders.
2. No conviction is possible for an offender under 16 years of age.
3. Minimum age of criminal responsibility was set at 10 years.

Brazil

Since 1921, due to the reforms brought about by a juvenile court judge, Jose Candido de Albuquerque Mello Matos, the illegal behavior of people below 14 years of age was decriminalized and excluded from any process of law. At the same time, it was established that offenders between 14 and 18 should be submitted to legal procedures especially designed for that age group (Cavalieri and Rios, 1980:7).

Israel

Israel has extended the jurisdiction of its juvenile courts from 16 to 18 years and raised the age of criminal responsibility from 9 to 13 years (Hartjen, 2008).

The Youth Labour Law of 1953 defines a "child" as a person below 16 years and an "adolescent" as a person between 16 and 17 inclusive. . . .

The Apprenticeship Law of 1953 defines a "juvenile" as a person who has not yet reached the age of 18 (Reifen, 1980:57, 68).

Jamaica

The Juvenile Law makes provision for dealing with three categories of children up to the age of 17 years: those in need of care and protection, those beyond control, and those 8 years of age and over who commit offenses against the law. It was the responsibility of the juvenile court to determine whether a child brought before it fell into any of these categories. . . .

For offenders the Juvenile Law fixed the age of criminal responsibility at 8 years. It stated: "It shall be conclusively presumed that no child under the age of 8 years can be guilty of any offense." At 17 the offender passed out of the jurisdiction of the juvenile court (Cumper, 1980: 36, 38).

Nigeria

With regard to juvenile delinquency, and therefore juvenile justice, the Children and Young Persons Law is applied. The law itself is referred to as "An Ordinance to make provision for the welfare of the young and treatment of young offenders and for the establishment of juvenile courts." Under it a "child" means a person under the age of 14 years and a "young person" means a person who has attained the age of 14 years and is under the age of 17 years. Thus, no person under the age of 17 years who is apprehended by the police can be brought before a court of summary jurisdiction (Asuni and Jack, 1980:101).

The Philippines

Youth offenders, under Philippine laws, include children over 9 and under 15 years who are not delinquents; children under 18 years who are delinquent but are entitled to suspended sentence; and youths under 18 who also are delinquent and are not entitled to suspended sentence; and those 18 to 20 years, who while considered as adult offenders, may be entitled to probation before service of sentence; executive clemency even before the service of sentence; executive clemency even before the service of the minimum sentence; and parole after service of the minimum sentence (De Jesus-Amor, 1980:106).

Poland

According to Polish penal code, young people are classified into three categories: those under 13 years of age, those between 13 and 17 years of age, and a special category for offenders from 16 to 17 years of age. Children younger than 13 years of age do not bear any criminal responsibility. In their case the judge decrees a "non-lieu" and prescribes one of the educational measures stipulated in the penal code.

The line of conduct in the case of offenders 13 to 17 years of age depends on their mental and moral maturity. Young people 16 to 17 years of age can be held responsible for crime (Zabrodzka, 1980:41; Hartjen, 2008).

Saudi Arabia

Through the application of Islamic law, the kinds of punishment vary according to the age of the offender. Also, a child is considered to pass through three phases. First, the *unconscious phase* that continues until his seventh year. In this phase he is referred to as a "kid" and, as such, cannot be condemned for any transgression. . . . The second phase, called the *unfulfilled conscious phase,* is a period from the seventh to the eighteenth year. In it responsibility is limited to what is known as "punitive responsibility." Any series or number of crimes is treated and dealt with individually. . . . Crimes in this phase and any punishment given are not recorded against the offender and consequently have no adverse effect upon his future. . . . The *fulfilled conscious phase* begins at the end of the eighteenth year. At this age, the youth is held to be fully responsible for any crime he commits; punishment is determined according to Islamic law (Al-Athl, 1980:129–130).

Based upon your reading of this chapter, how do the cultural and legal definitions of *child, juvenile delinquent,* and *legal responsibility* in the United States compare with those of other countries outlined in this section? In your judgment, do the juvenile laws and penal codes of these other nations seem to favor the legal definition, the role definition, the societal response definition, or some combination of these definitions of juvenile delinquency?

Sources

Some of the references cited in this Cross-Cultural Focus were included in the five-volume set entitled *Justice and Troubled Children around the World,* edited by V. Lorne Stewart. New York: New York University Press. 1980. These author-contributors are listed alphabetically:

Al-Athl, Abdullah Mohammed. "Saudi Arabia." Vol. III, 117–140.

Asuni, Tolani, and Jack, David D. L. "Nigeria." Vol. IV, 91–105.

Cavalieri, Alyrio, and Rios, Jose Arthur. "Brazil." Vol. I, 1–17.

Cumper, Gloria. "Jamaica." Vol. III, 31–48.

De Jesus-Amor, Ester. "The Philippines." Vol. III, 103–116.

Nichols, Helen. "South Australia." Vol. III, 141–165.

Reifen, David. "Israel." Vol. I, 57–86.

Zabrodzka, Halina. "Poland." Vol. V, 33–53.

Hartjen, C. A. 2008. *Youth, Crime and Justice.* New Brunswick, NJ: Rutgers University Press.

Willing, Richard. 2000. When children kill, who takes the blame? *USA Today* (March 3): 3A.

Summary

In this chapter, we examined the multiple and complex definitions of juvenile delinquency. The definitions of delinquency fall into three broad categories: legal, role, and societal response.

The legal definition focuses upon the act committed by the youth. Every state has established statutes that define criminal behavior. The legal definition indicates that delinquency occurs when juveniles between a specified age range (usually 7 to 18 years) commit an act that would be considered a crime if committed by an adult. Criminal statutes are norms that have been formally codified by society. These laws reflect the prevailing values of a society, and prohibit behaviors viewed as being dysfunctional to the overall stability of society. Murder, rape, robbery, theft, and other criminal offenses threaten social order. The legal definition goes beyond this, however, as states also have enacted statutes that make it illegal for juveniles to commit certain acts that would not be considered criminal if committed by an adult. These status offenses are legally defined as acts of delinquency because they violate the normative role expectations associated with the juvenile status in our society. Consequently, while the drinking of alcoholic beverages, smoking, and truancy are not crimes when done by adults, they are viewed as threatening to youths and their successful internalization of society's cultural values and social norms.

We also explored the role definition of delinquency. This definition shifts the focus of delinquency away from the specific act and onto the actor. The role definition overlooks the occasional minor transgression against social norms, and views delinquency as being a persistent pattern of law-violating behavior by a youth. This definition focuses upon the status accorded to juveniles in our society and the social role expected to accompany that status. While there is little argument over the validity of the values reflected in laws forbidding murder, rape, robbery, theft, and other violent and property offenses, the values reflected in the laws creating status offenses are not uniformly supported.

The third major definitional category focuses upon the societal response definition of delinquency. This definition views delinquency as being a result of the reaction of a social audience to a particular actor and act. The observing representatives of society have the power to judge and impute a delinquent label to a youth whose behavior is perceived to warrant such a label.

As the interplay unfolds between the act, the actor, and the audience, different interpretations of what has happened and what is happening confound the implementation of any definition of juvenile delinquency. Therefore, efforts to make practical application of the definitions often appear ambiguous. The legal definition of juvenile delinquency is plagued by vague phraseology that permits subjective criteria as to what constitutes a delinquent act. The role definition is weakened by a lack of consensus about how much nonconforming, antisocial behavior is necessary to indicate commitment to a delinquent role and identity. The societal response or sociolegal definition is dependent upon some type of consensus on the part of a social audience that deviance has been committed and that something should be done about it.

Finally, we constructed an integrated sociolegal definition to be used for our purposes in studying the problem of juvenile delinquency. This definition encompasses the major elements of all three of the aforementioned definitions. While not without some problems and limitations, this synthesized definition provides a clear conceptual framework for our study of the delinquency problem.

In Chapter 2, we establish a solid sociological foundation for the study of juvenile delinquency. We explore the social nature of humans and discuss the basic social processes involved in establishing norms and defining conformity and deviance. Juvenile delinquency is a serious form of deviant behavior and a social problem about which U.S. society is concerned.

Concept Integration: Questions and Topics for Study and Discussion

1. Define and explain the following terms and concepts: juvenile, adolescent, adult, mens rea, social role, social status, ascribed status, and achieved status.
2. What is juvenile delinquency?
   - based on the legal definition?
   - based on the role definition?
   - based on the societal response definition?
   - based on an integrated definition comprised of legal, role, and societal components?
3. Who is a juvenile delinquent? How does a delinquent differ from the adult criminal? How does the delinquent differ from the occasional experimenter with nonconforming or antisocial behavior?
4. Define *status offense.* Should status offenses be part of the legal definition of delinquency? Why? Why not?
5. Use the dramaturgical analogy to help explain the interplay and relationship between the social norm, the act, the actor, and the audience, and some common form of youthful misbehavior such as truancy from school, shoplifting, or something of your choice or from your experience.
6. Outline the problems associated with each definition of juvenile delinquency. In your judgment, can any of these problems be resolved? If so, how?

Chapter 2

A Sociological Approach to Delinquency

READING OBJECTIVES

Reading this chapter will help you achieve the following objectives:

1. Define and understand the sociological perspective as it applies to the study of juvenile delinquency.
2. Perceive how our need for interaction and interdependence resulted in the development of human society.
3. Trace the origins and purposes of social norms—rules of conduct for members of social groups.
4. Define and give examples of mores and folkways as different kinds of social norms governing our behavior.
5. Explain the concepts of conformity and deviance as alternative responses to the behavioral expectations of society for its members.
6. Understand why societal response to the violation of norms (degree of punishment, reward, or ambivalence) may vary with the culture, time period, social status of the offender, and other factors.
7. Comprehend how some deviant behavior can be beneficial to society.
8. Understand why juvenile delinquency, as a form of deviant behavior, is considered a serious social problem.

INTRODUCTION

There are many ways of looking at any phenomenon. You are probably familiar with the old story about the three blind men who encountered an elephant for the first time. One of them ran his hands over the animal's broad side and described the elephant as like a wall. The second, as he felt one of the creature's huge legs, became convinced that the elephant is similar to a tree. Finally, the third blind man, as he handled the beast's flexible trunk, declared that the elephant resembles a large rope. We may be amused at the ludicrous conclusions of the three blind men, but they illustrate that people tend to "see" and interpret things within their own frame of reference that is based on limited personal experience and inclination. These diverse viewpoints are called perspectives.

The problem of accurately describing and explaining what we "see" is even more difficult when we look at human behavior. For humans and their conduct comprise the most perplexing yet interesting set of variables to fall under our scrutiny. Even intelligent and well-intentioned observers of acts or events do not always agree on what they have seen. A primary task of attorneys and judges in criminal and juvenile court proceedings is to disentangle contradictory versions from eyewitnesses of what actually happened, and why.

For example, in a hearing involving a 16-year-old male accused of attempted sexual assault of a female student in a crowded high school parking lot, his male companions excused their friend's behavior with "He was drunk and didn't know what he was doing." One adult in the neighborhood was even more tolerant and stated: "The kid didn't do anything out of the ordinary. Boys will be boys!" Another observer claimed that the girl was dressed seductively and "asked for it," adding that "a maladjusted and immature boy reacted accordingly."

On the other side in the case, a friend of the victim declared that the alleged offender suddenly attacked and began ripping at the victim's clothing without provocation. Another nearby witness characterized the defendant as "a born criminal and well-known thug in the community who should be put away for a long time!"

All of these conflicting opinions were stated with conviction. Yet the various claims that the accused sexual assailant was somehow unaccountable, moved by a normal hormonal "call of the wild," an emotionally troubled youth unable to resist temptation, or the outraged generality that such individuals "commit the crime because they are slime!" (Downey, 1993), are somewhat unconvincing. They all have oversimplified the issues related to normative conformity and deviant behavior, and they all suffer from the assumption that delinquency is a result of some individualistic biological or psychological aberration (see Chapter 4).

THE SOCIOLOGICAL PERSPECTIVE

Sociology may be defined as *the systematic and scientific study of human behavior, social groups, and society* (Thompson and Hickey, 2008). Practical applications of sociological knowledge have been made to countless social issues and problems, including the causes, consequences, and treatment of juvenile delinquency.

In the pursuit of sociological insights and research objectives, sociologists have been guided by a unique viewpoint or approach. This *sociological perspective* holds that human behavior is generally a social act that can be traced to powerful forces in the social environment surrounding each actor. Expanding on this position, Peter Berger (1963:23) suggests that "things are not what they seem" and that sociologists must have a broader vision that moves away from the particular to the general; from the narrow, familiar, and easy explanations of social life to the larger, interconnected, and more profound social environment.

C. Wright Mills (1959) called the sociological perspective a "sociological imagination." Armed with this view of the social world and human behavior, keen observers are free from the confines of convention, so-called common sense, and the apparently obvious. They are able to explore all kinds of fascinating factors and variables in the social background of an individual or group that may be related to behavior. Thus, a sociological inquiry into the case described earlier of the youth accused of sexual assault might begin with these probing questions:

1. What social and cultural values and attitudes about male and female sex roles may have contributed to what took place, and the disparate interpretations of the event by various onlookers? Why did none of the onlookers intervene on the young girl's behalf?
2. What is the young man's family background? Are his parents deceased, missing, or divorced? Do they have necessary parenting skills? Are there positive and reliable adult role models in the family and home?
3. What kind of socialization has the youth experienced? Were ideals and values favorable to law-abiding behavior instilled at an early age? On the other hand, has he been exposed to attitudes or examples that could encourage law violation?
4. Has he had a positive school experience? Was there a good relationship with teachers and other students? Does he have any kind of learning disability? Did he drop out of school prior to the incident? If so, why?

5. Has the youth's social class and/or racial identity negatively affected his social acceptability or self esteem? Does he have a fulfilling job? Does he perceive the world as a dangerous and hostile environment that offers him little opportunity for success? Are frustration, poverty, alienation, and crime endemic in his neighborhood?
6. Who are his friends and close associates? Does this young man belong to a gang or other group with a record of antisocial behavior? Are there subcultural influences on him that are in conflict with the behavioral expectations of the larger society?
7. What are his attitudes toward women, sex, and violence? How do these reflect larger social and cultural attitudes toward women, sex, and violence?

The answers to such questions as these—springing from a sociological approach to understanding juvenile delinquents and delinquency—will unfold throughout this book. Such knowledge regarding the social origins of misbehavior is not intended as an excuse or justification for the offender. Rather, an awareness of possible causal linkages between a person's social milieu and his or her illegal conduct should enhance the remedial and rehabilitative work for juvenile delinquents in the United States.

THE SOCIAL NATURE OF HUMANS

Shortly, we will turn our attention to norms or rules of conduct, the necessity for a large measure of conformity in society, and the seriousness of antisocial deviance. However, these important topics will be more meaningful if their discussion is prefaced by and grounded in a brief overview of the basic social needs and practices of our species. Human beings are social animals. Sociologists refer to this as the social imperative.

The Social Imperative

Many young people express a desire to disengage from "authoritarian teachers," "abusive and insensitive parents," or some other interpersonal conflict or unpleasant situation in the family, school, or community. However, on second thought, nearly everyone realizes the impracticality of such a course of action. Not only is it virtually impossible to escape all social contact with other humans, but, after reflecting on the loneliness and vulnerability of isolation, few people really desire to totally separate themselves from society. On the contrary, intrinsic to human nature, and resting upon each of us, is an irresistible social imperative that demands our participation in society.

Most species of animals and insects are social creatures. They band together in social groups for companionship and mutual aid as well as in response to the biological urges to propagate their kind and nurture their young. Thus, the bird gravitates to the companionship and security of its flock; the honeybee orients its entire life span to the hive and the swarm; the cow on the hillside lives in proximity to and association with her herd. Men and women are also social creatures, drawn and driven by powerful forces to communicate and cooperate with a social group in order to collectively enhance personal and species survival (Barash, 1982). However, the human social imperative is not solely a biologically or genetically programmed response as in the lower forms of animal life. Our compulsion toward sociality also is embedded in the cultural content of every society and consciously transmitted to each new generation as a learned response to our basic needs for social interaction and social interdependence.

Adolescents often demonstrate a powerful social imperative. They enthusiastically seek their peers and congregate in shopping malls, parking lots, and other public places designated by the group for informal social interaction. Indeed, teenagers especially, appear to find security and identity in the company of other youths. Studies of juvenile delinquency indicate that most illegal acts are committed in small groups.

Social Interaction

Social scientists argue that our credentials as human beings rest on more than biological similarities. Normal development of human nature and personality is dependent on prolonged and positive interaction with other people. For example, the early focus of Kingsley Davis (1948) and others on feral or "wild" children, who had been deprived of human companionship and socialization, sought to establish causal linkage between social interaction and "becoming human."

Eric Miller (1978) reported on the discovery of three small rural children, locked in a wire cage in their parents' backyard. County welfare officials described the children as unsocialized and uncivilized—naked, wild, covered with excrement, and unable to talk or feed themselves. In addition, a large number of contemporary researchers have gathered considerable evidence of an association between social isolation, psychological stress, and maladjustment. As one author summarized, "genetics provides the raw material; life molds the spirit and the soul" (Kantrowitz, 1997:8).

While very few of America's youth experience the literal isolation of feral children existing in attics, cages, or other lonely places, many *do* feel a kind of *symbolic isolation*—a desolate alienation from parents and other adults who do not understand them. Such a barrier to meaningful communication and social interaction between the generations has been cited as a seedbed for serious deviance and delinquency (Erikson, 1956).

Social Interdependence

The desire and willingness to participate with others in an interdependent social relationship acknowledges the vulnerability of the individual in dealing with a difficult and dangerous environment. Thus, the social imperative that moves us to join forces and collaborate with others expands our intellectual and technological resources for personal and collective survival. At the same time, membership in society improves the accumulation and transmission of cultural knowledge to succeeding generations.

One of the earliest and most convincing statements supporting the necessity for social interdependence among humans came from the zoologist Peter Kropotkin (1914:57) who concluded that "the vast majority of species live in societies and they find in association the best arms for the struggle of life." Kropotkin's classic work on the subject is appropriately titled *Mutual Aid*.

How does the teamwork necessary to win a football championship illustrate the concept of social interdependence?

© Corbis RF

Sociologists, too, have contributed major theoretical insights and empirical findings that support the idea of a social imperative as the compelling force in the formation of interdependent social relationships. Emile Durkheim ([1938] 1947) suggested that humans find resolution to chronic conflict through social organization. For example, if there is a growing density of human population in an area, the struggle for scarce resources is reduced through a division of labor or increased occupational specialization. In this way, Durkheim said, people can coexist and cooperate in a shared environment.

Robert Park (1936) perceived social interdependence as a kind of symbiotic or collaborative relationship between diverse individuals and segments of the population. Their competition is balanced with a pragmatic cooperation for the mutual benefit of all parties and groups involved. Park's conceptualization has had widespread application in explaining the development and social organization of human communities.

A large number of studies have verified that human societies everywhere are characterized by a pervasive and persistent web of social relationships. For example, Arnold Green (1972) reported how preliterate societies have well-established patterns of communal and collective behavior in the procurement of sustenance, religious practices, government, and other dimensions of social life. William Foote Whyte (1993), in his well-known *Street Corner Society*, found extensive social organization, primary group relationships, and social control mechanisms in lower-class urban slums that some earlier writers had suggested were lacking in such districts.

The consensus of these scholars is that human isolation is contrary to human nature and detrimental to the survival of the species. Consequently, we have gathered ourselves together to form families, tribes, villages, communities, cities, nations, and a wide variety of other social groupings. **Society** is the general term for *people living in social interaction and social interdependence.*

On a smaller scale, involving fewer people and less formal organization, social interdependence also characterizes the many groupings of young people at school or in their neighborhood. For example, the accomplishment of any collective task—whether it be students performing in the school band, children playing games at recess, or street gangs at war with rival groups—all require a strong sense of social interdependence and cooperation.

Social Organization

Social interaction varies in intensity and complexity, depending on the size of the group, the relationship of the participants, the environment, and the objective or purpose of the interaction. In other words, social interaction ranges from brief and superficial contact between strangers who wait on a street corner for a traffic light to change, to the secondary and instrumental relationship between store clerk and customer, to the more permanent and intimate interrelationships between marriage or business partners. It includes the relatively passive interaction of a theater audience or a class of students, as well as the dynamic collective behavior of a football team or an angry gang fight.

Seldom is social interaction as spontaneous and unstructured as it may seem on the surface. Nearly all social interaction between the members and groups that comprise a society is guided by an extensive and detailed network of social organization. Every social group and society organizes its members and their behavior into recognized and accepted patterns so as to ensure the smooth operation and continuity of its collective existence. Most people are willing to standardize their behavior in many ways and to relinquish some individuality in order to function effectively as a social unit.

NORMS

We have indicated already that most human behavior is social in that it takes other people into account, their expected responses to one's actions, and the shared meanings that members of the group place upon these actions. It follows that an important dimension of social organization is the vast array of rules that serve as guidelines for socially acceptable behavior. All of these *rules, standards, laws, regulations, customs, and traditions—the "do's and don'ts" of human conduct and social interaction*—are referred to as **norms** by social scientists. *Behavior that conforms or is in harmony with this code of rules* is said to be **normative**, or **conformity.**

Some societal norms are **prescriptive**—that is, *they "prescribe" certain kinds of behavior as acceptable or desirable*—such as the accepted practice in American society that men shake hands with each other when they are introduced, and the legal requirements that children must attend school until a certain age and that men must register with Selective Service for possible military conscription when they reach their eighteenth birthday. Another prescriptive norm is that we must wear clothing in public (although the style and amount of clothing may vary widely, for example, whether one is going to the beach or to the senior prom). Other norms are **proscriptive**—that is, *they prohibit certain kinds of behavior as unacceptable to society*—such as our laws forbidding assault and theft, and the less seriously enforced curfew ordinances in some cities that deny minors access to public places after a specific nighttime hour. Other examples of prohibitive norms that govern the behavior of youths in the United States are age restrictions on marriage and the consumption of alcoholic beverages.

SOURCES OF NORMS

Where did we get our system of norms? There are several contrasting and controversial theoretical viewpoints regarding the origin of norms. The two most widely discussed and accepted viewpoints are the models of **Social Consensus** and **Social Conflict**.

Social Consensus

Philosopher Thomas Hobbes ([1651] 1914:63) was convinced that the uncontrollable natural inclination of humans is predatory, that is each person is, "as a wolf to his fellow man." Hobbes believed that in the distant past, people willingly surrendered much of their independence to a central and absolute government in order to protect themselves from one another and so created an ordered, workable society. This *voluntary abdication of a measure of personal autonomy and submission to group norms in exchange for security supplied by a dominant power structure* is known as a **Social Contract**.

The theoretical viewpoint that societal norms are founded upon longstanding consensus among members of society about how to best organize behavior was more fully developed by Max Weber (1925), William Graham Sumner (1906), Kingsley Davis (1948), and others during the 20th century. These sociologists argued that the major rules of conduct are "traditional" in that they have deep roots in the historic cultural values of a people. Over time, and with continual usage in fulfilling basic needs of the society, these norms become well-established and institutionalized as "the right way to do things." As long as they work and do not become obsolete through advancing technology or social change, these norms tend to remain in what Durkheim ([1938] 1947) called "the collective conscience of the people." They are passed on from generation to generation through socialization.

Social Conflict

A contrary viewpoint on the origin of social norms was offered by Karl Marx ([1867] 1967), Friedrich Engels ([1848] 1964), and others who advanced the thesis that a great many norms are founded on the political and economic power of dominant owners of property who comprise a ruling class, rather than on the cultural consensus of the common people. Marx, with his orientation toward social class conflict, viewed the normative system of society as generated by the greed of the ruling capitalistic class in order to consolidate its ownership of the means of production and to control the working classes. This economic exploitation, according to Marx and Engels, would lead to an inevitable war of the classes and the overthrow of the dominant capitalistic system. Then, according to socialistic ideology, the norms of the new classless society would truly reflect the will of the people.

Class conflict as an original source of norms, especially laws, continues to have strong proponents (e.g., Chambliss, 1973a; Dahrendorf, 1959; Quinney, 1970). Dahrendorf (1959) focused on the differential distribution of authority and coercive power in social organizations that represent the various social classes. He pointed to the legislative and political generation of law and the selective enforcement of the law as exercises of the upper and middle classes to discriminate against the underclasses. Dahrendorf (1959:165) hypothesized that "the patterns of domination and subjection that exist in social organizational arrangements lead to systematic social conflicts of a type that is germane to class conflicts in the traditional (Marxian) sense of this term." This theme has been developed further by Chambliss (1973) and by Quinney (1970), who have argued that criminal statutes are one of the ways that the powerful in American society inflict their will upon the socially disadvantaged. For example, since statutes regulating the behavior of juveniles are passed by legislatures comprised of adults, and enforced and interpreted by adult police officers, district attorneys, and judges, the conflict model of the origin of norms has been utilized by some to help explain the phenomenon of juvenile delinquency.

Both theoretical explanations concerning the origin of norms—social consensus and social conflict—represent *ideal types.* **Ideal type** is a term coined by Weber (1947: 99–100) to describe *a kind of conceptual model, expressing in a pure, and therefore hypothetical, form the core characteristics of a pattern of conduct.* The usefulness of the ideal type is that it offers a point of reference for comparing actual conditions and deviations. In short, social consensus and social conflict models represent idealized, unrealistic norm-producing circumstances. More moderate theorists contend that, while there may be some historical instances in which social norms developed exclusively from one or the other of these two sources, most contemporary societies can trace their norms to a combination of these origins.

FOLKWAYS, MORES, AND LAWS

Sociologists classify norms into three categories on the basis of their importance to the social order, how seriously society regards their violation, and their degree of formality. William Graham Sumner (1906), by using societal reaction to nonconformity to measure the value or importance of norms, helped us to distinguish between two types of informal social norms: folkways and mores.

Folkways

Folkways are *informal agreements or understandings about what is considered appropriate and inappropriate behavior.* Folkways may be very old and entrenched in the culture, such as our tradition of singing the National Anthem prior to sporting events, or they may be relatively new, and indicate normative conflict with older norms (and older generations), as exemplified by the dress and behavior of some punk rock bands and rappers. Folkways may change or fluctuate as do fads and fashions in clothing. Some men have been embarrassed by their tardy discovery that the width in neckties and coat lapels of their outdated wardrobes was suddenly inappropriate attire. Similarly, the prescribed length for a woman's skirt changes almost annually. Folkways also include detailed rules of etiquette covering table manners, dating behavior, habits of grooming and cleanliness, language, and many other aspects of daily life.

Society does not usually consider the violation of a folkway a serious offense, and severe penalties are seldom administered. However, members of society show their displeasure in unofficial, informal ways. People whose eating habits are judged as uncouth and ill-mannered by society will not be arrested, though they may find themselves avoided by others and dining alone. Someone who wears a sweatshirt and jeans to a formal church wedding will not be excommunicated, but may be the target of direct or indirect ridicule. One's social group may be annoyed by such overt challenges to propriety but does not feel particularly threatened. This is the important difference, according to sociologists, between folkways and mores.

Mores

Important and seriously enforced societal norms are called *mores* (pronounced morays). **Mores** are *salient norms in that they are perceived as germane to the overall cohesion and survival of society.* Mores carry a moral connotation, and consequently, their violation is seen as threatening to crucial values. Norms against lying, cheating, and adultery are examples of mores. The patience and permissiveness that often characterize societal reactions to those who violate folkways are not extended to those who transgress important mores. Historically, society has shown little tolerance for adulterers (e.g., Hawthorne's *The Scarlet Letter*) or others who are considered to have committed serious moral transgressions that threaten dominant cultural values. The mores often are reflected in our most formal type of norms: laws.

Laws

Laws are *formal norms that are systematically written down in a legal code that defines their violation as criminal behavior and prescribes the method and degree of punishment.* More specifically, criminal laws (and juvenile laws) are codified bodies of statutes generated by a political authority or government to regulate the behavior of societal members and provide for punishment for the violators of the rules. Since these more important and serious rules are "regarded as a conserving force in the life of human beings, protecting what society stands for" (Birenbaum and Sagarin, 1976:16), formal law enforcement agencies of the state may be used in their enforcement. Laws forbidding theft and murder, reflect mores in the Ten Commandments and other religious dictates, as well as the criminal codes of the various states.

The universal application of all the laws to all the people belonging to a national society like the United States, and the interpretation of all behavior as conforming or deviant in relation to these laws, are not as simple or clear-cut as some might suggest. Most major social norms, or group-shared expectations, are designed to enhance, preserve, or accomplish those things generally considered to be of greatest value in the culture of the larger society. When a cultural value does not undergird a social norm or law, it becomes very difficult (if not impossible) to enforce the law consistently. For example, due to the zeal and political influence of a minority group of social reformers, the prohibition of the manufacture and sale of alcoholic beverages became a national law through the Eighteenth Amendment to the Constitution in 1919. However, it soon became clear that law enforcement officers and agents could not control the illegal manufacture, transportation, and sale of alcoholic beverages. Too many Americans had values contrary to the intent of the prohibition law and, in 1933, the Eighteenth Amendment was repealed.

General application of norms is sometimes made difficult by the population composition of a heterogeneous society. The United States contains many subgroups differentiated according to age, social class, occupation, religion, politics, and ethnic-cultural backgrounds. These groups often represent different circumstances and orientations and thus do not always share the same values and rules. Becker (1973) cited the example of Italian immigrants who, by continuing to make wine for themselves and their friends during the prohibition era, simultaneously were conforming to the standards of the Italian subculture and breaking the law of their new country.

Marginality

Robert Park (1928) was one of the influential scholars at the University of Chicago during the formative years of sociology in this country, and was one of the first to identify the plight of certain individuals and groups who experience only marginal and incomplete social assimilation. Stonequist's (1937) *The Marginal Man* pinpointed the second-generation immigrant as the classic example of this phenomenon. He traced this *marginality* to the abrasive cultural conflict experienced by the new ethnic minorities in the United States. The experience of divergent and often contradictory cultural norms has the potential for generating normative confusion, alienation, and, hence, deviant behavior in some individuals. Park, Stonequist, and others portrayed the **marginal person** as *being caught between two conflicting cultures.* The person's commitment is torn and fragmented between the two, and, consequently, the individual fails to fully identify with either of the groups in question. For example, many children of immigrants are exposed to the language and traditions of the "old country" in their homes and ethnic neighborhoods, as well as to the intense socialization of their U.S. school and youthful peer group. Therefore, they become marginal in the sense that they lack complete integration into either the larger society or the subculture. The marginal person, often with mixed and lowly status and identity, inhabits a frustrating social limbo between two societies and cultures. This marginal situation has been considered a contributing factor in causing some juvenile delinquency, and as we discussed in Chapter 1, and you will see in Chapter 6, the concept has been incorporated in some explanatory theories. In Chapter 17, we discuss how reducing adolescents' marginality might help reduce juvenile delinquency. While this cultural conflict between subgroups and the larger society may confound the definition of normative and deviant behavior, every society seriously endeavors to distinguish between behavior that conforms to prevailing norms of social life and behavior that deviates from those norms.

NORMATIVE BEHAVIOR: CONFORMITY

Earlier in this chapter we discussed the origins and purposes of norms as they affect our personal and collective survival. This point can be further clarified by focusing on the definition of **norms** as *group-shared expectations* for behavior. Every social group operates under some set of fundamental regulations which each member starts learning from the day of birth. Charles Cooley (1964) perceived **conformity** as being *the attempt to maintain a normative standard established by a social group*. His early insight, that compliance and conformity with social expectations can be explained by the human tendency to adopt imitatively the prevailing patterns of behavior around oneself, has been expanded and refined into the contemporary viewpoint among sociologists that the individual internalizes the customs of his or her society through a process called socialization. **Socialization** is *the effective transmission and internalization of culture content*. It includes learning to respond to social situations in socially acceptable ways. Every person, from earliest infancy, and through continual interaction with parents, siblings, peers, teachers, and many other members of the social group, is exposed to the values, attitudes, and behavioral practices that are expected and acceptable. The idealized objective of socialization is social control or conformity of individuals, although it is usually articulated as "getting educated," "being properly raised," or "brought up to be law-abiding." In this way, even the process whereby we "put society in man [*sic*]" (Berger, 1963) becomes an institutionalized norm. Social control is considered most effective when it is manifested as self-control in harmony with what is socially expected from others.

Through successful socialization, *most* of us conform *most* of the time to *most* of the important norms of our society. For example, although juvenile delinquency is

Conformity or deviance? Most everybody would agree that the two boys in this photo who are text messaging are conforming to teenage norms. How do you think most adults would respond, however, when they realize the boys are texting each other? How would you respond if you discovered the text message was in regard to a drug deal?

widespread, most teenagers are not tempted to assault or rob other people. As very young children, the majority learned to respect the person and property of others. This is not to say that *all* of our conformity is spontaneous and without complaint. Fear of punishment, penalties, and other negative sanctions can elicit pragmatic conformity as an assist to internalization. For example, not all students refrain from cheating on examinations or bullying their classmates because they love and respect their teachers and have an unquenchable thirst for knowledge and education! Their temptations along these lines are held in check by the prospect of retribution.

When the socialization of group-shared expectations is ineffectual in producing conformity, society has equipped itself with more direct and coercive techniques that may be applied to nonconforming individuals. These range from informal rebuke and ridicule at one extreme all the way to formal, state-imposed fines, imprisonment, and even capital punishment at the other. People are never totally free or independent to determine their own course of action, for society continually monitors and molds the behavior of each member.

In addition to eliciting our personal conformity, what we have learned about norms as group-shared expectations helps us predict much of the behavior of other members of society. For example, the majority of people learn while very young that the right to use the public streets and sidewalks is balanced with a personal responsibility to abide by certain social norms. We have learned to expect that under ordinary circumstances other individuals will respect us and our property. We may usually participate in public social life without fear of insult or physical assault. Those persons whom we meet also have learned to anticipate the same respect from us. We need not be personally acquainted with everyone who shares our community. Our group-shared social expectations—whether in the form of municipal ordinances, constitutional rights, religious dogma, federal or state laws, or simply tradition—usually function to preserve order on our streets and sidewalks, even among strangers.

The ability to control and predict human behavior, based on norms or group-shared expectations, pervades virtually every area of social life. And without doubt our dominant cultural values—manifested in norms, traditions, customs, laws, and group-shared expectations—are part of the "glue" that holds society together, contributing major support to social stability and social organization.

DEVIANT BEHAVIOR: NONCONFORMITY

Many persons find it disagreeable, inconvenient, or otherwise unsatisfactory to order their lives in harmony with behavioral norms of their society, and are tempted to deviate. If their socialization experience or other forms of social control do not restrain them, some of these persons will not conform to all of the norms. Realistically, everybody violates some social norm at some time. These nonconforming members of society and their deviant behavior are a major focus of study in sociology.

Deviant behavior is *conduct that is perceived by others as violating institutionalized expectations that are widely shared and recognized as legitimate within the society.* Simply put, deviance is the violation of norms. So, in sociological terms, deviant behavior involves a complex interplay between a social norm, a member of a social group whose actions are expected to be subject to that norm, and other members of the social group who observe the actor and define a particular behavior as nonconforming to a degree exceeding the tolerance limits of the majority.

Some people argue that societal norms or standards of conduct are nonnegotiable—that they should be treated as inflexible absolutes. Therefore, they have little patience or tolerance for deviant behavior. By taking the position that deviance is only disruptive and destructive to the social group, it becomes possible to classify everybody into one or the other of two opposing subgroups: the "Insiders" and the "Outsiders." Unfortunately, this kind of dichotomous thinking permits motivation and morality to be quickly and conveniently imputed to those on each side as they are adjudged good or bad, right or wrong, friend or foe, loyal and law-abiding or antisocial and criminal, a good kid or a juvenile delinquent. While this approach is convenient and can be applied to almost any person or issue, it oversimplifies the realities of social life. Even though our society is surrounded with a scaffolding of behavioral norms, most of these norms are less rigid than they may seem at first glance. Sociologists have discovered that the members of society display a paradoxical and generous amount of tolerance for much deviant behavior, depending on several important variables.

First, the nature of the offense can determine the level of society's tolerance for norm violation. In many instances, our tolerance for minor norm-breaking requires only that the offender acknowledge the transgression. For example, a breach of etiquette such as a sneeze in a public place requires only the phrase "excuse me" from the offender to remedy the situation. Goffman (1965) called this "remedial work." Even some formal laws, such as traffic ordinances (especially jaywalking), or many of the statutes governing juveniles (such as curfews) can be occasionally violated and, if no accident results, or no harm is perceived, the transgressors can usually pay a fine or receive a warning, and gain the sympathetic understanding of society since such experiences have happened to most of us.

A second factor that determines the level of society's tolerance for deviant behavior is the social status of the offender. The 17th-century political doctrine known as the Divine Right of Kings offers a classic illustration. James I of England and supporting royalists, in order to excuse and boost his shoddy reign, claimed that subjects are required by God not to resist their monarch but to passively obey him, even if, in their view, he is wicked (Figgis, 1922). In the 20th century, Edwin Sutherland (1961) pinpointed the reality of large-scale illegal acts committed by businessmen, corporation executives, and other middle- and upper-class professionals in the course of their occupations. He coined the term "white-collar crime" for such offenses as financial fraud, monopolistic practices, price fixing, and embezzlement, and contended that such professional malpractice enjoyed greater social tolerance. Offenders often go unpunished or are treated leniently because they share the same social class as those with power and authority in society. Similarly, it has been documented that many communities are often more tolerant of some of the activities and escapades of middle- and upper-class youngsters that would be designated as juvenile delinquency if carried out by lower-class youths (Myerhoff and Myerhoff, 1964).

A third element affecting the level of tolerance manifested toward deviant behavior is the cultural context in which it occurs. In other words, there is a paradoxical kind of **cultural relativity**, *an act that violates the norms of one particular society may represent approved conformity from the point of view of another social group* when it comes to tolerance toward many forms of deviance. This principle is especially helpful in understanding behavior and societal reactions to it in a heterogeneous society such as the United States, made up of a number of subgroups with their own distinctive values and norms. Groups such as teenage gangs, homosexuals, drug addicts, and some urban slum dwellers support subcultures whose values, beliefs, normative practices, and shared attitudes run counter to those to which the larger society subscribes. Thus, a given act, and the level of tolerance it receives, must be interpreted within the framework of the relevant cultural or subcultural system.

Fourth, tolerance for nonconforming behavior often has a temporal dimension. That is, types of behavior that are disapproved at one time may be tolerated and even encouraged at a later time in the same society. For example, in colonial America, youths in their early teens were allowed to carry guns, marry, and were expected to engage in a variety of adult behaviors that would be considered deviant today.

In one sense, the entire country has become more tolerant of children and their behavior. Prior to the 20th century, the violation of important laws by American children was considered to be criminal behavior, and children could be incarcerated with hardened adult felons, or even put to death. Today, in what most Americans consider to be a more enlightened society, there are special agencies, courts, and institutions to deal with juvenile delinquents. Our growing concern for the special problems of youths is detailed in later chapters of this book.

NEGATIVE ASPECTS OF DEVIANCE

By the time most individuals reach college age, they are aware of many negative consequences of deviant behavior, especially for the person regarded as deviant. The socialization experience of children and adolescents includes enough penalties, punishments, threats, and warnings regarding misconduct that the unpleasant personal "payoff" for many forms of deviance becomes relatively clear. So pervasive is this message that our cultural folklore is replete with familiar proverbs and dire forecasts concerning the certain and ultimate doom for those who pursue a course of willful deviant behavior. The theme is apparent in such common expressions as: "Those who play with fire will get burned"; "Those who live by the sword will die by the sword"; "Chickens always come home to roost"; "You made your bed, now lie in it"; and "They enjoyed the dance, but now must pay the fiddler."

BOX 2.1

CROSS-CULTURAL FOCUS: Conformity, Deviance, and Delinquency among Native Americans

There are less than 2.5 million American Indians* in the United States and, compared to the other more populous racial groups in the country, their juvenile delinquency is negligible. However, in states such as Arizona, New Mexico, North and South Dakota, and Oklahoma where they *do* represent a sizable minority, and where Native American cultural identity is still vigorously preserved, misconduct by Indian youths is of serious importance.

The delinquent acts which usually bring Native American boys to court are similar to those of other boys. Traditionally, the most prevalent offenses among young Native American males are drunkenness, petty theft, sex offenses, vandalism, and incorrigibility. Among young Native American females, the most common forms of illegal behavior are sex offenses, incorrigibility, and drunkenness.

> The crime rate on reservations has soared in the past decade. Homicides, assaults, robberies, kidnappings, and weapon and drug trafficking are among the crimes being reported in record numbers. This increased crime rate is attributed to the growing gang presence on reservations. . . . On the Pine Ridge Reservation of South Dakota, home to about 20,000 Lakota Sioux, authorities have acknowledged 3,500 known gang members. The gangs have brought a life of terror to this reservation. They exist primarily to deal in drugs. . . . [but] are responsible for 70 percent of the crimes. . . . Gangs are so prevalent at the local schools that most youth drop out; in fact, the graduation rate is a dismal 1 percent. (Delaney, 2006:139–140)

Young American Indians experience a higher victimization rate than the total U.S. population. "From 1976 to 1999, 7 in 10 Indian juvenile murder victims were killed by another American Indian" (Perry, 2004: iv).

Historically, the percentage of commitments to juvenile institutions in centers of large Native American population shows a marked overrepresentation of Native Americans. For example, in South Dakota, where Native Americans account for 5 percent of the population, 50 percent of the training school population is composed of them.

Alcoholism among some tribes and the illegal consumption of alcohol by many Native American teenagers are chronic social problems. Although drunkenness seems to be associated with many criminal acts (among all racial and ethnic groups), there is no evidence that Native Americans are inherently more susceptible to intoxication or to alcoholism. However, the historical and social experience of American Indians suggests some useful insights regarding their apparent vulnerability to excessive drinking:

> Drinking was heavy on the American frontier during the 19th century among farmers, trappers, and cowboys. It was these groups that the Indians came into contact with and from whom they secured their first alcohol. In addition, most Indians were unfamiliar with the use of alcohol and this inexperience, along with the encouragement of white men, led to excessive drinking. . . .
>
> Different tribal groups exhibit great variations in drinking behavior. . . . The Pueblo of the southwestern United States, for example, are abstainers. . . . There are some tribes, however, where there is a large proportion of heavy drinkers, such as the Ojibwa where researchers classified 42 percent of the adults as heavy drinkers (defined as being drunk 2–5 times a week) (Clinard and Meier, 1998:287).

The consensus among both Native Americans and others who have sought to account for the heavy drinking among Indians is that it began and has continued as a consequence of culture conflict, marginality, and anxiety experienced by the indigenous minority as the white man's ways were arbitrarily imposed.

Similarly, other forms of deviance among American Indians also have been traced to the marginality and loss of self-esteem and social identity of a people whose traditional lands and culture have been threatened by the dominant society. Jack Bynum (1987) compared and analyzed suicide rates among six American Indian tribal nations. Of special concern was the startling increase in suicidal behavior of children, adolescents, and young adults among the Navaho, Cheyenne, Sioux, and Shoshone-Bannock during the 1960s. Bynum concluded that the culture conflict and anomic burden of "the marginal man" were etiologically significant as younger generations of Native Americans often find themselves caught in a precarious social dilemma. Simultaneously socialized to commit themselves

(*Continued*)

to their traditional heritage and values as well as to the culture of the larger society, many young American Indians have found suicide a viable way of escape from an untenable situation.

The use of the hallucinogenic drug, peyote, as part of the ritual and religious experience of the Native American Church offers a classic example of the cultural relativity of conformity and deviance. Cocaine, peyote, and other such hallucinogenic drugs are legally classified as dangerous drugs in the United States and possession and consumption are generally forbidden by law. However, peyote has been used for over 100 years by many American Indian tribes as a cultural residual of the Ghost Dance religious movement.

> In the 1870s the prophet Wodziwob told of a vision in which the ancestors of Native Americans came on a train to Earth with explosive force, after which the earth swallowed up the whites. Members of a number of tribes joined in the movement in the hope of salvation from white oppression. . . . In the late 1880s there was a resurgence; the prophet Wovoka experienced a vision ordering him to found a new Ghost Dance religion. The religious fervor spread through the Plains tribes. Trancelike dances were a central part of the ritual; . . . Peyotism surfaced as the Ghost dance movement was being destroyed; it reflected another way of protesting white cultural pressures (Feagin, 1989:200).

Although the manufacture, sale, and possession of such hallucinogenic drugs are controlled by federal law, it is interesting to note that when peyote is used in certain religious ceremonies by the Native American Church, the practice is exempt from some of these legal controls. The substance is now generally recognized as contributing to the fulfillment of a basic need in some tribal societies and is accepted and integrated into the norms of those cultures. The American principle of religious freedom has now proven to be flexible enough to tolerate the use of peyote by particular people under special circumstances.

From your reading thus far, what cultural values help explain juvenile delinquency among Native Americans? How might these values contribute to, or help prevent, delinquency?

Sources

Bynum, J. E. 1987. Suicide and the American Indian: An analysis of recent trends. pp. 367–377. In Howard Bahr, Bruce Chadwick, and Robert Day (Eds.). *Native Americans today.* New York: Harper and Row, Publishers. (1972); and in *Applied Sociology.* J. E. Bynum (Ed.). Acton, MA: Copley, pp. 5–8. 1987.

Clinard, M. B. and Meier, R. F. 1998. *Sociology of deviant behavior.* (10th ed.). Fort Worth, TX: Harcourt Brace College Publishers.

Delaney, T. 2006. *American street gangs.* Upper Saddle River, NJ: Pearson/Prentice Hall.

Feagin, J. R. 1989. *Racial and ethnic relations* (3rd ed.). Upper Saddle River, NJ: Prentice Hall.

Perry, S. W. 2004. *American Indians and crime.* (ABJS Statistical Profile, 1992–2002). Washington, DC: U.S. Department of Justice.

* There are ancient aborigine peoples still residing in many modern nations whose dominant white societies arrived only in recent centuries. The Eskimos, American Indians, Australian aborigines, and other ancient peoples have all shared the problems associated with culture shock as they have struggled to survive the intrusive dominance of newer and technologically advanced societies. A serious residual of this culture conflict has been the surprising and complex deviance of the younger generations of native populations. In the context of this book, this brief focus on Native Americans is representative of all such indigenous societies.

Deviant behavior such as juvenile delinquency also has a number of negative consequences for society. These negative consequences include, but are not limited to:

1. ***Personal Harm to Victims.*** Deviance can hurt people. Violent acts such as murder, rape, assault, and robbery create obvious personal injury for their victims. Property crimes such as theft, auto theft, burglary, and arson, also cause pain, suffering, and financial loss for those who are victimized by them. While the majority of delinquent acts are nonviolent, many of them create physical and emotional harm for the victims, the perpetrators, and their families.
2. ***Personal Harm to Deviants.*** Members of society whose behavior is generally perceived as grossly nonconformist or antisocial will often suffer loss of trust, stigma, and reduced life chances for success.
3. ***Threatening of Norms.*** Any act of deviance involves norm violation, and hence potentially calls into question the norm being violated. When social rules and guidelines are broken, and if no discernible social harm is apparent, the norm may be judged to be unimportant. In some cases, when one rule is questioned, rules in general may be questioned. Juveniles, in particular, are likely to question rules that govern their behavior when they occasionally violate one of them and perceive no harmful consequences. For example, the teenager who has been warned about the serious consequences of smoking marijuana may try it and feel that it caused no apparent harm. This may lead the youth to also question the potential harm of drugs such as cocaine and heroin against which similar warnings were received.
4. ***Costs.*** Deviance can be extremely expensive for society in both the literal and figurative senses. A tremendous amount of money, time, and energy is spent every year for law enforcement, courts, probation and parole, institutions, programs, and agencies whose sole purpose is to control, treat, and prevent social deviance. Juvenile delinquency, for example, costs Americans hundreds of millions of dollars each year. Beyond the monetary costs, deviance can take a tremendous psychological, emotional, and social toll on the members of a society. When people are afraid to go out at night, or to live in certain areas of a city, or in other ways feel threatened, deviance costs society far more than dollars and cents.
5. ***Social Disruption.*** Deviance can be socially disruptive. When people do not know what to expect of their fellow human beings in a given situation, social interaction can be severely disrupted. Norm violation can lead to fear, anxiety, mistrust, and confusion for members of society.
6. ***Threatening of Social Order.*** Deviant behavior can threaten the stability and social order of a society. As indicated in the consensus model, societal members establish social norms in an effort to create and maintain a sense of social order. The violation of these norms, even in isolated cases, can threaten that order temporarily. Widespread norm violation can create havoc and threaten social stability, as in the cases of mobs, riots, and revolutions.
7. ***Self-Perpetuation.*** In some ways, deviance can create more deviance, and hence, be self-perpetuating. The old adage "Give 'em an inch, and they'll take a mile" reflects the widespread assumption that when one norm is broken, it is likely to lead to other norms being broken. Part of the reason that there are so

many norms regulating juvenile behavior stems from the view that youths must learn at an early age that rules exist and that they must not be broken. Otherwise, many believe that the violation of one rule will encourage the violation of norms by other people. Similarly, the punitive view of our criminal justice system is based upon the idea that when caught, a law violator must be punished in order to deter others from similar deviance.

Because of the negative consequences of social deviance, most members of society attempt to prevent, limit, and control norm violation as much as possible. When a particular type of deviance, such as juvenile delinquency, is viewed as uncontrolled, or worse yet, uncontrollable, it is likely to be defined as a major social problem, and society will mobilize in an effort to minimize its negative consequences.

POSITIVE ASPECTS OF DEVIANCE

It would be simplistic and unrealistic to terminate our discussion of deviant behavior with the assumption that *all* of the consequences of deviance are socially and personally destructive. On the contrary, some deviant acts may generate positive results for the group or society in which they occur.

Although all deviant behavior is nonconforming, not all deviant behavior is antisocial. In fact, sociologists have identified several forms of unorthodox and deviant behavior that, when generally recognized as beneficial to the social group or community, often elicit considerable tolerance. Emile Durkheim (1938) began this line of thought with his thesis the "Functional Necessity of Crime." Later studies by Robert Dentler and Kai Erikson (1959) and by Lewis Coser (1956) further developed the concept. Some positive functions of deviance include:

1. ***Reaffirmation of Norms.*** Often, the deviant is rejected and the group's norms are reaffirmed. In this way, the occasional violation may revitalize the collective conscience of the people. Just as we mentioned that norms may be threatened when norm violation occurs and no discernible harm is apparent, when deviance clearly causes social harm social norms are reaffirmed and strengthened. For example, the obvious harm caused by serious forms of juvenile crime lends support to prevailing social norms that regulate juvenile misconduct.
2. ***Social Solidarity.*** Nothing unites a group like a common enemy. In many cases, the deviant is rejected and the social group is united. Internal enemies, functioning as a built-in "out-group," can bring people together in a common defense of their community in much the same way as do external and hostile enemies. History is replete with tragic examples of crucifixions, lynchings, and witch hunts that united the larger society and enabled people to blame their fear and frustration on selected scapegoats.
3. ***Unity on Behalf of the Deviant.*** The reaction of the social group is not always punitive toward the deviant. Juvenile delinquency, for example, provides a variety of instances in which various social groups, agencies, and society as a whole unite not against delinquents, but on their behalf. Many acts of delinquency are viewed as being the result of unfortunate social circumstances experienced by the youths committing them, and individuals and groups often

unite in an attempt to alleviate those undesirable situations in order to help the delinquent.

4. ***Contrast Effect.*** The deviant offers a convenient and complementary contrast to those who conform. Sometimes public exposure and chastisement of deviants is one of the means used to make conformity meritorious. Perhaps the unspoken message in some condemnations is: "Our indignation over deviant behavior is evidence of our virtue, and proof that we would never commit such offenses!" More overtly, parents often point their fingers at youths in serious trouble with the law to warn their own children that if they don't behave, they may face a similar fate some day.
5. ***"Safety Valve."*** Some forms of deviance may serve as a kind of safety valve for society. Human society is comparable to a boiler under pressure that might explode from inner social, political, and economic tensions unless some "steam" is periodically drained off. Many forms of nonserious juvenile misconduct are viewed as relatively harmless events of youths "letting off a little steam." Comments like "boys will be boys," or "kids have to sow a few wild oats" represent the view that minor deviance entered into periodically by youths is "normal" and far preferable to following all norms rigidly until the pressure builds and ultimately leads to some serious type of deviant behavior.
6. ***Leadership.*** In some cases, deviant behavior can help develop and promote new social leadership. Group dynamics, ranging from gang fights to social movements, often require and generate leaders who excel in articulating group needs and organizing the efforts of the group to achieve their collective objectives. Occasionally someone on the order of Joan of Arc emerges, whose visionary and deviant behavior ultimately placed the 19-year-old at the head of the French Army! (Later, as Joan fell from favor, she was burned at the stake, thus also fulfilling for her society the second positive aspect of deviance outlined in this list.)
7. ***Social and Cultural Change.*** Deviance and deviants may encourage meaningful social and cultural change. This may include the work of innovative administrators who cut through bureaucratic "red tape" to serve fellow workers, eccentric but brilliant inventors, and even revolutionaries like Patrick Henry and George Washington, who helped bring about major social change. On a less dramatic scale, the first to try a new hairstyle, dress style, or other innovative fad or fashion is usually considered deviant.
8. ***Warning Device.*** Deviance also may serve as a warning signal. Rising poverty levels, divorce rates, levels of unemployment, and rates of juvenile delinquency—all in the same area of a city—may indicate defects in the social structure or organization of society. Astute political leaders, observing such indicators of impending social erosion, may then take preventive measures.
9. ***Variety and Excitement.*** Finally, some forms of social deviance reflect the wide variety of personalities, characters, cultural orientations, and behavior manifested by people who dare to be different. Imagine how incredibly dull human society would be if everyone was a total conformist, seemingly cut out by the same predictable, conforming "social cookie cutter." Juveniles, in particular, bore easily, and love nothing better than variety and excitement.

Deviance or conformity? Who decides?

© Toby Canham/The Image Works

The section of this chapter that dealt with conformity ended by stating that "norms . . . and group-shared expectations—are part of the glue that holds society together. . . ." At the same time, and paradoxically, deviation from those norms is also part of the glue that holds society together.

JUVENILE DELINQUENCY

Deviant behavior can become a social problem when it is continuous, chronic, widespread, and perceived by a significant part of the population as threatening to the general well-being of society. Juvenile delinquency is a form of deviant behavior because it involves the violation of norms by children and youths. This form of deviant behavior comes to national attention because many of the norms that are violated are deemed important enough that they have been codified into criminal and/or juvenile laws. It should be noted that many of the behaviors identified as juvenile delinquency are not criminal acts, but relatively trivial forms of deviance. The various criminal laws and juvenile statutes that are most frequently violated by youths in the United States are detailed in Chapter 3. Nevertheless, juvenile delinquency involves enough of the nation's young people in serious, antisocial behavior that it is perceived by a large segment of our society to be a major social problem. Consequently, it receives a great deal of attention from scholars, civic leaders, law enforcement officers, and the media. News articles such as the following arouse citizen concern over the problem of juvenile delinquency:

> **THIRD GRADE ATTACK PLOT ALLEGED**
>
> WAYCROSS, GA (AP) WAYCROSS, Ga.—Some third-graders plotted to attack their teacher, bringing a broken steak knife, handcuffs, duct tape and other items for the job and assigning children tasks, including covering the windows and cleaning up afterward, police said Tuesday. The plot involving up to nine boys and girls at Center Elementary School in South Georgia was a serious threat, Waycross Police Chief Tony Tanner said. (From Seattle *Times,* April 2, 2008)
>
> **CHILDREN CHARGED IN POISONING PLOT**
>
> LUCERNE VALLEY, CA Four sixth graders were arrested for allegedly planning to kill their teacher by spiking her Gatorade with rat poison. Sondra Haile, 54, never drank the poison because a child warned her that someone had put poison in her bottle, said Deputy Cheryl Huff of the San Bernardo County Sheriff's Department. (From *Skagit Valley Herald,* Sedro Woolley, Washington, February 5, 1997:A2)
>
> **PIZZA DELIVERY MAN SLAIN BY TEENAGE ROBBERS**
>
> PITTSBURGH, PA Jay Weiss, a 34-year-old man who worked for Chubby's Pizza, was killed by two teen-agers while delivering a pizza to them. As the man lay dying, the two boys sat on a curb and ate the pizza. (Thomas J. DiLorenzo, *USA Today*, June 25, 1997:13A)
>
> **TEEN SUSPECTS USED GUNS, KNIFE IN TRIPLE KILLINGS**
>
> TYLER, TX (AP) Four suspects including a 16-year-old family member are charged with the murders of the girl's parents, 13-year-old brother, and 8-year-old brother. Apparently the girl's parents forbid her to date her 19-year-old boyfriend, so she and the boyfriend and two other friends broke into the home in rural East Texas and killed the entire family as they slept. (from *Tyler Morning Telegraph,* March 2, 2008)

One might attempt to rationalize that since juvenile delinquency has some positive consequences for society, such as reinforcing the validity of violated norms, mobilizing society for its control, and generating jobs for the army of law enforcement personnel, the resolution or serious reduction of juvenile delinquency could be dysfunctional to society. However, society is not inclined to make these theoretical "trade-offs" in view of the serious crimes portrayed in these and similar headlines. Serious juvenile delinquency jeopardizes basic social values regarding the safety and security of persons and property.

Large numbers of U.S. citizens feel unsafe in their homes, neighborhoods, or workplaces. Many have even stopped going out at night for fear of violent crime. Sociologists who study the effect of media coverage of crime on the public report that attitudes about the safety of one's neighborhood and about going out at night vary directly with the rate of index crimes in that city. The crime reports that are most closely correlated with fear of crime are those describing sensational murders in one's own city—that is, murders that are reported on the front pages of newspapers and on television (Kornblum and Julian, 2008).

BOX 2.2

CONCEPT APPLICATION: "Deviance or Conformity?"

The fundamental sociological concepts discussed in this chapter will be a useful foundation for the study of human behavior in general, and juvenile delinquency in particular. The following anecdote relates an experience of one of the authors and provides additional examples and a concrete application of some of these important concepts.

I grew up in an agricultural valley of Central California and attended a small-town high school. It was a quiet rural environment characterized by close-knit, informal relationships where nearly everyone knew a great deal about everyone else—including such details as family and marriage connections, religious and political persuasions, number of acres owned by each family, and any past scandals.

Nothing really exciting ever happened in our community. The business district of the town was just three blocks long and included a post office, grocery store, feed store, hardware store, and two gasoline service stations. Church, school, and Grange activities satisfied the social needs of the community (the pool hall having been successfully closed by local ministers as a corrupting influence on the youth). My home town enjoyed a reputation as a very law-abiding place and the one elderly police officer had little difficulty in keeping the peace.

There was one night of every year, however, when the high school boys of our town abruptly changed the usual pattern of their behavior, rampaged through the town, and broke a dozen laws. Everyone in the community knew when it was about to happen because considerable preparation always preceded this deviant behavior. During September and October of each year, the high school boys collected spoiled fruit, vegetables, and eggs. The activity came to a climax on Halloween night, when about 75 youths drove pickup trucks, loaded with their overripe "ammunition," onto the deserted Main Street of the town. Then and there, for several hours, bands of beer-saturated boys fought pitched battles with rotten produce. Other citizens seldom dared venture onto Main Street during this annual melee. Even the old policeman was conspicuously absent. Any unwary motorists who blundered into the area on Halloween night had their automobiles pelted and smeared with tomatoes and eggs.

The boys carried out many mischievous pranks. For example, one year they discovered a loaded manure spreader parked nearby and, after hooking it to an old car, spread several inches of manure up and down the three blocks of Main Street. As usual, the following day two county sheriff's deputies arrived early at our high school with a truckload of rakes and shovels. All of the boys were dismissed from school for the day to clean up the town. Then our little community returned to its usual pattern of peaceful and predictable behavior—until the next Halloween.

In light of the chapter that you just read, were the high school boys violating social norms? List as many laws and regulations as you can that may have been violated. In your opinion, and in the judgment of their community, were the high school boys "juvenile delinquents"? Explain how their Halloween behavior was conforming to *another* group-shared expectation. Finally, point out how their "deviant behavior" may have had a positive function for the community.

Richard Fuller and Richard Myers (1941) helped establish the linkage between deviant behavior such as juvenile delinquency and a national social problem:

> Social problems are what people say they are. Two things must be present: (1) an *objective condition* (crime, poverty, racial tensions, and so forth) the presence and magnitude of which can be observed, verified, and measured by impartial social observers; and (2) a *subjective definition* by some members of the society that the objective condition is a "problem" and must be acted upon. Here is where values come into play, for when values are perceived as threatened by the existence of the objective condition a social problem is defined. (Cited in McKee, 1974:496)

Juvenile delinquency is a social problem. It is social in that it has to do with human relationships within society. It involves people, their ethical values, and their relations with one another. Juvenile delinquency is a problem because it is regarded as undesirable. Moreover, members of society believe they can and should do something about these discrepancies between social standards and the conduct of so many youthful citizens.

The sociological approach of this book capitalizes on sociologists' ability to clarify the underlying nature and causes of social problems such as juvenile delinquency. "While sociology is not about creating utopia" sociologists use systematic scientific study to understand society and social problems, and to apply that understanding "to formulate social policies that enhance the quality of life" (Thompson and Hickey, 2008:24).

Summary

This chapter began with an explanation of the sociological perspective that links a person's behavior with his or her society or social context. Applying this approach to juvenile delinquency, we perceive human behavior as a reaction to or reflection of socio-cultural values, family, peers, neighborhood, socioeconomic status, and many other dimensions of the offender's social experience.

The discussion of conduct norms, conformity, and deviance was initiated with a brief overview of our compelling social imperative—an inherent need and desire for social interaction and social interdependence with others. Thus, the foundation is laid for the development and organization of human society.

When people come together to form a society, acceptable forms of social interaction and patterns of behavior are recognized. This social organization is based upon the establishment of norms, both prescriptive and proscriptive, that serve as guidelines for behavior considered appropriate and/or inappropriate. The norms may arise out of general social consensus, or may emerge out of social conflict. Norms may take the form of folkways, which are informal yet very important guidelines for our everyday behavior. Or they may be more seriously enforced mores, which are considered vital to the survival of society. When these norms are formally codified into legal statutes governing behavior, we refer to them as laws.

The establishment of norms immediately creates the concepts of conformity (adherence to social norms) and deviance (norm violation). Through the process of socialization, societal members are taught to internalize the norms of society as their own and to generally conform to the attitudes, beliefs, and behaviors considered appropriate.

When individuals violate society's norms they are considered deviant and their behavior is often socially sanctioned. Most people view extremely deviant behavior as serious, and perhaps antisocial; and we discussed several negative aspects of social deviance, such as personal harm, threat to norms, costs, disruption, threat to social order, and the encouragement of other forms of deviance. On the other hand, there also are some socially positive aspects of deviance. These include the reaffirmation of norms, promotion of social solidarity, uniting on behalf of (or against) the deviant, contrasting deviance with conformity, providing a "safety valve," establishing leadership, bringing about social and cultural change, acting as a "warning device" to society, and providing variety and excitement. Therefore, just as conformity plays an important role in maintaining society, so does social deviance.

Juvenile delinquency is a specific form of social deviance and is regarded as a major social problem in the United States. Members of our society are concerned, and in many cases alarmed, at the extent of law violation involving American youths. This book treats juvenile delinquency as a social problem, and contends that in order to be more clearly understood, it must be viewed in its broadest sociocultural context.

Concept Integration: Questions and Topics for Study and Discussion

1. What is the sociological perspective of human behavior? How is it applied to the study of juvenile delinquency?
2. What evidence can you cite from your reading of this chapter or from your own experience to support the idea that humans need social interaction and social interdependence?
3. What is social organization? How are social norms related to social organization?
4. Identify and explain the differences between the three subcategories of social norms. Can you give at least one example from your own experience of each?
5. Explain the theoretical origins of our social norms.
6. What are the purposes or functions of social norms? Try to think of a norm you have encountered that seems to have no purpose or function for society.
7. What is the difference between conformity and deviance? In your judgment, is it fair for society to restrict some of our individual freedoms in order to achieve a general conformity to social norms?
8. Based on your reading of this chapter, and your own opinion, would it be possible and good for society to outlaw all deviant behavior? Briefly explain or justify your answer.
9. Why is juvenile delinquency considered deviant behavior? Is juvenile delinquency a social problem?

Chapter 3

Dimensions of Juvenile Delinquency

READING OBJECTIVES

Reading this chapter will help you achieve the following objectives:

1. Define various kinds of crime according to the common classification and criteria used throughout the United States.
2. Identify sources of the data and statistical information on juvenile delinquency in the United States.
3. Explain various data-collecting techniques that are used and the strengths and weaknesses of each methodology.
4. Understand how unreliable and/or invalid data or data-gathering procedures can lead to questionable findings and conclusions regarding the magnitude of juvenile delinquency.
5. Trace the general dimensions of the delinquency problem with official FBI and juvenile court statistics on the incidence and trends of juvenile crime in the various offense categories.
6. Conceptualize, analyze, and critique a composite Delinquent Profile based on arrest statistics and on a summary of many characteristics of the "average" juvenile delinquent.
7. Explain why the amount and kind of juvenile delinquency vary, according to age, sex, race, place of residence, and other characteristics of offenders.

INTRODUCTION

In 1930, a voluntary national program for the collection of crime statistics was initiated by the International Association of Chiefs of Police (IACP) and the United States Federal Bureau of Investigation (FBI). The resulting annual reports on criminal activity in the United States have revealed seriously and consistently high rates of juvenile delinquency. The *First Annual Report of the National Institute of Law Enforcement and Criminal Justice* (U.S. Department of Justice, 1974a:15) reported that "during the 1960s, the arrest rate for juveniles increased six times faster than for adults." By 1970, juveniles under the age of 18 accounted for one-fifth of all arrests for violent crime and for more than half of all arrests for burglary. In 1974, The National Advisory Commission on Criminal Justice Standards and Goals identified juvenile delinquency as a critical, high-priority, national concern:

> The highest attention must be given to preventing juvenile delinquency, minimizing the involvement of young offenders in the juvenile and criminal justice system, and reintegrating them into the community. (U.S. Department of Justice, *Standards and Goals for Juvenile Justice*, 1974:3)

The media continually focus on crimes committed by U.S. youths, especially those crimes of a violent and sensational nature such as drive-by shootings, school shootings, and gang activities. Today, youths commit delinquent acts ranging from vandalism and breaking and entering to vicious assaults; they even record them on their cell phones or digital cameras, sometimes placing them on YouTube or other Internet outlets.

It is not surprising that the national problem of juvenile delinquency receives constant attention from the media, law enforcement personnel, criminologists, and other scholars in the social and behavioral sciences. Without minimizing the gravity of youthful crime, it should be pointed out that much of what we read or hear on the topic in the news media is selective reporting of those aspects of juvenile delinquency that capture public attention. Obviously, headline or feature stories of juvenile gang wars raging in the streets or of a maniacal teenager committing mayhem in a school sell more newspapers than a report that the vast majority of juvenile arrests are for property crimes, vandalism, and juvenile status offenses such as the violation of liquor laws (*FBI*, 2008). Equally lacking in sensationalism are the data-based findings that only 7 to 10 percent of delinquents are chronic and violent offenders, and this hard-core group commits up to 63 percent of all serious and violent juvenile crime (Snyder and Sickmund, 2006).

In order to more fully comprehend the magnitude of juvenile delinquency in the United States, we review the methods by which information on crime is acquired, various kinds and incidence of criminal activity, current trends, and characteristics of offenders as indicated by available official and unofficial statistics.

JUVENILE DELINQUENCY DATA

Statistical data and quantitative information are collected in order to provide fresh insights into juvenile delinquency in the United States. If this social problem is to be more fully understood, prevented, or controlled, accurate up-to-date information must be available to answer such questions as: How many juvenile offenses and arrests occur each year? What kinds of juvenile misbehavior are most common from year to year? What trends can be extrapolated from the past and the present, and projected for the future? Is there a "typical" juvenile delinquent? If so, what are his or her social, economic, and demographic characteristics?

Validity and Reliability

The methods and procedures used to collect and analyze data determine their accuracy and, in turn, the usefulness of the findings. For example, it is impossible to identify all the children and youths who have violated a juvenile statute or whose behavior could be interpreted by others as delinquent. Even if this prodigious task could somehow be accomplished, administering a questionnaire or conducting an interview in every case would be too expensive and impractical. Consequently, most research efforts to measure the amount and kinds of delinquent behavior utilize information collected by law enforcement agencies about known offenders. Conversely, such data are limited in informing us about the offenses and traits of delinquent youths who are not apprehended.

Other investigators into juvenile delinquency have implemented sampling strategies in which a relatively small number of known delinquents or other subjects are selected and surveyed on the assumption that they are representative of a much larger population. However, if the respondents who comprise the "sample of representative delinquents," for example, are conveniently gathered from Chicago street gangs, the findings would not give an accurate picture of all of the juvenile delinquency in Chicago, much less the rest of the United States. Validity and reliability are two precise concepts that will help us understand these common problems and errors in research methodology.

VALIDITY A measure has **validity** when it *in fact measures what it is supposed to measure.* A finding or conclusion is valid if it accurately reflects factual evidence. As an example, suppose Professor Smith at University A decides to interview a sample of students about their possible participation in unreported or undetected delinquent activities. The professor may be careful to randomly select subjects so that they are representative of all students attending the university (this is a very difficult task since every student must have an equal chance of being included in the sample). However, during the interviews, if the professor directly or indirectly, consciously or unconsciously, indicates expected or desired responses to the questions, there is a chance that the students will tell the professor what they think he wants to hear. Consequently, the findings will be invalid. In addition, if the students feel intimidated by the investigator's attitude, questions, or presence, they may be inclined to understate their involvement in delinquent behavior. So, besides a random sample, other factors in the survey instrument, the subjects, and the lack of anonymity in the situation can affect the validity of the results.

RELIABILITY A measure has **reliability** when *it yields the same results upon repetition of the measuring procedure or replication by other investigators.* For example, suppose that another teacher at a different school, Professor Jones at University B, hears or reads about Professor Smith's research at University A on unreported and undetected delinquency. Professor Jones decides to conduct a similar investigation to see how many students at her institution committed various kinds of unreported and undetected crime. Jones also wants to see if her findings agree or disagree with Smith's.

In order to make a fair comparison of the findings from the two studies, the survey conditions, methodology, and subjects must be as nearly identical as possible. Professor Jones therefore uses the same survey questionnaire used by Professor Smith at University A. She also carefully selects her subjects with the same random sampling procedures and makes every effort to ensure that the sample of students at University B is as similar as possible in background to those surveyed by Smith at University A. It follows that if, after replicating Professor Smith's study, Professor Jones' findings are essentially the same, we may conclude that the survey instrument or measuring procedure is reliable—that is, it can be relied upon to yield similar results when used by different, independent researchers at different places and points in time.

In summary, validity and reliability are related, and both are enhanced if survey questions are structured so that they can be readily understood by the subjects and elicit informative, straightforward answers. Additionally, validity and reliability are reinforced if subjects are systematically and consistently selected in the same way each time data are collected. Comparisons should be made only between two or more samples or of a single sample at different points in time, if variables such as age, race, sex, and social class have been *controlled* or held reasonably constant and similar, from group to group and from time to time.

These general principles of social science research methodology will be useful in our later evaluations of juvenile delinquency data and concomitant findings and conclusions. They are appropriate considerations with regard to truancy, homicide, unreported crimes, or any other statistical dimension of juvenile delinquency.

OFFICIAL SOURCES OF DELINQUENCY INFORMATION

Two agencies of the federal government have long-established programs designed to collect and summarize juvenile crime statistics on a national scale into periodic reports. They are the FBI and the Office of Juvenile Justice and Delinquency Prevention.

FBI Uniform Crime Reports

Since 1930, the FBI has been compiling arrest data on crime and delinquency from a network of city, county, and state law enforcement agencies across the country. The numbers and kinds of reported offenses, the numbers and kinds of offenses resulting in arrest, and characteristics of offenders such as age, sex, race, and place of residence form the basis of the FBI compilations. Each year, the FBI summarizes data into statistical tables and issues a *Uniform Crime Report* for the information and use of law enforcement officers and others concerned with the national crime problem.

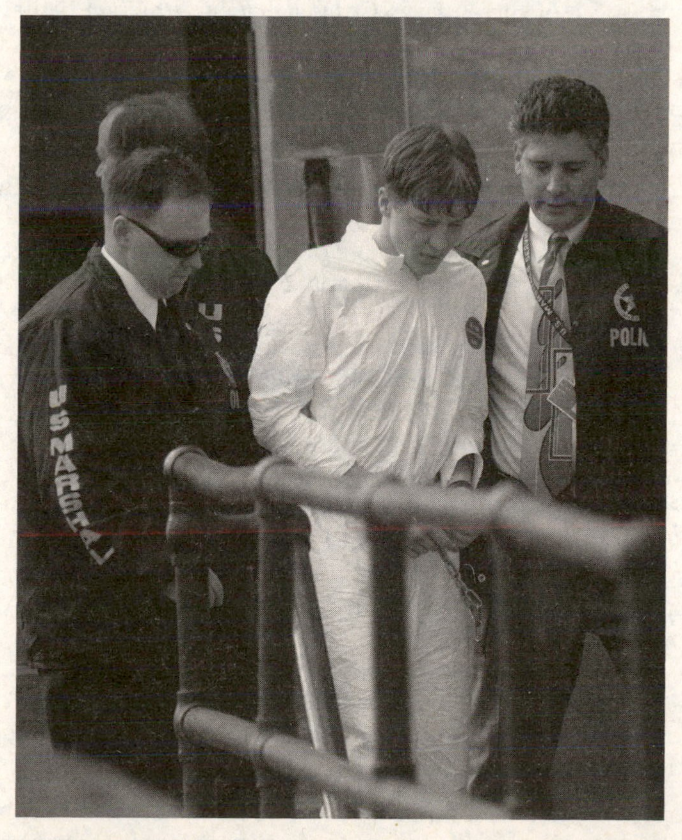

Federal officials rarely become involved in juvenile cases, but the federal government provides the most comprehensive official source of data on delinquency with the *Uniform Crime Reports*. What are some of the strengths of UCR data on delinquency? What are some of the weaknesses?

The FBI Uniform Crime Reporting Program is designed to attain three basic objectives:

1. To measure the extent, fluctuation, distribution, and nature of serious crime in the United States.
2. To measure the total volume of serious crime known to the police.
3. To show the activity and coverage of law enforcement agencies through arrest counts and police employee strength data. (*FBI* 2008:2)

In addition, the division of arrest data into "ages under 18" (and even more specific age categories) and "ages 18 and over" categories is of tremendous help to law enforcement personnel and researchers using FBI *Uniform Crime Report* data to separate juvenile delinquency from adult crime, according to the legal definition of delinquency presented in Chapter 1 (see Table 3.1). The most current FBI Uniform Crime Report data can be found on www.fbi.gov; however, even with the instantaneous availability of information on the Internet, most recent UCR data are usually a minimum of one year behind, despite "preliminary" reports that come out quarterly.

A major strength of the *Uniform Crime Reporting Program* is that *standardized definitions* of the main kinds of crime are utilized by *all law enforcement agencies* reporting from the various states. This is why the annual FBI compilations are called *"Uniform Crime Reports."* The definitions for the first eight UCR categories are as follows:

1. ***Murder and Nonnegligent Manslaughter.*** The willful (nonnegligent) killing of one human being by another.
2. ***Forcible Rape.*** The carnal knowledge of a female forcibly and against her will. Assaults or attempts to commit rape by force or threat of force are also included.
3. ***Robbery.*** The taking or attempting to take anything of value from the care, custody, or control of a person or persons by force or threat of force or violence and/or by putting the victim in fear.
4. ***Aggravated Assault.*** An unlawful attack by a person upon another for the purpose of inflicting severe or aggravated bodily injury.
5. ***Burglary.*** The unlawful entry or attempted entry of a structure to commit a felony or theft. (A felony is any offense punishable by death or imprisonment.)
6. ***Larceny–Theft.*** The unlawful taking, carrying, leading, or riding away of property from the possession or constructive possession of another. Attempted larcenies are included.
7. ***Motor Vehicle Theft.*** The theft or attempted theft of a motor vehicle.
8. ***Arson.*** Any willful or malicious burning or attempt to burn, with or without intent to defraud, a dwelling house, public building, motor vehicle or aircraft, personal property of another.

Because of their seriousness, frequency of occurrence, and likelihood of being reported to the police, *these eight crime categories were chosen as the basis for the Uniform Crime Report Index* and are referred to as **Index Offenses**. The index is useful for charting and analyzing changes in the volume of crime in its various and most serious forms from year to year.

TABLE 3.1 **Total Arrests: Distribution by Age and Crime Categories (Arrests by Age, 2007 [11, 936 agencies; 2007 estimated population 225, 518, 634])**

Offense Charged	Total All Ages	Ages under 15	Ages under 18	Ages 18 and over	Under 10	10–12	13–14	15	16	17
TOTAL	10,698,310	461,937	1,649,977	9,048,333	13,357	93,571	355,009	326,311	405,753	455,976
Total percent distribution[1]	100.0	4.3	15.4	84.6	0.1	0.9	3.3	3.1	3.8	4.3
Murder and nonnegligent manslaughter	10,082	103	1,011	9,071	1	6	96	131	294	483
Forcible rape	17,132	914	2,633	14,499	8	235	671	447	576	696
Robbery	96,720	5,601	26,324	70,396	72	784	4,745	5,353	7,229	8,141
Aggravated assault	327,137	13,662	43,459	283,678	460	3,320	9,882	8,146	10,231	11,420
Burglary	228,846	18,589	61,695	167,151	631	3,939	14,019	12,580	14,498	16,028
Larceny–theft	897,626	71,314	229,837	667,789	1,804	15,542	53,968	45,808	54,513	58,202
Motor vehicle theft	89,022	4,917	22,266	66,756	33	512	4,372	5,181	6,143	6,025
Arson	11,451	3,204	5,427	6,024	349	1,013	1,842	926	720	577
Violent crime[2]	451,071	20,280	73,427	377,644	541	4,345	15,394	14,077	18,330	20,740
Violent crime percent distribution[1]	100.0	4.5	16.3	83.7	0.1	1.0	3.4	3.1	4.1	4.6
Property crime[2]	1,226,945	98,024	319,225	907,720	2,817	21,006	74,201	64,495	75,874	80,832
Property crime percent distribution[1]	100.0	8.0	26.0	74.0	0.2	1.7	6.0	5.3	6.2	66
Other assaults	983,964	70,038	181,378	802,586	2,194	17,638	50,206	35,952	39,029	36,359
Forgery and counterfeiting	78,005	294	2,353	75,652	26	56	212	281	599	1,179
Fraud	185,229	886	5,690	179,539	56	132	698	867	1,464	2,473
Embezzlement	17,015	49	1,288	15,727	6	12	31	58	396	785

(Continued)

TABLE 3.1 (*Continued*)

Offense Charged	Total All Ages	Ages under 15	Ages under 18	Ages 18 and over	Under 10	10–12	13–14	15	16	17
Stolen property; buying, receiving, possessing	92,215	4,136	16,889	75,326	79	667	3,390	3,509	4,366	4,878
Vandalism	221,040	34,342	84,744	136,296	1,668	8,647	24,027	16,723	17,187	16,492
Weapons; carrying, possessing, etc.	142,745	10,577	33,187	109,558	438	2,524	7,615	6,251	7,604	8,755
Prostitution and commercialized vice	59,390	147	1,160	58,230	16	14	117	184	315	514
Sex offenses (except forcible rape and prostitution)	62,756	5,574	11,575	51,181	264	1,525	3,785	2,037	1,983	1,981
Drug abuse violations	1,386,394	21,506	147,382	1,239,012	273	2,207	19,026	25,053	40,562	60,261
Gambling	9,152	226	1,584	7,568	7	12	207	283	428	647
Offenses against the family and children	88,887	1.237	4,206	84,682	112	234	891	804	1,026	1,138
Driving under the influence	1,055,981	398	13,497	1,042,484	196	16	186	537	3,169	9,393
Liquor laws	478,671	9,592	106,537	372,134	115	619	8,856	16,210	30,465	50,270
Drunkenness	451,055	1,400	12,966	438,089	75	82	1,243	2,119	3,118	6,329

[1]Because of rounding, the percentages may not add to 100.0.

[2]Violent crimes are offenses of murder and nonnegligent manslaughter, forcible rape, robbery, and aggravated assault. Property crimes are offenses of burglary, larceny-theft, motor vehicle theft, and arson.

How does breaking down the number of arrests of those under age 18 into more specific age categories help give researchers a more accurate picture of juvenile delinquency?

Source: FBI, 2008. *Crime in the United States, 2007: Uniform Crime Report*. Washington, DC: U.S. Government Printing Office, Table 38.

JUVENILE ARRESTS FOR SPECIFIC OFFENSES The first four Index Offenses—murder, forcible rape, robbery, and aggravated assault—are often grouped together and referred to as "violent crimes." **Violent crimes** are *those that are directed against a person.* The last four Index Offenses—burglary, larceny–theft, motor vehicle theft, and arson—are combined under the heading of "property crimes." **Property crimes** are *nonviolent crimes directed against property.* By looking at data for persons under the age of 18, we can determine the percentage of arrests for violent and nonviolent crimes comprised by juveniles (usually around 15–16 percent and 27–28 percent, respectively). The UCR Program considers a juvenile to be an individual under 18 years of age regardless of state definition. The program does not collect data regarding police contact with a juvenile who has not committed an offense, nor does it collect data on situations in which police take a juvenile into custody for his or her own protection—for example, neglect cases (FBI, 2008).

Table 3.1 is a sample UCR table that indicates the numbers and percentages of arrests for violent crimes attributed to persons under 18 years of age and persons age 18 and over. The FBI arrest records in Table 3.1 show that the probability is much higher that youths will be arrested for property crimes than for violent crimes. Overall national trends in juvenile delinquency as well as the longitudinal trends for specific juvenile offenses are analyzed in a later section of this chapter.

STATUS OFFENSES A large proportion of law-violating behavior by U.S. youths falls into those vague areas collectively referred to as "status offenses." In contrast to crimes—specific and punishable offenses whether committed by adults or juveniles—status offenses are violations that are applicable only to juveniles. They cover such behavior as school truancy, the purchase and consumption of alcoholic beverages, knowingly associating with immoral persons, running away from home, being beyond parental control, and curfew violations. While status offenses vary from place to place and in the consistency and seriousness of law enforcement, they are considered violations of the codified laws of a state or municipality as are traditional crimes such as assault and robbery. The difference is that the conduct described as a status offense is illegal only if the offender happens to have the social and legal status of a "juvenile," defined in most jurisdictions as a person under 17 or 18 years of age. In New York state, a status offender is defined as a child under 16 who does not attend school or "who is incorrigible or ungovernable or habitually disobedient and beyond the lawful control of parents or other lawful authority" (Diegmueller, 1987:15). Critics argue that such legal definitions and codes of conduct are sufficiently variable and vague as to result in great disparity in law enforcement and thereby attach undeserved criminal stigma to many thousands of young people.

Status offenses, as an appendage to criminal law especially designed for wayward youths, appeared very early in United States jurisprudence, reflective of traditional concern for child rearing and character development. Such laws, while often appearing as arbitrary and intrusive, were based on the state's generally accepted role as *parens patriae.* This Latin phrase imputes to the state the ultimate parental authority over citizens who demonstrate a need for protection and direction because of age, infirmity, immaturity, or some other condition that limits personal responsibility. Although the juvenile status is idealistic in origin, the widespread application of juvenile status ordinances prior to 1965 resulted in the incarceration of a tremendous number of children and youths. For example, "Wisconsin researchers found that nearly 41 percent of

Drinking is one of the more common status offenses for teenagers. These boys can legally drive a car at 16, join the military at 18, but cannot legally consume alcohol until 21. How do these different "coming of age" requirements lead to marginality and delinquency?

© Corbis RF

the state's detained youths were status offenders. Studies conducted in Arizona, California, Utah, and Delaware produced similar findings" (Diegmueller, 1987:14).

Since the mid-1960s, through a series of landmark decisions from the United States Supreme Court (detailed in Chapter 14), society has become more sensitive to juveniles' legal rights. Reforms have been instituted that soften the treatment and adjudication of status offenders. There is growing support for the idea that the majority of status offenders should not be arrested and that their cases should be removed from the juvenile justice system. These advocates contend that the juvenile court should be reserved for youths who commit more serious offenses. Nevertheless, the annual *Uniform Crime Reports* reveal that many thousands of youngsters are arrested for status offenses each year (see Table 3.1). The differential treatment sought for the youngsters in these categories is epitomized in a sign on the office wall of Doug Gibson, Executive Director of a Youth Crisis Center in Oklahoma City (Manley, 1979:23): "HUCK FINN WAS A STATUS OFFENDER." To those who recall Mark Twain's story, Huckleberry Finn as a truant and runaway was indeed a status offender. Moreover, as is shown in a later section of this chapter, most of us were probably status offenders at one time or another!

MALE AND FEMALE INVOLVEMENT IN JUVENILE DELINQUENCY Uniform Crime Reports also divide the number of arrests of persons under age 18 into separate categories for male and female offenders. Each year, male juveniles are arrested, on

TABLE 3.2 Juvenile Arrests: Distribution by Sex, Crime Index Offenses, and Other Selected Offense Categories (9,746 Agencies; 2007 Estimated Population: 187,132,870)

Offenses	Number of Arrests under age 18	Percent Male	Percent Female
All Offenses	1,330,889	70	30
Crime Index			
Violent Crimes[1]	56,662	82	18
Property Crimes[2]	266,920	65	35
Other Selected Offense Categories			
Vandalism	71,884	86	14
Prostitution and commercialized vice	728	23	77
Weapons: carrying, possessing, etc.	26,345	91	9
Drug abuse violations	117,686	83	17
Liquor law violations	101,752	64	36
Curfew and loitering law violations	107,482	70	30
Runaways	82,218	40	60

[1] Violent crimes are offenses of murder, forcible rape, robbery, and aggravated assault.
[2] Property crimes are offenses of burglary, larceny–theft, motor vehicle theft, and arson.

What conclusions do you draw about sex, gender, and juvenile delinquency from the data presented in this box?

Source: FBI, 2008. *Crime in the United States, 2007: Uniform Crime Reports*. Washington, DC: U.S. Government Printing Office. Adapted from Table 35.

average, between two and three times more often than females (see Table 3.2). This sex and gender variation in crime rates is consistent in virtually all societies. This male–female disparity continues in those cases that are processed by juvenile courts and among young people who are institutionalized as a consequence of their delinquent behavior. An exception to the pattern of higher arrest percentages for males is the incidence of arrests of females under 18 years of age for prostitution. This finding seems to suggest a form of sexual discrimination in law enforcement since "commercialized vice" requires customers as well as prostitutes. The status offense of running away from home is another exception to the male–female disparity in arrest statistics. Running away continues to be an especially common recourse of young females in situations that appear untenable to them, and the rates and percentages for this offense are relatively stable from one year to the next.

Nationally, between 1998 and 2007, the number of juvenile arrests generally declined for most crime index categories. The *proportional* decrease in arrests of males below age 18 was much larger than the *proportional* decrease in arrests of females in that same age category. These data from the *Uniform Crime Reports* suggest that the proportional differences between male and female delinquency may be narrowing in some major offense categories (Carr and Alfieri, 2006; FBI, 2008).

While longitudinal trends in arrests of young females for these offenses are tenuous, they are interpreted by some observers as indicative of a steady breakdown of the double standard for male–female behavior that long dominated Western cultures (Adler, 1975). The hypothesis that the proportional upsurge in female participation in delinquency is traceable to the equal opportunities implicit in the feminist movement has been challenged by Josefina Figueira-McDonough's study (1984) that found only a weak and partial link between feminist orientation and delinquency in a sample of girls. At the same time, the conclusion by Meda Chesney-Lind and Randall G. Sheldon (1998:239) that "female delinquency has changed little in the past two decades . . .[and] what changes we have seen in girls' misbehavior have been in minor and traditional female offenses" has been refuted by data presented in the *FBI Uniform Crime Reports* since 1991 (see Poe-Yamagata and Butts, 1996).

There is evidence that much of the difference in delinquency rates between the sexes is a product of variations in parental restrictiveness, values, socialization, and cultural opportunities and expectations experienced by young males and females (Hagan, Gillis, and Simpson, 1985).

Girls and boys do not inhabit the same worlds, and they do not have the same choices. This is not to say that girls do not share some circumstances and qualities with boys (notably class and race), but even the manner in which these affect the daily lives of young people is heavily mediated by gender (Chesney-Lind and Shelden, 1998:241–242).

But the role of women in crime is expanding into traditional male areas. Socialization experiences are changing for women. If the trends of female crime continue, female crime will represent an increasing segment of total crime. Therefore, the focus on female crime is indeed vindicated and should not be abandoned (Forsyth and Foster, 1993:139).

The statistical picture of male–female offenses has changed in recent decades. Slowly at first, and then at an accelerated pace, role restrictions have been lifted for many women, and more options have become available. At the same time, female participation in crime and delinquency has increased. Between 1981 and 1997, the arrest rates for female juveniles increased twice as much as the increase in arrest rates for juvenile males. More specifically, female arrest rates for weapons law violations nearly tripled during that same time period, while the male rate nearly doubled. According to Freda Adler (1975:1), "the phenomenon of female criminality is but one wave in this rising tide of female assertiveness." This trend of increasing female involvement in crime and delinquency has persisted into the 21st century.

Statistics compiled in the United States, Italy, France, Germany, and Russia all show a marked rise in violent crimes committed by women in recent decades. Several experts have related this increase in aggressive criminal behavior to the emancipation of many women from their traditional passive and subordinate roles in male-dominated societies. Leon Salzman (1980), clinical professor of psychiatry at the Albert Einstein College of Medicine, reported that there was no biological reason for females to be less aggressive, except that being aggressive had no meaning in a woman's life until she had the same possibilities as a man.

THE RACIAL AND ETHNIC FACTORS IN JUVENILE DELINQUENCY The term **racial group** applies to *those minorities, and corresponding majorities, that are classified according to obvious physical differences* (Schaefer, 2009). Among the obvious attributes used to differentiate and classify racial groups are skin color, facial features, and hair color and texture.

According to the U.S. Bureau of the Census classification scheme, there are at least four races represented in the population of the United States. Whites, although a numerical majority, may be traced to over a score of different national origins in

TABLE 3.3 Juvenile Arrests (Under Age 18): Distribution by Racial Groups and Major Crime Index Categories

	Number	Percent	Number	Percent
	White		Black	
Arrest totals	1,100,427	67.0	505,464	30.8
Index crimes	243,503	62.3	138,113	35.3
Violent crimes[1]	34,810	47.5	37,151	50.7
Property crimes[2]	208,693	65.7	100,962	31.8
Nonindex crimes[3]	856,924	59.0	367,351	25.3
	American Indian or Alaskan Native		Asian or Pacific Islander	
Arrest totals	20,504	1.2	16,135	1.0
Index crimes	4,590	1.2	4,881	1.2
Violent crimes[a]	631	0.9	649	0.9
Property crimes[b]	3,959	1.2	4,232	1.3
Nonindex crimes[c]	15,914	1.1	11,254	1.0

[1] Violent crimes are offenses of murder, forcible rape, robbery, and aggravated assault.
[2] Property crimes are offenses of burglary, larceny–theft, motor vehicle theft, and arson.
[3] Nonindex crimes include all other forms of crime and status offenses listed in the FBI Uniform Crime Reports (see Table 3.1).

Based on data presented in the table, why do so many people view the "typical" juvenile delinquency as member of a racial or ethnic minority?

Source: Based on data derived from FBI, 2008. *Crime in the United States, 2007: Uniform Crime Reports.* Washington, DC: U.S. Government Printing Office, Table 43.

Europe. The black segment of the population traces its origins to a wide spectrum of ancient African nations. United States citizens of Asian or Pacific Islands backgrounds have roots reaching back to China, Japan, Korea, and many other diverse cultures and nationalities. American Indians and Alaskan Natives are descendants of the original and indigenous populations of the geographical areas now included in the United States. Blacks, Asians–Pacific Islanders, and American Indians–Alaskan Natives are numerically smaller groups than whites and are considered to be racial minorities.

The racial background of juvenile delinquents has received considerable attention from law enforcement agencies and criminologists. This focus was intensified by the discovery that racial minorities do not always manifest the same level of delinquency involvement as do members of the dominant racial group. For example, official FBI Crime Reports consistently show that young blacks are disproportionately overrepresented in juvenile arrest statistics (see Table 3.3). For example, while black youths comprise only about 15 percent of the juvenile population, they account for over one-half of the arrests for violent offenses under 18 years of age (FBI, 2008).

Each year, white youths are more likely than black youths to be arrested for property crimes, accounting for almost two-thirds of all property crime arrests of persons under age 18. At the same time, the relative difference in the population sizes of the two racial groups indicates that black youths account for an unusually high proportion of arrests for violent crimes. The great majority of violent assaults by African Americans are committed against members of their own racial group (FBI, 2008).

Each year, the official tabulation of participation in delinquency by young American Indians–Alaskan Natives and Asian–Pacific Islanders is proportionately insignificant. Their population sizes, as well as the number of arrests made among them, are very small compared with the much larger white and black populations and the delinquency involvement of youngsters from those two groups (see Table 3.3).

Minority groups that are designated by **ethnicity** are *differentiated from the dominant group on the basis of cultural rather than physical differences* (Schaefer, 2009). Millions of people, representing every other nation on earth, have immigrated to the United States. Over time, as they learned and accepted the language, norms, and beliefs of the dominant culture, most of these new citizens and their descendants were assimilated and "Americanized." However, some groups have retained a residual of pride in their "old country" heritage, reflected in ethnic values, traditions, and practices that have been perpetuated to distinguish particular subcultures within the United States.

As in their studies of racial backgrounds, criminologists have found that official statistics on juvenile delinquency also vary with ethnicity. Of special importance in this regard is the large ethnic minority classified by government agencies as Hispanic or Latino, which includes anyone of Spanish, Mexican, Puerto Rican, Cuban, or other Latin American background in the United States. The Hispanic segment of the population totaled 25 million in the 2000 census and is growing five times faster than the non-Hispanic population. About 36 percent of the Hispanic population in the United States is under 18 years of age, compared with 25 percent of the non-Hispanic population. Official data indicate that Hispanic young people also account for a disproportionately larger share of juvenile arrests (FBI, 2008).

You are cautioned to avoid racial and ethnic stereotypes of criminal involvement based on statistical summaries. Although the arrest rates for African Americans and Hispanics are higher than those of other groups, as we will see later in this chapter, these findings are moderated, by self-report studies which suggest that the discrepancy between white and black involvement in juvenile crime is not as pronounced as indicated by arrest statistics. Some of the racial differences in official arrest data may be traced to differential treatment accorded the races by law enforcement and the juvenile justice system.

The most plausible explanations point to social forces that negatively impact upon many members of these minority groups which tend to generate delinquent behaviors. Parallel findings from other sources concur that the rates of delinquency for Chinese Americans, Japanese Americans, and Jews, for example, are lower than the rates for the rest of the population.

PLACE OF RESIDENCE AND ARREST STATISTICS For as long as arrest statistics have been compiled in the United States, arrests have been highest in the large cities, moderate in small cities, and lowest in rural areas. This numerical pattern partially reflects the fact that a larger part of the population has lived in urban areas for well over a century.

While the number of offenses cleared by arrest still reflects a heavier urban concentration, the gap in arrest rates between cities, suburban communities, and rural areas has been narrowing. Numerous studies suggest that this changing geographical pattern of arrests reflects the centrifugal expansion of urban population and concomitant social problems into the smaller communities ringing the central cities

(Hurley, 1994; Weeks, 2008). The tendency toward the equalization of arrest rates between large cities and the suburbs also may indicate a greater sensitivity of law enforcement agencies and the public to the incidence of crime and delinquency in middle-class, suburban districts.

Urban and suburban youngsters are very similar in the kinds of crimes for which they are arrested, with each group closely paralleling on Index offenses. In contrast, rural youths are more likely to be involved in less-serious crimes and status offenses than their urban and suburban counterparts. Several sociological theories of urban delinquency are presented in Chapters 5 and 12.

Juvenile Court Statistics

The National Juvenile Court Statistical Reporting Program was initiated in 1929 by the Children's Bureau, a division of the United States Department of Labor, which began issuing annual reports on cases of children processed through a sample of juvenile courts. These reports included juveniles who had violated state laws or municipal ordinances, as well as children who were dependent or neglected and who required special proceedings to determine custody or adoption, permission for medical treatment, and other miscellaneous conditions. In short, the Juvenile Court Statistical Reporting Program furnished an index of the general nature and extent of the kinds of problems brought before the juvenile courts. For our purposes, we will consider just those juvenile court proceedings that focus on delinquent behavior. In 1975, the Juvenile Court Statistical Reporting System was transferred to the National Center for Juvenile Justice and Delinquency Prevention in the United States Department of Justice. The practice of publishing periodic summary reports has continued.

From its inception, the Juvenile Court Statistical Reporting Program has had a two- to four-year time lag between the collection of data and the actual publication and presentation to the public of annual reports. Even with the creation of their Web site (www.ojjdp.ncjrs.org), the time lag has not improved significantly, with the most recent juvenile court statistics often being three or four years old. For the most recent available juvenile court statistics, go to http://www.ojjdp.ncjrs.gov/ojstatbb/njcda/. The snail's-pace compilation and publication of such vital data is a considerable obstacle to analysts and authors.

Methodology

Cases of young people accused of law-violating behavior can be referred to juvenile court intake by law enforcement agencies, social agencies, schools, parents, probation officers, and victims. However, law enforcement officers are the primary source of referral, accounting for three out of every four delinquency cases petitioned to juvenile courts.

Juvenile courts operate a two-track system for processing delinquency cases. Which track is selected for a given case depends upon the seriousness of the offense, the number of previous contacts the youth has had with the police, quality of evidence, the subjective opinion of screening personnel, and other variables. In general, the choice is between informal or formal disposition.

In an informally handled (or nonpetitioned) case, court intake personnel make a decision to divert the matter away from the court system, thus operationalizing a less punitive approach. In most nonpetitioned cases, the youth is released, often with a warning. He or she may be referred to another agency for counseling, voluntary community service, or a restitution program to compensate victims.

More serious delinquency cases are assigned to the formal track that begins with the filing of a petition, affidavit, or other legal instrument used to initiate court action. These petitioned cases are scheduled on the official juvenile court calendar for adjudication by a judge. In a formal hearing, if a judgment of delinquent is reached, the court is asked to assume jurisdiction over the youth. Final court disposition may involve a fine, restitution, probation, institutionalization, or some combination of these sanctions.

Traditionally, national estimates of juvenile court activity have been based on data encompassing both petitioned (formal) and nonpetitioned (informal) cases. In recent years, however, the responsibility for juvenile court intake screening has become more diversified. In some jurisdictions, city and county government agencies other than the juvenile courts provide screening and diversion services that formerly were an exclusive function of the juvenile courts. Consequently, the multiple definitions and conceptualizations of delinquency at the screening level—impacting especially on those cases selected for nonpetitioned, informal treatment—eroded confidence in the estimates of the number and characteristics of juvenile offenders processed through the juvenile justice system. Moreover, questions were raised regarding the legitimacy of including nonpetitioned cases diverted away from the juvenile courts—often by other agencies—in annual summaries of juvenile court activities. Consequently, beginning in 1985, national summaries and projections of juvenile court activities have been based only on petitioned or formally adjudicated cases of delinquency and status offenses (Snyder, et al., 1989).

The National Juvenile Court Archive, *Juvenile Court Statistics Databook*, and *Easy Access to Juvenile Court Statistics: 1985–2004* provide detailed portraits of the approximately 1.6 million annual juvenile cases, including the offenses involved, sources of referral, demographic characteristics of offenders, detention practices, and case dispositions. All of these sources, and more, can be accessed on the Internet by typing their titles into any major search engine.

Although annual compilations of juvenile court data were originally intended to measure the workloads of the nation's juvenile courts, the expanded and refined methodology and nationwide network of participating juvenile courts also has provided another overview of the magnitude and more serious dimensions of juvenile crime in the United States.

Findings

Annually, courts with juvenile jurisdiction formally process approximately 1.5 million cases of juvenile delinquency. Delinquency cases encompass juveniles charged with the eight Index Offenses against persons and property, as well as drug law violations, and public order offenses, such as disorderly conduct and public drunkenness. Many status offenses such as running away, truancy, ungovernable behavior, and liquor law violations are also included in the total number of cases.

Consistently, the large majority of young people involved with juvenile courts are male, usually with about a three-to-one ratio (see Figure 3.1). When the volume

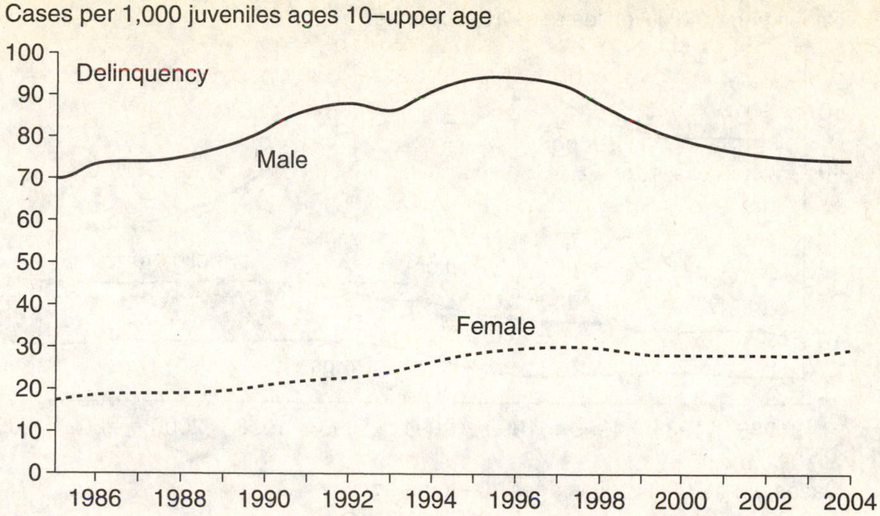

FIGURE 3.1 Sex Characteristics of Delinquency Cases Petitioned to U.S. Juvenile Courts. Although the delinquency case rate is much higher for males than females, the female rate increased more than the male rate between 1985 and 2004.

How do you explain the consistent disparity in the proportion of males compared with females petitioned to Juvenile Courts each year?

Source: Stahl, A., Puzzanchera, C., Livsey, S., Sladky, A., Finnegan, T. A., Tierney, N, and Snyder, H. N. 2007. *Juvenile Court Statistics 2003–2004.* Pittsburgh: National Center for Juvenile Justice, p. 14.

of delinquency offenses are controlled for type of crime, it is found that an almost identical percentage of males are responsible for crimes against persons, property crimes, and public order offenses. Yet, as previously discussed, each year the number of delinquency cases involving females increases at a higher rate than those involving males (see Figure 3.2).

Status offense cases processed by juvenile courts fall into a very different pattern of male–female participation. Females are adjudicated for a little over 40 percent of all status offense cases. When status offense cases are categorized by specific types, females account for approximately 45 percent of cases involving truancy and ungovernable behavior petitioned to juvenile courts and approximately 60 percent of runaway cases.

White youths are the subjects of adjudication in approximately two-thirds (66 percent) of all delinquency cases (see Figure 3.3). When the racial background of delinquency case offenders is tabulated for specific crime categories, white youths are petitioned to juvenile court for 59 to 70 percent of crimes against persons, property crimes, drug violations, and public order offenses. Although whites represent nearly two-thirds of all cases disposed of by juvenile courts in the United States, the number of nonwhites brought before juvenile courts is much larger than their proportional share of the national population (see Figure 3.3).

The preponderance of white involvement over nonwhite involvement in juvenile court proceedings is even more pronounced in the adjudication of status offenders. According to *Juvenile Court Statistics*, white youngsters account for 70–75 percent

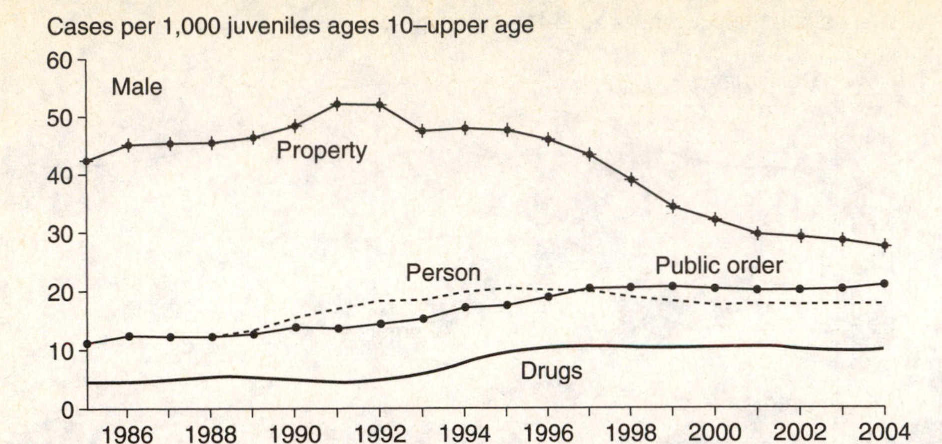

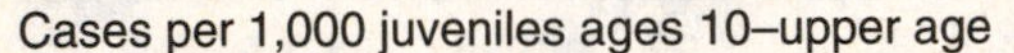

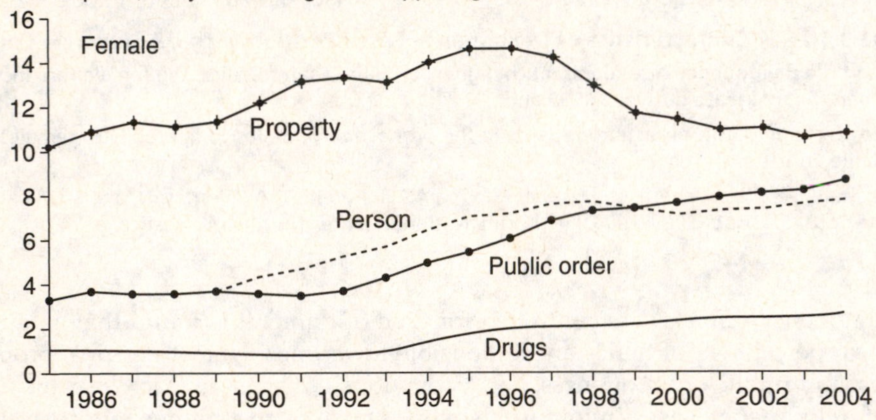

FIGURE 3.2 Sex Characteristics of Cases Petitioned to Juvenile Courts by Type of Crime. Do you see any interesting trends or patterns for males or females that indicate changes in cases petitioned to court?

Source: Stahl, A., Puzzanchera, C., Livsey, S., Sladky, A., Finnegan, T. A., Tierney, N, and Snyder, H. N. 2007. *Juvenile Court Statistics 2003–2004*. Pittsburgh: National Center for Juvenile Justice, p. 14.

of all runaway, truancy, and ungovernable behavior cases processed through the courts.

Occasionally, a delinquency case is transferred to criminal court if the offense is especially serious and the offender is deemed to have adult responsibility (see Chapter 14). The number of such delinquency cases transferred to criminal court jurisdiction has increased dramatically since the 1980s, but juvenile cases transferred to criminal courts still only represent just 1 percent of all petitioned delinquency cases (Stahl, et al., 2007).

The findings reported here regarding the number and categorization of delinquency and status offenders processed through U.S. juvenile courts are in general harmony with findings based on arrest statistics in the FBI *Uniform Crime Report* for the corresponding years.

Racial profile of delinquency cases:

Race	1985	2004
White	73%	66%
Black	25	31
Amer. Indian	1	2
Asian/NHPI	1	1
Total	100%	100%

Racial profile of delinquency cases by offense:

Race	Person	Property	Drugs	Public order
2004				
White	59%	68%	75%	66%
Black	39	28	22	32
Amer. Indian	1	2	2	1
Asian/NHPI	1	2	1	1
Total	100%	100%	100%	100%
1985				
White	59%	75%	79%	77%
Black	39	23	19	21
Amer. Indian	1	1	1	1
Asian/NHPI	1	1	1	1
Total	100%	100%	100%	100%

Between 1997 and 2004, delinquency case rates declined for youth of all racial groups: 20% for American Indians,17% for whites, 16% for blacks, and 2% for Asians/NHPI

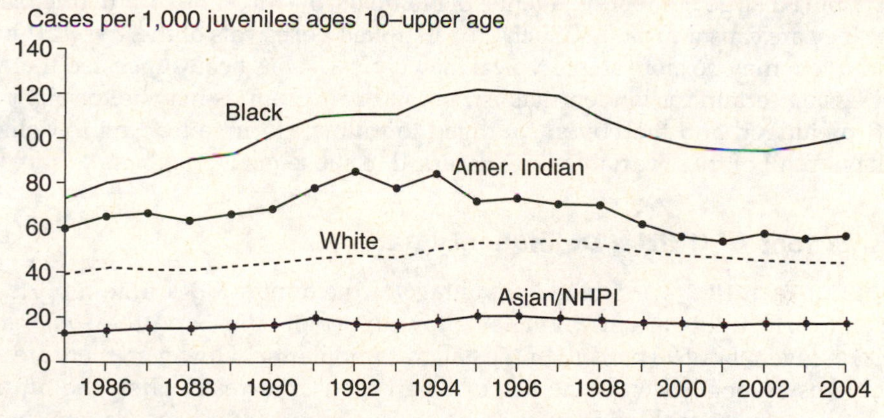

FIGURE 3.3 Racial/Ethnic Characteristics of Cases Petitioned to U.S. Juvenile Courts. Between 1997 and 2004, delinquency case rates declined for youth of all racial groups: 20% for American Indians, 17% for whites, 16% for blacks, and 2% for Asians/NHPI.

What significant trends/patterns can you discuss in cases petitioned to Juvenile Courts related to race and ethnicity?

Source: Stahl, A., Puzzanchera, C., Livsey, S., Sladky, A., Finnegan, T. A., Tierney, N, and Snyder, H. N. 2007. *Juvenile Court Statistics 2003–2004.* Pittsburgh: National Center for Juvenile Justice, pp.19–20.

THE COMPOSITE DELINQUENT PROFILE: TYPICAL OR STEREOTYPICAL?

By combining the findings and conclusions based on the two national official sources of juvenile delinquency data, it is possible to construct a composite picture of the "typical" delinquent. According to annual arrest statistics compiled by the FBI and the records of delinquency and status offense cases petitioned to juvenile courts, this composite juvenile delinquent is disproportionately male, between 15 and 18 years of age, and although most likely to be white, has a disproportionate likelihood of being a member of a racial or ethnic minority. The delinquent is also likely to have a prior record of both status and criminal offenses. Juvenile offenders reflect a higher incidence of unstable home life because of parental separation, divorce, desertion, or death. They are also often characterized by chronic poverty, little motivation or success in school, and few occupational opportunities. The probability is statistically high that officially defined juvenile delinquents reside in urban, lower-class, slum neighborhoods. A strong link also appears between the violent behavior of some juveniles and their having been exposed to extreme abuse and violence within their own families. Consequently, these are the youths that are most likely to be labeled "at risk" (Capuzzi and Gross, 2007).

Such composite summaries—based on statistical probabilities and averages of arrested and/or adjudicated youths—portray an oversimplified and distorted image of juvenile delinquents and the delinquency problem. The next section demonstrates that the generalizations that comprise the "composite" or "typical" delinquent are based on data that have several serious deficiencies. A vast number of delinquents do not fit the statistical model. In addition, several studies have sparked vigorous debate over the so-called correlates of delinquency. While gender, social class, race/ethnicity, and the quality of family life remain statistically significant in describing a large number of juvenile delinquents, one must be careful not to assume that they are causal variables. Such broad-stroked portrayals of the "typical" juvenile delinquent may be more stereotypical than typical. It has been suggested that youths possessing certain easily identifiable traits and backgrounds may be socially profiled and prejudged and thereby encouraged to follow a course leading to delinquent behavior. All of these variables are discussed in subsequent chapters.

Limitations of Official Delinquency Data

ARREST STATISTICS A decided advantage of the annual FBI crime reports is that juvenile arrest data are now available for almost all cities, and the *Uniform Crime Reports* cover about 96 percent of the nation's population. However, there are several problems associated with the use of data based on arrests. First, the number of arrests is a questionable index of crime and delinquency because law enforcement motives, techniques, and success vary from time to time and from place to place. For example, a low arrest rate may indicate little criminal or delinquent activity in a particular community. It also can mean that the police force is inadequate, inactive, or ineffective in that area. Conversely, a high arrest rate may mean that there is a high level of criminal and delinquent activity in a particular city. It can also mean that the police are making arrests on slight pretext or pursuing a highly publicized "war on crime and delinquency" for political purposes, or it could simply reflect the fact that the more police on the streets, the more arrests that will take place.

Researchers also note that conclusions based upon official statistics should be tempered by the observation that law enforcement may be more rigorous in lower-class neighborhoods inhabited largely by racial and ethnic minorities (Siegel, 2009). Smith and Visher (1981) examined variations in police arrest practices. They found that the decision to take a suspect into custody is influenced by such extralegal factors as the dispositional preferences of victims, the race and demeanor of the suspect, and the presence of bystanders. "Specifically, members of socially disadvantaged groups such as blacks and Hispanic youths are more likely to be taken into custody independent of the seriousness of their behavior" (Smith and Visher, 1981:167). The point is that while the FBI has attempted to standardize definitions of various crimes for law enforcement personnel and agencies participating in the *Uniform Crime Reporting Program,* no method has yet been devised to standardize the subjective decision-making processes involved in making arrests that can statistically inflate or deflate the participation of some groups in crime and delinquency (Gaines and Kappeler, 2008).

A second fundamental problem with *UCR* arrest statistics is that they tell us nothing about juvenile crime that is undetected, unsolved, or unreported. According to popular belief, the police, astute television detectives, and federal marshals "always get their man." On the contrary, there is overwhelming evidence that the number of arrests and court referrals reveals only the visible tip of the crime/delinquency iceberg.

THE DARK FIGURE OF CRIME AND DELINQUENCY *Many violent and even more property crimes go unreported.* These incidents are referred to as the **dark figure of crime and delinquency**. Some victims fail to report assaults and thefts because they feel that these are "private matters" or that the police can or will do nothing about them. Juveniles often get into fights or scuffles that could result in arrest but are never brought to public attention. How much teenage shoplifting goes unreported? Probably most of the status offenses and less serious instances of juvenile delinquency never become a matter of public record or concern. Many thousands of juveniles are confronted daily by parents, teachers, neighbors, and law enforcement officers who administer informal warnings, censures, punishments, or other controls over nonconforming youthful behavior. Such informal procedures are especially characteristic of small towns and rural areas, as illustrated by the youthful Halloween disturbance described at the end of Chapter 2.

JUVENILE COURT STATISTICS One of the more serious and chronic problems encountered with annual compilations of juvenile court data is the lack of representation from several states. Each year, either some states fail to submit reports or irregularities and errors in recording the characteristics and dispositions of cases processed through their juvenile courts make their data partially unacceptable. Although the procedures used to generate national estimates of court activity control for the size of a community, the volume of cases referred to reporting courts, the age, race, and offense characteristics of those cases and other factors, no procedure can completely overcome the fundamental threats to validity caused by the absence of a random sample in which every case has an equal chance of being included in the data. According to the National Crime Prevention Council (2007), the most comprehensive juvenile court statistics come from only about 2,000 of the more than 3,000 juvenile courts in the United States.

A second factor affecting the validity and reliability of juvenile court statistics is the apparently insurmountable problem of variation in definitions and coding categories for criminal offenses among data suppliers. These inconsistencies in reporting procedures generate a difficult heterogeneity and overlapping in national data.

How do juvenile court statistics contribute to our understanding of the extent of delinquency? Why do these statistics not give us the full picture?

© Imageworks

A third dilemma confounding the use of juvenile court statistics centers on the estimating procedures used by the National Center for Juvenile Justice in projecting from the sample of reporting courts, the total court activity, and populations served in given areas. Periodic changes in boundary lines, population size, and composition of many juvenile court jurisdictions make longitudinal comparisons of court activity tentative and often conjectural.

Over half a century of recording and reporting of juvenile court case dispositions passed before steps were taken to correct or reduce the effects of those basic methodological flaws. Consequently, a number of years of consistent data gathering and analysis will be needed before the National Juvenile Court Reporting System Program can achieve a high degree of longitudinal and comparative credibility, beyond recent years. Thus, while official surveys of juvenile court proceedings are helpful in measuring court caseloads at a given time, the incomplete and estimated nature of the data invalidate their use for making comparisons between years and between some states and communities.

The fourth limitation of juvenile court statistics is that every new referral of a juvenile to a court is regarded as a case. Therefore, a youth referred to a court three times during the course of a year is counted as three cases. While this procedure is appropriate for measuring caseloads, it contributes to inflation of the data if used to measure the number of juvenile delinquents in a given area. On the other hand, many youths are petitioned to a juvenile court as a single case—but having committed multiple offenses. The inclusion of such cases tends to deflate the reported number of juvenile offenses in each court jurisdiction.

UNOFFICIAL SOURCES OF DELINQUENCY INFORMATION

Self-Report Studies

Some of the limitations of the FBI *Uniform Crime Reports* and the *Juvenile Court Statistics* as indices of the scope and nature of the national delinquency problem, especially the dark figure of delinquency, are overcome by self-report studies. Rather than rely on official reports of arrests and court dispositions, many researchers draw samples of various populations and directly inquire through survey questionnaires or interviews about their respondents' previous delinquent behavior. This approach, aimed at adolescents and young adults not identified by law enforcement agencies as juvenile offenders, is designed to reveal and measure undetected and unreported instances of juvenile delinquency.

Although over a decade old, the most comprehensive and useful study of this type to date is the National Longitudinal Survey of Youth 1997 (NLSY97).

> The first wave of NLSY97 interviewed a nationally representative sample of nearly 9,000 youth who were between the ages of 12 and 16 at the end of 1996. The interviews were conducted in 1997 and early 1998. The survey asked youth to report whether they had engaged in a variety of delinquent or other behaviors that may lead to future delinquency. (Puzzanchera, 2000b:1)

Findings from the NLSY97 were astonishing. For example, one in seven 12-year-olds had engaged in assaultive behaviors, and one in four had purposely destroyed property.

Self-report studies show that delinquent behavior is far more common than is indicated by official data. Findings from repeated self-report studies can be generalized to apply to the entire population:

> Evidence indicates that over 90% of all Americans have committed some crime for which they could be incarcerated. The observation does not deny that crime may be more concentrated in some groups, but only that it is unlikely to be absent in others. (Bohm, 1986:197)

Self-report surveys can be expensive and time-consuming, and the absence of an ongoing unbiased national sample presents a virtually insurmountable methodological problem. In spite of these limitations, such studies support the contention that official statistics fail to completely measure the volume of delinquency and the incidence of many specific offenses.

Table 3.4 summarizes data from two self-report surveys, independently administered by the authors to over 600 undergraduate students attending two state universities in 2006. A majority of the subjects were white, and they were almost equally divided between males and females. Because they were not randomly selected, no assumption can be made that these students represent the total population of youth at risk of committing delinquent behavior or even the overall student population at their schools. Nevertheless, even within these limitations, some remarkable findings emerged.

TABLE 3.4 Self-Reported Delinquent Behavior by Students at Two U.S. Universities

Type of Offense	University A $N = 305$		University B $N = 320$	
While Under Age 18, Did You Ever:	YES (%)	NO (%)	YES (%)	NO (%)
Get arrested?	4.6	95.4	4.1	95.9
Break into a place?	12.1	87.9	14.4	85.6
Shoplift?	37.7	62.3	36.6	63.4
Steal something worth less than $100 (do not include shoplifting)?	5.9	94.1	4.1	95.9
Steal something worth more than $100?	2.9	97.1	2.2	97.8
Beat up or hurt someone on purpose?	33.1	66.9	29.1	70.9
Get into fist fights or brawls (don't include what you counted in item 6)?	31.8	68.2	32.8	67.2
Ruin, break, or damage someone else's property on purpose?	28.8	71.2	30.0	70.0
Take a car without owner's permission?	12.7	87.3	16.3	83.7
Have sexual intercourse?	78.6	21.4	80.1	19.9
Violate curfew?	80.9	19.1	87.8	12.2
Skip school without parents' knowledge?	71.4	28.6	70.0	30.0
Defy parents (do not include skipping school and curfew violations)?	68.5	31.5	60.1	39.9
Purchase and/or consume alcoholic beverages *or* illegal drugs?	84.2	15.8	89.7	10.3

Source: Bynum. J. E., and Thompson, W. Unpublished data from self-report surveys in two U.S. universities, 2008.

Take this self-report survey. Are you part of the "Dark Figure" of crime and delinquency?

BOX 3.1

CONCEPT APPLICATION: "Undetected and Unreported Delinquency: The Missing Statistics"

The following experience was related in a paper submitted to one of the authors by a female student enrolled in a Juvenile Delinquency course. I was a juvenile delinquent. Juvenile delinquency to me is like a disease. It grows inside of you and becomes an obsession. It takes over everything you do. I can write about my experience now with some objectivity because it is over. But I still feel pangs of guilt and regret for some of the things I have done and tried to do.

It does not seem likely that a delinquent could come from a respectable, conservative, upper middle class family with every kind of advantage available to an adolescent. But it can happen and happen very easily, even to a girl like me from that kind of background.

I was a victim of the busing system in my state. Not that the idea of desegregation and busing is totally bad, but in many cases it can cause more harm than good—especially with younger kids who must be separated from their familiar neighborhoods and other family members that might restrain them from getting in trouble. I was forced to catch a bus at seven o'clock every morning to travel to a high school twelve miles away from my home while my older brothers attended a high school less than a mile away.

My delinquent phase started when I was in the eighth grade. First I was pressured by my peers to try smoking cigarettes. I haven't kicked that habit yet. Next came the pot smoking. "Oh, I'll try it just this once," I could hear myself saying. Some harder drugs came next. Speed, quaaludes, reds, yellow jackets, and black mollies were names I heard and used regularly. Soon I was up to a $50 to $100 weekly drug habit. All this by the time I was a sophomore in high school. And nobody knew, except for my few so-called connections. Certainly not my parents who thought that I was a perfectly well-adjusted high school student. Both of them worked and they placed top priority on their careers and material success. They assumed that if they supplied a comfortable home, nice clothes, and a healthy allowance, I had everything I needed—especially since I didn't complain about anything or tell them about my "private" life. Somewhere in the back of my mind, I was confident that I could get out of the new lifestyle I was following before I developed any serious habits.

My grades began to suffer, especially when my friends and I began to skip school regularly. And I soon learned how to do a reasonable forgery of my mother's name on notes excusing my absences from school for "illness" or other lies. A large group of us regularly took off from school together and hung around in shopping malls, video arcades, and alleys.

The vandalism, things we did for fun, came later. I was never really involved, but always around. But one too many times, I was there and we got caught, just for smashing some windows for kicks. One trip to the "pokey" was enough for me. No report to our parents was made, thank God. I was literally "scared straight."

Of course, there were always unusual happenings at school. For instance, I can remember a shooting in the cafeteria. One guy just pulled a gun on another and shot him in the hand. Many fights occurred. I was even subjected to one once. I was just banged up a bit. And to think it was all over a lousy cigarette. I lost. I didn't have a menthol one. After that, I carried a knife. And, in a desperate moment, I could or might have been forced to use that knife.

Needless to say, there was always the talk of prostitution and promiscuity. Talk of the "tricks" the night before always fascinated and horrified me at the same time. Luckily, I never contacted that realm of delinquency.

Not all of my experiences in high school were bad. Some teachers really cared. I grew out of my juvenile delinquency phase. In a way I'm glad of what I experienced but I wouldn't want anyone else to go through it. I learned some important lessons. I learned the value of constructiveness, and I will do something good in my life. I was a lucky delinquent. I'm no longer involved in drugs of any kind. Now my education is everything. Plus the fact, that I grew up. Now I'm aged nineteen going on thirty-five, a decent, conservative, well-adjusted, upper middle class college student.

As a review of this chapter, what characteristics of the young woman in this account are contrary to those derived from official arrest statistics to typify the "average" juvenile delinquent? Do you agree that this self-reported, delinquent experience is evidence that much delinquent behavior goes undetected, unreported, and does not result in arrest? Did you ever participate in any illegal act prior to your eighteenth birthday that, if detected or reported, could have led to your arrest?

While one-third of the 625 subjects at the two universities had shoplifted and had damaged property and inflicted physical harm to others, and well over three-fourths had purchased and/or consumed alcoholic beverages, and 13 to 16 percent had taken an automobile without the owner's permission, less than 5 percent of the subjects had ever been arrested for any reason while under the age of 18! These figures are close to national arrest statistics. Based on information derived from self-report studies, we can conclude that juvenile delinquency is much more common and widespread than official statistics would lead us to believe. The similarity of findings from University A and University B and with those from other self-report studies confirms a reasonable degree of reliability for this measuring technique.

Research conducted by Maynard Erickson and Lamar Empey (1963) demonstrated how data generated from self-report studies can be combined with official statistics on arrests and court referrals to produce a more complete account of juvenile delinquency. They found that court records revealed which juvenile offenders demonstrated persistent patterns of more serious misbehavior, thus facilitating societal identification of juveniles who may have incorporated the delinquent role more decisively into their lifestyles. At the same time, self-report studies help us to more precisely comprehend the magnitude of delinquency among young people in general.

Critics of self-reports question the honesty of respondents who may falsify their answers to make themselves "look good" by denying that they committed delinquent acts when they actually have done so and the honesty of respondents who may exaggerate their true delinquent acts (Jesness, 1987). Such objections to self-reports are largely overcome by the use of anonymous questionnaires, which tend to frustrate subjects who may view the survey situation and their responses as a status-gaining opportunity. Also, it can be assumed that if respondents falsify information, as many are likely to exaggerate their delinquency as are likely to deny it. Hence, these falsifications will offset each other within a large sample.

Travis Hirschi (1969) countered the suspicion about respondents' dishonesty with data derived from police records and his own self-report study of those same youths. He found a strong similarity between the numbers and kinds of self-reported offenses of incarcerated juvenile delinquents and those listed in their official records. While this finding supports arguments for the validity of both measures, Hirschi (1969:64) contended that police records are *less* valid than self-reports as a measure of delinquency:

> As defined, every delinquent act committed by a person is witnessed by him; he cannot commit delinquent acts without knowing it (otherwise, there is nothing to explain). Obviously, the police do not have such omnipresence. . . . In short, the records of the police are, on a priori grounds, a weaker measure of the *commission* of delinquent acts than presumably honest self-reports.

In addition to aiding researchers in ascertaining the actual dimensions of juvenile delinquency, self-report studies also challenge the widely held view that since African Americans and Hispanics are overrepresented in official statistics, they must have a stronger proclivity toward delinquent behavior. Summarizing several self-report studies, Arnold and Brungardt (1983:152) concluded that "analyses consistently indicate that whites' offenses are so similar in number and type to those of the minority groups that the official data appear to be highly distorted. . . . [The] differences revealed do not approach the magnitude of the differences in official data."

Thus, while we cannot claim the absence of empirical documentation (national arrest and juvenile court statistics) that underclass and minority youths are more likely to be involved in delinquency than their middle-class white counterparts, self-report studies make the argument of the so-called correlates of delinquency more problematic and less conclusive.

Michael Hindelang and his associates (1979) reviewed the research literature on traditional correlates of delinquency and found that studies that use official records and those utilizing self-report surveys typically have measured different types of behaviors; official data tend to reflect more serious offenses, while self-report studies tend to measure much more common and less serious types of behavior. In other words, the notion that official and self-report methods produce discrepant results with respect to sex, race, and social class is largely illusory because the two methodologies tap different domains of behavior. They noted:

> other evidence from victimization surveys, studies of the reliability and validity of self-reports, and studies of biases in criminal justice processing, suggest that both official data and self-reports provide valid indicators of the demographic characteristics of offenders, *within the domain of behavior effectively tapped by each method.* [italics in original] (Hindelang, et al., 1979:995)

Victimization Surveys

Another useful source of juvenile delinquency information is victimization surveys conducted by the United States Department of Justice and a number of private researchers. These studies focus on victims and their recollections of crimes, the circumstances, and the offenders. Some of the variables included are the approximate age, sex, race, and other demographic characteristics of assailants and victims, relationship between victim and offender, types of crime, and the circumstances surrounding the crime.

The most ambitious victimization surveys have been conducted by the Law Enforcement Assistance Administration of the Department of Justice, beginning in 1972. This agency, together with the Census Bureau, operationalized an ongoing National Crime Survey to measure the victimization of persons aged 12 and over, households, and commercial establishments. Twice each year data are obtained through interviews with a representative national sample of about 49,000 households (containing approximately 100,000 individuals over age 12), from which rates of victimization for persons and households are generated. Currently, the National Crime Victimization Survey (NCVS) focuses on the personal crimes of rape, robbery, assault, and larceny, and the household crimes of burglary, larceny, and motor vehicle theft (U.S. Bureau of the Census, Statistical Abstract, 2008). Both of these data sources can be accessed online.

Like self-report studies, victimization surveys have the advantage over arrest and juvenile court statistics in offering an avenue through which to explore and estimate the extent of unreported crimes, especially when victims are allowed to respond anonymously. Law enforcement officers and researchers are convinced that vast numbers of offenses are not brought to the attention of police. For example, forcible rape is grossly underreported. Many rape victims may shrink from the embarrassment of reporting and detailing the experience to the police and in open court. Thus, like self-report studies, victimization surveys are more likely to uncover information about more serious types of unreported crimes. Although there is some variation from city to city in victimization rates, the surveys of both national and city samples have produced findings in agreement with self-report studies; that is, only about half of all crimes are reported to the police (Empey and Erickson, 1966; *Dallas Morning News*, 2003:3A).

The usefulness of such surveys is as an adjunct to arrest statistics in achieving a more complete picture of crime and delinquency.

Victimization studies also have supplied important and frightening facts about the victims of crime. Citing Bureau of Justice statistics, Parade (1987b:15) announced that "it's downright dangerous to be a teenager in this country. . . . teens are more than twice as likely as adults to be the victims of rape, robbery, assault and crimes of violence. In the violent-crime category, for example, more than 60 of every 1,000 teens were victims . . . compared to 27 of every 1,000 adults." There is a predominant pattern of teenagers killing other teenagers who are acquaintances (68 percent) by using a firearm (74 percent) (Finkelhor and Ormrod, 2001:1). At the same time, teenage victims of personal crimes are least likely to report crimes to the police, compared with other age groups (Criminal Victimizations in the United States, 2006, 2008).

A major limitation of victimization data collected by the National Crime Surveys is that the victims are the only source of information. For maximum validity, their perceptions and conclusions regarding such factors as the race and age of offenders should be made just after the crimes have been committed. It is understandable that judgment could be faulty and distorted by reason of the stress associated with the crime. In addition, victims have personal contact with offenders only in such crimes as rape, robbery, assault, and personal larceny, whereas the majority of crimes against persons and property are outside these categories. Thus, while systematically gathered reports from victims help researchers to determine the magnitude and trends of some crimes by incorporating measurements and projections of the unreported dimension, doubts remain about the complete accuracy and specificity of the victims' reports (McDermott and Hindelang, 1987).

A second criticism of victimization surveys centers on the long list of serious crimes that are excluded. For example, murder, kidnapping, forgery, driving under the influence of drugs, and status offenses are seldom included on victim questionnaires. Edward Wells and Joseph Rankin (1995:287) acknowledge that the NCVS is not equally reliable for all types of victims and offenses and that "young persons are less reliably represented in the NCVS due to such factors as sampling frame of the survey, form of the questionnaire, interview, and wording of questions." In spite of these shortcomings, Wells and Rankin provide a strong defense of victimization surveys as a useful supplement to compilations of arrests and other official and unofficial sources of crime data.

THE MAGNITUDE AND TRENDS OF JUVENILE DELINQUENCY

In view of the recognized limitations of the data with which they must work, social scientists, criminologists, law enforcement officers, and others who seek to measure crime and delinquency may be tempted to agree with Mark Twain, who exclaimed, "There are three kinds of lies: lies, damned lies, and statistics" (Wheeler, 1976:7). Nevertheless, the conjunction of official and unofficial data, especially when gathered over a period of years, *does* present a fairly clear pattern of juvenile delinquency. In total, American young people account for a large and often disproportionate share of the national crime problem.

At the same time, the trend of rising juvenile crime in the United States ended during the decade of the 1990s—at least temporarily. Between 1998 and 2007, arrests of youths for violent offenses and property offenses consistently declined over

TABLE 3.5 Longitudinal Comparisons and Trends of Arrests of Persons Under Age 18 For Crime Index Offences

	Number of Persons Under Age 18 Arrested		
Offense Charged	**1998**	**2007**	**Change (%) 1995–2007**
Murder	983	753	–23.4
Forcible rape	2975	2,034	–31.6
Robbery	18,439	19,550	+6.0
Aggravated assault	42,358	33,314	–21.4
Burglary	70,171	48,903	–30.3
Larceny–theft	258,540	175,561	–32.1
Motor vehicle theft	29,882	15,289	–48.8
Arson	5,407	4,391	–18.8
TOTALS			
Violent crimes[1]	64,755	55,651	–14.1
Property crimes[2]	364,000	244,144	–32.9
Crime Index totals	428,755	299,795	–30.1

[1] Violent crimes are offenses of murder, forcible rape, robbery, and aggravated assault.
[2] Property crimes are offenses of burglary, larceny–theft, motor vehicle theft, and arson.

What trends and patterns strike you the most when comparing delinquency data from 1998 to 2007?

Source: Based on data derived from FBI, 2008. *Crime in the United States, 2007 Uniform Crime Report*. Washington, DC: U.S. Government Printing Office. Table 33.

14 percent (see Table 3.5). The most pronounced reductions (over 50 percent each) were in murder, larceny–theft, and motor vehicle theft (FBI, UCR, 2008).

Although criminologists, sociologists, and other authorities in the field have not reached consensus for the significant decline in juvenile arrests, several partial and promising interpretations of the data have been suggested. Scholars have variously credited more vigorous law enforcement, proactive and preventive social programs aimed at youths at risk of becoming delinquent, enhanced economic and occupational opportunities, and smaller proportions of the national population in the delinquency-prone adolescent years. Although each of the above arguments is supported by some evidence, a conclusive causal explanation for the decline in juvenile arrests must await additional data and investigation.

However, a word of caution is in order. Despite more than a 10-year decline in the number of juvenile arrests, it is premature to declare the resolution of this serious social problem. With over 1.5 million persons under age 18 still arrested each year, it is clear that juvenile delinquency remains a challenging phenomenon in the United States.

In addition, short-term, statistical reversals have occurred in the past and often turned out to be temporary anomalies before prevailing demographic, economic, and social factors returned arrest data to the more dominant and longitudinal pattern and direction. Also, the reality of self-report data confirms that recorded delinquent behavior through arrest and juvenile court statistics represents only a small portion of youthful law-breaking and that a vast reservoir of "unofficial" delinquency remains.

ADDENDUM: A BALANCED PERSPECTIVE ON YOUTH

After struggling through a chapter such as this—under an avalanche of crime data on young people—a more balanced and complete portrayal of American youth is appropriate. Deviants and their behavior are more visible and reportable news because the public is titillated by nonconformity. Thus, we need to remind ourselves that even though approximately 1.5 million youths are arrested each year, over 35–40 million other young people between 10 and 17 years of age are *not* arrested each year. The great majority of American youth do not come into serious conflict with the behavioral expectations and law enforcement agencies of society. In fact, there are many instances every day of young people responding in supportive, responsible, even heroic ways, to the highest and noblest values and standards of civilized society. The two brief stories that follow are examples of this generally underreported phenomenon:

> **Teen Saves Child From Creek**
>
> PORTLAND (AP)—A teenager jumped into a frigid creek and saved a 4-year-old boy who was spotted floating face-down. Chris Cottrill, 17 . . . stripped off his outer clothes, plunged into the creek and pulled the boy onto a concrete bank. Cottrill then performed cardiopulmonary resuscitation on the child until paramedics arrived. "I started yelling at him, 'Come on! Stay with me!' " Cottrill [said]. "I hope . . . that his parents know that whatever the outcome, I tried to save him." (*Ashland Daily Tidings*, 2000:B1)
>
> **S.F. Teen Runs Toward Responsibility, Aids Columbine Victim**
>
> DENVER—While he was watching the Columbine High School tragedy unfold from his San Francisco home . . . 15-year-old Rashad Williams decided he had to do something to help [He] did just that, handing shooting victim Lance Kirklin a check for $18,000 . . . Kirklin, 16, was among 22 students who were injured in the rampage. He was shot five times at close range, including once in the face, and nearly bled to death . . . Kirklin's jaw was shattered and he faces at least four more reconstructive surgeries. His medical bills are expected to top one million dollars and he has no health insurance.
>
> [Rashad Williams,] a freshman at San Francisco's Archbishop Riordan High School, who runs the 400- and 800-meter events for his school's track team, sought sponsors in Kirklin's name and entered the 7½-mile Bay to Breakers Race in May. . . .
>
> Williams raised $14,000 in the race. In the weeks that followed, checks worth an additional $4,000 poured in. . . .
>
> Williams' mother, Sheila Burton-Harris, said she was not surprised. "This is nothing new to us. Rashad will give money to a student who doesn't have lunch money; he'll give $5 to a homeless person just after he's gotten it from me." (*San Francisco Examiner*, 1999:A9)

Despite continuing high rates of delinquency and lurid news accounts, it is impossible to be pessimistic about America's youth when we still produce young people like Chris Cottrill and, Rashad Williams!

BOX 3.2

CROSS-CULTURAL FOCUS: Juvenile Delinquency in Russia

Before the 1990–1991 economic and political upheaval in the former Soviet Union, and the new experimentation with democracy, there was little open discussion of crime and delinquency in that communist nation. In response to inquiries from visiting journalists and researchers from abroad, Soviet police and state officials were often defensive and denied that such problems existed in any magnitude in the Soviet Union. Trapped in the uneasy logic of Marxist–Leninist doctrine, these spokesmen had little choice in the matter. According to socialistic ideology, poverty, greed, exploitation, and other social causes of crime are eliminated as society progresses toward a communistic utopia.

It was in this stultifying system that David Shipler found himself in the 1970s. He was the Moscow Bureau Chief for the *New York Times*, and in the best tradition of American news reporters, he was in pursuit of the facts regarding crime and juvenile delinquency in the Soviet Union.

> "Crime statistics are a state secret," I was informed by the Ministry of Internal Affairs after weeks of unsuccessful attempts to get an interview there. News items on violent crime are kept off television. General-circulation newspapers never report crimes when they occur, only selected cases after they have been solved, when some moral point or sociological analysis can be made. . . . The instinct is to protect the society's image, and the rationale is to avoid publicity that could make the violence contagious. (Shipler, 1989:230)

Undaunted, Shipler set out to pierce the shroud of official state dogma and discover the scope and details of crime in the Soviet Union. After many months of conversations and interviews with Russians from all walks of life, and after exhaustive research through law libraries and other specialized publications, Shipler developed a frightening picture of crime as a major and growing social problem in that nation. Much of it involved an epidemic of murders, rapes, beatings, muggings, and burglaries committed by teenagers from 14 to 18 years of age. The reliability of Shipler's findings was supported by an earlier but much briefer account of runaway juvenile crime in Russia by Hedrick Smith (1985:194):

> When I was in Irkutsk, the rector of the university there told me that the most rapidly growing faculty was the law faculty because so many Siberian cities were requesting lawyers. One reason was, it turned out, that police forces wanted law-trained university graduates to help cope with juvenile delinquency.

The causes of the spiraling incidence of serious juvenile crime in the Soviet Union since World War II are strikingly similar to those often cited to explain American social problems since the beginning of the 20th century. Soviet criminologists have pinpointed major demographic and social changes associated with rapid industrialization and urbanization. Millions of vulnerable village folk must adjust to urban life, and as old values and stabilizing relationships become obsolete, divorce rates escalate and family control is weakened. The disorientation and anonymity of the mass society is conducive to nonconformity behavior (Hollander, 1990).

Even high-ranking government officials appeared to be ignorant or unconcerned about the magnitude of juvenile crime in the Soviet Union. Shipler found that even the head of the Central Committee's Department of Education, S. P. Trapeznikov, was unable to get any crime statistics. Prior to the new "openness" introduced by President Gorbachev in 1990, the

(*Continued*)

Soviet Union was organized to discourage negative reporting, even within official ranks. Consequently, there was a national effort to suppress any bad news that might reflect negatively on the state or agencies and officials at lower levels.

> Among those who conceal data to avoid bringing criticism on themselves are school teachers and principals. In Irkutsk, after two boys had raped a girl, the high school's principal and teachers tried to hush up the crime, a teachers' journal reported, dismissing it as a "childish prank" and pleading with the victim and her parents to drop charges. . . . It turned out that principals avoided reporting all crimes so that their schools would not be listed as performing poorly. Local police commanders also suppressed statistics. . . . "If I were to send in to the city militia headquarters the genuine figures about crime in my district," the commander of the 130th was quoted as saying, "I would not last a day in my job. That is what they all do; I am not the only one. Juvenile crime is a scourge in Moscow and in other cities as well." (Shipler, 1989:243–244)

In Moscow, a special task force was organized by concerned city officials and citizens to measure the true magnitude of crime and juvenile delinquency within the city and to probe for possible causes. When the group's work was completed and a report submitted, the findings were clearly unwelcome and summarily dismissed. Trapeznikov, head of the Central Committee's Department of Education, called the picture "exaggerated," rejected any relationship between crime and poverty, and branded the report "antisoviet."

As the individual nations that once comprised the Soviet Union move into the 21st century and intensify their experiment with capitalism, they are caught in the vortex of rapid and often traumatic social change. Reports continue to proliferate that the political collapse of the Soviet Union has been followed by widespread unemployment and family impairment. For example, Candice Hughes (1993) graphically describes the lifestyle of thousands of children and teenagers who are ignored, neglected, and abused by their parents—and roam the streets of Moscow as juvenile offenders. These Russian youths, lost in a tide of social change, are characterized as cynical, hedonistic, and committed to the pursuit of money through any illegal means that might be available. Russian authorities now openly express their concern and hope that revitalized families, schools, and social welfare agencies can soon effectively address their growing juvenile delinquency problem. Russia has created an Office of Juvenile Affairs to deal with the special problems of 14- to 18-year-olds who violate the law (Hartjen, 2008).

How do you think the breakup of the former Soviet Union along with advances in technology and media reporting of crime and delinquency have affected the secrecy that once surrounded juvenile delinquency there?

Sources

Hollander, P. 1990. A converging social problem: Juvenile delinquency in the Soviet Union and the United States. *British Journal of Criminology* 9 (April): 148–166.

Hartjen, C. A. 2008. *Youth, Crime, and Justice: A Global Inquiry*. New Brunswick, NJ: Rutgers University Press.

Hughes, C. 1993. Boys' life on the streets in Moscow. *Fort Worth Star–Telegram*, September 19, 1993: Section AA, p.1.

Shipler, D. K. 1989. *Russia: Broken idols, solemn dreams* (2nd ed.). New York: Time Books (a division of Random House, Inc.).

Smith, H. 1985. *The Russians* (3rd ed.). New York: Time Books (a division of Random House, Inc.).

Summary

This chapter focused on the challenging task of measuring the magnitude of juvenile delinquency in the United States in response to such questions as:

1. Approximately how many people under age 18 are involved in crime/delinquency each year?
2. What kinds of offenses are most common among American young people?
3. How do variables such as gender, race, ethnicity, and place of residence affect the incidence and kinds of juvenile offenses that are committed?
4. What are the trends in juvenile delinquency? Is it increasing or decreasing?

Evolving from these concerns, two national, data-gathering programs were instituted. The FBI collects, summarizes, analyzes, and reports arrest data from a network of city, county, and state law enforcement agencies and compiles this information in its annual Uniform Crime Reports. These FBI reports include the incidence of juvenile arrests for various crimes and tabulate for such variables as age, gender, race, and place of residence. The second official source is the National Center for Juvenile Justice and Delinquency Prevention of the Department of Justice, which collects and summarizes data on case dispositions submitted from juvenile courts across the nation. Annual reports on Juvenile Court Statistics also identify and summarize court dispositions by type of offense and a limited number of demographic variables.

Other sources of systematically collected data on juvenile delinquency include self-report studies and victimization surveys. Self-report studies are usually questionnaires directed at samples of the population, in which subjects are asked about their participation in delinquent and/or criminal activities. The advantage of self-report studies is that they identify and measure some of the vast amount of the "dark figure of crime," undetected and unreported criminal and delinquent behavior. Victimization surveys are designed to accomplish the same objective. However, the subjects are asked to indicate crimes perpetrated against them and their property and, if possible, to describe the offenders by age, sex, and race. The most ambitious victimization survey is conducted on a regular basis and targets a representative sample of housing units in the United States. The U.S. Department of Justice supervises this survey and issues annual reports of findings.

All of these data-gathering programs suffer from serious methodological limitations regarding validity and reliability. For example, arrest statistics are subject to distortion due to variable law enforcement techniques and success in different jurisdictions. Some data are incorrectly tabulated and reported. In addition, arrest data present a picture only of offenders who were apprehended. Juvenile court data have been plagued by nonprobability sampling techniques, reporting irregularities and fluctuating court jurisdictions. Self-report studies and victimization surveys have been criticized for biased samples and inflated or deflated reports that limit generalizations to larger populations.

In spite of these shortcomings, the accumulation and combination of all these data on delinquent behavior over a long period of time present a consistent conclusion that American young people account for a disproportionately large amount of criminal activity. According to official statistics, underclass, minority group males are the most overrepresented groups among juvenile delinquents—a finding that has been moderated by unofficial statistics. While most juvenile delinquency is composed of status offenses and property crimes, there are a large number of violent crimes against persons. Over the past decade, there has been a fairly steady downward trend in the number of juvenile arrests and juvenile court cases in the United States.

Concept Integration: Questions and Topics for Study and Discussion

1. Define each of the first eight crime categories of the *FBI* Uniform Crime Report. Why are they of major significance? Do you know anyone who has committed any of these major offenses? Do you know a victim of any of these crimes? Was the offense reported and the offender arrested?
2. Explain how information on crime and delinquency is collected for the *FBI* Uniform Crime Reports, the National Juvenile Court Statistical Reports, self-report studies, and victimization surveys. What are the advantages and limitations of each of these data-gathering techniques?
3. List and explain each of the variables that comprise the composite profile of the "typical juvenile delinquent." Is this a reliable and valid portrayal of juvenile delinquents in the United States? Explain your answer.
4. Discuss the statistical evidence of delinquent behavior among racial minorities. How can we explain the high rates of juvenile delinquency among such minority groups by looking at their social environments and economic backgrounds?
5. What are the most recent trends in crime and delinquency as reported in this chapter?
6. Discuss the statistical evidence of delinquent behavior by female juveniles. How can we explain the increasing rates of delinquency by young females in recent years?

Part II

CAUSES OF JUVENILE DELINQUENCY

INTRODUCTION: Theory and the Etiology of Juvenile Delinquency

In Part One, we defined juvenile delinquency as "illegal conduct by a juvenile that reflects a persistent delinquent role and results in society regarding the offender as seriously deviant." Even though a large proportion of juvenile delinquency is composed of such relatively trivial status offenses as running away from home, chronic school truancy, and curfew violation, a persistent pattern of youthful involvement in serious crimes against persons and property qualifies juvenile delinquency as a national social problem.

Now, after our discussion in Part One of what is delinquency and who are delinquents, we are ready to investigate the why of juvenile misconduct. In other words, how do we explain seriously deviant and antisocial behavior by young people? The study of **etiology**—*the cause(s) of an event, phenomenon, or behavior*—is a common inquiry and exercise in the scientific community and many academic disciplines. For example, the quest to explain biological variations in certain animal species prompted Charles Darwin to develop the theory of evolution. Similarly, Isaac Newton's observations of falling objects led him to conceptualize the law of gravity and other theoretical principles regarding cause and effect in the physical world. The application of the scientific method of investigation and theory building in the social sciences is somewhat more complicated than in the biological and physical sciences because of the incomparable complexity of human subjects and the ethical considerations involved in subjecting them to fully controlled laboratory test conditions. Nevertheless, within these limitations, sociologists and other students of human behavior are on the same etiological quest to explore, identify, understand, and explain the cause(s) of social phenomena. Serious efforts to establish valid and reliable findings and conclusions involve an objective, systematic approach to observation, data collection, and the testing of hypotheses. Finally, if findings and conclusions warrant, the ultimate result of the research enterprise may be the generation of explanatory theories.

In popular usage, the term *theory* means a "hunch" or a calculated guess that explains why some event occurs or the possible relationship between cause-and-effect variables. To the lay person, a theory often suggests mere speculation, based on unfounded assumptions and little factual data, concerning an event or a form of behavior. For example, in hypothetically reconstructing events leading up to an automobile accident, an onlooker might speculate, "My theory of what happened is that the driver fell asleep and ran off the road."

To the scientist or researcher, the term *theory* means much more than an off-the-cuff guess or estimate. To these scholars, a **theory** is *a tested and established general statement that systematically and objectively relates concepts or variables together to explain events or behavior.* If a theory is valid, it correctly predicts that identical relationships, events, or behaviors will occur in the future if the conditions and circumstances are identical.

A large number of scholars from many disciplines, utilizing many approaches and methodologies, have attempted to develop causal theories explaining why some juveniles become delinquent. There has been considerable variation in the adequacy of these theories as they have been exposed to continual scrutiny and testing. In some cases, theories of delinquency have been modified, expanded, or discarded as inadequate explanations. Other theories have survived relatively intact as useful contributions to delinquency etiology. The chapters comprising Part Two present the more interesting, prominent, and useful theories of deviant behavior in general, and juvenile delinquency in particular.

Chapter 4 begins with an overview of 18th-century philosophical speculations regarding the causal origins of criminal behavior. There follows a more detailed discussion of the 19th-century biological determinism and the "born criminal" suggested by Cesare Lombroso, the 20th-century constitutional typology and the "mesomorphic delinquent" described by William Sheldon, and others who argued that criminal and delinquent behavior can be traced to genetic and physiological factors. The chapter continues with a discussion of more current and methodologically sophisticated efforts to establish causal linkage between biology and juvenile delinquency, as well as some controversial insights offered by sociobiology. We then survey the early and contemporary concepts and contributions of psychiatrists and psychologists in explaining juvenile delinquency. These psychogenic theories and the medical model perceive the delinquent's misbehavior as symptomatic of an underlying neurological or learning disability or some form of emotional or personality maladjustment. Psychoanalysis and projective tests—as techniques for probing the unconscious dimension of the human mind—are also explained.

Chapters 5, 6, and 7 provide an extensive treatment of the major sociological theories of juvenile delinquency, including social strain, cultural transmission, social learning, social control, social labeling, and conflict theories. These sociological explanations share and amplify in various ways the basic premise of those who pursue sociological investigations and theory construction—that delinquency and most other human behaviors emerge as part and product of those human groups, interactions, and relationships that comprise the individual's social context and environment. Each section of these chapters concludes with a synopsis of contributions and criticisms of the various sociological theories of juvenile delinquency.

Chapter 8 covers rational choice, deterrence, and feminist theories and projects theory building into the future. New research investigations have been proposed that may produce significant new contributions to explaining juvenile delinquency.

Chapter 4

Classical, Biological, and Psychogenic Explanations of Juvenile Delinquency

READING OBJECTIVES

Reading this chapter will help you achieve the following objectives:

1. Explain the 19th-century effort of Cesare Lombroso to link biological or physical characteristics with criminal behavior.
2. Compare and contrast the "rational individual responsibility for behavior" of the Classical School of Criminological Thought with the "biological determinism" of the Positive School of Criminology.
3. Describe the 20th-century research of William Sheldon and of Sheldon and Eleanor Glueck who tried to establish a causal relationship between body type and juvenile delinquency.
4. Discuss several areas of investigation that focus on abnormal chromosomal and electroencephalograph patterns, diet, physical appearance, other biological variables, and sociobiology as possible causal backgrounds for some antisocial behavior.
5. Critique the weaknesses and limitations of theories of deviant and delinquent behavior that are based on biological and physiological variables.
6. Explain the psychological concepts of the unconscious and personality as motivating sources of human behavior, including juvenile delinquency.
7. Describe some of the techniques and tools used by psychiatrists and psychologists, such as psychoanalysis and projective tests, to trace symptomatic conduct disorders to deeply hidden mental stress and conflict.
8. Be aware of some major limitations and weaknesses of the psychogenic approaches to identifying and explaining the causes of juvenile delinquency.

INTRODUCTION

In Part One, we examined the questions "What is juvenile delinquency?" and "Who are delinquents?" Our understanding of the issues and answers raised by those initial questions form the foundation for the discussions in Part Two of the theoretical causes of juvenile delinquency. In other words, there was a logical need to define the *What* and the *Who* of juvenile delinquency before we consider the *Why.*

Many explanations of misconduct have been suggested. From the dawn of recorded history, philosophers, theologians, political leaders, and social thinkers have conjectured that deviance and antisocial behavior might be traceable to demons, original sin, or people's insatiable and self-serving lust for power, gratification, and material possessions. The "age of science" offered a plethora of additional explanations—all claiming to be based upon scientific reasoning. Biological and psychogenic theories and the medical model of what causes crime and delinquency emerged from this new scientific approach to explaining human behavior.

THE LINK BETWEEN BIOLOGY AND BEHAVIOR: MYTHS AND FOLKLORE

The notion that there is an intrinsic relationship between human physical traits and behavior is very old. For example, Franz Joseph Gall (1758–1828) speculated that mental faculties and traits of character, such as acquisitiveness, benevolence, destructiveness, spirituality, combativeness, and imitativeness, are manifested in separate portions of the brain. **Phrenology**, as Gall's system was called, *contended that there is a positive relationship between these specific cerebral functions and the formation or shape of the human skull.* Although phrenology has been disproved, the belief was popularized by practitioners claiming to ascertain these mental characteristics and behavioral propensities by measuring the shape, irregularities, and protuberances of the skull.

THE CLASSICAL SCHOOL OF CRIMINOLOGICAL THOUGHT

The first organized inquiry regarding criminal deviance emerged in the 18th century. Charles Montesquieu (1689–1755), Cesare Beccaria (1738–1794), Jeremy Bentham (1748–1832), and other Enlightenment writers propounded a "naturalistic" approach to explaining criminal behavior by contending that the only acceptable explanations for human conduct are to be found in humans themselves, thus launching the Classical School of Criminological Thought. Classical theorists were guided by the assumption that humans are rational, reasoning individuals who weigh and control their actions and destinies. The focus was upon the criminal as totally responsible for personal behavior. Consequently, according to Graeme Newman's *The Punishment Response* (1978), appropriate punishment "to suit the crime" would not only encourage the reformation of offenders, but discourage criminality in the general populace. Punishment was thought to be appropriate under most circumstances and for most offenses because it was assumed that crimes were the result of *free will* based on conscious, reasoned decisions.

While the classical position did not differentiate between children who violated laws and adult offenders, the later Neoclassical School recognized that not all persons are equally rational and responsible for their behavior. Consequently, "judges were allowed some discretion in dealing with the young, the mentally disturbed, and those confronted with unusual circumstances that decreased responsibility" (McCaghy, et al., 2006:9). Nevertheless, the Classical–Neoclassical approach has been criticized for overlooking how society is a major force in shaping human behavior, including criminality. Even if the questionable assumption of equal rationality among humans is valid, social inequality is a pervasive reality. An individual's decision to engage in criminal activity is based on much more than the simple equation and anticipated balance of pleasure minus pain. Levels of poverty, alienation, social status, and numerous other forces and factors also must be taken into account.

THE POSITIVE SCHOOL OF CRIMINOLOGY

The first efforts to apply scientific and systematic research methodology to establish the principle of biological determinism as the fundamental cause of criminal behavior occurred in the late 19th century. Implicit in the deterministic model is that a given thing cannot simply appear out of nothing or nowhere; it is determined or caused by some other thing, event, or phenomenon in the environment. This approach attracted a number of 19th-century researchers and theorists, including some early criminologists, who applied various forms of biological determinism to crime and juvenile delinquency (Albanese, 1993).

Cesare Lombroso (1835–1909), an Italian-army physician often referred to as the "father of criminology," measured the jawbones, skulls, hands, and other physical traits of a group of prisoners and proposed that criminals are biological throwbacks to an earlier, more primitive stage of human development (Ferrero, 1911). The ideas of Lombroso and his followers formed the basis of the **Positive School of Criminology** and constituted a reaction to the earlier Classical School. Whereas Classical School theorists had assumed that humans are rational and endowed with free will, positivists denied the existence of free will and argued that each person is born with an innate propensity toward certain forms of behavior. In other words, just as people inherit specific physical traits, reflective of their genetic background, so, too, the positivists contended, some people are motivated by an inborn tendency toward behavior that may be criminal according to the standards of society.

Lombroso (1911:365) concluded that there is a *born criminal type*, "bestial" in appearance, and characterized by "low cranial capacity; retreating forehead; highly developed frontal sinuses; . . . early closing of the cranial structures; . . . tufted and crispy hair; and large ears . . . [and] relative insensibility to pain." In short, Lombroso identified the *born criminal* as one whose body structure and criminal behavior are dual manifestations of an underlying **atavism**, that is, *a biological throwback to a savage, lower phase of human evolution*. Such persons (*Homo delinquens*), he reasoned, are biological and social misfits in a society of modern people (*Homo sapiens*) whose civilization includes extensive behavioral restrictions.

Cesare Lombroso is often referred to as the "father of criminology." Do his theories contribute to our understanding of delinquency today? If so, in what ways? If not, why?

Lombroso later refined and expanded his original thesis of the born criminal to include other types whose antisocial behavior he traced to biological or physiological traits. For example, the *insane criminal,* may be linked to diseases or abnormalities of the mind. The *criminaloid* was different from the born criminal only in that his predatory conduct was less savage and more occasional. Lombroso described the *criminal by passion* as characterized by a romantic sensitivity and capacity for altruistic motives in the commission of crime—and thus contrasting sharply with the born criminal.

The premises, methodology, and conclusions of Lombroso and the Positive School of Criminology have been subjected to intense scrutiny and criticism by subsequent investigators, who cite the weaknesses of descriptive data, broad generalizations from few cases, and the absence of comparative control groups of nonprisoners (Goring, [1913] 1972). At the same time, Lombroso has been applauded for at least implementing a rudimentary scientific approach to criminology and for acknowledging the impact of sociological causes of crime interacting with inherited traits and tendencies to produce antisocial behavior (Wolfgang, et al., 1972). The Classical and Positive Schools of criminological thought influenced more contemporary theories discussed in Chapter 8.

TWENTIETH-CENTURY CONSTITUTIONAL TYPOLOGIES

Biological explanations of crime and delinquency fascinated many investigators. William Sheldon and associates (1949) equated personality and character with body type and contended that youths with a certain physical appearance inherit enhanced potential for delinquent behavior. According to Sheldon, three distinct body types can be identified and characterized:

1. ***Endomorph.*** Physically characterized as having a rotund, soft, fleshy body. The endomorph tends to be easygoing, gregarious, and self-indulgent in temperament.
2. ***Ectomorph.*** A slender and fragile body, with small features and weak appearance. The ectomorph tends to be a loner, introspective, and emotionally high-strung.
3. ***Mesomorph.*** The body is generally muscular and firm, with a strong frame and resilient constitution. The mesomorph tends to be energetic, impetuous, and insensitive.

Sheldon compared 200 boys referred by social agencies and courts to a center for problem children in Boston with 4,000 college males and found the center's children to be more mesomorphic. He concluded that although mesomorphy does not predestine youths to delinquent behavior, it is the constitutional background most favorable to delinquency, since mesomorphs have the emotional makeup and physical resources to "translate impulse into action" and to become a predatory person (Cohen, 1966:51).

In 1950, Sheldon and Eleanor Glueck, a husband–wife team of researchers, reached similar conclusions. The Gluecks compared 500 white male delinquents with 500 white male nondelinquents and agreed with Sheldon that mesomorphs apparently possess higher delinquency potential than youths having other body types. They stressed that while a mesomorphic body does not make delinquent behavior

Sheldon's body type

Do these body-types tell us anything about potential delinquency today?
(Illustration by Marilyn R. Thompson)

inevitable, the aggressive, muscular youth seems more likely to relieve his tensions and frustrations in ways that society defines as troublesome and delinquent (Glueck and Glueck, 1950).

Broad generalizations from the Sheldon and Gluecks studies cannot be made, since both suffer from serious methodological problems (Clinard and Meier, 2008; Cohen, 1966). For example, black, middle-class, female, and more intelligent delinquents are conspicuous by their absence. Furthermore, the studies based their findings on the small proportion of youngsters who had been caught and were under treatment. Those who have been apprehended represent the unsuccessful delinquents. They tell us nothing about the successful ones! Finally, if mesomorphy represents a constitutional predisposition to delinquent behavior, what of the millions of persons who fit this body type but are not delinquent?

While the limitations of the constitutional typologies are formidable, Sheldon and Eleanor Glueck made their argument for the connection between biology and behavior more convincing when they extended a linkage to social variables. Their statement that "A physical characteristic may be socially defined and treated in ways which encourage criminal behavior" is a noteworthy contribution (Hartl, et al., 1982:557–558). Observations and perusal of juvenile court procedures and records indeed reveal that those youths who are aggressive, socially assertive, nonsubmissive to authority, and mesomorphic in physique, are those most likely to be arrested and committed to a correctional institution. This topic is expanded in Chapter 7 in a discussion of how society assigns the delinquent label.

THE CONTINUING SEARCH FOR THE BIOLOGICAL CONNECTION

Many criminologists, researchers, and theorists continue to search for a direct link between biology and human behavior. Although findings are often discredited or inconclusive, several lines of investigation warrant our attention.

Genetic Crime Causation: The XYY Hypothesis

Can crime be in the genes? Each human cell has 46 chromosomes. Upon conception, each parent donates 23 gene-carrying chromosomes concerned with the transmission and development of hereditary characteristics. These chromosomes combine into 46 chromosomes in the offspring. Among the 46 chromosomes is a set that determines sex. The female has two X chromosomes, referred to as XX. The male has one X and one Y chromosome, referred to as XY. The X chromosome, because it is inherited from the mother, is believed by some to convey gentle and passive traits; the Y chromosome, inherited from the father, is thought to carry tough and aggressive traits. Normal males, then, described as 46XY, are those in whom gentle and tough characteristics supposedly balance each other.

Occasionally, a male will have an extra Y chromosome, indicated by the symbol 47XYY. Although males with this chromosomal abnormality comprise only about one-seventh of 1 percent of the male population, the existence of an extra Y chromosome has led to the XYY hypothesis: "Men cursed with this rare cellular structure are predisposed to violent, antisocial acts" (Rosenberg, et al., 1982:6).

> The major characteristics of these people are that they are somewhat mentally challenged, have too much acne on their faces, stand taller than the average normal male, and—most importantly—have a strong tendency to be unusually aggressive. Thus it has been theorized that the extra Y chromosome can drive the XYY male into committing a dangerous, violent crime such as murder. (Thio, 2006:79)

The XYY hypothesis fueled a rash of speculation and some research efforts to collect supporting data. Richard Fox (1971) studied inmates of prisons and mental institutions and found that as many as 3 percent displayed the 47XYY characteristics, compared to an estimated frequency for the abnormality of 0.13 percent among the population at large. In addition, several highly publicized violent crimes between 1942 and 1968 were thought to have been committed by individuals with an XYY constitution. Richard Speck, who in 1966 murdered eight nurses in Chicago, was alleged to have the 47XYY trait. Not to be overlooked is the fact that the vast majority of murderers do not have an XYY chromosome pattern. Moreover, the sample of prisoners who have been tested is biased, since many criminals are not confined in institutions and therefore not subject to chromosomal analysis. Nor is the true prevalence of XYY in the general population known. Put differently, no one can tell how many XYY men are noncriminals and serve as model members of their communities.

Social scientists point out that the suspected connection between biology and behavior is more complex than it appears. Even though an extra Y chromosome may have the potential to lead its carrier to violent behavior, sociocultural factors supply the triggering mechanism and determine whether the potentiality will become an actuality. As one geneticist admits:

> A social mechanism is entirely possible. Large, possibly slightly retarded, males may be ridiculed . . . and may respond aggressively. In any case, it would appear that of the total amount of violence in our society only a very small part is contributed by XYY individuals. (McClearn, 1969:1003)

Concerned over popularized speculation and gross generalization that "crime is in the genes" (Wilson and Herrnstein, 1985), more cautious criminologists continue to question research methodology and suggest that we may be seeing bad research rather than bad genes (Walters and White, 1989; Gibbons, 1990).

Diet and Deviant Behavior

One area of contemporary research into possible organic causes for misbehavior is the apparent association between dietary deficiencies and biochemical irregularities which cause some youngsters to become hyperactive, unruly, and delinquent. There is evidence that children who develop poor nutritional habits can grow into disturbed adolescents and violent adults (Rimland and Larson, 1981). "Because their bodies are smaller . . . and because their minds and bodies are still developing, children are especially vulnerable to the dietary risks we all experience" (Reed, et al., 1983:118).

The popular overconsumption of junk foods and refined carbohydrates by youths in the United States is suspected by researchers as a culprit in stimulating some aggressive and antisocial behavior. Not only can such foods quickly raise blood sugar levels, but they may impair the brain's ability to perceive, process information, and regulate behavior. Lonsdale and Shamberger (1980) examined a group of children whose marginal malnutrition was traced to a junk-food diet high in sugar. The effects included reduced self-control and troublesome behavior.

Criminologists Alexander Schauss and Clifford Simonsen, along with University of Puget Sound chemistry professor Jeffrey Bland (1979), conducted an analysis of the diets of chronic juvenile offenders. They found that on average the juveniles ingested 32 percent more sugar than a control group of children who were behaviorally disordered but had no criminal record (Reed, et al., 1983). An experiment was conducted by Stephen Schoenthaler and Walter Doraz (1983) in which refined sugar was drastically reduced in the diets of 276 incarcerated youths. Honey and molasses were substituted for sugar, fruit juices took the place of beverages with high sugar content, and so forth. In a short while the dietary modifications apparently resulted in behavior modification among the subjects. Schoenthaler and Doraz (1983)

Junk food and high-sugar-content soft drinks are staples in American teenager's diets. Some researchers have linked diet to unruly and delinquent behavior, while others view the possible link as tenuous, or nonexistent. What do you think?

reported that physical assaults, fighting, thefts, and various other forms of disobedience were reduced by nearly 45 percent.

A study conducted by scientists at the Massachusetts Institute of Technology raised some doubts about the premise that the consumption of high-sugar products by children is the sole or determining culprit in producing unacceptable behavior (Matthews, 1983). These researchers think that it is the colossal amount of caffeine children ingest in soft drinks and iced tea that causes hyperactivity. Caffeine also interferes with the way the brain processes stimuli. Another contradictory opinion has emerged from controlled experiments conducted by Richard Milich and William Pelham (1986) on the effects of sugar ingested by school children. They found little support for the suggested relationship between diet and antisocial conduct. The popularity of energy drinks loaded with caffeine among today's teenagers may warrant more sophisticated investigation into the possible link between caffeine and social conduct.

Studies continue in the quest for a subtle but direct link between diet and deviant behavior. Food additives and preservatives are now suspected of causing numerous allergic reactions including hyperactivity, learning disability, and aberrant behavior. While commercial food producers are dismayed and challenge such findings, research inquiries regarding causal links between diet and criminal or delinquent behavior should be encouraged.

Brain Malfunctions

Since 1971, the administration of the electroencephalograph (EEG) test to criminal and delinquent offenders has aroused considerable interest. The theory holds that the brains of some deviants emit electric waves of abnormal frequency. While some findings tenuously support this contention, much more refined and systematic research needs to be done in this area.

Similarly, many studies searching for connections between attention deficit/ hyperactivity disorder (ADHD), brain damage, and delinquent behavior have produced inconsistent and controversial findings. For example, Lee Robins (1978) and James Satterfield (1978) found high incidences of hyperactivity among the delinquent children in their studies. This hyperactivity, or *hyperkinesis*, is characterized not only by frenetic activity but often by learning disabilities, extreme aggressiveness, and the inability or refusal to distinguish between right and wrong. The conclusion that this deviant behavior has a biological connection is based on the hypothesis that some of these hyperkinetic children may be suffering minimal brain damage due to birth injury and/or heredity. Other researchers (Broder, et al., 1978, 1981; Conrad, 1975; Johnson and Kercher, 2007) disagreed. These investigators not only challenged the basic premise of "minimal brain damage" as a valid diagnosis, but found no evidence supporting such a biological connection with deviant or delinquent behavior, and suggested that juveniles with ADHD may not be able to handle social strain (see Chapter 5) as well as other youths.

Another avenue of inquiry has focused on the association between learning disability and youth crime. A 1975 survey of all youngsters admitted to correctional institutions in Colorado found that an astonishing 90 percent had some form of learning disability (Poremba, 1975). The learning disability known as dyslexia has come under special scrutiny. **Dyslexia** is *a brain malfunction whereby visual signs are scrambled.* For example, the dyslexic child might see the letters and words on this page in reverse order or perhaps upside down. Consequently, average skills in reading, spelling, and arithmetic are impossible to attain if the malady remains undiagnosed. Teachers sometimes misinterpret the learning difficulties of apparently healthy children as laziness. Sometimes dyslexic children are assumed to be retarded; as their frustration and alienation deepens, they often become emotionally maladjusted, hostile, and delinquent (Eitzen and Baca-Zinn, 1997). A growing public awareness of dyslexia and its implications about learning and disciplinary problems for afflicted children has led to the creation of special diagnostic and educational programs in most states.

More current research in this area seeks to synchronize events from both nature and nurture that may be related to violent and delinquent behavior in some youths. In the 1990s, several investigators found statistical support for the thesis that children who have experienced traumatic birth complications plus early rejection by their mothers are likely candidates for violent criminality later in life.

A 1993 National Research Council report indicated that adult violent offenders displayed certain personality features as children, including hyperactivity, risk-taking, acting impulsively, poor attention span, low IQ, and low empathy. They also tended to be abused or neglected and lacked parental nurturing. The report also lists neurobiological factors linked to poor school performance and poor relationships with other children, which are then linked with later aggressive behavior. Key among these are childhood head injuries, inadequate prenatal care, and ingestion of lead paint (Friend, 1994:5D).

In 2003, researchers at the University of Pittsburgh and Carnegie Mellon University reported that they found higher lead levels in the body to be substantially associated with juvenile delinquency (Patterson, 2003a:2C). Among other areas of investigation into brain disorders as they relate to juvenile and adult criminality include a focus on brain tumors (Kletschka, 1966), epilepsy which may be related to diminished self-control (Pollock, et al., 1983), and the effects of environmental pollution on the brain and concomitant high delinquency and crime rates in urban areas (Londer, 1987).

It is expected that the hypothesized ecological connections with brain malfunctions and delinquency will continue to be challenging research topics.

SOCIOBIOLOGICAL EXPLANATIONS

One of the more imaginative and controversial directions for scholarly inquiry on the biological basis for deviant behavior lies in the relatively new field of **sociobiology**, a *hybrid discipline that combines ethology (the naturalistic study of whole patterns of behavior), ecology (the study of the relationships of organisms to their environment), and genetics in order to derive general principles concerning the biological properties of entire societies and explain social behaviors among animals and humans* (Wilson, 1978).

Sociobiologists maintain that social behavior is a product of evolutionary history and genetics. Just as Charles Darwin traced the evolution of physical traits, sociobiologists attempt to do the same for social behaviors. It is generally accepted that some of the social behaviors that promote survival of the species are passed on to offspring through inherited genes. This involves temperament and personality traits as well as physical characteristics. Thus, for male animals, physical traits that assist in the hunt, such as quickness and motor skills, are supplemented by an aggressive disposition. For females, the biological ability to become pregnant is supported by nesting and nurturing instincts.

Despite the fact that no one has yet isolated any of those genes in humans, some sociobiologists have made wholesale transfer of the conclusions regarding the assumed life-and-death genetic struggle of lower animals to human beings. For example, they explain kinship ties, social bonding, and the incest taboo as reflecting unconscious inborn needs to protect and perpetuate one's own genetic endowment. Similarly, according to some sociobiologists, several million years of human biological–genetic evolution have made us aggressive, acquisitive, and apparently amoral at times, since these characteristics and behaviors can enhance gene survival. Thus, through sociobiological reasoning, another deterministic explanation has been made for what ordinarily appears as deviant, criminal, and delinquent behavior. Others insist that heredity and environment both play a role in explaining delinquency with genetics perhaps providing certain propensities toward delinquency that environmental factors may either mediate or help promote (Guo, et al., 2008). Box 4.1 pursues the heredity/environment debate in delinquency.

BOX 4.1

CONTROVERSIAL ISSUE: Heredity versus Environment and the Study of Twins and Adopted Children in Scandinavia

Numerous efforts are being made to utilize sociobiology in the study of deviant behavior. For example, Sarnoff A. Mednick (1977), in harmony with the sociobiological perspective, argued that law-abiding behavior must be learned and that it is not inherent in people to conform to the normative behavioral expectations that prevail in their social group. Furthermore, he indicated that the vast majority of cases of deviant and criminal behavior can be traced to socioeconomic and situational factors that temporarily neutralize the socially learned avoidance of punishment. Nevertheless, there remain a very small number of deviant individuals whose antisocial behavior falls into a consistent pattern and for which there is no apparent social cause. Mednick's research concentrated on that minority of offenders and suggested that their habitual misconduct is caused by an autonomic nervous system that is biologically unique to them. Their autonomic nervous system (ANS) recovers very quickly from threats and fear of social punishment for misdeeds, thus reinforcing their ability to inhibit previously learned conformity responses:

> As Mednick points out, his is a learning theory. It is a *social* learning theory to the extent that people's behavior is influenced by previous reactions of others. It is a *biological* theory to the extent that biological factors (in this case, the ANS) regulate the efficiency of the learning process. (McCaghy, et al., 2006:43)

As new sociobiological findings accumulate and are extended to explain human behavior and conduct, we may expect renewed controversy and debate between extremists in both the heredity and environment camps. As one scholar put it:

> Unfortunately, most of the debate concerning genetic aspects of human behavior has been highly emotional and, hence, extremist in each direction. On the one hand, many social scientists advocate that human beings are born as *tabula rasa*, blank slates with infinite potential to become anything at all, depending only on experience. On the other end of the spectrum is extreme genetic determinism, in which free will and the capacity for self-betterment are denied, and we are literally prisoners of our heredity. As usual in such outlandish debates, the truth doubtless lies somewhere in between. (Dobzhansky, 1976:169) [italics in original]

Other leading scholars in sociobiology have taken a moderating and compromising position. Barash (1982:146) cautiously declared that sociobiologists are justified in assuming an influence of genetics in human behavior although not necessarily a controlling influence. Guang Guo, Michael Roettger, and Tianji Cai (2008) found that certain genetic markers may be significant predictors of serious and violent delinquency when added to a social control model of delinquency. On the other hand, most social scientists feel that any conclusions regarding the validity of sociobiology are premature and must await the empirical testing and theoretical scrutiny to which all established theories have been subjected.

For over 50 years, the study of twins has suggested a tantalizing avenue of inquiry for researchers pursuing the illusive relationship between human biology and antisocial behavior. Twins offer unique opportunities to identify, separate, compare, and contrast the effects of heredity and environment.

Twins are classified into two categories. *Fraternal twins* are no more similar than single-birth siblings; *identical twins* result from the double fertilization of a single egg and have exactly the same genetic blueprint and look much alike.

(*Continued*)

Criminologists have been motivated by the assumption that if delinquent behavior is an inherited propensity, twins should be similar in such conduct since they share a common genetic makeup. It soon became apparent, however, that this approach contained a serious methodological flaw. Steffen Dalgard and Einar Kringlen (1976) argued that because of their uniformities, twins are treated as twins by society. Twins almost always are reared together in the same family, they share the same social experience at school, and they elicit the same societal responses from their community. Consequently, the similar behavior of twins—delinquent or otherwise—may result from their social environment as well as from genetic inheritance.

In order to resolve this dilemma and control social influences in testing the hypothesis that serious deviant behavior has a genetic basis, researchers turned to the study of adopted children. In 1971, the Mednick group analyzed the records of criminal behavior for 1,146 male adoptees and their biological and adoptive fathers. In the 1980s, these researchers began a similar but larger study of over 14,000 male and female adoptees. This latter study also included the records of criminality of biological and adoptive mothers and fathers. The methodology was strengthened in both studies as adoptees were matched carefully for age, gender, place of residence, and occupational status of fathers with nonadoptee control groups of equal size. The many interesting findings and conclusions that emerged from the Danish studies of Mednick and his colleagues included the following:

1. They found that 31 percent of the biological fathers of convicted male delinquents had criminal records compared to just 13 percent of the adoptive fathers of the same youth group (Hutchings and Mednick, 1977).
2. The biological mothers of convicted female adoptees were significantly more likely to have more criminal convictions to their credit than the adoptive mothers of the same cohort of young female adoptees (Mednick, et al., 1986).

The Mednick group concluded from their extensive adoption studies that there is an important and persistent relationship between criminal parents and the criminal behavior of their biological offspring. The fact that the children in their samples had been separated from their natural parents and raised by adoptive parents underscores the *possibility* of a genetic connection (Mednick and Gabriella, 1984).

Social scientists have continued to criticize adoption research on methodological grounds. As yet, they argue, the complex and confounding effects of nature and nurture are not disentangled and adequately controlled. For example, there was wide variance in age at adoption of subjects. Ideally, all adopted subjects should have been removed as very young infants from their biological parents and other elements of their original social environments. Even more disturbing to validity is the fact that the Danish adoption agencies went to considerable pains to match biological and adoptive parents on socioeconomic status and other important social variables, thus effectively duplicating and perhaps reinforcing the original social milieu of many subjects.

A more recent research investigation focused on 311 adult, same-sex twins in Australia. This unique group of respondents controlled for many hereditary and environmental variables and offered insights into juvenile use of marijuana as a "gateway drug" to adult use of harder drugs such as cocaine, heroin, and LSD. It was found that those individuals who used marijuana before age 17 were two to five times more likely than their co-twins to develop alcohol or drug dependence as adults. Because this study involved twins, the findings suggest that genetics play a subordinate role in drug use (Lynsky, et al., 2003).

What do the studies of twins and adopted children tell us about the heredity versus environment debate? Why is it more productive to think in terms of heredity *and* environment as opposed to heredity *versus* environment?

Sources

Dalgard, O. S., and Kringlen, E. 1976. A Norwegian twin study of criminality. *British Journal of Criminology* 16, 213–232.

Hutchings, B., and Mednick, S. A. 1977. Criminality in adoptees and their adoptive and biological parents: A pilot study. In S. A. Mednick and K. A. Christiansen (Eds.). *Biological bases of criminal behavior.* New York: Gardner Press.

Lynsky, M. T., Heath, A. C., Bucholz, K. K., Slutske, W. S., Madden, A. F., Nelson, E. C., Statham, D. J., and Martin, N. G. 2003. Escalation of drug use in early-onset cannabis users vs co-twin controls. *Journal of the American Medical Association* 289, 4 (January 22).

Mednick, S. A., and Gabriella, W. F. 1984. Genetic influences in criminal convictions: Evidence from an adoption cohort. *Science* 224, 25 (May):891–894. (© 1984 by the American Association for Advancement of Science.)

Mednick, S. A., Moffitt, T., Gabrielli, W., and Hutchings, B. 1986. Genetic factors in criminal behavior: A review. In D. Olweus, J. Block, and M. Radke-Yarrow (Eds.). *Development of antisocial and preschool behavior.* Orlando, FL: Academic Press.

Barash, D. P. 1982. *Sociobiology and behavior* (2nd ed.). New York: Elsevier.

Dobzhansky, T. 1976. The myths of genetic predestination and of tabula rasa. *Perspectives in Biology and Medicine* 19:156–170.

Guo, G., Roettger, M. E., and Cai, T. The Integration of Genetic Propensities into Social-Control Models of Delinquency and Vioence among Male Youths. *American Sociological Review* 73 (August):543–568.

McCaghy, C. H., Capron, T. A., Jamieson, J. D., and Carey, S. H. 2006. *Deviant behavior: Crime, conflict, and interest groups* (7th ed.). Boston: Allyn and Bacon.

Mednick, Sarnoff A. 1977. A biosocial theory of the learning of law-abiding behavior. In S. A. Mednick and K. O. Christioasen (Eds.). *Biosocial bases of criminal behavior.* New York: Garden Press.

THE PSYCHOGENIC APPROACH AND THE MEDICAL MODEL

In the 19th century, scholars accumulated new knowledge about human anatomy, physiology, neurology, chemistry, and general medicine that had far-reaching implications for the scientific study of human behavior. The discovery of an organic basis for many physical illnesses led to the further discovery of an organic basis for some mental illnesses (Reid, 2008). This latter finding lent impetus to the development of psychiatry and psychology as academic disciplines and led to the *medicalization* of deviance. **Psychiatry** is *a medical specialty concerned with the diagnosis, treatment, and prevention of disordered or abnormal behavior.* After completion of their initial medical school education, some physicians take further specialized training in psychiatry in order to become professional psychiatrists. Because psychiatry is a subarea of medicine, psychiatrists apply a **medical model** to delinquency which views crime and delinquency as a social pathology analogous to physical or mental physical illness. Delinquency is viewed like an "illness" with identifiable "symptoms" needing diagnosis and treatment.

An easy application of this medical model to deviant behavior of juveniles was popularized in the late 19th century when The Child Savers, an influential group of social reformers, used such terms as *disease, illness,* and *contagion* to describe adolescent crime. They promoted the idea that criminals were the natural product of biological heritage and corrupt urban environments. The Child Savers, together with some prominent penologists of that time, "presupposed that crime was a symptom of 'pathology' and that criminals should be treated like irresponsible, sick patients" (Platt, 1977:45).

Psychology is *a behavioral science that investigates and associates mental processes with behavior.* Psychologists try to understand why people act the way they do by exploring how they grow up, how they react to and cope with stress and change, how their personalities develop, and how they become disturbed or get into trouble. "Unlike psychiatry, which is a medical specialty devoted to the understanding and cure of mental disease, psychology has a broader task, ranging from the laboratory study of simple behavior in animals . . . to the complicated behavior of human beings in social groups" (Rehm, 1983:593).

Although psychiatry and psychology are independent fields of study, they have much in common. Both focus on individuals and perceive human behavior as originating in the mind. Extreme deviance or delinquency is seen by psychiatrists and psychologists as overt symptoms or behavioral expressions arising from underlying personality or emotional maladjustments and as alternatives to mental illness (Halleck, 1971).

In addition, psychiatrists and clinical psychologists "devote much of their effort to helping disturbed, troubled, and mentally ill people" (Rehm, 1983:593) and share many diagnostic and treatment techniques. In view of the extensive common ground shared by professionals in these two disciplines, psychiatric and psychological contributions combine to form the *psychogenic approach* to juvenile delinquency.

THE DISCOVERY OF THE UNCONSCIOUS

The pioneering work of Sigmund Freud (1856–1939) laid the foundation for the contemporary psychogenic approach to understanding and explaining human behavior. Freud was trained in medicine and neurology, but his interest in the aberrant behavior associated with mental illness led him to conclude that biological, physiological, and genetic attributes cannot adequately account for human behavior. He demonstrated that much human conduct is not consciously motivated. Freud identified a deep, unconscious dimension of the human mind as the motivating source of many acts (Freud, 1961). The **unconscious** may be defined as *a subterranean mental reservoir of unfulfilled needs, desires, and feelings accumulated throughout life and not ordinarily available to conscious thought.*

According to Freud, humans suffer mental conflict because of desires and needs that are repressed into the unconscious mind, often during childhood development of personality, identity, and acceptable social roles. Thus, while an individual's behavior may appear to be illogical and even abnormal, the troublesome conduct is actually a purposive expression of unresolved problems and needs submerged in the subconscious mind.

THE FORMATION OF PERSONALITY

The concept of personality is an intriguing focus for the study and explanation of human behavior by those employing the psychogenic approach. **Personality** refers to *the unique organization of relatively stable psychological traits possessed by an individual, as revealed by one's interaction with people, events, situations, and other components of the environment.* For example, "enthusiastic," "energetic," "fun-loving," and "idealistic" are some descriptive personality traits that seem to characterize many young people. But if a youth is cheerful and upbeat one day and sad or depressed the next day, we would have some difficulty in ascertaining a dominant personality pattern. A psychologically healthy person maintains a certain consistency of personality that is apparent in the day-to-day presentation of self.

Freud and his colleagues contended that the normal adult personality has three fully developed components: the *id*, the *ego*, and the *superego*. Each of these three dimensions of the human personality performs critical, complex, and interrelated psychic and social functions for the individual.

At birth, the infant's personality is largely unidimensional, dominated by the **id**—*a set of primitive, self-centered impulses and instincts.* The sensuous and hedonistic id seeks immediate gratification and has no sense of time or reality. During the first few years of life, the individual develops an ego and a superego. We may conceive of the **superego** as *an antithetical or opposite force that restrains the impulsive id.* The superego is developed in the individual through socialization and represents socially conditioned and culturally learned moral values and a sense of right and wrong. It includes the formation of conscience and an ego ideal (Regoli and Hewitt, 2003:145). Whereas the id clamors for self-satisfaction, "the ego ideal represents what we should do and the conscience gives us guilt feelings when we do 'wrong' " (Yablonsky and Haskell, 1988:355).

The **ego**, in Freud's model, is *that part of the personality or self that arbitrates between the demands of the id and the socially sensitive and idealistic superego.* The more pragmatic ego is designed to unify extreme personality positions into balanced, behavioral responses to stimuli. If successful, it directs behavior toward satisfaction of urges consistent with social and physical reality.

After several decades of criticism as speculative and erroneous, Freudian psychology declined as a popular explanation for human behavior. However, since 2000, Freud has received new credit from scholars in the field as a major contributor to psychogenic explanations. Moreover, personality testing has become a staple in attempting to diagnose and treat delinquency.

> Right or wrong, Freud's theories revolutionized modern psychology and changed the way we think . . . Freud's legacy is the idea that, by observing the patient's symptoms, the therapist can discover the cause. Even today that notion lies at the heart of psychotherapy. (Adler, 2006:48)

FREUDIAN THEORY AS AN EXPLANATION OF CRIME AND DELINQUENCY

Freud's theoretical contributions regarding the mental or psychic origins and motivations for human behavior have been adopted, adapted, expanded, and applied by numerous other psychiatrists and psychologists to the inner conflicts, personality maladjustments, emotional problems, and feelings of insecurity, inadequacy, and inferiority among their patients. In addition, Freud's insights have guided countless psychogenic efforts to identify and explain the causes of such conduct disorders as sexual deviations, alcoholism, drug addiction, crime, and juvenile delinquency.

As a common example, Freud and many neo-Freudians have argued that crime is an outgrowth of the repressed, unconscious, emotional traumas of childhood (Samenow, 1984; Sykes, 1980:8). According to this view, most crime is a result of an imbalance in the offender's ego between uncontrolled drives (the id) and society's expectations about behavior (the superego). Often, the problem is ascribed to an overly strict superego in which the offender, as a child, was socialized with a supercharged, unconscious sense of guilt. In such cases, as drives are repressed, pressures build up until the drives become manifest in abnormal and dangerous ways. Freud (1961) contended that children and adults often misbehave in order to be punished, which then temporarily relieves their guilt. On the other hand, much deviant and delinquent behavior has been credited to a deficient or underdeveloped superego, which fails to intervene or restrain the selfish, antisocial impulses of the id. These individuals were also inadequately conditioned to internalize "the socially adequate responses which society requires them to integrate into some form of 'conscience' " (Eysenck, 1979:13).

In both examples, the psychiatrist or clinical psychologist would look to the subject's early childhood relationship with parents for explanatory causes of the disordered behavior. It is suggested that the socialization imposed by overly strict or overly permissive parents can create in their offspring a mental condition in which the ego is insufficient to perform its assigned task of mediating between the id and the superego.

PSYCHOANALYSIS

In addition to substantiating the existence of the unconscious and introducing the concepts of the id, ego, and superego in personality formation, Freud and his followers also developed various techniques for probing and examining the unconscious forces and motives that energize human behavior:

> The most ambitious and intensive form of psychotherapy is represented by Freudian psychoanalysis . . . The intention is to afford the individual insight into the unconscious motivation of his [or her] behavior and to allow the development of a "healthy" personality structure. Frequently, the aim is not the removal of the symptom, rather it is to solve the unconscious problems which have led, according to psychoanalytic theory, to the development of a particular symptom. (Feldman, 1978:234)

Psychiatrists and psychologists have continued to develop instruments designed to elicit the unconscious, subjective responses of their patients. Prominent among them is a wide variety of projective tests.

The Medical Model: Delinquent Acts as Symptoms

A basic tenet of the psychogenic approach and the medical model is that delinquent acts are symptoms of **psychopathology**: *some internal neurological disorder or deeply hidden personality disturbance.* Applying the medical model, psychiatrists consider delinquent acts or symptoms as "the sick or hurt child's cry for help." The psychoanalytic literature contends that overt delinquency is an indirect appeal for help in resolving some internal conflict (Shoemaker, 2005).

Several psychogenic theorists and practitioners have looked with suspicion upon a number of other common childhood activities besides outright delinquent behavior which, if carried to excess, may be viewed as symptoms of some underlying emotional disturbance or personality maladjustment. William Healy and

Augusta Bronner (1957), Raymond Kuhlen (1952), and others associated bed-wetting, nail-biting, interest or activity in sports, nervousness, and movie attendance with personality deviations and possible delinquency. This medical model approach is discussed further in Chapter 14, and prevention and treatment strategies based upon these alleged predelinquency symptoms are discussed in Chapter 16. Critics of these suggestions contend that the preoccupation with so-called behavioral symptoms as indicators of predelinquency not only blurs the boundaries for socially tolerable behavior, but can also place virtually everyone under suspicious scrutiny.

Conduct Disorders and Risk/Needs Assessment

The insistence that delinquent behavior is an external symptom of an inner psychopathological disturbance is a major point of psychological theory and debate with many social scientists. This psychogenic theme is demonstrated in the *Diagnostic and Statistical Manual of Mental Disorders* (DSM-IV-R) of the American Psychiatric Association (2000). For example, in the manual, the term **conduct disorder** is used to *describe the behavior of adolescents who manifest a repetitive pattern of actions that violate the rights of others and major conduct norms*. Youths with conduct disorders usually exhibit their unsettling and often threatening behavior in a social setting and may include bullying and cheating in games and school work.

> Although the adolescent may project an image of toughness, self-esteem is usually low. Angry outbursts, low frustration tolerance, irritability, and reckless behavior are frequent characteristics. School achievement in reading and language skills is below the expected ability and age level. (White, 1992:314)

Specific criteria suggested by the American Psychiatric Association (2000) for the use of clinicians in the diagnosis of conduct disorders include at least three of the following during a period of six months:

1. Frequent lying.
2. Running away from home overnight twice or one runaway without returning.
3. Frequent truancy from school or for older adolescents, absence from work.
4. Stealing without confrontation with the victim on more than one occasion (e.g., shoplifting).
5. Vandalism and destruction of property.
6. Breaking and entering into houses, cars, or buildings without permission from property owners.
7. Deliberate fire-setting activity (arson).
8. Cruelty to animals.
9. Frequent initiation of physical fights.
10. The use of weapons in physical fights on one or more occasions.
11. Stealing with physical confrontation of victims in muggings, purse snatchings, extortions, and armed robberies.
12. Forcing another person into sexual activity, such as rape or prostitution.
13. Physical violence and cruelty toward people. Even homicidal assault can occur in the later stages of conduct disturbance.

The consistent application of the medical model by the American Psychiatric Association is reflected in the usage of such terms as *conduct disorder*, *diagnosis*, and *the later stages*. The recommended diagnostic formula of "at least three of the following during a period of six months" presents an overwhelming temptation to social scientists who ask: "Why a minimum of three offenses before the adolescent is diagnosed as having a conduct disorder?" Surely one rape or two armed robberies within any period of time ought to qualify anyone for a "diagnosis of conduct disorder"!

OTHER PSYCHOGENIC EXPLANATIONS OF JUVENILE DELINQUENCY

Though Freudian and neo-Freudian theories probably have been the most influential, several other prominent psychogenic explanations of crime and delinquency merit discussion. There is considerable overlap among these theoretical constructs, and their difference is often a matter of emphasis. Underlying all of the biological and psychogenic approaches is a fundamental belief that criminals and delinquents are aberrant individuals, possessing some quirk of mind or body that is not manifest in the rest of the population.

Early Theories of Feeblemindedness

A bridge between the biological explanations and the psychogenic theories of crime and delinquency may be seen in the studies of feeblemindedness during the early decades of the 20th century. Just as Lombroso (1911), Sheldon, et al. (1949), and other biological determinists argued that some individuals are constrained to antisocial behavior by a genetic or physiological predisposition, Goddard (1920), Healy and Bronner (1926), and other psychologists contended that mental deficiency is a primary cause of crime and delinquency. This interest was further stimulated by the popular studies of the Juke and Kallikak families that purported to trace inherited feeblemindedness and criminal tendencies through several generations (Dugdale, 1910; Estrabrook, 1916; Goddard, 1927). These assumptions have been subsequently discounted.

BOX 4.2

CONTROVERSIAL ISSUES: The Debate over Television Violence, Childhood Personality Development, and Delinquent Behavior

The television set is on an average of eight hours a day in the typical American home, but the duration may double that on the weekends. One-third of all children live in a home where the television is on all the time during waking hours (Churnin, 2006). So what does that have to do with juvenile delinquency? Maybe nothing. Maybe a lot.

A study conducted by the American Psychological Association indicated that the child who watches two to four hours of television a day will have witnessed 8,000 murders and 100,000 other acts of violence before leaving elementary school (Huston and Donnerstein, 1992). What impact does viewing all that television violence have on the psychological and social development of young children? Nobody knows for sure, but there is mounting evidence that viewing violence and aggression on television may be linked to aggressive behavior in youths.

Social psychologist, Albert Bandura, was one of the first to study this possible link with his classic "Bobo Doll" studies of the 1960s. Experiments with the Bobo Doll (a child-sized inflatable doll weighted at the bottom) found that children learn and imitate aggressive and violent modes of play from watching television, as children repeatedly beat, punched, and kicked the Bobo doll after viewing similar behavior on television (Bandura, 1963; Bandura, et al., 1963). Other studies have also shown that there is a relationship between media violence and aggressive behavior, especially when viewers believe that the perpetrator was rewarded in some way by the violence, as is often the case in television and movies (American Academy of Pediatrics, 2001; Boyle, 2005; HND, 2003).

Dr. Leonard Eron of the University of Illinois conducted research that spanned over three decades and chronicled the lives of the same people. He concluded: *The more hours of television the children watched when they were 8 years old . . . the more serious were the crimes they were convicted of by the time they were age 30, and the more aggressive they were under the influence of alcohol, and the more severely they punished their own children.*

According to this 30-year study, the most risky age for television violence is during the first 10 years of a child's life. "Until children reach the double digits," says Eron, "they find it very difficult to differentiate between what's real and what's not real on TV" (Oldenberg, 1992).

According to Dr. Centerwall of the University of Washington, television is directly responsible for 10,000 homicides, 70,000 rapes, and 700,000 injurious assaults every year—roughly about half of all serious crimes. According to Dr. Centerwall's long postulated theory that 10 to 15 years after a society embraces television, expect a dramatic increase in murders and other serious crimes. That is just enough time, he notes, for the first generation weaned on television to reach adulthood and move into their most crime-prone years (Oldenberg, 1992). Neil Hickey observed that "more televised violence than at any time in the medium's history is flowing into American homes. It is coming from many more sources than ever before—from video, pay-per-view, and cable, as well as from the broadcast network and stations. The overwhelming weight of scientific opinion now holds that televised violence is indeed responsible for a percentage of the real violence in our society. What is new is that psychologists, child experts, and the medical community are just now beginning to treat televised violence as a serious public health issue—like smoking and drunk driving—about which the public needs to be educated for its own safety and well-being" (Wheeler, 1993:98–101).

Additional support for these concerns over violence in televised programs has come from a three-year study conducted by a team of researchers at four universities. The research was financed by the cable television industry. A 1998 report on the project statistically verified that the number of violent programs appearing in prime time has increased significantly in recent years. Moreover, Barbara Wilson, a senior researcher on the study and a communications professor at the University of California at Santa Barbara pointed out that nearly 75 percent of violent scenes on television contained no remorse, criticism, or penalty for the violence which sends "the message that violence is condoned" (*San Francisco Chronicle*, 1998:A-3).

These and other findings have led the American Psychological Association to conclude that viewing violence on television or other mass media promotes aggressive behavior, particularly in children (Ritter, 2003:2).

Industry rebuttals to warnings and threats of government regulation of television suggest a bitter and complex constitutional fight. They contend that television, like the print media, have certain inalienable rights embedded in the First Amendment to the U.S. Constitution, which guarantees that Congress will not interfere with the freedoms of religion, speech, and publishing the news. With this in mind, television apologists counter, government regulation would amount to censorship. In their view, self-policing by the television industry is the only viable option.

(*Continued*)

It also should be noted that not all research supports the purported link between television violence and aggressive behavior. Robert Hodge and David Tripp (1986), for example, argue that the link is exaggerated and that even young children realize that television violence is not real and view it only as entertainment. Others even suggest that watching media violence and playing violent video games could have a cathartic effect, providing a vicarious outlet for violence and aggression in place of a real one (Brown, 1990; DeFleur, 1983).

What psychogenic concepts and theoretical explanations of juvenile behavior are illustrated in the research cited in this box? What position do you take on the possible relationship between television violence, childhood personality development, and delinquent behavior? Does violence in the media merely reflect the violence in American society? Or, as suggested by the research in these studies, does viewing violence in the media help create and promote violence and aggression in American society?

Sources

American Academy of Pediatrics. 2001. Media violence. *Pediatrics* 108 (November):1222–1226.

Bandura, A. J., Ross, J. D., and Ross, S. 1963. Imitation of Film-Mediated Aggressive Models. *Journal of Abnormal and Social Psychology* 66:3–11.

Bandura, A. J. 1965. Invluence of models' reinforcement contingencies on the acquisition of initative responses. *Journal of Personality and Social Psychology* 1:589–595.

Boyle, K. 2005. *Media and violence: Gendering the debates.* Thousand Oaks, CA: Sage.

Brown. H. N. 1990. Can violent films help troubled teens? *Dallas Morning News*, March 11:4C.

Churnin, N. 2006. Tot TV comes with parental guidance. *Dallas Morning News*, May 25:1A.

Defleur, M. 1983. *Social Problems.* Boston: Houghton-Mifflin.

HND. 2003. Media violence predicts aggressive behavior. *Health News Digest* http://www.healthnewsdigest.com/

Huston, A. C. and Donnerstein, E. 1992. *Big world, small screen: The role of television in American society.* Linconln: Universityof Nebraska press.

Oldenberg, D. 1992. "Primal Screen," *Washington Post*, April 7.

Ritter, M. 2003. Children–TV violence link has effect. Associated Press. *Compuserve News*, March 10:2.

San Francisco Chronicle. 1998. No regret, no remorse. *San Francisco Chronicle*, April 17:A-3.

Wheeler, J. L. 1993. *Remote Controlled.* Hagerstown, MD: Review and Herald Publishing Association.

Such conclusions rested heavily upon the early application of measures of intelligence to institutionalized juvenile offenders. These were developed for the measurement of an individual's IQ, which is the ratio of a person's Mental Age (MA) to Chronological Age (CA). Thus, an IQ score of 100 means that one's MA and CA coincide at the national average. The higher the IQ, the brighter the individual; the lower the IQ, the more pronounced the retardation is assumed to be.

Many psychologists replaced the idea that delinquents are somehow biologically defective with the notion that they are mentally defective. From this perspective, juvenile delinquents are viewed as retarded or lacking the mental capacity to know the difference between right and wrong or they cannot foresee serious consequences of misbehavior for themselves and for others or they cannot avoid being seduced into crime by others.

In more recent decades, psychologists, educators, and other scholars have expanded their knowledge of how sociocultural variables and learning opportunities affect the accumulation of information by different individuals and groups and of how test construction and administration procedures affect responses to so-called intelligence tests. In addition, the ability of IQ tests to indicate or predict delinquent behavior has been challenged. IQ measurements of incarcerated or institutionalized offenders are a biased representation of the criminal and delinquent population since the subjects are those who were caught and convicted. Such scores tell us nothing about those who are successful in their deviance and avoid detection or apprehension. The preponderance of empirical evidence also fails to support the proposition that delinquents are less intelligent than the general population (Samenow, 1984:19). Instead, it would be more accurate to say that low IQ scores often are related to poor educational opportunities, and the likelihood of being officially identified as a delinquent is much greater in the most deprived socioeconomic groups whose educational opportunities are drastically circumscribed (Menard and Morse, 1984).

A contrary view was espoused by Travis Hirschi and Michael Hindelang (1977) and by Rolf Loeber and Thomas Dishion (1983) who reviewed research and literature on low IQ scores and delinquent behavior. These investigators pointed to low IQ scores as a key foundational variable for many youths that, when combined with negative circumstances in the home, neighborhood, and other elements of the social environment, can generate an indirect connection between mental incompetency, low self-esteem, and delinquency.

Neurological Abnormalities

It was a natural development for psychiatric research and theory as a medical specialty to advance the premise that some offenders may be suffering from a brain abnormality or some form of neurological damage. This psychogenic approach has linked criminal and delinquent behavior with congenital brain defects, a mental impairment induced by a tumor, or the residual neurological effects of an earlier injury.

Numerous cases have been cited in which deviant and antisocial behaviors are credited to pressures, lesions, and other injuries to those vital areas of the cerebrospinal system that are associated with intellect, emotion, inhibition, and self-control. Not infrequently, the "problem child" with a conduct disorder is found to have suffered from a severe trauma to the brain at an earlier stage of development (Roth, 1968). Douglas (1960) found significant correlation between premature birth (associated with a greater incidence of minor brain damage than normal birth) and "bad behavior" of school children as rated by their teachers.

Antonio Damasio (1999) and his associates at the University of Iowa College of Medicine identified two rare cases in which brain injuries during infancy prevented people from learning normal rules of social and moral behavior. As adults they showed no guilt or remorse for bad conduct because, it was assumed, their previous brain injuries prevented their normal socialization. In light of a sample of just two cases, this study must be considered exploratory rather than conclusive. Much additional work needs to be done on the possible linkage between neurological damage and subsequent antisocial behavior.

In their ongoing search for empirical evidence linking mental processes and malfunctions with antisocial behavior, psychiatrists and neurologists have turned to sophisticated medical technology to measure and interpret brain activity. One method of studying nervous system functioning is to record the electrical activity of the brain. The summated electrical activity of the neurons in the brain is so great that it can be recorded through electrodes attached to the outer surface of the head. Such recordings are known as *electroencephalograms* (EEGs). Some researchers believe that EEG data suggest that the brains of many criminals and delinquents do not function normally. They point out that antisocial behavior may develop following the appearance of brain tumors, head injuries, or the onset of diseases like encephalitis and epilepsy and that the incidence of abnormal EEG waves is greater among persons who chronically violate important social norms than among conformists (White, 1981). Thus far, however, the findings based on the use of electroencephalographic examinations are contradictory (Shah and Roth, 1974).

More research comparing larger groups of representative juvenile offenders with nonoffenders needs to be conducted before there can be general acceptance that neurological abnormalities offer a credible explanation for juvenile delinquency. Although there are some instances in which *violent* offenders suffer from some mental anomaly (Pincus, 1979), research has yet to demonstrate consistent correlations between neurological disorders and delinquency. Nor is there convincing evidence of a general association between mental retardation, epilepsy, or the constitutional aspects of personality with juvenile delinquency (Krisberg and Austin, 1978). A more balanced viewpoint accepts the fact that brain abnormalities are found in many cases of violent misbehavior, although this is rarely the single causal factor. Rather, neurological defect, damage, or malfunction, when joined with negative factors in the home and other segments of the social environment, contribute to the development of delinquent propensities in some individuals (Narramore, 1966).

Flawed Personality: Psychopathology and Sociopathology

Theories and research findings of psychiatrists and psychologists have increased our understanding of why people behave as they do. As discussed earlier, the development and dynamics of human personality have been their most fruitful areas of inquiry, as extensions or alternatives to Freud's early and basic conceptualizations.

The basic unit of personality organization and psychogenic analysis is the personality trait. A **personality trait** is *a distinguishing feature, quality, or disposition of mind or character.* Personality traits include such emotions and associated behaviors as anxiety, fear, anger, religiosity, cheerfulness, and so forth. Each individual's personality probably contains most personality traits to a greater or lesser degree.

Some of the relevant work in this area has focused on the identification, description, and causal explanation of the psychopathic personality. The **psychopath** *has a "flawed personality" in the sense that he or she has failed to internalize some of the major values and norms of society.* As a result of this incomplete or unsuccessful socialization, the superego part of the personality that monitors the individual's deportment as "conscience" is defective and impotent. The psychopath lacks self-control or internal restraints in the face of temptation and shows little genuine guilt or remorse for crimes committed (McCall, 1999; Rabin, 1961). The term **sociopath** is replacing the older term "psychopath" and thus implicitly recognizes that social forces are also involved in the development of the condition.

Hervey Cleckley (1988), in *The Mask of Sanity*, pointed out that whereas most people suffer from anguish and guilt for wrongdoing, sociopaths (or psychopaths) are loose and easy. They have little sense of regret and cannot seem to learn from experience. Often, they have superficial charm and above-average intelligence. But they keep doing wrong. Starting out perhaps as truants and juvenile vandals, they may proceed along criminal paths through theft, robbery, rape, or murder to become the classic recidivists who are released only to be reinstitutionalized. This emphasis on failed childhood socialization leading to aggressive and predatory adolescence often characterizes the contributions of developmental psychologists (Bandura and Walters, 1959).

DISTINCTIVE PATTERNS OF CRIMINAL THINKING In addition to investigating psychoses and antisocial personality disorders, psychologists continue to search for traits that can be studied as potential sources of crime and delinquency. One approach is to give batteries of tests such as the Minnesota Multiphasic Personality Inventory (MMPI) and other personality tests to both criminals and noncriminals. These tests contain questions about the beliefs, values, attitudes, feelings, and habits of the subjects. The purpose is to distinguish between criminal and noncriminal personality traits and profiles. As yet, no distinguishing and consistent criminal personality type has been isolated (Johnson, et al., 1979:34–35).

Samuel Yochelson and Stanton Samenow (1977) suggest that some criminals show distinctive thinking patterns and character traits early in life that become more conspicuous with age. The "criminal child" (and later the adult criminal), they say, is hyperactive, egocentric, a chronic liar, and able to counter fears of punishment and pangs of conscience with a unique "shutoff mechanism." Most surprising of all, many habitual offenders—those who have murdered, raped, and stolen, who have committed countless crimes from their youth—thought they were good people undeserving of punishment (Hernon, 1980).

This controversial approach is sometimes implemented through extensive interviews in an effort to determine what the offender was thinking prior to and during the time when the crime was committed. It has been well documented, however, that when adult and juvenile "offenders discuss what they were thinking while committing a crime, they often seek to slant what they reveal so it is socially acceptable" (Zastrow, 1992:46). Psychologist Samenow (1984:17), in *Inside the Criminal Mind*, underscored this problem in acquiring reliable information from offenders:

> When they are interviewed after being apprehended, criminals invariably relate a tale of horrors about their early lives. They seize upon any hardships in their lives, real or made-up, to justify their acts against society. By portraying themselves as victims, they seek sympathy and hope to absolve themselves of culpability.

Adolescent Identity Crisis

The concept of an "adolescent identity crisis" not only builds on the earlier theoretical constructs of the subconscious and personality development, but incorporates a strong sociological element with its emphasis on adolescent role confusion

How might the identity crisis, unfulfilled aspirations, and isolation experienced by many adolescents lead to delinquency?

and behavioral experimentation (this is further explored in Chapters 8 and 11). Part of the popularity for this theory must be credited to Erik Erikson (1956; 1968), who presented a convincing picture of delinquent behavior as a reflection of the inadequacy felt by many young people as they seek to establish new self-identities and social acceptance to go along with their newly acquired biological maturity.

According to Erikson (1968:50), a psychologically healthy adult has successfully integrated the self and social aspects of identity. Such an individual has achieved an **ego-identity**, *a persistent "sameness and continuity" within oneself that coincides with a consistently shared fundamental character and meaning with others.* Ego-identity is acquired during the formative adolescent years as youths mature and experiment with various poses and roles until they "find themselves" and their new roles and statuses in society.

Erikson contended that it is normal for "gaps" to exist in the personalities of young people that can lead to an identity crisis for some. Until these gaps are "filled in" by experience, the youth's personality pattern and behavior may be unpredictable at times, reflecting a state of **ego-diffusion**, which is the opposite of ego-identity. This *personality presentation of diffusion or inconsistency in ethics, roles, loyalties, and behavior* is characteristic of many adolescents and often worries and irritates adults who may have forgotten their own adolescent angst.

Sometimes the significant adults in a youth's life (parents, teachers, and others) misinterpret a young person's desire and need to experiment with trial roles and to disengage from total adult authority in a quest for self-identity and adulthood. When adults are confronted with what they perceive as a vacillating, rebellious teenager, they may overreact with stern, corrective measures designed to reform and restructure the young person's life. Misinterpretation and overreaction to minor adolescent nonconformity by the significant adults in the life of the youth may, according to Erikson, precipitate a serious alienation of the youth and reinforce the tendency to choose a negative and antisocial role.

The ultimate choice of a delinquent role can be exacerbated by the availability of antisocial role models in the youth's environment. Dorothy Rogers (1977) pointed out that as youngsters experiment with different roles, they often fantasize an ego-ideal. The **ego-ideal** is *a personality, character, or image to which the youth may aspire.* While youths are testing their independence from traditional authority figures, they may admire and seek to emulate persons whose behavior is the antithesis of parental expectations:

> flamboyant crooks, lurid heroes and heroines lend glamour to erotic or vicious behaviors and afford a measure of catharsis for tendencies ordinarily repressed. Such figures . . . represent the romantic longings of almost everybody's adolescence.
>
> Even gangsters may serve as worthy ego-ideals. (Rogers, 1977:196)

Numerous psychologists continue to research and explore the adolescent identity crisis (Browning, 2007; Ganiere and Enright, 1989).

Insufficient Moral Development

The early Freudian concept of superego development provides an important foundation for more contemporary studies of moral development and delinquent youth. For example, Jean Piaget (1948) focused on mental cognition—how people think and understand—proposing that children develop their cognitive awareness and reasoning in four identifiable stages as they grow older and have a wider experience with their society and the world. Each successive stage of biological and mental maturation involves an increased ability to deal with reality. The newborn infant, according to Piaget's experiments, relies totally on sensory contact in dealing with its environment. By about age two, the child is mastering a growing vocabulary and can mentally distinguish between physical or objective reality and things that cannot be sensed directly. In a few years, usually about age eight or nine, the child has the intellectual skill to perceive numerous causal connections in his or her surroundings; that is, to understand how and why things happen. Finally, in Piaget's model, the maturing adolescent is capable of more complex and abstract thought. For example, the youth no longer sees that one must obey rules just because they are expressed and enforced by parents, teachers, or the police. At this stage of mental and moral development, the youth has personally internalized and subscribed to a set of moral values and precepts.

Lawrence Kohlberg, building on Piaget's work, presented an elaborate theory of moral development that suggests psychogenic implications and explanations for crime and delinquency. Kohlberg (1981) declared that mental comprehension of right and wrong and corresponding behavior develop in childhood through three distinguishable, sequential, and evolving levels or stages.

Level 1 ***Preconventional Level of Moral Development.*** This elementary phase of mental and moral reasoning characterizes childhood between the ages of 4 and 10. The child is responsive to the rules of right and wrong as defined by his or her parents, teachers, and other personal authority figures. The child's moral judgments and subsequent conduct are based on self-interest, and acts are interpreted as good or bad in terms of physical gratification or punishment.

Level 2 ***Conventional Level of Moral Development.*** This intermediate stage of mental and moral reasoning prevails among adolescents (and most adults, according to Kohlberg). At this level, the individual is less egocentric and more sociocentric as his or her world and orientation expands. Through internalization of social norms, the individual now shares the common desire to support and protect the existing social structure. This perspective can function to guide mental and moral decisions.

Level 3 ***Postconventional Level of Moral Development.*** In this final and advanced stage of moral reasoning, the individual's judgment and ethical decisions have matured and transcended the personal and social demands that determined past behavior. At this highest level, one's approach to moral decisions of right and wrong are autonomously based on universal principles of justice that one has cognitively discovered and adopted along with a world view of humanity and of right and wrong (Muuss, 1996).

The mental and moral development ideas of Piaget and Kohlberg have been the basis of considerable speculation and some research in the ongoing quest to find out why some young people turn to delinquency and some do not. For example, Scott Henggeler (1989) reported that the majority of juvenile delinquents in research samples were clustered at the lowest level of Kohlberg's moral development scale in which behavior is motivated by self-gratification and a pragmatic avoidance of deviance for fear of punishment. On the other hand, nondelinquent youth were more likely to rank at higher levels of moral reasoning, characterized by idealism, generosity, empathy for others, and a universal concern for justice. The tentative conclusion is that juvenile delinquents may be more prone than nondelinquents to commit illegal and antisocial acts because they have insufficient moral development.

Again in 1983, Kohlberg and his associates extended the moral development model by suggesting that increased maturity provides "an insulating effect against delinquency," thus theoretically accounting for the fact that most delinquents eventually grow out of their delinquency (Jennings, et al., 1983:311).

The mental and moral development theories of Piaget and Kohlberg have been challenged on several grounds. First, many key terms and concepts lack definitional consensus. For example, *morality* and *rules* cannot be separate from their cultural or subcultural context, which can supply different meanings for different groups. Second, Piaget and Kohlberg may have made some questionable assumptions concerning the mental processes of *thinking* and *learning*. Not only are these processes impossible to observe and difficult to test, but other researchers indicate that there is no certainty that the transition from one cognitive level to another is as patterned or well correlated with chronological age as suggested by Piaget and Kohlberg. Moreover, the relationship between thinking and behavior is not as clear-cut and consistent as suggested by the moral development theorists. Finally, Kohlberg's methodology has been faulted for two intrinsic biases: "First, his emphasis on college learning as a prerequisite for critical thinking as well as moral maturity has been called elitist. Second, his levels of moral maturity have been described as sexist [since his subjects were mostly young boys]" (Thornton and Voigt, 1992:52).

PREDICTORS OF YOUTH VIOLENCE

In 2000, the Office of Juvenile Justice and Delinquency Prevention concluded a two-year analysis of research on risk factors and the development of serious and violent juvenile offending careers. The study group identified several personality and behavioral characteristics among boys that are correlated with later violent behavior (Hawkins, et al., 2000):

1. ***Hyperactivity, concentration problems, restlessness, and risk taking.*** A longitudinal study in Sweden found that 13-year-old boys with restlessness and concentration difficulties were five times more likely to be arrested for violence by age 26 than youths without these traits (Klinteberg, et al., 1993). Another study (Farrington, 1989) revealed that the tendency to fidget and frequent talkativeness predicted academic difficulties and later violence.
2. ***Aggressiveness.*** Many researchers note that aggressive behavior measured from ages 6 to 13 consistently predicts later violence among males. One study found that two-thirds of boys with high teacher-rated aggression scores at ages 10 to 13 had criminal records for violent offenses by age 26 (Loeber and Hay, 1996; Stattin and Magnusson, 1989).
3. ***Beliefs and attitudes favorable to deviant or antisocial behavior.*** Among males, dishonesty, antisocial beliefs and attitudes, and hostility toward police have been found to predict later violence. Relationships between these predictors of violence and actual violence are less consistent for females (Williams, 1994).

Faithful to the medical model, the psychiatric response to this syndrome of predictors of future violent and delinquent behavior includes an arsenal of psychiatric drug therapies. "Pediatricians and child psychiatrists are increasingly turning to pharmacology as the treatment of choice for depression, attention disorder, severe anxiety, obsessive-compulsive disorder, manic depression, and other conditions diagnosed in young patients" (Goode, 2003:1A, 12A). The number of children and adolescents receiving prescriptive medications was two to three times higher in 1996 than in 1987. Prozac, a mood stabilizer, was approved in 2003 as a treatment for depression in youths aged 7 to 17. However, "the long-term effects of such drugs, particularly on the developing brain, are largely unknown" (Goode, 2003:12A).

CRITICISMS AND LIMITATIONS OF THE BIOLOGICAL AND PSYCHOGENIC APPROACHES

Biological, psychiatric, and psychological theories of criminal and delinquent behavior have been helpful to our understanding and treatment of many conduct disorders and many individual delinquents. However, as with other causal explanations, they are not without their theoretical and methodological weaknesses.

Critiques of Theoretical Assumptions and Concepts

Biological determinism, or the position that perceives human behavior as genetically programmed, has elicited vigorous opposition from those espousing the view that human conduct is, in general, culturally relative. Austin Turk (1969) spoke for many social scientists by arguing that validation of biological-predisposition hypotheses would require us to agree that there are persons born to commit certain acts that will invariably be criminal, anywhere and everywhere. On the contrary, Turk (1969:10–11) contends

> There is apparently no pattern of human behavior which has not been at least tolerated in some normative structure. While there do seem to be universal categories of norms (e.g., norms limiting the use of violence) no specific explicit or implicit rule has ever been shown to be present in all human societies . . . From the absence of universal norms it follows that research on the etiology of any specific form of "criminal" behavior must inevitably be culture-specific and time-bound, because the phenomenon under study will change from culture to culture.

In addition to the criticism that sociobiology does not take culture into account and that culture is dominant over most genetic, inherited, behavioral tendencies, other opponents contend that the application of animal instincts to human beings is nothing more than a grossly imperfect transfer by analogy. Thus, sociobiologists assume that they are animals and we are animals; all species are the result of a long evolutionary process; therefore, the same inherited survival needs and instincts that characterize other primates also may be invoked to explain human behavior. Critics of sociobiology argue that these assumptions are simplistic in light of the sophistication and complexity of the human organism and human societies. They point out that the essential principles and hypotheses of sociobiology are scientifically untestable and therefore remain nothing more than interesting speculations. One attempt to overcome some of these shortcomings has led to the development of **human ontogenetics**, *a new discipline that deals with the development of the human individual as a biosychosocial unit from conception until death.*

Marshall Clinard and Robert Meier (2008:51) criticized psychogenic explanations of deviant behavior by stating that they "blur the line between 'sickness' and simple deviation from norms." In other words, the medical analogy comparing delinquent acts with physical ailments lacks generality and is unconvincing, since only a small proportion of juvenile misconduct can be traced to an organic cause, of either the mind or the body. The metaphor of the delinquent act as a symptom of underlying emotional maladjustment is seldom grounded in reality and, in fact, glosses over individual responsibility for behavior. It also ignores the fact that almost every adolescent commits some form of delinquency and that it may be more pathological to totally abstain from delinquency (Brezina and Piquero, 2007). In addition, Clinard and Meier (2008:69) disagree with the assumption that "adult behavior and personality are almost wholly determined by childhood experiences, most of them in the family, whereas evidence suggests that behavior varies according to social situations and social roles and that personality continues to develop throughout life."

Sue Titus Reid contended that the psychogenic terms are vague, so vague that they may be described as the unknown. No operational definitions for such concepts as *id*, *ego*, *superego*, or *unconscious* are given (Reid, 2008). Finally, there is no consensus or agreement among psychiatrists and psychologists concerning the objective criteria to be employed in assessing degrees of mental well-being or mental aberration.

Critique of Research Methodology

The methodological problems associated with most studies applying the psychogenic approach to the analysis of criminal and delinquent behavior are well summarized by Reid (2008). The research has been based on samples that are too small, that have usually been selected from among psychiatric patients and often from among institutionalized subjects, and the use of control groups has not been adequate. The focus on the individual seldom generates group patterns of behavior and prevents generalization. And, as discussed earlier in this chapter, projective techniques are open to the subjective interpretation of the analyst.

The notion that there is a personality trait or type that is peculiar to criminals and/or delinquents has come under close scrutiny. Gordon Waldo and Simon Dinitz (1967), for instance, reviewed all 94 psychological explanations published between 1950 and 1967. They found little evidence that personality traits could predict delinquent involvement. Tannenbaum (1977) reviewed personality studies from 1966 to 1975. He found that "personality tests, per se, are no better predictors of criminal personalities than were those of ten years ago" (Albanese, 1993:48).

Theorists who contend that some psychological factor makes delinquents different from nondelinquents have difficulty in explaining the preponderance of conforming behavior by those who possess the suspected psychological trait. At the same time, self-report studies consistently show that most people have committed delinquent acts sometime during their lives (Klein, 1987). With these data-supported findings before us, it seems futile to try to find an explanation for widespread behavior based on an alleged psychological abnormality, for, by definition, *abnormal* means *unusual*, or *out of the ordinary*.

Gwynn Nettler (1984:28) reported how efforts to expand the legal defense of insanity to include all those personality and emotional weaknesses and defects that afflict human beings have encountered skepticism and disagreement from the legal and psychological professions:

> While 77 percent of the psychiatrists expressed confidence in their expert testimony in criminal trials, only 44.5 percent of the lawyers expressed confidence in psychiatric expertise . . . As might be expected, the two professions disagreed also on the relationship between serious

> criminal activity and mental illness . . . [While] *half* of the psychiatrists believed that "anyone who commits a serious crime is mentally ill" or "most people who commit serious crimes are mentally ill," only a *third* of the lawyers agreed. (Nettler, 1984:28)

There is also a growing public complaint that psychogenic (and biological) explanations of crime and delinquency are being used by many offenders to reject personal responsibility for their antisocial behavior. It has become common, these critics argue, for theories tracing misbehavior to some irresistible force or factor in the culprit's psyche or genetic blueprint. In some cases, presenting offenders as "victims" has served as a courtroom defense for horrific crimes. Examples in recent years include the following:

- The campus strangler of a female student whose attorney suggested that his client was just acting out his unconscious anger and unfulfilled needs.
- The Los Angeles mob that brutally attacked and critically injured a passing truck driver claimed they were caught up in the contagious excitement and spontaneity of the moment.
- The infamous "Twinkie Defense" that contended that the murderer of the San Francisco mayor and city supervisor was less culpable because of a dietary biochemical imbalance.
- The gang leader whose violent and criminal lifestyle was credited to low self-esteem.
- The 17-year-old in Mississippi who testified that demons drove him to kill (also known as "the devil made me do it defense").

To sociologists, the critical dilemma of the biological and psychogenic approaches are that they attempt to explain juvenile delinquency and many other forms of deviant behavior on the basis of individual characteristics, while explanations about how individuals developed those characteristics are often social. Thus, they take a circuitous and often erroneous route to the more viable causal variables. For example, psychoanalytic theory emphasizes inherent drives and emotional stress, but social interaction with parents and others during childhood and adolescence can produce an imbalance between those drives and learned social expectations about behavior. Though biological and psychogenic explanations may help in the treatment of individual cases, increasingly, criminologists have turned to societal forces for explanations of behavior.

Summary

We began this chapter by exploring some of the myths and folklore that attempted to link biology to behavior. We pointed out how many of these attempts led to unfair stereotypes.

The 18th century gave rise to the Classical School of Criminological Thought, which assumed that crime and delinquency was the result of the exercise of free will and logical, rational thought. The Neoclassical School modified the assumptions of the classical theorists by allowing for extenuating circumstances and recognized that not all people are equally rational. This allowed for some discretion and differential treatment for young offenders or adults who were adjudged mentally incompetent.

In the late 19th century, the Positive School of Criminology, through the leadership of men like Cesare Lombroso, attempted to scientifically link biological and physiological characteristics to criminal behavior. This biological determinism laid the foundation for 20th-century research which attributed character, personality, and delinquency potential to the shape of one's body. As the search for a biological connection to delinquency continued, research has been conducted on many biological variables such as genetics, diet, and brain malfunctions (Fishbein, 1990).

In an attempt to link biological determinism with the contributing influence of social and cultural factors, sociobiological explanations for delinquency emerged. Sociobiologists insist that social behavior is a product of evolutionary history and genetics. Hence, delinquent behavior is viewed as being genetically programmed into certain individuals. Social scientists acknowledge that genetics, biology, and physiology may all play a role in understanding juvenile delinquency; however, they insist that it is the manner in which these traits are manifested and dealt with in a social and cultural context that explains deviant behavior.

We then defined and explained the psychogenic approach to crime and delinquency. The fields of psychiatry and psychology were defined, pointing out their similarities, areas of overlap, and significant differences.

Sigmund Freud's concepts regarding the "unconscious" and personality formation were reviewed. Freudian theory was applied to crime and delinquency, attempting to explain these forms of deviant behavior as resulting from problems in personality development. This medical model approach to delinquency contends that delinquency is a symptom of deeply embedded psychological problems. It is further suggested that if identified early enough, and corrected, future delinquency and criminality can be avoided.

Other psychogenic explanations included feeblemindedness, neurological abnormalities, flawed personalities (such as the psychopath or sociopath), insufficient moral development, and the adolescent identity crisis. There are a number of theoretical and methodological weaknesses in the biological and psychogenic approaches to juvenile delinquency. Suffering from questionable theoretical assumptions, and small and nonrepresentative samples, they fail to provide empirically tested and supported causal explanations for delinquent behavior. While they provide some useful insights, only a few delinquents seem to suffer from organic brain disorders or seriously maladjusted personalities. The majority of juvenile delinquents are physically and psychologically similar to the nondelinquent population.

From a sociological perspective, the psychogenic theories fail to view delinquency in its broader social context and to acknowledge the impact of the many social and cultural factors that influence and shape human behavior. In Chapter 5, and throughout the remainder of this book, we turn to these social and cultural variables in order to more fully understand juvenile delinquency.

Concept Integration: Questions and Topics for Study and Discussion

1. Reexamine the research of Lombroso, Sheldon, and the Gluecks. Identify and critique their methodology, findings, and conclusions.
2. What are the main assumptions of the Classical School of Criminological Thought and the Positive School of Criminology? What are the differences between these two early approaches to explain criminal behavior?
3. Discuss and explain the hypothesized links between the following variables:
   a. The XYY chromosome and criminal behavior.

   b. Abnormal EEG patterns and deviant or criminal behavior.
   c. Diet, biochemical irregularities, and misbehavior.
4. Define and explain sociobiology. How does this field of study attempt to bridge the social and biological sciences? What contribution may sociobiology make toward an understanding of human behavior?
5. What did the Gluecks mean by their statement: "A physical characteristic may be socially defined and treated in ways which encourage criminal behavior?" Give several examples.
6. Briefly define the psychogenic approach to explaining and interpreting human behavior and list its shortcomings and limitations.
7. Based upon your reading of this chapter, briefly outline the contributions of Sigmund Freud, Erik Erikson, and Lawrence Kohlberg. Compare and contrast the ideas of Freud and Erikson regarding the development of human personality as they may relate to juvenile delinquency.
8. What do psychiatrists mean when they say, "The delinquent act is the hurt child's cry for help"? Do you agree with them? Why or why not?
9. What is a psychopath (or sociopath)? Have you known or read of anyone who seemed to manifest this particular kind of personality? Could there be other explanations for his or her behavior besides personality maladjustment?

Chapter 5

Sociological Explanations of Juvenile Delinquency

Social Strain and Cultural Transmission Theories

READING OBJECTIVES

Reading this chapter will help you achieve the following objectives:

1. Define and explain the sociological perspective in explaining human behavior in general and juvenile delinquency in particular.
2. Understand the principles and purposes of theory building as it applies to the explanation of delinquent behavior.
3. Define and explain specific sociological concepts and theories of deviant and delinquent conduct and the major categories of Social Strain or Anomie Theory and Cultural Transmission Theory.
4. Apply these sociological theories of human behavior to explaining juvenile delinquency.
5. Summarize contributions and limitations of the sociological theories of deviance and delinquency discussed in this chapter.

INTRODUCTION

Sociology is a comparatively young academic discipline, yet its influence upon modern criminology and contributions to theoretical explanations of deviant behavior have been more extensive and enduring than the preceding theories of biological determinism and psychological maladjustment. Despite some meaningful contributions to our understanding, the biological and psychological explanations neglect *the* most prominent aspect of deviance, that is, like any other human activity, deviant behavior is inherently social in nature. For an individual to be deviant or delinquent, he or she must be involved with other people.

Sociologists, in explaining and interpreting human behavior, maintain that human behavior is intrinsically social and that "social facts should be explained by other social facts and not by psychological, biological, or any non-social facts" (Durkheim, 1950:18–22). More specifically, sociological explanations stress that juvenile delinquency emerges from the complex network of social groups, institutions, and human interrelationships that exist in a society. Therefore, in order to better understand juvenile delinquency, we must examine it within the social context in which it occurs. While sociologists are not unanimous in pinpointing the exact causes of juvenile delinquency (or any other kind of nonconformity or deviance), the inseparable social nature of human behavior is a common thread throughout all sociological explanations of delinquency.

Before we present major sociological theories of juvenile delinquency in Chapters 5, 6, 7, and 8, it is important to briefly define theory and explain its purpose.

THEORY

The study of **etiology**—*the cause(s) of an event, phenomenon, or behavior*—is a common exercise in the scientific community and many academic disciplines. Ideally, systematic and controlled observations, data collection, and the testing of hypotheses result in valid and reliable findings that then can be stated in a theoretical explanation of what has occurred (Lastrucci, 1967). In other words, a **theory** is *a general statement that accurately relates cause-and-effect variables so as to explain events or behavior.* Thus, sociologists, in their pursuit of theoretical explanations of delinquency, have linked youthful misconduct to the home, family, neighborhood, school, peer group, and a host of other variables found in the juvenile's social milieu.

Sociologists agree that causation is present if three conditions are met (Cole, 1980). First, causation can occur only if the independent variable exists *before* the dependent variable. That is to say, the "cause" must precede the "effect." For example, it has been theorized that young people exposed to dominant adult criminal elements in their neighborhoods have increased opportunity to learn and participate in delinquent behavior. In other words, the presence and availability of adult criminals as role models are the causal independent variables that exist before the emergence of delinquent behavior, the affected or dependent variable, in this line of reasoning.

Second, if causation exists, then change in the independent variable also affects the dependent variable, but in a different way. Thus, if a youngster is removed from the old neighborhood and surrounded by a preponderance of neighborhood models and influences favorable to law-abiding behavior, the youth would be less likely to commit delinquent acts.

Finally, causation cannot be established until researchers have ruled out the influence of other possible independent variables. The way to do this is to analyze the effect(s) of each possible independent variable, keeping constant all other possible independent variables. Referring back to the previous example, perhaps the degree of stability and cohesiveness of a child's family and home environment is the true independent variable that determines whether the youth will participate in delinquent activities, and not the older established criminal elements that exist in the neighborhood. It is conceivable that a strong and secure family and home life may insulate many children from becoming juvenile delinquents, regardless of their neighborhood environments, whereas children from fragmented and dysfunctional families may gravitate toward the available criminal models in their areas.

It is much more difficult to identify and control for possible antecedent or intervening variables that can confound conclusions regarding causality in social science research than in the laboratory conditions of the chemist or physicist. It follows, then, that sociological theories explaining the cause(s) of juvenile delinquency (or other social phenomena) are more tentative and subject to continual scrutiny, verification, and possible modification. As Schur (1973: 170–171) noted, "In their interminable search for 'causes,' sociologists have produced no definitive 'solution' to delinquency problems. They have, however, alerted us to many misconceptions and blind alleys, and begun to show us the direction that policy might sensibly take."

Moreover, sociological theories of delinquency do not readily lend themselves to micro-level and macro-level division and classification.

> Microlevel analysis focuses on the day-to-day interactions of individuals and groups in specific social situations. Macrolevel analysis examines broader social structures and society as a whole. (Thompson and Hickey, 2008:17–18)

While it may be convenient to divide social phenomena into these two categories, it is important to understand that theories of juvenile delinquency, more often than not, are mixtures of micro-level and macro-level sociology.

In seeking logical organization of a myriad of sociological theories, it is also tempting to separate them into broad social structure and social-process categories. *Social structure* refers to the way that society is put together, its institutional arrangements and functions, and the hierarchy of social classes and how they relate to one another. And, indeed, some crime and delinquency can be traced to weaknesses and conflicts in social structure. *Social process* refers to the dynamic interaction between and among individuals and groups as they relate to peers, family, school, and other social institutions and agencies. Without question, some juvenile misconduct evolves from the negative and unproductive personal relations of some youths with processes and institutions of society. However, the etiological or causal roots of juvenile delinquency cannot be placed neatly in social structure and social-process categories. For example, in this chapter we will see that Sutherland's Theory of Differential Association involves not only the social learning of criminal values and techniques in intimate groups, but also the availability of such alternative socialization in underclass neighborhoods of economically disadvantaged residents. Likewise, as is detailed in Chapter 6, radical theorists such as Karl Marx and his followers perceived criminal deviance as a logical and legitimate reaction of outraged workers against the manipulation and economic system of the dominant ruling class. Clearly, Radical Theory contains elements of both social structure and social process. In the absence of stronger organizing criteria, we have chosen to systematize our presentation of sociological theories of delinquency with a typology containing six categories of overarching substantive similarities. In other words, we have examined the sociological theories for similarities in sociological content, explanatory approach, and focus on delinquency etiology.

In order to conceptually understand the various sociological explanations of juvenile delinquency, we have divided them into seven major categories—organized and presented in four sequential chapters:

1. Social strain theories
2. Cultural transmission theories
3. Social learning theories
4. Social control theories
5. Labeling theories
6. Conflict theories
7. Maturation, rational choice, and deterrence theories

While typologies such as these are useful for organizing and presenting a mass of data or information, it must be acknowledged that the theoretical categories that supply the framework for Chapters 5, 6, 7, and 8 are neither exhaustive nor mutually exclusive. Thus, they share the common weaknesses of virtually all typologies in the social and behavioral sciences. In attempting to group together major theoretical explanations of juvenile delinquency that share a major conceptual basis, it becomes clear to the astute reader that the real world of cause and effect of human behavior cannot be so easily packaged in discrete categories. As demonstrated in all such endeavors, the etiological theories often merge, overlap, and build on each other. Moreover, these sociological theories are presented in only approximate order of chronological development. In fact, sometimes the theories were formulated simultaneously as the research and intellectual products of contemporary scholars.

The first two types of sociological explanations—social strain theories and cultural transmission theories—are presented in this chapter. The other five kinds of sociological theories are discussed in Chapters 6, 7, and 8.

SOCIAL STRAIN THEORIES

The theoretical explanations of deviance and delinquency that are grouped together in this category share an underlying assumption that nonconforming behavior arises out of social circumstances in which individuals or groups experience normative confusion or disruption. Confronted with a new, traumatic, or frustrating social situation (social strain), some people respond in a deviant and perhaps criminal manner.

Durkheim's Concept of Anomie

Emile Durkheim, in his landmark study of suicide ([1897] 1951), developed the concept of **anomie** to characterize *the condition of a society or group with a high degree of confusion and contradiction in its basic social norms.* Durkheim traced the unusually high suicide rates during periods of serious economic depression, severe political crises and upheavals, rapid societal change, and other unstable social conditions, to the absence or reduced efficacy of normative regulation during such times. Under such conditions, Durkheim hypothesized, the usual rules that restrain us from committing socially unacceptable acts can become weakened or suspended for some members of society. In this state of anomie, it is difficult for some individuals to know what is expected of them. In extreme cases, such persons may be "free" to take their own lives. Durkheim contended that unusually high suicide rates could be predicted from a careful study of prevailing social conditions.

Merton's Theory of Anomie

Suicide is just one form of deviant behavior. In 1938, Robert K. Merton modified and expanded Durkheim's concept of anomie into a general theory that helps explain many different kinds of deviant behavior (Merton, 1957). As a result of this conceptual connection with Durkheim's early work, Merton's more fully developed Strain Theory of deviant behavior is often referred to as Anomie Theory. Very few sociological theories are broad enough in basic concepts and assumptions to encompass a wide spectrum of deviant behaviors with any degree of specificity. A general theory is like an umbrella. Just as several different individuals may find shelter under a shared umbrella, so Merton's general theory of anomie offers an organized framework of logical explanations that can be applied to several kinds of deviant behavior, including juvenile delinquency.

Merton perceived anomie as a state of dissatisfaction arising from a sense of discrepancy between the aspirations of an individual and the means that the person has available to realize these ambitions. In his essay on anomie, Merton observed that Americans are exposed to powerful socialization processes that stress the success ethic. Consequently, nearly everyone internalizes the culturally approved goal of "getting ahead," that is, making money, accumulating material possessions, and achieving high social status based on money and occupation. At the same time, American society gives a clear message regarding culturally approved means to achieve these lofty objectives. We are encouraged to strive for them as society says we should—attend school, work hard, save money, lead lives of virtue, thrift, patience, and deferred gratification—and ultimately we hope to realize our dreams of material success and enhanced social status. However, Merton maintained that some people, particularly among the disadvantaged lower classes,[1] unhappily realize that they will not be able to achieve those idealized goals through the legitimate means that society endorses. They may lack the academic background to attend college, and the only jobs available to them may be unskilled, low-paying "dead-end jobs" that lead to neither promotion nor financial security. Yet, the desire to fulfill the internalized objectives persists. This juxtaposition of idealized, socially approved goals, and the reality of reduced life chances and opportunities for achievement in the socially approved ways, places many individuals in a state of helpless and hopeless frustration or *anomie*. Denied legitimate opportunities, the rules of the game may have diminished importance. What really matters to such anomic individuals is not how one "plays the game" but whether one "wins." Under such circumstances, some persons will turn to illegitimate means to attain the culturally approved goals. However, Merton contended, not everyone who experiences anomic frustration over blocked goals will resort to criminal behavior. Other avenues of adaptation are also open. Merton's Typology of Modes of Adaptive Behavior is an innovative contribution and is the heart of his general theory of deviance.

In his Typology of Modes of Adaptive Behavior, Merton identified five possible behavioral patterns for individuals as they respond to culturally approved goals and institutionalized means for achieving those idealized objectives in American society (Figure 5.1). Merton stressed that these are role adaptations and not personality types. People may readily shift from one of these roles to another.

	Individual Adaptations	Culturally Approved Goals	Institutionalized Means of Achievement
I.	Conformity	(+)	(+)
II.	Innovation	(+)	(−)
III.	Ritualism	(−)	(+)
IV.	Retreatism	(−)	(−)
V.	Rebellion	(−,+)	(−,+)

FIGURE 5.1 Merton's Typology of Modes of Individual Adaptive Behavior.

Note: (+) signifies "acceptance" by the individual.
(−) signifies "rejection" by the individual.
(−,+) signifies "rejection of existing goals and means and the substitution of new goals and means" by the individual.

Can you think of examples other than those given in the text that fit Merton's adaptation strategies? Why is it important to understand that Merton was referring to adaptations and not personality types?

Source: Merton, R. K. Social structure and anomie. *American Sociological Review* 3 (1938):676.

[1] *Underclass* is the more acceptable term today. However, in order to maintain consistency in usage and avoid confusion, we use the term *lower class* when discussing or referring to older, classic studies.

The first adaptation is *Conformity,* which encompasses most members of our society. This adaptation accepts the culturally approved success goals and has available the institutionalized work ethic for achievement. Thus, this adaptation conforms to societal expectations.

The other four possible adaptations represent deviant responses to the disparity between cultural goals and institutionalized means in the context of anomic strain. Adaptation II is *Innovation* and characterizes situations where people who subscribe to the typical cultural goals of monetary and material success realize they lack the socially approved and legitimate means to achieve those goals. They become dissatisfied, frustrated, and anomic and resort to innovative, norm-violating behavior to achieve the coveted cultural goals. This adaptation to blocked goals is often a criminal or delinquent response (Bernard, 1990).

Behavioral Adaptation III is *Ritualism* and involves rigid adherence to culturally approved methods for getting ahead and making progress. However, like caged squirrels on a treadmill, their overconformity isn't going to "pay off." In time, perhaps these persons realize that the attained level of achievement will not equal the level of aspiration or effort. They experience feelings of despair and anomie, and modify or abandon the idealized cultural goals, but persist at a ritualized, unfulfilling line of work.

Adaptation IV is *Retreatism.* Here, in anomic frustration, this adaptation abandons both cultural goals *and* the institutionalized means for attaining them. In a sense, these people give up in the struggle to reach the seemingly unreachable goals

What influence might this individual have as a potential role model for inner-city lower-class youths?

via unrewarding methods and retreat from a social system and culture that imposes such unreasonable "ends" and "means." This adaptation is reflected by runaways, transients, drug users, and alcoholics who turn their backs and seek escape from the struggle for material success and other socially approved values.

The fifth behavioral adaptation is *Rebellion*. In this case, angry over the anomic situation experienced, this adaptation rejects both the culturally approved goals and the institutionalized means of achievement. In their place are substituted new goals and new means of achievement. This call for a new social order is a typical response of the social reformer or revolutionary.

Cohen's "Delinquent Boys"

Albert Cohen (1955) elaborated upon Merton's anomie explanation of deviant behavior with his more specific theory that a large amount of delinquent behavior results from blocked goals and "status frustration." According to Cohen, lower-class boys want to achieve success and higher social status, just like middle- and upper-class boys. Yet, due to their unpromising social circumstances, they find that they are blocked from achieving status (especially in school). Essentially, Cohen reported, lower-class boys who aspire to increased social status in a dominant, middle-class value system can respond in one of three ways:

1. The "college-boy" response
2. The "corner-boy" response
3. The "delinquent-boy" response

The "college-boy" response roughly corresponds to Merton's Conformity mode of adaptation. In this case, lower-class youths accept the challenge of the middle-class value system and, through higher education and deferred gratification (foregoing small, immediate rewards for larger, long-term rewards), attempt to achieve social status by conforming to middle-class expectations. This response is chosen by comparatively few lower-class boys, according to Cohen, because their limited financial resources make chances for college graduation and occupational success extremely low.

Probably the most common response in Cohen's scheme is the "corner-boy" response, which involves the youths' withdrawal into a subculture of working-class boys who share a mutual set of values by which status can be gained within the group without having to conform and compete with middle-class society. This is analogous to Merton's Retreatism mode of adaptation to anomic conditions. While this group is not specifically delinquent in its purpose, the boys who choose this response often become involved in delinquent activities (especially status offenses such as truancy, smoking, and alcohol consumption).

The final response in Cohen's typology is the "delinquent boy." Boys in this group—manifestly similar to the youths who make Merton's Innovation and Rebellion adaptations—become frustrated with their inability to gain status through conventional means. Consequently, they develop what Cohen referred to as a delinquent subculture, whose values and behavior are antithetical to those espoused by the middle class. Paradoxically, in acting out their subcultural values, these boys find themselves in harmony with the expectations of their group but are perceived as nonconforming delinquents by the larger society.

The similarities between the theories of Merton and Cohen are striking. At least one major difference, however, is that Merton viewed criminal deviance as practical and utilitarian in nature, whereas Cohen (1955:25) saw delinquency as more "non-utilitarian, malicious, and negativistic."

Cloward and Ohlin's "Delinquency and Opportunity"

Richard Cloward and Lloyd Ohlin (1960) added to the social strain approach with their concept of "illegitimate opportunity." Like Cohen, they accepted Merton's view that lower-class juveniles generally internalize the standard success goals. They also agreed with Merton and Cohen that the blockage of these goals can lead to status frustration and place some youths in a position of untenable strain. This situation can result in a sense of alienation and anomie in which those affected may turn to delinquent, illegitimate means to achieve an increment in status. It is at this point that Cloward and Ohlin moved their theoretical formulation beyond those suggested by both Merton and Cohen.

Cloward and Ohlin contended that while lower-class juveniles have differential opportunities for achieving success through *legitimate* means, they also have differential opportunities for achieving it through *illegitimate* means. They pointed out that there are some areas in which illegitimate opportunities for youth to acquire success and status are not readily available. In such surroundings, some juveniles may be totally frustrated with their locked-in lowly status and lack of opportunity to achieve the idealized success goals. Lacking even deviant or delinquent opportunities, their frustration is unrequited and their aspirations remain unfulfilled. In situations where there *are* illegitimate opportunities, Cloward and Ohlin saw response to anomic frustration as being group oriented. However, the type of delinquent response depends upon the *kind* of illegitimate opportunity available to the youths. Thus, in contrast to Cohen who saw blocked goals leading to a rather standard delinquent gang response, Cloward and Ohlin delineated three possible delinquent subcultural responses. In other words, while anomic status frustration over blocked goals could well be a common denominator in groups of lower-class boys scattered throughout a city, the particular form of collective, delinquent response any given group might make would depend on the kind of delinquent opportunity available to the group.

Cloward and Ohlin presented three types of juvenile gangs, each characterized by different kinds of delinquent activities:

1. The crime-oriented gang
2. The conflict-oriented gang
3. The retreatist-oriented gang

The first response of underclass youths to their collective sense of unjust deprivation and alienation involves such criminal activities as theft, fraud, and extortion. The criminal orientation of this group is elicited and orchestrated by adult criminal elements that operate in the neighborhood or district in which this group of disenchanted and anomic youths reside. In the perceived absence of a legitimate opportunity structure, they become vulnerable to the influence of adult criminals whose activities and prosperity have high visibility in the area. The adult criminals are in a position to serve as viable role models and mentors for youths feeling the disappointment and frustration of blocked avenues to success. According to Cloward and Ohlin, the criminal alternative and the opportunity for enhanced social status lead these boys into instrumental delinquency, in which they serve as "apprentice criminals" under the direction and control of adult professionals.

The second anomic response is the formation of a conflict-oriented gang. Cloward and Ohlin suggested that youthful gangs that turn to fighting and violence as primary means of securing status live in areas where both conventional and criminal opportunities are either absent or very weak. In other words, the conflict-oriented activities of these street gangs develop under conditions of relative detachment from all institutionalized systems of opportunity and social control, either legitimate or illegitimate. These are neighborhoods where opportunities for upward social mobility are essentially nonexistent, where conventional law enforcement agencies are weak, and where opportunities to participate with adult criminals in their illegal but successful operations are also absent. In such areas, frustrated and discontented youths often seek to establish their own status hierarchy in conflict with one another and with society.

Cloward and Ohlin termed the third kind of delinquent response as the retreatist-oriented gang. While this response is a *group* reaction to social strain engendered by blocked success opportunities, it is similar to Merton's fourth Mode of Individual Adaptation, disengagement and retreatism from larger society. Cloward and Ohlin depicted members of retreatist gangs as overwhelmed with feelings of failure, despair, and normlessness. These youths withdraw into the restricted world of their group and center their attention and activity upon the consumption of drugs in quest of physical or emotional "highs." In this way, they not only demonstrate their contempt for the normative standards of conforming society, but mask their sense of failure. As with the other two types of delinquent gang responses, the development of the retreatist group and its characteristic behavior depends upon the presence of certain opportunity structures in the members' environment. There must be easy access to sources of drugs and the lore of drug use in the area where the potential gang members live. The genesis of a drug subculture in lower-class neighborhoods is often aided by "rapid geographical mobility, inadequate social controls, and other manifestations of social disorganization" (Cloward and Ohlin, 1960:178).

One of the most innovative ideas put forward by Cloward and Ohlin centers on how youths are recruited or motivated to abandon the quest for material success and social status and adopt a retreatist orientation. Just as it requires some opportunity and aptitude to achieve societal goals in the culturally approved ways, youths also must have a measure of opportunity and certain physical or organizational abilities in order to acquire success through crime or delinquency. Therefore, Cloward and Ohlin suggest, youths failing in both legitimate and illegitimate approaches to material success and social status are *double failures.* These double failures are most likely to demonstrate their anomic frustration in a retreatist gang response.

Contributions of Social Strain Theories

Social strain theories view deviance and delinquency as a result of the social structure in which they occur. Juveniles who grow up in communities where access to culturally approved goals by conventional means is denied, and where a large degree of social disorganization is present, find themselves in situations where social norms governing behavior are not clearly defined. It follows, according to social strain theories, that these youngsters may discover that delinquent activities supply opportunities to achieve social identity and social status.

For many years, Social Strain Theory, with its fundamental postulates of anomie and social disorganization, dominated sociological explanations of deviant and delinquent behavior. It is an inherently sociological approach, and because official arrest statistics seem to support the idea that juvenile delinquency is primarily a lower-class phenomenon, strain theory offers a great deal of explanatory power. A number of researchers have rallied in support of social strain theories as basically correct in a broad sense, if not in all particulars (Bernard, 1990; Menard, 1995). At least one study indicates that general strain theory may have explanatory power for ethnic minorities, especially Hispanics, who due to the acculturation process are exposed to unique types of strain that may increase the likelihood of delinquency (Perez, et al., 2008). And another suggests that delinquency previously associated with attention deficit/hyperactivity disorder (ADHD) and other biological and psychological maladies may actually be more a result of the strain experienced by those with the afflictions (Johnson and Kercher, 2007).

Strain theories of delinquency contribute to an understanding of the relationship between the status frustration experienced by lower-class youths and poor performance in school. For example, Polk and Schafer (1972) indicated that poor school performance and the feelings of frustration due to blocked educational opportunities of economically disadvantaged youths have been linked to juvenile delinquency (this phenomenon and its relationship to delinquency is further explored in Chapter 10).

Although Merton made no direct application of his anomie theory to juvenile delinquency, it is regarded as one of the most influential and useful formulations in describing and explaining the process behind many forms of deviant and delinquent behavior. A number of other social scientists were quick to recognize the potential of Merton's general theory of deviance in explaining why at least some juveniles become delinquent (Farnsworth and Leiber, 1989).

Perhaps the greatest contribution of strain theories has been in their application to gang delinquency (discussed in detail in Chapter 12). Cohen, Cloward and Ohlin, and others applied the basic assumptions of anomie and strain theories to help explain the formation and activities of juvenile gangs. Irving Spergel (1964), for example, studied lower-class gangs, and while his typology of gangs differed from the one constructed by Cloward and Ohlin, he documented that juvenile gangs indeed tend to specialize in certain types of delinquent activities.

While debate continues over whether lower-class youths internalize middle-class aspirations and goals as assumed by the proponents of strain theory, and while most juvenile delinquency does not involve juvenile gangs, strain theories emphasize the importance of socioeconomic status, neighborhood environment, and adaptation to social structure as important variables in understanding delinquency. These contributions provide insight into some types of juvenile delinquency, especially those related to the activities of lower-class gangs.

Robert Agnew (1992, 1995) offers a more expansive application of social strain explanations of delinquent behavior. Agnew's General Strain Theory counters some persistent criticisms and more appropriately appears at the end of the next section.

Criticisms and Limitations of Social Strain Theories

A number of weaknesses in the explanatory arguments of strain theories have been advanced. For example, the anomie theory of deviance, while useful in explaining some kinds of lower-class nonconformity, makes some questionable assumptions about the situation of lower-class people. It assumes, first, that people from the lower social classes develop about the same level of aspiration for themselves as do people from the more favored classes. Studies of lower-class subjects show that this is not necessarily the case and that lower-class people tend to develop a fairly realistic assessment of their lowered life chances and adjust their expectations accordingly (e.g., Han, 1969).

Another apparent assumption of anomie theory that may be faulty is the generalization that structural frustration causes delinquency (Agnew, 1984). Sanders (1981:31) challenged this assumption by asking, "Why is it that only a relatively few members of the lower socioeconomic strata commit delinquent acts frequently? Why are boys ten times more likely to engage in delinquent acts than girls in the same social position?"

Travis Hirschi (1969) pointed out that most delinquent boys eventually become law-abiding adults, which is a potential source of embarrassment to the strain theorists. Indeed, most delinquents do come to terms with society as they mature. They do *not* graduate into a life of adult crime. Typically, as they mature, they abandon juvenile crime and misbehavior. But their eventual reform cannot be explained by changes in the lower-class conditions that purportedly forced them into their initial deviance.

In *Delinquent Boys* (1955), Cohen's main focus was on the nonutilitarian behavior of lower-class juveniles. It was at this point that Sykes and Matza (1957) cast doubt upon Cohen's theory by contending that the delinquent gangs they studied stole in order to get money for entertainment, which demonstrated that they were impractical adolescents, rather than "nonutilitarian."

Cohen's point that lower-class youths make a delinquent response as a frustrated attack upon middle-class standards also has been targeted for criticism. Kitsuse and Dietrick (1959) argued that the initial motives of youths for joining gangs and participating in delinquent activities are many and varied, ranging from self-preservation in the neighborhood to the desire for friends.

Cloward and Ohlin's theory of Differential Opportunity also has been subjected to sharp criticism. The main complaint has been that the theory's emphasis on a set of delinquent subcultural reactions to perceived lack of economic opportunity ignores other major factors in delinquency causation. For example, Bordua (1962) charged that Cloward and Ohlin had a tendency to ignore the life histories of their delinquent subjects. The delinquents of Thrasher, Cohen, Miller, and other theorists were presented as having family, school, and other background experiences that affected their subsequent delinquent behavior. "On the other hand, Cloward and Ohlin's delinquents seem suddenly to appear on the scene sometime in adolescence, to look at the world, and to discover: 'There's no opportunity in my structure!'" (Bordua, 1962:255).

Cohen (1966) pointed out that Cloward and Ohlin suggested a false dichotomy between "legitimate opportunities" and "illegitimate opportunities." He argued:

> the same things are typically, and perhaps always, both. [For] example, identical firearms can be used to kill deer in season; or deer, policemen, and estranged spouses out of season. It is one of the most fundamental

> and pervasive dilemmas of social life that all legitimate power, whether over things or people, can be used to implement or to violate social norms. (Cohen, 1966:110)

Cloward and Ohlin's contention that youthful gangs specialized in criminality, fighting, or drug use also has been challenged. Numerous studies have shown delinquent gangs to be engaged in a wide variety of illegal activities (Kulik, et al., 1968; Short, et al., 1963).

Another common complaint regarding the Theory of Differential Opportunity centers on the rather rigid typological structure (a criticism also shared by Merton's Anomie Theory and most other behavioral typologies). Lemert (1967), Short, et al. (1963), and Bordua (1962) all contended that the assignment of groups to one or another category is too mechanistic, that is, much gang delinquency in working-class areas is more spontaneous and unstructured than Cloward and Ohlin would have us believe.

A persistent criticism of traditional Strain Theory is that while suggesting helpful explanations of underclass delinquency, it fails to offer any direct insights into delinquency in the middle and upper classes. This may be a moot point since most strain theorists never claimed etiological generality beyond the lower class.

Perhaps a more telling deficiency in Strain Theory is the shortage of viable applications to female delinquency of any class. Ruth Triplett and Roger Jarjoura (1997:287) point out that "although gender and social class are two of the best known correlates of crime and delinquency, criminologists have shown surprisingly little interest in exploring how these variables intersect in the etiology of deviant behavior." Their findings add significant details to the idea of blocked goals leading to individual strain and possibly illegal conduct—for females as well as males. More specifically, Triplett and Jarjoura (1997:287) "suggest that gender and class are both important factors shaping educational expectations and through them, the likelihood of delinquency involvement." John Hoffman and Susan Su (1997) found that stressful life events have similar impact on delinquency and drug use among both females and males.

AGNEW'S GENERAL STRAIN THEORY

The last two complaints regarding the apparent failure of traditional Social Strain Theory to account for the delinquency of females and middle- and upper-class youths have been countered by Robert Agnew's (1992; 1995; 2001) General Strain Theory of delinquency. . Agnew views strain as more than just a disjunction between goals and means. He sees crime and delinquency as adaptations to stress. Agnew (1992;2001) identified three major sources of stress that leads to social strain:

1. Discrepancy between means and goals or between expectations and actual outcomes. This type of stress is most closely related to Merton's conception of anomie.
2. Loss of something positive in one's life. For juveniles, this could be loss of a parent, loved one, or the breakup with a boyfriend or girlfriend.
3. Presence of negative circumstances or events. These could be environmental (e.g., slum living conditions) or more personal stress related (e.g., victim of sexual abuse or criminal victimization).

How has strain theory helped explain delinquency among Chinese youths?

Agnew's General Strain Theory inspired a series of research studies supporting his thesis that juvenile males and females in all classes can experience delinquency-generating social strain (Agnew, et al., 2002; Brezina, 1996; Mazerolle, 1998; Menard, 1995). In addition, these investigators addressed the issue of why some youngsters express their anomic frustration in acts of delinquency, while others—experiencing the same negative circumstances and prospects—do not turn to antisocial deviance. Agnew and his supporters contend that the kind of response that an anomic individual will make depends on what he or she brings to the situation: specifically, motivation, self-esteem, social support, level of anger, and fear of punishment. Box 5.1 shows how strain theories can help explain delinquency in China.

CULTURAL TRANSMISSION THEORIES

Another line of theory building was established in 1938 with a focus on the contradictory and often competitive cultural content of different social groups. The underlying assumption was that the heterogeneity of the population associated with 20th-century industrialization and urbanization resulted in an inharmonious mixture of ethnic, religious, political, and social-class subcultures, each with its own distinctive beliefs, traditions, values, norms, and behavioral expectations. Moreover, it was assumed to be self-evident that the proximity of these diverse segments of the urban population would lead to unavoidable culture conflict as each group judged its own standards as correct and normal and those of other groups as deviant and delinquent.

BOX 5.1

CROSS-CULTURAL FOCUS: Social Strain and Juvenile Delinquency in China

Social strain theories were developed by American criminologists to explain American crime and delinquency. To date, most research utilizing strain theory has been conducted in the United States or other Western capitalist societies. After all, at the center of Merton's Anomie theory is the internalization of capitalistic goals such as success, money, and material acquisitions. Strain theories have been particularly useful in helping explain lower-class delinquency, since they are based on the assumption that lower-class youths internalize capitalistic goals, but then find their legitimate means for achieving those goals blocked by a variety of structural variables. More contemporary generalized strain theories have expanded the concept of strain beyond economic goals and the blockage of culturally approved methods for achieving them, to the more general interpersonal strain and frustration experienced by youths in their everyday lives including distress over appearance and the frustration they encounter in an adult-structured world (Agnew, 1992). These theories, too, were developed by Americans to explain American delinquency.

How would strain theories fare in explaining delinquency in a dramatically different, primarily socialistic culture, and emerging market economy such as that of China? Ruth Liu and Wei Lin (2007) asked just that in their study of over 2,000 Chinese middle-school students in the city of Fujian, in the southeastern part of China.

Liu and Lin contended that Chinese adolescents may be more susceptible to some forms of strains than others. There is tremendous emphasis on academic success in China. Chinese children who do not succeed in school are not only considered unlikely to be successful later in life, but also bring dishonor and disgrace upon their families. Sociological research has found some linkage, at least anecdotally, between suicides among Chinese youths and the overwhelming pressure on them to succeed in school (Lee, 2004). Also, there are noticeable differences in the opportunities provided to young Chinese males as compared with females. Success and performance demands on adult males are much higher than on adult females, so consequently, boys are simultaneously pushed much harder to succeed as youths and are provided more opportunities to do so than their female counterparts. This led Liu and Lin to study the differential effects of strain on Chinese boys and girls.

Liu and Lin's research findings supported the tenets of strain theories of delinquency and showed remarkable similarities with research conducted in the United States despite the overwhelming cultural differences. Chinese boys reported higher levels of strain and frustration than Chinese girls. Consistent with strain theories, Chinese boys were far more likely than girls to become involved in delinquency. The boys also expressed more deviant attitudes, more delinquent friends, and lower sense of self-control. Through the use of multiple regression analysis, Liu and Lin also found that specific types of strain were more related to delinquency than others. Specifically, strain associated with status achievement (the type of strain experienced more by boys than girls) had the strongest link to juvenile delinquency. Chinese girls experienced more interpersonal strain over physical well-being and relationships, a type of strain less related to delinquency. In these regards, the apparent support for strain theories of delinquency is similar among Chinese youths and American youths.

How have social and economic changes in contemporary China made adolescents' experiences there more similar to those of American youths than in the past? Based on your study of juvenile delinquency thus far, are these changes likely to lead to more or less juvenile delinquency in China? What should the Chinese, and for that matter, Americans do to help reduce the strain experienced by adolescents to help reduce involvement in delinquency?

Sources

Agnew, R. 1992. Foundation for a general strain theory of crime and delinquency. *Criminology* 30:47–87.

Lee, Y. 2004. Mental health concerns resurface in the Chinese community. http://news.ncmonline.com/news/view

Liu, R. X. and Lin, W. 2007. Delinquency among Chinese adolescents: Modeling sources of frustration and gender differences. *Deviant Behavior* 28 (September–October):409–432.

Sellin's Theory of Culture Conflict

Thorsten Sellin, a criminologist, laid important groundwork for this theoretical approach to explaining criminal and delinquent behavior, with the publication of *Culture Conflict and Crime* (1938). Sellin, in explaining fluctuating crime rates in different parts of urban society, noted that values, customs, and standards of conduct were not uniform throughout the population. On the contrary, many districts and neighborhoods of American large cities represent the ethnic culture of foreign countries more than the general culture of the United States. Additionally, the various social classes also occupy their own subcultural "islands" where their distinctive beliefs, norms, and behaviors prevail.

If these different groups were not in direct geographical and social contact with each other and with the larger society, their behavior would not be subject to comparison and evaluation so closely. However, because such diverse groups coexist in proximity to one another, chronic and abrasive culture conflict often ensues. Thus, Sellin concluded, culture conflict creates great potential for misunderstanding and antagonism, especially among the subordinate, lower-class groups regarding what is conforming behavior and what is deviant behavior. Even the definitions of crime and delinquency can become culturally relative and subject to interpretation within the cultural context of particular groups and neighborhoods in which assimilation into the dominant society is incomplete (Cole, 1993). You will note that many of Sellin's ideas fit well with the conflict theories discussed in Chapter 7.

Burgess' Concentric Zone Theory

Considerable evidence of the distinctive spatial patterns and concentrations of minority groups, social classes, and specialized land uses was amassed during the 1920s and 1930s by sociologists Robert Park, Ernest Burgess, R. D. McKenzie, and others in the forefront of human ecology, a newly emerging sociological subarea. For example, Burgess (1925), using Chicago as his model, demonstrated the variation in naturally formed urban areas, each occupied by a particular part of the population and reserved for a particular land use, such as commercial, lower-class housing, middle-class housing, and so forth. Burgess hypothesized that these population groupings and specialized land uses develop as a series of concentric zones spreading out from the dominant and dynamic city center and that this spatial pattern characterized the industrial city of his time.

Burgess pinpointed Zone II as an urban environment especially conducive to a wide variety of individual maladjustments and social problems, including crime and delinquency. Zone II, the *Zone of Transition*, was so designated because it was the area most subject to rapid change. Population was ever-shifting as waves of new and impoverished immigrants settled first in the crowded tenements to begin their American experience. Many of the neighborhoods in Zone II reflected the cultural and ethnic identity of groups of inhabitants from Ireland, Poland, Italy, and other foreign countries (Figure 5.2).

Zone II was also called the Zone of Transition because it lay between the more prosperous and expanding commercial center of the city and the more established residential areas of blue-collar workers in Zone III. Consequently, encroachments,

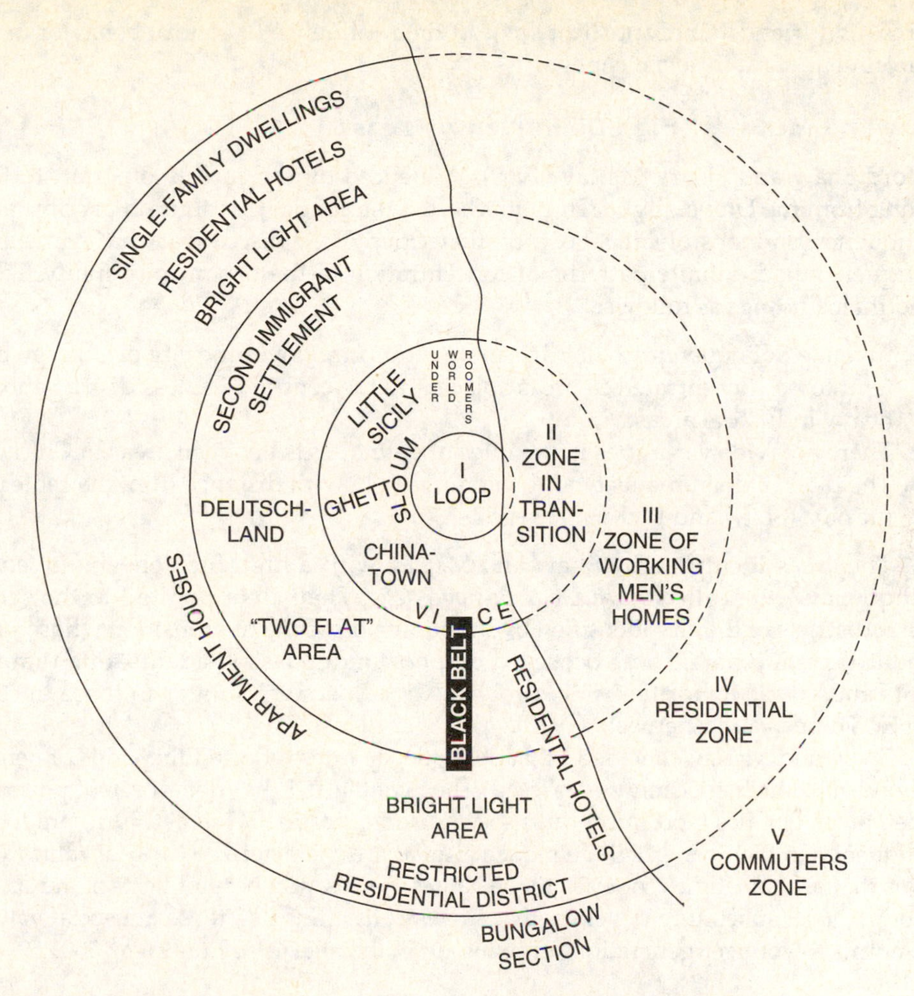

FIGURE 5.2 Burgess's Concentric Zone Pattern of Urban Development and Subareas.
How does the concentric zone pattern identified by Burgess fit your city? Does your city/home town have a "Zone of Transition"? If so, are crime and delinquency rates high there?

Source: Burgess, E. W. "The Growth of the City: An Introduction to a Research Project." In Park, Burgess, and McKenzie (Eds.), *The City.* University of Chicago Press (1925), pp. 47–62. Reprinted by permission.

invasions, and successions of new groups of people and new land uses, and other forms of social change, were most obvious and traumatic in Zone II. To people living in such an area, nothing seems to be permanent, as society is in a continual cycle of settlement and resettlement, of disorganization and reorganization.

A number of researchers investigated these urban dynamics of social disorganization, industrialization, population movements, and changes in neighborhoods to determine their influence on crime and delinquency. For example, W. I. Thomas and Florian Znaniecki (1927) examined social disorganization in a Polish neighborhood of Chicago. They noted the failure of existing social rules and norms to control behavior, and they documented their observations that the home, neighborhood, church, and friendship groups lost some of their influence to control behavior in an environment of rapid social change.

Shaw and McKay's "High Delinquency Areas"

Clifford Shaw and Henry McKay (1969), influenced by the early ecological studies coming from the University of Chicago, charted the spatial distribution of crime and delinquency on maps of Chicago and other cities. They discovered that crime and delinquency had definite patterns of concentration in the urban community. They listed their findings as follows:

1. Juvenile delinquents are not distributed uniformly over the city of Chicago but tend to be concentrated in areas adjacent to the central business district and to heavy industrial areas.
2. There are wide variations in the rates of delinquents between areas in Chicago.
3. The rates of delinquents tend to vary inversely with distance from the center of the city. (Shaw and McKay, 1931:383–385)

The areas identified by Shaw and McKay with a high incidence of juvenile delinquency were called *High Delinquency Areas*. Their data pointed to the same central districts of the city identified by Burgess as the Zone of Transition whose substandard, slum housing was occupied by poor underclass residents, often immigrants and ethnic minorities, with problems of adjustment similar to those uncovered by Thomas and Znaniecki (1927).

Shaw and McKay concluded that delinquency rates reflected the kinds of neighborhoods in which children were raised. They contended that deteriorated, poverty-ridden areas of cities tend to produce social disorganization which, in turn, produces delinquency. In their view, high delinquency areas are characterized by local values and norms that are sometimes contrary to the values, norms, and best interests of the larger society. A local subculture develops that successfully transmits these antisocial values and norms to younger generations growing up in the area. (See Lundman, 2001:59–62)

Cultural Efficacy Theory

Robert Sampson and his colleagues (1999; 2003) expanded upon earlier social ecology and cultural transmission theories and insisted that more than poverty, social disorganization and lower-class values lead to the development of high crime and delinquency areas. They contended that areas of cities develop **collective efficacy**, *a group's shared belief in its ability to successfully complete tasks and its extent of social cohesion and trust.* This collective efficacy leads to informal social control (refer to control theories in Chapter 6), and increases the likelihood that people will band together, intervene, and stop others' criminal and delinquent activities as well as build informal support networks. Where social efficacy and social cohesion are low or lacking, crime and delinquency flourish.

Miller's Focus on Lower-Class Culture

Walter Miller (1958) offered a different explanation of adolescent misbehavior as a product of its cultural context. Miller's theory disagreed with the reactive subculture theories of Cohen and of Cloward and Ohlin, which portrayed groups of lower-class

How might strain and cultural transmission theories shed light on these youths' everyday experiences and help explain why they might become involved in delinquency?

© Corbis RF

delinquents responding in anomic frustration to their blocked access to idealized, middle-class, success goals. Rather, Miller proposed that lower-class culture contains an effective body of values, norms, and behavioral expectations in its own right. Moreover, children and youths from lower-class families and neighborhoods internalize their culture content just as thoroughly as young people from the middle class learn their culture. It follows, Miller argued, that much of what Cohen, Cloward and Ohlin, and others interpreted as a lower-class, delinquent reaction to the unfair imposition of middle-class values was actually a reasonable reflection of lower-class values.

Miller's theory cites successful lower-class socialization as the origin of aggressive and antisocial conduct. According to Miller, delinquency results not from a lack of commitment to middle-class cultural values, but from commitment to lower-class cultural values. Thus, lower-class conformity does not harmonize with the behavioral expectations of the dominant middle class.

Miller identified six "focal concerns" or "values" that have high priority for young males:

1. ***Trouble.*** Chronic anxiety over possible confrontation with law enforcement personnel and the consequences of illegal behavior. Staying out of "trouble" is a major, practical concern of many lower-class people.

2. ***Toughness.*** The exhibition of physical prowess; fearlessness; masculinity. Miller saw this kind of posturing as extremely important to lower-class boys who come from female-based households (dominant mothers and absent fathers) and who are trying to establish a male identity. Thus, they equate femininity with weakness.
3. ***Smartness.*** Display of verbal agility; quick-wittedness; ability to outsmart.
4. ***Excitement.*** Thrill-seeking; taking a chance; fighting over women.
5. ***Fate.*** A tendency to trust in luck; to assume that what will be, will be.
6. ***Autonomy.*** The need to feel independent and free from external authority.

Miller believed that such class-specific focal concerns or values develop because the social classes are segregated from each other spatially, economically, and socially. Hence, youths develop values and behaviors distinctive of their own class. The internalization of lower-class values combined with a need to demonstrate their "manhood" can, according to Miller, cause some young males to defy authority and participate in fighting and other activities that, in turn, could be interpreted by middle-class people as a predisposition to juvenile delinquency.

Contributions of Cultural Transmission Theories

Cultural transmission theories offer significant contributions in data, concepts, and fresh insights that help explain juvenile delinquency. Each one is like a different lens on a microscope that reveals new and fascinating details regarding culture and subculture as they relate to delinquent behavior.

Sellin's Culture Conflict Theory recognized the pluralistic nature of society in the United States. Rather than viewing society as a homogeneous entity wherein unchallenged, universal norms prevail, Sellin emphasized the diversity of groups and subcultures within larger society. Many of these ethnic and social-class subcultures come into contact with one another in the urban environment—a contact sometimes made unpleasant and abrasive by conflicting codes of conduct. Crime and delinquency as a precipitate of culture conflict between dominant and subordinate social groups is detailed.

Burgess (1925) paid careful attention to ecological space relationships as human groups interact in a crowded, heterogeneous, urban environment. He pointed to the ethnic enclaves in Chicago and other large cities that generate and reinforce subcultures with territoriality, social identity, and solidarity. The more entrenched and resistant the subculture is to assimilation, the greater the likelihood of normative conflict, especially for younger generations in subordinate subcultures. This was the idea behind the concept of "the marginal man" suggested by Burgess' colleague, Robert Park (1928), who followed by Everett Stonequist (1937), traced the alienation and delinquency of many children of immigrants to their marginal social status and identity as they are caught between two conflicting cultural systems. These second-generation residents of the ethnic area were exposed to the norms, traditions, and language of the "old country" in their homes and neighborhood and, at the same time, experienced the socialization of their American school and peer group. Thus, they became "marginal"—without complete commitment or assimilation into either of the conflicting cultures.

Shaw and McKay (1969) incorporated an ecological dimension from Burgess into their criminological scrutiny of Chicago. They identified distinctive spatial patterns of crime and delinquency that corresponded with specific ethnic and social-class areas, particularly in the inner city. Perhaps Shaw and McKay's greatest contribution was the discovery that High Delinquency Areas of Chicago retained that statistical reputation in spite of major changes in the ethnic composition of the population in the areas. Repeated collection, examination, and comparison of population and crime data for those troubled areas revealed that they were inhabited by successive waves of poor immigrants from various European countries. Over time, older immigrant groups improved their economic standing with better jobs, experienced a measure of assimilation, and moved further out from the central city into more stable and affluent residential areas. Their places in the old, least desirable neighborhoods were taken by the most recently arrived immigrant groups. As each ethnic group escaped from inner-city blight and poverty, it manifested lower rates of juvenile delinquency, while rates remained high in the old areas adjacent to centers of commerce and heavy industry, irrespective of the ethnicity or national origin of the new residents. From this, Shaw and McKay (1969) concluded that delinquency-producing factors are inherent in the socioeconomic conditions of the community, not in the racial or ethnic composition of the population.

Miller (1958) embarked in a different direction in making his contribution to Cultural Transmission Theory. His focus on lower-class culture identified a set of basic values that can activate lower-class, adolescent behavior that, in turn, may be perceived as overly aggressive and delinquent by middle-class people. Miller did not justify lower-class gang delinquency; rather, his analysis adds to our understanding of *why* lower-class youngsters become delinquent. While such behavior may reflect a culturally relevant quest for manhood, it is still often dangerous and undesirable. David Brownfield's research (1990) found empirical support for Miller's contention that such esteemed attributes as toughness and autonomy are particularly strong predictors of delinquent behavior.

Criticisms and Limitations of Cultural Transmission Theories

Social strain theories strongly suggest that social disorganization often characterizes individuals and groups living in high delinquency areas. This assumption has been seriously questioned. A number of more recent studies have concluded that lower-class neighborhoods are not without social organization. Rather, their social organization is *different* from that found in middle-class areas.

Shaw and McKay implied that social disorganization was most prevalent in areas in which local institutions were unable to control the behavior of local residents. Certainly, many of the families, schools, churches, and formal law enforcement agencies often appear weak and impotent in high delinquency areas. The strength of local organizations is to a large extent a function of local participation, and participation in such organizations is most likely among people who have positive feelings about their neighborhoods (Bursik, 1984:403). On the other hand, in areas of oppressive poverty, status deprivation, and urban blight that withers hope, local residents may give up on traditional institutions and develop a form of social organization more realistic to their prospects and satisfying to their needs. William Foote Whyte's *Street Corner Society* (1993) and similar studies indicate that there is a high degree of social organization in slum neighborhoods. While the nature of that social organization is different from that found in larger, middle-class society, it is no less meaningful and viable to participants. Jane Jacobs, in *The Death and Life of Great American Cities* (1961:55, 57), described the more casual and less structured social organization of inner-city neighborhoods:

> Reformers have long observed city people loitering on busy corners, hanging around in candy stores and bars and drinking soda pop on stoops, and have passed a judgment, the gist of which is: "This is deplorable. If these people had decent homes and a more private . . . outdoor place, they wouldn't be on the street!"
>
> This judgment represents a profound misunderstanding of cities. It makes no more sense than to drop in at a testimonial banquet in a hotel and conclude that if these people had wives who could cook, they would give their parties at home. The point of both the testimonial banquet and the social life of city sidewalks is precisely that they are public.
>
> Formal types of local city organizations are frequently assumed by planners and even by some social workers to grow in direct, common-sense fashion out of announcements of meetings, the presence of meeting rooms, and the existence of problems of obvious public concern. Perhaps this growth is so in suburbs and towns, but not so in cities. Formal public organizations in cities require an informal public life underlying them, mediating between them and the privacy of the people of the city.

Delinquency area studies also have been criticized by other researchers on the ground that official statistics of arrests and court appearances, used to measure the amount of delinquency for such areas, are biased because of more rigorous law enforcement, compared with more affluent, middle- and upper-class suburbs (see Chapter 3).

Another complaint regarding the logic of the High Delinquency Area thesis is that such urban areas may be *collectors* of deviants rather than the *generators* of deviant behavior. In other words, the socioeconomic conditions and social disorganization of the local community may not be the primary causal variables of crime and delinquency in the area. This argument holds that the real antecedent variable is the preexisting condition or propensity to illegal behavior in some persons prior to their movement into the high delinquency neighborhood. For example, the district of cheap bars and saloons commonly referred to as "skid row" does not produce alcoholics. Rather, many people who have a serious drinking problem gravitate to skid row because they can merge without difficulty into an area subculture and lifestyle similar to their own. Similarly, "the red light district" does not produce prostitutes. Many prostitutes move there to find a supportive subculture and other people who share their values and behavioral expectations. The same reasoning can be applied to some of the criminal and delinquent elements that inhabit high delinquency areas. It is conceivable that they brought with them certain character flaws or social circumstances in their families that were conducive to juvenile delinquency as they settled in the area.

Walter Miller's "Lower Class Culture as a Generating Milieu of Gang Delinquency" (1958) has been limited by a lack of generality. More specifically, the "focal concerns" and "female-based households" described by Miller do not equally characterize the lower-class residents of black, Hispanic, Irish, and Italian enclaves in American cities.

Miller's thesis and other theoretical explanations of lower-class delinquency share an inability to generalize to just *one* lower-class racial or ethnic group. Some Strain and Cultural Transmission theorists have portrayed an oversimplified, homogeneous picture of lower-class values and behavior that fails to adequately take into account the diversification of culture and dynamics of social-class mobility *within* certain groups. For example, since the 1960s, there has been a bifurcation of lower-class black America into an underclass that seems unlikely to escape and an upwardly mobile middle class (Lemann, 1986). Thus, two contrasting versions of black life have emerged.

On the one hand, poverty is even more deeply entrenched for many blacks and is characterized by extraordinarily high and rising rates of unemployment, school dropouts, welfare dependence, single mothers, crime, and delinquency. This *underclass* (a nomenclature also shared by portions of the white and Hispanic populations) has been defined by Michael Morris (1989:125) as "a segment of the poor who are not only economically deprived, but who manifest a distinctive set of values, attitudes, beliefs, norms, and behaviors. . . ."

Miller's observations have been applauded for identifying some focal concerns of the underclass. On the other hand, they are hardly an adequate depiction of those members of the black lower class who are demonstrating higher achievement and lower delinquency rates; who are now moving out of the ghettos and into the middle class. "The clearest line between the two groups is family structure. Black husband–wife families continue to close the gap with whites; their income is now 78 percent as high" (Lemann, 1986:33). In view of the more pronounced heterogeneity of the lower class, Miller's (1958) formulation has lost some contemporary relevance for the lower class. Moreover, it can be argued that Miller's so-called lower-class focal concerns are reflected in the values of juveniles in general, especially adolescent males. Valuing staying out of trouble, toughness, smartness, excitement, fate, and autonomy are hardly unique to the lower class. Box 5.2 departs from emphasis on lower class focal concerns to explain possible links between television violence and delinquency.

BOX 5.2

CONCEPT APPLICATION: Searching for Causal Explanations of Contemporary School Shootings

Over four decades ago, Walter Miller (1958) identified "trouble, toughness, smartness, excitement, fate, and autonomy" as highly regarded, lower-class, cultural values. Miller suggested that the acting out of these "focal concerns" represents the achievement of manhood and respect to many lower-class males (Anderson, 1998). On the other hand, these attitudinal and behavioral traits may be interpreted as delinquent by police officers and other members of more favored classes.

Recently, in the wake of numerous violent attacks by young males in U.S. schools, Miller's theoretical concepts may have a fresh and broader application. A common theme and clue has emerged in many of these shocking

(Continued)

reports: a number of these angry young gunmen were obsessed with a reckless, fatalistic desire to publicly display toughness and autonomy and to get even for some real or imagined insult. In many cases, their violent bid for recognition and reputation was triggered by an accumulation of what they considered disrespectful and degrading taunts. Many of the reputed perpetrators apparently felt like outsiders. They were kids who were out of the mainstream—unhappy, searching for their place, and suffering ridicule (Witkin, et al., 1998:16, 17).

The 1999 carnage at Columbine High School offers a classic example:

> LITTLETON, COLORADO: They were so different from their peers, who ridiculed them for wearing black trench coats even in the summer. . . . Students are beginning to describe how a long-simmering rivalry between the sullen members of their clique and the school's athletes escalated and ultimately exploded in . . . [the] week's deadly violence that left more than a dozen dead and 22 wounded at Columbine High School. (Johnson and Copeland, 1999, 1A0)
>
> A suicide note, purportedly written by one of the attackers, was defiant and ominous: "Your children who have ridiculed me, who have chosen not to accept me, who have treated me like I am not worth their time are dead. THEY ARE (expletive) DEAD. . . . I may have taken their lives and my own—but LET THIS MASSACRE BE ON YOUR SHOULDERS UNTIL THE DAY YOU DIE. . . . You may think the horror ends with the bullet in my head, but you wouldn't be so lucky." (*Ashland Daily Tidings,* 1999:A1)

There is growing evidence that the phenomenon of explosive high-school violence is occurring in other parts of the world.

> UPPER NAZARETH, ISRAEL: Educators say they are alarmed by youngsters drawing knives instead of settling disputes verbally, or at worst, with their fists. . . .
>
> The first killing took place . . . during a break at the Yigal Alon High School. A group of boys were standing in the yard, and one asked another for a lick of his ice cream. A ninth grader, Yevgeny Yakobovich . . . quipped that the boy with the ice cream wouldn't share because "he is fat and a miser."
>
> The boy who was teased decided to take revenge and rallied four friends. The five went home after school to pick up knives, a baseball bat and a pair of brass knuckles, then headed to the park where Yevgeny liked to play.
>
> They stabbed, beat, and kicked Yevgeny until he slumped on the ground. . . . Police said the suspects returned to their homes and went to sleep, as though nothing had happened. ("Teen Violence Leaves Israel Looking for Answers" in *Dallas Morning News,* 1999:8A)

Several of the theoretical explanations of youthful crime presented in Chapters 4 though 9 of this book, including Walter Miller's focus on cultural values, offer helpful insights concerning these current reports of high-school violence.

Perhaps the most exciting implication of this new application of Miller's concepts is the expansion of so-called lower-class values to encompass some hostile, antisocial posturing and behavior of middle-class youth. Such an application garners a larger measure of generality for Miller's causal explanation. Peter Jennings (1999) underscored this point by pointing to the cultural context of violence: "Boys don't cry; but they are encouraged to be tough, manly, and to fight back" (Jennings, 1999, ABC, "Boys at Risk"; Pollack, 1999).

"Copy-cat" student attacks continue to threaten U.S. schools. For example:

> CONCORD, NORTH CAROLINA (December 17, 2003): Teenager arrested for planning to blow up his high school and school buses with

home-made napalm. His "Corpse List" of twenty names included his name.

LANCASTER, CALIFORNIA (December 18, 2005): Two teenagers taken into custody for plotting a school massacre. Their notebook contained pictures of Columbine High School killers Eric Harris and Dylan Klebold, murderer Charles Manson, and a scrawled message: "When I'm God, everyone dies!"

NORTH POLE, ALASKA (April 22, 2006): The arrest of six seventh-graders marks the nation's second breakup of an alleged Columbine-style attack this week. Five Kansas teenagers suspected of planning a shooting rampage at their high school were arrested Thursday, the seventh anniversary of the massacre in suburban Colorado. Authorities reported that the Alaskan seventh graders had been bullied by other students and were seeking to retaliate. (ABC Television News, April 23, 2006).

A more detailed discussion of current school violence, together with suggestions for prevention and control, can be found in Chapter 11, Schools and Delinquency.

Based solely on the reading of this chapter, what theories could you apply to help explain school shootings?

Sources

ABC Television News, April 23, 2006.

Anderson, E. 1998. *The code of the streets.* New York: W. W. Norton.

Jennings, P. "Boys at Risk." *American Broadcasting Company,* November 15, 1999.

Johnson, K., and Copeland, L. "Long-simmering feud may have triggered massacre." *USA Today,* April 22, 1999:A1.

"Suicide note contains more death threats." *Ashland Daily Tidings* (Oregon), April 24, 1999:A1.

"Teen violence leaves Israel looking for answers." *Dallas Morning News* (Texas), June 12, 1999:8A.

Pollack, W. 1999. Cited in "Researchers say American boys are brought up to be tough." *Ashland Daily Tidings* (Oregon), August 21, 1999:A1.

Witkin, G., Tharp, M., Schrof, J. M., Toch, T., and Scattarella, C. "Again." *U.S. News & World Report,* June 1, 1998:16–18.

Summary

This chapter introduces sociological explanations of juvenile delinquency, focusing on two prominent groups of theories: social strain and cultural transmission. Strain theories share the underlying assumption that nonconforming behavior arises out of social circumstances in which individuals or groups experience normative confusion or disruption. Based on Durkheim's concept of anomie, Robert Merton developed a theory of delinquency based on a typology of modes of individual adaptive bahavior to social strain. Albert Cohen elaborated further developed strain theory with his theory of "delinquent boys," and Richard Clward and Lloyd Ohlin pointed out that delinquency is directly related to legitimate and illegitimate opportunities for youths to realize their goals in socially acceptable or unacceptable ways. Agnew's general strain theory of delinquency is a contemporary version of strain theories that responds to some of the criticisms and weaknesses of earlier strain theories.

Cultural transmission theories of delinquency focus on the contradictory and often competitive cultural content of different social groups. Thorsten Sellin's theory of culture conflict provides a basis for early cultural transmission theories as does Ernest Burgess' concentric zone theory of urban development. Clifford Shaw and Henry McKay charted the spatial distribution of crime and delinquency, identifying "high delinquency areas" from a social ecological perspective. Walter Miller's contribution to the cultural transmission came in the form of six lower class "focal concerns" that he believed helped explain the high rates of delinquency among lower class youths.

The strain theories and cultural transmission theories of delinquency add important insight into possible causes of juvenile delinquency, especially among lower class boys. As research began showing these theories inadequate to explain delinquency among middle and upper class youths and among females, other sociological theories emerged to do so. Two of those schools of thought are explored in the next chapter which deals with social learning and social control theories of delinquency.

Concept Integration: Questions and Topics for Study and Discussion

1. Explain the sociological perspective regarding human behavior and social phenomena. How does it differ from the biological determinism and psychogenic explanations presented in Chapter 4?
2. What is a theory as the term is used by social scientists and the researchers?
3. List the major assumption(s) underlying the social strain theories of delinquency etiology. Identify and discuss several prominent sociologists and their respective concepts and contributions to the social strain approach. What are some of the weaknesses and limitations of social strain explanations?
4. List the major assumption(s) underlying cultural transmission theories of delinquency etiology. Identify and discuss several prominent sociologists and their respective concepts and contributions to the cultural transmission approach. What are some of the weaknesses and limitations of cultural transmission theories ?
5. Compare and contrast the problems of first- and second-generation immigrants in the United States. How do these problems help explain juvenile delinquency in these groups?
6. What are the similarities and differences between Merton's Theory of Anomie, Cloward and Ohlin's Theory of Differential Opportunity, and Miller's concept of Lower-Class Culture as a Generating Milieu of Gang Delinquency?

Chapter 6

Sociological Explanations of Juvenile Delinquency

Social Learning and Social Control Theories

READING OBJECTIVES

Reading this chapter will help you achieve the following objectives:

1. Understand more fully the overlapping of typologies of sociological theories accounting for juvenile delinquency.
2. Define and explain specific sociological concepts and theories of deviant and delinquent conduct under the two major categories of Social Learning theory and Social Control theory.
3. Apply these sociological theories of human behavior to help explain juvenile delinquency.
4. Summarize the contributions and limitations of the various sociological theories of deviance and delinquency discussed in this chapter.

INTRODUCTION

This chapter continues our discussion of major categories of sociological theories to explain juvenile delinquency. This chapter covers social learning and social control theories. As stated in Chapter 5, there is unavoidable overlap in sociological theories, both historically and etiologically. In many instances, the earliest theorists to pursue a particular approach were contemporaries who often built on, expanded, or reapplied each other's work. In addition, their common quest for causal explanations of juvenile delinquency often entailed the same variables and focused on youthful misconduct in the United States. In this chapter we turn our attention to Social Learning Theories and Social Control Theories.

SOCIAL LEARNING THEORIES

The social learning approach to explaining crime and delinquency is dominated by the assumption that virtually *all* human behavior is socially learned. Consequently, deviance, like conformity, must be learned through the complex process of socialization. **Socialization** refers to *a process in which we learn and internalize the attitudes, values and beliefs, and norms of our culture and develop a sense of self* (Thompson and Hickey, 2008:83–84). In other words, socialization is learning to function as social beings and to participate in group life in a society. Social learning theorists view juvenile delinquency as another pattern of learned behavior that some juveniles are taught through social interaction with the family, peer group, and other major agents of socialization.

Sutherland and Cressey's Theory of Differential Association

One of the most popular and durable of the social learning theories is the Theory of Differential Association developed by Edwin Sutherland and Donald Cressey (1943). They stated that most criminal/delinquent behavior is learned through contact with criminal elements and patterns that are present, acceptable, and rewarded in one's physical and social environment. Sutherland and Cressey argued that this is why juvenile delinquency rates vary among social groups and neighborhoods. In more stable and prosperous neighborhoods, the socialization of the young is largely dominated by values that stress conformity to middle-class standards and respect for law enforcement agencies (Browning et al., 2005). On the other hand, in a high delinquency area, delinquent behavior may be an integral part of the area culture. In the presence of a "criminalistic tradition," youths have the opportunity to associate with those who can teach them alternative and illegal behaviors. Thus, Sutherland and Cressey called their explanation of juvenile delinquency the Theory of Differential Association. They summarized their theory with a set of nine propositions:

1. Criminal behavior is learned.
2. Criminal behavior is learned in interaction with other persons in a process of communication.
3. The principal part of the learning of criminal behavior occurs within intimate personal groups.
4. When criminal behavior is learned, the learning includes (a) techniques of committing the crime, which are sometimes complicated, sometimes very simple; and (b) the specific direction of motives, drives, rationalizations, and attitudes.
5. The specific direction of motives and drives is learned from definitions of the legal codes as favorable or unfavorable.
6. A person becomes delinquent because of an excess of definitions favorable to violation of law over definitions unfavorable to violation of law.
7. Differential associations may vary in frequency, duration, priority, and intensity.
8. The process of learning criminal behavior by association with criminals and criminal patterns involves all the mechanisms that are involved in any other learning.
9. While criminal behavior is an expression of general needs and values, it is not explained by those general needs and values, since noncriminal behavior is an expression of the same needs and values. (Sutherland and Cressey, 1978:80–83)

The sixth proposition is at the heart of Differential Association Theory: "A person becomes delinquent because of an excess of definitions favorable to violation of law over definitions unfavorable to violation of law." The picture is one of a youth subjected to a variety of influences; some endorse the rejection of the law and suggest deviant behavior, others uphold the normative standards of society and recommend conformity. By analogy, the youth is activated like a balance scale, as the two antagonistic forces of socialization strive for supremacy. On one side are placed the "definitions favorable to violation of law"—perhaps the negative influence of a street gang or delinquent peers; on the other side are placed those "definitions unfavorable to violation of law"—perhaps the positive influence of parents and teachers. According to the reasoning of Sutherland and Cressey, if the definitions favorable to law violation outweigh the definitions unfavorable to law violation, the balance scale is tipped and the youth slips into juvenile delinquency. However, the struggle for supremacy in directing an individual's behavior between the two accumulating and antithetical definitions is subject to several subtle and complex nuances. As Sutherland and Cressey stated in their seventh proposition: "Differential associations may vary in frequency, duration, priority, and intensity." Thus, the actual point of commitment to either a conforming or a deviant career will vary widely among individuals.

Auto theft has a high incidence rate among teenage males. How would differential association and other social learning theories help explain this youth's behavior?

The core propositions of Differential Association Theory continue to gain interest and support from contemporary research. For example, Tia Kim and Sharon Gato (2000) empirically documented that peer delinquency is the strongest predictor of Asian American adolescent delinquency, and Allison Payne and Steven Salotti (2007) found that both social learning and social control theories helped explain and predict both crime and drug use among college students.

Glaser's Concept of Differential Identification

Daniel Glaser (1956) supplemented Sutherland and Cressey's Theory of Differential Association by adding the concept of Differential Identification. Viewing Sutherland and Cressey's theory as too mechanical and inflexible, Glaser emphasized an individual's ability to make choices and take on social roles. He contended that it is not merely association with criminals or delinquents that is important, but the *extent* to which the individual *identifies* with those who are involved in criminal and delinquent patterns of conduct: "During any period, prior identification and present circumstances dictate the selection of the persons with whom we identify ourselves" (Glaser, 1956:441).

According to Glaser, criminal or delinquent role models can be real or imaginary, nearby or far away, thus allowing for human ability to identify with certain individuals (and learn from their behavior) without direct association. For example, the mass media, notably television and motion pictures, have come under continuous scrutiny and sharp attack as a powerful socializing agent that can influence some children to seek to replicate the violence they have seen on the screen. As far back as 1971, the Surgeon General's Advisory Committee concluded that children whose parental attitudes on violence, prior socialization, and emotional makeup predispose them to imitate or to be incited by violent content on television were most likely to try to transfer the fictionalized aggression into real life. In this context, and from the perspective of Glaser's differential identification, the fantasized heroics and aggression of *Rambo*, *The Terminator*, or even roboticized *Transformers*, can become viable role models for some youngsters. (See Box 4.2 for an analysis of television's influence on children.)

Akers' Theory of Differential Reinforcement

Ronald Akers is one of the principal theorists behind the view that deviant (and delinquent) behavior is learned and acted out in response to rewards and reinforcements that are available in the individual's environment. Burgess and Akers (1966) noted that Sutherland and Cressey failed to specify the learning process in their Theory of Differential Association and therefore sought to improve the theory by incorporating some basic concepts from B. F. Skinner's (1938) operant conditioning. In their synthesis of sociology and psychology, Burgess and Akers said that people are motivated to behave in certain ways if they have been rewarded for doing so. Likewise, they are discouraged from repeating a behavior for which they have been punished or denied positive reinforcement. Akers collaborated with others in refining the Theory of Differential Reinforcement into a series of propositions that detail the process of learning and performing deviant behavior through interaction with individuals and groups who have the power to bestow gratification, social status, and other commensurable rewards (Akers, et al., 1979; Lanza-Kaduce, et al., 1982). Moreover, Akers recognized the impact of public acclaim and reward of selected individuals for certain kinds of behavior. These individuals may then serve as role models for many others who, in experiencing vicarious reinforcement, are also encouraged to imitate the rewarded behavior (Akers, 1985).

Contributions of Social Learning Theories

The social learning approach to explaining delinquency has enjoyed considerable support from many sociologists. Its emphasis on the socialization process as well as the influence of peer and reference groups identifies the sources of delinquent behavior as social in nature. Numerous studies support the basic concepts of the social learning approach, especially as proposed by Sutherland and Cressey's Theory of Differential Association (e.g., Payne and Salotti, 2007; Reiss and Rhodes, 1964; Short, 1957; Thompson, et al., 1983). Going beyond scientific studies, the basic postulates of social learning theories also appeal to many "common sense" assumptions about human behavior. For example, they reflect the popular view that "good character is a good habit that must be taught." The old axioms that "one rotten apple can spoil the barrel" and "birds of a feather flock together" imply that individuals' behavior is influenced by those with whom they associate and identify.

Social learning theories have had wide application to juvenile delinquency. An especially helpful aspect is the understanding of the sociological and psychological dynamics of drug and alcohol use and addiction.

> Sutherland's development of the principle of differential association to account for the "specific direction of motives and drives" has been particularly pertinent to the study of drug and alcohol use among adolescents. Primary group associations and favorable attitudinal definitions have emerged as the key causal factors. (Orcutt, 1983:221)

Research conducted by Richard Johnson and associates (2006) confirmed the supposition that the best predictor of the extent of a youth's involvement in delinquent behavior is the number of his or her delinquent associates. Their findings also support the view that differential association with situational pressure to join others is most relevant to adolescent drug use. The introduction to illegal drugs and persistence in their use is part of an individual's social experience. The further linkage with delinquency was argued by W. D. Watts and Lloyd Wright (1990), whose statistical correlations revealed that self-reported alcohol, tobacco, marijuana, and other illegal drug use were all significantly related to both minor and major delinquency for groups of Mexican American, black, and white males.

In a study on marijuana use, James Orcutt (1987:354) further supported the Differential Association Theory and concluded that the theory can be readily and empirically tested, and "perhaps no other theory of deviance can generate such exact conditional predictions about the initiation of any deviant act."

A study by Karen Heimer (1997), using data from a national sample of males, found strong support for learning theories of delinquency. Her "results show that violent delinquency is a product of learning definitions favorable to violence, which itself is determined directly and indirectly by association with aggressive peers . . ." (Heimer, 1997:799).

Schicor (1983) also applauded the generality of theories that employ socialization as an explanatory factor in human behavior. He contended that socialization is an acceptable and meaningful approach to an understanding of delinquency whether one is looking at societies dominated by capitalistic or by socialistic political ideology.

Criticisms and Limitations of Social Learning Theories

Despite much support, the social learning approach to explaining illegal behavior by juveniles is not without weaknesses. Several of the criticisms are shared by other theoretical contributions discussed in this chapter, such as the questions raised by Jack Gibbs (1966) and others that the relationship between delinquency and association with other delinquents may in fact be just the opposite from Sutherland and Cressey's view. It may well be that as delinquents are rejected by the conforming segments of society they are forced to seek association with each other. From this perspective, high delinquency areas and delinquent groups *do not generate* delinquency, but merely *collect* and concentrate it. Thus, the social learning theories may not explain the original causes of crime, but simply describe a process whereby criminality is transmitted and perpetuated in some delinquents (remember the cultural transmission and ecological theories from the Chapter 5).

Critics also have questioned the generality of social learning theories (a charge that can be leveled at almost any sociological theory, since exceptions to explanatory schemes are legion!). In this instance, it has been argued that social learning theories do not cover crimes of impulse or passion, or delinquencies springing from emotional maladjustment.

Another flaw in social learning theories and other explanations involving delinquency areas is that even in areas with the highest crime and delinquency rates, there are many nondelinquents. It has been suggested that some children are insulated from primary contact and intimate association with neighborhood delinquents by their unaggressive dispositions and/or careful parental supervision. In addition, many other juveniles are only episodically or superficially involved in delinquent activities. In any case, the fact remains that deteriorated, poverty-stricken inner cities containing lower-class minorities and criminal elements do not produce delinquency in *all* young people residing there.

BOX 6.1

CONCEPT APPLICATION: Grand Theft-Auto

Each year, nearly half of all motor vehicle thefts in the United States are committed by persons under the age of 18 (FBI, 2008). Charles McCaghy and his associates (1977), in their comprehensive study of "Auto Theft: Offender and Offense Characteristics," found that while some middle-class youths are motivated to steal cars for fun and joyriding, urban lower-class black youths are responsible for most auto thefts, for economic profit. These youths often steal cars so they can be stripped and the parts sold, or so the intact vehicles can be sold on the black market. T. W. Burke, in his "Armed Carjacking: A Violent Problem in Need of a Solution" (1993), reported on the escalating danger to motorists from this type of criminal behavior. Burke estimated that 60 percent of all armed carjackers are under 21 years of age with the most common offender being a young male in his late teens or early 20s. Although the first President Bush, in response to public alarm, signed an "Anti-Car Theft Act" in 1992 making armed carjacking a federal offense, the incidence of such violence continues to be very high. In 1993, the assault and murder of several vulnerable tourists during carjackings prompted the German government to advise German citizens traveling abroad to avoid Florida.

The following anecdote was related to one of the authors by a student enrolled in one of his off-campus extension courses.

"Going into the Automobile Business"

If I had not known otherwise, Mike could easily have been mistaken for one of the typical male college students who regularly sit in my classes at the state university. He was 23 years old; naturally gregarious with a disarming grin; wanted to get more education and ultimately a good job; and he liked football, girls, and automobiles—*especially automobiles.*

But we were not on the university campus, nor was Mike a typical 23-year-old student. I was

(*Continued*)

teaching a university extension course at a federal reformatory and Mike was serving a 10-year sentence for "Grand Theft: Auto." He was assigned to assist me with the logistics of the classroom such as inmate attendance at my lectures, seating arrangements, distribution of books, paper, examinations, and other supplies, and so forth. Consequently, we had numerous opportunities to talk, both formally and informally, and an unusual degree of trust and rapport was established.

I soon learned that although Mike was a high school dropout, he was bright and articulate. Moreover, he was streetwise and very cynical. During the last 11 years he had "graduated" from adolescent play group to youth gang to professional auto theft ring; from school yard to city streets to prison yard. He asserted proudly: "I can get into nearly any car without breaking a window and I can start almost all of them without a key." At first, such declarations sounded like just so much bravado and bragging, but later when I had the opportunity to review Mike's official records, it became clear that he was a very professional automobile thief. His file record dated back to age 12 and was filled with documentation of confrontations with police and juvenile courts, and a multitude of suspected, alleged, and proven crimes against society.

Based on our series of discussions, I was able to reconstruct the course of events that brought Mike to the federal reformatory. He had grown up in the underclass slum neighborhoods of East St. Louis and Chicago. The family was poor, characterized by his father's unemployment, with five people living in three small rooms and sharing a toilet and tub with two other families. They wore second-hand clothing that didn't fit; and they were often cold, hungry, frustrated, and angry. Mike played in the streets of his neighborhood with boys of similar backgrounds.

Mike reported that high school was a particularly trying ordeal for youths from the poorer neighborhoods:

> There were dudes there who had plenty of money, wore nice clothes, and even drove cars to school. My ol' man didn't even own a car. We walked everywhere, or rode the bus if we had the fare. The teachers always gave us that bull—— about getting an education, working hard, and being successful. Man, it was unreal! I got out of there as soon as I could. Besides, I was flunking anyway.

On the streets of the city, Mike found other boys with similar experiences who shared his feelings of rejection, alienation, and hopelessness. Then, one day, he recalled:

> We spotted a parked, unlocked car with the keys just hanging there. It was like an invitation! We looked and laughed and someone dared me to get in. Well, I wouldn't have done it, but the guys were all watching me. So, I got in, and so did they. I was just fourteen, but I could drive it. We decided to borrow it for a while, circle around the high school, and try to pick up some girls. However, something went wrong. The car swerved over a curb and got banged up. Somebody saw us, and the cops picked me up. Later, a judge put a judgment against my father to pay for the damage. And he pulled out of the family after that.

There were other joyriding experiences for Mike and his friends. It was never hard to find a car in which some negligent driver had left the ignition key and the boys could not resist the temptation to "cruise the streets" and enhance an otherwise boring day or night.

At about age 16, Mike began associating with a street gang in his neighborhood. He described how the gang was inclined to "steal anything that wasn't nailed down." Sometimes they stole food from grocery stores "because they were hungry, or just for the hell of it." One distracted the clerk, while another filled his pockets and sneaked out the door. This same technique was used in clothing and hardware stores for merchandise they could sell or trade on the streets. Mike specialized in automobile parts—hubcaps, tires, and stereos. A couple of older gang members showed Mike how to "hotwire" an automobile and thus start it by bypassing the ignition switch. The boys also discussed which types of cars were easiest to steal, and the older youths told Mike that the "high dollar" cars were best to steal, because "they were easy to resell, and the owners always had enough insurance" to cover their losses.

Mike complained bitterly about social conditions in his old urban neighborhood. There were few job opportunities and "the poor got no help and no respect," he said:

> Even though I had a few dollars and better clothes, even my own family and the neighbors called me a "no good thug." So, finally, I decided to have the game as well as the name, and got more involved in illegal activities. And, at least I had the guys in the gang who appreciated me.

As Mike grew older, however, many of those he knew best in the gang started dropping out. Some got married, several took jobs, some went to jail or joined the military, and one or two even went back to school. Mike took a different course:

> As for me, I had made friends with some older men in the area who were into the rackets, you know, some were "hustling prostitutes," others were pushing drugs, or into gambling. But the ones that really appealed to me were in the "used car business." They made lots of money and drove big cars. I hung around their "garage" and got acquainted.

As Mike described it , the "garage" was a basement with painted-over windows and a large automobile door that opened off a back alley. It was "open" only from midnight until dawn. When Mike was about 20, he was invited to "go into the automobile business" with the men at the garage. It was a professional auto theft ring comprised of eight men with a highly specialized division of labor: two of them were the "pickups" who cruised side streets and unattended parking lots near theaters and bars. They would locate automobiles they wanted, preferably large and expensive. With special tools and sets of keys, they were usually able to open and drive off the automobile with minimal difficulty. Mike became one of these "pickup men."

Three other men were garage "mechanics." Their job was to change odometer readings, license plates, and even engine and body manufacturers' identification numbers. They could repaint an automobile and have it out of the door in less than 24 hours. Another man had the task of producing or procuring false registration documents. The other two men had the responsibility of transporting and selling the stolen and altered automobiles, often many hundreds of miles away in other states.

The scheme was successful for a long time until, as Mike summarized his career in the "automobile business," "one guy got caught, and in order to get a lighter sentence for himself, he rolled on us, led the cops to the garage, and we were all picked up."

As you reflect on this case study, consider the various sociological explanations of deviant and delinquent behavior presented in Chapters 5 and 6. How do they fit as causal explanations for Mike's juvenile delinquency and criminal career? Which theories seem most applicable to Mike's case?

Sources

Burke, T. W. (1993). Armed carjacking: A violent problem in need of a solution. *Police Chief* 60 (January):18–24.

Federal Bureau of Investigation, 2008. *Crime in the United States: Uniform crime reports—2004.* Washington, DC: U.S. Government Printing Office.

McCaghy, C. H., Giordano, P. C., and Henson, T. K. (1977). Auto theft: Offender and offense characteristics. *Criminology* 15(3):367–385.

David Matza (1964) offered another interesting alternative to Sutherland and Cressey's Differential Association Theory and other causal explanations of this kind. Contrary to those theorists, Matza contended that deviants do not consistently give moral support to one another by approving deviant acts. He pointed out that most delinquents share with nondelinquents the view that their antisocial behavior and that of their peers is wrong. Thus, the idea that the purposeful teaching and learning of delinquent values and techniques occur as more experienced delinquents communicate with youthful novices is misleading. Even among adult criminals, there is often a measure of respect for and acknowledgment of the legitimacy of major social norms. We seldom hear of criminals, incarcerated or otherwise, endorsing and encouraging kidnapping, assassination, child molestation, and other serious offenses. In fact, many times, persons imprisoned for a particularly shocking or heinous crime must be isolated from other inmates for their own protection.

In spite of efforts to revise, clarify, and expand Sutherland and Cressey's original Differential Association Theory by Glaser (Differential Identification), Akers (Differential Reinforcement), and others, the most valid criticism remains. A large number of researchers have expressed difficulty in operationalizing the variables involved in order to empirically test social learning theory (Gottfredson and Hirschi, 1990; Short, 1960; Strickland, 1982; Warr, 1993). For example, the reasoning behind the concept of a "criminalistic tradition" is somewhat circular; that is, a *criminalistic tradition* is viewed as creating high rates of crime and delinquency, yet the only way we can identify it is by identifying an area as having high rates of crime and delinquency. Crime and delinquency rates are measurable; criminalistic tradition is not (Reiss and Rhodes, 1964).

SOCIAL CONTROL THEORIES

Whereas the sociological approaches already discussed (as well as the biological and psychological explanations in Chapter 4) have attempted to answer the question "What causes delinquency?" the social control approach also asks, "What causes conformity?" Albert Cohen (1966:1) succinctly stated the inseparable nature of deviance and conformity:

> Why do so many people insist on behaving in certain ways despite rules to the contrary? Or, to turn the question around: Why, despite the manifest convenience and utility of violating rules, do so many people insist on complying with them so much of the time? Our view is that these are two ways of putting the same question, because in order to explain why men [*sic*] behave, we would have to know those circumstances that make the difference between complying with rules and not complying, and in order to explain why men [*sic*] do not behave, we would have to know the same.

While the search for answers to these two questions may lead down similar paths (looking at environment, family, peers, social class, and the socialization process), the assumptions behind the theoretical approaches are vastly different. In the previously explored theories is the central idea that deviants are somehow inherently different from conformists. This leads to the assumption that juveniles can be divided neatly into two distinct categories: *delinquents* and *nondelinquents*. This division seemingly is supported by official data showing that of those young people arrested and processed through the courts for delinquent behavior, a disproportionate number are from lower-class minority groups. The delinquent/nondelinquent notion is reinforced when we recall that much of the theory that we have studied thus far in explaining the presence and persistence of juvenile delinquency rests heavily on those statistical findings. Consequently, while offering many valuable insights into anomie, culture conflict, subculture response, and the social learning of delinquent behavior, those theories suggest that delinquency is largely a lower-class phenomenon and is clustered together with other social problems such as poverty, unstable family life, and central-city slum neighborhoods.

With increasing frequency, social scientists and criminologists are declaring that the delinquent/nondelinquent dichotomy is an oversimplification of juvenile behavior regarding social norms. It has become apparent that young people cannot be easily classified into those two opposite types. As Cloward and Ohlin (1960:37-38) stated:

> Deviance and conformity generally result from the same kinds of social conditions. People are prone to assume that those things which we define as evil and those which we define as good have their origins in separate and distinct features of society. Evil flows from poisoned wells; good flows from pure and crystal fountains. The same sources cannot feed both. Our view of this phenomenon is different.

This broader and more refined perspective on the origins of juvenile delinquency is supported by unofficial data. Self-report and victimization studies show that a great deal of juvenile delinquency is undetected, unreported, or informally handled. In fact, there is considerable evidence that the majority of youths commit the same illegal acts for which only a small minority are officially categorized as delinquent. For example, a 2002 self-report survey of a large sample of British youth between the ages of 11 and 17 revealed that 50 percent of the respondents had committed vandalism, shoplifting, or binge drinking of alcoholic beverages within the previous year (*Dallas Morning News*, 2002). Some researchers contend that delinquency is so common, abstention from delinquency may be the statistical abnormality that needs to be studied and explained (Brezina and Piquero, 2007).

Social control theories discussed in this section include a focus on conformity as an approach to identifying and explaining the causes of deviance and juvenile delinquency. The social control approach does not view deviance as abnormal. All of us, from this perspective, contain the potential to commit deviant acts. The reason, then, that people do not commit deviant acts is seen as a result of effective restraint or *social control*.

Reckless' Containment Theory

Walter Reckless (1961) considered conforming and nonconforming behavior as two alternative responses to the control system that regulates human conduct. The control system was perceived by Reckless as a double line of defense that protects society against serious deviance. One protective barrier is socialized into each member of society and is comprised of such personal attributes as *self-control, self-concept, and internalization of social norms.* This defense barrier is called **inner containment** and represents *the ability of the person to resist temptations to deviate and to maintain normative loyalty.* The strength of inner containment varies from individual to individual.

The social group or society to which one belongs supplies the other line of defense. This barrier to serious deviance is external to the individual and is called **outer containment**—*the formidable array of legal demands and prohibitions that keep most people within the behavioral bounds of their society—backed up by official law-enforcement agencies.* The ability of the formal laws that comprise outer containment to control behavior also can vary from person to person or from group to group.

Together, this double defense line is called **Containment Theory** and, when functioning adequately, is designed to control the individual and protect society from deviant or antisocial behavior. Applying this theory to delinquency, Reckless contended that the barriers of inner and outer containment are subjected to the onslaughts of powerful "push factors" within the individual and "pull factors" within the individual's social environment. **Push factors** are *such variables as mental conflict, anxiety, alienation, and frustration.* **Pull factors** are *such variables as membership in a street gang or participation in a criminal subculture.* If there is some weakness in this carefully balanced control system, conformity will give way to deviance and even delinquent behavior.

According to differential association theory, how might casual conversations like this one help youths develop "favorable definitions toward the law" and perhaps help prevent delinquency? How might this photo be interpreted to prevent delinquency in relation to social control theories?

Sykes and Matza's Techniques of Neutralization

Gresham Sykes and David Matza (1957) argued that much delinquency occurs because many young persons, under simultaneous pressure from society to conform and from a peer group or subculture with conflicting values and norms urging them to deviate, will extend a set of psychological defense mechanisms to justify delinquent behavior. Thus, they rationalize their actions with a set of sliding, situational ethics. Sykes and Matza appropriately called their explanation of the delinquency process **Techniques of Neutralization**.

According to Sykes and Matza, juvenile delinquents are neither members of a deviant subculture that adheres to a totally different set of norms, nor are they victims of anomie or norm confusion as a result of social disorganization. On the contrary, most juveniles who commit delinquent acts know what the norms are, and for the most part, have respect for those norms. Sykes and Matza contended that most delinquents experience a sense of shame or guilt for their actions. Why then do some juveniles refrain from delinquency or commit only a few sporadic acts, while others repeatedly violate the laws? The answer, Sykes and Matza indicated, rests with juveniles' ability to rationalize their actions in such a way as to neutralize their negative impact (from the point of view of the delinquent offender). As they stated, "It is our argument that much delinquency is based on what is essentially unrecognized extension of defenses of crime, in the form of justifications for deviance that are seen as valid by the delinquent but not by the legal system of society at large" (Sykes and Matza, 1957:667).

Specifically, Sykes and Matza cited five major techniques of neutralization:

1. ***Denial of Responsibility.*** The delinquent contends that delinquent acts are due to forces beyond one's control (e.g., environment, family situation, poverty). This leads to what Sykes and Matza described as a "billiard ball" conception of self in which some juveniles see themselves as "acted upon" rather than "acting."
2. ***Denial of Injury.*** The delinquent insists that although a law was violated, nobody was hurt. Acts of vandalism and theft become interpreted as mere pranks. Victims are often insured and thus compensated for their losses. Since much juvenile misconduct is defined by adults as harmless or normal, the youth can appeal for social support for this neutralization technique.
3. ***Denial of the Victim.*** Even if the delinquent must accept responsibility and admit that someone was hurt (as in cases of assault), often the delinquent reinterprets the wrongful act as some form of rightful retaliation. The victim may be depicted as one deserving of injury. The urban "sport" of "gay bashing" (assault on homosexuals) by juvenile gangs is often justified by participants on the basis that the victim was a "pervert" and therefore deserved punishment.
4. ***Condemnation of the Condemners.*** The delinquent may shift the attention away from personal actions to the motives or behaviors of those who show disapproval. This "turning of the tables" is used to put accusers on the defensive and demonstrates the tactical stance that "the best defense is a good offense." For example, parents scolding a child for curfew violation may be reminded that they too on occasion come home late without notifying the family. Many parents are faced with this neutralization technique in regard to youthful behaviors such as drinking or smoking, in which the parents themselves may engage.

5. ***Appeal to Higher Loyalties.*** The delinquent argues that the social expectations and demands of smaller groups (friends, gangs, siblings, etc.) must take precedence over the social expectations of society. Conformity to peer pressure or doing something "for the good of the group" can neutralize the negative aspects of the act committed.

Sykes and Matza, in their initial exposition of Techniques of Neutralization in 1957, did not fully develop the linkage between background factors and the repertoire of justifications so readily available to delinquents when confronted with their misdeeds. Consequently, the listed techniques of neutralization appeared to many readers as transparent excuses for criminal responsibility. In a subsequent paper, Matza and Sykes (1961) expanded and reinforced their argument by maintaining that juveniles also subscribe to a "subterranean" adult value system, "which tacitly encourages the pursuit of thrills and irresponsibility among juveniles. This underground system of values . . . also contributes to adolescent justifications for delinquency by allowing one to charge that 'Everyone is doing it, so why can't I?'" (Shoemaker, 2005:159).

Matza's major work, *Delinquency and Drift* (1964), contains his fully developed version of Control Theory. He expanded neutralization and expressed the view that since most juvenile delinquents conform most of the time, they evidently are able to alternate loyalty between different sets of norms—between conformity and nonconformity. In other words, juvenile delinquents experience a kind of "episodic release" from normal moral restraints that permits them to intermittently act out the deviant role. Matza presented a picture of the delinquent as occasionally free to "drift" with ease between conformity and nonconformity.

An almost classic illustration of "episodic release from normal moral restraints" occurred in Hazleton, Iowa, in 1999. On the night of March 14, forty teenagers from the rural Amish community attacked the farmstead of a terrified Amish family. The typically religious and traditionally conservative youths overturned buggies, broke windows, and damaged furniture in their sudden rampage. County sheriff's deputies finally restored order and issued numerous citations for drunkenness and criminal mischief. A court sentenced four Amish teenagers to 90 days in jail. Many shocked residents of Hazleton had difficulty explaining the unusual delinquent behavior of the Amish young people. However, non-Amish old-timers recalled that occasional hell-raising by the sober Amish youth is not too surprising: "Some of their parents and grandparents did the same thing when they were young" (Associated Press: *The Dallas Morning News*, June 19, 1999:5A).

From Matza's perspective, delinquents are not propelled into their deviance by irresistible biological forces, psychological maladjustments, or even social circumstances, but instead casually "drift" into it through an ongoing mental process of temporary negation of conventional normative expectations. Virtually every juvenile commits delinquent acts, just as every juvenile commits acts of conformity. According to Matza, the juveniles most likely to violate major norms repeatedly are those who most successfully rationalize their delinquent acts through the techniques of neutralization. Thus, conventional social restraints and mechanisms of social control are temporarily and effectively overcome by many juveniles.

Hirschi's Social Bond Theory

One of the most tested theories of adolescent crime was presented by Travis Hirschi in his book *Causes of Delinquency* (1969). Unlike many earlier theorists, Hirschi (1969:34) did not set out to explain why some juveniles violate the law, but sought to explain why some do not. Hirschi attacked strain theorists for depicting delinquents as typically lower-class gang members, forced into delinquency by the frustrating realization of underachievement of common societal goals. Likewise, Hirschi rebuked the cultural transmission theorists for their standard picture of the "innocent foreigner" who, in a failed attempt to understand and obey what are perceived as the irrelevant rules of society, turns to deviant but more satisfying norms of a subgroup.

The main building block of Hirschi's theoretical construction is the *social bond* that attaches a person to the basic values and expected behaviors of society. In general, the social bond is established early in childhood through a natural attachment to parents, peers, teachers, and others who manifest and model the expected conformity and respected sanctions. Quite simply, according to Hirschi, if the social bond is firmly intact for an individual, there will be no pattern of delinquent behavior. Conversely, if the social bond is weakened or absent, juvenile delinquency can be expected.

More specifically, Hirschi enumerated and detailed four elements of the social bond that tie an individual to conventional society and thus prevent juvenile delinquency.

1. ***Attachment.*** This emotional dimension of the social bond explains conformity as emanating from sensitive regard and respect for one's fellow human beings. It signifies how much one cares about other people.
2. ***Commitment.*** This component of the social bond encompasses an individual's pursuit of idealized and conventional objectives, such as the development of an occupational career and establishment of a reputation for virtue. The ideological commitment to such enterprises functions as a buffer against nonconformity.
3. ***Involvement.*** An individual's preoccupation and heavy investment of time and effort in conventional pursuits ensure conformity by reducing one's availability for deviant activities.
4. ***Belief.*** This entails one's perception of the moral worth of societal norms. If laws are perceived as right and proper, they probably will be respected; if the individual entertains doubts about the viability or validity of social norms, it is likely that he or she will violate them.

Hirschi asserted that there is wide variation among people on the degree of their attachment, commitment, involvement, and belief in conventional behavior and thus variability in their individual ability to resist deviant and delinquent conduct. He said that delinquents tend to have relatively weak social bonds and consequently feel little remorse for violating generally accepted social standards.

Religiosity and Juvenile Delinquency

The idea that "religious beliefs and practices can inhibit criminal deviance," or—stated conversely—"the lack of religious involvement can enhance the likelihood of criminal behavior," represents persistent, intriguing, and controversial hypotheses.

The long debate over the possible impact of religiosity on criminal and delinquent conduct has ebbed and flowed within the context of Social Control Theory. On one side of the issue, some criminologists and sociologists have contended that there is little empirical support for the suggested inverse relationship between religiosity and criminal deviance; that findings are contradictory and spurious—strongly influenced by peer groups, types of crime, and other intervening variables (Merton, 1957; Schur, 1969; Sutherland and Cressey, 1978). "A few early scholars even maintained that, rather than inoculating adherents against waywardness, religion actually promotes crime" (Evans, et al., 1996:44).

On the opposite side of the issue, a number of criminologists and sociologists contend that there is growing evidence that the absence of religion in the lives of criminal and delinquent offenders contributed—at least in part—to their antisocial behavior (e.g., Burkett and White, 1974; Ellis, 1987; Jensen, 1981). Emile Durkheim ([1897] 1951) supported this position when he posited "that religion is a crucial integrative mechanism for maintaining social order and fostering common beliefs and values" (Benda, 1997:163).

In agreement with this latter contention that religious socialization and commitment of young people can reinforce social bonding to community standards and stem the tide of juvenile delinquency, a myriad of social control policies and programs have been suggested. These new initiatives range from alliances between police and street preachers in approaching youth gangs (Woodward, 1998) to resurrecting the concepts of sin, shame, and repentance in juvenile courtroom proceedings (Alter and Wingert, 1995), to posting the Ten Commandments in schools (*Medford Tribune*, 1999:A1). All of these hopeful efforts are based on the supposition that an infusion of personal morality, responsibility, and respect for the life and property of others can be successfully integrated into human character, personality, and behavior.

Contributions of Social Control Theories

The social control approach is more eclectic than some of the other approaches to explaining delinquency. For example, Reckless' Containment Theory embodies some ideas shared by the social learning approach in that inner containment most logically develops through the process of socialization in interaction with positive influences in one's social environment (Sutherland and Cressey, 1943; Reckless, et al., 1956). Harjit Sandhu (1977:58), in an enthusiastic endorsement of Containment Theory, also referred to its eclectic quality:

> A most useful theory, the one that explains the largest amount of criminal and delinquent behavior, is the containment theory of Reckless. It not only combines both the sociological and psychological theories, but also fills in the gap between the two. It satisfactorily answers the persistent question: Who succumbs and who remains immune to crime when exposed to a crime-provoking situation? It takes into account both the macro and micro levels of explanation.

Reckless and various associates conducted several intensive longitudinal studies of boys in a high delinquency area who did not become delinquent (Dinitz and

Reckless, 1972; Reckless, et al., 1956; Scarpitti, et al., 1960). They sought to establish a relationship between the level of a child's self-concept and the development of successful inner control in resisting the temptation to become delinquent.

Reckless and Dinitz asked school teachers of 12-year-old white boys to nominate "good" and "bad" boys. In subsequent interviews with these boys, researchers found that the "good boys" also perceived themselves as good boys, planned to complete high school, and looked upon their friends and families in a favorable light. In contrast, the "bad boys" already had developed an unfavorable self-image. They did not plan to graduate from high school. Moreover, they did not like their families and assumed that they and their friends would get into trouble.

Four years later, in a follow-up study of the same subjects, it was found that their previous self-concept assessments were significant predictors of future behavior and events: "nearly all of the good boys were still in school and had had little or no trouble with the law. On the other hand, 39 percent of the bad boys had been in a juvenile court an average of three times" (Sandhu, 1977:49).

Regarding such findings, Dinitz, et al. (1962:517) observed: "We believe we have some tangible evidence that a good self-concept, undoubtedly a product of favorable socialization, veers slum boys away from delinquency, while a poor self-concept, a product of unfavorable socialization, gives the slum boy no resistance to deviancy, delinquent companions, or delinquent sub-culture."

A study by Thompson and Dodder (1986) reported successful operationalization of inner and outer containment variables in a manner conducive to empirical investigation. Factor analysis of data collected from a varied sample of 677 subjects from public high schools and juvenile correctional institutions generally supported Reckless' theory. Control of delinquency potential was related to favorable self-image, goal orientation, frustration tolerance, internalization and retention of norms, availability of meaningful roles, and reinforcement. A major finding was that Containment Theory provided valuable explanatory insights into delinquency across three of four race and sex categories (for white males, white females, and black males).

Sykes and Matza's *Techniques of Neutralization* (1957) and Matza's expanded construction in *Delinquency and Drift* (1964) have received mixed reviews and partial support from other theorists and researchers in the field. Nevertheless, Matza's assumption that juvenile delinquents casually and intermittently fluctuate their loyalty and behavior between conformity and deviance seems reasonable and convincing (Goodman, 1962). In a study of institutionalized females, Regoli and Poole (1979) found support for the argument that delinquents drift into and out of delinquent behavior. Their findings offered evidence that the internalization of values supporting conformity had taken place but that some individuals were episodically released from moral constraint so they could engage in delinquency. They also found support for Matza and Sykes' "subterranean values" concept that delinquent conduct reflects hidden and more permissive adult values (Regoli and Poole, 1979:53). Earlier research (Krisberg, 1974; Short and Strodtbeck, 1965) also found general acceptance of middle-class, conventional values among juvenile gang members, which is consistent with Sykes and Matza. Heith Copes' (2003) study of auto thieves found his subjects using neutralization techniques consistent with Sykes and Matza's original conception of the theory.

Control or containment theories, more than the other explanations of delinquency presented earlier in this chapter, have provided points of departure for empirical testing. Hirschi (1969) offered a rigorous definition of delinquency suitable for quantitative research and then proceeded to conduct research to test his social bond theory. His research methodology was systematic and thorough as he surveyed a broad sample of youths from a California city and, with reference to rates and kinds of delinquency, examined the basic bonding elements that tie individuals to society. The empirical evidence was consistent with Hirschi's theory as he demonstrated how variation in the strength of these ties is associated with the commission of delinquent acts. More specifically, Hirschi found that juvenile delinquents were not as attached to parents, peers, and teachers as were nondelinquents. Delinquents were less involved in conventional behavior and were less conforming than nonoffenders. One of the most important conclusions emerging from Hirschi's study was that his social bond theory cuts across social classes. Hirschi found that the lower-class child is no more likely to commit delinquent acts than the middle-class child. Furthermore, Hirschi contended that a broken home and a working mother have very little significance for delinquency (Hirschi, 1969).

A number of subsequent researchers have generated support for Hirschi's theory. For example, Michael Hindelang (1973) enhanced the predictability of Hirschi's theory by partially replicating the finding that variations in the strength of social bonding are linked to the likelihood of delinquent behavior. A revised model of Hirschi's social bond theory was operationalized in a research project conducted by Michael Wiatrowski, et al. (1981) and indicated that large correlations do exist between Hirschi's four bond elements and participation in delinquent conduct. Rick Linden (1978) questioned the view that separate theories are required to explain the delinquency of lower- and middle-class boys and turned to Hirschi's theory which does not postulate class differences. He tested Hirschi's theory with data derived from a large sample of white boys attending public junior and senior high schools in Contra Costa County (California). The data combined information from school records, police records, and from a questionnaire administered to the subjects. Linden found that the nature and amount of self-reported delinquency did not vary greatly by social class, nor did the amount of official delinquency. He concluded that Hirschi's theory "explained both the self-reported and official delinquency of boys from different classes equally well suggesting that a general theory of delinquency involvement is possible" (Linden, 1978:428). LeGrande Gardner and Donald Shoemaker (1989) examined and compared Hirschi's social control theory as it applied to urban and rural youth. They found that weak or incomplete social bonding, as conceptualized by Hirschi, is significantly associated with delinquency and generally in the predicted direction for both subgroups.

Marianne Junger and Inike Marshall (1997) used Social Control Theory to model the self-reported delinquency in a sample of 788 Surinamese, Moroccan, Turkish, and Dutch boys (all living in the Netherlands). Multivariate analyses found that the key propositions of the social bond (as stated by Hirschi) are interrelated in the same way among all four ethnic groups. "The variables most consistently related to delinquency among the four subsamples are beliefs in conventional values, virtual (family) supervision, (school) conflict, and participation in unconventional leisure activities" (Junger and Marshall, 1997:79).

Barbara Costello (2000), in her "Techniques of Neutralization and Self-Esteem," empirically tested several key hypotheses of Hirschi's Social Control Theory. Using data from the Richmond Youth Survey, Costello found supporting evidence for Hirschi's prediction that the strength and focus of a delinquent's bond with conventional society will affect the likelihood and success of neutralization (the temporary setting-aside of those basic values and ethics that ordinarily direct the individual toward conformity rather than deviant behavior). The youth's ability to neutralize the expectations of the larger society also influences the quality of his or her self-esteem.

> Children who are attached to their parents are less likely to use police-related neutralizations, but delinquents who do use these neutralizations have higher self-esteem. . . . Delinquents who are more strongly attached to their parents are also less likely to use general neutralizations, but these neutralization techniques do not lead to higher levels of self-esteem. . . . (Costello, 2000:308)

Studies utilizing control theory in combination with social learning theories have also been successful in shedding light on explaining and predicting delinquency (Payne and Salotti, 2007; Thompson, et al., 1983). Self-control (inner containment), in particular, has been found linked to crime/delinquency in several studies (e.g., Kerley, et al., 2008; Kobayashi, et al., 2008). Control theories have also been found compatible with sociobiological theories where it is contended that genetic predispositions toward aggression or violence may be overcome by social control (Guo, et al., 2008).

Can you apply Hirschi's Social Bond theory to this photo?

Criticisms and Limitations of Social Control Theories

Social control theorists' explanations of juvenile delinquency have drawn fire from proponents of other approaches. Cohen and Short (1958) struck at the heart of Reckless' Containment Theory by rejecting the notion that delinquency is an inherent potentiality in all human beings. In other words, the idea suggests greater biological determinism and more freedom from deviant influences in the environment than is sociologically tenable for some. Matza, who prefaced his own version of control theory in *Delinquency and Drift* (1964) with a critique of hard biological, psychological, and sociological determinism, also rejected uncontrolled human nature as the sole source of delinquent behavior. Matza sought to resolve the motivational dilemma of Social Control Theory by perceiving the offending behavior not as a simple response to human nature, but as a response to the temptation of certain circumstances facing adolescents. Matza utilized the concept of "will" which may be activated by an individual's realization that the deed can be accomplished without apprehension or by the need to demonstrate daringness to others. Thus, temporarily free from conventional restraints and willfully motivated, the youth can "drift" into delinquency. Nevertheless, Matza's theory also has not been spared criticism. With his combination of will and drift, Matza may have constructed a contradiction in terms and a semantic quagmire that confounds more than clarifies. With the exercise of will, the casual drift into delinquency seems overstated. If "drift" accurately describes the process, the concept of "will" is much too strong in conjunction. It is difficult to have it both ways.

Hirschi (1969:230) has been a forthright critic of his own social bond theory:

> The theory underestimated the importance of delinquent friends; it overestimated the significance of involvement in conventional activities. Both of these miscalculations appear to stem from the same source, the assumption of "natural motivation" to delinquency. If such natural motivation could legitimately be assumed, delinquent friends would be unnecessary, and involvement in conventional activities would curtail the commission of delinquent acts.

Marvin Krohn and James Massey (1980) examined the overall and relative effects of the elements of Hirschi's social bond theory on four separate measures of deviance using data from a sample of 3,065 adolescents. While the magnitude and direction of the observed relationships moderately supported the theory, Krohn and Massey found that elements of the bond were more predictive of less serious forms of deviance than they were of more serious forms. Their findings also suggested that commitment to academic pursuits and commitment to extracurricular activities had different effects on deviant behavior for males than for females. Overall, the variables used by Hirschi to measure attachment were slightly stronger in predicting male delinquency than they were for female delinquency. In conclusion, Krohn and Massey acknowledged sufficient support for the theory's major hypotheses but called for further research and evaluation for needed reinforcement of generality.

BOX 6.2

CROSS-CULTURAL FOCUS: Criminality among the Children of Immigrants in Western Europe

The population dynamics and composition of the United States have always included a strong immigrant factor as successive waves of new residents have arrived from other parts of the world. Their chronic marginality, strain, conflict, and other problems are a recurring and productive theme for students of juvenile delinquency in this country. In general, second-generation immigrants—the adolescent children of the original newcomers—have been credited with more than their proportionate share of juvenile crime (Sellin, 1938; Sheu, 1986).

Traditionally, immigration into the industrially developed nations of western and northern Europe was considered a temporary labor arrangement with most incoming residents from southern and eastern Europe commonly idealizing an ultimate return to their homelands. However, soon after World War II, many of these "foreign" enclaves of alien groups took on a more permanent character. By 1970, they had put down roots and produced children—the so-called second-generation immigrants. In recent years, criminologists in the host countries of West Germany, France, Great Britain, the Netherlands, Sweden, and Switzerland have focused their research interest in the criminality of immigrants on the children of parents who came from eastern European, Mediterranean, African, and Asian nations. Martin Killias (1989) performed a valuable service to scholars by collecting and reviewing these scattered empirical studies and identifying similarities, differences, and patterns in findings and conclusions.

Killias structured his comparative analysis around three fundamental questions: (1) Do second-generation immigrants suffer from differential treatment at the hands of police and court personnel? (2) Do youths from immigrant families engage in crime more frequently than native-born youths with deeper historic roots in the nation? (3) What are the most viable explanations for higher crime rates among second-generation immigrants?

Regarding the issue of possible police and court discrimination directed against ethnic and racial minorities that could artificially inflate their delinquency statistics, only studies from Great Britain and Holland were available to Killias. While these data were inconclusive, he found little support for the thesis of unfair police and adjudication practices against the children of immigrants.

In answering the second question concerning the incidence of delinquent behavior by second-generation immigrants in northern and western Europe, Killias found a close correspondence with the earlier prototype of such phenomena in the United States. History does indeed repeat itself, at least in the statistical picture emerging from studies in France, Britain, West Germany, Sweden, and Switzerland. Not only has juvenile crime increased significantly in these countries since World War II, but Killias verified that the children of immigrants contributed much more crime than their proportionate share of the population.

> British as well as German studies also suggest that there may be considerable variation among immigrant youths according to the origin of their parents, although the German subsamples are too small to allow any firm conclusions in this regard. . . . But Asians are regularly cited for their low official crimes rates, in Britain . . . as well as elsewhere. (Killias, 1989:18)

The third question raised by Killias, "How do we account for the higher crime rates among second-generation immigrants?" also suggested a return to the American experience for an explanation. After rejecting Sellin's (1938) culture-conflict perspective explaining juvenile delinquency by second-generation immigrants, Killias turned to the "values and attitudes among immigrants and their position within the host

(*Continued*)

country's social structure" (Killias, 1989:20). Based on research conducted in Switzerland, Killias concluded that an application of strain theory offered the most promising explanation. Investigators found that the original, parent-generation immigrants reduced their levels of aspiration and frustration by continuing to utilize the standard of living in their home country as a point of reference in evaluating their current situation. On the other hand, their children, the second-generation immigrants, were much more likely to refer to living conditions in their country of residence when assessing their achievements and possibilities. It follows that their level of discontent and crime rate increased accordingly.

Based on your reading of this chapter and previous chapters, how might you explain higher rates of juvenile delinquency among children of immigrants?

Sources

Killias, M. 1989. "Criminology among second-generation immigrants in Western Europe: A review of the evidence." *Criminal Justice Review,* 14 (1) Spring, 1989:13–26.

Sellin, T. 1938. *Culture conflict and crime.* New York: Social Science Research Council.

Sheu, C. J. 1986. *Delinquency and identity: Juvenile delinquency in an American Chinatown.* Albany, NY: Harrow and Heston.

Concept Integration: Questions and Topics for Study and Discussion

1. What are the advantages and shortcomings of typologies? Outline several typologies with which you are familiar, including the typology of sociological theories of juvenile delinquency that was used to organize this chapter.
2. What is the difference between microlevel sociology and macrolevel sociology? How do these concepts apply to sociological theories of juvenile delinquency?
3. List the major assumption(s) underlying the social control theories of delinquency. Identify and discuss several prominent sociologists and their respective concepts and contributions to the social control approach. What are some of the weaknesses and limitations of the social control explanations?
4. List the major assumption(s) underlying social learning theories of delinquency. Identify and discuss several prominent sociologists and their concepts and contributions to the social learning approach. What are some of the weaknesses and limitations of the social learning approach?
5. Return to Box 2.2. Do you see any evidence of "neutralization" in the Halloween behavior depicted there? How about in Box 6.1 and Mike's description of "going into the automobile business?"

Chapter 7

Sociological Explanations of Juvenile Delinquency

Labeling and Radical/Conflict Theories

READING OBJECTIVES

Reading this chapter will help you achieve the following objectives:

1. Define and explain specific sociological concepts and theories of deviant and delinquent conduct under the major categories of Labeling Theory and Radical/Conflict Theory.
2. Apply these sociological theories of human behavior to explaining juvenile delinquency.
3. Summarize the contributions and limitations of the various sociological theories of deviance and delinquency discussed in this chapter.
4. Perceive how Labeling and Radical/Conflict theories offer insights into increasing delinquency by racial and ethnic minorities and females.

INTRODUCTION

Part Two of this book focuses on the biological, psychological, and sociological explanations of juvenile delinquency. Much of our discussion is on the testing and refining of these causal theories by researchers in the field. It is important to confirm the validity of proposed theories of delinquency causation if we ever hope to control this serious social problem. Later in the text, you will see how some of these theoretical constructs and concepts have become the foundations of prevention and treatment programs for antisocial deviance and juvenile delinquency.

In previous chapters, we identified major groupings of sociological theories of delinquency. In Chapter 5 we introduced Social Strain and Cultural Transmission theories. The subjects of Chapter 6 were Social Learning and Social Control theories. Now, in this chapter, we turn our attention to Labeling and Radical/Conflict theories.

LABELING THEORIES

One of the most popular sociological explanations of juvenile delinquency and other forms of deviance is based on how society perceives, judges, and reacts to the behavior in question. It is appropriate to preface our explanation of Interactionist Theory—or Labeling Theory, as this formulation is commonly known—by briefly reviewing social status and social roles, and how we acquire these dimensions of personal identity (see Chapter 1 for a more thorough treatment).

Social status is *an individual's prestige position in relation to others in his or her social group or society.* Social status also can refer to the prestige position of a group in relation to other groups. The level of social status or prestige held by a person is determined by the social group as every member is ranked from high to low. Some status or prestige is automatically **ascribed** to a person as *a consequence of biological characteristics such as sex or age.* Individuals also may receive some unearned and vicarious status based upon the wealth and power of their parents. Some social status can be changed or **achieved** *through personal effort*, especially in an open-class society that encourages its members to strive for upward social mobility. Considerable social status may be derived from one's level of education and occupation.

The level of social status assigned to an individual also may be modified by taking on new roles. Thus, the prestige position held by a person is founded not only on

"Dear, now would be a good time to tell him that this type of behavior may eventually lead to a clash with the criminal justice system and subsequent criminal labeling."

From Sense and Nonsense About Crime: A Policy Guide by S. Walker. © 1985 by Wadsworth Inc. Reprinted by permission of Brooks/Cole Publishing Co., Pacific Grove, CA 93950.

inheritance and personal achievement, but also on the social role(s) one occupies. A **social role** is *the set of behavioral expectations that accompanies a particular status*. As people grow older and have new experiences, society often changes their social statuses and assigns new roles to them. For example, your life course will probably encompass the successive roles of child, sibling, adolescent, college student, spouse, parent, grandparent, and retiree, to name just a few. With each role assignment (and related status position), society hands the individual a rather carefully structured "script" containing behavioral expectations to be fulfilled.

When each of us is made aware of our role assignments and the behavioral expectations associated with those roles, we usually comply. To conform to the social expectations of our group or society is much easier than to digress from them. Societal judgments regarding role assignments and the behavioral expectations regarded as appropriate for those roles are powerful forces and influences on people. Thus, it becomes normative and, in some cases, mandatory for people to comply with the role "labels" that have been applied to them. The fundamental sociological principles of social status, roles, and expectations comprise the foundation for the Labeling Theory of deviant and delinquent behavior. For, even a deviant role can be assigned by society to some persons who, in the judgment of society, seem to warrant such a negative label. Labeling Theory concentrates less on deviant acts themselves and instead focuses on the actor and the audience and their perceptions of each other (Gibbs, 1966). Howard Becker (1963:9) described labeling as an interactive process: "Social groups create deviance by making the rules whose infraction constitutes deviance. The deviant is one to whom that label has successfully been applied. Deviant behavior is behavior that people so label."

For example, if a person becomes known as an alcoholic, prostitute, juvenile delinquent, or by any other negative label or reputation, the social status or prestige position of that individual is ranked accordingly. Moreover, with the label goes a new role and set of social expectations. The person is expected to behave in harmony with the social role assignment. In other words, labeling is a public declaration of one's social identity—of what society perceives and expects the individual to be. Thus, in one sense, societal labeling is being publicly "branded." It is extremely difficult to escape the label—whether rightly or wrongly applied—because it not only imputes a social identity, but also leads to a redefinition of the relationship and expectations between the person labeled and the other members of society. Labeling

Theory contends that the causal explanation for much juvenile delinquency, as well as a large share of the responsibility, can be traced to society itself.

Early Contributions to Labeling Theory

Labeling Theory has its roots in some of the early ideas of social psychologists Charles Horton Cooley and W. I. Thomas. Cooley ([1902] 1964), in his classic concept of the **Looking-Glass Self**, observed that *an individual's self-evaluation and self-identity are a reflection of one's perception of other people's reactions to his or her conduct*. Broadly applied to adolescent behavior, juveniles use those with whom they interact, like a mirror that reflects back an image (a social identity), which is then internalized as part of the youths' self-concept. If juveniles perceive that others view them as delinquent, they are very likely to accept that label.

W. I. Thomas (1931) contributed the concept of **Definition of the Situation**, which essentially means that *when people define a situation as real, it becomes real in its consequences*. This concept further illuminated the process whereby certain acts are socially defined as deviant or delinquent and the juvenile who commits an act so defined becomes labeled as "delinquent." This is similar to Robert Merton's idea of the **Self-fulfilling Prophecy** as a catalyst for eliciting future behavior of the prescribed kind. According to Merton (1968), *when the members of a social group define a person or event in a certain way, they may in fact shape future circumstances and activities so that the anticipated and projected behavior comes to pass*.

Tannenbaum's Concept of "Tagging"

In 1938, with the publication of *Crime and Community* by Frank Tannenbaum, an innovative application of the labeling perspective was made to criminology. Tannenbaum emphasized the treatment of the offender that makes a habitual criminal out of the accidental or occasional one. Thus, the greater evil lies in the societal treatment, not in the original act. Tannenbaum (1938:17–19) called this demonization process *tagging* and pointed out that:

> There is a gradual shift from the definition of the specific acts as evil to a definition of the individual as evil, so that all his acts come to be looked upon with suspicion. In the process of identification his companions, hangouts, play, speech, income, all his conduct, the personality itself, become subject to scrutiny and question. From the community's point of view, the individual who used to do bad and mischievous things has now become a bad and unredeemable human being. . . . The young delinquent becomes bad because he is defined as bad and because he is not believed if he is good. . . . The process of making the criminal, therefore, is a process of tagging, defining, segregating, describing, emphasizing, making conscious and self-conscious; it becomes a way of stimulating, suggesting, emphasizing, and evoking the very traits that are complained of.

The process of **tagging** led to Tannenbaum's (1938:8, 20) somber conclusion: "The adult criminal is usually the delinquent child grown up. . . . *The person becomes the thing he [sic] is described as being.*"

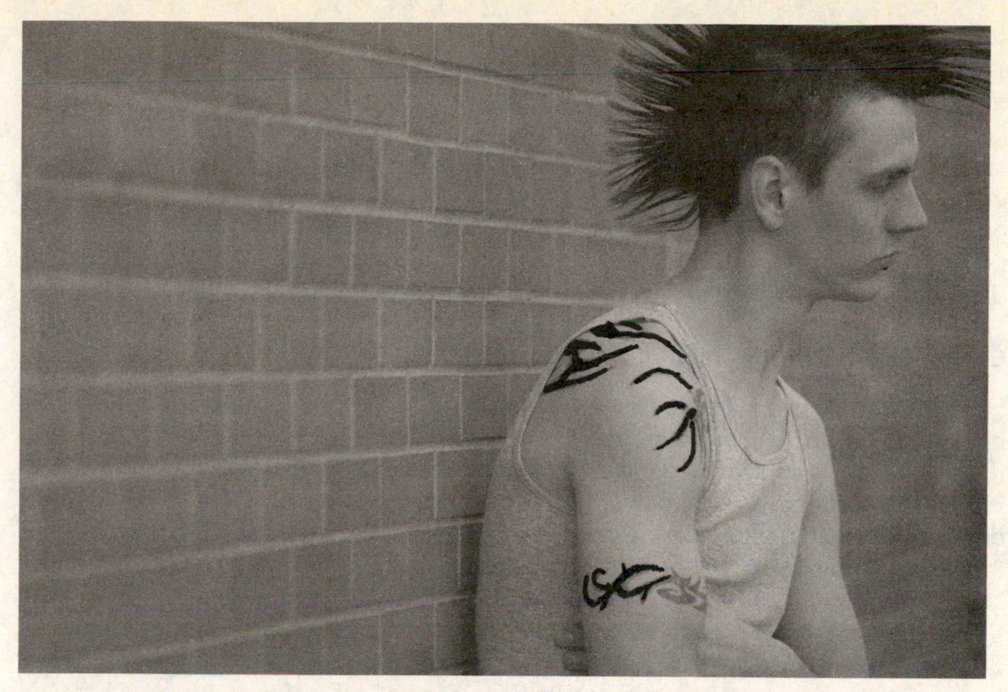

This student is waiting outside the principal's office for a conference. Do you think the principal may label him before he ever speaks a word? What would you guess the conference is about? Would it surprise you to discover the young man was going in to ask the principal for a letter of reference to a prestigious Ivy League school?

Lemert's Primary and Secondary Deviance

As we have unfolded the development of each theoretical explanation of deviance and delinquency, we have tried to demonstrate how successive theorists have added to the accumulating store of insights, concepts, and knowledge until the full theoretical formulation eventually takes shape and comes into view. Nowhere is this process of theory building more obvious than in the emergence of the labeling perspective of deviance and delinquency. While the modern labeling approach is often attributed to the work of Edwin Lemert (1951), it is obvious that he stood on the shoulders of numerous earlier theorists, as he synthesized and refined their work as a foundation for his own contributions.

Lemert's expansion of Labeling Theory was in his concern for the consequences of an individual being labeled on future behavior. Remember, Cooley indicated that an individual's evaluation of self is a reflection of other people's reactions. It follows that if the labeled person believes in the societal label, then the process of labeling can be a critical determinant of the subsequent deviant or conforming career of the individual.

In discussing the dynamics involved in becoming a juvenile delinquent, Tannenbaum implied that there is a progression between two types of criminal or delinquent acts. One is the *first* act, which the child considers as innocent but which adults define as delinquent. The second is the *final* behavior, which both the child and adults define as delinquent. Lemert made explicit the distinction between these two behavioral steps in deviance. He called the first one *primary deviation* and the second, *secondary deviation*. **Primary deviation** occurs when *an individual may commit a deviant act (or several deviant acts), but does not internalize the deviant self-concept and continues to occupy the role of conformist.* **Secondary deviation** occurs when *an individual's self-concept is altered and the deviant role is personally assumed.*

The labeling approach to explaining juvenile delinquency has the potential of going beyond the questions of how society defines, labels, and punishes the deviant, or how people alter their social expectations and responses to the person. The theory poses the question of how the revised self-concept of the socially labeled and stigmatized individual can lead to the emergence of stable patterns of deviance.

Becker's Developmental Career Model

Howard Becker is one of the leading proponents of the labeling perspective. In his book *Outsiders* (1963), he propounded the view that deviance, like beauty, exists in the eye of the beholder. No act is intrinsically deviant but must be defined as such. He emphasized that societal perception of an act as deviant can impute a generalized deviant role to the individual. Everett Hughes (1945:357) described this process as taking on a **master status**—*a status that "tends to overpower, in most crucial situations, any other characteristics which might run counter to it."* As Becker (1963:34) said, "Treating a person as though he were generally rather than specifically deviant produces a self-fulfilling prophecy. It sets in motion several mechanisms which conspire to shape the person in the image people have of him [*sic*]." Thus, taking on a master status quite often leads to what Edwin Schur (1973) called **role engulfment**—*becoming caught up in fulfilling the particular role expectations that accompany the master status to the exclusion of the many other statuses and roles a person may occupy.*

Perhaps Becker's major contribution to Labeling Theory was his introduction of the notion of a developmental process that precedes the attainment of a deviant or delinquent identity and career. Becker's (1963) study of marijuana users prompted him to outline an unfolding sequence of steps that could lead an individual to unreserved commitment and participation in a deviant career.

Becker argued that the identity of being a "confirmed marijuana user" develops over time. It has history and longitudinal development. For example, Becker found that the developmental process for becoming a confirmed and consistent user of marijuana included the following sequence of related steps or stages: (1) the person must have access to the drug, (2) he or she must experiment with it, and (3) the individual must continue its use. Each of these steps toward the final condition involves subtle changes in the individual's attitudes and perspective, as well as behavior. Becker (1963:23) noted:

> Each step requires explanation. . . . We need, for example, one kind of explanation of how a person comes to be in a situation where marijuana is readily available. . . and another kind of explanation of why, given the fact of its availability, he [*sic*] is willing to experiment with it in the first place. And we need still another explanation of why, having experimented with it, he [*sic*] continues to use it. . . . That is, no one could become a confirmed marijuana user without going through each step.

Circumstances that determine movement along a particular path include characteristics of both the person and the situation. The personal component involves an individual's susceptibility and vulnerability to the drug; the situational component in the developmental process consists largely of feedback from other actors, who witness it, and how they respond to the individual's use of marijuana (Cohen, 1966). According to Becker and other labeling theorists, it is within a given social situation and context that the user of marijuana can encounter sanctions and a labeling experience that can stimulate further progress and development of a deviant career.

The developmental model suggests considerable explanatory power for many other forms of deviant and delinquent behavior besides the use of marijuana. In addition, Becker's formulation helps to moderate the rigid delinquent–nondelinquent dichotomy by perceiving delinquent behavior at various stages of development, intensity, and commitment.

Contributions of Labeling Theory

A significant contribution of the labeling approach to juvenile delinquency is its analytical division of nonconforming behavior into primary and secondary deviance. Of equal importance is its focus on the societal perception and reaction to the initial deviant act and the subsequent revision in self-concept that enables the actor to continue into a more stable pattern of deviant behavior. As Matza (1969:89, 164, 196) pointed out:

> we see how the effort of society to remedy or control deviance ironically becomes a factor in producing deviance. This paradoxical development runs against common sense, which usually sees social control efforts as an effective response rather than a cause of deviant behavior.

Wide application of the labeling perspective has been made in critiques of law enforcement procedures and the juvenile justice system. Piliavin and Briar (1964:214) contended that many dispositions made by police officers in cases of suspected juvenile offenders are based on intuitive character assessments which, in turn, are founded on the youth's group affiliations, age, sex, race, grooming, dress, and demeanor:

> the official delinquent, as distinguished from the juvenile who simply commits a delinquent act, is the product of a social judgment, in this case a judgment made by the police. He is a delinquent because somebody in authority has defined him as one, often on the basis of the public face he has presented to officials rather than of the kind of offense he has committed.

The labeling process that occurs during police/juvenile encounters on the streets is further discussed in Chapter 13.

Similarly, Cicourel (1968) used a labeling approach to show differential treatment between lower- and middle-class families in the administration of justice. He indicated that ad hoc interpretations and imputations of character, family life, and future possibilities—often retained in official and unofficial files by schools, police departments, and courts—not only negatively and unfairly label some youths, but also predestine them for future litigation. William Chambliss' (1973b) research highlighted this point even more (see Box 7.1).

More specific research investigations of the "pre-delinquent label" have uncovered several differential racial and gender effects. Adams, Johnson, and Evans (1998)

BOX 7.1

CONCEPT APPLICATION: The "Saints" and The "Roughnecks"

In the 1970s, William Chambliss (1973) conducted a longitudinal participant observation study of delinquency in a small town that demonstrated the power of both official and unofficial labeling. Chambliss studied two juvenile gangs—one called the "Saints" comprised of eight youths from respectable, middle-class homes and another referred to as "Roughnecks" that consisted of six youths from lower-class families. He discovered that although the Saints had never been arrested, they were involved in just as much and many of the same types of delinquency (although less violent offenses) as the Roughnecks, who had been arrested numerous times. Moreover, despite their delinquency involvement, the Saints' reputations in the community and among teachers and school administrators remained positive, with much of their delinquency viewed as "pranks and mischief." Members of the Saints seemed to internalize the nondelinquent label and also viewed themselves as "good" boys. On the other hand, the Roughnecks' reputation was that they were "a bad bunch of boys headed for trouble," and they too, had clearly embraced that label (Chambliss, 1973b:27–28).

Over the period of his observation, Chambliss noted that the Saints, despite their delinquency, continued to view themselves as "nondelinquent," simply out to have a good time and to "raise a little hell"—a view that seemingly comported with both official and unofficial labels of them. Conversely, the Roughnecks became highly visible delinquents, openly flaunting their hostility toward the law and "respectable" members of the community. Chambliss' findings not only underscore the importance of labeling, but also lend credence to the conflict theories, as you will see later in this chapter, and in Box 7.2, which shows how labeling often has a social-class basis.

Did your high school have a group of "Saints" and "Roughnecks"? Can you think of other examples when you saw the impact of labeling? Is there a self-fulfilling prophecy when "pre-delinquent" or "delinquent" labels are placed on youths?

Source

Chambliss, W. J. 1973. The Saints and the Roughnecks. *Society* 11:24–31.

found that negative, informal labels have a greater delinquency-causing impact among black than among white youths. Jeffrey Victor (2004) found that girls who have a supportive emotional bond with their mothers or a grandmother were less likely to develop low self-esteem and were insulated from the delinquency effects of derogatory stereotyping. Research shows that some labels have an enduring quality shaping perceptions, not only of individuals, but of themes and stereotypes that can be quite resilient over time (DeVenanzi, 2007).

Edwin Schur emerged as another outspoken proponent of the labeling perspective on delinquency. In his book *Radical Non-intervention* (1973), he asserted that we must rethink the delinquency problem. The label of delinquency has been so overused and so widely applied that it covers everything from talking back to parents and truancy, to forcible rape and first-degree murder. As Schur pointed out, both the terms *juvenile* and *delinquent* are ascribed statuses. That is to say, they are labels assigned to some youths by the society in which they live. Schur insisted that so-called delinquents are neither internally nor externally different from nondelinquents except for the fact that they have been officially processed by the justice system and so labeled.

A less radical labeling viewpoint of criminal and juvenile justice procedures has been set forth by David Kauzlarich (2009). He asserted that criminologists and legal authorities have long attempted to distinguish between those acts of **mala in se**—*considered inherently evil* (such as murder and rape) and **mala prohibita**—*those considered evil only because they are prohibited* (such as gambling and alcohol consumption by minors). The labeling approach provides valuable insights into the latter category, as a vast number of the acts committed by juveniles that come to be labeled as delinquent clearly fall under it. The wide variety of acts which become treated as status offenses for juveniles are not considered evil in and of themselves but merely have been labeled as inappropriate behavior for juveniles.

Additional support for the labeling argument has been derived from the research of David Ward and Charles Tittle (1993:60) whose findings suggest that "sanctioning and labeling of norm violators significantly affects the likelihood that an offender will develop a deviant identity and that such identities significantly affect the likelihood of recidivism." However, they caution that the traditional labeling process is just one of several ways that recurring deviance may be produced. Moreover, labeling may be more relevant in explaining minor acts of deviance and delinquency than for major offenses.

Ordinarily, the labeling explanation of crime and delinquency focuses almost exclusively on the negative effects impacting the offender. A growing body of literature has analyzed the modified self-identity and subsequent patterns of secondary deviance emerging from initial social assessments of deviants and their primary misconduct. J. Scott Kenny (2002) extended this interactive labeling process to include the victims of crime. His unique approach focused on the consequences of differential societal reactions of sympathy offered by friends, family, and community to victims suffering the loss of a loved one through murder. Similar to findings from studies on social labeling of criminal deviants, Kenny found that primary and secondary deviance, modification of personal identification, and role accommodation "each have their conceptual counterpart in the experience of victims" (Kenny, 2002:235).

Criticisms and Limitations of Labeling Theory

The reviews of Labeling Theory are mixed and sometimes contradictory. The weaknesses cited by critics are diametric opposites to the strengths referred to by proponents. For example, much has been made of Labeling Theory's focus on societal reaction as a key factor in producing deviance (e.g., Becker, 1963; Erikson, 1964). In response, Gibbs (1966) suggested that the approach is defective in that it tends to deny the existence of deviance as any reality apart from the process of social adjudication of deviance. Gibbs indicated that this approach cannot tell us why one person rather than another commits deviant acts. He argued that the usefulness of the approach is in its understanding of the societal response to deviance, while leaving the original or primary deviance unexplained. However, labeling theorists like John Kitsuse (1972) have countered that Labeling Theory was never intended as an explanation of primary deviation from societal norms.

David Bordua (1967:48) challenged the depiction of societal reaction as a force totally external to the passive (and often innocent) actor, moving the actor to a secondary and more stable pattern of deviance. He pointed out that juvenile delinquents often have coveted, encouraged, and cultivated such labels as "tough" or "bad" for themselves as a matter of pride. Gang members often flaunt their presence and stage confrontations with police because their subsequent arrests are often sources of "rep" among their peers (Werthman and Piliavin, 1967). On the other hand, punishment, societal labeling, and stigmatization for wrongdoing can be effective in deterring many offenders from pursuing a course of continual law violation. It is *not* axiomatic that those guilty of primary deviance and subjected to the labeling process will move on to secondary deviance (Akers, 1985).

As a counterbalance to Barry Glassner's (1982:75) contention that "during the past few decades, more sociological research has derived from the labeling perspective than from any other model of deviance," a number of sociologists complain that "labeling theory lacks empirical verification and that therefore its pronouncements should be considered with caution" (Bordua, 1969:121). Moreover, L. N. Robins (1975) argued that it is unlikely that the proponents of the perspective will subject Labeling Theory to empirical study since they are the sociologists most suspicious of "hard" data. He contended:

> In short, labelling theorists believe that deviance in a society is largely the product of attempts to measure or record it. Like Archimedes, who realized he would have to stand outside the earth if he were to move it, the sociologist accepting labelling theory has nowhere to stand from which he or she can observe the "natural" rates against which the size of the distortion in official rates and rates based on interviews can be measured, to estimate the impact of labelling. (Robins, 1975:21)

Labeling Theory has been used to indict the juvenile justice system, charging that police, courts, and other agencies tend to negatively evaluate and label some suspected delinquents, thus increasing their likelihood of further involvement in secondary deviance. This contention was disputed by Foster, Dinitz, and Reckless (1972), who found that labeling by the juvenile justice system during an early stage of processing did not produce changes in self-concept or increased delinquency by their subjects. Similarly, Terence Thornberry (1979) found that the handling of delinquent youths in a stern manner generally did not result in greater criminality, as Labeling Theory suggests. Along the same line, Bordua (1967:154) and Gibbs (1966:50) charged that labeling theory does not take into account the positive aspects of societal reaction to deviant or delinquent behavior. Many children and youths are diverted from further misbehavior and delinquency by the serious and even threatening response of parents, teachers, and police officers to an initial offense. Even an uncomplimentary label and dire predictions about where a delinquent course can lead has deterrent value for many juveniles. This has led to the development of what some call *shaming theory*, or **reintegrative shaming**, *where judges require juveniles to publicly acknowledge their wrongdoing and perhaps perform a somewhat degrading or humiliating public service to account for their deviance* (Braithwaite, 1989). This is discussed again in Chapters 15 and 16).

Research on the logic and explanatory power of Labeling Theory continues to generate mixed and contradictory findings. For example, Lawrence Sherman found inconsistent support for the hypothesis that "the process of repeatedly being arrested and labeled affects individuals' self-image and later behavior such that they come to accept this definition of themselves" (Sherman and Berk, 1984; Sherman, et al., 1992). "Sherman's work showed . . . not everyone who is labeled comes to see him or herself in that way and increase his or her deviant behavior. This probably reflects the fact that each of us has many components to our self-identities" (Stockard, 1997:138–139).

RADICAL/CONFLICT THEORIES

Conflict Theories of delinquency are sometimes referred to as *Radical Theory* because they dramatically depart from more established and accepted criminological theories. Such revisionist approaches have a recurring history in sociology and often are precipitated by major social problems and a growing conviction among some theorists that the existing explanations of what is happening and why are incomplete or inaccurate. For example, during the 1960s and early 1970s, the civil rights struggle, Vietnam War, and other social upheavals became catalysts that sensitized many people to the gross suffering and glaring inequities among human beings and led to the questioning of dominant economic, social, and criminological theories. A number of sociologists and criminologists expressed their discontent with the theoretical status quo by calling for fundamental revision of explanations of deviant and criminal conduct (e.g., Chambliss, 1974; Quinney, 1974; Turk, 1969). This radical new criminology focused on the generation of laws and legal institutions by affluent and politically influential groups that not only perpetuate their elitist power and position but also discriminate against the underclass with a criminal label. The radical/conflict theorists complained that traditional criminology emphasized the categories set up by the criminal law and "the kinds of common crimes believed to be associated with the poor and powerless" (Michalowski, 1985:314, 315).

Consistent with the labeling perspective, radical/conflict theorists view adult crime and juvenile delinquency as labels that are selectively applied to specified individuals and groups whose behavior is disturbing to those who are in a position to attach such labels and implement social sanctions. However, labeling theorists usually focus on the microsociological context of interaction and postulate that the deviant label and role can be imputed in communities of any size and for a multitude of reasons. On the other hand, radical/conflict theorists take a macrosociological approach by contending that the criminal or delinquent label arises from conflicts between different social classes as their vested interests and values clash and as law enforcement is differentially applied to these social classes.

The Marxian Heritage

The philosophical roots of radical/conflict theories of deviant and delinquent behavior can be traced to the writings and conflict perspective of Karl Marx ([1867] 1967). Marx saw capitalism as an evil economic system that intensified and perpetuated the separation and ranking of social classes. He contended that by virtue of their ownership and control of the means of production, the *bourgeoisie* (capitalist class) were able to maintain their power, materialistic and hedonistic lifestyle, and domination over the disadvantaged *proletariat* (working class).

In his writings, Marx pointed to a growing awareness and alienation among workers of the world as they toiled to maintain productivity and profit for their capitalist overlords. Karl Marx and Friedrich Engels ([1848] 1964) developed a conflict interpretation of human society, behavior, and social phenomena in which they called for the revolutionary overthrow of capitalistic, political, economic, and social structures and the radical reorganization of society. They pointed to an inevitable war of the classes in which the downtrodden and pauperized proletariat would revolt and ultimately establish a classless society in which people could not be exploited to satisfy the greed of a small, wealthy, and powerful upper class.

Although Marx did not focus his Conflict Theory explicitly on explaining crime or delinquency, many subsequent scholars expanded and applied his basic thesis to those phenomena. Radical/Conflict theories of delinquency generally agree with Marx that the unequal distribution of wealth and power is the major causal explanation behind norm-violating behavior. The theoretical contributions of Richard Quinney, David Greenberg, and Herman and Julia Schwendinger are extensions of the Marxian argument and examples of Radical/Conflict theories of crime and delinquency.

Quinney's Social Reality of Crime and Delinquency

Richard Quinney emerged in the 1970s as one of the most prominent spokespersons for radical/conflict criminology in the United States. According to Quinney (1975), crime and delinquency can best be understood in relation to how a society creates its criminal laws, defines crime and delinquency, and what practices it implements to control its citizens. He distinguished between what he called the "official reality of crime," which purports that law violation threatens social order and public safety, and the "social reality of crime," which reflects the less visible definition that any act that threatens those in power is legally prohibited and considered criminal or delinquent.

Quinney's (1975:37–41) theory of criminal behavior contains definite undertones of Marxian class conflict and was summarized in six propositions:

1. ***The Official Definition of Crime:*** Crime as a legal definition of human conduct is created by agents of the dominant class in a politically organized society.
2. ***Formulating Definitions of Crime:*** Definitions of crime are composed of behaviors that conflict with the interests of the dominant class.
3. ***Applying Definitions of Crime:*** Definitions of crime are applied by the class that has the power to shape the enforcement and administration of criminal law.
4. ***How Behavior Patterns Develop in Relation to Definitions of Crime:*** Behavior patterns are structured in relation to definitions of crime, and within this context, people engage in actions that have relative probabilities of being defined as criminal.
5. ***Constructing an Ideology of Crime:*** An ideology of crime is constructed and diffused by the dominant class to secure its hegemony.
6. ***Constructing the Social Reality of Crime:*** The social reality of crime is constructed by the formulation and application of definitions of crime, the development of behavior patterns in relation to these definitions, and the construction of an ideology of crime.

It is clear from the context of Quinney's *Social Reality of Crime* (1970) that his use of the term *crime* encompasses juvenile delinquency as well as illegal conduct by adults. It follows that the six propositions comprising the nucleus of Quinney's theory represent an explanation for the definition and creation of crime *and* delinquency, as well as the societal responses. Quinney views criminal and delinquent behavior as largely resulting from repressive efforts of the dominant class to control subordinate classes.

In his book *Class, State, and Crime,* Quinney (1980) outlined two broad categories of criminal activity. The first is what he called *crimes of economic domination and repression.* These crimes include the unlawful acts committed by members of the ruling class in order to maintain their social supremacy. These activities, according to Quinney, involve the constant efforts of government and law enforcement officials to criminalize those behaviors of the working class which appear to threaten the existing social order. In order to control the masses, Quinney argued that the lower class must be coerced or duped into believing that laws that repress them actually protect them.

Quinney called the second type of criminality *crimes of accommodation and resistance.* These are crimes committed by members of the working class in an effort to survive the oppression of the ruling class. Expanding on Marxian theory, Quinney postulated that in a capitalist society, the poor and powerless are forced into crime for survival. Predatory and parasitic property crimes such as vandalism, theft, burglary, and robbery are explained as resulting from the impoverished situation of the underemployed, the unemployed, and the unemployable (Bartol and Bartol, 1989:275).

Quinney's Radical/Conflict theory can be applied to juvenile delinquency in two important ways. First, it implies that activities and conduct by youths which are perceived by adults as threats to the authority and privileged status enjoyed by adults are those most likely to be defined and punished as delinquency. Second, it indicates that underclass and minority youths are more likely to be involved in activities that are seen as threatening the existing social order, and hence, far more likely than their white middle- and upper-class counterparts to be punished by legal authorities (see Box 7.2).

Greenberg's Focus on Adolescent Frustration

David Greenberg (1977) applied Conflict/Theory to juvenile delinquency by linking it to the high level of frustration experienced by many adolescents in a capitalist society. As Robert Merton (1957a) pointed out in his Theory of Anomie (Chapter 5), in a country like the United States, there is tremendous pressure on everyone to achieve certain culturally approved objectives. There is a general consensus that these objectives are money, material possessions, and other symbols of economic success. Greenberg added that the precise nature of these success goals depends upon one's place in a rigidly structured and age-graded life course. Adolescents, for example, are subjected to uncompromising peer pressure to conform to certain prescribed codes of appearance and behavior. At the same time, pressures from older generations and larger society in the form of laws requiring school attendance and minimum-age work regulations restrict the opportunities of teenagers in the job market and lock them into their unfulfilling age-status roles. Based upon this situation, Greenberg identified several sources of potential frustration among adolescents in a capitalistic society that can motivate many to delinquent conduct:

> ***Lack of Money.*** Most prominent among adolescent frustrations can be the lack of money by the poor to participate socially, or at least symbolically, with more affluent teenage members of the youth subculture. The absence of funds for

BOX 7.2

CROSS-CULTURAL FOCUS: British "Hooligans": Labeling, Social Class, and Delinquency in Great Britain

One of the most disparaging and stigmatizing labels in the United Kingdom is that of *hooligan*. First used by the British press during the latter part of the Victorian era, the term is still widely used by royalty; Members of Parliament; police officers; judges; and members of the upper, middle, and working class to refer to rowdy youths, youth gangs, vandals, and other juvenile delinquents and young criminals (Schwarz, 1996). Today, *hooliganism* is most associated with rowdy, young football (soccer) fans who paint their faces and bodies in team colors, drink heavily, yell and spit at opposing players and fans, and often wreak havoc on pubs and neighborhoods near stadiums and underground stops after matches (Frosdick and Marsh, 2005).

Augusto De Venanzi (2008:203) contends that the hooligan label developed out of a strong need for middle-class Victorians to label and stigmatize what "they perceived to be a declining aristocracy and a degenerated working-class." Over a period of time, the term came to refer to a "criminal class" that was routinely vilified and denigrated by "proper" Victorian society and the press. As the label became popularized, the media attached it to almost any criminal act, and anytime adolescent boys or young men were seen in groups on the streets, it was assumed that they were hooligans up to no good. As most street crimes became attributed to hooligans, a "moral panic" was created that allowed the aristocracy and police to exert more social control over the working class through social, legislative, and judicial means.

Steven Humphries (1997) pointed out that public perception that hooligans were unemployed youths who roamed the streets wreaking havoc and committing street crimes was not accurate as many young men who were labeled as hooligans were actually gainfully employed in a wide range of semi-skilled and unskilled jobs in factories and mines. Nevertheless, the label *hooligan* took on such a powerful meaning that it not only shaped attitudes toward individuals tagged with it, but legitimated the ruling class's efforts to exert even more formal and informal social control over the entire working class and underclass.

How does the creation and application of the "hooligan" label in the United Kingdom exemplify tenets of labeling theory? How could you apply Radical/Conflict Theories to explain its uses?

Sources

De Venanzi, A. 2008. Social representations and the labeling of non-compliant youths: The case of Victorian and Edwardian hooligans. *Deviant Behavior* 29 (April):193–224.

Frosdick, S. and Marsh, P. 2005. *Football hooliganism*. UK: Willan.

Humphries, S. 1997. *Hooligans or rebels? An oral history of working-class childhood and youth 1889–1939.* Oxford: Cambridge University Press.

Schwarz, B. 1996. Night battles: Hooligan and citizen. In Nava, M. and O'Shea, A. (Eds.). *Modern Times: Reflections on a century of English modernity*, pp. 101–127. London: Routledge.

popular clothing, cosmetics, recorded music, and automobiles may lead to shoplifting, burglary, automobile theft, or perhaps dealing illegal drugs in order to get these items. These pressures may be negligible for youths fortunate enough to have parents who are sympathetic and economically able to fulfill the needs and desires characteristic of their children's age and status position in society. On the other hand, Greenberg argued, less affluent, minority and lower-class youths may feel compelled by their economically disadvantaged situation to engage in juvenile delinquency.

Lack of Respect. A second source of adolescent frustration is failure to achieve respect in school. A weak academic performance or aptitude coupled with stigma imposed by teachers and classmates may be interpreted by a youngster as valid appraisals of his or her worth as a person and ultimate chances for success. Such a demoralized youth, according to Greenberg, is a prime prospect for antisocial and delinquent behavior. Such negative school experiences are more commonly found among members of the underclass.

Lack of Employment. A third source of economically determined juvenile misconduct is the inability of huge numbers of lower-class youths (and sometimes middle-class youths) to find gainful employment. Greenberg suggested that unemployed and underemployed males are especially vulnerable to anxiety regarding their "manhood" and are likely to feel a critical inadequacy in fulfilling social expectations associated with the adult male role. This frustration may lead to an overemphasis on toughness and lead to aggressive acts, including fighting, assault, rape, and even homicide.

Schwendingers' Instrumental Theory

Radical/Conflict theories in the Marxist tradition contend that a person's status position in the social-class structure is the key factor in explaining illegal behavior. Capitalism, according to Marx and those who espouse this theoretical approach, generates competitiveness, acquisitiveness, and the exploitation of others, and reinforces the division and mutual antipathy of the "have" and "have not" social classes. Each member of society is assigned membership somewhere in the stratified social-class system based upon his or her success in controlling and/or accumulating the profits and products of economic endeavors. Thus, radical/conflict theorists argue, the stage is set for all kinds of illegal behavior resulting from the alienation of many lower-class individuals and groups. Official arrest and court statistics seem to confirm that crime and delinquency are largely lower-class phenomena. On the other hand, radical/conflict theorists suggest that a capitalistic system, which encourages a certain amount of surplus labor and unemployment, together with the legal system and law enforcement, is organized to ensure such an outcome.

Herman and Julia Schwendinger (1985) extended these basic premises from the Marxist conflict perspective in developing their own innovative theory. While affirming that delinquency still can be explained by a youth's social-class status, the Schwendingers (1985:3) added that significant amounts of "criminality can be found among youths in all stations of life." As noted in Chapter 3, self-report studies support this contention, by indicating that middle-class youths are about equally involved in delinquent conduct as members of the lower class.

To this, the Schwendingers added their main theoretical insight: parents' social class is not the most important variable in determining the delinquency potential for adolescents. Rather, the youths' relative status position among other teenagers is the best predictor of delinquency. Herman and Julia identified several relatively exclusive, stratified status formations—or distinctive social networks formed by the youths themselves—which roughly correspond with some of the more traditional

Do these girls fit one of the Schwendingers' categories of students? If so, which one? If not, how do you think their dress reflects their social status? Would you view them more as conformists or deviants? © Photoedit Inc.

social classes. These stratified formations of youth tend to be based upon common values, interests, and activities, and separate members of one social network from other youth groupings. The Schwendingers outlined the following prominent social networks among American youths:

1. *Socialites,* which may be referred to as "elites," "frats," "soshes," or "preppies" that are generally comprised of upper middle class, college-bound youths.
2. *Greasers,* also called "hoods," "homeboys," "thugs," or "hodads." This group is largely comprised of lower-class and minority youths.
3. *Intellectuals,* members of this group are often called "brains," "bookworms," or "nerds."

Not all youths neatly fit into one or another of these categories. There can be considerable overlap of individuals who comfortably interact with more than one group. There likely will be some individuals who do not readily identify with any of these social strata or networks in a given school or community. There is also considerable crossover based on a blurring of socioeconomic background. For example, athletes may be identified as "jocks," and those interested in skateboards may be known as "skaters" regardless of the socioeconomic status of their families. Nevertheless, in spite of such irregularities, the Schwendingers posited that virtually all youths find some specific clique with which they can identify.

The theoretical formulation developed by Herman and Julia Schwendinger to explain juvenile delinquency is called **Instrumental Theory**. This theory describes misbehavior as motivated by calculated and selfish designs upon the victims—not dissimilar from the rationalizations of the "greedy bourgeoisie" described by Karl Marx. The delinquent has a utilitarian attitude regarding the illegal act as well as of the victim as a "legitimate" object of exploitation ("What is in it for me?") (Carey and McAnany, 1984:138).

Moreover, the Schwendingers' instrumental theory conceptualized delinquency as importantly linked to a youth's social network, contending that members of some stratum formations are more likely to become delinquent than others and that delinquent conduct manifested by members of one stratum or social network may vary significantly from the kind of delinquency most common in other groups. For example, youths with economically deprived backgrounds are not only more likely to become involved with the network identified as "greasers," but are apt to participate in theft, burglaries, and perhaps violence (especially if they join a gang). On the other hand, middle-class youths who are identified as "socialites," while perhaps equally delinquent, are more likely to engage in truancy, vandalism, shoplifting, and less violent forms of law violation. These ideas are consistent with Chambliss' study of Saints and Roughnecks discussed in Box 7.1. Thus, in another sense, membership in a particular stratum or subgroup has an "instrumental" function—serving as a vehicle for a social identity and enhancing opportunity and motivation for various specialized activities—even juvenile delinquency. Youths identified as "intellectuals," regardless of their parents' social class, are less likely to become involved in serious illegal behavior.

Contributions of Radical/Conflict Theories

In our study of various theoretical perspectives and approaches that explain human behavior, we must be cautious that some viewpoints are not summarily rejected simply because personal biases and preferences interfere with objective considerations. Radical criminology is in danger of such a fate because it is philosophically linked with **Marxist Conflict Theory** and boldly calls for revolutionary revision of the political and economic institutions that are assumed to define crime and delinquency in support of upper-class domination of the underclass. The United States has a long history of costly political and military confrontation with socialism, communism, and other dimensions of Marxist activism, and it may be difficult for some to conceive of any positive contributions from Radical/Conflict theories to our understanding of juvenile delinquency. However, Radical/Conflict Theory offers several helpful insights into the causes of delinquency.

A major contribution of Radical/Conflict theories is that they call attention to the lack of power and resultant alienation experienced by young people living in any society dominated by adults. Juvenile statutes, for the most part, reinforce expectations for children and youths to conform to norms which reflect adult values about appropriate behaviors. When those norms are violated, youths are confronted by a juvenile justice system which is similarly dominated by adults. Many young people feel powerless in this adult world. In Marxian terms, these juveniles experience a growing alienation, class consciousness, and class cohesion, much like any other powerless group of people (this idea is pursued in Chapter 11).

Radical/Conflict theories also underscore the prejudice and discrimination experienced by youths who are members of racial and ethnic minorities. Radical/Conflict theorists argue that minority youths are subjected to differential and unequal treatment at the hands of school officials, law enforcement officers, and juvenile court judges. An awareness of their social handicaps, in a perceived conflict with a hostile society, can enhance the attractiveness of illegal means to attain economic success to some underclass and minority youths. The economic determinism behind some juvenile crime was graphically illustrated to one of the authors during field research on urban street gangs. During the course of the investigation, there was an opportunity to briefly interview several youths after their conviction for possession and selling of crack cocaine. Although high-school dropouts, they were very "street smart" and mercenary about their profession as drug dealers. In response to a naive inquiry regarding why they did not pursue their formal education and seek an honest job, one 17-year-old youth answered with a question: "How much money did you make last year?" Momentarily thinking that his response was tangential and unrelated, the researcher asked: "What does my income have to do with the illegal activities for which you have been convicted?" "Well," he countered, "I made over $100,000 last year, doing my thing; and no income taxes. How much did you clear?!" It seems that some of our most popular and traditional theories of juvenile delinquency have underemphasized the importance of class conflict and economic determinism which are central tenets of Radical/Conflict Theory.

An example of the relatively new interest in and influence of the radical/conflict approach to explaining crime and delinquency can be seen in the heated debates it has sparked among criminologists and sociologists. Its support by some scholars is evidenced by the formation of a learned society known as the Union of Radical Criminologists. This group holds meetings, circulates newsletters among its members, and focuses on research that applies the conflict perspective and radical theory to the study of crime and juvenile delinquency.

Another contribution of these theories is that they force more conventional criminologists and sociologists to consider alternative theoretical explanations for deviance, crime, and delinquency. Crime and delinquency (in the minds of radical/conflict theorists) often are contrived nomenclatures imputed to underclass offenders who are actually the victims of the system rulers. By shifting the focus away from individual delinquents and on to the macroscopic social, economic, and political forces which create and enforce the laws defining delinquency, these theories encourage society to examine and question the juvenile justice system. Even if these theories do not provide a comprehensive explanation for delinquent behavior, such an examination and critical analysis of the juvenile justice system can be very useful.

Criticisms and Limitations of Radical/Conflict Theories

As with other theoretical schools of thought put forward to account for juvenile delinquency, Radical/Conflict theories not only offer significant insights but have been subjected to critical evaluation. James Short (1990:135), for example, observed that capitalism and socialism have much in common and their dichotomous division into "good" and "evil" systems is not as simple as radical/conflict theorists suggest:

> All advanced industrial and postindustrial societies "reproduce surplus labor" and capitalist and socialist nations alike apparently undergo similar changes in crime patterns in various stages of development. Profitability and competition in international markets motivate capitalist, socialist, and mixed economies. . . . Thus, while many of the facts upon which Marxist and other "radical" theories are based are generally accepted, much debate centers on specific interpretations. Although the levels and types of unemployment and the levels of alienation of labor vary a great deal among nation-states, they are more or less constant features of capitalist, socialist, and mixed economies in today's economically interdependent world.

Lamar Empey and Mark Stafford (1999:499) noted the failure of Radical/Conflict Theory to empirically test its propositions as an important limitation of its explanatory power:

> It has failed to explain why age and sex continue to be better predictors of crime than social class. And it has failed to indicate why, contrary to all of the lessons of history, sociology, and anthropology, delinquency can be expected to disappear in a truly socialist society—why such a society could be expected to avoid the disorienting, often crime-producing conditions that all advanced societies—capitalist and noncapitalist—are now experiencing. In terms of traditional scientific standards, at least, the theory has been deficient.

Other analysts have pointed out that the theoretical causes of delinquency are not solely rooted in socioeconomic class conflict. Rather, there is considerable, legitimate overlap with Radical/Conflict theories of key variables from other theoretical orientations. The concept of lower-class alientation, for example, must be shared with social strain and cultural transmission theories.

David Schicor (1983) contends that "socialization"—so useful in social-learning theories—is a meaningful approach to understanding juvenile delinquency, whether looking at capitalist or socialist societies. Although Marxian and radical theorists must rely heavily on socialization as a causal factor in accounting for cultural materialism and lower-class inability to fulfill such expectations, they have tended to discount the importance of this basic concept. The reason, according to Schicor, is the overpoliticization of delinquency research by some Marxian and radical theorists. The idea of socialization (the internalization of societal norms and values by members of society) "is conservative in the sense that it is meant to support and maintain the status quo and is not intended to support or further social change" (Schicor, 1983:95).

Finally, while it has been often repeated and appeals to logical supposition, a direct link between economic conditions and crime has never been systematically established. Marxian theory contends that the lower classes feel exploited and alienated and consequently strike out at those who are repressing them. The greater involvement of lower-class individuals in highly visible street crimes such as homicide, assault, robbery, burglary, larceny–theft, and automobile theft seems to support this assumption.

Which theories might explain how the status frustration experienced by these youths might lead to delinquency and possibly even violence?

© Getty Images

What is puzzling, however, is why the great majority of victims of these crimes also are members of the lower class.

Richard Quinney (1975) attempted to address this question by suggesting that the reason violent and property crimes committed by the poor against the poor are so heavily policed and punished is because they threaten the general social order. Moreover, Quinney argues that the ruling class fears that victimization will spread beyond the lower class and into their ranks. Still, Radical/Conflict theories and the class-conflict perspective do not adequately explain why members of the lower class vent their frustrations and aggression against poor people of similar economic circumstances.

Summary

In this chapter, we look at two theoretical orientations that take a different approach to explaining delinquency than those in previous chapters: labeling and radical/ conflict. In Chapter 1, when we defined juvenile delinquency, we discussed the importance of the act, the actor, and the audience. Labeling theories focus their attention on the *audience.* More specifically, labeling theories look at how the labels societal members place on individuals shape those people's personal and social identities and influence their behavior. Cooley's *looking-glass self* and Thomas' *definition of the situation* provided basic sociological foundations for the labeling approach to juvenile delinquency.

Frank Tannenbaum was one of the first criminologists to apply the labeling perspective to crime and delinquency with his concept of *tagging,* indicating that defining a person as criminal/delinquent and then treating him or her according to that "tag/label" may, in fact, produce the very thing society was trying to prevent. This concept is compatible with Merton's *self-fulfilling prophecy*, which basically warns that "saying it's so, makes it so."

Edwin Lemert differentiated between *primary deviance,* in which individuals may commit a delinquent act, or even several delinquent acts, but not internalize the deviant label, and *secondary deviance* in which an individual is labeled as delinquent and takes on the deviant role. It is important to understand that Lemert was not referring to the number of times a person commits a deviant act, but to what extent being labeled as a deviant affects a person's self-concept.

Howard Becker proposed a developmental career model of deviancy that described the process by which people go from being viewed as specifically deviant to generally deviant. Deviance often becomes a *master status,* one which subsumes all other statuses and leads to *role engulfment,* where the delinquent role overpowers all other roles of the youth.

Labeling theories expands our way of defining and explaining deviance by looking at the important role played by a social audience. They are particularly useful in explaining secondary and career deviance.

The radical/conflict approach to delinquency looks at the laws themselves, and how they serve to protect and enforce the values of an elite ruling class. Based on a Marxian heritage, Quinney distinguished between official definitions and what he called the social reality of crime and delinquency. Greenberg expanded these ideas to illustrate how adolescent frustration helps propel many, especially lower-class youths, into delinquency. The Schwendingers' *instrumental theory* pointed out that parents' social class and social status might be less related to delinquency than the relative deprivation and powerlessness felt by some youths in comparison to others.

Contributions of the Radical/Conflict theories are their acknowledgement of the importance of social class on values and behavior, and the fact that those who make and enforce the rules often do so in order to protect their own vested interests. On the other hand, Radical/Conflict theories are difficult to empirically test, and they provide no explanation for why the victims of lower-class offenders are so often members of the lower class themselves.

Concept Integration: Questions and Topics for Study and Discussion

1. List the major assumptions underlying social labeling theories of delinquency. Identify and discuss several prominent sociologists and their concepts and contributions to the social labeling approach. What are some of the weaknesses and limitations of the social labeling approach?
2. List the major assumptions underlying the Radical and Conflict theories of delinquency. Identify and discuss several prominent sociologists and their respective concepts and contributions to the Radical/Conflict theory approach. What are some of the weaknesses and limitations of these explanations of juvenile delinquency?
3. How do the labeling theories fundamentally differ from the sociological theories discussed in Chapters 5, 6, and 7? How are they compatible with some of those theories?
4. How does the radical/conflict approach to delinquency differ from the sociological theories discussed in Chapters 5, 6, and 7? How is it compatible with some of those theories?

Chapter 8

Sociological Explanations of Juvenile Delinquency

The Ongoing Process of Integrative Theory Building

READING OBJECTIVES

Reading this chapter will help you achieve the following objectives:

1. Review and summarize the past development of biological, psychological, and sociological theories offering causal and deterministic explanations for juvenile delinquency in the 17th through the 20th centuries.
2. Examine *short-term hedonism* (e.g., delinquent behavior for pleasure) as an understudied motivation for juvenile crime and as a possible contributing factor to new theoretical formulations.
3. Understand and explain Maturation Theory and Life Course Theories and how they fit into a sociological framework for explaining juvenile delinquency.
4. Explain and link Rational Choice Theory and Deterrence Theory as contemporary throwbacks to the original assumptions of full personal responsibility for illegal behavior and strong punitive response from society that undergirded the 18th-century Classical School of Criminological Thought.
5. Summarize some of the differences between male and female delinquency and outline some of the contributions of feminist theories to the explanation of juvenile delinquency.
6. Comprehend the potential and analytical direction of newly emerging *integrated theories* that seek to bring together and build on overlapping causal variables from older theories established by diverse and often conflicting perspectives and disciplines.
7. Look to the future as scholars continue their quest for a general theory (or *grand theory*) that would fully explain the causes of juvenile delinquency and thus open the door to an ultimate solution to this serious social problem.

INTRODUCTION

At the outset of Part Two, we defined a **theory** as *an established, general statement that systematically and objectively relates concepts and variables together to explain events or behavior*. In Chapters 4 through 7, we have followed the sequence of major theoretical explanations of juvenile delinquency developed by scholars from various perspectives and disciplines.

Chapter 4 briefly outlined the pretheoretical Classical School of Criminological Thought that dominated corrections and penology during most of the 17th and 18th centuries. During that period, law enforcement professionals as well as the general public were guided by the oversimplified assumption that humans make rational and cognitive choices regarding conformity and deviance from social norms. It follows from this reasoning that other variables, such as personal mitigating circumstances, would have only negligible influence on the decision-making process. Consequently, individual offenders were perceived as fully responsible for their subsequent criminal conduct. This prevailing viewpoint was reflected in rigorous law enforcement and sanctions from the criminal justice system of that period.

As systematic and empirical research methodology was introduced into criminology in the 19th century, the classical position was replaced by the emerging

Positive School of Criminology. While the focus was still on the individual offender, Cesare Lombroso (1835–1909) and other influential writers of that time presented fragmentary evidence to support their thesis of a *born criminal type*, Lombroso and his followers argued that the physical appearance and predatory behavior of many criminals were indicative of an underlying atavism—an earlier, more primitive stage of human evolution. Although Lombrosian criminology has been discounted by later researchers with better data, the concept of biological determinism has been refined and expanded today into other promising areas.

Chapter 4 also discussed the psychogenic and medical model approaches, continuing the focus on the individual offender in explaining criminal and delinquent behavior. Psychiatrists and psychologists, led by the pioneering work of Sigmund Freud (1856–1939), began probing the unconscious dimension of the human mind in the search for sublimated motives, unresolved needs and conflicts, and earlier traumatic experiences that were hypothesized to cause abnormal personality patterns and antisocial deviance. Since the latter half of the 19th century, a great many kinds of juvenile delinquency have been linked by psychogenic professionals to various forms of personality maladjustment and mental illness. This psychological determinism has had a telling impact on the adjudication of criminal offenders in the United States with arguments of *diminished responsibility* for many and the *insanity defense* for a few. As the reader will see in later chapters, these psychogenic assumptions are also reflected in many treatment strategies for juvenile offenders—with mixed results.

Chapters 5, 6, and 7 provided an outline and analysis of the major theoretical constructs that comprise major sociological explanations of juvenile delinquency. The categories we have created are not absolute, discrete, exhaustive, or mutually exclusive. Instead, we have grouped together various sociological theories which generally share common assumptions and concepts. Rather than attempting to adhere to any single theoretical approach, such as Social Strain, Cultural Transmission, Social Learning, Social Control, Social Labeling, or the Radical/Conflict perspective, we have introduced each one as offering reasonable causal explanations for juvenile delinquency, together with appropriate summations of contributions and weaknesses.

We also have avoided the temptation to attempt the development of a single general theory to explain all delinquents and all the acts defined as juvenile delinquency. Even without total synthesis, the various approaches and the specific theories and concepts presented here can, in combination, shed a great deal of light on the social problem we call juvenile delinquency. Going beyond the limitations of the biological and psychological approaches, the sociological explanations show delinquent behavior to be a complex social phenomenon. Delinquency is a social act, from the very inception of the norms which govern juveniles to the social institutions which affect juveniles, the environment in which juveniles live, the socialization to which they are subjected, and the process whereby their actions are judged by others as conforming or deviant. Juvenile delinquency does not exist in a social vacuum. Each of the sociological approaches contributes a measure of understanding to some of the dynamic social factors involved in delinquency etiology. Subsequent chapters will present several treatment techniques and programs designed to counter or correct these external social forces causally related to youthful delinquency.

In this chapter, we present contemporary sociological theories of juvenile delinquency. These theories are integrative in nature with some combining elements of biology and psychology with sociological variables (e.g., Maturation Theory), while others harken back to the Classical School of Criminological Thought (Rational Choice and Deterrence Theory). Still others integrate various aspects of several of the sociological theories discussed in previous chapters. We begin this chapter with one of the more obvious, and perhaps more startling, theoretical propositions: delinquency is fun!

SHORT-RUN HEDONISM: "DELINQUENCY IS FUN!"

Although investigators have long observed the game element and the pleasure experienced by many youngsters participating in illegal activities (Shaw and McKay, 1931; Thrasher, 1927), the possible importance of this hedonistic dimension as an explanatory variable is a more contemporary suggestion. For example, Richards, et al. (1979) found that their middle-class subjects readily identified delinquency as "play" and "fun." Box 8.1 looks at the phenomenon of juveniles videotaping their acts of delinquency and posting them on the Internet for fun and entertainment.

BOX 8.1

CONCEPT APPLICATION: The *Jackass* Scrapbooks

In 2002, *Jackass: The Movie* managed to shock and nauseate theatergoers with a new level of outrageous content, while grossing a new high in film revenues in its first week. The film was little more than a sequence of loosely connected scenes in which actors and amateur stunt men perform dangerous and even death-defying antics. For instance, actors are shown engulfed in flames, narrowly escaping staged automobile crashes, and engaged in violent physical combat. The heart-stopping escapades first premiered on MTV's *Jackass* show. Not surprisingly, *Jackass: The Movie* was so successful at the box office that it spawned a sequel, *Jackass Number Two*, that hit movie theatres in 2006. Bloggers described *Jackass Number Two*, as more fun and more daring than the first movie because "the stunts were more stupid and dangerous and the actors could have actually been killed" (www.jackassmovie.com, 2008).

This kind of programming apparently has been interpreted by many teenagers as a dare and challenge to their own "indestructible bravery," as well as an avenue to easy money if they can market the documentation of their similar escapades. Despite warnings in the program and in the movie and oblivious to personal safety, a number of youths have recklessly staged fights, started fires, and participated in close encounters with speeding automobiles—with tragic results:

> While his friends stood by with a video camera running, a 15-year-old boy from Bellevue, Washington soaked his shirt in rubbing alcohol and lighted it in what the teens claimed was a "Jackass" copycat stunt. But it went terribly wrong. The boy suffered first-degree burns over his face and upper body. His friends had planned on selling the videotape. (Conroy, 2002:1)

The transition of the *Jackass* concept from reckless self-destruction to delinquent vandalism and assaults on society soon followed. The violence turned inward became violence turned outward as the young people involved became amoral, irresponsible, and out of control. Their pursuit of thrills and excitement became emotionally addictive as targets for attack changed from mailboxes, empty houses, and automobiles to transients and other vulnerable people.

(*Continued*)

Adolescent psychologist David Walsh describes this transition as "a slippery slope of insensitivity . . . a progression of growing cruelty to animals and people" (ABC, *20/20*).

In the hands of young vandals and assailants are the ubiquitous home video cameras and personal cell phones that have proven to be convenient means of documenting their outrageous and predatory behavior and posting their exploits on the World Wide Web. These youths refer to the practice as "scrapbooking" their lives and deeds—as proof for bragging rights to friends. Police confiscation of these video films also supplies prime evidence against offenders for specific crimes.

The explanation offered by apprehended teenagers for their wild, destructive sprees is that they were young and stupid and that "It is fun to break things." Dr. Walsh adds, "Thinking is not what is going on here. . . . They are emotionally driven" (ABC, *20/20*).

What theoretical explanations in this chapter and previous chapters might help explain the *Jackass* phenomenon and the desire for teenagers to record their delinquent episodes and put them on YouTube, Facebook, and other publicly available sites?

Sources

ABC. 2002. *Scrapbooking.* 2002, (Reporter: Arnold Deaz; Editor: Tom Marcylus). November 11, 2002.

Conroy, C. 2002. *Jackass* copycat: Teen badly burned. *(Compuserve)*, November 13, 2002:1.
www.jackassmovie.com, 2008.

Jack Katz, in his *Seductions of Crime: Moral and Sensual Attractions of Doing Evil* (1996), contended that criminal behavior cannot be fully understood or explained without grasping how it is experienced by or what it means to the actor. If we grasp the subjective interpretation of the experience, Katz argues, we find that crime has a sensual, magical, creative appeal that is lacking in most conventional, law-abiding acts. The "central problem" for criminologists, Katz (1996:4) argues, "is to understand the emergence of distinctive sensual dynamics." Doing evil, he writes, is motivated by a quest for moral transcendence, righteousness in the face of challenge, boredom, humiliation, or chaos. Deviance has authenticity, Katz believes, an attractiveness that uplifts, excites, and purifies. To understand crime as a strictly rational pursuit, as the desperate need to wallow in self-flagellation, as the manifestation of a mental disorder, or the enactment of straightforward cultural or subcultural dictates, is to miss the point spectacularly. Deviance is the existential pursuit of passion, a "lucid" enterprise, with clear-cut winners and losers, a fevered, out-of-one's-head experience, a world of beauty all its own, accessible only to the righteous, the daring, the members of a kind of soulful elite (Goode, 1990:7).

The extension of delinquency theory based on these suggestions (though requiring additional research validation) is relatively obvious, straightforward, and potentially embarrassing to some established theorists who may have underestimated the obvious allurement and pleasure associated with criminal deviance. One of the authors of this book made this serendipitous discovery when interviewing youthful gang members in California cities. In response to inquiries regarding their motivation for involvement in criminal conduct, a majority cited the usual social and psychological justifications. In addition, some of the more candid and articulate informants enthusiastically alluded to the unparalleled adrenalin rush and emotional high connected with the risk of their illegal activities (Bynum, 1996). Tim Delaney

Many municipalities have ordinances against riding skateboards on sidewalks and other public areas. What theory (or theories) might help explain this type of delinquency?

Jacksonville Journal Courie/The Image Works

(2006:112) has confirmed this observation: "Some people simply find delinquency and gang behavior exciting, fun, and thrilling."

Some scholars might deny that Katz's reasoning points to a new direction in theory building to account for deviant and delinquent behavior. Rather, they might contend that the hedonistic aspects of misconduct are already incorporated in existing social learning and cultural transmission theories, as well as implicit in some elements of the psychogenic approach. Nevertheless, as we have mentioned before, most sociological theories overlap with others, and the notion of "crime is fun" as a basic value (to the participants) is at least a helpful insight into the inexplicable deviance of some youths who say they committed crime "just for the hell of it!"

Neuroscientists have reintroduced biological determinism in accounting for the puzzling and often deviant behavior of adolescents (Crenson, 2001). Research at the University of North Carolina at Chapel Hill and at the University of Massachusetts Medical School in Worcester indicates that reckless driving, drug use, and vulnerability to unwholesome and even criminal influences can be traced to a normal stage in the adolescent's brain development. "Beginning around age 11, the brain undergoes major reorganization in an area associated with things like social behavior and impulse control. . . . Because their brains are not yet mature, adolescents do not handle social pressure, instinctual urges, and other stresses the way adults do" (Crenson, 2001:1B).

James Q. Wilson offers a more sociological explanation for unrestrained and explosive juvenile delinquency. Wilson suggests that our young people have not been effectively socialized by parents and society and lack the moral resources to consistently determine "right" from "wrong."

> The moral relativism of the modern age has probably contributed to the increase in crime rates. . . . It has done so by replacing the belief that responsibility is personal with the notion of social causation and by supplying to those marginal persons at risk for crime a justification for doing what they might have done anyway. (Wilson, 1997)

If these findings persist after continued investigation, they may help explain the wild and delinquent conduct of many youths, as well as why the vast majority of young people later abandon their deviant behavior as they mature into adulthood.

MATURATION AND LIFE COURSE THEORIES Just as new prospects for theoretical development may be emerging regarding chronological age as an important biological determinant in the genesis of delinquency, similar attention is being focused on the age of offenders, their social development, and the termination of their delinquent careers. While juvenile delinquency may be an advance predictor for many youths who later become adult criminals, it is also true that most delinquent youngsters change for the good. Sociologists, criminologists, and considerable data agree that young people typically seem to mature and "grow out" of their deviant behavior—usually without the assistance or sanctions of law enforcement or other control agencies of society.

One of the longest standing and most agreed-upon facts is that age and crime are related. The very young and the very old rarely break the law. Law violation occurs most frequently among those aged 15 to the mid-20s and then begins to decline again (see Chapter 3). Consequently, this so-called age-curve illustrates that the older the delinquents and criminals become, the less likely they will be to continue their law-violating behavior. Virtually all criminologists, whatever their theoretical persuasion, appear to operate with a common image of the age distribution (Hirschi and Gottfredson, 1983). The influence of age and cessation of crime has generally been referred to as the "maturation effect" (Blumstein, et al., 1986; Hirschi and Gottfredson, 1983). Walter Reckless (1961) summed up this phenomenon as "crime is like a fast rising storm which peaks during adolescence and young adulthood, blows strongly for awhile and eventually subsides in middle age." Official data tend to bear this out (see Chapter 3).

Robert Sampson and John Laub, in their study *Crime in the Making* (1994), found that delinquents who reform do so because they get attached to a structured social institution. They described how juveniles' attachment to conventional society changes over the life course and noted that there are often several *pathways* and *turning points* along the way. High school graduation can be one such life-changing event; strong ties to a job or a spouse can reduce one's criminal behavior to about zero. This theoretical approach is very compatible with Hirschi's social bond theory discussed in Chapter 6. A research-based counterpoint to this conclusion was suggested by Peggy Giordano and associates (2002), but there is considerable support from cultural transmission and social control theories as well as maturation and life-course theories for this notion.

Terrie Moffitt (1993; 2003) used life-course theory to distinguish between what she called *life-course persistent offenders* and *adolescence-limited offenders*. The former

What sociological theory might help explain why this 17-year-old went from a couple of appearances in juvenile court when aged 12 and 14 for minor offenses to now serving as a legislative intern?

© Images Works

refers to those who engage in antisocial behaviors at an early age and persist throughout their entire life course, often graduating in severity of deviance as they grow older. The latter, who are more typical, include those, who like most of us, commit some form of delinquency during their adolescent years, but whether detected and corrected or not, usually refrain from doing so and do not go on to commit more serious offenses as adults.

The maturation effect, or Maturation Theory as it has been called, and life-course theories warrant further study as they integrate biological, psychological, and numerous social components to explain delinquent behavior and conformity. There is considerable speculation among theorists over why and how most offenders later come to terms with society and conform as they mature and grow older. In this respect, these theories may have important implications for the social control of serious deviance.

MAKING DECISIONS FOR DELINQUENCY: RATIONAL CHOICE THEORY

One of the most interesting and popular theoretical developments in juvenile delinquency is credited to Derick Cornish and Ronald Clarke (1986) and others, and begins with the premise that delinquent acts do not spontaneously and emotionally occur in a cognitive vacuum. Rational Choice Theory (in contrast to psychologist Walsh's conclusion in Box 8.1: "Thinking is not what is going on here.") takes the position that youths usually access a less emotional and more logical decision-making process that weighs the potential benefits and costs *before* acting on the delinquent impulse and opportunity.

Felson (1986:121) argued that in order to understand criminal opportunity, we need to know the decisions made "by offenders, targets, and guardians as well as the situations of physical convergence that result from these decisions." He notes that human choice enters at many steps in the process. Choice theorists indicate that law-violating behavior occurs when an offender decides to take a chance violating the law after considering his or her own personal situation (need for money, learning experiences, personal values, need for peer approval) and situational factors (how well the target is protected, whether people are at home, etc.) (Cornish and Clarke, 1986). The decision to commit a crime or enter into a delinquent lifestyle is a matter of personal decision making (Kennedy and Baron, 1993:105).

This explanatory insight supplied by Rational Choice Theory strikingly parallels the position of the pretheoretical Classical School of Criminological Thought back in the 18th century (see Chapter 4). The idea that criminal and delinquent behavior is based on a cognitive selection process by offenders is a contemporary resurgence of the thoughts of the English philosopher Jeremy Bentham and the Italian jurist Cesare Beccaria over 200 years ago. "Both Bentham and Beccaria referred to the process as hedonism, or the choice of behavior that would maximize an individual's pleasure and minimize personal pain" (Clinard and Meier, 2008:73). According to Rational Choice Theory, offenders make conscious decisions about whether to engage in criminal or delinquent behaviors and what tactics to use to commit the offense. These decisions are primarily couched in economic terms as to whether the reward from the act outweighs the effort and potential consequences (Williams and McShane, 2004). Again, similar to the original classical position, the contention of Rational Choice theorists that criminal behavior generally rests on a foundation of preliminary thought and evaluation tends to impute responsibility and accountability more directly and fully to the offender. In this way, some proponents may downplay the importance of biological, psychological, and sociological determinants of crime and delinquency. Rational Choice Theory also implies that potential punishment becomes part of the calculation as to whether to commit delinquency or refrain from it.

THE PUNISHMENT RESPONSE: DETERRENCE THEORY

The 18th-century classical position and the neoclassical theme presented in Rational Choice Theory also share the assumption that responsive and vigorous punishment should discourage most offenders from repeating their crimes. At the same time, proponents believe that rigorous sanctions for law violation will likely inhibit other potential criminals and delinquents from embarking on such a course. This perspective, known as Deterrence Theory, encompasses a spectrum of contemporary "get tough" treatment policies and programs, ranging from the reinstatement of corporal punishment in schools to demands that youths indicted for serious crimes should face adult Criminal Courts and the possibility of more severe penalties, including capital punishment. The deterrent effects of such uncompromising societal responses are thought to strike directly at the recidivism of chronic offenders and serve as a warning to other possible law violators in the general population. Such a deterrence policy and program have been endorsed by Ernest van den Haag (1975), a professor of jurisprudence at Fordham University, and numerous others.

Deterrence theorists differentiate between **specific deterrence**, *which are punishments that discourage an individual from committing similar acts in the future*, and **general deterrence**, *which discourages others from committing similar acts.* General deterrence is preferable to specific deterrence—otherwise, every individual criminal or delinquent must be caught and punished in order to deter further crime or delinquency. In order for punishment to have general deterrence value, it must be highly visible and socially recognized.

A ghastly application of swift and severe "punishment to suit the crime" (without other considerations) has been portrayed on public television in a few extremist countries. Convicted thieves are shown suffering brutal amputations and brandings—without anesthetic. "As a device to intimidate political opposition and reduce crime, the mutilations may be tragically effective" (*Time*, 1995:46).

Rational choice and deterrence theories have found current support in the United States among a segment of the public that has become disheartened by the continuing high rates of crime and delinquency and the many failures of rehabilitation. In the face of frightening and highly publicized violence and destruction carried out by occasionally rampaging young people, some people have discounted the validity of flawed inheritance, maladjusted personalities, dysfunctional families, and disadvantaged social circumstances as legitimate causes of such deviance. In other words, an exasperated and vociferous minority has overgeneralized and oversimplified cause and effect and declares that a strong punishment response from a victimized society is the natural and just reward for rational offenders freely choosing illegal and antisocial behavior.

The emergence of Rational Choice Theory and accompanying Deterrence Theory parallel a "get tough" attitude toward crime and delinquency. While proponents of this perspective add some new insights into the cause and control of crime and delinquency, they also regress some 200-plus years to breathe new life into the assumptions and arguments of the old Classical School of Criminological Thought. Consequently, it comes as no surprise that many of the 18th-century weaknesses of this viewpoint take on new relevancy.

Evaluation of Rational Choice and Deterrence Theories

Continuing research applications of Rational Choice Theory have resulted in mixed and tenuous generality. Thus far, like many other theoretical explanations of crime and juvenile delinquency, the rational choice formulation does not fully and adequately account for a broad spectrum of criminal conduct. Unlike buying "one size fits all" socks, the complex variability of motives among offenders defies the theoretical quest for a common cause. The generality of Rational Choice Theory is further limited by the fact that most of its support is based on studies of the thought patterns and criminal activities of adults, not juveniles (Shoemaker, 2005). The decision-making process of an immature and inexperienced youth that precedes the commission of an illegal act is different enough from that of an adult to warrant examination. While a teenager might choose to steal an automobile for joyriding with friends, the same theft has a different meaning for a professional carjacker with criminal profit in mind.

Critics have also charged that Rational Choice Theory and Deterrence Theory have oversimplified the assumed motivational process behind criminal and delinquent behavior by dichotomously dividing rational choices into "good" or "bad" and "right" or "wrong" decisions. This either/or approach thus enables society to dispense more immediate and uncompromising sanctions. "Rationality makes perhaps the most sense, not as an all-or-none condition, but as a matter of degree. Everyone makes choices, but some people choose among more and better options than others. . . . [One] may expect some progress by viewing rationality along a continuum rather than [as] a categorical variable" (Clinard and Meier, 2008:74).

Rational Choice Theory may be most useful in explaining the causes of some delinquency when combined with established sociological theories that more fully acknowledge the deterministic impact of situational factors (see Chapters 5 through 7). Not only do complex background and triggering factors vary widely among offenders, but individuals also are not equally rational in choosing to refrain from or participate in delinquency.

Similarly, the wholesale and rigorous sanctions espoused by many deterrence theorists as a punitive response to offenders and a warning to potential lawbreakers also tend to ignore the dysfunctional biological, psychological, and socioeconomic "baggage" that handicaps so many youths and helps to propel them into delinquency. In Part Four, we will see how the U.S. Juvenile Justice System has a basic commitment to consider such factors as "possible mitigating circumstances" in many cases of juvenile delinquency.

EXPLAINING FEMALE DELINQUENCY

As noted in Chapter 3, juvenile delinquency is predominantly a male phenomenon. Males dominate both official and unofficial statistics in almost every crime category with a few exceptions (e.g., status offenses such as running away from home, incorrigibility, and sexual promiscuity, or relatively minor property offenses like shoplifting). Nevertheless, as we also noted in Chapter 3, female delinquency has increased dramatically over the past few decades and is, in fact, increasing at a more rapid rate than male delinquency. Also, females are becoming more involved in serious delinquent and criminal offenses such as assaults, robberies, burglaries, and other Index Offenses. Almost any of the theories discussed in Chapters 4 through 7 can be applied to females, but virtually all of them were developed by men to explain the delinquent behavior of boys. Moreover, most of the research designed to test these theories was conducted on males, and in studies where females were included, many of the theories lost much of their explanatory power. Biology, personality development, poverty, social disorganization, family problems, school problems, socialization, self-control, labeling, and all the other variables explored in the previous chapters affect girls' behavior as much as they do boys', but few, if any, delinquency theories discussed to this point shed meaningful light on the phenomenon of female delinquency. Consequently, scholars are turning their attention to the national trend of rising delinquency and crime among females, and revising versions of earlier theories and developing new theories of explanation.

SEX, GENDER, AND DELINQUENCY

In order to discuss the impact of sex and gender on delinquency, it is important to define and differentiate the two concepts, which often are used interchangeably, but have distinctive meanings. **Sex** is *based on biological and physical differences between males and females;* **gender** *refers to a cultural understanding of what constitutes masculinity and femininity in a society.* Consequently, biological theories emphasize biological and physiological differences between the sexes (e.g., hormones, physical development, etc.), whereas the psychological and sociological theories focus on differences in cultural expectations for boys and girls and how they shape personality development and individual and group behavior.

Recall from Chapter 4 that Cesare Lombroso attributed much criminality to *atavism* (evolutionary throwbacks) and studied the physical differences between offenders and nonoffenders. In his book *The Female Offender*, Lombroso (1895) contended that there were very few differences between female offenders and female

Guns and violence are not just for boys. What insights into increased female delinquency, especially violence, are provided by feminist theories of delinquency? Are there other theories that might also explain this phenomenon?

nonoffenders and that basically, women were less intelligent, weaker, more jealous, more childlike, and more spiteful and deceitful than men. He thought that females were largely incapable of violent or sophisticated crimes and that their criminality (primarily theft and prostitution) was linked to sexual issues. Although contemporary biologists and criminologists discount Lombroso's theory, contemporary biological explanations for female crime and delinquency focus on the differences that testosterone and estrogen have on human behavior. Similarly, early psychological theories often linked females' behavior to sexuality. For example, in his book *The Criminality of Women*, Otto Pollack (1950) contended that women's sexual immaturity and deceitful personalities linked to hiding sexual arousal and menstruation lead them to commit sneaky crimes and that men often covered for them in order to protect them. Again, contemporary psychologists and criminologists reject Pollack's assertions, but even today, many psychological theories of personality development are laden with sex and gender stereotypes. Not surprisingly, we will focus most of our attention on sociological explanations of delinquency and the impact of gender roles on females' behavior.

SOCIOLOGICAL THEORIES AND FEMALE DELINQUENCY

Social strain and *cultural transmission* theories discussed in Chapter 5 focused almost exclusively on male delinquency explaining how pressure on males to achieve societal goals often created social strain which led to delinquency. For strain theorists, masculinity was at the core of delinquency, and the types of stress and strain experienced by lower-class females were largely ignored. Delinquency on the part of females was attributed to the inability of a few girls to meaningfully adapt to their "natural" roles as nurturers, caregivers, and eventually as wives and mothers. Meda Chesney-Lind (2004) and others point out that Merton, Cloward and Ohlin, Cohen, and other major strain theorists were "locked into the gender roles of the times." Similarly, cultural transmission theories and social ecology looked exclusively at male delinquency and crime patterns and assumed that females in those areas were limited or prevented from offending because of custom and tradition—that is to say, the inflexible gender roles of that time.

Social learning theories emphasize socialization and peer influence. While these theories can be used to explain female delinquency, they too, were primarily developed for, and tested on, males. Gender roles are all about socialization as masculinity and femininity—behaviors considered appropriate for boys and girls—are not genetically transmitted but must be socially taught and learned. Part of traditional male socialization has been aggressiveness, assertiveness, dominance, and competitiveness, all characteristics that can lead to delinquent behavior. Conversely, traditional female socialization emphasized passivity, cooperation, nurturing, and submissiveness, traits less likely to get girls in trouble with family, school, or the law. Social control theories also emphasize socialization (e.g., inner containment) and a strong social bond as insulators against delinquency, and while they help explain the predominance of delinquency among males, when tested with female subjects, their explanatory power has waned (e.g., Thompson, et al., 1983).

Labeling and *conflict* theories make more substantial contributions to understanding female delinquency. Since girls traditionally have been involved in committing more status offenses than serious crimes, it can be readily seen how the applying of a deviant label by parents, teachers, or especially peers, could lead to the internalization of that label and secondary deviance. For example, Schur (1984) pointed out, if a high-school girl gets labeled as a "tramp," "easy," or "promiscuous," it might be almost impossible for her to live down that reputation, even if she is not sexually active. Since she is probably highly curious about sex, and sexual hormones are peaking, it is easy to see how she might decide to go ahead and become sexually active, because her moral character is already under question. Deviant labeling on the part of parents and school officials can lead to status offenses such as truancy, running away, and other acts that might lead to a girl ending up in juvenile court. Conflict theories have even more application as males have historically occupied a privileged position in American (and most) societies. Meda Chesney-Lind and Randall Shelden (2004:119) noted, "Many girls adapt to their disadvantaged positions by their involvement in 'accommodative' and 'predatory' criminal behavior (e.g., shoplifting, prostitution, drug use)." Viewing females as a minority class can help explain their involvement in crime and delinquency. In some cases, girls may have two, three, and even four strikes against them (e.g., age, race, sex, and social class), which combine to propel them toward some of the same types of delinquency as impoverished and/or minority males (Chesney-Lind and Shelden, 2004). The *radical/conflict* perspective gave rise to the feminist theories of delinquency.

FEMINIST THEORIES OF DELINQUENCY

Feminist theories *study, analyze, and explain social phenomena from a gender-focused perspective*. This approach, used by both women and men, emphasizes the fundamental importance of gender for understanding society, social relationships, and human behavior. Eclectic in their approach, feminist theories reflect and synthesize much of the rich diversity among other theoretical perspectives in sociology (Beasley, 1999; Delamont, 2003; Thompson and Hickey, 2008). Feminist theorists argue that gender is incorporated into the basic social structure of society and that traditional gender roles may give one sex (males) advantages over the other (females), prohibiting females from reaching their full potential. A major interest of feminist theorists is the intersection of race, class, and gender and how these variables may be related to crime and delinquency.

Kathleen Daly and Meda Chesney-Lind (1984) contend that feminist criminology differs from traditional criminology in five important ways:

1. Gender is a social and cultural creation and is not simply derived from a difference between the sexes.
2. Gender helps to order social life and social institutions.
3. Gender constructs of masculinity and femininity are linked to men's economic, political, and social dominance over women.
4. Knowledge is gendered. That is, it reflects men's views of the natural and social world.
5. Females should be at the center of sociological and criminological inquiry as opposed to being on the periphery or viewed as a "special subcategory" of males.

Freda Adler (1975) offers the liberation hypothesis as a feminist explanation for why females have been historically underrepresented in crime and delinquency and why their offense rates are climbing. According to the **liberation hypothesis**, *females have not committed as much crime and delinquency as males in the past, because rigid gender roles provided fewer opportunities for them to do so. As gender roles change and more gender equity is achieved, girls and women will have more equal opportunities to violate laws*. As discussed in Chapter 3, both official and unofficial statistics seem to bear this out. Each year, more girls are showing up in the FBI *Uniform Crime Reports* for Index Offenses and other crimes once thought the exclusive domain of males. Shocking videos are appearing on YouTube and MySpace and in the nightly news depicting girls in aggravated assaults and other violent crimes. Research on girls in gangs indicates that where females once were relegated to being in auxiliaries of male gangs or limited to providing sexual pleasure or other subordinate roles, girls now are active gang members committing many of the same crimes as their male counterparts (Miller, 2001; 2002).

Feminist scholars point out that while the types of offenses committed by males and females may be becoming more similar, they still differ markedly, and moreover, their pathways to committing those offenses are highly gendered. Box 8.2 indicates that this may be true not only in the United States, but in other parts of the world as well. Mary Gilfus (1992) and Peggy Giordano and her associates (2002) found that women involved in street crimes quite often started out as victims of crime. Many prostitutes, for example, are runaways who fled homes where they were sexual-abuse victims. On the streets, they may become involved in drug sales, petty theft, muggings, and even armed robberies related to their prostitution. Even runaways who do not turn to prostitution and street crime may appear before juvenile judges, be remanded to state custody, and end up engaging in criminal activities both in and out of foster homes or institutional settings.

Meda Chesney-Lind (2004) counters some of the arguments of the liberation hypothesis by asserting that females are not necessarily becoming more violent, despite the fact that they may be showing up in more violent crime data. Chesney-Lind contends that some status and property offenses are being relabeled as violent offenses, and in the case of domestic violence, whereas police used to only arrest the male participants unless it was obvious that the woman was the assailant, it is now more common for police officers to arrest all parties involved. Another example would include the zero tolerance policies of schools. In the past, a girl who had a small pocketknife or pepper spray attached to her key chain would have been ignored. Today, she could be expelled from school and adjudicated as a delinquent in possession of a dangerous weapon (see Chapter 10). Chesney-Lind also points out that the sexism that has dominated American society and the juvenile and criminal justice systems led the public and researchers to overlook the violence of females in the past, whereas today it is being singled out for jurisprudence and research. This poses the question: Are females more violent today? Or, are we just more cognizant of female violence?

Feminist theories have opened new vistas for research into female delinquency. With their eclectic and integrative approach, as well as their emphasis on sex, gender, age, and social class, they may also shed new light on male delinquency as well.

BOX 8.2

CROSS-CULTURAL FOCUS: The Double Standard in Delinquency: Not Just an American Tradition

In her book *The Female Offender: Girls, Women, and Crime*, Meda Chesney-Lind (1997:2) points out that criminology has long suffered from what Jessie Bernard has called the "stag effect." Criminology has attracted male (and some female) scholars who wanted to study and understand outlaw men, hoping perhaps that some of the romance and fascination of this role will rub off. As a result, among the disciplines, criminology is almost quintessentially male.

As feminist scholars note, most scientific disciplines (including sociology and criminology) primarily have involved male scientists conducting research on male subjects and then developing theories to explain human behavior that are generalized to both males and females (Scheider, 2000). This academic sexism may have been in part because with the exception of prostitution, both official and unofficial data reveal that crime is predominantly a male activity. Similarly, when prostitution and some of the status offenses, such as incorrigibility and running away from home, are excluded, males dominate delinquency data as well as the juvenile courts and detention facilities. Still, variables such as the so-called chivalry factor, where females are suspected less and treated more leniently by police, along with myths and stereotypes from the time of Lombroso forward—that females are less capable of committing crimes—have thwarted a thorough investigation and understanding of female crime and delinquency not only in the United States, but around the world.

Joan Sangster (2002) attempts to explain why juvenile delinquency among girls is a persistent theme in popular contemporary media in English Canada. She notes that Canadian media portray wayward girls in numerous mythological and sensationalistic ways that often have stereotypical sexual overtones. Moreover, any problems that girls get into with the law are generally framed within a context of bad family experiences. The lack of solid social scientific research on female delinquency in Canada makes it difficult to puncture these myths and stereotypes.

Focusing on family problems for explanations of female delinquency is a common theme in China as well as the United States and other Western countries (Liu and Situ, 2006). While numerous studies on American delinquency focus on the family as a primary insulator against delinquency (see control theories in Chapter 6), family influence is seen as even more profound in China, especially on girls' behavior. The most powerful role models in Chinese society are males. Chinese children in general, and girls in particular, grow up in a very protective environment with very strict conformity to norms taught and expected. If girls vary from normative expectations, sanctions can be very harsh. Consequently, Chinese girls, like American and Canadian girls, often experience a double standard: First they are beneficiaries: not expected to commit deviant or criminal acts, and hence, less likely to be labeled delinquents; then, they are victims: once labeled deviant, more subject to harsh sanctions, more likely to be more severely punished by families, courts, and correctional facilities.

An examination of the history of American juvenile delinquency and the juvenile justice system shows that family, school, police, and the courts have been paternalistic toward girls—a stance that has led to a double standard of juvenile justice. While this double standard has reinforced the notion that delinquency is primarily a male problem, it also has created a system where the most common girls' delinquent behavior such as incorrigibility and running away from home are often "sexualized" and "judged inappropriate" and consequently dealt with more harshly than some of the more criminal offenses of males (Benekos and Merlo, 2004:223).

Given some of the myths, stereotypes, and the "double standard" surrounding female delinquency, how can some of the theories presented in this chapter be useful in shedding new light

(*Continued*)

on this subject? Can you think of other areas in the social sciences that might also benefit from the feminist approach to delinquency?

Sources

Benekos, P. J. and Merlo, A. V. 2004. *Controversies in Juvenile Justice and Delinquency*. Cincinnati, OH: Anderson/Lexisnexis publishing.

Chesney-Lind, M. 1997. *The Female Offender: Girls, Women, and Crime*. Thousand Oaks, CA: Sage.

Liu, P. W. and Situ, Y. 2006-11-01. "The Impact of Family Environment on Juvenile Delinquency in China and the USA" *Paper presented at the annual meeting of the American Society of Criminology (ASC), Los Angeles Convention Center, Los Angeles, CA Online*. 2008-10-09 from http://www.allacademic.com/meta/p125660_index.html.

Sangster, J. 2002. *Girl Trouble: Female Delinquency in English Canada*. Ontario: Between the Lines.

Scheider, M. C. 2000. Moving past biological determinism in discussions of women and crime during the 1870s–1920s: A note regarding the literature. *Deviant Behavior* 21 (September–October):407–427.

BACK TO THE FUTURE: INTEGRATIVE THEORIES AND PROSPECTS FOR THEORY BUILDING

The integration and unification of theoretical concepts and contributions from a broad spectrum of approaches into one overarching explanation of juvenile delinquency has been a tantalizing and controversial objective for many sociologists (Williams and McShane, 2004). The formulation of a general theory of etiology that encompasses multiple racial, ethnic, environmental, gender, and social-class variables in accounting for delinquency is no small task. Thus far, it has been an impossible task. Nevertheless, a number of serious efforts have been made by sociologists to develop the ultimate and definitive theory explaining why some children become juvenile delinquents while others do not. Some have suggested expanded versions of their favorite theories as fulfilling this objective. Still others have sought to blend portions of some theories into overall eclectic approaches with varying scope and success. A few examples will illustrate the many scores of efforts along this line.

Gottfredson and Hirschi's General Theory of Crime and Delinquency

A proposed general explanation of crime and delinquency that is generating a lot of interest among contemporary criminologists is that of Michael Gottfredson and Travis Hirschi (1990). You may remember that we spent considerable time in Chapter 6 looking at Hirschi's Social Bond Theory, one of the social control theories of delinquency. While Gottfredson and Hirschi's general theory contains some elements of the social bond, it differs markedly from that theory. Gottfredson and Hirschi contend that most of the earlier theories of crime and delinquency either focus too much on individual pathologies (e.g., biological, psychogenic, medical model) or too much on social pathologies (e.g., social disorganization, social ecology, poverty). Their view is that in general, both juvenile and adult offenders lack "self-control." Low self-control, however, is not genetic or psychopathological but is the result of faulty socialization by the family and school. Lack of self-control coupled with opportunities for committing crimes leads to the commission of anti-social acts. Once developed, low social control continues, as does the associated deviant behavior. While some argue that Gottfredson and Hirschi's General Theory of Crime and Delinquency is not truly integrative (Williams and McShane, 2004), you should recognize elements of some of the psychological (personality development), strain (differential opportunities), social control (attachment), social learning (socialization) theories, and even labeling, in its mix.

Other Integrative Theories of Delinquency

Delbert Elliott and David Huizinga (1985) partially integrated traditional strain, social control, and social learning theories into a synthesized perspective to account for delinquency and drug use. They postulated that "involvement with and commitment to delinquent peers is the most proximate cause of delinquency and drug use and mediates the influence of weak bonding to parents, school, and conventional norms" (Ellioitt and Huizinga, 1985:85). Jeffrey Segrave and Douglas Hastad (1985) used self-report data from a sample of high-school students to develop three-path analysis models showing that variables derived from strain, cultural transmission, and social control theories explain significant, though small, proportions of the variance in male and female delinquency.

Paul Vowell and Frank Howell (1998) investigated the linkages among several popular theories in the delinquency literature—social disorganization, strain, and social control theories—as well as their causal effects on delinquent behavior. In their study of 8,338 public high-school students in Mississippi, "social disorganization is measured by observed indicators of juveniles' perception of neighborhood deterioration. Social strain is operationalized through perceptions of blocked opportunity, whereas social control is measured through the respondents' reported level of attachment, commitment, and involvement in school" (Vowell and Howell, 1998:361). The effects of the latent variables of race and place of residence as they relate to the three theoretical approaches were estimated separately.

Another useful approach toward the integration of major sociological theories of delinquency was initiated by Hennessey Hayes (1997) who analyzed a sample of data derived from a National Youth Survey. Hayes incorporated elements of labeling, differential association, social learning, and social control theories into a model designed to help explain both initial and continued delinquency. Hayes (1997:177–179) reasoned that:

> social controls, such as those provided by the family, significantly affect the development of delinquent peer associations and the associating with delinquent peers increases the likelihood of primary delinquency. . . . Thus, newcomers may be socialized within delinquent peer groups and may learn new delinquent norms and values, which serve to heighten the likelihood of engaging in delinquent behavior. . . . More frequent involvement in delinquency then may increase the likelihood of being observed by members of conventional groups and finally may elicit an informal reaction (informal parental labels).

The effects of parental labels in this study were most dramatic in the maintenance of delinquent peer relationships, which further increased the likelihood of secondary delinquency.

Terrence Thornberry (1987) combined elements of Social Control Theory and Social Learning Theory. Thornberry's *Interactional Theory* contends that delinquency can best be explained by the interaction of a juvenile's attachment to parents, commitment to school, belief in conventional values, and association with delinquent peers. Research has shown that combining these elements from social control and social learning, especially differential association theory, can be productive in explaining delinquency, especially among males (Thompson, et al., 1983; Thornberry et al., 1985).

Charles Tittle (1995) developed what he called *Control Balance Theory*, which uses a number of other theories, all related to the balance of control a juvenile experiences in his or her life—that is the extent to which a youth has control over oneself and over others in relation to the control others have over him or her. According to Tittle, if a youth has a deficit balance of control, he or she will act in a way to gain greater control. A surplus of control results in deviant acts to extend that control. Youths who interact with those they believe have power over them may feel the need to strike back and act either in a predatory or defiant manner to exert control. Tittle's theory provides an interesting model for criminologists to test in the future.

A commonly acceptable "grand theory" of juvenile delinquency has not yet emerged. There are still numerous unanswered questions regarding the validity and reliability of these theoretical suggestions. More methodologically sound, empirical testing needs to be conducted. For now, predictability and generality remain tentative for these promising theoretical offerings (Osgood, et al., 1988).

Considerable interest in formulating a general theory of social deviance which encompasses juvenile delinquency was generated by a panel of scholars who gathered in Albany, New York, in 1987. The participants included Ronald Akers, Jack Gibbs, Travis Hirschi, James Short, Terrence Thornberry, and a number of other distinguished sociological theorists. The objective of the Albany conference was to bring together leading scholars in the field of deviance to address some of the more important issues surrounding the integration of competing theories. For example, Short (1990:7; 1998:28) suggested that the considerable overlap among academic disciplines in their shared interest in delinquency and delinquents could offer a rationale and fertile common ground for the integration of theoretical explanations.

Several promising interdisciplinary approaches to the etiology of deviant and delinquent behavior have been made within the last two decades. Especially noteworthy is the resurgence of interest in the role of heredity and sociobiology in determining criminality. Hans Eysenck's intriguing thesis incorporates psychological and sociological elements in his conclusions regarding "genetic determinism" in the study of personality differences and similarities between twins and adopted children. In asserting that genetic factors may be partially responsible for antisocial conduct,

> Eysenck's theory could best be termed as a "biologically-rooted conditioning theory" (Eysenck, 1980). He maintains that individuals refrain from law breaking to the extent that they are adequately socially conditioned

> and acquire an internalized conscience. . . . Thus, the undersocialization of the conscience is the key to antisocial and criminal behavior. (Kraska, 1989:2)

Alan Booth and D. Wayne Osgood (1993) turned their attention to the influence of varying levels of the male hormone, testosterone, in contributing to antisocial behavior in a large sample of men. They found "a significant and moderately strong relationship between testosterone and adult deviance, and this relationship . . . is largely mediated by the influence of testosterone on social integration and on prior involvement in juvenile delinquency" (Booth and Osgood, 1993:93). In other words, testosterone is one of a complex constellation of biological and social factors that are causally involved in subsequent deviant behavior.

As previously noted, a current and innovative theoretical integration has been offered by Robert Agnew (2005). According to Agnew, crime is causally related to five clusters of personal and environmental variables organized into interacting life domains of self, family, school, peers, and work. The core propositions of Agnew's candidate for a general theory of crime and delinquency await more testing and validation.

One of the most ambitious efforts toward an integrated and general theory of crime and delinquency has moved from the planning stage to implementation. The Program of Research on the Causes and Correlates of Delinquency is a massive and methodologically sophisticated investigation that focuses on these research questions:

> Why do some children and adults who share similar characteristics and experience similar life circumstances become criminals while others do not? How are drugs and crime intertwined in the development of criminal careers? At what age and developmental stage do we have the best opportunity to intervene with programs to decrease the number of individuals who progress to more serious antisocial behavior and criminology? (National Institute of Justice, 1990:2)

The longitudinal series of studies began in 1993 and focuses on seven cohorts of individuals from birth to age 18. The initial group includes 1,000 boys and 1,000 girls from urban neighborhoods. Funded thus far by the National Institute of Justice and the MacArthur Foundation, the 10-year project may ultimately cost $80 million (Geyelin, 1992:B6).

The research agenda for the program integrates biological, behavioral, and sociological perspectives and contributions in tracking the individual and social factors impacting on the development of pro- and antisocial behavior. The project director is Felton Earls, professor of human behavior and development at the Harvard School of Public Health. Co-director is Albert Reiss, professor of sociology at Yale University (Browning, et al., 1999:1).

Scholars and theorists from many academic disciplines, as well as law enforcement agencies and personnel, look forward to the findings and conclusions from this massive study. If enough interest continues to be generated toward the integration of divergent theoretical explanations of social deviance, some day a more eclectic theory of juvenile delinquency causation may become a reality.

Summary

This chapter began by taking a very different look at delinquency with the theory of short-run hedonism, which points out that many forms of delinquent behavior are simply viewed as "fun." Maturation and life course theories look at how adolescence and passage from one life stage to another can help lead to delinquency, which may, in turn, be "outgrown" as juveniles enter into adulthood and another life stage. Rational Choice Theory returns us to the foundation of the Classical School of Criminological Thought, seeing delinquency as involving rational choices to conform or deviate from the law.

We learned in Chapter 3 that juvenile delinquency is a male-dominated phenomenon. Hence, most delinquency theories and research are provided by male social and behavioral scientists studying male behavior. Nevertheless, sex and gender play an important role in explaining delinquency, especially as we see females becoming increasingly involved in delinquency and crime. Feminist theories of delinquency focus on the importance of sex and gender regarding the types of research questions that are posed and how those questions are answered.

As delinquency research progresses, we see more attempts to integrate components of various theories in an effort to provide a more general theory of juvenile delinquency. While these efforts have not produced a single theory that can explain all forms of delinquency, they show the value of the theory-building process and how by combining elements of various theories, perhaps a more thorough understanding of juvenile delinquency can be developed.

Concept Integration: Questions and Topics for Study and Discussion

1. Review, compare, and outline the basic concepts, explanations, and limitations of major causal theories of delinquency presented in Chapters 4 through 7.
2. Based on the reading of this chapter, do you think that crime is fun? Why or why not? To what extent might this explain some types of juvenile delinquency?
3. Focusing directly on this chapter, list the major assumptions underlying the Rational Choice Theory of delinquency etiology and the Deterrence Theory of societal response. What are some of the criticisms and limitations of these two theories?
4. List some of the differences between male and female delinquency. Why did previous theories focus almost exclusively on male delinquency? How can feminist theory help fill this theoretical void?
5. Evaluate the future for theory building in the areas of crime and juvenile delinquency. Do you have a theory explaining delinquent behavior that has not been discussed in Chapters 4 through 8? What are the strengths and weaknesses of your theory?

Part III

JUVENILE DELINQUENCY IN A SOCIAL CONTEXT

INTRODUCTION: Collective Behavior and Social Groupings

Part One of this book explained the sociological perspective and emphasized the social nature of juvenile delinquency. In Part Two we presented major theoretical explanations for delinquency. Now, in Part Three, we look at juvenile delinquency within the social context of collective behavior. **Collective behavior** refers to *behavior motivated and influenced by an individual's membership in or identification with a social group.* There are a variety of social groups that impact upon human behavior. Three of the most important and readily identifiable are primary groups, secondary groups, and reference groups. A **primary group** is *a relatively small intimate group characterized by face-to-face interactions.* A **Secondary group,** on the other hand, tends to be a *somewhat larger group characterized by more formal interactions that are usually organized for a specific purpose.* A **reference group** is *a group with which an individual has a strong sense of identification regardless of his or her actual membership in the group.* The four chapters in Part Three look at examples of these types of groups and explore their relationship to juvenile delinquency.

Chapter 9 looks at the family—a primary group which is typically the first social group that teaches an individual basic attitudes, values, beliefs, and appropriate behaviors. This chapter traces the historical development and changing role of the traditional American family. We emphasize the family's role in influencing juveniles' behavior and summarize the importance of social variables such as social class, family size, birth order, and the nature of family interaction in terms of their relationship to juvenile delinquency. The effect on children of mothers working outside the home is explored, and various techniques of parental discipline are reviewed in regard to their theoretical link to delinquency. Research on the assumed link between single-parent families and delinquency is summarized and discussed, and the chapter ends with an overview of the family's role in delinquency prevention.

In Chapter 10, we look at the secondary group of the schools, develop the concept of the school as a social arena, and emphasize its role as a major agent of socialization transmitting dominant attitudes, values, and beliefs of society to American youths. We explore how schools act as "screening devices" in distributing academic credentials, and how, in some situations, they may become a "combat zone" for those who socially interact there. We look at the relationship between schooling and delinquency, and conclude the chapter by exploring ways in which schools might become more actively involved in delinquency prevention.

Chapter 11 explores the phenomena of youth subcultures, which serve as important reference groups for adolescents, have widespread influence on American teenagers, and provide many possible links to juvenile delinquency. The important sociological concepts of **culture, subculture,** and **counterculture** are defined, and the origin, development, and perpetuation of youth subcultures are placed within a sociological context. Distinctive elements of youth subcultures such as values, dress, grooming, fads, and language are described along with their possible relationship to juvenile delinquency. The influence of mass media on American youths is discussed and serious social problems linked with youth subcultures—running away, prostitution, teenage drug usage, and permissive sexual practices leading to increased numbers of teenage pregnancies—are explored.

Chapter 12 deals with one of the most misunderstood dimensions of juvenile delinquency—gangs. Youth gangs are among the more difficult types of social groups to categorize. As we discuss in Chapter 12, some contend gangs constitute primary groups, others view them as loosely constructed secondary groups, and still others see them as more closely resembling a reference group for some inner-city youths. As we point out in Chapter 12, this has led some researchers to categorize them as a fourth type of social grouping, the **near group**. As a near group, gangs rest on a continuum between the extremes of an unorganized mob at one end and the primary group at the other, and are *characterized by diverse membership, loose organization, ambiguous leadership, and impermanence.* While most delinquency does *not* involve juvenile gangs, juvenile delinquency is much more likely to take place within a group context than to be the act of an isolated individual youth. In this chapter we look at the phenomenon of "predatory youth" and the subtle social processes which occur when the play groups of some children evolve into full-fledged juvenile gangs. The organization of gangs is viewed from a sociological perspective, and motivations for joining a gang are explored. The participation of females in gang delinquency is summarized, and some of the major sociological theories that focus on explaining the formation of juvenile gangs are reviewed.

As you read Part Three, keep in mind the discussion of the basic social nature of juvenile delinquency presented in Part One, as well as the many theoretical explanations for the causes of delinquency presented in Part Two. Apply them to the material presented in these four chapters. You should note that while none of the theories presented in Part Two can fully explain *all* of the types of delinquency discussed in Chapters 9, 10, 11, and 12, they can provide valuable insights into the roles played by the family, the schools, the youth subculture, and juvenile gangs in relationship to juvenile delinquency.

Chapter 9

The Family and Juvenile Delinquency

READING OBJECTIVES

Reading this chapter will help you achieve the following objectives:

1. Understand the changing role of the family in U.S. society.
2. Identify how the family acts as a primary agent of socialization for youth in our society.
3. Explain how family variables such as social class, family size, the nature of family interaction, and parental discipline relate to juvenile delinquency.
4. Summarize the research relating single-parent families to delinquency.
5. Understand the impact of parental discipline upon youths and how various techniques of discipline may relate to delinquency.
6. Explore how the family may serve as an insulator against juvenile delinquency.

INTRODUCTION

Part Three of this book explores juvenile delinquency in a social context and how membership in social groups and collective behavior impact upon human behavior. This chapter discusses one of the most important social groups in which juveniles participate—the family. For most juveniles, the first social group to which they belong is their **family of origin**—*the family in which the child grows up,* and today, in Western nations like the United States, *usually consists of only the parents and children.* This concept of family need not be limited to biological relatives, and would include adoptive parents and their children. In other words, we are referring to the first family setting to which the child is exposed, and which serves as the primary socializing agent for the youth. This family also may be referred to as the **family of orientation**.

THE CHANGING ROLE OF THE FAMILY

The shift in American society from being predominantly rural to predominantly urban after the Industrial Revolution had tremendous impact upon the family institution. As Marcia and Thomas Lasswell (1991:10) pointed out, "Although the dramatic move away from the farm was not the result of changing ideas about love, marriage, and the family, it certainly had a profound effect on all of these." Preindustrial families served as schools, churches, job-training, and welfare agencies for children (Simons, et al., 2004). Today, these roles have been abdicated to other social institutions.

Agrarian America often is depicted as being characterized by the **extended family** *in which several generations (which may include parents and their children, grandparents and other close relatives) lived under one roof, shared and cooperated in the economic, social, and psychological support of the family.* There is some question whether the extended family was actually the predominant type of family or not. Research indicates a lack of evidence that early families in the United States typically followed the extended family pattern. According to Rudy Seward (1978:44), "The extended family was the exception rather than the rule." Whether it was extended or not, there is agreement that the family was much larger in agrarian America. Children typically grew up in the same household as their parents. Families were usually large, hence, family rules had to be negotiated among several people. If the family was an extended one, the oldest male usually assumed the role of head of the household, and was viewed as the ultimate source of power and discipline.

Often steeped in misinformed nostalgia, this earlier version of family life was not idyllic, as is sometimes portrayed in novels and movies, or in the minds of those who lament the decline of the family as they envision it. Life was tough in preindustrial America and families faced a variety of problems on a daily basis, not the least of which was their very survival. However, there were aspects of family life in preindustrial America that limited the likelihood that youths would get into trouble with law enforcement officials. While children were growing up, they rarely found themselves lacking supervision from adults or older siblings. There almost always was a parent, grandparent, or some other adult around to set limits on a child's behavior, or to mete out punishment should these limits be exceeded. Another important factor was the cultural attitudes toward childhood and adulthood during that time. In agrarian America the role expectations for children and adults were fairly explicit. Children were assigned chores and expected to help around the house and farm (or store if they happened to live in town), but were exempted from responsibilities associated with adulthood. When children reached an age when they were physically and mentally capable of assuming the work responsibilities of adults (usually somewhere after the onset of puberty), they began to be treated as adults by family, friends, and the community. This clear transition from child to adult resulted in changing role expectations for youths who began to make plans for marrying and starting families of their own. The marriage ceremony symbolically marked the *rite of passage* into adulthood. The concept of adolescence had not been developed; hence, the marginality experienced by juveniles today did not exist.

That is not to say that young people did not violate norms in preindustrial U.S. society. They certainly did. However, most norm violations were handled by the family through parental discipline. If minor violations occurred outside the home, they were usually handled informally, as local constables typically knew everybody in the community and either disciplined the youngsters themselves, or reported the behavior to their parents. When serious violations occurred, one of two things was likely to happen: either the child's parents were held legally accountable for their child's actions; or the child was held responsible and treated as an adult (Reid, 2008).

INCREASING IMPORTANCE OF THE NUCLEAR FAMILY AND THE CREATION OF "ADOLESCENCE"

The shift from an agricultural to an industrial society, and the concomitant transition from rural to urban residence for the majority of our citizens, had lasting impact upon family size and structure. Urban life put new demands on the family, many of which were not compatible with the traditionally larger or extended family pattern. For example, families went from being units of production to units of consumption. Families also needed to be located near industries, and if necessary be mobile enough to move should the father's place of employment change. A result was that families became smaller. As Rogers (1985:228) noted:

> At one time adults considered adolescents as an economic asset, useful in performing numerous household chores or in earning their keep.

> However, household appliances, urbanization, and labor laws have taken away most of the tasks that children used to perform, and some parents find children an economic burden.

As economic and social constraints acted upon the family, the large nuclear or extended family pattern gave way to the smaller **nuclear family** as the norm. The nuclear family was *limited to the husband and wife and their children, and was characterized by smaller size, greater independence for its members, and more geographical and social mobility.* Along with this transition to smaller nuclear families the characteristics previously mentioned in regard to extended and larger nuclear families were dramatically altered. The number of adults and older siblings available in the nuclear family to supervise the behavior of children was diminished. As the small nuclear family emerged, typically one parent (the father) went off to work, leaving only one adult (the mother) to supervise the children.

Further complicating the situation was the emergence of the concept of **adolescence**—*a socially created life stage between childhood and adulthood.* No longer were role expectations clearly delineated for adults and children. The enactment of child labor laws prohibited children from working in factories, and with the emergence of the concept of adolescence, routine chores and responsibilities were no longer assigned to physically capable youth. Instead, for a period of one's life (roughly from about 10 to 16 years of age) youths found themselves in a social paradox where they were neither allowed the tolerance of behavior granted to children, nor afforded the rights and responsibilities associated with adulthood (Lesko, 2000). "Appropriate" behavior for teenagers became ambiguous, leading to the marginality of the juvenile status. Adolescence came into its own during the periods of the Great Depression and World War II, as older youths left school for part-time and full-time jobs to help support their families. The marginality of adolescence was increased because despite the fact that these youths were assuming adult roles, they were not afforded the rights, privileges, responsibilities, and status of adulthood (Klein, 1990). As the normative expectations for youth became less clear-cut, the void gave rise to what many refer to as the youth subculture as adolescents struggled for a sense of identity and a set of attitudes, values, and beliefs to which they could adhere (see Chapter 11).

Contemporary society presents the family with an ever-changing set of circumstances, causing families to be redefined, restructured, and realigned in a variety of ways. Researchers disagree as to what relationship these changes may have to juvenile delinquency, but studies consistently show that the family is among the most influential factors in delinquency (Patchin, 2006; Simons, et al., 2004). Divorce, changing sex roles, working mothers, increased leisure time, economic pressures, and the increasing expectation for upward social mobility have all exerted numerous pressures on the family and the individuals within it.

Of the aforementioned changes, the effects of mothers working outside the home and divorce have been the most researched regarding their possible connections to juvenile delinquency. These two variables have received so much attention from researchers that they will be discussed later in separate sections of this chapter.

THE FAMILY AS AN AGENT OF SOCIALIZATION

Socialization refers to the *process whereby individuals learn and internalize the appropriate attitudes, values, beliefs, and behaviors of a particular culture.* This complex social learning process has appropriately been referred to as "people-making" by family therapist Virginia Satir (1972).

Socialization is a lifelong process. Everybody with whom an individual comes in contact can influence the socialization process, but for the most part, sociologists contend that the major agents of socialization consist of the family, school, church, peer group, and mass media. Debate arises over which of these agents of socialization exerts the most influence; however, in almost all cases, the family is the first agent of socialization with which a child comes in contact. As Robert Bell (1983:437) pointed out, "In most cases the important agency for transmitting the culture is the immediate family . . . it gets [children] first, keeps [them] longest and is [their] major source of cultural imperatives." Larry Bumpass (1984:621–622) concluded it is "the 'family of orientation' that serves as the reference point for the transmission of social values." Thus, the family has the first opportunity to socialize the individual to the particular set of ideas, values, beliefs, and behaviors that family members deem appropriate (Gubrium and Holstein, 2006; Hulbert, 2003).

Further, while the family cannot totally control outside influences upon its members, it can have significant impact in shaping the extent to which a child will be exposed to the other major agents of socialization. Whether a child attends church, and if so, what kind, is usually determined by parents early in the child's life. Likewise, the decision to own a television and how much and what type of viewing will be allowed is at least initially a prerogative of the family. The child's first peer group is usually not chosen freely, but is often determined by the parents' choice of friends. The first play group of most children consists of the children of their parents' adult friends and neighbors. Once children venture outside the home their initial peer group is determined by the geographic boundaries of the immediate neighborhood. Thus, parents' choice of residence (or socioeconomic circumstances which dictate place of residence) largely determine the initial peer group for most children. Neighborhood characteristics can also greatly influence a youth's likelihood of becoming involved in delinquent activities (Elliot, et al., 1996; Liberman, 2007). One major longitudinal study concluded that parental socialization and adverse neighborhood conditions combined to be the strongest predictors of low self-control and higher rates of delinquency (Pratt, et al., 2004). While school attendance is required by law, the choice of private versus public, church-related versus secular, or in which school district a child lives is largely determined by the parents.

One of the most important ways in which a family socializes its young members is through *role modeling.* Social learning theorists contend that an important part of learning social role expectations occurs through the observation and subsequent identification with and imitation of those who already fill those roles (e.g., Bandura and Walters, 1963). Consequently, a significant part of the socialization of children consists of them observing their parents and older siblings in everyday social interaction. While parents instruct their children in regard to the "dos" and "don'ts" of social behavior, the children also learn by watching their parents and older siblings. A substantial amount of the delinquency literature indicates that juveniles whose parents and/or older siblings violated the law, committed violence, or committed other forms of deviance are more likely to become involved in illegal and deviant behavior (e.g., Barnes, et al., 1986; Heimer, 1997; Hogan and Kitagawa, 1985; Lauritsen, 1993; Patterson, 2002; Simons, et al., 2004). While biological theorists might cite these studies as verification that criminality is inherited, from a sociological perspective the studies emphasize the importance of social environment, social learning, socialization, and role modeling.

There is considerable evidence that juveniles learn their attitudes toward the law, law enforcement officials, and law violation from those with whom they associate (e.g., Sutherland and Cressey, 1978). The social group from which children are likely to learn their first attitudes toward the law is the family. Thus, the early childhood socialization process cannot be over-estimated in its importance in developing the foundation of attitudes, values, and behaviors likely to lead to conforming or law violating behavior in adolescence and young adulthood. Evidently, the family influence and its importance in early socialization are significant in virtually all societies (Haviland, et al., 2008; Schicor, 1983).

WORKING MOTHERS AND JUVENILE DELINQUENCY

The phenomenon of large numbers of married women working outside the home is a relatively recent one, but researchers cannot seem to agree on what the specific nature of the impact of this phenomenon has been upon the children in the family. When "Rosie the Riveter" stepped into the factory to take the place of her husband, who had marched off to war, the event was viewed as temporary. The results, on the other hand, were long lasting. Women proved that they were capable of working in factories alongside men, or in place of them. They also, however, were expected to return home to perform all of their "wifely" and "motherly" duties, such as cleaning, cooking, and childrearing, which were not expected of their male counterparts. To a large extent, this expectation remains today. If women with young children are employed outside the home, their family responsibilities are often considered paramount and the job, while important, comes second (Hochschild, 1997).

Over the decades since World War II, women increasingly assumed their place in the employment market and have gone to work outside the home in record numbers. Many researchers on the family view this phenomenon as being one of the greatest changes that has occurred in the traditional view of marriage. In 1900, only one out of five women was employed outside the home, and most of them were single; however, by 1970, more than half (54%) of all women between the ages of 45 and 54 were in the labor force, and the number of working married women with children under the age of 6 more than doubled between 1960 and 1975 (Bell, 1983:265–267). Claire Brindis (1986:6) reported that over 50 percent of all mothers were in the labor force, including women with children under the age of 6 who were the most likely to be considered full-time homemakers.

Today, over 70 million American women and over 75 percent of mothers between ages 25 and 54 work outside of the home, although for the first time in 40 years, the percentage has stabilized (Porter, 2006; U.S. Bureau of Census, 2008). One of the major problems faced by working mothers is finding adequate child care for their children. The number of working women with children is large, and there were over 13 million preschoolers in child care (Neubauer, 2007; Vedantam, 2001).

The changing structure and size of the U.S. family means that in most cases there are no other adult family members available to care for the children in the home. Some mothers who cannot afford daycare make arrangements with nonworking mothers to watch their preschoolers or to watch their school-aged children for a brief period of time before or after school. However, in many cases, the children must fend for themselves. The phrase **latchkey children** is used to describe the numerous *school-aged children who return home after school to an empty house.* The U.S. Bureau of the Census estimates that there are approximately 7 million grade-school-aged children left unsupervised after school (Belsie, 2000; Smith, 2000).

Despite the rhetoric associated with the detrimental effects on children of working mothers, there has been little research linking higher rates of delinquency to the children of mothers working outside the home. In fact, Sheldon and Eleanor Glueck (1968), Travis Hirschi (1969), Mary Reige (1972), and Paul Recer (1999) all found insignificant differences in rates of delinquency when comparing children of working mothers to those whose mothers did not work outside the home. Another study indicated that working mothers often make a point of spending more time with their children when they are home in order to compensate for the time away from them (Hill and Stafford, 1979). And, in a nationwide poll, 41 percent of mothers employed outside the home indicated that they believe they spend more time with their children than their mothers did with them (CNN, 1993). Moreover, studies show that day care has far less effects on infants and children than their experiences in the home (NY Times News Service, 1996; *Washington Post,* 1997). At least one study, however, indicated that toddlers who spend time in child care facilities are more likely to be aggressive and defiant when they enter kindergarten (Vedantam, 2001). Still, time spent in day care has not been linked to delinquency, and according to a study conducted by the National Institute of Health:

> **The bottom line is this:** The over-all conclusions from the bulk of these "scientific studies" tell mothers what they've known all along: Daycare remains a viable option for those who choose to work outside of the home with one caveat: *The one-on-one time you spend with your child while not at work, a loving home environment and family values are still the determining factors deciding a child's ultimate ability for socialization and a successful academic career* (Neubauer, 2007).

There also is the notion that the *quantity* of time spent between parents and children may be less important than the *quality* of the time spent. Parents who consciously make up for lost time with children because of work may attempt to enhance the quality of interaction during what limited time they do have with their children (Gubrium and Holstein, 2006; Neubauer, 2007; Vander Ven, 2003). Finally, research also indicates that children of mothers who work outside the home are more likely to participate in meaningful after-school activities (Lopoo, 2007). As suggested by Hirschi (1983), these contributors to a "social bond" may be more effective in reducing the likelihood of delinquency than merely the mother's presence in the home.

OTHER FAMILY VARIABLES AND JUVENILE DELINQUENCY

The importance of the family in socializing its young members is without question. Much less clear is which variables within the family context are related to the problem of juvenile delinquency. While the possibilities are almost infinite, at least four

Dual-income households are the norm today. Are children of working mothers more or less likely to become involved in delinquency? What other variables must be considered?

© Michael Newman/Photo Edit

variables have emerged in delinquency research that provide the basis for various theories of delinquency causation: social class, family size (and birth order), the nature of family interaction, and parental discipline.

Social Class

The first social status of a child is that of the family. Whether a child is born into an impoverished family, a blue-collar working class family, a middle-class professional family, or a wealthy family is totally beyond the child's control, yet has profound impact upon his or her life. This *ascribed status* affects choice of neighborhood, attitudes and values, parental discipline, education, career choices, and even life expectancy (Hogan and Kitagawa, 1985; Leiber and Mack, 2003; Pagani, et al., 1999; Sampson and Laub, 1994; Silverman and Dinitz, 1974).

Lower-class juveniles are more likely to be arrested than middle or upper-class youths; hence, they comprise more than their proportionate amount of the official data on delinquency. Several sociological theories of delinquency causation attempt to explain why lower-class youths might be more prone to commit delinquency than their middle and upper-class counterparts. Self-report studies, however, indicate that delinquency exists among all social classes, but that lower-class youths are more likely to be officially processed. Lower-class youths are more likely to come into contact with the police. They are also more likely to be arrested and petitioned to juvenile court; if petitioned, they are more likely to be adjudicated delinquent and, if adjudicated delinquent, more likely to receive a severe disposition by the court

BOX 9.1

CONTROVERSIAL ISSUE: "Latchkey Children: Independence or Neglect?"

Brandon and Mica step off the school bus at approximately 4:00 p.m. every day. They wave goodbye to their bus driver and all their friends on the bus. Then they walk two blocks to their home. When they reach their house, Brandon, who is the older of the two at age 12, reaches into his shoe to retrieve his house key, unlocks the door for his 8-year-old sister, and they go inside. After relocking the door, Brandon and Mica proceed through their daily ritual. Brandon pours each of them a glass of milk while Mica unwraps the cookies, brownies, donuts, or similar snack that was left for them on the kitchen counter earlier that morning. They retire to the family room where Mica watches her favorite cartoon show and Brandon begins working on his homework.

Brandon and Mica are not orphans; nor are they victims of a broken home, severe neglect, or any other form of child abuse. Rather, they are part of the legions of "latchkey" children who return home from school each day to an empty house to await the arrival of their parents, both of whom work outside the home. Their mother teaches at the high school, and arrives home around 4:30 p.m. each day, approximately 30 minutes after the two children. If their mother must attend a meeting, run an errand, or is otherwise delayed, the two children are sometimes in the home alone until approximately 5:30 p.m. when their father, who teaches at the local university, usually arrives.

Brandon and Mica have been carefully schooled in their role of latchkey children. Their mother and father have established some basic house rules regarding their activities while in the home alone. They are not allowed to play outside or have house guests, are forbidden from cooking, and do not answer the door under any circumstances. If the phone rings, they take a message, informing the caller that their mother is "in the shower" and cannot come to the phone at the moment. Their mother's and father's work phone numbers are posted near each of the telephones right below the emergency 911 number, and right above the phone number of their next-door neighbor, who is usually at home in the afternoon.

Brandon and Mica's parents are concerned about their children's welfare, and fear the possibilities of harm coming to their children while home alone. Their mother's greatest fear is that of fire, and despite the presence of smoke alarms in every room, the practiced fire drills, and other precautions taken, she worries that if a fire breaks out, the children would panic. Their father's major concern is the possibility of personal harm which might come to the children from walking in on an intruder, or from someone noticing that the children walk home alone from the bus stop every day at the same time.

On the positive side, Brandon and Mica's parents have noticed a growing sense of independence and responsibility on the part of the two children. Brandon is mature for his age, and takes the responsibilities associated with his role as the older sibling quite seriously. He is confident of his ability to take care of himself and his younger sister for the brief period that they are alone each afternoon. He has begged his parents not to hire a babysitter, although his parents continue their search for somebody to stay with the children during that period of time. Mica also has shown increased confidence in her own abilities, and no longer relies on her mother or father to perform minor tasks for her when she is capable of doing them for herself.

Brandon and Mica are far from unique. They happen to be from a middle-class background with well-educated parents, both of whom are pursuing professional careers. Many other children are in the same situation. Others come from lower-class backgrounds where their parents are employed in unskilled or semiskilled occupations. There are as many possible scenarios as there are social situations for families, but one common element seems to permeate today's American family: more and more of them rely upon two paychecks. Either by choice or by necessity, many American families are characterized by the dual-income

(*Continued*)

phenomenon and, consequently, the number of children who must spend a portion of the day in the home alone without adult supervision is growing.

Some researchers lament the phenomenon of "latchkey children" as being a form of child neglect, and predict that children left alone in the home even for a brief period of time are more likely to become juvenile delinquents. On the other hand, some research has indicated that the children of working mothers tend to be well adjusted and no more likely to become delinquent than children whose mothers stay at home.

What do you think? Should children be left alone in the home without adult supervision? If so, at what age should parents allow their children to be in the home unsupervised? In your opinion, are "latchkey children" more or less likely to become involved in delinquency? How do you feel about the case of Brandon and Mica? Are they being neglected, or are they becoming independent and learning to assume responsibility?

(Cox, et al., 2008). Whether lower-class youths commit more delinquency, or are merely more likely to be caught and processed, the family's social class emerges as an important variable. Likewise, whether middle- and upper-class youths actually commit less delinquency, or are just less likely to be apprehended and adjudicated, the importance of their social status cannot be denied.

The family's social class also affects the socialization experienced within the family. Walter Miller (1958) argued that lower-class values were different from those of the middle and upper class. He viewed the focal concerns of the lower class as involving *trouble, toughness, smartness, excitement, fate,* and *autonomy,* all of which he contended led to gang delinquency. While Miller's assertions are questionable in that these same focal concerns may be emphasized by juveniles in general, regardless of social class, few would argue that social class does not impact upon one's set of values.

Other researchers have linked social class to different types of parental discipline and other aspects of family interaction and have indicated that other family factors such as relative deprivation, family size, amount of supervision, and styles of discipline may mediate some of the effects of social class (Strong, et al., 2007). From a sociological perspective, socioeconomic status is an important determinant of social behavior.

Family Size and Birth Order

Psychologists and sociologists long have emphasized the importance of parents in personality development, but research indicates that the number of siblings and the child's place in the birth order are also importantly related to delinquency (Kidwell, 1981). Hirschi (1969) indicated that large families tend to lack financial resources, discipline, and adequate socialization. Walter Toman (1970:45) agreed: "After all, as families get larger, children turn to each other for what they cannot get from parents." Michael Rutter (1980:155) attempted to more directly relate family size to problems which might lead to delinquency:

> First, large family size is quite strongly associated with overcrowding and socioeconomic disadvantage. Secondly, there is probably less intensive interaction and less communication between the parents and the children in large families if only because parental time has to be distributed more widely.

> Thirdly, parental discipline and supervision may be more difficult when there are a lot of children to look after. Fourthly, some of the children may have been unwanted. Fifthly, in some cases the lack of family limitations may reflect general parental qualities of inadequate foresight and planning.

Numerous arguments could be raised regarding Rutter's assertions. For example, although rural families tend to be larger than urban, place of residence is an intervening variable. Urban delinquency rates are much higher than rural. To date, family size consistently emerges as an important variable in delinquency studies and seems most consistent with social learning theory (see Chapter 6) in that exposure to sibling delinquency is almost always related to delinquent conduct (Brownfield and Sorenson, 1994). However, family size appears to be a relevant variable for further research as to its possible relationship to juvenile delinquency.

The Gluecks (1968), Nye (1974), McCord, et al. (1959), and Sulloway (1998) saw birth ordinal position as an important variable associated with the likelihood of delinquency. Their research suggested that the first child tends to relate well to adults and experiences the undivided attention of parents for a period of time. Research has shown first-born males to have higher than average IQs (Schmid, 2007), but as we noted in Chapter 4, the relationship between IQ and delinquency is tenuous. First-born children apparently accept their parents' ways of doing things much more readily than do later-born children. Bell (1983:456) even contended that "parents attach greater importance to first-born than to later-born children." Loretta Blerer (1980) and Sulloway (1998) also concluded that first-born children were less likely to become involved in delinquency because they tend to relate well to adults and internalize rules and regulations established by parents. The first-born also may act as a "third parent" to younger siblings, thus identifying more strongly with adult roles than subsequent children. The later child, however, tends to be intensely competitive and feel a strong "need not to conform" in order to contrast with the "conservative older sibling" (Blerer, 1980:52).

The youngest child also seems somewhat more insulated against delinquency. The youngest child benefits from the experience parents have gained in childrearing while also gaining from the experience of having older siblings as role models. Bell (1983:456) pointed out that the older sibling "who is further along in the socialization process but still relatively close in age actions to the younger sibling, may be a more effective agent of socialization than the much older adult parents." The "baby" of the family typically receives a great deal of attention from parents and older brothers and sisters, which may make the youngest child less likely to become involved in delinquency.

Middle children sometimes get "lost" in the childrearing process. They are not usually given the responsibility and meaningful roles assigned to the oldest child, and also are not granted the tolerance and freedom from responsibilities afforded to the baby of the family. Hirschi (1969; 1983), Nye (1958; 1974), and McCord, et al. (1959) all found middle children to be more likely to be delinquent. It may be that middle children feel relatively deprived of parental attention as compared to the oldest and youngest children, and perceive getting in trouble as one method of gaining attention from adults (Sulloway, 1998).

Family size and position in the birth order impact upon the socialization process and are relevant variables to be considered in the study of delinquency. In the ongoing argument of heredity versus environment, it is often ignored that different children in the same family experience different *social* environments. When answering questions about why children of the same parents (and hence, same environment) have such different personalities, Blerer (1980:52) stated, "The fact is that it is *not* the same environment: each child, depending upon his [or her] birth order position is born into an environment that is entirely different from that into which any of his [or her] siblings is born." Lasswell and Lasswell (1991:323) confirmed "that the addition of each child changes the family structure . . . not only does each sibling change the parents' relationship . . . but also the children's relationships." Dalton Conley (2005) noted that in addition to birth order, siblings also create a "pecking order" in the family that greatly influences personality, behavior, likelihood of success, and likelihood of delinquency. The extent to which family size, birth order, and pecking order are related to delinquency poses interesting prospects for future sociological research.

Family Interaction

The dynamics of family interaction include infinite possibilities, and vary between and within families, depending upon which family members are involved and what circumstances surround the given situation. However, there are certain identifiable types and patterns of family interaction between parents and children which appear on a fairly consistent basis throughout much of the research on the family and delinquency. Parental rejection, for example, has been shown to be an important factor leading to delinquency (Simons, et al., 1989; Simons, et al., 2004), as has parental coercion and shaming (Zhang and Zhang, 2004), whereas strong attachment to, and involvement with family have been consistently linked to non-delinquency (Patchin, 2006).

Family violence has been shown to be even more consistently related to problematic youth. Murray Straus and his associates (1980) indicated that violence ranging from spanking and shoving to shooting and stabbing has become a common element of social dynamics in an increasing number of American families. It has been estimated that annually over 50 million Americans are victims of physical violence at the hands of family members. The California Commission on Crime Control and Violence Prevention indicated that millions of American children are violently abused, molested, or seriously neglected by their parents each year (Strong, et al., 2007)). Family violence does not only involve parents abusing children; it is estimated that "138,000 children use a gun or knife on a sibling each year" (Lasswell and Lasswell, 1991:382). The Family Violence Prevention Fund (2006) estimates that anywhere between 3.3 and 10 million children witness some form of family violence each year.

Numerous studies have linked violence within the family (especially abuse by one or both parents) to juvenile misbehavior and delinquency (e.g., Gelles and Straus, 1979; Gil, 1970; Kratcoski, 1982; Sampson and Laub, 1994; Steinmetz and Straus, 1973; Straus, et al., 1980). The violence-begets-violence theme suggests that children who are socialized in a family environment in which violence is the norm are much more likely to commit violent behavior and to perceive violence as a viable solution to problems (Hamner and Turner, 1985; Nofziger and Kurtz, 2005; Straus, et al., 1980). Some researchers contend, however, that the link between child maltreatment and delinquency may be somewhat exaggerated (Zingraff, et al., 1993). Yet studies show that victims of mistreatment as children are more likely to become involved in drug usage and other forms of delinquency (Ireland, et al., 2002).

Besides the issue of physical violence, the overall relationship between parents and children appears relevant to understanding delinquency and its relationship to home environment. Numerous studies indicate that parental conflict and other aspects of family stress are linked to adolescent behavior—especially delinquency (e.g., Acock and Demo, 1999; Ambert, 1999; Plunkett and Henry, 1999; Simons, et al., 2004). David Abrahamsen (1960:43) pointed out that "homes racked with a great deal of tension . . . may produce a great deal of hostility and arguing which threatens family cohesiveness and could lead to delinquency." McCord, et al. (1959:83) contended, "Quarrelsome, neglecting families actually had a higher crime rate than homes in which permanent separation disrupted the family" and suggested that homes characterized by neglect and conflict were more likely to produce delinquents than those broken by divorce. August Aichorn (1969:164) indicated that in homes where youths are confronted with constant bickering and quarreling, they often leave the home and take "refuge in the streets." As we shall see in Chapters 11 and 13, when juveniles take to the streets, their likelihood of involvement in delinquency and with the police is great. Stephen Cernkovich and Peggy Giordano (1987) concluded that patterns of interaction within the family are more important in explaining delinquency than structural factors such as family size and broken or intact homes. Social control theorists contend that attachment to parents is a significant element of the "social bond" and extremely important in insulating a child against delinquency. Hirschi (1969:88) indicated that children who had developed a strong social bond with their parents were more likely to feel the "psychological presence" of their family when out in the social world. He viewed "affectional identification, love, and respect" as important delinquency inhibitors (Hirschi, 1969:91). Later research confirmed that the social bond with parents was an important variable in family interaction for reducing the likelihood of delinquency (e.g., Cernkovich and Giordano, 1987; Gove and Crutchfield, 1982; Jensen, 1972; Rosen, 1985; Simons, et al., 2004; U.S. Department of Justice, 1999a,b). Some source for optimism can be found in a nationwide poll that showed that 75 percent of American teens said they got along "very well" or "extremely well" with their parents (AP Washington, 2003c:6A).

Parental Discipline

An acknowledged role expectation in U.S. society is that parents will discipline their children. The nature, type, and extent of the discipline vary a great deal, as do attitudes about what constitutes appropriate disciplinary measures.

In colonial America, children were viewed as the property of their parents (especially the father), and virtually any disciplinary method deemed appropriate by the parent was permitted. Corporal punishment was used regularly, as the "spare the rod and spoil the child" school of childrearing dominated. In fact, some colonies enacted "stubborn child laws," which allowed parents to kill their children for serious or continuous misconduct (Straus, et al., 1980). The severity of discipline legally sanctioned in colonial America is documented in a law from one of the colonies which read:

> If any child or children above 16 years old of competent understanding, shall curse or smite their natural father or mother, he or they shall be put to death unless it can be sufficiently testified that the parents have been

very unchristianly negligent of the education of such child . . . if any man have a rebellious or stubborne [*sic*] son of sufficient years and understanding, that is to say, 16 years of age or upwards, which shall not obey the voice of his father or the voice of his mother, yet when they have chastened him will not harken unto them . . . such son shall be put to death, or otherwise severely punished. (Calhoun, 1960:42)

While such extreme measures were rare, general attitudes regarding the disciplining of children supported the unquestioned authority of the parent. As time passed, attitudes toward children changed, and laws were passed to protect children. Corporal punishment was still used, but laws prohibited excessive physical abuse. Today, attitudes toward parental discipline are varied, but every state has laws designed to protect children from parental abuse. Discipline in the U.S. family ranges from corporal punishment to no punishment at all, with everything in between. In general, parental attitudes have become more tolerant with less severe methods of punishment being used. Strong and associates (2007:375–377) summarized contemporary childrearing strategies into the following categories:

1. ***Authoritarian.*** Typically require absolute obedience; parents maintaining control seems most important; "Because I said so" is typical response to child's questioning of authority. More typical of lower-class and working-class families.
2. ***Permissive.*** Child's freedom of expression and autonomy are valued; parents are sometimes manipulative using such terminology as "do what we want you to do because you want to do it"; typical of middle-class families.
3. ***Authoritative.*** Relies on positive reinforcement and infrequent punishment; encourages autonomy within reasonable limits; more typical of upper-middle and upper-class families.

Parental discipline is involved in the concept of delinquency in a variety of ways. If nothing else, in virtually every state parents can petition their own children to juvenile court for refusing to obey them. Usually handled under the umbrella of "incorrigibility," this type of misbehavior is treated as a status offense.

Beyond the possibility of parents bringing the court's attention to their own child's misbehavior, parental discipline influences the development of the juvenile in a multitude of other ways which lead to or prevent delinquency. For example, Larzelere and Patterson (1990) as well as Sampson and Laub (1994) found that the apparent effects of socioeconomic status on delinquency could be significantly mediated by parental monitoring and consistency of discipline.

When strict discipline takes the form of corporal punishment, however, it may contribute to behavioral problems as opposed to deterring them. A study showed that 61 percent of Americans believe that spanking is condoned as a regular form of punishment for young children (Brandon, 2002). Research indicated that in the 1970s and 1980s, over 90 percent of parents reported they spanked their 3-year-olds, whereas fewer than 9 percent admitted spanking their children between ages 2 and 11 in 2007 (Scelfo, 2007). It's hard to determine if that fewer parents were actually spanking, or were just less willing to admit it, but the difference between over 90 percent and less than 9 percent is staggering.

A study released by the American Medical Association showed that the more a parent spanks a child, the worse that child acts over time (Schulte, 1997). Another in-depth study conducted at Columbia University's National Center for Children in Poverty indicated that spanking leads to temporary compliance, but long-term defiance and aggression (*Washington Post*, 2002). While another study showed that parents who use physical punishment are the most likely to produce neighborhood and school bullies (Ahmed and Braithwaite, 2004). Nevertheless, the debate over the relative pros and cons continues among American parents (Davis, 2003). When a California legislator proposed banning spanking of children under age 4, a national uproar erupted, but Governor Schwarzenegger pointed out that his native Austria and 15 other European nations banned all corporal punishment of children in 1989 (*L.A. Times*, 2007).

While parental violence is linked to delinquency, strict discipline by parents is not. McCord, et al. (1959) and Sampson and Laub (1994) found that consistency in discipline was more important in insulating against delinquency than the method used. Tommie Hamner and Pauline Turner (1985) suggested that parents adhere to the following guidelines if punishment is to be successful:

1. Before punishment is administered, the child should know clearly what the expectations for his [or her] behavior are and what consequences will occur if these expectations are not met.
2. Punishment should follow the act immediately.
3. Punishment needs to be deserved and understood.
4. Punishment needs to be related to the act.
5. Punishment should be administered within a context of love and respect. (Hamner and Turner, 1985:45)

Hirschi (1983:15) further emphasized the importance of parental discipline: "The parent who cares for the child will watch his [or her] behavior, see him [or her] doing things he [or she] should not do, and correct him [or her]. Presto! A socialized decent human being."

Admittedly, Hirschi may have oversimplified the complex art of disciplining children, but his point may be valid. Paying attention to their children's behavior, and then doing something about misbehavior, represents a basic element of the socialization process and the internalization of norms supporting conforming behavior. He pointed out some potential problems that might enter into the socialization process and thwart the prevention of delinquency:

1. The parents may not care.
2. The parents may care, but may not have the time or energy to monitor the child's behavior.
3. The parents may care, may monitor the behavior, but may not see anything wrong with it.
4. The parents may care, may monitor the behavior, may view it as wrong, but might not have the inclination nor the means to impose punishment. (Hirschi, 1983:15)

Regardless of the reasons, when parents fail to discipline their children, the burden is likely to shift to other agents of social control such as school, police, and the courts.

Research concludes that spending time with children, good communication, supervision, monitoring behavior and holding youths accountable are the most effective delinquency-prevention tools for parents. Also, positive reinforcement for desired behavior is a more effective form of discipline than punishment for undesired behavior (Larzelere and Patterson, 1990; Simons, et al., 2004; Strong, et al., 2007).

SINGLE-PARENT FAMILIES AND DELINQUENCY

There has been much debate over the relationship between broken homes, single-parent families, and juvenile delinquency. **Broken home** usually *refers to any family situation in which one of the parents is not present on a permanent basis.* **Intact home** *is used to describe a family situation in which both parents are consistently present in the home.* **Single-parent family** *describes a family in which only one parent is present on a permanent basis.*

A common theme in much of the earlier literature on juvenile delinquency was that broken homes contributed to delinquency causation. Since the family usually serves as the primary agent of socialization, a logical assumption was that any disruption in the family institution, especially something as significant as divorce, was likely to have negative impact upon the socialization process. Thus, social learning theories and social control theories linked broken homes and single-parent families to delinquency.

The number of marriages in the United States ending in divorce increased dramatically during the 20th century. Only about 5 percent of all marriages in the 1860s

A divorced father picks up his daughter for a weekend visitation. Is there a meaningful link between "broken homes" and delinquency? What other factors must be considered?

ended in divorce (Preston and McDonald, 1979) while about 50 percent of marriages today terminate through divorce (Kim, 2000). According to *Enrichment Journal* on the divorce rate in America: The divorce rate in America for first marriage is 41%; The divorce rate in America for second marriage is 60%; The divorce rate in America for third marriage is 73% (www.divorcerate.org, 2007). As divorce rates increased, so did speculation about the impact of divorce upon juveniles and its assumed relationship to juvenile delinquency.

Empirical research on the relationship between single-parent families and delinquency has provided mixed results and led to a variety of interpretations and conclusions. Ivan Nye (1958) contended that the broken home had a stronger relationship to status offenses (especially truancy and running away) than to serious delinquency. John Johnstone's (1978) and Joseph Rankin's (1983) research, some 20 and 25 years later, essentially came to the same conclusion. Research by Thomas and associates (2000) indicated that single-parent family structures were directly linked to sexual risk taking and indirectly linked to alcohol use and abuse. Nye (1958) concluded that the broken home was related to delinquency among girls more than for boys. Susan Datesman and Frank Scarpitti (1975) also viewed divorce as having differential impact on boys and girls, with the relationship to delinquency being stronger for girls. Rachelle Canter (1982a,b), on the other hand, contended that boys were as affected as girls by the breakup of their parents. One study by the Office of Juvenile Justice and Delinquency Prevention suggested that almost any form of family disruption could be linked to delinquency (Bilchik, 1999).

Talcott Parsons (1947) promoted the idea that divorce was particularly dysfunctional for the development of young males because it created anxiety about their masculine identity. He viewed that anxiety as leading to **compulsive masculinity,** or *an overemphasis on what were considered "manly" characteristics,* which was likely to result in antisocial behavior. Jackson Toby (1965) amplified this theme 20 years later, and contended that compulsive masculinity was likely to develop in families where the father was absent. Compulsive masculinity, he claimed, was linked to delinquency, especially violent behavior. Ira Silverman and Simon Dinitz (1974) agreed that the absence of a male role model led to exaggerated masculinity and in an attempt to assert their masculinity, many young males commit delinquency—a finding supported by the research of Pagani and associates (1999) who found boys from single-parent families were more likely to engage in fighting. Barbara Cashion (1982) refuted these assumptions, however, indicating that her research findings on female-headed families showed that delinquency was not higher among juveniles in homes where the father was absent when the variable of socioeconomic status was controlled. Among other factors, children from broken homes generally experience a loss of socioeconomic status, which might contribute to their delinquency (Li and Wojtkiewicz, 1992). Research also suggests that broken homes may lead to other problems later in life, such as psychiatric illnesses and addictions (Ross, 2003). The sex of the single parent may also be significant, as one study found that children from single-mother families had lower delinquency rates than children from single-father families (Demuth and Brown, 2004).

Other research on delinquency has questioned the relationship between single-parent families and delinquency, especially the assumption that broken homes *cause* delinquency. Studies suggest that juveniles from single-parent families are treated differently by juvenile courts (Singer, 1993; Smith, 1955). Thus, studies linking broken homes to delinquency which used youths who had been adjudicated delinquent, and especially studies which used institutionalized samples, were called into question. Monahan (1957) confirmed that youths from broken homes were much more likely to be referred to juvenile court, while those from intact homes were more likely to be dismissed during intake. Further, he found that juveniles from single-parent families were more likely to be institutionalized than placed on probation (Monahan, 1957). A study of Massachusetts youths found that while prior record, nature of offense, and other legal variables were important factors in disposition, many social caseworkers viewed single-parent families as less capable of handling delinquents, and, consequently, were more likely to recommend that they be placed in some type of juvenile facility (Isralowitz, 1981). Youthful offenders from single-parent families are also more likely to be remanded to adult courts and face grand jury indictments than are juveniles from intact homes (Cox, et al., 2008; Singer, 1993).

Karen Wilkinson (1974) indicated that the variable of broken home fluctuated in its importance to sociological research on delinquency. She suggested that perhaps the reason that sociologists emphasized the broken home in delinquency causation more at some times than at others is because the relationship between broken homes and delinquency has indeed been different during different periods of time. Wilkinson went on to say that if the concept of broken home is going to be utilized in sociological theory it must be refined. She suggested that it is likely to have a different impact upon a juvenile if the home is broken as a result of the death of one of the parents as opposed to divorce or desertion. Richard Hardy and John Cull (1973) confirmed that the loss of a parent through death was not nearly as likely to lead to delinquency as the loss of a parent through divorce or separation, and a longitudinal study conducted by Cambridge University showed that family disruptions caused by parental conflict were more likely to lead to delinquency than disruption due to death (Juby and Harrington, 2001). Wilkinson (1974) pointed out that if the broken home factor in delinquency is going to be meaningful, it must be incorporated into a broader theory of delinquency causation such as Hirschi's (1969) control theory.

The relationship between single-parent families and delinquency is, at best, ambiguous. With divorce rates so high, it might be argued that single-parent families have become the norm. If not the norm, at least the negative attitudes and stigma associated with divorce have been reduced greatly and divorce has become much more socially accepted (Strong, et al., 2007; Thornton, 1985). Whether the increased number of homes split by divorce has caused increased delinquency is debatable. If social agencies such as Big Brothers/Big Sisters and day care centers can help fill the void in a child's life caused by the absence of one of the parents, the juvenile may be no more likely to engage in delinquency than would a child from an intact home. Further, it might even be argued that the juvenile who has experienced a divorce receives more adult supervision and has more adult role models. Statistics indicate that most of those who divorce soon remarry, and it is estimated that one-third of all children under age 18 now live in blended, or step-families with an increase of nearly a million every year (Jaffe, et al., 2008).Children of divorced parents are likely to have two families, not one, and four adults involved in the socialization process as opposed to two.

Some research emphasizes the nature of the relationship between parents and children as being more importantly related to delinquency than whether the home is broken or intact (e.g., Cernkovich and Giordano, 1987; Simons, et al., 2004). Lawrence Rosen and Kathleen Neilson (1982:134) concluded that "the concept of broken home no matter how it is defined or measured, has little explanatory power in terms of delinquency." A study by Margaret Farnworth (1984) came to essentially the same conclusion. Homes characterized by tension, even in two-parent families may produce situations which could lead to delinquency (Abrahamsen, 1960:43). McCord, et al. (1959) suggested that homes characterized by neglect and conflict were more likely to produce delinquents than those broken by divorce. Suzanne Steinmetz and Murray Straus (1973) reaffirmed that idea in a study indicating that children who experienced family violence were more likely to commit violence than those who had not. With increasing divorce rates, it is likely that the possible relationship between single-parent families and delinquency will continue to capture the interest of researchers, but all the evidence suggests that one parent doing a good job of parenting and bonding with the child is better than two parents who do not.

THE FAMILY AND DELINQUENCY PREVENTION

How one perceives the role of the family in delinquency prevention is linked to one's view of the role of the family in delinquency causation. The disparate findings of sociological research in this area suggest that a multicausal approach needs to be taken which assesses the variety of ways in which the family impacts upon its individual members.

Many of the problems of juvenile delinquency appear related to the marginal status accorded adolescents in American society. One of the ways in which the family might attempt to prevent delinquency is to create clearly defined and meaningful social roles for its younger members. Societal and parental expectations should be consistent, well defined, and clearly articulated to children. Whether both parents are present in the home or not appears less important than the quality of the relationship established between the child and the parent(s) who is/are present.

Parental supervision and consistency in discipline also appear to be important insulators against delinquency. Much of the controversy over the relationship between single-parent families and delinquency causation may be mediated by looking at the extent of parental supervision. Donald Fischer (1983) concluded that high parental supervision is a significant variable in lower delinquency rates even under other adverse social conditions, and other studies have indicated that unsupervised youths are far more likely to get into trouble than those who are well-supervised (Agnew and Peterson, 1989; Simons, et al., 2004). One parent who is intimately involved in the supervision of the child's behavior may be more effective in preventing delinquency than two parents who show little or no interest in their children's behavior or who are distracted from their parental responsibilities by marital stress. While studies linking single-parent families, physical and emotional abuse, and other family problems to delinquency causation create much controversy, there is almost irrefutable evidence that a stable family life characterized by love, concern, consistency in discipline, and adequate parental supervision is related to less likelihood of delinquency. Allen Liska and Mark Reed (1985:558) concluded that parents "are the major institutional sources of delinquency control"; Larzelere and Patterson (1990) and former U.S. Attorney General Janet Reno concurred that direct parental

How does quality family time with children help prevent juvenile delinquency?

© Kevin Dodge/Masterfile Corporation

supervision is the best insulation against delinquency (Cass, 1993). Box 9.2 provides a view of the family's role in delinquency prevention. Cross-cultural studies indicate that the family is a strong insulator against delinquency in other countries, as well as in the United States (Bush, et al., 2002).

The family serves as the first social group to which a juvenile belongs. While church, school, mass media, and peers influence the values and behavior of youths, the family usually has the first opportunity in the socialization process. No doubt, the changing role of the family has altered its preeminence in socializing its young members. Many of the functions formerly fulfilled by the family have been abdicated to other social groups and agencies. Yet, the family still plays a fundamental role in shaping the attitudes, values, beliefs, and behaviors that may promote or prevent future law violation (AP, Chicago, 1997; Hulbert, 2003).

The social bond between juveniles and their families appears to be one of the most effective insulators against delinquency (Simons, et al., 2004; U.S. Department of Justice, 1999a). As U.S. society has become more industrialized, urbanized, and bureaucratized, the juvenile's attachment to the family has become difficult to maintain. In today's urban environment, a multitude of sociocultural influences exist which potentially weaken a juvenile's commitment to family. In Chapter 11, we discuss some of the competing values experienced by juveniles in the social and cultural milieu in which they interact.

As indicated at the beginning of this chapter, the family has undergone and continues to experience dramatic changes. There is no solitary version of *the* family.

BOX 9.2

CROSS-CULTURAL FOCUS: The Role of the Family in Preventing Delinquency: United States, China, and Japan

Former U.S. Attorney General Janet Reno contended that strong parenting may be the only "cure for crime," and established what she called a "national agenda for children" in an effort to reduce crime and delinquency in the United States (Cass, 1993:A7). Asian countries such as China and Japan, have always viewed the family as the cornerstone in delinquency prevention (Foljanty-Jost, 2004; Liu and Lin, 2007; Liu and Situ, 2006). Strong family role models and respect for parents and other elders are important values seen in creating a strong family bond and insulating youngsters against delinquency. Despite immense cultural differences between China and Japan, in both countries, family comes first. These strong family bonds, most Chinese and Japanese citizens believe, help account for much lower rates of delinquency found in those two countries than in the United States. As these traditional Asian countries become more "westernized" it is feared by some that their delinquency rates will climb, and some data, at least in Japan, support that assumption (Foljanty-Jost, 2004).

So many studies over the past four decades have linked delinquency to family problems in the home that, in 1990, the Office of Juvenile Justice and Delinquency Prevention cited the need of "preserving families to prevent delinquency" as one of its top priorities (National Institute of Justice, 1992; U.S. Department of Justice, 1992). Three community-based programs across the United States were cited as exemplary and proposed as models for other communities and states to replicate. They included *Targeted Outreach,* a delinquency intervention program designed and operated by the Boys and Girls Clubs of America; *Court Appointed Special Advocates,* a program that ensures that courts are familiar with, and mindful of, the needs of neglected and abused children; and *Permanent Families for Abused and Neglected Children,* a training and technical assistance project of the National Council of Juvenile and Family Court Judges (U.S. Department of Justice, 1992). Parents Anonymous, perhaps the oldest child abuse prevention organization in the United States, is committed to strengthening families and reducing delinquency. They offer mutual support groups, parental leadership training, and a host of other specialized services and information to families. Research shows that involvement with Parents Anonymous leads to better parenting skills, reduction in physical and emotional abuse, improved self-esteem, better social interaction, and reduced delinquency (Rafael and Pion-Berlin, 1999).

These programs, and thousands of others across the country today, acknowledge the central role the family can play in delinquency prevention, and how local communities can intervene and help youths whose families are not fulfilling that role. As one juvenile court judge noted:

> If we're going to make any inroads into the criminal justice system, it's going to be with the juveniles. That's exactly why they are having to spend billions of dollars on new prisons now, because they ignored the juveniles.

Most experts agree, whether practitioners or academic researchers, that any significant effort to reduce and prevent juvenile delinquency must start with the family (Simons, et al., 2004). While American family structures and interactions differ dramatically from those found in Asian countries, delinquency prevention efforts focusing on the importance of family are not that different.

Based on the reading of this chapter, and your own experiences, how can the family help prevent juvenile delinquency? Despite cultural differences, can American families use some of the same delinquency prevention strategies as those found in China and Japan?

Sources

AP, Austin. 1993. "Rate of violence among Texas kids at a high point." *Dallas Morning News,* August 21:41A.

(*Continued*)

Cass, Connie. 1993. "Reno pushes strong parenting as cure for crime." *Fort Worth Star Telegram,* September 19:A7.

Foljanty-Jost, G. 2004. *Juvenile delinquency in Japan: Reconsidering the crises.* Boston: Brill.

Liu, P.W. and Lin, W. Delinquency among Chinese adolescents: Modeling sources of frustration and gender differences. *Deviant Behavior* 28 (Sept–Oct), 2007:409–432.

Liu, P. W. and Situ, Y. , 2006-11-01 "The Impact of Family Environment on Juvenile Delinquency in China and the USA." *Paper presented at the annual meeting of the American Society of Criminology (ASC), Los Angeles Convention Center, Los Angeles, CA Online.* 2008-10-09 from http://www.allacademic.com/meta/ p125660_index.html.

National Institute of Justice. 1992. "Breaking the cycle: Predicting and preventing crime." *National Institute of Justice Journal* 225 August: 28–29.

Rafael, T., and Pion-Berlin, L. 1999. Parents Anonymous: Strengthening families. *Juvenile Justice Bulletin,* April, 1999.

Simons, R. L., Simons, L. G., and Wallace, L. E. 2004. *Families, Delinquency, and Crime.* Los Angeles: Roxbury.

U.S. Department of Justice: Office of Juvenile Justice and Delinquency Prevention.

U.S. Department of Justice. 1992. "OJJDP model programs 1990: Preserving families to prevent delinquency." *Juvenile Justice Bulletin* April:1–4.

Rather, the institution of the family is in a continuous process of transition. Bumpass (1984:621) reported: "In 1980, only three-fifths of all children lived in the simple family composed of once-married parents, less than half will live out their childhood in this status. In this context, we must rethink our conceptualization of the family in sociological research."

Today, with large numbers of children living in single-parent families, blended families, and other alternative family forms, in order to more thoroughly assess the family's impact upon juvenile delinquency, the changing role of the family will have to be more fully understood within its broadest sociological context.

Summary

The role of the family in the United States has changed a great deal over the past 200 years. The extended or large nuclear family that fulfilled the necessary economic and social functions in a predominantly agrarian society gave way to the smaller more mobile nuclear family as the United States became more urbanized and industrialized.

The family serves as one of the most important agents of socialization in our society, and the first agent to which most people are exposed. A child's initial attitudes, values, and beliefs typically are learned from family members. Additionally, a child's first play group, place of residence, exposure to religion, and a variety of other experiences primarily are determined by the family of orientation.

There has been tremendous interest in and much disagreement about the impact on children of having mothers who work outside the home. Each year, more women with children of pre-school and school age join the U.S. work force. A major problem associated with the increased number of working mothers is the lack of adequate child care facilities available in the United States. This situation has given rise to the phenomenon of "latchkey children" who must spend some time in the afternoons left unsupervised until one or both parents return home from work. Much speculation has occurred regarding the potentially increased likelihood of delinquency among these unsupervised youths. When children are left unsupervised for long periods of time, their opportunities for engaging in delinquent behavior are increased. Research indicates, however, that if working parents are aware of the potentially negative impact of both parents working outside the home and spend "quality time" with their children when possible, that adequate socialization can overcome the negative aspects of temporary lack of supervision.

Some important family variables have been shown to be related to delinquency. Social class, family size, birth order, family interaction, and parental discipline all impact upon a juvenile's likelihood of becoming delinquent.

For many years a causal link was believed to exist between single-parent families and delinquency. Data indicated that children of single-parent homes were apparently more likely to commit delinquent offenses. However, subsequent research has indicated that the apparent relationship between broken homes and delinquency may be spurious, and better explained by other variables such as lack of supervision and differential treatment by members of the juvenile justice system.

Because of the significant impact the family has upon children, it potentially can play a vital role in delinquency prevention. Adequate socialization and the development of a strong social bond are important dimensions of the family's delinquency prevention role. The family also can reduce the marginality experienced by adolescents by providing meaningful familial roles and responsibilities. In short, the family's impact upon juveniles cannot be overestimated, and consequently, should remain a major research focus for sociological inquiry into the social problem of juvenile delinquency.

Concept Integration: Questions and Topics for Study and Discussion

1. In what ways does the type of family (extended or nuclear) a juvenile experiences affect the likelihood of his or her becoming delinquent?
2. How does the socialization process in the family impact upon the likelihood of a youth becoming delinquent?
3. An increasing number of mothers work outside the home today. In your opinion, are the children of working mothers *more* or *less* likely to become delinquent? Why?
4. How do family variables such as social class, family size, birth order, family interaction, and parental discipline relate to juvenile delinquency?
5. Define the following terms: extended family, nuclear family, family of orientation, role modeling, latchkey children, broken home, and intact home. How does the understanding of these terms and concepts help us in understanding juvenile delinquency?
6. In what ways can the family become more involved in delinquency prevention?
7. Think of your own family situation when you were growing up. What type of family did you live in (extended or nuclear)? In what ways did your family help prevent you from becoming delinquent? What family situations did you experience which potentially could have promoted delinquency on your part? As a parent, how would you go about trying to prevent your children from becoming delinquent?

Chapter 10

Schools and Delinquency

READING OBJECTIVES

Reading this chapter will help you achieve the following objectives:

1. Describe and explain the role of the school as an agent of socialization in our society.
2. Identify ways that schools act as a *screening device,* helping to channel students into future failure or success.
3. List ways in which schools have become a *combat zone* or arena of confrontation between many students and their teachers and school administrators.
4. Describe how the bureaucratic structure of our schools has helped create and perpetuate juvenile delinquency.
5. Identify specific ways schools can become actively involved in delinquency prevention.

INTRODUCTION

Education is one of the basic social institutions and is largely responsible for the transmission of culture, including values and norms, to members of society. Because of this important socialization function, our society requires that every child attend school for a specified period of time. It follows that virtually every American has an early experience in elementary and secondary school. However, the quality and extent of that educational experience varies among our young people.

Most U.S. children make a relatively easy transition from home to school if the significant adults in these social environments share common values and norms. However, a large number of young people arrive at school painfully aware of the differences between their socioeconomic status and that of their classmates and teachers. They soon learn that teachers and administrators have the authority and responsibility to teach and enforce standards of conduct that are difficult for them to understand and accept. Thus, the school may become an arena of conflict and confrontation for many youths as they develop delinquent patterns of behavior.

THE SCHOOL AS AN ARENA

An **arena** is *a public place where individuals or groups are pitted against each other in struggles to determine dominance and often survival.* According to ethologist Robert Ardrey (1966), **arena behavior** is a *struggle for both status and territory* and is common in most animal species, including humans. Thus, examples of arena behavior include the battles between male elk during the mating season, ancient gladiator contests, many athletic events, and such collective violence as fights between rival street gangs and wars between nations. In the context of our study of juvenile delinquency, the public schools often become an arena where delinquent youths first encounter a society that opposes and resists their behavior.

SCHOOLS AND THE SOCIALIZATION PROCESS

The school is usually the first social institution beyond the family to be entrusted as a major agent of socialization for children. The school's socialization responsibilities are twofold: the transmission of cognitive skills, and the transmission of normative culture.

In the contemporary United States, the teaching of basic cognitive skills has become almost exclusively the domain of the schools. While a great deal of controversy may surround *how* cognitive skills should be taught, there is virtually unanimous agreement that they *should* be taught. The teaching of the three Rs (readin', 'ritin', and 'rithmetic) as well as other basic skills is clearly the primary responsibility of the schools.

The role of the school in the transmission of normative culture is not so clear-cut, however. The teaching of normative culture involves the transmission of values, norms, attitudes, and beliefs. According to Emile Durkheim ([1906] 1956:71–72):

> [Education] consists of a methodological socialization of the younger generation. . . . It is the influence exercised by adult generations on those that are not ready for social life. Its object is to arouse and to develop in the child a certain number of physical, intellectual, and moral states that are demanded of him[/her] by the political society as a whole and for the special milieu for which he[/she] is specifically destined. . . . From the egotistic and asocial being that has just been born, [society] must, as rapidly as possible, add another, capable of leading a moral and social life.

Two basic questions arise in regard to the school's attempt to promote the internalization of cultural attitudes, values, and beliefs. First, which specific attitudes, values, and beliefs will be taught? Second, how does the school go about teaching them?

The United States is an extremely diverse, culturally pluralistic society composed of many ethnic, religious, economic, and social-class subgroups. These various subcultural groups view life from a wide spectrum of value perspectives. Since compulsory attendance laws require that every child attend school for a specified period of time, the widest possible range of cultural values is represented among the student population as they enter school. On the other hand, the school officials who are charged with the socialization task are a much less culturally diverse group. For example, teachers tend to come from white, middle-class, Protestant backgrounds. Numerous studies have indicated a strong bias favoring the promotion of middle-class values in our public schools (e.g., Cicourel, 1968; Farkas, et al., 1990; Jencks, et al., 1972; Kozol, 1991; 2006). The vastly divergent backgrounds of students in contrast to the predominantly middle-class experience of their teachers can lay the groundwork for unfortunate social confrontations and nonproductive learning situations.

In a study of Chicago public schools, Howard Becker (1952) documented teachers' preferences for white middle-class children. In a much more shocking exposé, in his book *Death at an Early Age* (1967), Jonathan Kozol described the cynicism, prejudice, and outright racism he saw lower-class black students subjected to by white, middle-class teachers in the public schools. And 25 years later, in his book *Savage Inequalities,* Kozol (1991) found that the disparities between predominantly black schools and predominantly white school districts had grown greater rather than smaller. In 2006, Kozol contended that American schools represented a form of Apartheid. Aaron Cicourel (1968) argued that misbehavior, especially delinquent acts, from lower-class youths elicited more severe responses from teachers and school administrators than the same behavior from middle- and upper-class youths. He indicated that school officials tended to view delinquency on the part of students of middle and higher socioeconomic status as out of character and only situational.

Later studies noted similar findings that students from middle-class family backgrounds were more likely to have internalized the values of competitiveness, politeness, and deferred gratification which lead to success in the public school experience (e.g., Braun, 1976; Jencks, et al., 1972). Carl Braun (1976), for example, found that teachers' expectations were influenced by noncognitive variables such as physical attractiveness, socioeconomic status, race, gender, name, and older siblings. His research indicated that teachers expected lower achievement from students who belonged to minority groups, came from economically disadvantaged homes, were physically unattractive, had unusual or unattractive names, or had older brothers or sisters who had been unsuccessful in their school experience. Other research confirmed that teachers' perceptions of students' work habits and conformity to behavioral norms were most directly linked to grades (Farkas, et al., 1990). Undeniably, a student's family background (especially socioeconomic status) has been linked to educational aspirations (Alwin and Thornton, 1984; Astone and McLanahan, 1991; Hurn, 1978; Jencks, et al., 1972), and educational aspirations appear highly related to educational achievement and success in school (Hurn, 1978; Johnson and Elder, 2002).

JUVENILE DELINQUENCY AND THE SCHOOL EXPERIENCE

Thus far, our discussion has focused on the attempt to socialize students to the dominant value system in the United States and how that relates to a successful school experience. This takes on additional meaning for understanding delinquency when we view the relationship between the school experience and the process of becoming a juvenile delinquent. Studies indicate that poor performance in school and negative school experiences are significantly related to juvenile delinquency (e.g., Arum and Beattie, 1999; Brownfield, 1990). That relationship is far more complex than it may appear, however. As pointed out in the Societal Response definition of delinquency, in order for juvenile delinquency to take place, a social audience must react to an actor and an act, and make an evaluation of them in regard to social appropriateness. As further developed by the Labeling Approach, some group must react to the juvenile's behavior and apply the negative label of "delinquent" if the juvenile is going to be considered a juvenile delinquent by society. The variable of social power becomes relevant if there is disagreement over the appropriateness of the act. Individuals, groups, and/or social agencies with the power and authority to label juvenile behavior as wrong and place the label "delinquent" on juveniles so that the label becomes a part of their identity are critical in creating the "juvenile delinquent." The schools have that power in our society.

Harry Gracey (1977) described how from their first day of school, children are subjected to authoritarian adults who arbitrarily judge students' behavior as "right" or "wrong" and label students as "good" or "bad" based on those judgments. Referring to kindergarten as "academic boot camp," Gracey contended that the primary purpose of kindergarten is not so much the preparation for the academic experience to come in future grades (as contended by most teachers and administrators), as it is to socialize children into fitting into the bureaucratic structure of the school system. Gracey (1977:217) stated: "The unique job of the kindergarten in the education division of labor seems . . . to be teaching children the student role. The student role is the repertoire of behavior and attitudes regarded by educators as appropriate to children in school."

Gracey found that learning classroom routines and submitting to rules and authority are the main elements of the student role. To a large extent, successfully fulfilling the student role means "doing what you're told and never mind why" (Gracey, 1977:225). Hence, those students who are most obedient, whose personal values either agree with or have been successfully subjugated to the teacher's, are most likely to be labeled "good students" and have a successful school experience.

In his book *Creating School Failure, Youth Crime, and Deviance,* Delos Kelly (1982) illustrated how the school's initial labeling has lasting impact on the child's entire educational career. Those students who disobey, question authority, refuse to suppress their own values (values gained from early childhood socialization in the family) are more likely to be labeled "bad students" and be unsuccessful in school. Ironically, this early application of the label "delinquent" (or "predelinquent" for younger children) may encompass students at both ends of the intellectual continuum. In other words, students with the least academic potential, along with the most intellectually curious and innovative students, may be the most likely to violate normative expectations of teachers, and end up labeled as "problem students." According to the Labeling Approach, this negative label has impact upon a juvenile's self-concept and may influence future behavior which culminates in the **self-fulfilling prophecy.** Students who are labeled early in their educational career as "dumb," "slow," "mean," or "troublemaker" may engage in types of behavior expected to accompany those student roles. Conversely, students labeled as "bright," "gifted," "polite," and "obedient" are likely to conform to the positive expectations entailed in those roles. A possible example of this may be revealed in the findings that participation in school athletics serves as an insulator against delinquency for some students (e.g., Hastad, et al., 1984; Segrave and Hastad, 1984).

Of course, not all negative labels are initiated at school. Parents, neighbors, police, and juvenile courts also may judge certain children to be more problematic than others. Consequently, negative labels and poor self-concepts can be brought from outside the school. In fact, Allen Liska and Mark Reed (1985) contended that parents, not the schools, were the major institutional sources of delinquency control. They found that "for most adolescents in high school, the good opinion of teachers and school administrators may be less important than that of their parents" (Liska and Reed, 1985:558). The extent to which these factors affect the educational process is not clearly understood, but there is some evidence that they may negatively impact upon the school experience. For example, Kelly (1977) showed that juvenile delinquents, or at least those who had been officially identified by the legal system, were at a significant disadvantage in the classroom, and subsequent research indicates that many youths, after spending time in juvenile custodial facilities, do not reenter school, which often leads to more delinquency (Roy-Stevens, 2004).

SCHOOLS AS A SCREENING DEVICE

One of the important functions of the educational institution in our society is to acknowledge academic performance and intellectual development through awarding academic credentials. In this sense, schools are designed to serve as a *screening device.* Ideally, everybody in our society is supposed to be provided equal access to our educational system. This supposition is, of course, highly questionable, since we know that individuals have been denied equal access to education on the basis of race, ethnic background, and other social variables. Nevertheless, it is widely proclaimed in American society that the opportunity for education is a right, and not a privilege. Though everybody is supposedly given equal access to the academic credentials offered by our educational system, it has never been expected that everybody would attain them equally. As Peter and Brigitte Berger (1975:188) indicated, "Since the educational system contains an endless series of hurdles, it is important that not all should succeed in it; it is predetermined that some (indeed, many) should fail to reach the top." Those who have the most potential, work the hardest, and learn the most are viewed as having legitimately earned higher academic recognition than the rest. We logically conclude that our high school graduates are smarter and more diligent than those who dropped out, but not as smart and diligent as those who have earned college degrees. Likewise, bachelor's degrees signify something different from master's degrees, and master's degrees signify something different from doctoral degrees. The assumption is that everybody aspires to the highest level of academic certification (a highly questionable assumption), but the schools screen out those who are not qualified, so that only the most "deserving" attain the highest credentials (an even more questionable assumption). These academic credentials, in turn, are then used in a variety of ways which affect occupation, income, housing, and virtually all components of lifestyle and social status (Collins, 1971).

The basis for this "screening device" may very well be variables other than intelligence, diligence, and academic performance. Edgar Friedenberg (1959;1971) made a strong case that academic credentials do not certify ability, but the acceptance of larger society's dominant values and norms. Friedenberg contended that

Why do so many juveniles who get into trouble at school also get into trouble with the police?

© Corbis

academic credentials, more than intelligence and academic performance, signify an individual's willingness to endure the rules. In this sense, he argued that schools preserve the status quo by guaranteeing that those who fail in school also fail in society—a point substantiated by research (e.g., Monk-Turner, 1989). From this perspective, it is no wonder that failure in school and juvenile delinquency are closely related. This phenomenon is not limited to the United States (see Box 10.1).

BOX 10.1

CROSS-CULTURAL FOCUS: Self-Concept and Delinquency among Chinese Schoolchildren

Americans typically perceive Chinese youths as bright, passive, and above all, respectful to their teachers and parents. Rarely do we think of China as having a delinquency problem, and little research appears in U.S. journals on this phenomenon. Young criminal offenders have become a major concern in contemporary China, however. Chinese law provides that youths under the age of 16 are held criminally liable only if they have committed homicide, robbery, arson, or some other serious offense which greatly threatens social order. Most youthful offenders commit relatively minor infractions and are handled through neighborhood tribunal committees and other local administrative agencies. The handling of juvenile cases and the operation of youth reformatories in China falls under the supervision of the Ministry of Education.

In China, as in the United States, schools not only teach cognitive skills, but also play an important role in the overall socialization process. Students are expected to show great deference and respect to their teachers, and strict conformity to rules is as important as high academic performance. In this way, Chinese schools act as a screening device, and professors Kwok Leung and Sing Lau (1989) indicated that the relationship between poor school performance and delinquency in China is not appreciably different from that experienced in the United States.

Leung and Lau studied 1,668 seventh- and ninth-grade students in Hong Kong in an effort to determine the relationship between academic performance and self-concept, and the relationship between poor self-concept and delinquency. They summarized that youths who were unsuccessful and frustrated in school often turn to peers for their major source of approval as opposed to parents and teachers. In this peer reference group, they usually seek out and find others who share similar frustrations in school and support delinquent values and behavior. Findings from this study suggest that consistent with studies of U.S. students, peer approval had a stronger influence on self-concept and the promotion of delinquent behavior than the countervailing influence of teachers and parents combined.

Ruth Liu and Wei Lin (2007) pointed out that there is tremendous pressure placed on Chinese youths to achieve academically in schools. Failure in school equates to failure in life. This pressure to perform academically places a tremendous amount of strain on Chinese youths, and poor academic frustration can produce the type of status frustration that is likely to lead to delinquency.

Sources

Leung, K., and Sing L. 1989. Effects of self-concept and perceived disapproval of delinquent behavior in school children. *Journal of Youth and Adolescence* 18 (August):345–359.

Liu, R. X. and Lin, W. 2007. Delinquency among Chinese adolescents: Modeling sources of frustration and gender differences. *Deviant Behavior* 28 (Sept-Oct):409–432.

Worder, R. L., Sarada, A M., and Dolan, R. E. *Criminal justice and public security in China: A country study* (4th ed.), 1988.

Mark Colvin and John Pauly (1983) pointed out that socioeconomic status of a child's family has been linked to school "tracking," which to a large extent determines a student's immediate peer group. **Tracking** refers to *an educational strategy in which students considered to be roughly equivalent in intelligence, based upon standardized tests, previous academic performance, and other criteria, are placed in the same classroom,* and can have important impact on a child's academic achievement (Gamoran, 1992; Stanford University, 1994). Students in a particular "track" often resemble each other in a variety of ways other than academic abilities. Sometimes, students who have reputations as "behavioral problems" may be placed in the same class, and placed under the supervision of a teacher with the reputation of being a strict disciplinarian. Colvin and Pauly indicated that the initial bond to the school is developed at home by the family, but may be reinforced or weakened by the immediate peer group at school. If placed in a social setting in the school where a student is surrounded by delinquent peers, "this type of association continues the pattern of reinforcement toward more sustained delinquent behavior" (Colvin and Pauly, 1983:543).

A variety of social cliques form in the school environment. J. Milton Yinger (1982:274) pointed out that the "standard high school subcultures, with their emphasis on sports, fun, and a modicum of learning, are quite different in sociological meaning from groups oriented to truancy, petty theft, masculine hyperaggressiveness, and gang combat." Yinger attributed the youth's fear of failure as part of the motivation to join deviant groups.

High school represents a *defining moment* in most young people's lives. School hallways are becoming increasingly an arena of "haves" and "have-nots" and students from less affluent homes and neighborhoods find they are often relegated to lower social standing in school (Johnson, 1998; Kozol, 1991, 2006). In large part, a youth's status and social identity are connected to school performance. Carl Werthman (1976) compared the identity needs and materials available to adults and to youths. In our society, adult status and identity are typically gained through occupations and affluence. Young males (especially from lower classes), without access to the materials with which to build male identity and social status, will use whatever materials are available in their environment. They may assert their autonomy by fighting with other students or rejecting the rules and authority of the school. The adult authority figures and the normative structure of the school offer a situation of confrontation and risk in which the youth can gain a measure of identity and status from peers. On the other hand, the aggressive, rebellious stance is interpreted by school officials as a predisposition to delinquency and the stage is set for further confrontation and struggle. Research suggests that if these males work while in school, although they may be able to buy some of the material possessions that enhance their status, they may still be more likely to become involved in delinquency (Wright, et al., 1997).

Walter Schafer and Kenneth Polk (1976) reported another possible dimension of the school's role in projecting youths into delinquent behavior. They pointed out that educators often perceive a correlation between educational deficiencies and behavior problems and therefore categorically define some youngsters as "stupid" or "bad." As these children become aware of this negative evaluation, their alienation is deepened and they increase their truancy and other forms of delinquency. The possible link between low intelligence and/or learning disabilities and juvenile delinquency is unclear. The hypothesis that "academic competence is linked to delinquency by way of success in and attachment to the school" has been very popular (Hirschi, 1969:115). Travis Hirschi and Michael Hindelang (1977) contended that IQ is an important but frequently ignored variable in juvenile delinquency. Margaret Farnworth and her associates (1985) indeed found that intervention prior to school entry that improves academic potential and future school performance for children categorized as "high risk" for school failure may in fact reduce the likelihood of delinquency. However, they contended that the impact of the preschool intervention was independent of IQ scores. At least two important studies reveal a seeming direct link between low IQ and delinquency. Moffitt and Stouthamer-Loeber (1993) found a significant relationship between low IQ scores and delinquency when controlling for variables of race and social class, and McGloin and Pratt (2003) linked low IQ to early onset of delinquency and extent of delinquency.

Much of the apparent link between low IQ, learning disabilities, poor school performance, and juvenile delinquency has been seriously challenged. For instance, Lane (1980) reviewed the research examining the connection between juvenile delinquency and learning disabilities, and explained that no clear relationship has been established between the two. A study of 12- to 15-year-old boys, separated into groups of learning disabled and nonlearning disabled, indicated no more delinquency on the part of the learning disabled than the others (Broder, et al., 1981). Paul Broder and his associates (1981) however, found that the learning disabled group members were more likely to be adjudicated delinquent by juvenile courts. Scott Menard and Barbara Morse (1984) reported similar findings. They argued that the IQ–delinquency hypothesis lacks empirical support and adds nothing to delinquency theory. They indicated that the correlation of IQ with delinquency is not because IQ exerts a causal influence on delinquent behavior, but because, in the schools, it may be selected as the criterion for differential treatment. Another study found that while learning disabled and nonlearning disabled students engage in essentially the same behaviors, learning disabled children are treated differently and are more likely to be considered delinquent (Keilitz, et al., 1979).

Dropout and delinquency rates vary across communities, and socioeconomic status, race and ethnicity, and other social and economic variables have been shown to be importantly related to both (Figueira-McDonough, 1993; McNeal, 1997). School dropouts have a hard time finding jobs, and girls who drop out are more likely to become pregnant than those who stay in school (Cantelon and LeBoeuf, 1997). Delbert Elliott (1966) expanded on the problems experienced by some youngsters at school and the alternative responses open to them. His and later studies (Elliott and Voss, 1974; Jarjoura, 1996), showed that while in school, lower-class boys had higher rates of delinquency, but as suggested by strain theories, after lower-class boys dropped out of school and took a job, their delinquency rates dropped dramatically. Conversely, middle-class boys' delinquency increases when they drop out of school (Jarjoura, 1996). Colvin and Pauly (1983) provided additional insight into why this may occur. While in school, lower-class boys experience a great deal of failure. Failure in school may have made these boys "more receptive to the influence of delinquent groups in which they learn specific attitudes, motives, and skills to produce patterned delinquent behavior" (Colvin and Pauly, 1983:524). Out of school, these lower-class boys moved into a setting where they could experience some success. Terence Thornberry and his associates (1985) questioned the methodology of these studies, however, and by using longitudinal data from a Philadelphia sample they determined that dropping out of school was positively related to delinquency and later crime over both the short and the long term. Their study indicated more support for the Social Control Theory approach, in that the severing of the social bond with the school apparently resulted in increased delinquency. On the other hand, subsequent studies continue to question the relationship between dropping out of school and later delinquency involvement (Figueira-McDonough, 1993; Jarjoura, 1993; 1996), and one study even suggests that secondary education related to occupational training lowers the likelihood of delinquency and adult crime (Arum and Beattie, 1999). Contemporary research suggests that early onset of delinquency, especially committing delinquent acts before age 10, is more likely to lead to dropping out of school than dropping out of school leading to delinquency (Beuhring, 2006). Leon Botstein, president of Bard College, argues that high schools have become obsolete and are an "infantilizing" experience, needlessly prolonging the marginality of adolescence when many of the young people there are capable of meeting the responsibilities of adulthood (Epstein, 2007). He offers a controversial solution to the truancy problem: abolish high schools! His proposal is to create a K-10 educational system divided into two parts: elementary (K–5) and secondary (6–10). After students complete the 10th grade, they should be allowed and encouraged to either go to work, enter national service, further their education in vocational or technical fields, or attend college (Epstein, 2007).

David Hawkins and Denise Lishner (1987) developed a theoretical model which illustrates how the aforementioned school experiences may be related to juvenile delinquency (see Figure 10.1). The series of arrows in Figure 10.1 show how each of the school-related risk factors is directly and indirectly linked to juvenile delinquency among males. The figure also illustrates both direct and indirect interrelationships among the variables. Finally, the model depicts how these risk factors are also related to dropping out of school. It is important to note that there is no direct relationship indicated between dropping out of school and increased juvenile delinquency among males. Rather, consistent with the research of Elliott (1966) and Elliott and Voss (1974), the model suggests that both delinquency and dropping out are the result of similar negative school experiences. This supports the " . . . contention that school experiences themselves are factors in delinquent behavior, which, when removed, no longer contribute to [delinquency]" (Hawkins and Lishner, 1987:186). It also supports research findings that dropping out of school may be viewed as the culmination of a long-term process of academic disengagement (Alexander, et al., 1997).

One form of delinquency which grows directly from problems in school is that of truancy. Each school day, thousands of students miss school without a bona fide excuse (Baker, et al., 2001; Reid, 2002). In some cities, truancy rates run as high as 30 percent, and there is mounting evidence that juveniles who skip school are more likely to get involved in alcohol, drugs, gangs, and violence (Baker, et al., 2001; Garry, 1996). Students who are having difficulty in school are most likely to be truant. As Jacob Getzels (1977:74) put it:

> What can be more tormenting than to be confronted day after day with a situation in which the language, and value codes seem different in inexplicable ways from those to which you are accustomed—and more a situation in which you cannot succeed and from which you are not permitted to escape without threat of severe punishment?

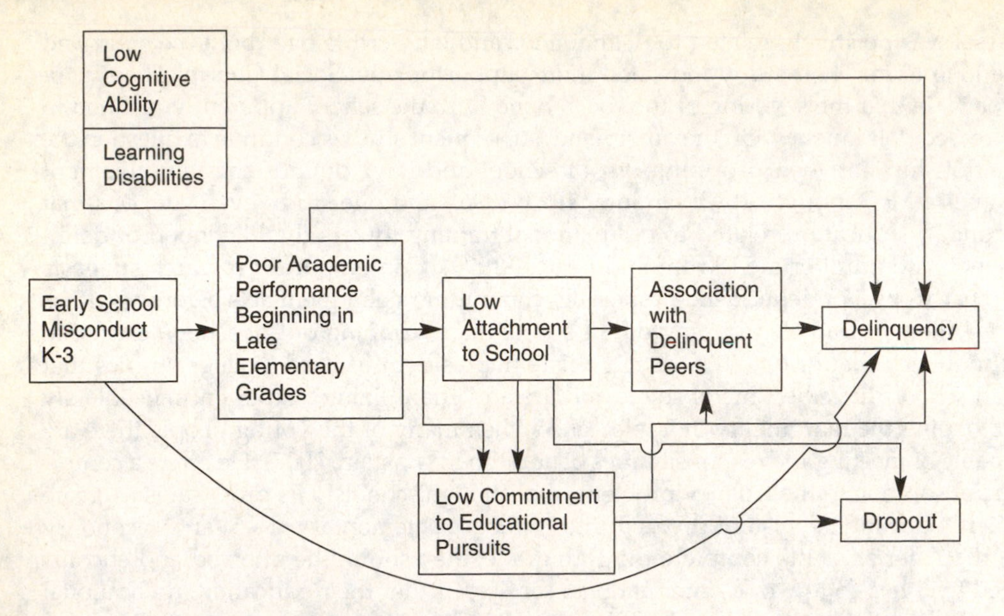

FIGURE 10.1 School-Related Risk Factors for Individual Delinquency Among Males.
How might you apply some of the sociological theories from Chapters 5, 6, 7, and 8 to this figure? For example, could you use Hirschi's Social Bond theory to explain parts of this diagram?

Source: J. David Hawkins and Denise M. Lishner. "Schooling and Delinquency." Pp. 179–221 in Elmer H. Johnson (Ed.), *Handbook on Crime and Delinquency Prevention.* Westport, Connecticut: Greenwood Press (1987), p. 185.

One of the ways that schools act as a screening device is to (perhaps unintentionally) drive away those students who cannot succeed there. As these students grow more frustrated, they are much more likely to skip school. Gayle Zieman and Gerald Benson (1980) interviewed junior high school boys who had histories of truancy, and found that they perceived the school as a place of discomfort associated with confrontations and lack of success. Most states have a compulsory attendance law up to a certain age (usually 16) and students below the legal age for dropping out are delinquent by virtue of their truancy.

Beyond the act of truancy making the juvenile a delinquent, the juvenile is also likely to get into other kinds of trouble while wandering the streets when school is in session (OJJDP, 2008). While this may not be the case when older students drop out to take full-time jobs (Elliott, 1966), it is probable that younger students who skip school to frequent pool halls, video arcades, shopping malls, or simply roam the streets, are likely to get involved in other forms of delinquency beyond their truancy. In some cities, police routinely make daytime sweeps of shopping malls searching for truant youths (NBC Nightly News, 1997). By virtue of being on the streets or in malls during school hours, the juvenile is highly visible to police and may be picked up, questioned, and possibly searched. In these cases, the general behavior of the youth which earned a reputation or label of being "smart aleck," "out of control," and "bad" at school is also likely to compound potential problems with the police. As several studies point out, the demeanor of juveniles as perceived by the police becomes one of the most significant variables in determining how the police handle the case (Lundman, 1996a,b; Piliavin and Briar, 1964).

SCHOOLS AS "COMBAT ZONES"

Failing grades, truancy, and dropping out are only some of the responses available to students who do not succeed in the school system. Another way they can respond to the value conflict, frustration, and damage to self-concept that they experience is to fight back. As William Glasser (1978) pointed out, students who cannot cope with an unsuccessful school experience feel they have two options: drop out, or go to school and cause trouble. Compulsory attendance laws can limit those options to the latter, turning some schools into what amount to "combat zones."

One of the prominent psychological explanations of human violence which was developed in the 1930s is the *Frustration–Aggression Hypothesis.* According to John Dollard and his colleagues (1939), frustration arises when an individual is unable to reach some desired goal. This frustration is then vented in the form of aggressive behavior. While there is disagreement over the causal link between frustration and aggression today (especially over the early assumption that frustration *must* lead to aggression), it is generally agreed that frustration certainly *can* lead to aggression. Likewise, Merton's Anomie Theory contends that juveniles who cannot pursue culturally prescribed goals through socially approved means become frustrated and often pursue a deviant adaptation strategy to the situation. General strain theory goes further to link strain, stress, and frustration to delinquency. Given this, it is not totally unexpected that when students find themselves at odds with the school system, are negatively labeled, and cannot achieve success through the approved standards, they will become frustrated. That frustration may be relieved by dropping out (if they are allowed to), or it may be vented through wreaking havoc on the school, teachers, and other students.

Vandalism and Destruction

Juveniles sometimes strike back at the schools with vandalism and destruction. William Sanders (1981:101) reported that schools are the most common target of **malevolent vandalism**—*"activity in which property is destroyed out of malevolent motives on the part of the perpetrators."* The school becomes the target of vandalism because of the juveniles' contempt for the institution. Paul Chance (1984) indicated that vandalism is primarily a result of not liking school and feeling disliked by teachers and administrators. Estimates of the total annual cost of school vandalism in the United States ranged between $100 million to $600 million over 25 years ago (cited in Neill, 1978:305). Today, no comprehensive figures on school vandalism are even kept, but it is safe to assume that the figure is much higher. Vandalism is a property offense and generally not considered to be a violent act. But in this situation we are not referring to the petty types of vandalism that routinely occur at most schools, such as seniors spray painting the year of their graduating class on the sign in front of the building. Although even those types of acts can be costly, they are engaged in for fun and mischief. Rather, we are referring to massive attacks on school property.

James Truckenmiller (1982) identified students' perceived lack of access to educational success as one of the variables most predictive of vandalism. Later studies confirm a link between frustration in school and destructive behavior (Horowitz, 2003). School districts are acutely aware of the problems associated with school vandalism, and many have taken steps to create programs in an effort to reduce it. G. Ray Mayer and coworkers (1983) reported the results of a 3-year study of 20 schools from 12 school districts which showed that educators could take positive steps to reduce vandalism and other forms of inappropriate student behavior. Patricia Stagliano and Irwin Hyman (1983) found that implementing student conduct codes, student–teacher–community task forces, community training, and legislation requiring the monitoring of school vandalism had all met with at least some success.

Violence and Personal Attacks

Vandalism is not the only form that violence takes in the schools. Sometimes the frustration and anger felt toward the educational system are directed against the teachers and administrators who represent it. Ron Halvorsen and Donald Hawley (1973:56) described the "combat conditions" of teaching in some of the poorer sections of Brooklyn:

> The school tool shed had a telephone in it, and if things got too difficult an instructor could make a run for it, lock himself in, and then telephone for help. In one classroom the students suspended the teacher out of a fifth-floor window, threatening him, "Teach, if you assign any homework today, we're going to drop you."

A study of 253 classroom teachers in the Los Angeles public school system in the 1970s indicated that 28 percent of those teachers had suffered physical assault (Bloch, 1978). It went on to describe how the reactions to long-term stress among these 253 teachers were similar to combat neurosis. And, in 1991, assaults on teachers became so common in the state of Florida that three state legislators introduced a bill to allow teachers to zap unruly students with electric "stun guns" (AP, Tallahassee, FL, 1991). A massive study of delinquency in schools conducted at the turn of the millennium indicated that 42 percent of teachers had been the targets of obscene gestures or threats; 28 percent had been victims of personal property damage; and approximately 1 percent had been physically attacked by a student (Gottfredson, et al., 2000).

A Senate subcommittee report on juvenile delinquency concluded that school violence in the form of vandalism and attacks on people was definitely on the increase (Bayh, 1975). A similar subcommittee report found that the types of crimes found in the public schools encompassed virtually every type of crime found on the streets, including fatal beatings, stabbings, and even rapes of both students and teachers (U.S. Senate Subcommittee on Delinquency, 1977:7–10). The same report found that an alarming number of students were arming themselves with knives and guns for personal protection.

A National Institute of Education report in 1978 indicated that over a quarter of a million secondary school students were physically attacked by other students each month, and blamed some truancy problems on students' fear for their personal safety (Okaty, 1991). A subsequent study by the U.S. Department of Education estimated that 3 million violent crimes and thefts occur per year in U.S. public schools—an average of 16,000 crimes per day (Johnson, 1993). And, an APA Commission report estimated that kids carry an estimated 270,000 guns to school every day (Fields,

1993). Fear of violent attacks is increased when fatal shootings or stabbings over something as trivial as a cigarette lighter are reported (AP, Webbers Falls, OK, 1997). A 2000 study indicated that violence and personal attacks were higher in middle schools than high schools with 41 percent of middle school students saying they had been threatened, hit, or beaten by another student at school (Gottfredson, et al., 2000). A U.S. Department of Education study showed that slightly over 12 percent of the nation's students reported being the victims of a violent or property crime while at school (Addington, et al., 2002). In 2003, that percentage dropped to less than five, and students were twice as likely to be victims of violence away from school than at school (AP Washington, 2005c).

School violence peaked in the United States during the 1992–93 academic year, but a series of tragic shootings in American schools during the late 1990s focused worldwide attention on schools as "combat zones." A 16-year-old boy rumored to be part of a Satanic cult shot nine of his high school classmates fatally wounding two in Pearl, Mississippi, in October of 1997, and only two months later three students were killed and five others wounded in a shooting at Heath High School in West Paducah, Kentucky. Americans were still reeling from the shock of these two school shootings when in March of 1998, two boys, aged 11 and 13 killed four girls and a teacher and wounded ten other students during a false fire alarm at a middle school in Jonesboro,

Arkansas. A month later, a science teacher was shot to death and two students were wounded at an eighth-grade dance in Edinboro, Pennsylvania. The following month, May of 1998, saw two fatal shootings within two days as an 18-year-old honors student killed a classmate in a high school parking lot in Fayetteville, Tennessee, and a 17-year-old boy in Springfield, Oregon, opened fire at a high school, killing two and wounding 20 others, after having murdered his parents in their home. On April 20, 1999, two students entered Columbine High School in Littleton, Colorado, clad in black trench coats and armed with several high-powered weapons and bombs. Before the rampage ended, 12 students and a teacher had been shot to death, 23 students had been wounded, and the two boys had turned the guns on themselves and committed suicide. Police estimated that if the killers had successfully discharged the bombs as planned, hundreds of students and teachers would have been killed or seriously wounded.

Four years later, a 14-year-old Red Lion, Pennsylvania, boy took three handguns to school and killed the principal before turning one gun on himself and committing suicide. That same school had witnessed a principal, two teachers, and 11 students attacked with a machete in 2001 (AP, Red Lion, PA, 2003). In 2006, Sheriff's deputies in Riverton, Kansas, foiled a plot to "celebrate" the seventh anniversary of the Columbine shootings in which five teenage boys were arrested in possession of guns, ammunition, and knives after discussing plans to massacre classmates at school on the popular Web site MySpace.com (AP Riverton, KS, 2006).

These events, like others that preceded them and still others that followed, reminded Americans that children are not safe from violence even when at school. They also signaled a change in the nature of school violence. Prior to these mass shootings, violence in schools tended to be more one-on-one and motivated by some particular incident between the two students involved. Today, violence is more likely to be gang-related (Howell and Lynch, 2000), or as in the cases just cited, these violent incidents involved large numbers of victims and were much more random in nature. Thus, although the number of specific violent incidents in schools actually decreased during the years 1993 to 2000, the numbers of students killed or injured in such incidents and the sensational nature of the violence in many of these episodes dramatically increased. Also, the media's portrayal of school violence in both rural and urban areas greatly affected public awareness and political responses to school violence (Menifield, et al., 2001).

Data on school crime are difficult to collect and assess because schools' disclosure of crime information varies from one school district to another. Although colleges and universities are now required to compile campus crime statistics and release them to the public, no similar requirements exist for U.S. elementary and secondary schools. In 1993, President Clinton proposed that a campus-by-campus computerized crime report should be compiled by all schools, kindergarten through 12th grade, so that parents would be aware of potential threats to their children's safety while at school, and after the tragic shooting at West Paducah High School in 1997, President Clinton directed the U.S. Department of Education and Justice to prepare an annual report on school safety (1998). In 2000, as he left office, Clinton was pleased that reports indicated a significant decrease in school violence between 1992 and 2000, a trend that continued through 2005 (U.S. Department of Education, 2005; U.S. Department of State, 2000). School safety remains a vital concern, however, and in 2007, the first National Student Safety and Security Conference was held where school officials, law enforcement personnel, and community leaders met to share best practices on promoting school safety and reducing violence in schools.

BOX 10.2

CONCEPT APPLICATION: Bullying and School Violence

In 1999, 5.1 percent of 12- to 18-year-olds reported that they had been "bullied" at school (Addington, et al., 2002), but a study conducted by the National Institute of Child Health and Human Development indicated that as many as one in three students in grades six through ten experience bullying at school (Tanner, 2001). Sometimes the bullying, even with very young children, goes beyond threats, as in the case of seven fifth graders who were caught trying to poison a classmate by putting pills, glue, lead, and chalk in her drink (AP, Denver, 2003). In its more serious forms, the bullying can be linked to assault and other acts of violence. National data indicate that school bullying is increasing and becoming more severe (Mayo Clinic staff, 2007).

School bullying is usually defined as behavior that involves bigger or stronger students picking on, harassing, or trying to coerce weaker students into doing something that they don't want to do. Research shows that younger students (grades one to eight) and boys are most likely to be victims of school bullying, but no student is exempt. Shortly after being crowned Miss America 2002, Erika Harold traveled across the United States speaking to student groups about the physical and emotional consequences caused by school bullying and told students that she and a friend were bullied and harassed so mercilessly in high school that they had to transfer schools (*People*, 2002).

Often, the bullying begins at home, continues at school, and ultimately, may be carried over to the workplace when the adolescent bullies become adults (Ahmed and Braithwaite, 2004; Furedi, 2003).

School bullying often has been ignored with the pervasive attitude that "kids will be kids and this is just going to happen" (Tanner, 2001:12A), but as one school official noted, "these are not just 'kids being kids', but are violent attacks against young people" (Bergmann, 1987:A8). The serious consequences of school bullying gained national attention when, in 1999, two students at Columbine High School in Littleton, Colorado, went on a shooting rampage that left 12 students (14 including the two shooters who turned the guns on themselves) and one teacher dead, and 23 others wounded. Subsequent investigation indicated that the two boys had been teased, taunted, and harassed by students at the high school and had made a videotaped message indicating that the schoolhouse slaughter was their means of getting revenge. On the seventh anniversary of the Columbine massacre, six middle school students were arrested in Anchorage, Alaska for plotting an attack on fellow students and teachers that they claimed picked on them (AP, Anchorage, 2006). Several other school shootings have been attributed to bullying (e.g., Crary, 2001), and research shows that being bullied at school can lead to depression, low self-esteem, criminal activities, and even suicide among adults (Tanner, 2001).

Increased school violence, including numerous shootings, has prompted school officials across the nation to take steps to reduce school bullying and its potentially dangerous consequences. As early as 1987, the National School Safety Center emphasized the need for awareness of the widespread problem of taunting and violent assaults on school playgrounds and, along with Harvard University, sponsored a "Schoolyard Bully Practicum" for teachers and administrators. Studies in England and Norway show that intervention programs on the part of schools can reduce bullying by 30 to 50 percent (Tanner, 2001), and some states, including Colorado, Minnesota, and Oklahoma, have passed legislation to create programs to reduce bullying in their schools (Crary, 2001; Hamilton, 2002).

(*Continued*)

Although school bullying can probably never be totally eliminated, school officials realize that efforts must be made to intervene on behalf of victims before serious harm is done. These efforts may reduce some school violence and the overall delinquency and crime rates as well, as both the numbers of victims and perpetrators of school bullying decrease.

Were you ever a victim of school bullying? What can school officials do to help reduce school bullying? Would reducing school bullying help reduce delinquency?

Sources

Ahmed, E. and Braithwaite, V. 2004. "What, me ashamed?" Shame management and school bullying. *Journal of Research in Crime and Delinquency* 41 (August):269–294.

AP Denver, 2003. Fifth graders tried to poison girl, police say. *Dallas Morning News,* January 18:18A.

Addington, L. A., Ruddy, S. A., Miller, A. K., DeVoe, J. F., and Chandler, K. A. 2002. *Are America's Schools Safe? Students Speak Out: 1999 School Crime Supplement.* Washington, DC: U.S. Department of Education.

Bergmann, R. 1987. Purdy: Few bullies in Manteca. *Manteca Bulletin,* June 9:A8.

Crary, D. 2001. Shooting prompts look at bullying. http://newsroom.compuserve.com/nr/edit.../shooting.asp&PageView=NAT&CoView=&BTM=

Furedi, F. 2003. Bullying as a social problem in Great Britain. In J. Best and D. R. Loseke (eds.), *Social problems: Constructionist Reading.* New York: Aldine de Gruyter: 13–20.

Hamilton, A. 2002. With law, Oklahoma joins anti-bully fight. *Dallas Morning News,* May 6:1A;8A.

Herndon, L. 1993. Bullies can make a kid's life miserable—but don't despair. *The Oregonian,* August 26:A1.

Mayo Clinic Staff. 2007. Bullying: Help your child handle a school bully. Mental Health (April) http://www.mayoclinic.com/health/bullying/MH00126

People. 2002. Bully pulpit. http://people.aol.com/people/magazine/magazineheroes/0,11369,364971,00.html

Roberts, J. 1988. School yard menace. *Psychology Today* 22 (February):52–56.

Tanner, L. 2001. "Study: 1 in 3 kids deals with bullying. *Dallas Morning News,* April 26:1A; 12A.

Joan McDermott (1983) examined research on crime and the fear of crime and victimization in the school and community. She suggested that crime and the fear of crime should be viewed in a community context since schools which experienced high rates of crime tended to be located in high-crime neighborhoods. A longitudinal study of 532 young black males and their parents in Philadelphia substantiated McDermott's assumption. In that study, it was found that both the juveniles and their parents had extremely high rates of fear about the boys being victims of crime in the school environment (Savitz, et al., 1978). Over one-half of the boys indicated that they had been the victims of robbery, assault, or extortion. Even those who had not been victimized personally expressed a great deal of fear. These youths indicated that they feared being mugged, robbed, and even murdered in school rooms, school hallways, school yards, streets, playgrounds, recreation centers, movie theaters, dance halls, and on public transportation. The study found that parental and juvenile fear of school-based crime was alleviated by truancy, joining gangs for protection, and even relocation to safer schools in safer neighborhoods (Savitz, et al., 1978). The U.S. Department of Education surveys students annually to determine the extent of

What does research indicate about the possible links between school bullying and delinquency?

© Getty Images

crime and the fear of criminal attacks at school. This survey shows that since the highly publicized school shootings (especially Columbine), students are more fearful of becoming crime victims at school (Addington, et al., 2002). Sociological research indicates that to be understood and prevented, school violence must be viewed as related to neighborhood, community, and larger societal factors (Lawrence, 2007).

Whether high crime neighborhoods lead to crime in the schools, or crime in the schools leads to high crime neighborhoods, has developed as an interesting sociological question. One study found that geographic proximity to a high school increased the likelihood of crime in neighborhoods in San Diego (Roncek and LoBosco, 1983). In fact, that study indicated that residential areas adjacent to public high schools experienced more crime than areas that were more than a block away from those same schools. Dennis Roncek and Donald Faggiani (1985) replicated that study in the city of Cleveland, and discovered similar findings. These studies suggest that crime and violence in the schools, like any other social problem, must be viewed within their broader sociological context, as opposed to being viewed as isolated acts. Crime does not occur in schools in isolation from crime in the rest of society (Lawrence, 2007).

Overgeneralizations are dangerous, and it would be a gross exaggeration to conclude that very many of today's youths are violent sociopaths ransacking the schools and terrorizing administrators, teachers, and fellow students. Nevertheless, the increasing rates of truancy, vandalism, and student violence indicate a significant problem for our schools in regard to juvenile delinquency.

School Safety and "Zero Tolerance"

In many communities, parents are not sitting idly by while their children are being robbed, bullied, and assaulted at school. For example, at Arlington High School in Indianapolis, things became so bad that some concerned fathers formed a group known as "Security Dads" who with the cooperation of school officials took it upon themselves to spend several hours per day patrolling the halls and campus in order to provide a safer environment for their children to attend school (Whittemore, 1992). The Indianapolis story is but one example of how parents can make a difference, and experts agree that parents can make schools safer by simply spending more time there with their children (Greer, 1993).

School officials are aware of the necessity to provide a safe and secure environment for students, faculty, and all those who enter the school domain. In some schools this has prompted the stationing of full-time uniformed police officers or security guards within the schools. Other schools require all students, school personnel, and visitors to pass through metal detectors upon entrance to school buildings, while still others conduct random checks for weapons, drugs, or other forms of contraband and potentially dangerous items. Additionally, a number of schools prohibit the use of backpacks or book bags that might be used to conceal a weapon or some other dangerous or controlled substance. In an effort to reduce crimes and violence in schools, approximately 95 percent of school districts participate in a federally funded Zero Tolerance program whose aim is to establish schools as "gun-free" and "drug-free"

What impact has "Zero Tolerance" school policies had on delinquency?

© Marilyn R. Thompson

zones (Lawrence, 2007). Although it may be defined somewhat differently by various school districts, **zero tolerance** generally refers to *school policies that prohibit the possession, use, sale, or supply of any type of weapon, alcohol, or illegal drug on school premises or at any school-related functions.*

These programs, for the most part, have enjoyed widespread public support, but they have not been without their problems and critics. Some argue that the presence of uniformed and armed guards in school buildings conveys the wrong image for students, and may inadvertently create a more hostile and potentially violent atmosphere. Others argue that students' constitutional rights are violated when they are required to pass through metal detectors or are subjected to random stops and searches for weapons or drugs without probable cause. Research compiled throughout the 1990s indicated that there was virtually no difference in drug usage between schools that randomly tested for drugs and those that did not (*New York Times*, 2003a). And, in some high-profile cases, the zero-tolerance policies of some schools have received widespread media attention for their bureaucratic absurdity as children have been suspended over the possession of nail clippers, mouthwash, or over-the-counter pain relievers (Thompson and Hickey, 2008). The American Bar Association called for a ban of zero-tolerance policies, indicating they had become "a one-size-fits-all solution" to school problems and had redefined "students as criminals" (Williams, 2001:1A). Nevertheless, school administrators often find themselves in a difficult situation when faced with the need to provide an open, inviting, and pleasant learning environment while at the same time trying to ensure that schools are safe and secure. A National Study of Delinquency Prevention in Schools found that although nearly all U.S. schools had delinquency prevention programs in place, less than half were deemed effective, and that bureaucratic and organizational problems prohibited meaningful delinquency prevention in schools (NIJ, 2004).

SCHOOL AS BUREAUCRACY

Beyond the outright hostility some students express toward the school as a result of their failure, or their inability to relate to the dominant values being expressed there, is the more subtle problem experienced by students in regard to dealing with the bureaucratic structure of the school. Max Weber ([1922] 1968) indicated that **bureaucracy** as an *ideal type* is typified by *a clear-cut division of labor; a hierarchy of authority; an elaborate system of rules and regulations; people treated as "cases," not as "individuals"; and a clear-cut career pattern for those working within the bureaucracy.* Clearly, the public schools meet the criteria for bureaucracy.

The bureaucratic elements that may create the most significant problems for students are those regarding the elaborate system of rules and regulations and the fact that people often are treated as cases rather than individuals. No school could operate without a set of rules and regulations. However, in some situations, the schools, at least as perceived by many of the students, have adopted so many rules and regulations that it becomes impossible to abide by all of them. Further, it seems that in some cases, the rules take precedence over the people who must enforce and abide by them. Rules for the sake of rules are likely to be broken for the sake of breaking them.

Students who feel they are being treated like numbers, rather than people, are likely to develop a sense of alienation in the school environment. The assembly line model of education which has dominated our educational philosophy since the industrial revolution has led to viewing schools as analogous to factories. Thus, incoming students are seen as raw materials to be shaped, molded, and transformed into finished products (i.e., productive citizens) by those trained and skilled to do so (the teachers). Students' views of teachers and teachers' views of students are affected by the roles they are forced to fulfill within the bureaucratic structure. Students often are amazed to discover that their teachers have a life outside the bureaucratic structure of the school.

The depersonalization, and, in some cases, the dehumanization of the educational process in contemporary U.S. society have taken their toll on young people. Standardized testing, tracking, technological teaching devices, and a variety of other developments in education undoubtedly have made positive contributions to the educational endeavor. However, on the negative side, it must be noted that these developments also have led to increased bureaucratization of the schools. A major nation-wide report showed that reliance on standardized testing and increased bureaucratization of the schools have led to declining teacher morale and increasingly unruly students (AP, Washington, 2003a). The students, forced to survive in this bureaucratic structure, may find themselves unable or unwilling to cope with it, and hence become involved in a variety of nonconforming activities leading to delinquency.

SCHOOLS AND DELINQUENCY PREVENTION

Because of the school's significant role in the socialization of U.S. youth, a large part of the responsibility for preventing delinquency falls upon the school system. To a large extent, educators and administrators have interpreted this responsibility as meaning they should be on the lookout for those youths most likely to cause trouble, commit delinquent acts, and become adult criminals. This emphasis on individual pathology as an explanation for deviance has been nonproductive and unsuccessful, and the use of standardized tests for predicting potential problem students has come under increased fire. Despite the widespread use of standardized personality inventories, aptitude tests, achievement tests, and tracking, the problem of delinquency has increased rather than diminished. As pointed out in the earlier discussion on the labeling processes in the schools, these developments in education have, if anything, compounded the problems of delinquency rather than alleviated them. As more potential delinquents are identified, labeled, and acted upon, more actual delinquents are produced.

Perhaps one of the most enlightened discussions of this problem and suggestions for modification is provided by Delos Kelly (1982:122): "If change is to come about, then I believe that it must begin with the educational system. Not only is this one of our basic social institutions but most children spend at least ten years or more within the system; they also spend many hours each day in school. The same does not exist with many families or the community." He points out that the problems of stereotyping, labeling, degrading, tracking, and programming failure into certain students must be stopped. Kelly (1982: 123–124) calls for an all-out resocialization of parents, teachers, educators, and students in regard to the success–fail philosophy of the schools.

The teacher plays a significant role in any strategy of changing schools in such a way as to eliminate some of the problems of delinquency. Eliminating failure and making students feel accepted and cared for are viable approaches to solving many of the discipline problems in the public schools, and teachers play the most vital role in implementing any school-based strategy for delinquency prevention (Glasser, 1978; Kimbrough, 1986). According to Carl Werthman (1976), when faced with situations in the classroom which threaten serious disruption, the teacher can respond in one of three ways. The teacher can simply overlook any activities other than learning which take place in the classroom, and attempt to teach those who are willing to learn. Rarely do serious problems erupt, because the teacher fails to acknowledge the activities of those who are trying to disrupt the educational process. A second strategy is for the teacher to participate in the disruption. Minor disruptions, such as jumping to the window to see a passing firetruck or discussing last night's homecoming game, do not have to elevate into teacher–student confrontations if the teacher is flexible enough to allow the students these minor distractions for a brief period and then direct them back to the desired classroom activity. The third response is for the teacher to confront any activities which do not directly relate to the learning planned for the class. This confrontational approach indicates that the teacher sees extraneous activities not only as disruptive, but as direct challenges to adult authority in the classroom. When the teacher responds in this fashion, an adversarial situation is created in which, if the teacher is to maintain control of the classroom, he or she must win each and every encounter. While some situations may not allow for the first two options (such as fights and other situations which threaten others), the tendency for a teacher to choose the third response is viewed by the students as overreaction, and may in fact lead to problems in the classroom rather than reduce them. Thus, the reactions of teachers to potentially disruptive situations in the classroom cannot be overestimated as potential ways of reducing delinquency in the schools.

As with the family (see Chapter 9), consistent and fair discipline may be one of the most effective delinquency prevention tools to be used by teachers and the schools. The National Association of School Psychologists (2003) recommends that effective school discipline is that which:

- is designed to teach and instruct;
- focuses on how to do better and not on what went wrong;
- makes a direct connection between the misbehavior and the consequences;
- is done in private, not before an audience (especially other students);
- is done with benevolence and respect; and
- never involves name-calling, shouting, yelling, or berating.

Kenneth Polk (1975; 1984) viewed the educational institution as one of the most important elements in delinquency prevention and control. He contended that the number of marginal youths is growing, not only because less successful students have an unpleasant school experience, but also because their future occupational aspirations are severely limited. He proposed that to counter the alienation experienced by these youths, they must be engaged in useful work and be more thoroughly integrated into the school community. William Pink (1984) concurred, viewing effective schools as the most cost-efficient delinquency prevention program. He contended that the current educational system perpetuates a two-trajectory system where the low-trajectory youths (less successful students) are not only ill prepared academically, but also meet with failure in the out-of-school world, creating social situations which generate delinquency and other forms of deviance. Leon Botstein maintains that schools increase rather than decrease the marginality of adolescents, and that serious revisions must be made to reduce delinquency and develop productive citizens (Epstein, 2007).

J. David Hawkins and Joseph Weis (1980) also acknowledged the school's importance in delinquency prevention, and viewed the school's role as going beyond academic and intellectual development. They suggested that the school must provide more alternative educational options, such as enhanced skill training. This suggestion was supported by a study which showed that students who received meaningful occupational education in high school were less likely to be incarcerated later as adults (Arum and Beattie, 1999). Hawkins and Weis also suggested that the school take a more active role in the social development process, including education in civil and criminal law. Emphasizing the social context in which the schools operate, they argued for more student input into the educational process and urged schools to draw upon student leaders to exert peer influence in delinquency prevention. They pointed out that the student leaders should not be merely the academic leaders, but also the informal leaders of various social groups and cliques. Consistent with social control theories, research shows that a strong bond to school is one of the most effective tools in delinquency prevention (Eith, 2005).

Barry Krisberg and James Austin (1978) further emphasized the social nature of the educational process and outlined some ways in which schools could reduce delinquency. They suggested that schools might enter into agreements with local communities to enhance their partnership role with the entire community. Their suggestions included utilizing local artisans, craftspersons, and other professionals in the community as guest lecturers. They also suggested revising the curriculum to include local internship programs and viewing the local community as a learning resource. Local museums, libraries, universities, scientific establishments, businesses, and industries all should be viewed as places of learning and instruction. Enhanced school–community relations would better integrate school and community in the educational process and reduce the view that schools are socially set apart from the rest of the world. Further, a number of studies suggest that schools must become more involved in *all* aspects of a student's life, including family, interaction with other private and social institutions, and other interests outside of school (e.g., Fagan and Pabon, 1990). As a result, many school districts are developing comprehensive delinquency prevention plans in cooperation with parents, the police, local businesses, and other available local, state, and federal agencies (Lawrence, 2007).

Summary

The educational system did not create youthful misbehavior and juvenile delinquency. The main sources of delinquency reside in the features of society; however, schools as social arenas can either aggravate or reduce the problem according to the way they dispense rewards and punishments to students, provide access to opportunities for success, and react to the problems of students. In this chapter we illustrated some of the ways in which the schools as public arenas are interwoven into the phenomenon of juvenile delinquency. The schools usually represent the first social institution (outside the family) with which the child must contend.

The major role of the school is socialization. For the schools, this process involves not only teaching the necessary cognitive skills expected of all citizens, but also teaching what are considered to be appropriate attitudes, values, beliefs, and behaviors. Children's ability to conform to normative expectations of teachers and administrators and adapt to the student role is critical in helping to determine success within that institution.

Success within the educational system is importantly linked to success in the larger society. Those who fail, create problems, cause trouble, and cannot achieve success in school are those who are most likely to be labeled "delinquent," and also to subsequently fail in life. The succeed/fail orientation of the educational system often acts as a "screening device" which may alienate the unsuccessful students to the point of truancy or dropping out. Those alienated students who choose to remain in school may do so at great costs to the schools, administrators, teachers, and other students, who become the victims of their violence and vandalism.

While schools cannot be blamed for causing juvenile delinquency, they may play an important role in reducing and/or preventing it. Schools are an integral part of society and the single social institution in which juveniles spend the largest portion of their time. From a sociological perspective, if members of society want to make a serious effort to reduce many of the problems associated with juvenile delinquency, the schools must play a major role.

Concept Integration: Questions and Topics for Study and Discussion

1. Explain how the school acts as a major agent of socialization in our society. Should schools attempt to socialize students in regard to normative aspects as well as cognitive aspects of culture? If so, how can they best do that? If not, why not?
2. Academic credentials have become extremely important in our society. Discuss some ways in which schools determine what level of credentials a student should receive. Should a student's willingness to conform to school rules be a factor in determining academic success? Why? Why not?
3. What is meant by referring to the school as a "combat zone"? What might be done to alleviate some of the conflict in the schools?
4. Schools have become increasingly bureaucratized in recent years. What positive outcomes has bureaucratization had on the schools? What has been the negative impact?
5. What can school teachers and administrators do to help reduce and prevent delinquency in the schools?
6. Discussion topic: Should states require compulsory school attendance? If so, why? If not, why not?

Chapter 11

The Youth Subculture and Delinquency

READING OBJECTIVES

Reading this chapter will help you achieve the following objectives:

1. Define subculture and explain what is meant by the concept of youth subculture.
2. Explain those aspects of American society which may lead to the creation and perpetuation of a youth subculture.
3. Identify specific attitudes, values, beliefs, behaviors, and norms characterizing the youth subculture.
4. Understand how participation in a youth subculture may result in committing delinquent acts such as running-away, prostitution, drug use, teen sex, and various other forms of delinquency.
5. Identify elements of the youth subculture which may constitute countercultures (e.g., teenage Satanism and hate groups which may be involved in serious forms of delinquency and violent crimes).
6. Explore ways in which the youth subculture might be utilized to help control and prevent juvenile delinquency.

INTRODUCTION

Every generation of adults worries about the future of society being turned over to its children. History is replete with the theme of elders believing that the younger generation has abandoned the most important attitudes, values, and beliefs of their parents and that each succeeding group of youngsters almost ensures that society's ruin is imminent. Likewise, as children grow into young adults, they marvel at the "old fogeyness" of their parents, teachers, and other older members of society. They wonder how adults survived so long while being so ignorant, out of touch, and old-fashioned. These disparate views have led to a *generation gap* between adults and juveniles that has spawned both social speculation and scientific research into the phenomenon often referred to as the **youth subculture**.

In Chapter 9, we looked at the family as the most important primary group to which people belong. We discussed the prominent role that the family plays in socializing its members to internalize the culture of society. We indicated, however, that as children grow up, they also become exposed to a variety of other socializing agents, including church, school, peers, and mass media. Chapter 10 focused on the powerful influence of the school and how it may contribute to, or help prevent, juvenile delinquency. In this chapter, we explore the ways in which the youth's movement outside the family and the school into a larger social world may lead to the development of social ties to other youths embarking upon the same process. This sense of identity along with a variety of other social factors contributes to the formation of a youth subculture, some elements of which may contribute to the youth's likelihood of committing acts regarded as deviant by adults.

CULTURE, SUBCULTURES, AND COUNTERCULTURES

Culture is *the entire body of shared and learned beliefs, values, attitudes, traditions, normative expectations, and other forms of knowledge that is passed on from one generation to the next within a society*. Within the dominant culture of larger society, there exists a variety of

subcultures *which share most of the attitudes, values, and beliefs of the overall culture; however, they also adhere to certain attitudes, values, beliefs, and norms unique to them, somewhat setting them apart from larger society.* Hans Sebald (1997:205) referred to culture as "*a blueprint for behavior of a total society*" and subculture as "*the blueprint for behavior of a smaller group within the society.*" He illustrated the concept by saying, "there are subcultures for narcotic addicts, longshoremen, inmates in prison, Texas oilmen, those in the world of fashion, jazz musicians—and adolescents" (Sebald, 1997:205).

As long as the smaller group accepts and conforms to most of the norms of larger society while maintaining its uniqueness, it is usually considered to be a subculture. However, *when the subculture differs to the point that it rejects the overall attitudes, values, beliefs, and norms of larger society and offers a substitute normative system*, it becomes a **counterculture**.

Some debate has been waged as to whether U.S. youths constitute a subculture. A number of social and behavioral scientists contend that there *is* a youth subculture and that in order to understand most juvenile behavior (including delinquency), it is necessary to put it in its subcultural context (e.g., Bennett and Kahn-Harris, 2004; Best, 2006; Coleman, 1960; Schwendinger and Schwendinger, 1985; Wilson, 2006). Some even contend that the youth subculture is in direct conflict with the larger culture created and maintained by adults and hence, constitutes a youth counterculture (Roszak, 1969; Yinger, 1960; 1982). Chapter 12 explains the concepts of deviant and delinquent subcultures and focuses upon gang membership as a counterculture that pits juveniles against the mainstream of adult society. In this chapter, we discuss the concept of a youth subculture in the United States in its broadest sense and explore its possible relationship to certain types of juvenile delinquency.

THE CREATION OF A YOUTH SUBCULTURE

Throughout this book, we have emphasized the marginal status accorded U.S. youths. Ralph England (1967) contended that the beginnings of the youth subculture can be traced to the rapid urbanization and industrialization which occurred during the 19th century. He indicated that the status of youth became marginal—neither adult nor child. He saw the 20th century as reinforcing the development of the youth subculture in a variety of ways. After World War II, the United States experienced the creation of a distinct youth culture separated from adults and children. England viewed this youth subculture as based on the values of hedonism and materialism and supported by enough money to express those values socially. When those values lead to behavior disapproved by adults, delinquency can be the result (England, 1967).

David Gottlieb and associates (1966: *ix*) agreed that "there is general agreement among many students of adolescent behavior that the emergence of distinct youth cultures is related to the emergence of industrialization." According to Gottlieb and his associates, in a modern industrial society, there is a prolonged period of adolescence which lacks a clearly defined rite of passage into adulthood. This helps create an adolescent subculture with distinctive attitudes, values, and behaviors. This notion is supported by research on the rise of a Japanese youth subculture (see Box 11.1). Ernest Smith (1962) also linked the marginal status of adolescence to the formation of a youth subculture. He indicated that "the absence of transitional rituals and the prolongation of dependence of American youth lead to parent–youth conflict" (Smith 1962:21).

There probably always has been some type of conflict between teenagers and their parents in U.S. society. However, the concept of adolescence and the marginal status of juveniles were not traditional in American society. Rather, as America experienced the shifts from rural to urban and agrarian to industrial, the role expectations for youths became much less clear. According to Dorothy Rogers (1985:8),

> various factors have conspired collectively to designate adolescence as a discrete age stage. First, children inevitably became more separated from adults as society moved from a rural to an urban environment. Second, as cultures became more complex, the stages became increasingly refined, with a definite step-like transition from infancy to adulthood. While some societies ritualize the shift from youth to maturity, those lacking such rites have instead a *youth culture*, or institutionalized adolescence.

BOX 11.1

CROSS-CULTURAL FOCUS: Japanese Youth Subculture, Skinheads, and Counterculture

For several decades, Japanese youths have become increasingly "Westernized" as they have adopted American and Western European fashion trends, hairstyles, music, and other cultural phenomena. Particularly popular in Japan is the American "cowboy look" comprised of tight-fitting Levi or Wrangler jeans, snap-button shirts, cowboy boots, and cowboy hats (Kawamura, 2008). Also, with brands such as Sony, Nokia, and others originating in Japan, it is no surprise that Japanese youths have plunged full tilt into the technological world of computers, cellular phones, CD players, and other high-tech gadgets that dominate the American youth subculture. Ninety percent of Japanese youth between the ages of 10 and 14 own video games, around 70 percent of them sing karaoke to American songs, one-half to two-thirds of all Japanese teenagers smoke cigarettes, and 85 percent of those between the ages of 16 and 18 say they feel rebellious. While these elements of change among Japanese youths have elicited some concern from their parents, teachers, and older members of Japanese society, for the most part they have been viewed as relatively harmless. Other elements of the "new" Japanese youth subculture are more disconcerting to adults, however, and have led to a noticeable increase in the amount of delinquency and crimes committed by Japanese youths. One alarming phenomenon in the Japanese youth subculture is the increasing number of young people in Japan who identify themselves as "skinheads."

There are basically two types of skinheads in Japan: "trads," or traditional skinheads, and "SSS," which refers to Skinhead Samurai Spirit. Both groups tend to either shave their heads entirely or wear "one-clips," referring to using the number-1 guard setting on a set of hair clippers to crop the hair close to the head. The shaved head in Japan, however, does not necessarily conjure up the negative images that it might in the United States, Great Britain, or Western European nations, because Japanese monks, Japanese soldiers, and even Samurai warriors have traditionally shaved their heads. Similarly, the popular Levi jeans and black Dr. Marten's boots ("Docs") do not necessarily set Japanese skinheads apart from the larger youth society for disapproval or negative sanctions. Rather, it is the behavior and activities of the Japanese skinhead subculture, and some would argue counterculture, that elicit the disapproval of Japanese adults and attract the attention of Japanese police.

A large number of Japanese skinheads buy, use, and sell illegal drugs. Finding the money to

(*Continued*)

support drug habits often leads to other illegal activities, such as prostitution, burglary, petty thefts, and even robbery. While dark ales and British beers seem to be the drink of choice among Western-world skinheads, wine and sake are the preferred drinks of their Japanese counterparts, especially the SSS. Japanese youths tend to be far less violent than American youths, and this is also true of Japanese skinheads in their delinquent and criminal activities. It is common, however, for the skinheads to get into fights, although often they simply fight among themselves.

A final defining characteristic of the Japanese skinheads is their taste in music. Initially partial to Jamaican reggae, Japanese skinheads made a transition to heavy metal and "punk" music, and later to Oi!/Punk, which is characterized by loud instrumentals and vocals that emphasize oppression, toughness, and rebellion.

The Japanese skinhead movement is relatively small, but nevertheless of much concern to Japanese adults, the government, and law enforcement. As the subculture, or counterculture, gains popularity, youthful crime rates in Japan climb proportionately—a mark of "Westernization" that most Japanese citizens would just as soon did not take place.

Why do countercultures often recruit their members from the youth subculture? How has "Westernization" affected Japanese youths? Are there some positive as well as negative influences? If so, what are they?

Sources

Comsia, A. J. 2003. Skins, Punks, and Other Japanese I Know. *Japan Ink: An Online Journal of Japanese Studies*. http://www.earlham.edu/~japanink/japanink_skins+punks.html.

Freire, Dan. 2003. Japanese Skinheads: The Meaning of a Subculture. www.clas.ufl.edu/users/murphy7312/JPT3500file/JPT.Projectfile/Jpt/Skinhead.html

http://www.youthlink.jp/youth

Kawamura, Y. 2008. Understanding Japanese youth subcultures through fashion: 1995–2006. *Current Perspectives on Fashion and Textiles*. http://www.hio.no/content/view/full/57358.

Kersten, J. 1993. Street youths, *Bosozaku* and *Yakuza:* Subculture formation and societal reactions in Japan. *Crime and Delinquency*, 39 (July):277–295.

A youth subculture is not unique to U.S. society (as Box 11.1 indicates), but certain characteristics of our culture seem to be particularly linked to the formation and perpetuation of such a subculture (Lesko, 2000). James VanderZanden (1986:38) indicated that Western societies have "postponed the entrance of their adolescents into adulthood . . . [and] have spawned conditions favorable to the development of unique cultural patterns among their youth." James Coleman (1960:337) suggested this same analysis: "Industrial society has spawned a peculiar phenomenon, most evident in America but emerging also in other Western societies: adolescent subcultures, with values and activities quite distinct from those of the adult society—subcultures whose members have most of their important associations within and few with adult society."

ROLE OF THE YOUTH SUBCULTURE

Social and behavioral scientists who support the idea that a distinctive youth subculture exists in the United States are *not* suggesting that U.S. youths constitute a delinquent subculture. Rather, they argue that youths, especially teenagers, experience social conditions that may alienate many of them from their parents' generation and many of their parents' traditional social values. This feeling of alienation can be manifested in a variety of ways, most of which would not be considered delinquent. We will look at some of the specific elements of the youth subculture which might contribute to some forms of delinquency. At this point, we turn our attention to the social situation of American youths and why they tend to experience alienation from the adult world and why that sense of alienation leads to the formation of a strong sense of identity and cohesion with other youths.

Erich Goode (2007:84–85) described a subculture as a group whose members:

1. interact with one another more frequently and more intimately than they do with members of other social categories;
2. [have a] way of life, and . . . beliefs [that] are somewhat different from members of other social categories; and
3. think of themselves as belonging to a specific group, and they are so defined by those who do not share this trait.

American youths fit this description. A subculture is not a primary group. Unlike the family, the youth subculture is not characterized by intimate face-to-face interaction. Although many ethnic, religious, social-class, and other subcultures often are reinforced by spatial proximity and direct interaction, the existence of a widespread youth subculture indicates that value sharing does not require direct contact or primary social interaction. Unlike some of the smaller street gangs and other juvenile groups (clubs, fraternities, sororities, etc.) which depend upon the interpersonal contact among members for transmission of values, norms, and social support, a subculture may be widely distributed geographically and without interpersonal contact. However, if a subculture is to perpetuate itself, there must be mechanisms for transmitting its values among members and from one generation to another. Our massive and technologically sophisticated communications network contributes the necessary cohesiveness among youths by affording instant awareness of news and issues relevant to young people, innovations in dress and language, and the rapid sharing of values and norms across the country (Bennett and Kahn-Harris, 2004).

Hans Sebald (1997) pointed out that there is not a uniform adolescent subculture, but a very diverse one. He established that important differences exist in youth peer cultures based upon socioeconomic status, age, race, ethnicity, and rural or urban residence. However, he contended that despite these differences, there is a sense of unity among virtually all teenagers. "They know they belong together and observe norms and values not necessarily consistent with the adult world's folkways and mores" (Sebald, 1997:204).

Why do subcultures form? What purposes does a youth subculture serve for adolescents? Sebald identified eight commonly-agreed-upon functions provided by subcultures in general and showed how these functions are specifically fulfilled by the youth subculture. According to Sebald (1997:208–209), subcultures provide:

1. ***Common Values and Norms.*** Typically, youth subcultural values are different from those of children and those of adults.
2. ***A Unique "Lingo."*** Youths speak an argot that is often only partially understood and approved by adults.
3. ***Distinct Forms of Mass Media.*** For example, certain movies, magazines, television programs, and music appeal primarily to the youth subculture.

4. ***Common Styles and Fads.*** This is especially evident in styles of dress, grooming, and makeup.
5. ***A Sense of Belonging.*** Thinking of and referring to one's peer group in terms of "we" instead of "they."
6. ***Unique or Distinctive Status Criteria.*** Adolescents tend to choose different standards for selecting leaders or earning prestige.
7. ***Social Support.*** Teenagers provide one another with a sense of understanding and support for behavior that may violate adult norms.
8. ***Gratification of Specific Needs.*** There are some basic needs of teenagers which larger society prohibits (e.g., sexual activity) and which are provided for in the youth subculture.

Identifying with a youth subculture alleviates some of the frustrations experienced by juveniles as a result of their marginal status in society. It also provides group support for norms and values that run counter to those of their parents, teachers, and other adults. Membership in the youth subculture also provides a sense of identity and belonging for juveniles (White and Wyn, 2008). Although today's teenagers may have less in common with each other than teenagers of some past generations, they still are very strongly peer-driven and the need to belong is considered crucial. The sense that other people are in the same situation as they and understand their problems serves as an important symbolic expression of a sense of belonging for American teenagers. Researchers who most strongly contend that there is a youth subculture tend to focus on three assumptions:

1. Adolescents suffer a certain amount of turmoil and stress due to their uncertain position in the social structure.
2. A teenage subculture develops as a social reaction to this uncertainty and it has a widespread and powerful pattern among American adolescents.
3. The adolescent subculture provides a sense of security during the period of adolescent discontinuity. (Sebald, 1997:199–201)

Consequently, the formation of a youth subculture serves as an important frame of reference for teenagers to enhance personal and social identity and give meaning to their lives. Again, the marginal status of juveniles in U.S. society plays an important role in assigning importance to the youth subculture. Very few meaningful social roles are provided for adolescents in the adult world.

DISTINCTIVE ELEMENTS OF THE YOUTH SUBCULTURE

The persistent conflict between adult and juvenile values contributes to the ongoing phenomenon of the youth subculture. Theodore Roszak (1969:1) proclaimed, "The struggle of the generations is one of the obvious constants of human affairs." This struggle takes place in a variety of arenas. We have already discussed the schools (Chapter 10). Part Four of this book looks at other public arenas in which the confrontation between adults and youths is manifested (the streets and courts). Here, we identify some of the elements of the youth subculture which distinguish it from the larger society and set the stage for potential confrontation with adults. Juveniles differentiate themselves from adults in a multitude of ways, but that differentiation is most clear-cut in regard to values.

Youth Values

Values are *beliefs and ideas that are held in high esteem by a particular group*. There is great diversity within the juvenile subculture reflective of the pluralism found in the larger society. Variables such as race, age, sex, socioeconomic status, and even geographical location impact upon youth values as they do upon those of adults. There are, however, some consistent areas in which adults and juveniles differ in their value judgments. Two of the most notable are in regard to attitudes toward sex and drugs.

A large amount of research has been conducted on teenagers' attitudes and behaviors related to premarital sex and the use of drugs. Since both of these activities are illegal for juveniles, they are explored in some detail in the next section of this chapter, which relates the juvenile subculture to the problem of juvenile delinquency. In this section, we confine our treatment of youth values to a brief discussion of some of the values of young people which differ from those of adults and which may contribute to the cleavage between the generations.

The contention that youths adhere to a particular set of social values that are different from those of most adults is not to imply that there are no similarities in the value systems of youths and their parents. After all, children are first socialized within the context of their family and learn their first values from their parents and older siblings. Consequently, most youths, especially those with middle-class parents, are socialized to the dominant values of society (Adler and Adler, 2002). Cultural pluralism notwithstanding, most teenagers understand the norms of larger society and feel a sense of guilt when they violate them (Sykes and Matza, 1957). How, then, do the values of the youth subculture come into conflict with those of their parents and other adults? It has been suggested that the differentiation of youth values is largely symbolic and resides not so much in conflicting ideology, as in conflicting lifestyle.

In an earlier chapter, we discussed sociological theories that contended that a great deal of delinquency can be attributed to the existence of delinquent subcultures (e.g., Cohen, 1955; Miller, 1958). These theorists contended that delinquent subcultures tend to be comprised of lower-class youths who take dominant middle-class norms and turn them "upside down" (Cohen, 1955). While there is debate over the general explanatory power of these subcultural theories, they may provide insight into the basic value system of U.S. teenagers. Gary Schwartz and Don Merten (1967) suggested that the major subcultural elements of adolescent social life are in the symbolic aspects of their values, beliefs, and standards. "The distinctiveness of the youth subculture is not necessarily that their norms and values are fundamentally at odds with the adult world, but that their evaluative system which provides cultural meaning for their life is vastly different" (Schwartz and Merten, 1967:453).

In other words, many of the distinctive values of the youth subculture are not all that different from the values they were taught by their parents. Rather, the difference resides in the ways that teenagers express those values in their behavior. For instance, Talcott Parsons (1942) used the automobile as an example in which youths take basic social values and reinterpret them in a way that is socially meaningful to them, but leads to behavior that is at odds with the norms prescribed by adults. By the 1930s, the automobile had become a basic part of U.S. culture. Virtually every family owned one, and adults highly valued the automobile for its utilitarian purpose—transportation. American youths also highly valued the automobile, but for very different purposes. The automobile, approved and sanctioned by adults for transportation, was used by juveniles for entertainment, drag racing, and other activities frowned upon by adults (Parsons, 1942). By the 1960s, the automobile had taken on even more importance for teenagers, becoming, perhaps, the most important symbol of the youth subculture, providing prestige, a place for dating and sexual activities, and a hobby for many teenage boys (Best, 2006; Sebald, 1997).

There are several other basic social values that parents teach their children that the youth subculture expresses in ways that may lead to conflicts with parents, teachers, law enforcement officials, and other adults. For example, *independence* is a basic value in American society. Liberty, freedom, and independence are concepts taught to children from birth. However, when teenagers assert their independence, they often meet with disapproval from adults. Adults usually conceive of independence, freedom, and liberty in a more nationalistic and abstract sense. When juveniles speak of independence, freedom, and liberty, they typically mean freedom from parents, school, and other adult authority figures and rules. Thus, it is not the value which conflicts with adult society, but the behaviors chosen for expressing it which lead to youths being viewed as deviant.

Another basic middle-class American value is *conformity*. While parents encourage individuality, they insist that it be tempered with the ability to get along with others, to be part of an accepted group, and to conform to normative expectations. Evidence suggests that juveniles value conformity as much as their parents, and perhaps even more. Again, the problem does not lie in internalizing the value, but in exhibiting it in behavior. In fact, the youth subculture is probably a result of the strong desire on the part of young people to conform with one another.

A multitude of studies indicate that one of the strongest motivations for behavior among juveniles is their desire to gain and maintain acceptance with their peers (e.g., Clasen and Brown, 1985; Schwendinger and Schwendinger, 1985; Sebald, 1997; Smith, 1962; White and Wyn, 2008). Gerald Pearson (1958:88) stated, "A fundamental evidence of the existence of youth culture is the compulsive conformity required of its members." Smith (1962:9) explored the phenomenon of the **clique**, *a small primary group within the youth subculture*, and indicated that the clique "sets norms that are often the highest authority for its members and may take precedence over both family and other adult norms." Schwendinger and Schwendinger (1985:106–107) described various youth cliques such as "greasers," "jocks," "surfers," "squares," "intellectuals," and "nerds" and pointed out that whatever the particular clique membership, all were characterized by extreme peer pressure to conform to a particular set of attitudes, values, beliefs, and behaviors. Americans were shocked by a video released in May 2003 that showed graduating senior girls at a middle-class suburban Chicago high school dousing junior girls with spoiled food and feces. As a part of this initiation ritual, "some girls were beaten and kicked, leading to the filing of criminal charges and civil lawsuits." Today, MySpace, Facebook, and YouTube are filled with examples of hazing rituals and other examples of pressure on youths to gain their peers' acceptance.

The peer pressure to conform provides a strong sense of esprit de corps and social identity for juveniles. Thomas Cosner and Gerald Larson (1980) contended that the youth subculture is a reaction to the increased demands of the larger society for juveniles to conform while mediating much of the tension and rebellion experienced as a result of their status. This need to conform to and identify with the youth subculture hinges on adherence to its values. Bennett Berger (1963) contended that the youth subculture is not merely a function of one's chronological age. Rather, it is a distinctive set of attitudes, values, beliefs, and behaviors which focus on hedonism, irresponsibility, and expressiveness. Support for the notion that the youth subculture is not totally based on age may be seen in a quote from 1960s "Yippie" leader Jerry Rubin, who, in his forties, declared, "We ain't never, never gonna grow up . . . we're gonna be adolescents forever!" (*Time*, 1986:24). The hedonism and irresponsibility on the part of middle-class youths in the United States has received widespread attention in the sociological literature on the youth subculture. Lamar Empey (1982:202) summarized some of the research on youth subcultures by pointing out that while there are questions as to the "uniqueness of adolescent subculture, most theorists suggest that it helps to produce an adolescent world of hedonism and irresponsibility, and the more adolescents are involved in it, the more likely they are to be delinquent."

In summary of youth subculture values, Sebald (1997) proposed that American young people are socialized to some basic cultural values which contradict each other. He described some of the "dichotomous values with which juveniles must come to grips" as including *competition* versus *cooperation*; *work* versus *leisure*; *piety* versus *freethinking*; *individualism* versus *conformity*; and *sexuality* versus *chastity* (Sebald, 1997:145–150). It may well be that identity with a youth subculture provides a temporary social frame of reference for teenagers within which to handle these value discrepancies. Hence, a feeling of group support allows juveniles to validate their behaviors based upon their interpretation of appropriate values and behaviors.

Tattoos

Tattoos have become a widespread symbol of the youth subculture (Kosut, 2006). Once primarily the trademarks of sailors, prostitutes, motorcycle gangs, prison inmates, and other social outcasts, tattoos have become a symbolic mainstay of today's youth subculture, and tattoo parlors can be found on small-town squares and in middle-class urban and suburban shopping malls. It is estimated that somewhere between 12 million and 20 million Americans, almost one-fourth of all those between ages 18 and 50, have tattoos, and for generation X, tattoos are what identity bracelets were for their Baby Boomer parents' generation.

Although tattoos often symbolize rebellion on the part of youths, since many states have laws that people under the age of 18 must have parental permission to get a tattoo, they have become such a widely accepted part of the youth subculture that they are now being sported by class presidents, valedictorians, athletes, cheerleaders, and chess-club members. Teenaged girls tend to get designs on the lower parts of their backs just above the buttocks and on their ankles, while boys go for the more traditional tattoos on biceps, forearms, and backs. Almost all school districts ban students from having visible tattoos, so students have become adept at getting tattoos strategically placed on their bodies so that they only show when they want them to be seen. Many youths sport more than one tattoo, leading one researcher to declare that "tattoos are like potato chips. . . . you can't have just one" (Vail, 1999:253). Other researchers illustrate how middle-class adults and their children have used a number of legitimation techniques to redefine tattoos to fit within their conventional values and

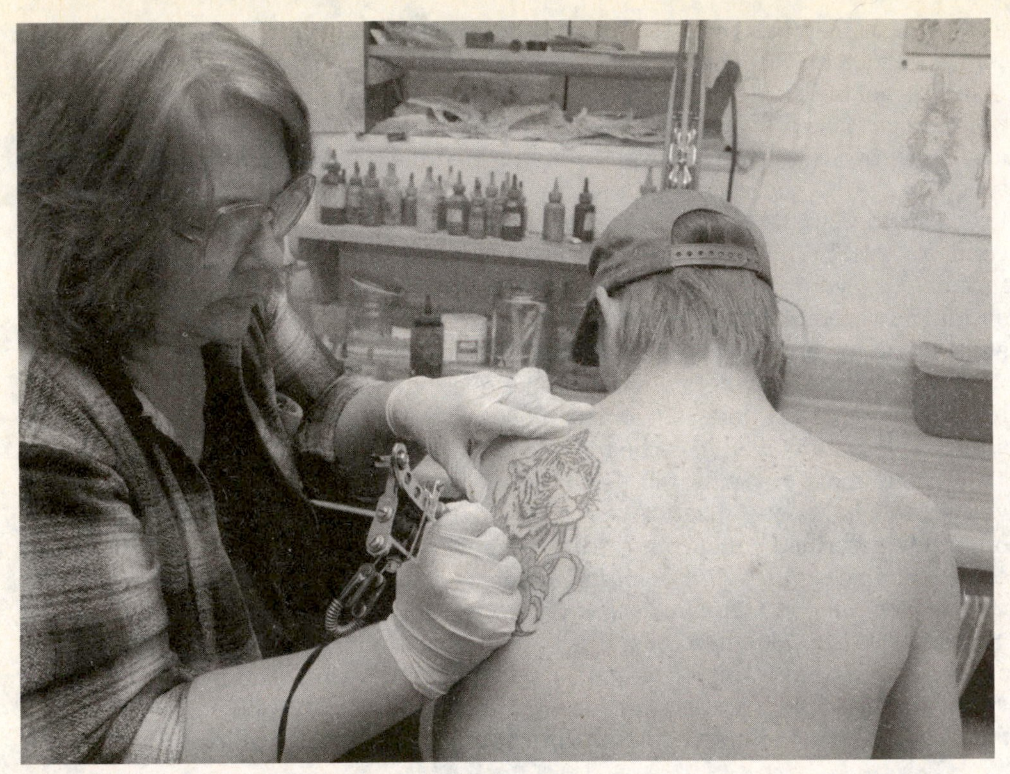

Tattoos have become important symbols in the youth subculture. Do they reflect deviance or conformity, or both? At what age should youths be allowed to legally get tattoos? Should it be considered delinquency if they get one before that age? If so, what should be the consequences?

norms, some simply for artistic purposes, while others have important social, political, and religious meanings (Atkinson and Young, 2008; Bridges, 2006; DeMello, 2000; Irwin, 2001; 2002; Kosut, 2006; Parker, 2003; Sullivan, 2001).

Despite tattoos becoming more commonplace even among middle-class adult culture, many youths who were tattooed in their late teens and early twenties marry and start their careers and then regret their "badges of rebellion" and seek to have them removed—a process that is far more painful and expensive than getting the tattoo in the first place (Marin, et al., 1995). Unlike many other aspects of the youth subculture (e.g., hair and clothing styles), tattoos serve as a more permanent reminder of youthful fads and what may have been poor judgment.

Dress, Grooming, and Fads

Some of the ways teenagers express their identity within a youth subculture can be found in their norms regarding dress, grooming, and various fads. VanderZanden (1986:38) indicated that the "unique cultural patterns among youth . . . find expression in fads having to do with musical recordings, entertainment idols, and dance steps, personal adornment and hair styles." The distinctive and often faddish dress of teenagers sets them apart from their adult counterparts. It simultaneously unifies members of the youth subculture while distinguishing them from the larger culture (Coker, 1993; Richards, 1988). Dress, grooming, and personal appearance become the most important vehicles by which juveniles can symbolize their status.

England (1967) indicated that after World War II, a large market of goods emerged aimed primarily at the youth culture in the United States. Adherence to the normative expectations of youths regarding dress and other material possessions (cars, athletic equipment, stereos, cosmetics, etc.) demands access to a certain amount of money. Nancy Needham (1986:16) estimated that Americans under the age of 18 spent more than $70 billion annually on everything from breakfast cereal to name brand clothing. The importance to conform to peer expectations regarding these items has not diminished. According to research conducted by Harris Interactive, Americans between ages 8 and 21 (approximately 57 million youths) spend roughly $172 billion annually with about 15 percent of that spending taking place online (Greenspan, 2003). Consequently, many parents have been confronted by a teenager demanding the purchase of a particular brand of athletic shoe, MP3 player, or some similar gadget, when a much less expensive brand would have been equally functional. Teenagers are bewildered by their parents' failure to understand that one item is "in" and another is definitely "out." This failure to recognize such a widely known and accepted "fact" only serves to underscore the so-called generation gap.

Juvenile hairstyles also accentuate the existence of a youth subculture and broaden the gap between parents and teenagers. James McAlexander and John Schonten (1989) contended that hair, more than any single body feature, is a central part of a person's identity. Further, they suggested that in a society lacking puberty rites, such as the United States, hairstyles may serve as a symbol of transition from childhood to adolescence and from adolescence to young adulthood. It seems almost axiomatic that when adults are wearing their hair short, teens will be wearing theirs long, and vice versa. In the mid-1960s, the Beatles launched a revolution in hairstyles for teenage boys. Crew cuts disappeared, and the "Beatle cut" swept across the United States much to the chagrin of parents, teachers, and other adults. Many schools passed dress and hair codes (it was at about the same time that the miniskirt became the style for teenaged girls) and the battle of generational values once again surfaced. Eventually, adults became more tolerant of the longer hair; ultimately, not only were teen rock stars wearing their hair longer, but so were middle-aged crooners, country and Western singers, and talk-show hosts. When lawyers, doctors, teachers, and "good ol' dad" followed suit, it was inevitable that the teenagers of America would make the move back to shorter hair. By 1990, "flat tops," "buzzes," "spikes," and other shorter (but deviant) hairstyles dominated the youth culture. One juvenile judge in Houston, Texas, believes that hair style is such an important part of a juvenile's identity that he offers to cut delinquents' sentences if they will agree to cut their hair in a more "mainstream" style (AP, Houston, 1993). Teen hairstyles also often create confrontations with school officials that may translate into delinquency (Anderson, 2008).

While styles of dress, grooming, and cosmetics vary by race, social class, ethnicity, and other social and demographic factors, juveniles seem to have much more in common with each other than they do with their parents or other adults (Lesko, 2000;

Sebald, 1997; Wein, 1970). As mentioned earlier, the youth subculture is not a small primary group within which all members interact directly with one another. Consequently, the youth subculture becomes dependent upon mass media to carry the message of current trends in style to teenagers across the country. This necessitates a communication network primarily aimed at adolescents to express and reinforce their particular values and norms. Those youths who feel the most committed to the youth subculture are most likely to express conformity to its norms.

Mass Media and Technology

Today's teenagers are no strangers to mass media and technology. Research shows that they spend only about 6 hours per week reading; whereas they spend almost 8 hours talking on the phone, 12 hours listening to music, almost 14 hours watching television, and not including e-mail, approximately 17 hours per week on the Internet (Greenspan, 2003).

What little reading teens do often does not include books. A perusal of any magazine rack indicates that this mass medium acknowledges the existence of a large youth subculture and makes every effort to cater to its tastes and styles. After World War II, a large number of magazines, books, records, movies, and television shows were aimed at the special interests of the huge youth market (England, 1967; Klein, 1990). Today, magazines such as *Teen*, *Teen Beat*, *Spin*, and *Rolling Stone* are aimed at youthful consumers and simultaneously dictate and reflect teenagers' preference in music. Likewise, *16*, *Seventeen*, *Glamour*, *Teen*, and other magazines cater to a juvenile audience, setting the pace for teen dress and hair styles. *Mad* magazine still satirizes adult life and appeals to the sense of humor of junior–high- and high-school students. All of those magazines, and a variety of others, influence and reinforce values of U.S. youth.

Television program producers, writers, directors, and commercial advertisers also recognize the large teen market and cater to its particular tastes and values. Numerous television programs are aimed at teenagers, using popular teenaged stars and models. Market researchers indicate that teenagers spend almost $200 billion annually, so advertisers aggressively stalk the youth market through all possible avenues. Frances Lawrence and associates (1986:434) found that adolescents on average watched 147 minutes of television daily—approximately 17¼ hours every week. Lawrence discovered that many of the attitudes, values, and beliefs of adolescents, especially regarding standards of dress and personal conduct, were formed by television. By the mid-1980s, cable television offered 24 hours every day of rock videos and music programming aimed specifically at the American youth market, and today, these programs are among the most popular with youths in the United States and around the world.

Since the late 1950s, rock music has become one of the most important symbols uniting the youth subculture in America (Kaiser, 1988). It has served as one of the most distinctive ways that youths express their values and rebellion against adult traditions and norms. Adults have always expressed concern over the lyrics and rhythms of popular teen music, and the rap music of the late 1980s and 1990s created such a furor that steps were taken to ban it in several states and at least label it as offensive in others (Lynxwiler and Gay, 2000) (see Box 11.2). A major study indicating that violent lyrics

BOX 11.2

CONTROVERSIAL ISSUE: Censoring Rock Music

Censoring Rock Music

Few things demonstrate the gap between generations more than preferences in music. In the 1940s, many concerned parents forbade their daughters to listen to "crooners" such as Perry Como and Frank Sinatra for fear that they would become so caught up in the romantic trance induced by the music that boys would take advantage of them. The 1950s launched rock 'n' roll and the driving beat and suggestive movements of the performers convinced many parents that the music would drive their teenagers into a sexual frenzy. Elvis Presley's first performance, especially his hip movements, on the *Ed Sullivan Show* was considered so suggestive that cameramen were instructed to show him only from the waist up. The 1960s spawned songs of protest against the Vietnam War and for civil rights, while the 1970s gave rise to "acid rock" and songs espousing free love and experimentation with drugs. The 1980s saw "heavy metal" reach its peak, and many adults were certain that it was connected with illicit drugs, satanic worship, adolescent suicide, and other evils. Popular bands and recording artists did little to dissuade parental fears as they used satanic symbols on their album covers, wore exotic makeup, performed with snakes and other animals, and covered their bodies with offensive tattoos. Each new trend in music popular with teenagers seemed more threatening than those preceding it, and in each decade, adults concerned about the negative impact of popular music on youths instigated movements to burn records, ban radio broadcasts, and censor certain musical artists and their performances.

The 1990s and dawn of the 21st century saw a renewed and more intense effort at censorship spawned by the popularity of rap music. Simply referred to by some as "filth" or "audio pornography" and by others as "attitude" filled with misogyny, anger, and hatred from the ghetto, rap music touched off a tidal wave of censorship efforts across the country. The governor of Florida banned performances by 2 Live Crew, one of the most popular and controversial rap bands, and several states followed suit by attempting to ban the sale of their album "As Nasty as They Wanna Be."

Other rap and heavy metal groups also generated much concern. Perhaps generating the most controversy has been hip-hop and the so-called gangsta rap. Ice-T's controversial song "Cop Killer" brought waves of protest from police organizations and the songs of N.W.A. (Niggaz With Attitude) and other rappers infuriated the public with their violent, sexist, and racist lyrics, and several radio stations refused to play their records. The pressing question is whether there is a relationship between violent rap songs and violence in the streets. One youngster convicted of murdering a police officer unsuccessfully used the defense that he was listening to the song "Cop Killer" and therefore should not be held accountable for the shooting. And critics of rap music point to the fact that life is imitating art far too often as a number of popular gangsta rappers have been indicted for violent crimes. Many of the rappers, however, insist that they are simply depicting life on the streets as they know it and that by shocking the white community with their songs, they may bring about desirable social change (Leland, 1993). As one youth confessed, "There's a lot of anger in my generation—you can hear it in the music" (Begley, 2000:55). One study concluded that listening to violent lyrics can lead to increased aggression (Anderson and Carnagey, 2003). Whatever its social impact, this form of urban music simultaneously frightens and attracts the American public and accounts for the sale of approximately 70 million albums per year (Vognar, 1998).

An Oklahoma legislator introduced a bill to put "warning labels" on objectionable records (Hinton, 1990), and an Arizona state senator introduced a "No ID, no LP" bill which would prohibit sales of recordings containing lyrics describing or advocating drug use, satanism, murder, or violence to anyone under the age of 18 (Burgess, 1990). At least 12 other states debated similar

(*Continued*)

legislation. Many of the legislators who favor labeling and censorship bills consider themselves fairly "hip" and admit that they resented earlier attempts to censor the popular rock-and-roll music that they enjoyed as teenagers. Viewing the new heavy metal and rap music as much more dangerous and threatening, however, they believe that their efforts are different.

Research conducted by Amy Binder (1993), however, suggests that attempts to censor heavy metal and rap music may reflect different motives. She analyzed the rhetoric in media accounts from 1985 to 1990 regarding the potential societal dangers of the two genres of music and found that although both focused on sex and defiance of authority, the racial compositions of the artists and audiences of the two brands of music primarily shape the way they are perceived. Binder argued that images and stereotypes of white youths greatly influenced the perceived dangers portrayed by the media as being associated with heavy metal music, whereas dangers associated with rap music were exaggerated by whites' fears of stereotypical portrayals of poor, angry, black youths.

Columnist Lewis Grizzard (1990:J-6) put these censorship efforts in perspective, pointing out that "nothing sells like controversy," and urged adults to take a different tack in fighting the offensive music—ignore it. He indicated that much of the music's attraction to teenagers was a result of the horror it generated for adults—their parents. Take away the controversy, he concluded, and the thrill will be gone and "your children will go back to dyeing their hair orange or whatever else they can think of to drive you crazy." Another journalist surmised that it is difficult to worry about song lyrics when our nation faces problems of domestic and international terrorism (Segal, 2002). Still another suggests that the widespread commercialization of the contemporary music scene may have done more to dilute its appeal to the youth subculture than previous efforts at repression and censorship (Moore, 2005).

Why do you think adults place so much emphasis on teen music? Should music be censored? What about other forms of media and technomedia—television, movies, the Internet?

Sources

Adler, Jerry and Jennifer Foote. 1990. The rap attitude, *Newsweek*, March 19:56–59.

Anderson, C. A. and N. L. Carnagey. 2003. Exposure to violent media: The effects of songs with violent lyrics on aggressive thoughts and feelings. *Journal of Personality and Social Psychology* 84 (5):960–971.

Begley, Sharon. 2000. A world of their own. *Newsweek*, May 8:53–56.

Binder, Amy. 1993. Constructing racial rhetoric: Media depictions of harm in heavy metal and rap music. *American Sociological Review* 58 (December):753–767.

Burgess, Mike. 1990. Arizona: 'No ID, no LP'. *Dallas Morning News*, March 25:43A.

Grizzard, Lewis. 1990. Parent–teenager dis-chord: Fighting dirty. *Dallas Times Herald*, March 25:J-6.

Hinton, Mick. 1990. Moore legislator seeking warning on records deemed objectionable. *Sunday Oklahoman*, February 24:1-A.

Leland, John. 1993. Criminal records: Gangsta rap and the culture of violence. *Newsweek*, November 29:60–64.

Lynxwiler, John, and David Gay. 2000. Moral boundaries and deviant music: Public attitudes toward heavy metal and rap. *Deviant Behavior* 21 (January–February):63–85.

Moore, Ryan. 2005. Alternative to what? Subcultural capital and the commercialization of a music scene. *Deviant Behavior* 26 (May–June): 229–252.

Segal, David. 2002. As rappers and rockers step up their assault, the censors retreat. *Sunday Oregonian*, July 7:F5.

Vognar, C. 1998. The rhyme and reason behind hip-hop's mainstream success. *Dallas Morning News*, September 6:J1–J5.

can lead to increased aggression in their listeners added fuel to the fire (Patterson, 2003b). In the early 21st century, rave, hip-hop, and gangsta rap represent much of what upsets adults about the youth subculture (Hug, 2006; Moore, 2005; Wilson, 2006).

Writers, producers, and directors of movies also have acknowledged the existence of a youth subculture and have attempted to capitalize on movies geared toward its values. Richard Corliss (1986) described some of the trends in youth-oriented movies over the past few decades. During the 1950s, the movies starring James Dean and Marlon Brando exemplified the rebellion of youth; the 1960s were dominated by beach party movies, and later by social protest films; the 1970s gave rise to teen "sexploitation" films such as the *Porky* series; and the 1980s witnessed what Corliss (1986) described as a revamp of the Andy Hardy movies—films characterized by kids struggling with values, drugs, sex, parents, and school. Corliss discussed the youthful stars such as Molly Ringwald, Anthony Michael Hall, Emilio Estevez, Judd Nelson, Andrew McCarthy, and Ally Sheedy, who became known as the "Brat Pack" by their young fans. The theme of youths struggling against parental authority also dominated many of the movies of the 1990s, and young stars like Drew Barrymore with on-screen and real-life struggles with drugs, sex, and other teenage and young-adult problems emerged as youthful role models. Jennifer Love Hewitt, Scott Wolf, and Sarah Michelle Gellar helped the youth subculture usher in the 21st century, when Mandy Moore, Jessica Alba, Scarlett Johansson, and a host of other young actors in their teens and twenties took over the reigns, only to give way to Miley Cyrus (aka Hannah Montana) and others.

No discussion of contemporary youth subculture would be complete without noting the influence of computers and the Internet. Families with children under the age of 18 are more likely to own computers than those without children, and preteens and teenagers use computers on a daily basis more than any other age group. Just under 90 percent of all school-aged children between the ages of 5 and 17 use computers daily, and Web sites such as MySpace and Facebook allow youths all over the world to chat with each other, exchange photos and personal information, and interact via the World Wide Web. YouTube has become one of the most popular sites for teens to post photos and videos—some of which depict them engaging in delinquent and criminal activities. In the 21st century, the Internet has become a powerful cyberforce, providing a forum for youths of all ages, races, and nationalities to share common values and experiences.

Language (Argot)

One of the most important ways that any subculture can symbolically distinguish itself from the larger culture is by adopting a unique language or jargon. American Old Order Amish speak German, Orthodox Jews speak Yiddish, and various ethnic groups adhere to the language of their homeland in urban subcultural enclaves like Chinatown and Little Italy.

Language also is a vehicle by which teenagers differentiate themselves from adults. According to some researchers, the most important symbolic element of the youth subculture is its distinctive language. Smith (1962:14) saw language as a means for teenagers to "exclude outsiders" and "intensify group identity." Yinger (1982:152–171) pointed out ways in which juveniles reverse language by using words to mean their exact opposite, such as using the word "bad" as a compliment to actually mean "good." For example, when one teenaged male tells another that his car is "really bad," he is paying him a high compliment.

One of the most thorough treatments of the distinctive language of the youth subculture can be found in Sebald's (1997) sociological analysis of adolescence. He contended that teens have created a unique **argot** (*specialized slang, or jargon*) to promote group cohesiveness and provide boundary maintenance. In the 21st century, youths continue to create their own forms of communication, especially when it comes to text-messaging and communicating on-line.

THE YOUTH SUBCULTURE AND JUVENILE DELINQUENCY

When people think of delinquents, listen to television news reports, or read newspaper headlines about delinquency, they are most likely to hear or read about rapes, robberies, murders, school shootings, and other violent offenses committed by youths. Youth crime is a major problem, and much of this book has focused on the typical street crime types of delinquency. Yet, the vast majority of youthful offenses are not serious violent crimes. Rather, a much larger proportion of juveniles who get into trouble with the law commit what would be considered misdemeanors if they were adults or not crimes at all (status offenses). Consequently, exploring the existence of a youth subculture which promotes values, attitudes, beliefs, and norms that often conflict with adult normative expectations may provide valuable insight into understanding status offenses and nonviolent crimes committed by youths.

Research dealing with the existence of a youth subculture consistently has linked it to middle-class delinquency, especially status offenses and nonviolent crimes (Shoemaker, 2005). It is unlikely that theoretical frameworks attempting to explain rape or murder are also going to explain the motivations for truancy, drug use, or premarital sex. The issue of truancy was addressed in Chapter 10; in this chapter, we provide a brief sociological analysis of juvenile runaways, prostitution, drug use, and premarital sexual behavior in relation to the youth subculture.

Juvenile Runaways

A vast literature has accumulated on the runaway phenomenon in the United States, and numerous theories have been postulated on why youths leave home and what can and should be done about it. Much of the research on running-away focuses upon home and family problems which place unusual stress upon the juvenile who finally decides to flee the home environment (e.g., Gullotta, 1979; Morgan, 1982; Roberts, 1981; Whitbeck and Simons, 1990), while others have examined the difference between **runaways**, *those who leave their home*, and **throwaways**, *those who are pushed out of their homes* (e.g., Adams, et al., 1985; Flowers, 2001).

Running away from home is a delinquent act. Each year approximately 100,000 juveniles are arrested for running away. Of course, not all runaways are arrested. Current estimates of runaways range from one-half million to 2 million (Flowers, 2001). Running away from home seems to increase during certain social, political, and economic conditions. Mona Wells and Harjit Sandhu (1986) pointed out that throughout U.S. history, periods of war and social upheaval have been accompanied by increased rates of running-away. Lipschutz (1977) also documented specific periods in history when there was an increased incidence of running-away. In the 20th century, the periods of the Great Depression (1930s), World War II (1940s), and the "Flower Child Era" (1960s) saw large waves of runaways in this country.

Wells and Sandhu (1986) concluded that the phenomenon of running away from home seems to result from a combination of "push–pull" factors such as problems at home and pressures of school combined with the allure of perceived freedom and independence. A counselor for runaways in Los Angeles summarized:

> Kids are not really running away . . . they are running to something they think is there which isn't there. They think it's just a groovy street scene . . . which of course, isn't true. There's nothing more revolting than the street scene, but they really don't know it. They think it's really an exciting thing. It's complete freedom, but they don't realize it's kind of hard to have freedom if you're out pan-handling for food. (Wein, 1970:201)

Jennifer James (1978; 1982) confirmed that many runaways are lured to the streets by the anticipation of excitement to be found there, but often become disillusioned with the life they find. While running-away is a delinquent act in itself, it is only one aspect of the problem which links running away from home to delinquency. As D. Kelly Weisberg (1985) indicated, many juvenile runaways wind up in jail or prison because they get involved in street crimes such as prostitution, drugs, theft, and violence. Drug usage has been found to be much higher among runaways (especially females) than other youths (Windle, 1989).

Many runaways were either abused or neglected by their parents (Kaufman and Widom, 1999). Once they leave home, runaways are vulnerable prey for pederasts, pimps, and others who spot them on the streets, show them some attention and apparent affection, and offer them a warm meal and a place to sleep. They become easy targets for prostitution (Flowers, 2001; Miller, 2006), child pornography (O'Brien, 1983), and other forms of victimization, especially violence and sexual abuse (Singer, 2006; Whitbeck and Simons, 1990). In *America's Runaways*, Christine Chapman (1976) discussed the problems that runaway youths face on the streets of major cities. These almost invariably include being taken advantage of by more "streetwise" adults. Tom Cox, of the Diggers Creative Society in Los Angeles (a group formed to help street youths), noted:

> A kid of fourteen can't cope with the streets. Even if they wanted to fool with the illegal part of it, they just can't manage it, they just can't make it. They are going to get busted, or they are going to get into some very bad situations where the people who are sheltering them have nothing to lose. In one case, there's a guy who collects fourteen-year-old boys and sends them out to earn money for him. (Cited in Wein, 1970:196)

Juvenile Prostitution

For both male and female juveniles on the streets, especially runaways, prostitution may become one of the few available routes to survival. Weisberg (1985:4) noted, "Since runaway episodes begin impulsively, the runaways seldom brought much money with them, and they frequently found themselves without resources for food and shelter. They might find shelter with strangers, but such as might well be conditioned on an exchange of services involving drug dealing or prostitution."

Frances Newman and Paula Caplan (1981) verified that a significant number of teenage prostitutes were runaways. Similarly, Patricia Hersch (1988:31) pointed out that "wherever we turn, teenagers are being used for sexual recreation by men—lots of men." Estimates are that two out of three teenaged prostitutes are runaways (Flowers, 2001). Each year, a little over a thousand people under age 18 are arrested for prostitution, and certainly that figure represents only the tip of the iceberg. Conservative estimates of the number of prostitutes under age 18 on the street range from 100,000 to 300,000 (Flowers, 2001; Miller, 2006).

When young girls run away from home, they make easy victims for pimps who prey on their vulnerability. Some of the juvenile prostitutes on the streets appear to have voluntarily entered into prostitution. James (1978) found that some female juvenile prostitutes were from affluent backgrounds but were attracted to street prostitution for the thrill and adventure of it. Many runaway youths conclude that prostitution means "easy money," even if not desirable. Many of Weisberg's (1985:57) subjects stressed that prostitution meant easy money, "with 'easy' referring to the short duration of the sexual encounter as well as the lack of difficulty in performing such employment." Some of the juvenile prostitutes indicated that they like "the absence of fixed working hours, leaving them to 'do their own thing'" (Weisberg, 1985:57).

The so-called voluntary nature of such prostitution may be nothing more than rationalization for the norm-violating behavior in which the youth is participating. For as Shirley O'Brien (1983:69) pointed out, "It is easy for children desperately in need to turn to pornography and prostitution to support themselves." And Weisberg (1985:78–79) concluded that runaways were most likely to fit into the category of "situational prostitutes" (temporarily entering into prostitution due to specific social and economic circumstances) as opposed to "vocational prostitutes" (entering into prostitution as a career). As O'Brien (1983:69) summarized, "Runaways who have been neglected and abused to a point that their home situation was more troublesome than whatever might be 'out there,' rationalize that food and shelter provided in exchange for sexual favors is better than living in an impossible home environment." Unfortunately, youths who were abused and neglected at home are also very likely to be abused and neglected on the streets and they often get arrested for a variety of street-related crimes (Flowers, 2001; Kaufman and Widom, 1999).

Juvenile prostitution (like adult prostitution) is not a form of deviance solely for females. Runaway boys are also quite vulnerable on the streets and often succumb to prostitution because they see it as a viable means of survival. Research by Calhoun and Weaver (1996), for example, indicates that many male runaways view prostitution as a "rational choice," after weighing the perceived benefits of financial gain, sexual pleasure, and control of work schedule against the potential liabilities of getting arrested, possibility of violence, sex with undesirable people, and the possibility of not getting paid for their services. Few if any of the young male prostitutes mentioned the fear of contracting AIDS as part of their mental equation when assessing the potential benefits and liabilities of street prostitution. Robin Lloyd (1976:211) estimated that there were approximately 300,000 male prostitutes under the age of 16 in the United States. Prostitution becomes an integral part of life on the streets for juvenile males (Hersch, 1988; Weisberg, 1985). Young males who run away from home find life on the streets extremely difficult and may find themselves exploited by adults for purposes of child pornography (O'Brien, 1983) and prostitution (Farley, 2004; James, 1982; Wein, 1970; Weisberg, 1985). The Tenderloin district of San Francisco attracts numerous runaways, and many young males congregate in that area as prostitutes. The area along Market Street from Mason to Tyler streets has become so well known for having male juvenile prostitutes that it is referred to as the "Meat Rack" (Weisberg, 1985:20).

Young male prostitutes, like females, may enter into prostitution for a variety of reasons. James (1982) found that the largest percentage of adolescent male prostitutes entered the trade out of economic necessity. Hersch (1988) estimated that male juvenile prostitutes often made $75 to $100 per night. On the other hand, an earlier study by Albert J. Reiss (1961) revealed that some male juvenile prostitution was primarily a form of "street hustle" highly supported among delinquent peers. Reiss described a situation in which delinquent males would hang around on the streets posing as prostitutes. When approached by older males, they would agree to engage in fellatio for a price. The boys viewed the older male's behavior as homosexual, while rationalizing that their own participation in the act was simply a form of sexual release for which they were paid. Sometimes, after the act, they would even beat the older male to signify their own revulsion at homosexuality. This type of behavior was viewed as very "macho" by the delinquent boys and never viewed as being a homosexual (Reiss, 1961). Similar activities occur in urban areas where "tough" local teenagers cruise the gay areas, participating in "fag bashing" or "rolling queers" for money. Sometimes, these juveniles sell sexual favors to the homosexuals before beating them.

Juveniles and Drugs

In September 1986, President Ronald Reagan, with wife Nancy alongside, appeared on national network television to "declare war" on drug use in the United States. A series of drug-related deaths of famous athletes and other celebrities, together with network news coverage of widespread drug smuggling and dealing in the United States, stirred public sentiment to be ready to "take up arms" in that war. Later, the first President Bush vowed to step up the war against drugs and sent American troops into Panama to capture drug kingpin Manuel Noriega. By 1990, drugs were viewed as America's most serious social problem, especially for youths. Every subsequent president has vowed to continue the "war on drugs."

Drug use is not new in the United States. James Inciardi (1986; 2004) traced opium use back to the 18th century. Later, opium, morphine, and even heroin were openly used for their medicinal values (Inciardi, 1986). The Harrison Act of 1914 regulated most addictive narcotics, and together with the Supreme Court decisions of *Webb* v. *U.S.*, *U.S.* v. *Behrman*, and *Lindner* v. *U.S.*, it became almost impossible for the estimated 200,000 narcotics users to legally obtain their drugs (Inciardi, 1986:15). Illegal drug markets and dealers emerged, and the nation had a drug problem.

For the most part, drug use was perceived as being associated with lower-class urban ghettos and adult derelicts. By the 1950s, it became linked with juveniles, but was viewed as an aspect of youthful rebellion, and was thought to be most associated with lower-class ghetto youths and juvenile gangs (Inciardi, 1986; 2004).

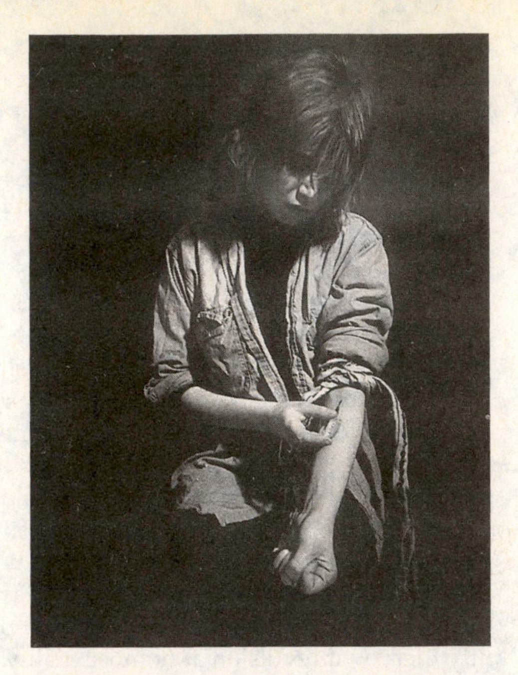

What role do illegal drugs play in the youth subculture? What does society do about the increasing abuse of legal drugs among teens?

In the 1960s and early 1970s, drug use within the youth subculture came to national attention. Harvard professor Timothy Leary openly advocated LSD use, and the so-called hippie movement preached free love and drugs as mind-expanding experiences. Drugs were linked to the youth subculture as one of the means by which juveniles could express their rebellion against the adult world (Smith, 1962; Sebald, 1997; Roszak, 1969; Wein, 1970). Marijuana appeared to be the drug of choice of the youth subculture, and popular motion pictures such as *Easy Rider* depicted youth cult heroes using drugs the way children might nibble on cookies.

The decade of the 1970s saw the drug-related deaths of rock stars Jimi Hendrix and Janis Joplin. Their music was considered wild by most parents and even some teens. Later, during that same decade, however, Elvis Presley, the King of Rock 'n' Roll, died, and a subsequent investigation indicated possible drug involvement. The 1980s saw numerous drug-related deaths of famous celebrities, many of whom had mass appeal among America's teenagers. John Belushi of *Saturday Night Live* and movie fame died of an overdose. Two very celebrated cases involved the airplane crash of Ricky Nelson (could the son of *Ozzie and Harriet* have been on drugs as news accounts alleged?) and the cocaine overdose of University of Maryland's All-American basketball star Len Bias just two days after he signed a lucrative contract with the Boston Celtics. Public awareness of a drug problem mushroomed; virtually everybody wondered just how widespread the problem was, especially among the nation's young people. The drug-related death of teen idol River Phoenix in 1993 fanned the flames of concern, as did the death of *Saturday Night Live*'s Chris Farley in 1998, and Heath Ledger's drug overdose in 2008.

Approximately 120,000 youths under the age of 18 are arrested for illegal drug usage each year (FBI, 2008), but this too is considered to represent only a fraction of the illegal drug usage among juveniles. For example, Coryl Jones and

Catherine Bell-Bolek (1986:5) cited a study indicating that 61 percent of students surveyed reported trying an illegal drug at some time, and 40 percent had used a drug other than marijuana. Evan Thomas (1986:64) cited a similar study indicating that at the time the survey was taken, 25.7 percent of the high school seniors surveyed had used marijuana within the preceding 30 days. Cocaine had been tried by 17 percent of the students surveyed in 1985 as compared to 10 percent in 1976 (Jones and Bell-Bolek, 1986:6). While some studies suggest that overall drug use declined during the 1980s (Greenwood, 1992), usage of lethal drugs such as "crack" and "ice" made inroads into the nation's high schools at an alarming rate (Gelman, 1990). A 2005 study revealed that 37 percent of youths had smoked marijuana, and about 9 percent had tried crack, cocaine, or ecstasy (McShane, 2005). In their analysis of the widespread drug use among juveniles, Jones and Bell-Bolek (1986) contended that it was a social event in most cases. They suggested that drug abuse was "a function of the adolescent's social interaction and experimentation with lifestyle" (Jones and Bell-Bolek, 1986:7). Similarly, Glassner and Loughlin (1987) pointed out that adolescent drug use almost always occurs in a social context, and while *peer pressure* may be too strong a term, certainly "peer interaction" is one of the most important influences. Other studies also found drug use among juveniles to be social in nature and cited peer influence as the most important factor (Brownfield, 1990; Kandel, 1985; McGee, 1992; Monti et al., 2005). Delbert Elliott and associates (1985) further underscored the influence of peers. They integrated Strain, Social Control, and Social Learning theories into a synthesized perspective to account for delinquency and drug use. They postulated that "involvement with and commitment to delinquent peers is the most proximate cause of delinquency and drug use and mediates the influence of weak bonding to parents, school, and conventional norms" (Elliott, et al., 1985:85).

Part of the allure of drugs for youths may be tied to their parents' abhorrence of them. Glassner and Loughlin (1987:1) succinctly pointed out that adolescent drug use scares adults. Evan Thomas (1986:65) indicated that "in the age of youth rebellion, the fact that parents were shocked by drugs was all the more reason for children to take them," and studies indicated that certain types of drug use became more widespread and socially accepted among juveniles (Beschner and Friedman, 1986). The existence of a youth subculture in which value is placed on breaking away from parents may be influential in drug acceptance. Jones and Bell-Bolek (1986:7) stated: "Even the identification of drug taking as a severe risk provides a fascination for the risktaking adolescent. For some adolescents, risk is not a deterrent, but a challenge."

On the brighter side, studies suggest that fewer teens view illegal drug usage as "cool," and government reports show that teen use of alcohol, tobacco, and illegal drugs actually decreased from 1998 to 1999 and again in 2001, 2002, and 2007 (AP, Chicago, 2003; AP, Washington, 1999a; Butterfield, 2002; *New York Times* News Service, 1999; Wire Reports, 2007a). Unfortunately, this good news was accompanied by reports that perhaps 3 million teens suffer from depression (Wingert and Kantrowitz, 2002), and that prescription drug use among people under age 18 reached an all-time high in 2002 (AP, New York, 2002). In 2005, for the first time, studies showed that more youths had abused prescription drugs, especially pain killers, than ecstasy, cocaine, crack, or LSD (McShane, 2005). Prescription drugs are the drug of choice for 12- and 13-year-olds (SAMHSA, 2008). Prescription drug abuse among teens became so popular that the youth subculture coined the term *pharming parties* to describe parties where teens take prescription pain relievers, antidepressants, diet pills, and other prescription drugs to get high instead of drinking alcohol (Doup, 2006).

Juvenile drug use is illegal; hence it constitutes delinquency. Even the use of drugs that are legal for adults, such as alcohol and nicotine (cigarettes) are deemed inappropriate for youths. The 1990s witnessed renewed interest in smoking and the use of tobacco products among teenagers—with boys tending to use the "smokeless" tobacco and girls smoking cigarettes and even cigars, but by 2005, teen smoking was on the decrease with use of alcohol and pain-killers increasing (AP, Washington, 2005a). Alcohol use has become normative among teenagers and by the upper grades in high school almost all have tried it, with many using it regularly (Gelman, 1990). Studies show that smoking, drinking, and some types of illegal drug usage are increasing among the nation's youth—especially among teen-aged girls (AP, Washington, 1998a,b; Griffin, 1999). Moreover, the use of alcohol, tobacco, and marijuana either singly or in some combination are all significantly related to each other and both minor and violent forms of delinquency (Dembo, et al., 1992; Elliott and Morse, 1989; Watts and Wright, 1990). Alcohol use is related to violence for both males and females (Bachman and Peralta, 2002). Research shows that the younger an adolescent is at the onset of drug usage, the more likely he or she is to continue to use them—especially if they associate with peers who use drugs (Zhang, et al., 1997). A juvenile subculture that encourages and/or promotes violation of parental norms is likely to accentuate drug taking and related forms of delinquency among its members.

Juveniles and Sex

Perhaps no subject sparks more interest among juveniles and provokes more fear among parents than premarital sexual activity. Smith (1962:5) suggested, "Probably the most important area within which adult norms attempt to dominate youth behavior is that of sex . . ." On the other hand, he contended that the youth culture often dominates adolescent behavior "particularly in relation to sex activities" (Smith, 1962:7). In a treatise on the youth subculture of the 1920s, Paula Fass (1977) discussed sex mores of the period and indicated that peer influence and conformity to peer culture were the most important guidelines youths considered in regard to sexual behavior. In her book *Barriers Between Women*, Caplan (1981) found that it was in the area of sexuality that mother–daughter relationships were most conflictual, but a 2002 study found that girls who were close to their mothers delayed sex (AP, Washington, 2002).

All sexual activities are illegal for juveniles. Since juvenile statutes prohibit premarital sexual behavior for both males and females, one of the status offenses for which juveniles can be adjudicated delinquent is that of promiscuity. Under Arizona law, for example, if a youth is under the age of 15, anything more amorous than kissing is a serious violation of the law and social workers, teachers, parents, or any other adults who are told of petting activities are legally required to report them to the police (Reuters, 1990). American society exhibits a double standard, however, more vigorously enforcing virtue among teenaged girls than boys. When four high school cheerleaders in the small town of Hempstead, Texas, were kicked off the cheerleading squad, one of their parents pointed out that the girls had not gotten pregnant by themselves, yet no boys were being punished in a similar fashion (AP, Hempstead, TX, 1993). Official data indicate that females are more likely to be brought to court for committing sex offenses than males (Chesney-Lind and Sheldon, 2004) but either sex can be petitioned to court for being sexually active. Adolescents must somehow balance the biological and physiological changes that are turning them into sexually potent young men and women against the traditional values of their parents which discourage adolescent sexuality and the laws of the state which make it illegal. Research suggests that the scales are not very well balanced.

A *Newsweek* poll in the year 2000 showed that about 47 percent of teens reported they had engaged in sexual intercourse prompting some researchers to refer to the 1990s as a "new sexual revolution" (Treas, 2002). Many teens report that their first sexual experience is in their own homes, often with their parents in the house (Browning, et al., 2005; Johnson and Thomas, 2002). Researcher Su Yates commented, "For many kids, you're considered out of it if you're not having sex—it's a rite of passage" (Sherman, 1986:199). The values of many youths toward premarital sexual activity differ from what most parental norms allow. Wein (1970:11) interviewed street youths in New York City and Los Angeles and concluded "Most kids seem to find the *idea* of premarital intercourse quite acceptable" [italics in the original]. Other studies suggest that the youth culture approves of more than just the idea. Elizabeth Stark (1986:28) found that among 15- to 17-year-olds, "almost half of the boys and a third of the girls were sexually active." In a study of college students, Carol Darling and J. Kenneth Davidson (1986) found that 84 percent of the females and 99 percent of the males had experienced sexual intercourse before marriage. They indicated that there was a "major increase over the past 15 years in the numbers of adolescent males and females engaging in heterosexual intercourse" (Darling and Davidson, 1986:403). Stark (1986:28) stated that "teenagers are becoming sexually active at younger ages." One poll showed that most teenagers were having sexual intercourse regularly by the eleventh grade (Gelman, 1990), and studies throughout the 1990s showed that one in five teens had sex before the age of 15 (*New York Times*, 2003b). One 15-year-old New Yorker explained, "A virgin today is not the same thing it used to be—A virgin might be someone who has only had oral sex" (Zeman, 1990:27). And, despite finding a slight drop in the sex rate among teenage girls, for the first time in 25 years, a 1995 study showed that half of all girls between 15 and 19 years of age have had sexual intercourse at least once (AP, Washington, 1996). Despite being blanketed with media images telling young girls to be sexy, however, the new millennium has seen a "new virginity" and abstinence movement among many teenagers. Since 1982 the federal government has spent $1.1 billion on funding abstinence programs, and research shows that youths who take an abstinence pledge are slightly less likely to engage in sex than those who do not (Ali and Scelfo, 2002; AP Austin, 2008; Harris, 2001; Housewright, 2001). Nevertheless, in the 21st century, one in five teens are sexually active before the age of 15 (*NY Times*, 2003b); more than half of 15–19 year-olds have had intercourse (Stein, 2008); teenagers still have unprotected sex (Johnson, 2004), and oral sex is very common among teens with more than half of 15- to 19-year-olds engaging in it (AP Washington, 2005b; Stein, 2008), but research shows that the idea that oral sex is a widespread epidemic among American youths is more myth than fact (Yabroff, 2008). The assumption that becoming sexually active at an early age leads to other types of delinquency later on, however, has been challenged by research findings (Begley, 2007).

Sexual activity among juveniles has led to at least one other social problem: teenage pregnancies—resulting in approximately half a million teenage girls giving birth each year (Gelman, 1990). Approximately one-third of young women in the United States become pregnant during their teens. A 1995 study showed that 11.2 percent of teenaged girls become pregnant with pregnancy rates highest among blacks (22 percent) and Hispanics (18 percent) (AP Washington, 1996). Teen pregnancy rates decreased during the first 5 years of the 21st century, but research suggests it was due more to new forms of birth control than abstinence from sex (*New York Times*, 2004), and then in 2006, teen birth rates increased again (Wire Reports, 2007b). Teenage pregnancy rates remain high and approximately 1 million teenage girls become pregnant each year in the United States. About 13 percent of U.S. births involve teen mothers and about 25 percent of teenage girls who give birth have another baby within 2 years (WHC, 2008). Research shows that a host of variables including self-esteem, attitudes toward school, educational aspirations, and religiosity, influence premarital sexual activity and how teenage girls resolve the problem of premarital pregnancy (Plotnick, 1992). Eric Sherman (1986:202) pointed to popular "television shows, music videos, and movies with names like *Losing It* and *The Last American Virgin* as leading adolescents to believe that *everyone* fools around." Yinger (1982:120) pointed out that when youths "misperceive that 'everyone else' is participating in a particular activity, they may be tempted to join the fictitious 'everyone else.' " Joyce Ladner, a professor of sociology at Harvard, indicated that teenage pregnancy "knows no color . . . it is not a black problem or a white problem," she stated. "It is an American problem" (Sherman, 1986:202).

YOUTH COUNTERCULTURES AND DELINQUENCY

Our discussion of delinquency associated with the youth subculture to this point has focused on nonviolent activities such as running away, prostitution, drugs, and premarital sex. As we noted at the beginning of this chapter, however, subcultures sometimes turn into *countercultures*—groups that reject society's values and norms and replace them with others that run counter to those of the larger culture. In Chapter 12, we take a look at the counterculture of juvenile gangs, but in this chapter we want to look at two aspects of the youth subculture that constitute juvenile countercultures and sometimes promote serious and violent criminal activities: teen-age Satanism and youth hate groups.

Teenage Satanic Groups

Sociologist Marcello Truzzi is quoted as saying that teenage sex no longer shocks parents—"the only thing left is the devil" (Lyons, 1988:163). Over the past several decades, teenagers have shown an increased interest in Satanism, and many popular rock and heavy metal groups have capitalized on this interest. With painted faces and eerie costumes these groups play live concerts and record tapes and compact discs that extol the virtues of animal and human sacrifices, sexual orgies, suicide, and even murder. Rumors abound that Satanic cults are responsible for everything from animal mutilations on Halloween night to human kidnapping and mass murders

(Frankfurter, 2006). Almost every popular television talk show has featured at least one segment on teenage Satanism; and one poll indicated that 63 percent of the respondents viewed Satanism as a "serious threat" to our society, while another 23 percent said it was "somewhat serious" (Zellner, 1995).

The extent of teenage Satanism is not known. The Church of Satan claims that annual sales of the Satanic Bible exceed a half-million copies, but some evidence suggests that law enforcement agencies, concerned parents, school officials, and fundamentalist Christians may account for as many sales as believers and practitioners (Zellner, 1995). Also, while teenage Satanists may indeed be involved in some serious criminal activities including kidnapping and murder, research indicates that teenage Satanists are far more likely to be "dabblers"—youngsters "who listen to rock and heavy metal music with occult themes, have an interest in Satanic imagery, and engage in fantasy role-playing games" (Zellner, 1995:87). One study divides teenaged Satanists into three categories:

1. Soft-core Satanists—Generally younger (12–16) who get involved in Satanism primarily to upset, provoke, and embarrass their parents.
2. Non-criminal hard-core Satanists—Begin as soft-core but as they become older (16–early 20s), they become more committed to Satanism as a religion,
3. Criminal hard-core Satanists—Typically have severe sociopathic tendencies. Commit crimes such as assault, kidnapping, sexual and physical abuse, animal and human sacrifices (Wooden, 1995).

Kathleen Lowney (1995) spent 5 years conducting participant observation and ethnographic interviews with members of an adolescent Satanic counterculture in the south known as "the Coven." Lowney's analysis of the group indicated that popular folklore and psychiatric explanations for adolescent Satanism are inadequate. Members of the Coven showed no evidence of being mentally ill. And, while they participated in delinquent activities such as underage smoking and drinking, minor vandalism, occasional truancy, and premarital sex—activities also engaged in by non-Satanic youths—they did not commit any serious crimes (Lowney, 1995).

Some youth countercultures *are* involved in serious crimes, however. Among them are the hate groups such as Skinheads, neo-Nazis, and others, who commit crimes of violence against homosexuals, members of racial and ethnic minorities, and various other groups who may become the targets of their hatred.

Youth Hate Groups

During the 1980s, the United States experienced an increase in the number of **hate crimes**—*crimes directed at people because of their race, ethnicity, religion, sexual orientation, or some other physical or cultural characteristic that sets them apart from the perpetrator*. These crimes often involve groups such as the Skinheads, Neo-Nazis, Ku Klux Klan, and others, and are most often committed by young men under the age of 20. These groups are usually comprised of disgruntled working-class and middle-class youths and are formed and maintained under a strong ideological commitment to some "cause" such as white supremacy, racial or ethnic purity, anti-Semitism, homophobia, or a return to some so-called idyllic past (Levin and McDevitt, 1993).

Why do hate groups such as skinheads, neo-Nazis, and others actively recruit youths?
© Mark Richards/PhotoEdit

While there are a number of hate groups in the United States today, probably the most visible and well known are the various groups that refer to themselves as *Skinheads*. Their distinctive shaven heads, elaborate tattoos, and black Doc Marten boots are copied from their British counterparts who emerged during the early 1950s in England. It is estimated that there are over 5,000 Skinheads in the United States today, and their crimes range from simple assaults and terroristic threats to serious felonies such as aggravated assault, forcible rape, and murder. By 1995, the increase in violent crimes committed by various hate groups had prompted 29 states to enact special hate crime legislation (Marowitz, 1991; Perry, 2001; Zellner, 1995).

Why do juveniles join hate groups? The answers vary by individuals, but sociologically, the most common explanations focus on marginality, alienation, and scapegoating (Zellner, 1995; Perry, 2001). We have discussed the problem of marginality experienced by adolescents who are no longer considered children, but not yet treated as adults, throughout this book. This marginality may be combined with strong feelings of alienation—a sense of futility and desperation—linked to family problems, school failure, and/or unemployment. This helps explain the appeal of a group that can point to the alleged "source" of these problems—members of minorities, or other vulnerable scapegoats—and offer an avenue for venting frustration and retaliating against the so-called culprits (Levin and McDevit, 1993; Perry, 2001; Zellner, 1995).

THE YOUTH SUBCULTURE AND DELINQUENCY PREVENTION

It should be pointed out again that the youth subculture has not thrown out all adult values and the vast majority of crimes and delinquency associated with it are nonviolent. Consequently, the same subculture that may promote some forms of juvenile delinquency also may serve as a potential preventive.

We have discussed the influence of mass media on juveniles. While movies, television programs, and other media aimed at youths might promote rebellious or delinquent behavior, they can also be used to present delinquency prevention messages. For example, rock and roll music has both influenced and reflected the values of the youth subculture. By the mid-1980s, while the themes of many popular rock songs encouraged engaging in sex, drug use, and rebellion against parents, some entertainers used that same forum to encourage young girls to "just say no" to sex. Although these songs were urging girls to limit their sexual behavior, they nevertheless reflected the overall tone of the youth subculture, and did not put parents' minds completely at ease. While teens are bombarded by the sexcapades of Britney and Paris, the most popular icon for preteen and teenaged girls is Miley Cyrus who promotes abstinence and a wholesome image.

During the late 1980s, and into the 1990s, organizations such as Students Against Driving Drunk (SADD) were filling the airwaves with messages against drinking and driving. Likewise, young celebrities made public service announcements on television urging teenagers to enter into contracts with their parents in which they agreed not to use alcohol and drugs, and by 1990, television had launched a major public service campaign against drug usage. Perhaps one of the most influential media efforts aimed at the youth subculture focused on encouraging youths not to start smoking. Again, teenaged celebrities warned youths of the dangers of smoking. More importantly, the campaign not only pointed out the dangers associated with smoking but also emphasized that it simply was not "cool" to smoke. While some people are skeptical of the impact of these public service announcements, research indicates that they are effective in changing juveniles' attitudes and behaviors in a positive fashion (Ingersoll, 1999).

The youth subculture and its heavy emphasis upon conforming to certain distinctive values, attitudes, beliefs, and norms undoubtedly contribute to certain forms of delinquency. This seems to be especially the case for status offenses and other nonviolent law violations. Thus, that same youth subculture may hold tremendous potential for delinquency prevention. Peer pressure to conform to the law can be just as strong and influential as peer pressure to violate it. While the World Wide Web hosts YouTube and other sites that may promote delinquency, it also hosts thousands of sites for teenage support groups, suicide prevention, runaway prevention, and a host of other potentially positive resources for troubled teens.

Finally, as suggested by maturation theory, much of the delinquency attributable to membership in a youth subculture is the type that is likely to diminish and desist as juveniles mature into adulthood. For example, many of the symbols of youthful rebellion—hairstyles, dress, and even tattoos (which are expensive and painful to remove)—are likely to be discarded as teenagers move into their 20s and 30s and assume the responsibilities of work, marriage, and parenthood (Marin et al., 1995).

Summary

We have reviewed a substantial amount of sociological literature documenting the existence of a youth subculture in U.S. society that perpetuates distinctive attitudes, values, beliefs, and norms that may lead some youths to delinquent behavior. The subculture developed during the latter part of the 19th century primarily as a result of industrialization, urbanization, and the increasingly marginal status of adolescents.

Youth values reflect early socialization by family, school, and church, but become more influenced by peers and mass media during adolescence. The values are consistent with the values of the adult culture but are manifested in many distinctive ways. Fashion, grooming, dress, music, fads, and language are a few of the observable vehicles by which youths symbolically differentiate themselves from their parents, teachers, and other adults.

While the youth subculture does not constitute a deviant subculture, some aspects of it can be linked to delinquent behavior, especially in the areas of running away, prostitution, drug use, and premarital sexual behavior. Research associates the youth subculture with middle-class delinquency, primarily involving nonviolent crimes and status offenses. But, as noted in this chapter, sometimes youth countercultures can be involved in serious delinquency and violent crimes.

The existence of a distinctive youth subculture is open to debate, but it seems clear that the marginal status of adolescents and the lack of any clear-cut rites of passage into adulthood in U.S. society have created a social situation that tends to bond youths in spirit if not in ideology. As a result, much of the youthful behavior reflects values supported by their peers and not by their parents or other adults. Friedenberg (1963:4, 9) asserted, "the young disturb and anger their elders, and are themselves angered and disturbed . . . the plight of the adolescent is basically similar to that of the emigrant in that he can neither stay what he was nor become what he started out to be." While questioning the existence of a distinctive youth subculture, William Arnold and Terrance Brungardt (1983) acknowledged that many youths are uncommitted to the normative system of adults.

Howard Becker (1963) surmised that rules about youthful behavior are made without regard to the problems of adolescence; hence, juveniles are "outsiders" who are often labeled deviant as a result of violating rules that have little or no meaning for them. This relative powerlessness in rulemaking may lead to social alienation, which could result in delinquency. The lyrics to a hit song of the mid-1980s seem to summarize the attitudes of many American youths, as the rock group Twisted Sister chanted:

> We're not gonna take it,
> No, we're not gonna take it,
> We're not gonna take it anymore.
>
> Quoted with permission from "We're Not Gonna Take It" sung by Twisted Sister. (From the album "Stay Hungry" produced by Tom Worman. Atlantic Recording Company, New York, 1984.)

While not all youths are rebellious in attitude, they can relate to the sentiment. Wein (1970:223) described an interview with a 16-year-old "chemistry whiz" on his way to a Rotary Club meeting. It may reflect the strong sense of unity among American teens:

Youth: "Being a part of the subculture I'm in, I don't believe what's going on."
Wein: "What subculture?"
Youth: "Oh, teenagers. Our little subculture."
Wein: "Is there anyone your age whom you would exclude from that?"
Youth: "Oh, probably not . . . you can't help but be in it."

Acknowledging the existence of a youth subculture and its powerful influence upon adolescent behavior is not the same as identifying all U.S. teenagers as belonging to a delinquent subculture. Rather, the much broader context of a youth subculture provides a meaningful sense of social identity for American youths. It also provides a social context in which adolescent nonconformity to both adult and child normative expectations can be viewed as acceptable. We have demonstrated ways in which that acceptance can promote certain types of juvenile delinquency. Given that fact, it is reasonable to assume that the youth subculture can also provide a significant influence for discouraging and preventing juvenile delinquency.

Concept Integration: Questions and Topics for Study and Discussion

1. Define culture, subculture, and counterculture. What is meant by the concept of youth subculture?
2. Is there a youth subculture in the United States? If so, what are some of the distinctive elements of it? If not, why does there seem to be a sense of unity among juveniles? Are there other explanations? If so, discuss them.
3. In what ways do youth values differ from those to which they were socialized by adults? In what ways are they similar? How do these similarities and differences create conflict between juveniles and adults?
4. How do the mass media contribute to the formation and perpetuation of a youth subculture? How do they possibly contribute to juvenile delinquency?
5. In what ways does participation in a youth subculture potentially lead to juvenile delinquency? Are there ways in which a youth subculture might be utilized for delinquency prevention?

Chapter 12

Juvenile Gangs and Delinquency

READING OBJECTIVES

Reading this chapter will help you achieve the following objectives:

1. Extend the sociological perspective to help you understand and explain group dynamics, that is, in what ways gang behavior is social in origin, social in content, and social in consequences.
2. Understand how neighborhood play groups can evolve into delinquent youth gangs.
3. Define and understand the concept of gang.
4. Comprehend the magnitude of the juvenile gang problem, that is, the number of gangs, number of gang members, and gang involvement in delinquent behavior.
5. List common motives for joining gangs and outline the general organization and roles within fighting gangs.
6. Understand more clearly the connection between the personal and collective social identity of gang members and their use of rituals, symbols, language, and graffiti.
7. Explore the compositional factors of gangs—social class, race or ethnicity, and gender—and link these factors to reasons why gangs are formed and the illegal activities of gang members.
8. Trace gang formation and behavior back to the theoretical causes and explanations developed by sociologists.

INTRODUCTION

The theoretical explanations of deviance and delinquency discussed in Part Two included the important perspective that human behavior is social in origin. In general, our conduct reflects the powerful influences and effects of our families, neighborhoods, communities, subcultures, and other social forces and groups in which we share membership and with whom we interact. More specifically, we looked at the causal linkages between a broad spectrum of social variables and delinquent behavior.

In earlier chapters, we focused on the family, school, and youth subculture as potential generators of alienated and delinquent youths. In this chapter, we turn our attention to juvenile gangs, whose delinquent behavior is not only social in origin but social in context; that is, they act out their misconduct within supportive and cooperative groups.

Predatory Youths: A National Alarm

> **TEXAS:** Four teenagers were hospitalized Saturday after being shot during a gang fight in Oakcliff Friday night. A group of high school students had rented a ballroom for a party when a second group of uninvited youths entered and began firing automatic pistols and a shotgun into the ceiling. "Then the youths lowered their guns and began firing at teens believed to be in a rival gang," police said. (*Dallas Morning News,* 1996:34A)
>
> **CALIFORNIA:** A show of disrespect led to the shooting of a 15-year-old Manteca boy in the Taco Bell parking lot late Tuesday night.

Police believe the shooting was gang related and don't have any suspects in custody. The victim said that he and two friends were cruising through the parking lot when two young men in a pickup truck "showed them disrespect by staring at them." The teen then reportedly got out of his car and confronted the two men. They exchanged words before a bullet was fired, striking the youth in the shoulder. The two suspects fled westbound and disappeared. (Tressel, 1993:A-1)

OHIO: The young people charged in a killing rampage that left six dead bragged about the slayings during a holiday dinner, a newspaper reported.

Melissa Gomez, who had been a member of the loosely formed group, [said] . . . that her friends held a Christmas dinner at which the talk quickly turned to the slayings.

She said Heather Matthews, 20, told her: "If you're going to run with us, you need to know what's going on and what's already happened."

She said Ms. Matthews showed off a new pair of tennis shoes and said: "Oh, I killed some girl at the phone booth for them."

Matthews and three other members of the group called the Downtown Posse were charged with murder and robbery in the three-day spree. DeMarcus Smith, 17, and Laura Taylor, 16, were charged with aggravated robbery in juvenile court. (*Daily O'Collegian*, 1993:3)

Although only a small proportion of juvenile crime in the United States is as violent as reported in these news excerpts or impacts so tragically on individual victims or society, such acts of collective violence are repeated often enough to warrant our serious concern and study.

THE SOLITARY DELINQUENT

As with many other forms of deviant behavior, some juvenile crime is committed by solitary individuals acting alone, and this phenomenon must be acknowledged. Opportunities arise for youngsters to make delinquent responses that do not require encouragement from peers or other influential persons. For example, occasional opportunities for crimes may appeal to some juveniles because they can be carried out alone and privately, without an accomplice or even a tolerant witness. Such solitary operatives seek to protect and maintain respectable ties and status within the nondeviant society (Goffman, 1986). Solitary delinquents also may be emotionally or socially maladjusted in some way. They avoid companionship and group interaction and express their frustration or anger in a delinquent, loner role:

> The solitary delinquent may be a social isolate, who is unable to make friends or who prefers to work or play alone. Throughout society there are people who do not make close affiliations with groups. If such a person is motivated toward delinquency . . . It is normal to act as an individual and not as a member of a clique or gang. (Cavan and Ferdinand, 1981:225)

Although nearly a third of those who come before the juvenile court have, for one reason or another, committed their delinquencies alone, little research has focused on the solitary delinquent. As a result, causal explanations are largely speculative.

Many sociologists, while acknowledging the statistical reality of solitary individuals, counter that the popularized picture of "the lone gunman," "the secretive alcoholic," or "the solitary delinquent"—acting out deviant behavior with little or no connection with other members of society—is an oversimplification. Theoretically, it is virtually impossible to conceive of any human behavior as occurring in a complete social vacuum, without an interlocking web of human interaction and totally devoid of social causes, social support, and/or social consequences. Applying this sociological principle to deviant or delinquent behavior, no act can be judged as conforming or nonconforming without a societal audience.

Sociologists often conceptualize each individual and his or her behavior as being at the hub of a social network (Mitchell, 1979). For example, consider the shoplifter. Although there are professional shoplifting gangs that prey upon retail merchants (see Box 12.1), much shoplifting involves single individuals, operating alone. However, many observers are oblivious to the social linkages between a solitary delinquent shoplifter and numerous other members of society who, while usually not responsible for the illegal behavior, are nevertheless related to it in some way. Figure 12.1 outlines the shoplifter's social network.

The model of the shoplifter's social network contains only some of the linkages and associations between the individual offender and other people. If we look closely at the apparently solitary actor, we can discern an abstract, dynamic, and complex social web that connects the individual and the behavior in question to a wide array

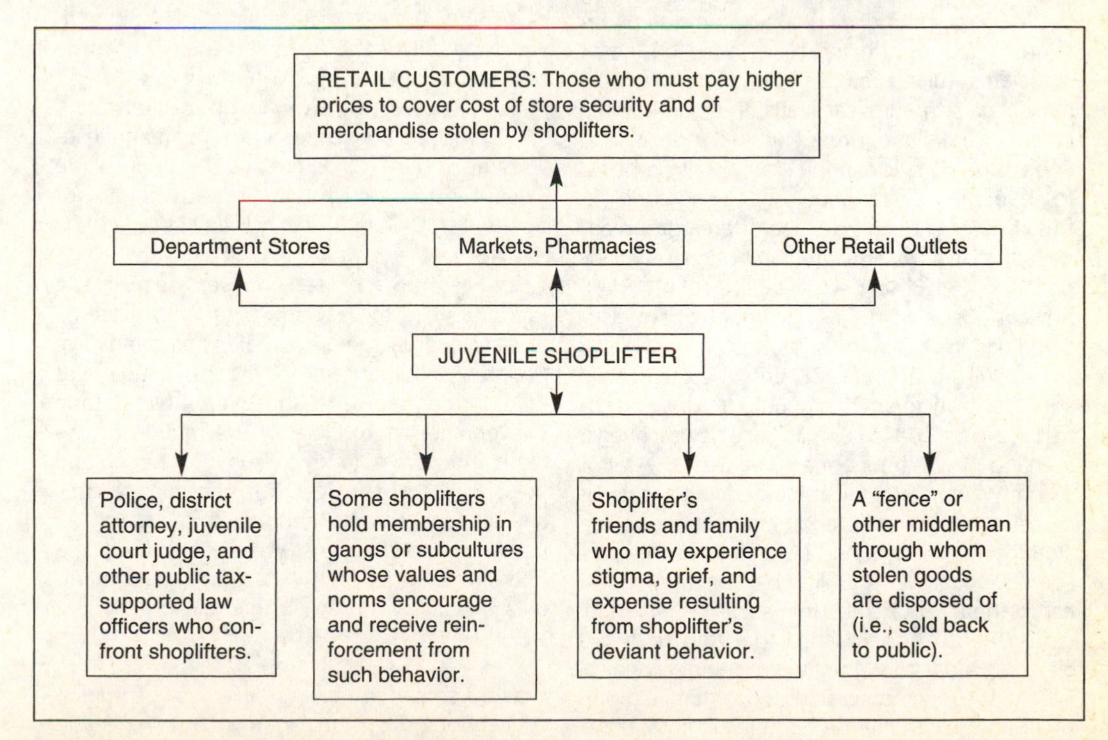

FIGURE 12.1 The Shoplifter's Social Network.

Have you ever thought of shoplifters as being part of a larger social network? How does this sociological approach help us better understand shoplifting in a group context?

BOX 12.1

CONCEPT APPLICATION: The Profit Motive: Group Shoplifting and "The Swarm"

In many cases, the youthful rationale for collective delinquency has moved away from the "fun and games" extension of the play group and the "fraternal hell-raising" of the street gang, to a purposeful economic motive. Several social scientists have begun using economic models to explain the mercenary and predacious emphasis of such gangs (Clarke and Cornish, 1985).

> These rational choice theorists argue that when faced with a choice, individuals calculate the costs and benefits of various options and, on the basis of these calculations, choose the most profitable option. Such economic models usually assign monetary values to the costs and benefits of various options. (Best and Luckenbill, 1994:226)

Some youth gangs have become semiprofessional groups of highly specialized "business" associates, fully committed to the pursuit of financial gain through car thefts, the marketing of illegal drugs, and other criminal operations. Shoplifting gangs are good examples. In contrast to shoplifting by individuals, discussed earlier in this chapter, shoplifting is also often a group endeavor, not only stimulated and encouraged by peer support (Rosenberg and Silverstein, 1969), but conducive to the development of sophisticated criminal skills and strategies.

William Cobb (1982) described a juvenile shoplifting incident that required considerable nerve, planning, and coordination. He described a scenario in which nine male juveniles, several of whom were known to the store security as previous shoplifters, gathered around a table in the clothing department and distracted security personnel while they shoplifted. In an attempt to catch them, all of the store security personnel (seven people) approached the boys to make clear to them that they were being watched. Meanwhile, on another floor of the store, a group of youths helped themselves to merchandise "secure in their belief that their nine confederates were keeping the store detectives busy" (Cobb, 1982:374).

Another highly organized and proficient juvenile shoplifting gang emerged on the East Coast. New Jersey police reported that a charismatic shoplifting mastermind organized about 20 boys into a gang of thieves for weekend excursions to suburban malls in four states. Each child netted up to $800 worth of designer clothes which were exchanged for money and drugs. As arrests were made, authorities found several boys carrying a typewritten manual that explains how to exchange old clothes from their knapsacks for new clothes in store fitting rooms, how to remove alarm devices from merchandise, and how to spot store detectives.

"Mostly you have to use common sense and act cool and you really shouldn't have any trouble," the manual says.

"If you see someone pick up a phone on your way out of the store and then hear some bells, those bells are for you," it reads. "Don't run or panic. Just calmly walk out of the store."

If a shoplifter gets caught, the manual advises, he or she "will be out in several hours. The juvenile justice system is such that you will not be held for very long." (*Daily O'Collegian,* 1987:8)

Even more brazen, but less secretive in their intent, is the "swarm assault" utilized by at least one Sacramento, California gang. The "swarm" is comprised of 10 to 30 young males who suddenly invade and overwhelm a lone convenience store clerk in the middle of the night. They are not only attentive to timing and the element of surprise, but neutralize alarms and security cameras, and focus on high-priced items of merchandise. After assaulting the clerk and plundering the store, the gang members quickly withdraw with their loot (KCBS, 1993).

How do shoplifting gangs differ from common conceptions of juvenile gangs today? Do you think most juvenile shoplifting occurs in gangs or is more likely to be carried out by the solitary delinquent or small primary group?

Sources

Best, J. and Luckenbill, D. F. 1994. *Organizing deviance* (2nd ed.). Englewood Cliffs, NJ: Prentice Hall.

Clarke, R. V., and Cornish, D. B. 1985. "Modeling offender's decisions." *Crime and Justice* 6: 147–185.

Cobb, W. E. 1982. "Shoplifting." Pp. 369–376. In L. D. Savitz and N. Johnston (Eds.). Contemporary criminology. New York: John Wiley.

Daily O'Collegian. April 17, 1987. Stillwater, OK: Oklahoma State University. P. 8.

KCBS Radio News Report. July 20, 1993. Sacramento, California.

Rosenberg, B., and Silverstein, H. 1969. *The varieties of delinquent experience*. Waltham, MA: Blaisdell.

of other persons and groups which in some way support, influence, or are affected by the behavior. These often inescapable connections and relationships may be voluntary or involuntary, formal or informal, primary or secondary, but the impact of deviant or delinquent behavior on other persons sharing a social network can be extremely negative and traumatic. Bottom line: most delinquency is not performed in isolation but takes place in some type of group context, even if only two or three juveniles acting in consort.

DYADS AND TRIADS

A **dyad** is *a social group comprised of just two persons;* a **triad** is *a group of three persons in social interaction.* These sociological descriptors for very small groups are the focal point of findings that have weakened common stereotypes of large groups or gangs of youths participating together in collective delinquency.

Paul Lerman (1967) used self-report techniques with 700 boys, aged 10 through 19, living in New York City. He determined that until the age of 14 or 15, most of the boys committed delinquent acts together with one or two close friends. At ages 16 through 19, more of the youths could be classified as loners, but paired and triad participation in illegal conduct continued to be the most dominant grouping. While the gang fight—in which squads of youths from opposing neighborhoods meet in armed and angry conflict—still occasionally occurs, most delinquent acts usually involve just two or three close friends, operating together in a less sensational manner. As Michael Hindelang (1976) emphasized, our revised concept of collective delinquency more accurately focuses on a small network of two or three trusted pals and peers (see also Gonzales, et al., 2005). They may well be members of a larger gang, whose values, norms, and behavioral expectations are far from altruistic, but most delinquency is acted out in much smaller social units than the gang.

A number of studies confirm that primary association with delinquent friends—in small groups or large gangs—is a major factor influencing a youth's subsequent delinquent behavior. Peer bonding "fosters the social learning of crime because delinquent friends are more likely to reinforce crime, model crime, and teach beliefs favorable to crime" (Agnew, 2005:52).

GROUP DELINQUENCY

In addition to the sociological principle regarding the social causes and consequences of human behavior, there is considerable documentation that most juvenile delinquency is committed by social groupings of varying size, purpose, and organization. One of the most extensive studies along this line of inquiry was conducted by Maynard Erickson and Gary Jensen (1977) who administered self-report questionnaires to 1,700 high-school students from three small towns and three urban schools in Arizona. The subjects were asked how many times during the past year they had committed each of 18 delinquent acts, and in how many of those times they had been in the company of others. The findings suggested that the youths generally engaged in delinquent behavior when they were with their friends. However, the tendency varied with the type of offense. Group violations were more common with drug offenses and least common with status offenses other than drinking alcoholic beverages and smoking tobacco. The study also found that females were even more likely than males to commit delinquent acts in groups.

The findings of Erickson and Jensen agreed with those of similar investigations carried out in other countries. For example, Brunner (1974) found that group membership and processes played a central role in juvenile crime in Germany and that between 80 and 90 percent of illegal behavior by juveniles involved groups of youths—particularly gang violence and drug abuse.

The group context of juvenile misbehavior should come as no surprise when we recall from Chapter 2 that we human beings share with most other species a strong social imperative that constrains us toward social interaction with others of our kind. Thus, most nonconforming, delinquent behavior—like most conforming, law-abiding behavior—has been widely observed and documented in social groupings (Gonzales, et al., 2005). LaMar Empey and Mark Stafford (1999:114, 116) concluded that "the gregarious and companionate character of law-violating behavior" is reflected in self-report studies of juvenile delinquency: "the preponderant majority of all delinquent acts are committed in groups—whether male or female, black or white, middle or lower class." Paradoxically, the initial social stimulant for potentially serious delinquent behavior by some children has been traced to innocent neighborhood play groups.

PLAY GROUPS

The natural, spontaneous, and initially innocuous emergence of neighborhood play groups among urban youngsters was well described in Frederick Thrasher's (1927:26) early study of gangs: "On a warm summer evening children literally swarm over areaways and sidewalks, vacant lots and rubbish dumps, streets and alleys. . . . This endless activity has a tremendous fascination . . . and it would be a marvel indeed if any healthy boy could hold himself aloof from it."

The play groups engage in all sorts of childhood games including "hide-and-go-seek," "pick-up basketball," and crap-shooting. These are natural groupings of participants who live in the same area and know each other as well as brothers. In time, as the youngsters grow older, more adventuresome, and more mischievous, such childhood games may become less satisfying. Building on the loosely organized alliances and innocent activities of the play group, some youths begin to experiment with more aggressive and predatory group behavior, directed toward youths outside

Research indicates that gangs often start out as neighborhood play groups. What sociological theories might help explain how these girls involved in harmless play might evolve into a delinquent gang?

the group and against society in general. Thus, the "game" is extended over time and territory to include higher stakes and involuntary victim-participants.

Fifty years after Thrasher's landmark study, in a *Time* magazine report (1977), a youth who attended a school for problem youngsters said: "Mugging is like playing a game; kids do it for the fun of it."

Clifford Shaw and Henry McKay (1931:251) also reported on the playful, game-like approach of juveniles at the beginning of their delinquent careers:

> When we were shoplifting we always made a game of it. For example, we might gamble on who could steal the most caps in a day, or who could steal caps from the largest number of stores in a day, or who could steal in the presence of a detective and then get away. We were always daring each other that way and thinking up new schemes. This was the best part of the game. . . . It was the fun I wanted, not the hat. I kept this up for months and then began to sell the things to a man on the west side. It was at this time that I began to steal for gain.

Since the family usually provides the first social setting for childhood play activities, siblings sometimes move on to engage in delinquent behavior together. Seattle, Washington, even had a one-family gang: seven brothers, aged 11 to 20, were arrested 192 times during a 9-year period, 1968 through 1976. Enough of the boys were always at liberty to keep up the family tradition (*Time*, 1977).

Ikuya Sato (1987) focused on this propensity among a great many youngsters to "play" as a prelude and accompaniment to delinquent behavior. He conducted an extensive review of major urban ethnographies describing the playful attitude and approach of youth groups seeking entertainment and excitement in the streets. The developing by-product often turned into juvenile crime. Sato suggests that this common, playful approach to misconduct by mischievous, daring, and thrill-seeking adolescents is an understudied characteristic of gang behavior. This aggressive play group, according to Sato, offers a promising conceptual framework for explanatory theory building and an alternative to the widely held views that juveniles are thrust into delinquency by their unfortunate circumstances or conformity to deviant subcultural values.

JUVENILE GANGS

Several studies have concluded that much juvenile delinquency consists of gangs committing crimes as social activities. For instance, Sarnecki (1983) suggested that committing crimes together satisfies juveniles' needs for togetherness and excitement. Notwithstanding, society shows little tolerance for serious misconduct by youth groups, even if interpreted as "social activities" fulfilling juvenile needs for "togetherness" and "excitement." For while gang members may view their predatory behavior as "fun and games," their victims see it as violent and frightening crime. From the viewpoint of larger society, there is a great difference between the neighborhood play group and the intimidating street gang. Despite the play group basis for the early association among some gang members, once they advance beyond the occasional and spontaneous prank to a conscious and deliberate pattern of illegal conduct, they become a threat to society.

What Is a Gang?

In its broadest sense, the term *gang* means *a group of persons assembled and acting or working together*. The term *gang* has often been used to signify a group of close associates or friends with no criminal or antisocial connotations. For example, a generation or so ago "the gang" could have signified a collegial and informal male group whose activities centered on social drinking, cardplaying, and sporting events. And, criminologists acknowledge, "Not all gangs are particularly bad, nor do all of them do bad things. Some gangs exist simply for the purpose of providing companionship" (Miller and Rush, 1996:*iii*).

Although criminologists, sociologists, and law enforcement agencies have given several decades of serious attention to juvenile gangs, the great variability among these gangs and the many dimensions of their behavior have confounded the development of an all-encompassing answer to the question, "What is a gang?" (Curry and Decker, 2003:2). However, Walter Miller (1975:1), after interviewing law enforcement and social service professionals who dealt with youth gangs in six large American cities, brought together some of the major variables into one of the better working definitions of the term *gang:* "A **gang** *is a group of recurrently associating individuals with identifiable leadership and internal organization, identifying with or claiming* *control over territory in a community, and engaging either individually or collectively in violent or other forms of illegal behavior."*

In later sections of this chapter, we address the multiple variations in gang objectives, orientation, and organization and offer theoretical explanations for their formation and behavior.

James Short (1987:16–17) extrapolated a useful set of definitional criteria from the gangs he studied with Fred Strodtbeck, contending gangs manifest the following characteristics:

1. recurrent congregation outside the home;
2. self-defined inclusion/exclusion criteria and continuity of affiliation;
3. a territorial basis consisting of customary hanging and ranging areas, including self-defined use-and-occupancy rights;
4. a versatile activity repertoire; and
5. organizational differentiation, for example, by authority, roles, prestige, friendship, or special interest cliques.

Such academic definitions fail to capture precisely what "the gang" means to its members. A 16-year-old gang member in Hartford, Connecticut, *was* able to summarize the camaraderie, esprit de corps, mutualism, and male bonding in his definition: "What is a gang? You look out for me and I look out for you—that's what makes a gang" (Ramos, 1989:7).

History of Youth Gangs

Antisocial and criminal conduct by members of juvenile gangs is not a new phenomenon. Nor does history exempt any Western nation from this form of deviant behavior. Cyril Burt (1925) reported that many troublesome and even dangerous delinquent gangs were present in England during the first quarter of the 20th century. The word *hooligan* came into common English usage in 1898 to describe the rowdy youths who participated in a regular pattern of civil disorder. The term was derived from the Hooligan gang which engaged in pitched battles with other youth gangs in London.

> The "Hooligans" adopted a uniform dress-style. Bell-bottom trousers with a buttoned vent in the leg, colourful neck scarves, a distinctive style of cap, boots said to be "toe-plated with iron and calculated to kill easily", ornamental leather belts with designs worked in metal studs, and a characteristic "donkey fringe" haircut. (Pearson, 1984:83)

Thrasher (1936:40) noted in 1936 that tens of thousands of poverty-stricken Russian youths were gravitating to gangs for survival: "Russia's ... neglected children are said to travel in gangs, winning a precarious living by stealing and finding shelter in deserted buildings and in Moscow and other cities in the sewers and catacombs."

James Inciardi (1978:34–36) documented the presence of youth gangs engaged in criminal activity in American cities during the 19th century:

> The earliest gangs consisted almost entirely of Irishmen. The Irish, emigrating to this country in vast numbers and lacking funds, education, and skills, were met with contempt by native New Yorkers and were forced

> into the city's worst slum—the Five Points district . . . and lacking other means of earning a living, many developed criminal careers.
>
> The Plug Uglies were formed in the mid-1820s and took their name from the giant plug hats which each member filled with rags and straw to protect their heads during gang battles. The Shirt Tails were so called because they wore their shirts on the outside of their trousers. . . . These gangs of the Five Points, Bowery, and Hell's Kitchen, which often included hundreds of men and boys, consisted of many small gangs grouped together and led by a supreme chieftain who commanded absolute loyalty. . . .
>
> The gangs of youthful and young adult criminals who made war on one another and terrorized the streets of New York were also evident in other cities. Philadelphia had its "Buffaloes," "Blood Tubs," "Rugs," and "Copper Heads"; Baltimore had its "Stringers"; and a group known as the "Crawfish Boys" plagued the streets of Cincinnati.

CONTEMPORARY YOUTH GANGS IN THE UNITED STATES

The first scholarly investigation of youth gangs in the United States was Frederick Thrasher's (1927) work in Chicago. Although Thrasher verified that a great many of the gangs were organized primarily for conventional participation in athletic, dancing, and other socially acceptable activities, many gang members were routinely involved in collective or individual delinquency.

Number of Gangs and Members

Although the United States has a long history of aggressive youth gangs taking to the streets to battle one another and the police and to prey upon the citizenry, the statistical magnitude of the gang problem was imprecise and often speculative. Nevertheless, during the 1960s, 1970s, and 1980s, several researchers made significant beginnings to measure the number of gangs and members in selected cities (Klein, 1995; Miller, 1975; Needle and Stapleton, 1983; Spergel and Curry, 1988). These scholars documented an alarming increase in gang activity spreading rapidly across the country and constituting a serious social problem.

In 1995, fortified by a national concern and funding, the Office of Juvenile Justice and Delinquency Prevention of the U.S. Department of Justice, established the National Youth Gang Center (NYGC). One of the major tasks assigned to the NYGC was to conduct periodic and methodologically sound, national surveys to obtain comprehensive data on American youth gangs. These annual surveys systematically collect information on reported gang composition and activities from a sample of law enforcement agencies in cities, counties, and communities of varying population size, in all parts of the nation. Data on motorcycle gangs, hate or ideology groups, prison gangs, and exclusively adult gangs were excluded from the survey. The rich database emerging from these ongoing NYGC surveys have validated earlier projections that large numbers of American youth are seriously involved in gangs and gang-related crime.

The 1997 National Youth Gang Survey summarized reports from 2,766 urban and suburban police departments and county sheriffs' departments (a 92 percent response rate). "From these data, it was estimated that 4,712 U.S. cities and counties experienced gang activity in 1997, down slightly from 4,824 in 1996. There were an estimated 30,500 gangs and 816,000 gang members in 1997" (Moore and Terrett, 1999:1).

By the year 2002, the national survey had identified a moderate decline in U.S. gang activity, with an estimated 21,500 gangs containing 731,500 members (Egley and Major, 2004). While this downward trend was encouraging, five years later the NYGS showed another upswing in gang activity estimating that approximately 785,000 gang members and 26,500 gangs were active in the United States (Egley and O'Donnell, 2008). There has been a tenfold escalation of gang problems since 1970 (Jackson, 2001). Youthful gangs continue to inflict enormous woes on our communities. The latest available data on number of gangs and gang members can be found at the NYGC website http://www.iir.com/nygc/.

Locale

Youth gangs have been active in all 50 states. Robert Park, in the Editor's Preface to Thrasher's study, reminded readers that "Gangs are not confined to cities, nor to the slums of cities. . . . Every village has at least its boy gang . . . composed of those same foot-loose, prowling, and predacious adolescents who herd and hang together, after the manner of the undomesticated male everywhere . . ." (Thrasher, 1927:*ix*).

However, Park's important generalization has been overshadowed by Thrasher's forceful portrayal of the inner city as the normal and natural habitat of the street gang. The contemporary image of the leather-jacketed, streetwise, and dangerous gangs roaming the inner city streets has prevailed, not only because of their high visibility, but also because of recurring news reports of their criminal activities and the public outcry for protection.

Criminologists and social scientists, supported by the official data on crime and delinquency, often have contributed to the stereotype of the youthful street gang as an inner city phenomenon with their conclusion that urban areas of blighted slum neighborhoods are the focal points of numerous social ills, including juvenile delinquency. The research of Shaw and McKay (1969) supported the belief that delinquency is especially associated with the normative confusion and corruption manifested in the high delinquency areas of large U.S. cities. These writers and numerous others argued that criminal and delinquent behavior is concentrated, encouraged, and reinforced by the prevailing customs and norms of such deteriorated areas (see Chapter 6 for a detailed discussion). The National Youth Gang Survey indicated that approximately 90 percent of larger cities reported having gang problems, while 51 percent of suburban areas, 33 percent of smaller cities, and less than 15 percent of rural areas reported problems with gangs (Egley and O'Donnell, 2008).

In the lower socioeconomic slum districts of the city, gang behavior can take on a spatial, ecological dimension as members relate and interact with each other and their mutual environment. It has been well documented that urban gang members generally demonstrate a territorial imperative in which they consistently identify and defend boundaries around their *turf*—the geographical area they intend to dominate. The gang territory may be the immediate neighborhood in which members reside or the area around a recreational center, store, school, park, or pool hall. The familiar range and sense of possession lend social and psychological security and much coveted status and identity to gang members. Similar to the citizens of formally organized nations, gang boys will defend their established boundaries against competing gangs from another area, and other outsiders who are perceived as threatening.

Motives for Gang Membership

Although a large number of gang members commit delinquent acts, they rarely cite that as a reason for becoming a gang member. Many gang members contend that they joined a gang out of fear of being alone and vulnerable in a tough neighborhood. Others expressed much the same rationale—that the gang offered an opportunity to develop and maintain a peer group, or friendship network. Certainly this is a natural human desire, especially for youngsters who see former associates from their play group and school affiliating with a neighborhood gang. Other reasons given by gang members for joining a gang include boredom, defiance of authority figures, loyalty to one's own racial or ethnic group, adventure, money from the drug trade, and poor relationships with parents and teachers. Thus, in a sense, the gang can represent a surrogate or substitute family for some youths who perceive a lack of rapport and positive interaction with their own biological families.

James Coleman's (1988) concept of "social capital" is especially relevant in explaining why some youth seem favorably or unfavorably inclined toward gang membership. **Social capital** *is a reservoir of resilience in some individuals that enables them to resist the allure of potentially damaging associates and activities.* Coleman outlined how social capital is acquired initially through nurturing, intergenerational relationships within one's family of origin, particularly through the presence of both parents in the home and the amount of quality time they spend with their children. This thesis has similarities to Social Learning Theory (see Chapter 6) in that the youth is more likely to extend internalized, conventional, family values into life in the larger society. On the other hand, the lack of social capital is an important deficit for both young men and women in their efforts to overcome pressures on the street toward participation in gangs and crime.

Other boys have suggested that gang membership was the only available avenue open to them to achieve some measure of respect and identity. This unfulfilled need can be especially pressing in lower-class neighborhoods where residents who lack status and recognition on the basis of occupations, material possessions, and educational achievements can find social support, security, and a sense of power within a gang of similarly situated persons (Bing, 1991). One gang in New York City is composed largely of deaf boys and young men between the ages of 13 and 35 who are drawn together by their common physical disability and perceived rejection by the larger society. They call themselves the Nasty Homicides and decorate their hangout and leather jackets with the slogan "Deaf Power"—a statement of unity and a challenge to all others. Like many other gangs, the Nasty Homicides is potentially violent. According to Short and Strodtbeck (1965), members of delinquent gangs tend to be characterized by a general *social disability*, lacking skill in interpersonal relations, social assurance, knowledge of the job market, and sophistication in their relations with girls. By displays of toughness and by committing crimes, these unskilled, unemployed school dropouts can assert their masculinity and feel successful in the eyes of friends in the gang (Zastrow, 1992). Short (1987b:31), in citing earlier research on gangs, observed that "The greater social skills possessed by gang leaders...and their supportive and nurturant style of leadership...confirm the value of group membership to gang members."

Lewis Yablonsky and Martin Haskell (1988) contended that motivation for gang affiliation is also related to the primary purpose of the specific gang in question. Gangs that focus on social activities such as athletic competition with other groups, dancing, and group discussions (or "bull sessions") attract youths who crave camaraderie and fellowship by engaging in generally innocent activities and seldom resort to serious crime. On the other hand, these authors noted, juvenile gangs whose major pursuit is the procurement of money and material possessions through theft and other illegal activities recruit members who are not only interested in such endeavors but have those skills of organization and guile that will be useful to the gang.

Yablonsky and Haskell's final type of gang was the violent-prone gang whose main function and activity centers on the planning and implementation of intragroup confrontation and conflict in defense of territory or status. New members are attracted into alliances and associations with the gang by the prospects of excitement and violence (Yablonsky and Haskell, 1988:260–264).

Karl Hill and his associates conducted a study of Early Precursors of Gang Membership (Hill, et al., 2001). They discovered that 10- to 12-year-old youths with marijuana available in their neighborhoods, learning disabilities, low academic achievement, and early exposure to violence were over three times more likely to join gangs between 13 and 18 years of age than were youths without those precursors. The potential of such findings is that knowledge of precursors may assist in preventive measures.

Initiation Rituals

Most gangs, whose members are informally organized and have only vague objectives, have no initiation ceremonies or rituals. Youths may become members by virtue of their living in proximity to other gang members or their hangout or interacting with gang members in a play group, at school, or on the streets. Thus, the role and status change from nonmember to member is a taken-for-granted, natural transition. However, researchers have discovered that some of the more aggressive gangs, in keeping with their ominous names and hostile posturing, do have formal and often violent initiation ceremonies for new members. An older study by Herbert Block and Arthur Niederhoffer (1958) cited a wide assortment of rituals and symbols, including jackets decorated with the gang's name and logo, distinctive and sometimes radical hairstyles, and scarification and tattooing sessions resulting in the permanent display of gang affiliation.

A longstanding practice among many lower-class gangs has been to initiate new members with an ordeal of hazing, which often takes the form of physical punishment called "cramping" or "the pink belly." The new applicant for membership is held by two of the older boys, while the rest of the gang take turns striking him in the stomach. If he "chickens out" of the ordeal, he is rejected for gang membership. A variation is putting the aspiring member inside a circle of gang members and demanding that he fight his way out. Some more predatory gangs require members to mug somebody—"getting paid," they call it (*Tulsa World,* 1990:A9). Contemporary gangs sometimes "jump in" new members where the initiate must stand up to a severe beating by the other gang members (Curry and Decker, 2003).

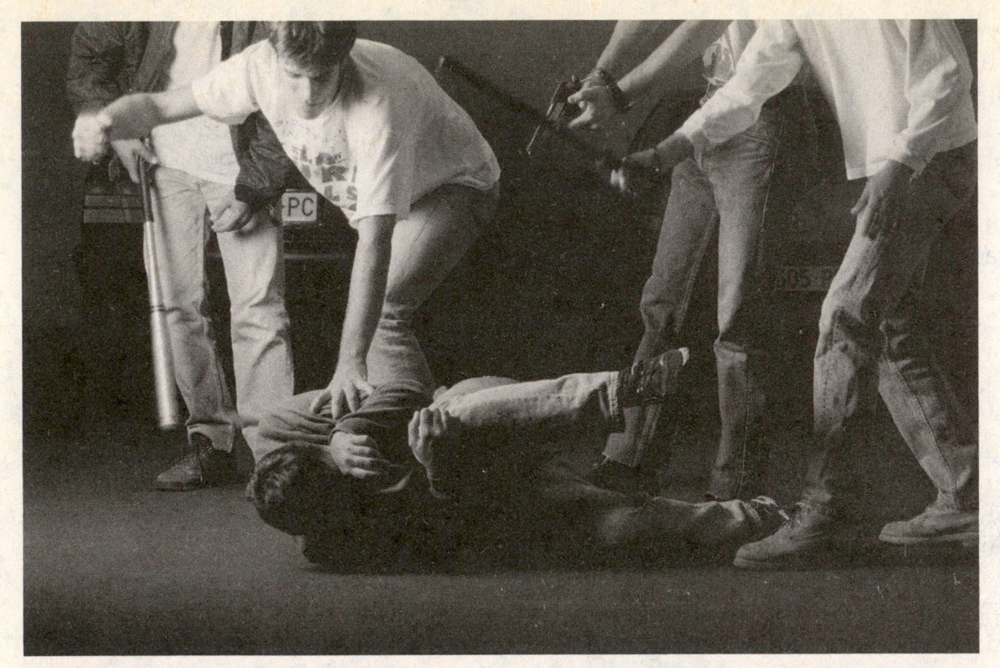

Gang rituals such as "jumping in" can be brutal if not sometimes fatal. What purpose do such gang initiations serve? Why might prospective members be willing to endure such brutality to become part of a gang?

The drive-by killing has been occasionally used as an initiation rite for the Crips and Bloods of Los Angeles. "From the comfort of a passing car, the itinerant killer simply shoots down a member of a rival gang or an innocent bystander" (Bing, 1989:51). While such initiation rituals appear cruel, bizarre, and senseless to the outside observer, they represent highly coveted badges of honor, courage, and membership to new gang inductees.

NBC *Dateline* (1993) reported that initiation into some San Antonio, Texas, girl gangs involves having sexual intercourse with someone infected with HIV (the virus precursor of AIDS). Another female initiation is called "rolling the dice" in which the digits on the dice determine the number of males with whom the new member must have sex. The slang expression used by the gang for this sexual initiation is "engine to caboose" (i.e., "first to last").

Gang Organization

Frederick Thrasher's (1927) observation that "no two gangs are just alike" is still valid. He indicated that "wide divergency in the character of its personnel combined with differences of physical social environment, or experience and tradition, give to every gang its own peculiar character. It may vary as to membership, type of leaders, mode of organization, interests and activities, and finally as to its status in the community" (Thrasher, 1927:45). While this complex variability among delinquent gangs confounds the formation of discrete, categorical types, there are some overarching patterns of social organization that can be identified.

In smaller, less goal-oriented youth gangs, one or two older, tougher, more articulate boys with forceful personalities may be the informally acknowledged leaders, who set the pace and determine the nature of the groups' activities. On the other hand, larger and more instrumental gangs have a functional organization, generally reflecting the nature of their orientation and activities. For example, the leadership of such well-known fighting gangs as the Egyptian Kings and Dragons, the Mau Maus, and the Jesters includes the president, vice-president, treasurer, a "light-up man" or "armorer" who maintains the gang's arsenal, and the "war counselor" who serves to identify enemy gangs and arranges for "rumbles" or fights.

Formal and informal alliances may be worked out between gangs that find some practical advantage or benefit in such alliances. Malcolm Klein (1964) identified such affiliations among several traditional gangs in Los Angeles. Typically, a "gang cluster" consists of three or four age-graded male subgroups plus a female auxiliary. Each subgroup maintains its own identity yet clearly affiliates with the overall cluster and its "generic name." In this way, several small and relatively weak gangs can muster a more formidable appearance through their alliance network, in confrontations with rival gangs. A few crime-oriented youth gangs have contacts and working agreements with adult criminals in their areas. This can have far-reaching implications. An exploratory study by John Irwin and Donald Cressey (1977) highlighted the situation in Illinois prisons where there is an importation of organization, roles, and norms from the streets of Chicago to the prison through gangs which retain their organization and identity inside and outside prison walls. Today, gangs operate openly in almost every penal institution.

Meetings and meeting places may be loosely defined by most smaller gangs and their members as "anytime" or "all the time," "anywhere" or "everywhere," and a centrally located street corner, shopping mall, or convenience store may serve as gang headquarters. At the other extreme, a few large gangs have become institutionalized in some cities. The Vice Lords in Chicago, for example, created an administrative board of directors comprised of representatives from subgroups within the "Vice Lord Nation." Regular weekly meetings were instituted, along with membership fees, and membership cards featuring the Vice Lords' logo—a top hat, cane, and white gloves (Keiser, 1969).

The Near Group

Lewis Yablonsky (1959) complained that most efforts to explain gang organization begin with the imprecise assumption that gangs fit the pattern of the traditionally defined sociological group. His research concluded that the delinquent gang is organizationally midway between the stability of the established group and the instability of the mob. Thus, the gang is a kind of social collectivity in its own right, with characteristics especially suited to meet the varied needs of its members.

> One way of viewing human collectivities is on a continuum of organization characteristics. At one extreme, we have a highly organized, cohesive, functioning collection of individuals as members of a sociological group.

> At the other extreme, we have a mob of individuals characterized by anonymity, disturbed leadership, motivated by emotion, and in some cases representing a destructive collectivity within the inclusive social system. (Yablonsky, 1959:109)

Yablonsky maintained that most delinquent gangs are midway on the group–mob continuum and thus are structurally neither groups nor mobs. He described the gang as a "near group" characterized by "diffuse role definitions, limited cohesion, impermanence, minimal consensus of norms, shifting membership, disturbed leadership, and limited definition of membership expectations" (Yablonsky, 1959:109).

Several other researchers have challenged parts of Yablonsky's generalization. Cohen and Short (1958) and other proponents of the gang subculture concept argued that many gang members share a remarkable consensus regarding norms and roles. Klein (1971) contended that the large majority of gang leaders are *not* sociopathic nor do they otherwise suffer serious emotional maladjustment.

John Hagedorn (1998), on the basis of his study of Milwaukee gangs, confirmed Thrasher's observation on the diversity of gang organization and cautioned against the pyramid stereotype of a hard core of sociopathic criminals leading a broad fringe of impressionable kids.

> Milwaukee's gangs come in a variety of forms and shapes, but none that looks like a pyramid. . . . Each age-group has its own "main-group," its leaders, and its "wanna be's.". . . The makeup of each of these age groups varies between gangs and over time within each gang. A "wanna be" this week may be in the "main group" next week. (Hagedorn, 1998:89, 90)

Gang Graffiti, Slanguage, and Symbols

Like most other enduring subcultures, street gangs are characterized by their unique and ever-evolving jargon or language. This *slanguage* is reflected in youth gang graffiti, which has been called "the newspaper of the streets" for gang members. Its presence is usually one of the first signs of street gang activity in a neighborhood. While graffiti is a chronic and unsightly eyesore to the larger community, it serves several useful purposes to gangs, including identifying territorial boundaries, giving a roster of members, advertising gang exploits, and communicating messages to rival gangs.

An understanding of graffiti is important to law enforcement officers who have the responsibility of surveillance and interrogation of gang members and to protect society from their illegal activities. Accurate interpretations of graffiti can help identify gangs operating in certain areas, identify the members through their monikers or nicknames, aid in monitoring gang challenges and rivalries, and assist in developing leads on suspects of gang-related crimes. Figure 12.2 is an example of Hispanic gang graffiti and its interpretation. For more contemporary examples, use any major search engine to search "gang graffiti."

The distinctive language employed by various gangs is a code that defies translation by nonmembers. In order to decipher the communication within and between gangs and their members, police intelligence units in many cities have compiled extensive lexicons or dictionaries of words and phrases commonly used by black,

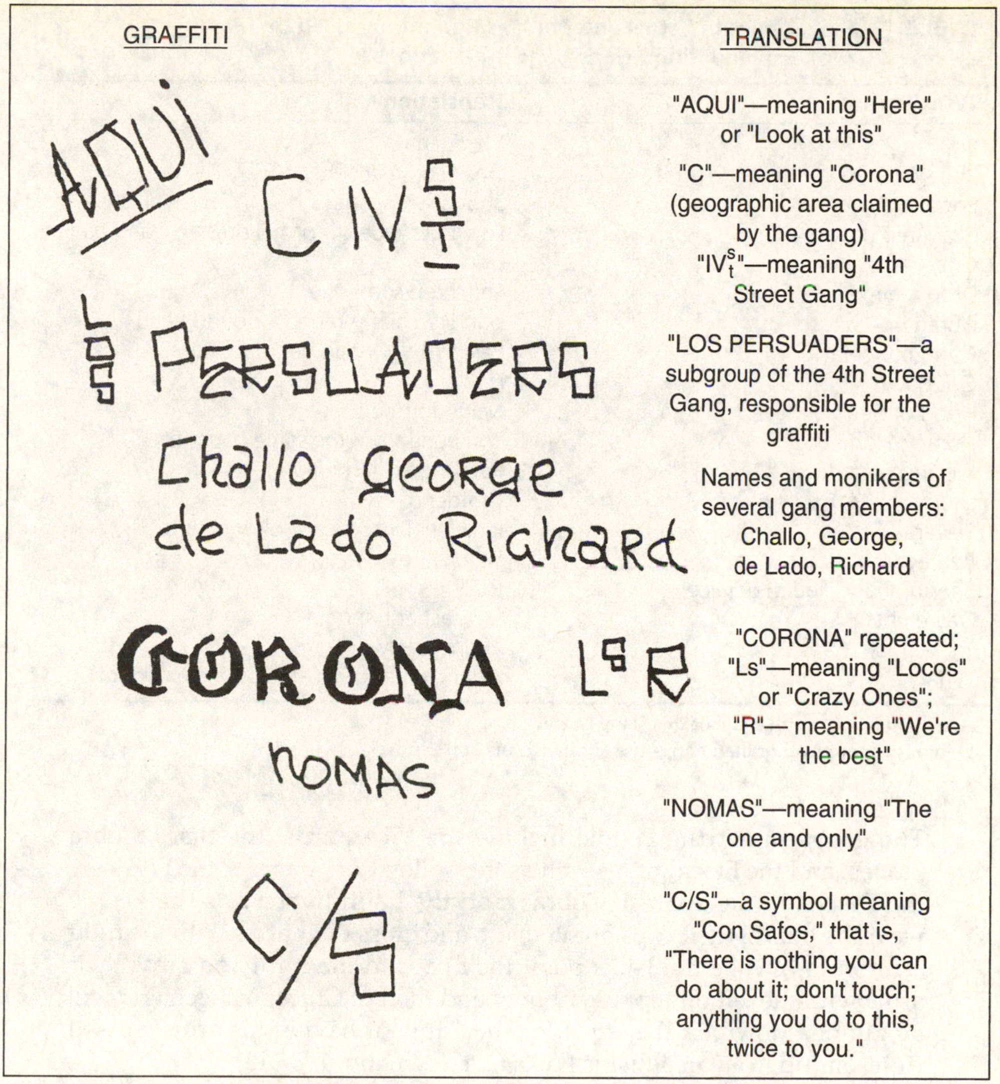

GRAFFITI	TRANSLATION
AQUI	"AQUI"—meaning "Here" or "Look at this"
C IV$^{S}_{T}$	"C"—meaning "Corona" (geographic area claimed by the gang) "IV$^{s}_{t}$"—meaning "4th Street Gang"
LOS PERSUADERS	"LOS PERSUADERS"—a subgroup of the 4th Street Gang, responsible for the graffiti
Challo George de Lado Richard	Names and monikers of several gang members: Challo, George, de Lado, Richard
CORONA L^{S} R	"CORONA" repeated; "Ls"—meaning "Locos" or "Crazy Ones"; "R"— meaning "We're the best"
NOMAS	"NOMAS"—meaning "The one and only"
C/S	"C/S"—a symbol meaning "Con Safos," that is, "There is nothing you can do about it; don't touch; anything you do to this, twice to you."

FIGURE 12.2 An Example of Hispanic Gang Graffiti and Translation.
Have you seen graffiti on walls, signs, and other places? Does it represent gang activity? What other forms of delinquency might it represent? How should communities go about combating gang graffiti?

Source: Castaneda, Esteban P., *Guide for identifying youth gang graffiti and tattoos.* Sacramento, CA: California Youth Authority, March 26, 1986:4.

white, and Hispanic gangs. Table 12.1 lists just a few examples from a lengthy police compilation of terms and phrases employed by Blood and Crip gangs.

More formally organized youth gangs also often have a complex system of identifying colors, clothing styles, hand signs, and body language (Savelli, 2005; Trump, 1998). In Chicago, for instance, there are two large families, or clusters, of interrelated and allied gangs: the People and the Folks.

TABLE 12.1 Examples of Terms and Phrases Commonly Used by Members of Crip and Blood Gangs and Translations

Term/Phrase	Translation
Bo	Marijuana
Bullet	One year in custody
Popped a cap	Shot at someone
Cragared down	Low rider type car or full dressed gang banger
Cuzz	Crip
Drop a dime	Snitch on someone
Durag	Handkerchief wrapped around head
Gang banger	Person involved in gang activity
Get down	Fight
Hood or Set	Neighborhood
Homey, Homeboy	Someone from the same gang; friend
Kicking back	Relaxing; killing time
Lady	Girlfriend
Player	Individual interested solely in girls
Red eye	Hard stare
Sherm, wack, liquid, or juice	P.C.P.
Tray eight	.38 caliber handgun
Trick, hook	Phoney sissy
What set you from?	Asking what gang are you a member of

Are you familiar with some of this slang/argot?
Do youth groups other than gangs use similar terms and phrases?

> The gangs under the People include the Vice Lords, the Black Cobra Stones, and the El Rukns, as well as the Valley Rocks; under the Folks are the Disciples, the Spanish Cobras, and the Latin Jivers. . . . The People wear the bills of their caps pointed left, and cross their arms with the right arm on top, while the Folks point their caps to the right and cross their arms with the left on top. Every now and then in Chicago a teenager will be gunned down on the street for the crime of having his arms crossed right-on-top in an area that is Folks turf. (Lemann, 1986:13)

COMPOSITION OF GANG MEMBERSHIP

The composition of a group or population of people refers to those common demographic traits that best describe or typify the group. Three population characteristics of gang members are discussed here that will contribute to our overall understanding regarding the formation and delinquent behavior of youthful gangs: social class, racial and ethnic composition, and female participation in delinquent gangs.

Social Class

Official crime reports indicate that juvenile delinquency is statistically concentrated in lower socioeconomic urban neighborhoods. While this conclusion may be tempered by a purported class bias among some law enforcement officers as reflected in arrest statistics, there is considerable evidence of the strong relationship between lower-class unemployment and poverty and a high incidence of property crime. Similar to juvenile delinquents in general, gang members are typically characterized as being from poor neighborhoods with substandard housing in which the residents have little hope for educational or occupational achievements.

A broader picture of social class and juvenile gang membership has emerged from several important studies that found definite groupings of young people in more affluent social classes who participate in delinquent activities. For example, Howard and Barbara Myerhoff (1964), in their observations of middle-class gangs, found youngsters informally and loosely organized for many socially acceptable activities. However, drag racing, drinking of alcoholic beverages, sexual activity, and other forms of deviant and illegal behavior often emerged. The middle-class subjects of the Myerhoffs' study generally lacked the alienated leadership and violent behavior often attributed to lower-class gangs. In addition, and again in contrast to the lower-class subjects targeted by most research on gangs, the middle-class youngsters did not demonstrate well-developed delinquent values, nor did they define themselves as delinquents or troublemakers. Rather, they fully expected to ultimately abandon their temporary deviant behavior and take conventional and law-abiding places in society. These optimistic feelings about the future were shared by the adults in their environment, thus eliciting more tolerance for middle-class juveniles than for lower-class or underclass youngsters.

THE STRAIGHT EDGERS In contrast to the middle-class gangs observed by the Myerhoffs, Edmund Vaz, and other scholars cited in this section, a middle-class, ideology-based gang has emerged. Between 1995 and 1998, an ultraconservative youth group named *The Straight Edgers* reacted violently against drug and alcohol use and against casual sex by many other youths in society. They take their name from a 1981 song, "Straight Edge," by Ian MacKaye of the band Minor Threat:

> I'm a person just like you,
> But I've got better things to do
> Than sit around and smoke dope . . .
> I've got a straight edge.

Extreme, hardcore Straight Edgers use chains, mace, knives, clubs, beatings, brawls, and vandalism to enforce their abstinent lifestyle in schoolyards, punk rock concerts, and shopping mall parking lots. In Salt Lake City, a crowd of Straight Edgers carved a large × on the back of a youth caught smoking marijuana. To underscore their self-styled wholesome lifestyle, Straight Edgers have adopted the × as their symbol, × being what music clubs stamp on the hands of patrons too young for alcohol (Levinson, 1998).

According to Arlene Levinson (1998:3A), "The typical Straight Edger in Utah is white, male, and middle class, ranging in age from the early teens to early 20s." The more extreme members of the movement are often strict vegetarians—rejecting all animal products—and are involved in violent crimes as part of the Animal Liberation Front.

Racial and Ethnic Composition of Gangs

Race and ethnicity are, of themselves, powerful forces that can draw people together into cohesive groups. Birds of a feather indeed flock together! Moreover, if the race or ethnicity of a group is associated in the minds of group members with social, economic, or political injustices they feel they have suffered, additional solidarity and commitment to group objectives can result. With this in mind, Davis (1978) argued that gang ethnicity should always be considered when the modalities and motivations of gangs are examined. Thus, race or ethnicity can serve as a unifying and sacred cause for some gangs—more symbolic and preeminent than their leather jackets and intimidating names (Moore, 1985). Howard Erlanger's study (1979) of the relationships between the subcultural values of the Hispanic American barrios in East Los Angeles, estrangement from the dominant white society, and gang violence offers a classic example of this phenomenon:

> . . . while subcultural values of the barrio may be different from those of the Anglo society and may exist independently of Anglo society, they do not directly require or condone violence. . . . [However], under situations of estrangement or alienation from the Anglo society brought about by discrimination or negative images of Chicano culture, young Chicanos may become collectively violent as they respond to the strong Chicano cultural emphasis on values such as courage and dignity for males. (Erlanger, 1979:235)

Erlanger described the deep resentment Hispanic Americans felt about the educational situation in East Los Angeles, in which their children were punished for speaking Spanish, even among themselves, in the schoolyard. Hispanic youths interpreted this as rejection by the Anglo society, and this scenario elicited a readiness to fight among some youthful barrio gangs. James Vigil (1997) briefly traces the emergence and evolution of Hispanic gangs in southern California and other parts of the nation. Beginning in the 1940s as a small number of neighborhood-based youth groups given to periodic outbursts of destructive behavior, these gangs became very deadly and violent street entities by the 1990s. Vigil (1997) estimates, however, that a still small number, between 4 and 10 percent, of Mexican American youth belong to gangs.

Chinese American youth gangs have a long history in major U.S. cities on the West Coast. Their criminal activities of extortion (selling of "protection") and the theft of goods and services from Chinese American merchants have become institutionalized due to the pragmatic tolerance of their victims (Chin, et al., 1992).

While Hispanics and African Americans constituted the majority of U.S. gang members in 1996 (Bilchik, 1999a:23), gangs continue to develop in every racial category. One of the more recent racial gang groupings is the Vietnamese, emerging from the relatively new, close-knit Vietnamese communities of California (Senate Subcommittee on Juvenile Justice, 1983; Wyrick, 2000a). These gangs are particularly violent, utilizing robbery, bombing, extortion, and murder as terror tactics. Several loosely organized Asian gangs in Sacramento, California, specialize in midnight attacks on the homes of other Asians, assaulting occupants and stealing money. This group of masked young people, after each three- or four-day rampage, quietly disbands and fades back into the general population.

Although the majority of gangs of racial and ethnic minority origin are homogeneous in composition, some demonstrate a degree of racial and ethnic integration in their membership, especially in neighborhoods where housing has been well integrated (Bilchik, 1999c). However, Kobrin and Peluso (1968) observed strikingly different levels of social status within the gangs for members of various races. The numerically dominant race carefully retained positions of highest prestige and power within the group.

Female Participation in Delinquent Gangs

Chapter 3 underscored the statistical evidence that juvenile delinquents are predominantly male. The same generality applies to gang membership. Traditionally, female involvement in gang delinquency has been more passive than active, with girls and young women functioning as support personnel to male members rather than as equal participants. James Short (1968:4) and numerous other writers aptly depicted these females and their secondary roles and statuses as a branch organization or female auxiliary:

> The gang world is dominated largely by males. . . . But girls are important, too, for many reasons: as sex objects, hustles to be exploited, sources of prestige among the boys with whom they are associated, and in their own right. "Female auxiliary" groups are not uncommon, and when they exist they perform many functions for boys' gangs and enjoy a degree of autonomy among themselves. Their names characteristically suggest their association with boys' gangs, e.g., Vice Queens (associated with the Vice Kings), Egyptian Cobrettes (associated with the Egyptian Cobras), and Lady Racketeers (associated with the Racketeers).

While auxiliary status has been the most common form of gang participation available to females, some gangs permit sexually integrated membership (Hardman, 1969). This phenomenon is more likely in middle-class, suburban gangs, whose youthful members have not been seriously alienated from middle-class norms and values and still aspire to middle-class educational and occupational objectives. This does not mean that females may not be members of lower-class urban street gangs, however. Anne Campbell (1991) estimated that approximately 10 percent of the growing gang population in New York City are females ranging in age from 14 to 30.

It now appears that a rapidly growing number of well-organized, crime-oriented female gangs are creating a major problem for law enforcement. A *CBS News* Report (1986) estimated that approximately 1,000 girls are involved in over 100 female gangs in Chicago alone. It was emphasized that these are not sister organizations or auxiliaries to male gangs, but independent female gangs. Similar to their male counterparts, these female gangs stake out their own "turf" or territory, adopt distinctive colors and insignia, and have physical confrontations and fights with rival gangs. The CBS Report documented one case in which a nonmember was badly beaten because she wore a yellow article of clothing and yellow happened to be the official color of a nearby female gang. Another juvenile, a 13-year-old girl, was shot in the head and killed by other gang members because they thought she was a police informant.

The authoritative National Youth Gang Survey extrapolated in 2006 that females accounted for approximately 11 percent of active gang members in the United States. Although numbers were highest in urban areas, the proportion of female gang members was highest in rural counties (Egley and O'Donnell, 2007).

Female gangs today, like male gangs, also vary considerably in motivation and kind of criminal involvement. The Sly Vixens and the Tiny Diablas are both centered in the Watts ghetto of Los Angeles County. The Sly Vixens are into heavy drugs and prostitution while the 14- to 19-year-old Tiny Diablas take a weekly collection to buy guns and contend that their gang "gives them a social structure and sense of identity they would not have otherwise" (Donovan, 1990:33).

Contemporary research on why young females affiliate with gangs offers mixed and inconclusive explanations. Anne Campbell's qualitative study of *The Girls in the Gang* (1991) found that membership in three New York City gangs appealed to lonely and alienated girls from transient and physically violent families. However, a quantitative study by Lee Bowker and Malcolm Klein (1983) weakened the previously accepted generalization that females commit delinquent acts or join delinquent gangs because they are socially maladjusted, come from broken and unhappy homes, and do not relate well to the opposite sex. This latter position is supported by Jody Miller's study, *One of the Guys: Girls, Gangs, and Gender* (2001). A comprehensive review of the literature by Joan Moore and John Hagedorn (2006) found that most studies show friendship, solidarity, self-affirmation, and a sense of new possibilities motivate young, inner-city females to join and remain in gangs.

GANG VIOLENCE

Law enforcement agencies, criminologists, and others who specialize in the study of juvenile crime generally agree that gang membership increases the likelihood of more serious delinquent behavior (Thornberry and Burch, 1997). The reason, according to Klein and Crawford (1968), lies in the cohesiveness generated in the group, as "macho" posturing, alienation, and the challenge of taking risks are shared and reinforced. It follows that the individual youth who might ordinarily be intimidated by law enforcement officers and reluctant to violate major social norms can become emotionally involved and committed to acts of bravado and delinquency in the context of the gang (Kennedy and Baron, 1993). But, here again, we must take into account the great variation among gangs in purpose, social class, level of perceived estrangement from the dominant society, and subcultural values.

Most gangs do not have crime as their dominant activity; offenses are committed spontaneously; and most members have temporary gang memberships and short criminal careers (Sarnecki, 1982).

Walter Miller (1966) sought to counter the popular media reports that urban gangs are massively, consistently, and continually involved in violent behavior. His research revealed that while theft and vandalism were common among gang members, violence was not a major activity of urban street gangs, nor a central reason for their existence. Only a small minority of gang members participated in violent crime. When violence did occur, it most frequently involved unarmed physical encounters between male antagonists, usually motivated to defend honor or prestige. "Generally, it was not 'ganging up' by malicious sadists on the weak, the innocent, the solitary. It did not victimize adult females. With few exceptions, violent crimes fell into the 'less serious' category, with the extreme or shocking crimes rare" (Miller, 1966:111).

During the years since Miller's research, the level and scope of gang violence has dramatically increased. In a later study, Miller (1975) reversed his former position with newer data showing that the rate of murder by youth gangs with firearms was higher than ever before.

R. B. Toplin's (1975:81) *Unchallenged Violence: An American Ordeal* supported the view that contemporary gangs engage in violence of greater severity than did gangs of past years: "During the 1950s, gangs fought with bottles, clubs, chains, knives, and fists. Now they fight with handguns, revolvers, and shotguns." Many combat-oriented gang members in the 1990s were equipped with such advanced automatic weapons as Uzi submachine guns and Chinese copies of the Soviet AK-47 assault rifle, which can be purchased on the streets of our cities.

Gang violence continued to undergo modifications in strategy and style. In his *Gang Bangers and Drive-bys* (1994), William Sanders describes how the drive-by shooting replaced rumbles as the primary form of gang confrontation. Using automobiles and mobile tactics with manufactured, high-quality weapons and the element of surprise, this form of gang violence is far more deadly than the street melees of the past. Gangbangs is a generic term for a variety of other gang violence including assaults rapes knifings, killings, and beatings.

Drive-by homicides began to decline in Los Angeles in 1993. Coincidentally, that was also the year that an organized crime syndicate nicknamed "The Mexican Mafia" issued an anti-drive-by edict in the belief that the practice threatened its lucrative drug trade by bringing unwanted attention to the neighborhoods. Many gangs further adapted with the "walk-up" or walk-by shooting in which the gunman attacks his targeted victim face-to-face. This was an easy transition, rationalized by the exaggerated and distorted sense of honor held by gang members: "If you are going to be a man and shoot somebody, at least have the guts to look them in the face and shoot them. . . . It is more honorable to kill at close range" (*Medford Mail Tribune,* 1996:8B). The decline in drive-bys did not stem the number of gang homicides which reached an all-time high of 807 in Los Angeles County in 1995.

In 1999, the Office of Juvenile Justice and Delinquency Prevention reported that "gangs played a role in almost 80 percent of the adolescent homicide incidents examined in Los Angeles" (Bilchik, 1999b:14).

Violence touches and terminates the lives of a very large portion of American young people, over and above the conspicuous and aggressive street gangs. This alarming point was underscored by Robert Blum (1987), Director of the Adolescent Health Program at the University of Minnesota, and published in the *Journal of the American Medical Association.* Blum's statistical analysis revealed that three of four 15- to 24-year-old Americans who die are victims of violence. Accidents, primarily auto accidents, account for 53.5 percent of the fatalities and remain by far the leading cause of death in that age group. But homicide deaths among young people have climbed 300 percent in three decades to become the number two killer.

Blum credited these grim statistics on homicide and other forms of violence to the increasing "juvenilization of poverty." He projected that within a few years, one of every five adolescents will live at or below the poverty level. Blum agreed with numerous social scientists that impoverished and hopeless youths are subject to more substance abuse, more adolescent pregnancy, higher school dropout rates, more crime, and higher death rates due to violence.

The Federal Bureau of Investigation has given top priority to a rapidly expanding criminal enterprise that has been labeled "America's Most Vicious Gang" (Dealey,

2006). The notorious "MS-13 Gang" originated among thousands of children of immigrants who fled the San Salvador civil war in the 1980s to settle in U.S. urban and suburban neighborhoods (Nightline Gang Report, 2005). They recruit new members from other Hispanic groups and, armed with guns, machetes, fanatical gang loyalty, and a brutal disregard for human life, MS-13 has become the dominant gang. Their criminal activities include robbery, car-chopping, smuggling drugs and illegal aliens, rape, and indiscriminate murder—often targeting police officers (Ragavan and Guttman, 2004). As an example of the gang's mindless violence, in 2002, MS-13 gang members "raped two deaf teenage girls in a Boston-area park. One girl was lifted from her wheelchair and slammed onto a park bench for the assault" (Dealey, 2006:2).

DRUG FRANCHISES AND GANG WARFARE

As discouraging and alarming as these reports of persistent and collective violence by young people may be, they have proved to be but a prologue for the escalating and bloody urban gang wars that erupted in 1987 and continues into the 21st century—though at a slightly reduced pace (Bilchik, 1999c).

This proliferation of street gangs and violence are sometimes driven by the economics of drug. Urban districts and perhaps entire cities are being franchised for the marketing of "crack" cocaine. Thus, the gangs have become the pushers and enforcers for the international drug trade.

Several California research investigations have reported that two prominent Los Angeles gangs were expanding their drug-trafficking operations to other cities. Verification came from the National Drug Intelligence Center in 1996: "Gangs claiming affiliation with the Bloods or Crips were reported in 180 jurisdictions in 42 states. . . . Chicago-based gangs were reported in 110 jurisdictions in 35 states" (Howell, 1998:11).

A nationwide perspective is offered by the 2006 National Youth Gang Survey which cited that on average, law-enforcement respondents estimated that 43 percent of the drug sales in their jurisdictions involved gang members" (Egley and O'Donnell, 2007).

Gang Rape

Gang rape is another form of violent crime that involves surprisingly large numbers of American youths. Multiple rape or group rape is almost as common as single rape. Menachem Amir's (1971) study of a large number of rape cases revealed that 43 percent were multiple rapes. The most significant fact about multiple rape, as shown by Amir's data, is that its perpetrators were largely adolescents from 10 to 19 years of age.

In 1989, a new term was added to our lexicon of fear and violence when six New York City youths described their predatory rampage through Central Park as "wilding." They were brought to trial in 1990 for allegedly brutalizing and raping a young woman jogger and leaving her for dead with a crushed skull (Kaplan, et al., 1990). The trial was later declared a "mistrial" and the youths were released.

Some psychiatrists interpret gang rape as an expression of latent homosexuality, arguing that the co-rapists have an unconscious wish to have sex with each other. Such an interpretation, according to Alex Thio (2006) makes as much sense as the

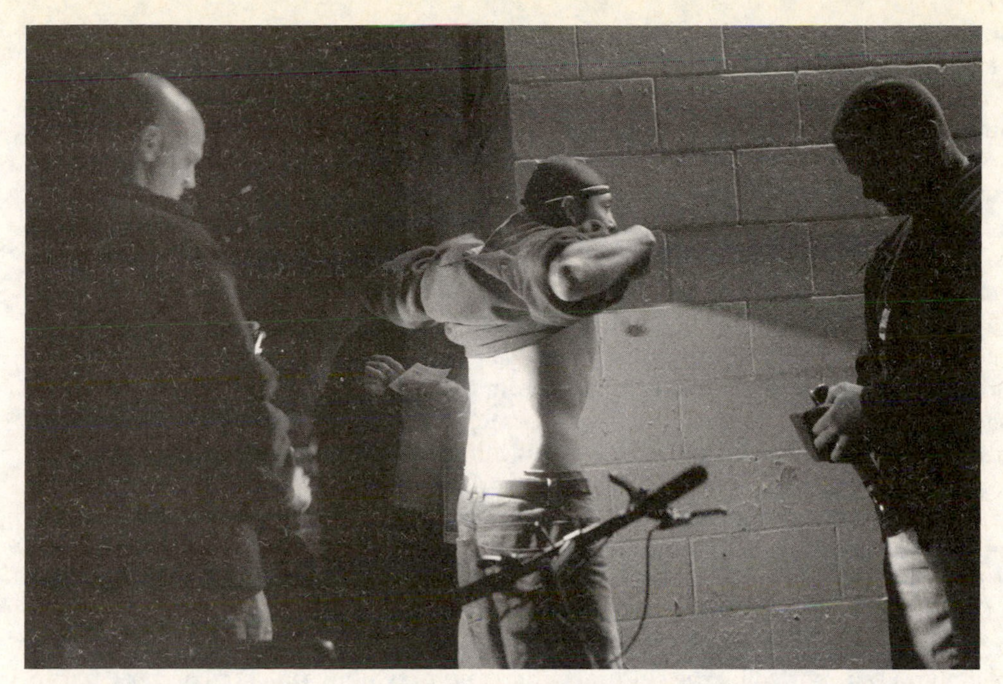

Suffolk County Police officers from the anti-gang unit check for tattoos and identity papers of possible gang members of Mara Salvatrucha 13 or MS-13. Does your hometown or city have an anti-gang unit? What other measures are cities taking to help cut down on gang violence?

suggestion that several men who rob a store together unconsciously want to rob each other. Actually, participation in a gang rape fulfills a social need rather than a sexual desire, particularly for youngsters who feel peer pressure to prove that they are not "chicken" (Groth and Birnbaum, 1979:115).

One of the startling byproducts of such acts of violence is the failure of many bystanders to heed calls for help from the victim. A vivid example was the 1983 gang rape of a young woman in a bar in New Bedford, Massachusetts. She entered the building to make a telephone call and promptly was assaulted by a group of young men: "Despite the presence of numerous patrons other than the several rapists, none intervened. Only after the victim ran naked into the street did a passing motorist provide assistance and summon the police" (Ritzer, 1986:461).

Although such widely publicized events are relatively infrequent, and are not limited to occurrence in large cities, they reflect an apparent pattern of apathy among many urban residents.

EXPLANATORY THEORIES OF GANG FORMATION AND BEHAVIOR: A SUMMARY AND SYNTHESIS

Chapters 4 through 8 are devoted to causal theories of juvenile delinquency. Chapter 5 contains a discussion and critique of several sociological theories related to the etiology of juvenile gangs. Now, in the context of this chapter, a brief review and summary of the most prominent explanatory theories of gang formation and behavior are appropriate.

The sociological examination and application of the related concepts of culture and subculture formed the foundation for some major theoretical explications of juvenile gang delinquency. In Chapter 11, we defined culture and subculture and discussed how American youth subculture can contribute to delinquency.

Once they had carefully defined culture and subculture, it was a short step for sociological theorists to turn their attention to deviant, criminal, and delinquent subcultures as explanatory social contexts for nonconforming or antisocial behavior.

Deviant subculture is *a term applied to any subgroup that deviates markedly from the generally accepted values, norms, and behavioral expectations of the dominant society.* Such nonconformists as "punk rockers," nudists, and religious snake handlers may be classified as members of deviant subcultures because they share with others some unusual beliefs, practices, and lifestyles that significantly set them apart. However, they are not ordinarily perceived by the larger society as major threats to the social order.

On the other hand, a **criminal** or **delinquent subculture** *manifests such extreme and negative nonconformity to the normative prescriptions of the larger society that its members are generally viewed as antisocial—against society.* Sutherland (1939), Shaw and McKay (1942), and other early sociologists/criminologists pinpointed the locus of many of these subcultures in high delinquency areas of central cities, where criminal behavior is supported by the cultural values and prevailing practices of those particular districts. Thus, juvenile delinquents often gain identification and encouragement from other delinquents and from criminal elements in their area with whom they associate. In that environment, such behavior is socially learned, expected, and rewarded. Such youngsters, with strong loyalties and emotional attachment to peers, have also learned to distrust established institutions and authorities. They clash with society because the values of their subculture are in conflict with the dominant laws of the land. Once these youths have become involved in lawlessness, their problems snowball, making it more and more difficult for them to stay out of trouble.

After World War II, the most important advances in understanding the causes of delinquency emerged from studies of urban youth gangs. Collectively, these theoretical formulations are sometimes referred to as *Theory of the Reactive Subculture,* though actually this is a group of theoretical constructs. They have in common the idea that misconduct is elicited in lower-class youths who have internalized middle-class cultural values and objectives of educational, occupational, and materialistic success and are frustrated in their achievement. For example, Albert Cohen (1958) advanced the theory that gangs develop a delinquent subculture, which represents solutions to the problems of some lower-class males. A gang gives them a chance to belong, to amount to something, to develop and demonstrate their masculinity, and to fight middle-class society. In particular, the delinquent subculture, according to Cohen, is an anomic response toward resolution of the status problems of lower-class boys.

The theoretical contribution of Richard Cloward and Lloyd Ohlin (1960), like Cohen's, is also a spinoff from Robert Merton's (1957) general theory of anomie as an explanation for deviant behavior. As discussed in Chapter 5, Cloward and Ohlin, while agreeing with Merton and Cohen that the disunion between cultural goals and the inadequate means available for their achievement can create strain for lower-class youths, argued that they still need to have the opportunity to break away from the dominant, middle-class values and turn to illegitimate means to achieve status and self-esteem. In other words, Cloward and Ohlin's Theory of Delinquency and Opportunity postulated that every youth who feels deprived and disadvantaged does not turn to the same alternative illegitimate avenues to success. Even delinquent opportunities may not be readily available in the frustrated youth's social environment. Moreover, not only does the quantity of delinquent opportunity vary from area to area and from neighborhood to neighborhood, but there is a quality differential as well. In recognition of that fact, Cloward and Ohlin suggested that there are three kinds of gang subcultures that can develop—the crime-oriented, the conflict-oriented, and the retreatist or drug-oriented. The type that emerges to satisfy the needs for group support and status among lower-class youth depends upon the available opportunity in their local communities.

A more contemporary investigation by Vowell and May (2000:42) found empirical support for Merton's classic Strain Theory and the postulate that "poverty status, perceived blocked opportunity, and gang membership are predictors of adolescent violent behavior."

Walter Miller (1958) disagreed with Cohen and with Cloward and Ohlin that the gang is a reactive subculture whose delinquent behavior is a compensation for lower-class failure to reach middle-class goals. Rather, Miller scrutinized lower-class culture for values that could reflect in behavior identified as delinquent by the dominant, middle-class society. Miller's study concluded that lower-class culture is characterized by six "focal concerns" or values that could easily be interpreted as troublesome opposition to middle-class values or a predisposition to delinquency. These lower-class cultural values are *trouble, toughness, excitement, fate, smartness,* and *autonomy,* which represent highly prized masculinity to lower-class boys. Paradoxically, the youth's socialized allegiance to those values can produce delinquent behavior and encourage gang membership.

Sociological theories of gang delinquency offer many valuable insights into social class differences, culture conflict, and subcultural response. They suggest that gang delinquency is largely a lower-class phenomenon and is typically clustered together with other social pathologies such as poverty, unstable family life, and inner-city slum neighborhoods. Box 12.2 indicates that urban youth gangs are not unique to the United States.

As detailed in Chapter 5, the subcultural theories of juvenile delinquency are not without their critics. Some have contended that the entire concept of a subculture of juvenile delinquency is meaningless when compared with more powerful and permanent familial, ethnic or racial, and social class value systems impacting upon young people. David Matza (1964) argued that juvenile delinquents, like all young people, spend only a limited amount of time with each other. They still go to their own homes; many attend school; some have jobs. There are prior and offsetting influences in place to counter the shared alienation that is assumed to lead to the procriminal values of the gang. If juvenile delinquents did belong to a viable delinquent subculture, Matza argued, then those who are caught would not be embarrassed or remorseful, as they so often are. Do these youngsters really have a set of values of their own, or do they actually believe in those of their parents, teachers, and other conforming authority figures with whom they are still in contact? Today's violent gang members, however, seldom show the embarrassment or remorse Matza found in the 1960s.

BOX 12.2

CROSS-CULTURAL FOCUS: Urban Youth Gangs in Russia

The following interviews with Russian police officers, youthful offenders, and other citizens were conducted by CBS news correspondents Harold Dow, Bernard Goldberg, Dan Rather, and Phil Jones. They are excerpts from a CBS documentary entitled "Moscow Vice" that was the televised topic of *48 Hours* on May 31, 1990.

Muscling In

Harold Dow, CBS News: Moscow in the spring. As hard-lined Communism continues to thaw, a new order is emerging here. But for now, no one knows the rules. Private businesses and cooperatives are flourishing, choice targets for the vanguard in Soviet crime. Nick has the power to enforce his own law. He's the leader of a Moscow street gang. . . . Nicholas, why do you have to stay strong?

Nick: Because if I don't stay strong, I won't be able to survive the competition. I protect businessmen, that's how I live.

Dow: Legitimate businesses are not the only prey of Moscow's racketeers. When state-run liquor stores close, black marketeers take up the slack, selling booze at inflated prices, and paying street gangs for protection.

Nick: I don't have to beat their face in, if someone doesn't want to pay, we just take his vodka and smash the bottles. Nothing criminal in that.

Dow: Nick and his boys are one of many gangs fighting to control turf. Today, they're setting off to meet a rival gang, competition trying to muscle in.

Nick: They wanted to take our daily bread. They came and started to demand money from the people that nourish us. We told them that we would destroy them if they tried to do that again. . . .

Wild Ones

Bernard Goldberg, CBS News: Ever since Gorbachev began lifting the Iron Curtain, all sorts of light has been flooding into the Soviet Union. In Moscow these days, kids can watch music videos, beamed in by satellite, from what the old men in the Kremlin used to call the decadent West. But there's also a darkness amidst the light, called juvenile crime. . . . Vera Kripinova and her 14-year-old daughter Elizabeth, [are] among Moscow's elite. They see the changes, and notice the darkness.

Ms. Kripinova: And lots of people steal because they think—they feel it will be worse in the future, so this is the time—the good time, for stealing. It's not only for children. It's a mentality.

Goldberg [to young prisoner]: Why are you here in jail?

Young Man: I have stolen sneakers.

Goldberg: Sneakers! Sneakers? It's one of the new, hot juvenile crimes in the Soviet Union: sneaker snatching. He traveled 900 miles to steal a pair. Now let me make sure I understand this. You got on a train, some place up the Volga River, traveled a day and a half to Moscow to steal somebody's sneakers? Why sneakers?

Young Man: Just fashion.

Elizabeth Kripinova: Just look at our kids—I go to school and I see that they—you know, they don't believe in anything, really.

Ms. Kripinova: Skeptical?

Elizabeth Kripinova: Yeah, they're very skeptical.

Goldberg: [Then there are] the wild ones, Moscow style. Wheelies in the night. Police call them the rockers. They live in the shadows of the new Soviet Union—part of it, but mostly apart from it. [to a group of rockers] Do you have any dreams? What do kids want to be? What do you hope for in this new Soviet Union?

Rocker: That's a very interesting question. The thing is that I don't think our generation has anything to dream about.

Goldberg: Whom do you look up to? Do you have any heroes?

Rocker: No, we don't have any heroes, no idols.

Goldberg: Have any of you, honest, been either the victims of crime or have actually committed crimes yourself?

Rocker: We've been victims since we were born. The thing is, first you're a victim and then you become a criminal.

Something Old . . .

Dan Rather, CBS News: A precinct in southwest Moscow. This night, like every night, these cops are on drunk patrol. [to officer] Do you get hardened to this?

Police Officer, Moscow: I haven't become indifferent to their suffering. I think about all of the sorrow that they bring their family members. It makes me very sad.

Rather: Eighty percent of the crime here is linked to alcohol abuse. Its effect may even be more devastating on Soviet society than drugs are in the United States. . . .

Something New

Phil Jones, CBS News: The drug war, Moscow style. . . . Andree Dahilenko is a 23-year-old American from San Francisco involved in Moscow's drug war.

Mr. Dahilenko: The situation with drugs here is probably similar to the situation with drugs in the United States, let's say in the 50s or 60s. When it wasn't around all that much. . . . This program was designed to help the kids stay off the street, stay away from drugs. Their life is so miserable, they consider that taking drugs takes away the pain. . . .

Interpreter: Mostly they're using opium, various amphetamines, chemical mixtures, poppy seed.

Jones: Officially, there are 8,000 registered drug addicts in Moscow, but everyone concedes that the number is much too low.

Sources

Adapted from "Moscow Vice," *48 Hours.* With News Correspondents Dan Rather, Bernard Goldberg, Harold Dow, Phil Jones, and Peter Van Sant. CBS Inc., © 1990. All rights reserved. Originally broadcast on May 31, 1990, over the CBS Television Network. Reprinted by permission of CBS archives.

Travis Hirschi (1969) also challenged the delinquent subculture theories by pointing out that while frightening and highly publicized gang crimes do occasionally occur, most delinquency is committed with one or two companions. Hence, the small dyadic or triadic relationship and interaction is an inadequate base for the development of a subculture or a set of delinquent values. Hirschi further concluded that there is no evidence that delinquent companions and gang membership precede delinquency. Rather, an attitude and interest favorably inclined toward nonconformity will lead a youth to experimentation with delinquent behavior and association with like-minded peers.

Other sociologists and criminologists have focused attention on alternative theoretical explanations of gang delinquency. For example, L. Thomas Winfree and his associates (1994) present a data-based argument that a variation of Social Learning Theory offers the most specific explication of the processes whereby one learns deviant behavior. They found that "gang members were distinguishable from nongang youths more in terms of variables derived from social learning than personal-biographical characteristics, including ethnicity, gender, and place of residence" (Winfree, et al.,1994:167). Winfree and his colleagues have suggested a possible alternative to Cultural Transmission Theories of gang delinquency.

Not to be overlooked is the renewed theoretical emphasis of many theorists on the unfortunate socioeconomic structures and circumstances in which millions of lower-class youths seem to be trapped. These scholars credit grinding poverty, dysfunctional families, negative school experiences, marginal racial and ethnic statuses, and crime-infested urban neighborhoods with transforming hopeless and helpless children into alienated and angry gangs of delinquents (Anderson, 1994). Too often, such youths demonstrate their total disregard for human life and contempt for the norms and justice systems of the larger society:

> **PROVIDENCE, R.I. (AP):** As stunned courtroom observers looked on, one of six Latin Kings gang members accused of murder, drug dealing, and extortion, stood up Thursday, unzipped his pants and urinated.
>
> Federal marshalls tackled George "King Animal" Perry and removed all the defendants from the courtroom. U.S. District Judge Mary Lisi called a recess and ordered Perry banished to a cell for the rest of the trial. (*Stockton Record*, 1997:A-4)

Such criticisms as these have undermined the popularity of the subcultural theories of gang delinquency. Yet the works of Cohen, Cloward and Ohlin, Miller, and others, while imperfect, are still viewed as having considerable explanatory power regarding lower-class juvenile gang delinquency. However, the failure of these subcultural theories to account for middle-class group delinquency has led to new research and theoretical explanations. In seeking the reasons why youths who have conventional role models and socialization, and abundant opportunities—all conducive to achieving middle class values—become nonconforming and delinquent, attention has been focused on the youth culture argument. As we indicated in Chapter 11, youth itself can be perceived as an age-graded subculture, complete with its own shared attitudes, values, language, symbols, tastes in music, and styles of dress, sharpened and focused by marginal social status and separation from meaningful participation in the larger society. Thus, the youth subculture, functioning as a catalyst for the expression of marginality and collective alienation, is a surprising explanation of illegal behavior among the affluent and promising children of the middle class.

Several innovative community programs for dealing with gang-related delinquency are presented in Chapter 16.

Summary

Americans are alarmed by what seems to be a massive amount of predatory youth. While delinquency is sometimes a solitary act, it is more often than not carried out in groups, from dyads and triads to juvenile gangs.

Juvenile gangs often evolve from neighborhood play groups. Frederick Thrasher (1927) was one of the first criminologists to define a gang, and that definition has been modified several times since. Gangs tend to have predictable demographic characteristics and research has identified some common motivations for joining a gang.

Gangs often have initiation rituals, and while some gangs are fairly loosely organized, others have very sophisticated organizational schemes resembling those of organized crime. Lewis Yablonsky's concept of the near group added a new dimension to understanding the dynamics of gang membership and leadership. Racial and ethnic gangs exist in most major cities as do female gangs. Whereas gang violence used to be largely over battles for turf, those turf battles today are more closely linked to drug dealing territories as opposed topride and territoriality in neighborhoods.

Many of the theories from earlier chapters can be directly applied to gangs. Attempts to reduce gangs and discourage gang membership are logical outgrowths of some of these theories.

Concept Integration: Questions and Topics for Study and Discussion

1. Imagine yourself as a youth living in a neighborhood contested by two rival street gangs. Would you join one of the gangs? Why or why not?
2. Although gangs are often thought of as having little redeeming value or positive function, can you think of any contributions that even a delinquent subculture can make to the social and psychological well-being of its members?
3. Diagram your own cultural and subcultural memberships and involvements. Be sure to include your social class, occupation (or major field of study in college), religious affiliation, and racial or ethnic group (if appropriate). Next, discuss how membership in any of these subcultures can influence a person's values, attitudes, perceptions of what is right and wrong, and behavior.
4. Compare and contrast the locale, racial/ethnic composition, and delinquent behavior of lower and middle-class youth gangs. How are gangs organized?
5. Based on your reading of this chapter, how do you explain the fact that even though there are serious violations of the law, middle-class youths do not generally consider themselves as delinquent or in trouble with society? Why is this view shared by the adults in their environment?
6. Define and give examples of the following terms and concepts: Theory of Reactive Subculture, Theory of Differential Opportunity, lower-class culture and focal concerns, the play group, gang, near group, graffiti, dyad and triad, female auxiliary, high delinquency area, gang composition, deviant subculture, social capital, delinquent subculture, social network, and gang rape.

Part IV

APPLIED THEORY: SOCIAL CONTROL AND THE JUVENILE JUSTICE SYSTEM

INTRODUCTION: Elements of Social Control

In this book we are studying the social problem of juvenile delinquency from a sociological perspective. In this section, we examine the social processes involved in attempting to control juvenile delinquency.

Sociologists seldom assume that any form of crime or juvenile delinquency can be totally eliminated. As indicated in Part One, norm violation occurs in every society, and, in fact, deviance can be both functional and dysfunctional in its consequences. In this section, we focus upon the juvenile justice system and social processes involved in efforts to control juvenile delinquency. **Social control** refers to *the ways in which society members attempt to regulate the actions of others and reduce the negative impact of behavior which violates social norms.*

Chapter 13 focuses upon juveniles' activities in the social arena of the streets and looks at their encounters with the police. Police discretion is discussed as well as the legal and extralegal factors that influence policing juveniles. The issues of due process and delinquency prevention are also addressed.

In Chapter 14 we examine the juvenile court. The historical background which set the stage for development of the juvenile court is described with emphasis upon the Child Savers movement which dominated social philosophy and policy toward juveniles in the late 1800s. Juvenile court procedures are described with a focus on the issue of due process in the juvenile justice system. Some of the major criticisms leveled at the juvenile court are summarized, with suggestions for reforming the juvenile court of the future.

In Chapter 15, we discuss the sociological concept of social control and summarize methods utilized by society in attempting to correct the behavior of juveniles. Our discussion includes elements of voluntary, informal, and **formal** measures of social control and how they are applied to the problem of delinquency. We explore juvenile probation, restitution, incarceration, and we look at the controversial issue of capital punishment for juveniles, the ultimate measure of social control that can be exerted by a society. Finally we discuss and evaluate programs that involve deinstitutionalization, community corrections, and diversion.

As you read these chapters, we urge you to keep in mind the sociological framework, concepts, terms, and knowledge that have been developed through your reading of the first three parts of the book.

Chapter 13

Juveniles and the Police

READING OBJECTIVES

Reading this chapter will help you achieve the following objectives:

1. To view the public streets as a social arena where juveniles come in contact with adults, especially the police, who may define them as delinquent.
2. Understand and analyze juveniles' encounters with the police and the attitudes and variables that affect that interaction.
3. Identify and explain at least two disparate role expectations involved in policing juveniles and the strain this places on police officers and the youths involved.
4. Understand the role of the police as part of the filtering process in the juvenile justice system in regard to the amount of discretion police officers have in handling juveniles and to summarize the legal and extralegal factors that influence this discretion.
5. Define due process and provide an overview of some of the constitutional and legal issues that influence the handling of juveniles by the police.
6. Identify and explore some of the creative and innovative community policing strategies that have been developed to enhance police–juvenile relations and some of the programs used by police departments in an effort to help prevent juvenile delinquency.

INTRODUCTION

Chapter 10 began with a definition and discussion of the concept of *arena,* and then discussed the public schools as an arena where juveniles come in contact with others who may disapprove of their behavior and may even perceive them as delinquent. Another important social arena in which juveniles interact is the streets. "Cruising," "dragging the strip," and "hanging out" bring juveniles by the hundreds of thousands out onto America's streets. In an effort to curb delinquency, many cities have implemented teen curfews to limit the nighttime activities of youths, but juveniles continue to see the streets as an important part of their social domain (Ruefle and Reynolds, 1995). These activities bring juveniles together not only with other juveniles, but also with a multitude of adults including people on their way to and from work, shoppers, local merchants, homeless "street people," vagrants, prostitutes, pimps, drug dealers, muggers, and, of course, the police. Encounters with any of these adults could result in a youth being identified as a delinquent, but when it comes to officially being labeled as a juvenile delinquent, the most important interaction that takes place in the social arena of the streets is when juveniles encounter the police.

JUVENILE ENCOUNTERS WITH POLICE

If juveniles spend much time on the streets, it is inevitable that they will at some time encounter the police. Younger children are often fascinated by police officers and usually wave to them as they drive by in their patrol cars, or stop and talk to them as they walk their beats. Police departments attempt to foster this respect and admiration of the police by sending officers to local elementary schools to talk to children, provide safety tips, and otherwise nurture the image of police as public servants, "helpers," and "friends." In some areas, police officers coach little league baseball and soccer teams to develop better relationships with children. In cities with professional sports franchises, police sometimes give youths football or baseball cards featuring the pictures of famous athletes on the front and helpful safety and crime prevention tips on the back. These efforts to enhance juvenile–police relations can be effective, and from childhood through the early teen years, youths generally view the police as "good guys" who can be counted on when they are needed (Bouma, 1969), or, at worst, have ambivalent attitudes toward police (Whitehead and Lab, 2006).

As they enter their mid-teens, however, juveniles' attitudes toward police change, and often become more negative. Many juveniles resent the authority that the officers represent and some may merely be conforming to peer pressure to "not like cops." Research shows, however, that teenagers' attitudes toward the police vary by race, ethnicity, gender, socioeconomic status, number of contacts with law enforcement officials, and exposure to violence and poverty (Whitehead and Lab, 2006; Winfree and Griffiths, 1977). Whites have been found to have more favorable attitudes toward police than African Americans and other minorities; girls tend to view the police more favorably than boys; and youths from middle- and upper-class families typically have a higher opinion of the police than do those from the lower class. Not surprisingly, the more negative contacts youths have had with police, and the more committed juveniles are to violating the law, the less favorable their attitudes are toward law enforcement officers (Giordano, 1976; Greene, 1993; Hoobler, 1973; Portune, 1971; Whitehead and Lab, 2006; Winfree and Griffiths, 1977).

Similarly, while police usually like small children and often go to great efforts to befriend them, they tend to be more suspicious of and less friendly to teenagers on the streets. As discussed in Chapter 11, teenagers often rebel against adult authority, and through their dress, hairstyles, language, and demeanor, may exhibit behavior that runs counter to a number of adult values and norms. Since police are adults, and more importantly, are charged with enforcing adult values and norms in the form of laws, it is not surprising that many juvenile encounters with the police become confrontational. Police may find youths' dress, hairstyles, language, and demeanor offensive, and many police officers acknowledge that they have a difficult time establishing rapport with juveniles (Dantzker, 2003). Consequently, what may begin as routine encounters between juveniles and police on the streets may turn hostile in a matter of seconds. If a youth in an automobile is stopped and asked to show a driver's license or proof of insurance, if his or her response or attitude is interpreted by the officer as being disrespectful or suspicious, the encounter may accelerate beyond a routine traffic stop. It could lead to a confrontation that might result in a search of the vehicle, and in the officer taking the youth to the police station. These extralegal factors that influence encounters between police and teenagers are explored later in this chapter when we discuss police discretion in handling juveniles.

Again, the sociological concept of *arena* is helpful in analyzing juvenile encounters with police as it sheds light on the struggle for dominance and superiority that often takes place on the streets. A 16-year-old girl summarized the confrontational nature of juvenile encounters with police on the streets: "Cops don't care. . . . They loud talk you and harass you. If you're in their custody, they can say and do anything they want to you. Even off-duty, they are still like that. They think they can do anything because they're the law" (Smallenger and Bartollas, 2008:396).

Because of the somewhat negative attitudes held by many police and juveniles toward each other, it is understandable that their encounters are often confrontational in nature and punctuated by bad feelings, mistrust, and even downright hostility and violence. All of these factors make policing juveniles a challenge.

POLICING JUVENILES

The police are the most visible symbol of the juvenile justice system and are on the "front lines" in identifying, controlling, and processing juvenile delinquents. Law enforcement officers often view policing juveniles as a "no-win" situation. Since many of the offenses by juveniles are petty in nature and, in the case of status offenses, are not even against the law if committed by adults, police are often accused of overreacting and harassing youths when they should be protecting society from more serious offenders. On the other hand, if police ignore youthful pranks, status offenses, or the minor vandalism of juveniles, they find that the public expects them to intervene, make arrests, and enforce the legal codes no matter how trivial the consequences of their violations..

Virtually everyone agrees that the police should arrest juveniles who commit serious offenses such as burglary, robbery, rape, assault, and murder, but even in these cases, officers often find their actions more highly scrutinized and open to criticism and even formal sanctions than when they arrest adults for the same offenses. For instance if an officer must use force to apprehend a juvenile suspect, he or she may be far more vulnerable to charges of excessive force or brutality than if the perpetrator were over the age of 18. Consequently, police officers often feel that they are caught in a "catch-22" situation when dealing with juveniles, because if they do not take proper precautions and treat the youths as potentially dangerous, they put themselves at serious risk. Yet, if they handle a juvenile in the same way they would an adult, the general public, and even superior officers and police review boards may "second-guess" their actions as being inappropriate because of the offender's age. A police officer expressed this sense of frustration to one of the authors: "I'm just never sure what to do when it's a kid. I mean, hell, a bullet from a gun fired from a 14-year-old is going to kill me just as dead as one fired from somebody who's 24. But I know if I draw my weapon on a kid, have to wrestle one down, or God forbid, have to shoot one, it could mean my career."

Another officer expressed similar concerns and the predicament the police often find themselves in when encountering juveniles on the streets:

> Lots of times when we're chasing a car or confront a suspect on the streets, we don't have any idea how old they are. . . . I mean, I've chased down cars, had the driver flee on foot . . . chased 'em half a mile while they turned and shot at me . . . tackled, handcuffed and arrested 'em while they're kickin', scratchin', cussin', and spittin' at me, only to find when I got 'em down to the station that they were only 14 or 15 years old.

Police frustrations in handling juveniles are compounded by the lenient treatment juvenile offenders sometimes receive from the district attorney's office or the courts. Studies show that many officers believe that much of their law enforcement efforts against juveniles are useless, because the juvenile justice system merely "slaps the wrists" of offenders, and turns them back on the streets before the paperwork is even completed (e.g., McCamey, et al., 2003; Skolnick, 1966; Walker, 1983; Whitehead and Lab, 2006).

In order to deal with the special problems of policing juveniles, Berkeley, California, established a special "youth bureau" in its department in the 1930s, and in the 1950s both a U.S. and an International Association of Juvenile Officers were established. A study by the U.S. Department of Justice (1993) showed that in 1990, 95 percent of the large police departments in the United States (departments with over 100 sworn officers) had specific written policy directives for the handling of juveniles and 89 percent of large departments had special units for policing juveniles. Sixty percent of large departments had special gang units; 79 percent had units for dealing with child abuse and 74 percent had special units for handling missing children. The study also revealed that approximately three-fourths of all state police departments and even many small municipal police and rural sheriff's departments had special units for handling juveniles (U.S. Department of Justice, 1993). Today, not only do most large police departments have special units for dealing with juveniles and gangs, but a large number of school districts hire police officers for full-time duty in the schools (Lawrence, 2007).

These **juvenile officers** often *receive special training in child development, adolescent psychology, sociology, and counseling, in order to better equip them to handle the unique problems associated with policing juveniles.* In some cases, becoming a juvenile officer may involve a promotion in rank or an increase in pay, while in others, it may result in ridicule and teasing from their fellow officers who refer to them as "kiddie cops" or the "diaper squad."

Because of special problems faced in policing juveniles, law enforcement officers, whether regular police or specially trained juvenile officers, sometimes must fulfill different roles and grapple with what style of policing will be most effective in handling youths. In general there are two major schools of thought on the matter: the *law enforcement role* and the *crime prevention role* (Birzer and Roberson, 2007; Walker, 1983).

Law Enforcement Role

The first police officers in the United States were volunteer citizens who served as town "watchmen," and "kept the peace" through their vigilance and the mutual cooperation of the community. By the early 1900s, however, a new image of the police had emerged that emphasized the "crime fighting" aspect of police work and focused on their role as law enforcement officers (Thurman, et al., 1993). This role contended that police officers should avoid becoming too closely associated with those whom they patrolled (Williams and Murphy, 1990). The **law enforcement role** requires that *police should concentrate on arresting juveniles who violate criminal laws* (Walker, 1983). In the strictest sense of this view, youths are viewed and treated by the police in the same way as are adults. In departments lacking specialized juvenile units, officers are more likely to adopt the law enforcement role in handling youths because their training and experience have been geared toward policing adults (Birzer and Roberson, 2007). Thomson and Fielder (1975) noted that when police departments changed their primary means of patrolling from officers on foot walking a beat to motorized patrol on motorcycles and in squad cars, policing shifted from an informal, social interactive role to a more formalized law enforcement model. This may be particularly true in regard to policing juveniles, as officers today are more likely to encounter youths in the area of the streets outside the context of neighborhood and family. While officers can still use discretion in handling minor offenses, their primary duty is viewed as enforcing the law, arresting criminals (regardless of age), and protecting society.

As described earlier, however, even when the police are acting in their law enforcement role, they sometimes are expected to handle juveniles differently. This produces a certain amount of **role strain** in that *the set of expectations accompanying one role (i.e., law enforcement officer) may be at odds with fulfilling the expectations of another role (i.e., a concerned adult acting on behalf of a child in trouble).* In some cases, this strain could even become pronounced enough to constitute **role conflict** *where the fulfillment of one role necessitates the violation of another.* Thus, in addition to being a law enforcement officer, when law violations involve a juvenile offender, the police also must attempt to carry out their duties in such a way as to protect the "best interests" of the child. Consequently, another major goal of policing juveniles is crime prevention.

Crime Prevention Role

When Sir Robert Peel formed the London Metropolitan Police Force in 1829, he indicated that the "duty of police is to prevent crime and disorder" (Inkster, 1992:28). Modeled after the British constables (see Box 13.1), the **crime prevention role** calls for police officers *to act as social workers, and even surrogate parents, to help juveniles to avoid situations which might lead to delinquency* (Walker, 1983). This role places additional demands on police officers beyond simply knowing the law, responding to criminal complaints, and arresting juveniles suspected of having committed delinquent offenses. Thus, the crime prevention role requires expanded training that includes: enhancement of communication skills (especially listening), public-speaking ability, problem-solving techniques, understanding of childhood and adolescent development, and conflict resolution and negotiation skills (Meese, 1993).

Contemporary policing of juveniles goes beyond answering calls to what is referred to as **broken windows policing** in which *police focus on crime and delinquency prevention by reducing criminal opportunities and social disorder.* For example, police break up groups of teens hanging out on street corners, implement policies to reduce and prevent vandalism, and otherwise try to dissuade unruly and delinquent activities by policing the environment as well as citizens. The idea is that law-abiding citizens often avoid such areas, prompting delinquents and criminals to become the only people there. Consequently, a vicious circle is created in which "hanging out," vandalism, and unruly behavior eventually lead to more serious property and violent crimes (Whitehead and Lab, 2006).

When acting in the crime prevention role, officers often assume a **loco parentis**, or *parental role* toward juveniles. In this role, the police anticipate that adolescents will "act up" from time to time, and prefer to handle minor indiscretions informally, reserving arrest and court referral only for serious criminal offenses.

Broken windows- going after minor crimes, if you get rid of small offenses you can prevent more serious offenses.

BOX 13.1

CROSS-CULTURAL FOCUS: ***Policing Juveniles in Great Britain***

The mainstay of British policing is the unarmed constable, or "Bobbie," who patrols the streets on foot in much the same way as his or her predecessors did almost two centuries ago. Nowhere is this type of policing more evident than in London where the Metropolitan Police Service is charged with protecting and serving London's 8.5 million residents and almost that many tourists and visitors every single day. The vast majority of London's police officers walk a "beat" in pairs interacting informally with the public, answering questions, giving directions, and occasionally springing into action to apprehend a criminal.

When British police officers encounter juvenile lawbreakers they emphasize their social service and crime prevention orientation over their law enforcement roles. Most acts committed by youths under the age of 15 are not punishable by law, so offenders in that age group are informally reprimanded or formally "cautioned" by the police and then turned over to their parents. Between the ages of 15 and 18, constables still prefer to handle offenders informally whenever possible, unless the offense is a serious one, or parents refuse to cooperate with the police.

As in the United States, juvenile crime prevention has become a major focus of policing in Great Britain. The *Children Act of 1989* authorized local police agencies to work with families, schools, and other social agencies to focus their law enforcement efforts with youths on delinquency prevention. Strategies have been devised to involve young people in a variety of community projects designed to keep them in school and out of trouble with the law. In London, a Youth Partnership Program was developed in which over 40 schools created Youth Crime Prevention Panels and over 22,000 elementary school children participate in 27 Junior Citizen Schemes and 15 police–community summer projects. A Volunteer Cadet Corps, involving over 300 youngsters aged 16 to 18, has been organized to involve teenagers in local community projects along with London Metropolitan police officers.

New Scotland Yard and other British police agencies are committed to diverting as many young first-time offenders from the criminal justice system as possible in order to avoid the stigma associated with arrest and prosecution. The British police and judicial system have come under much scrutiny and heavy criticism for being too lenient toward youthful offenders, and British constables have experienced increased public pressure to arrest juvenile delinquents. Over the past two decades, Great Britain has experienced an increase in crime rates, and approximately 25 percent of the known offenders are under the age of 17. Concerns over these trends have prompted the public to question some of the informal policing tactics used by the British police in handling juveniles, and constables now issue more formal cautions and place more youths in custody as a result.

Because the United States derives much of its culture and legal tradition from Great Britain, and many top-level law enforcement officials from both countries exchange ideas, information, tactics, and policing methods, it is not surprising that many similarities exist between the two countries regarding the policing of juveniles. Studies show that, as in the United States, British police officers have much discretion in how they handle youthful offenders, and a variety of legal and extralegal factors help determine the outcome of police encounters with juveniles. British police insist that youths be respectful, and the age, sex, race, attitude, and demeanor of the juvenile during the encounter have at least as much effect on police discretion as do the seriousness of the offense and previous police contacts.

Despite increasing pressure from the public to adopt a stricter law enforcement role in handling juvenile offenders, the vast majority of British police officers interviewed by one of the authors indicated that they believe that all but the "most serious" juvenile offenders will eventually "grow out" of delinquency and are best treated informally. Consequently, the British police both officially and unofficially express a solid commitment to the crime prevention role of policing.

(Continued)

Based on this reading how would you compare/contrast British policing of juveniles with that of American policing? What social and cultural differences can you think of that might help explain the two different approaches to policing juveniles?

Sources

Becker, J. K. 1973. *Police systems of Europe.* Springfield, IL: Charles C Thomas.

Holdaway, S. (Ed.) 1980. *The British police.* Beverly Hills, CA: Sage.

Holdaway, S. 1984. *Inside the British police.* New York: Basil Blackwell.

Sanderson, J. F. 1993. *Youth crime in London: Prevention through partnership.* London: Metropolitan Police Service.

Thompson, W. E. 1992–2008. Unpublished interviews with officers at New Scotland Yard, London Metropolitan Police Service, and Surrey Police Department, England.

Many Americans believe that the mere presence and visibility of police officers helps to prevent delinquency. An Associated Press poll showed that two-thirds of Americans questioned said that posting police officers in schools not only would help curb school violence but also would help reduce other forms of delinquency such as bullying and petty theft. Moreover, they believed that police officers would not only be additional adults in the school that children could turn to if they felt frightened or threatened in any way, but also would serve as positive role models for students (AP, Washington, 1999b).

Community policing has been an important tradition in Great Britain. What role can community policing play in policing juveniles in the United States?

POLICE DISCRETION IN HANDLING JUVENILES

One of the most salient issues related to policing juveniles is that of **police discretion**—*the wide latitude police officers have in deciding how to handle juvenile offenders.* During the course of everyday policing, officers face numerous situations where they must decide what is the most appropriate response to achieve the most desirable outcome for themselves, the police department, and the community they are sworn to serve (Stevens, 2003). Police discretion is so important because it is during the initial contacts between juveniles and police that decisions are made that determine whether the encounter will be handled unofficially, or that the juvenile will be detained and officially processed—thus contributing to the official data on juvenile delinquency as we discussed in Chapter 3. In this way, the police contribute to an important **filtering process,** *determining who does or does not become officially recognized as a juvenile delinquent.* Police catch a large number of juveniles in their huge "net," yet many juveniles are both intentionally and inadvertently allowed to slip through "holes" in the "net" as they are "filtered out" of the adjudication process and the juvenile justice system (see Figure 13.1). For example, of the over 677,000 youths processed by the police in 2006, approximately 1 in 5 (20.8 percent) were released (see Table 13.1). Stephanie Myers (2002) found that police took juveniles into custody only about 13 percent of the time.

Krisberg and Austin (1978:83) noted that police have five basic options in deciding what course of action to pursue with juveniles:

1. Release, accompanied by a warning to the juvenile.
2. Release, accompanied by an official report describing the encounter with the juvenile.
3. Station adjustment, which may consist of:
   (a) release to parent or guardian accompanied by an official reprimand;
   (b) release accompanied by referral to a community youth services agency for rehabilitation; or
   (c) release accompanied by referral to a public or private social welfare or mental health agency.
4. Referral to juvenile court intake unit, without detention.
5. Referral to juvenile court intake unit, with detention.

What determines which of these options will be exercised by police? First, whether all of these alternatives are available often depends upon community resources. Some states, counties, and local communities provide a wide variety of diversionary alternatives to police for dealing with juveniles. Others, however, provide few if any community resources. In times of economic hardship, budget cutting at state, county, and local levels, and other monetary restrictions, police options may be severely limited as social service agencies for youths are often among the first to be targeted for cutbacks or closure. Consequently, in some communities, for all practical purposes, viable police options may be limited to two: either release the juvenile outright or petition the juvenile to court.

Also, the overall political climate and changes in public policy play an important role in police discretion (Aaronson, et al., 1984; Lawrence, 2007). For example, public perceptions of youthful "crime waves," and fear of violence coupled with "get

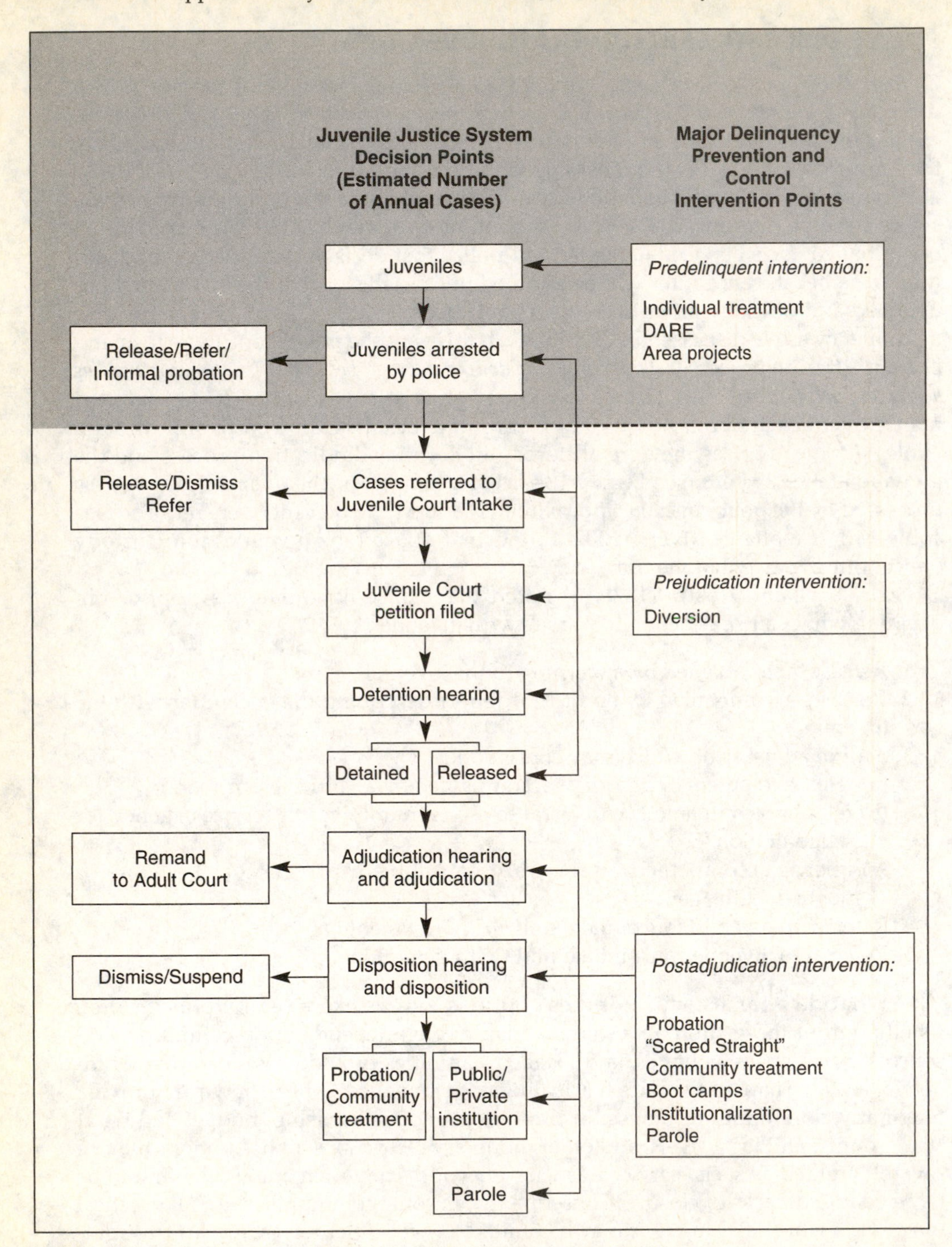

FIGURE 13.1 Filtering process in the Juvenile Justice System: The Police

Were you aware of this type of filtering process by police? Why aren't all juvenile offenders simply arrested and taken to jail?

Source: Adapted from Caseflow Diagram, Office of Juvenile Justice and Delinquency Prevention, <http://ojjdp.ncjrs.org/facts/case.jpg.html>.

TABLE 13.1 Police Disposition of Juvenile Offenders Taken into Custody

Population group		Total[1]	Handled within department and released	Referred to juvenile court jurisdiction	Referred to welfare agency	Referred to other police agency	Referred to criminal or adult court	Number of agencies	2006 estimated population
TOTAL AGENCIES	Number	677,346	140,758	469,670	3,639	8,021	55,258	5,314	118,700,928
	Percent[2]	100.0	20.8	69.3	0.5	1.2	8.2		
TOTAL CITIES	Number	577,182	127,939	369,912	2,951	6,469	42,911	3,986	86,098,095
	Percent[2]	100.0	22.2	68.8	0.5	1.1	7.4		
GROUP I (250,000 and over)	Number	153,785	51,833	98,960	655	771	1,566	33	22,004,970
	Percent[2]	100.0	33.7	64.3	0.4	0.5	1.0		
GROUP II (100,000 and 249,999)	Number	82,376	17,843	58,832	455	1,748	3,498	93	13,947,587
	Percent[2]	100.0	21.7	71.4	0.6	2.1	4.2		
GROUP III (50,000 and 99,999)	Number	104,091	19,484	75,723	450	1,041	7,393	229	15,568,963
	Percent[2]	100.0	18.7	72.7	0.4	1.0	7.1		
GROUP IV (25,000 and 49,999)	Number	79,611	13,779	56,571	651	1,731	6,879	371	12,869,843
	Percent[2]	100.0	17.3	71.1	0.8	2.2	8.6		
GROUP V (10,000 and 24,999)	Number	85,238	13,529	58,425	300	535	12,449	803	12,781,404
	Percent[2]	100.0	15.9	68.5	0.4	0.6	14.6		

(Continued)

TABLE 13.1 (continued)

Population group		Total[1]	Handled within department and released	Referred to juvenile court jurisdiction	Referred to welfare agency	Referred to other police agency	Referred to criminal or adult court	Number of agencies	2006 estimated population
GROUP VI (under 10,000)	Number	72,081	11,471	48,404	440	643	11,126	2,457	8,925,328
	Percent[2]	100.0	15.9	67.1	0.6	0.9	15.4		
METROPOLITAN COUNTIES	Number	21,928	2,842	14,835	277	289	3,685	671	8,374,812
	Percent[2]	100.0	13.0	67.7	1.3	1.3	16.8		
SUBURBAN AREA[3]	Number	285,130	48,227	198,068	1,237	3,058	34,540	3,275	57,971,585
	Percent[2]	100.0	16.9	69.5	0.4	1.1	12.1		

What important trends and patterns can you discern from these data? How would you explain them sociologically?

[1] Includes all offenses except traffic and neglect cases.

[2] Because of rounding, the percentages may not add to 100.0.

[3] Suburban area includes law enforcement agencies in cities with less 50,000 inhabitants and county law enforcement agencies that are within a metropolitan statistical area. Suburban area excludes all metropolitan agencies associated with a principal city. The agencies associated with suburban areas also appear in other groups within this table.

Source: FBI, Uniform Crime Reports, 2006. Washington DC: U.S. Government Printing Office 2007.

tough" policies of national, state, and local officials may preclude many of the alternatives usually left to police discretion. Still, on a daily basis, decisions made by the police at the time of the encounter with juveniles play the most important role in determining who will be officially processed as a delinquent (Dantzker, 2003).

Common sense would seem to dictate, and many people believe, that the nature of the offense committed by a youth determines how police decide to handle a case, and indeed that is a factor. However, research shows that a number of other legal and extralegal factors affect police discretion.

Legal Factors

There are a number of legal factors considered by police that help determine how they handle juvenile offenders. Research indicates that the most common legal factors that affect police discretion are the seriousness of the offense; number and extent of prior police contacts; the amount and nature of evidence linking the juvenile to the offense; and whether a complainant insists that formal action be taken.

SERIOUSNESS OF THE OFFENSE Juveniles who commit serious criminal offenses that would be classified as felonies or serious misdemeanors if committed by adults are more likely to be arrested, detained, confined, and petitioned to court than those who commit less-serious misdemeanors and status offenses (Black and Reiss, 1970; Krisberg and Austin, 1978; Lawrence, 2007; Lundman, et al., 1978; Piliavin and Briar, 1964; Terry, 1967; Whitehead and Lab, 2006). Not surprisingly, when juveniles are involved in a murder, the police almost always place them under arrest, detain them, and turn the case over to the district attorney's office. Likewise, forcible rape, aggravated assault, and robbery invoke serious formal responses from the police regardless of the age of the offender.

Yet the seriousness of the offense is only one factor that shapes police discretion in handling juveniles. Alleged felonies comprise only a small fraction of all police-juvenile encounters (most estimates are between 5 to 10 percent), with the vast majority of juvenile offenses being less-serious crimes and status offenses. Yet many of these less-serious infractions lead to serious consequences. Thus, several other factors influence police discretion in less-serious matters.

PRIOR POLICE CONTACTS Every police department keeps records of prior arrests and in today's computerized world of data collection, prior records can literally be at a police officer's fingertips in a matter of seconds. However, individual officers often carry a small notebook to keep track of contacts with juveniles whether they lead to official arrest or not, and warn youths that if they encounter them again, even for minor infractions, more serious steps will be taken. In some cases, these contacts may have represented nothing more than a police officer stopping a juvenile on the street and asking a few questions, or taking the youth home to his or her parents. Nevertheless, if the officer encounters this juvenile again, because of the previous contact, he or she may be treated much more seriously.

If a juvenile is taken to the police station for more extensive interrogation, an official record, or "rap sheet," is kept. Thus, even if a youth simply happened to be in the vicinity of a crime, he or she may become "known" to the police, and be treated

What legal and extralegal factors will help determine how the police handle these youths?
© Jonathan Nourok/PhotoEdit

more harshly in future police encounters. Aaron Cicourel (1968) found that prior contacts with the police often escalated what would have been a routine minor encounter with a juvenile resulting in an unofficial warning, into a formal police action ending in arrest and petition to court. Likewise, Terry (1967) found that while almost 40 percent of juvenile arrests involve first-time offenders, only about 7 percent of them are referred to juvenile court; conversely, chronic offenders and repeat juvenile offenders well known to the police were much more likely to be arrested and referred to court. Research suggests that seriousness of the offense and prior police contacts are two very important variables that determine police discretion in handling juveniles (Cohen and Kluegel, 1978; Lattimore, et al., 1995; Whitehead and Lab, 2006). Prior contacts with police are so important that many police departments have developed special policing tactics and programs designed to identify and target chronic offenders—a controversial issue discussed later in this chapter and in Box 13.2.

EVIDENCE Another factor in determining how police handle a juvenile is how compelling the evidence is linking the youth to the offense. Logically, police are reluctant to take actions against juveniles or adults if there is little or no tangible evidence linking them to an illegal act. In the majority of cases leading to the arrest of a juvenile, a police officer witnesses the commission of the delinquent act (Black and Reiss, 1970). Even in those cases, however, police still exercise wide discretion as to how to handle the case. In one study, it was found that only 13 percent of the suspects were arrested even when police saw them commit the offense (Black and Reiss, 1970). On the other hand, when someone else witnessed law violation and called the police, 19 percent of

BOX 13.2

CONTROVERSIAL ISSUE: Targeting Serious Habitual Offenders: Delinquency Prevention or Police Harassment?

Over the last three decades, research has shown that a disproportionate amount of juvenile delinquency, especially serious property and violent offenses, is committed by a small segment of the juvenile population. In some cases, as few as 5 percent of all juvenile offenders may be responsible for as much as three-fourths of serious juvenile crime. Moreover, in most cases, these juveniles' criminal careers usually begin when they are in their early teens. In response to these findings, various police departments have developed policing strategies aimed at targeting serious repeat offenders in an effort to "stem the tide" of serious juvenile crime.

In 1983, five cities were selected to implement pilot projects aimed at identifying, catching, and processing serious habitual juvenile offenders. The five cities were: Colorado Springs, Colorado; Oxnard, California; Portsmouth, Virginia; Jacksonville, Florida; and San Jose, California. The goal of the programs was *not* to catch and arrest *more* juveniles, but to identify and target the most serious juvenile repeat offenders in each community and to neutralize, or "incapacitate" them, by taking them off the streets (Bassett, 1993; Kline, 1993).

The SHO/DI (Serious Habitual Offender/Directed Intervention) project in Colorado Springs is typical of the programs established in each of the five cities. It required extensive cooperation among the police, the district attorney's office, probation services, and the schools. Law enforcement officials developed a complete profile of the 25 to 30 most serious repeat offenders in Colorado Springs. These profiles included detailed physical descriptions, summaries of modus operandi, case summaries, traffic offenses, police contacts, drug and alcohol involvement, complete delinquency and criminal records, probation information, and summaries of school records. After the most serious habitual offenders are identified, they are placed under intensive surveillance and arrested for even the most minor legal infraction. The district attorney then prosecutes to the fullest extent possible, and juvenile judges cooperate in either adjudicating the youths as delinquent and recommending incarceration, or in certifying the youths as adults to stand trial in criminal courts.

An evaluation of the SHO/DI program 10 years after its inception concluded that it was very successful in identifying, targeting, arresting, adjudicating, and incapacitating the most serious repeat offenders in the community (Kline, 1993). Overall delinquency rates were reduced and the most serious juvenile offenders were not allowed to "fall through the cracks" of the juvenile justice system.

While police officials and many members of the general public are delighted with SHO/DI and similar programs, the targeted juveniles, their parents and attorneys, and the American Civil Liberties Union raise some serious civil rights issues related to these police tactics. Their concerns are that, in effect, juveniles identified as serious habitual offenders are not only arrested and punished for offenses they have committed, but also are singled out and targeted for "special" policing—what some argue is tantamount to police harassment and invasion of privacy. Moreover, it is contended that when police encounter unsolved crimes with no substantial evidence or probable suspects, they simply reach into their SHO/DI file and pull out a "likely" suspect to go after. Also, attorneys and civil libertarians argue that these "targeted" youths are arrested and given very stiff penalties for very minor offenses that would be ignored by law enforcement officials if committed by other "nontargeted" youths.

Should police officers identify and target certain juveniles for differential law enforcement tactics? What are some of the benefits of programs such as SHO/DI? What are some potential problems associated with such a program?

Sources

Bassett, A. 1993. Community-oriented gang control. *Police Chief* 60 (February):20–23.
Kline, E. M. 1993. Colorado Springs SHO/DI: Working smarter with juvenile offenders. *Police Chief* 60 (April):32–37.

the suspects were arrested. This suggests that the presence of a complainant may also be an important variable related to the action taken by police.

COMPLAINANT The presence of an audience, complainant, or a victim also influences police discretion in handling juveniles. Smith and Visher (1981) found that the police were much more likely to intervene formally and arrest juveniles when there was an audience present, especially if that audience included an adult willing to sign a complaint. Of particular importance to police discretion is the attitude of complainants and victims if they are present. Studies show that when complainants and victims indicate an unwillingness to cooperate with prosecution or recommend that police handle the situation informally, police almost always comply with the request (Black and Reiss, 1970). On the other hand, when a complainant insists that formal action be taken, police are more likely to arrest the juvenile and take him or her to the station, even if they decide later not to petition the juvenile to court (Black and Reiss, 1970; Hohenstein, 1969).

While the presence or absence of an audience or victim willing to file a complaint represents a legal factor that influences police discretion in handling juveniles, the attitude of the complainant and his or her willingness or unwillingness to cooperate with the police demonstrates that a number of extralegal factors also affect police–juvenile encounters.

Extralegal Factors

In addition to the legal factors that we have discussed, a number of extralegal factors also have been shown to be related to police discretion in handling juveniles. The extralegal factors most commonly cited in research are: age; sex; race and ethnicity; socioeconomic status; willingness of parents to cooperate with the police; appearance, attitude, and demeanor of the youth; and the characteristics of the police officer involved.

AGE Age is a legal factor in determining how police handle juveniles in that each state defines juvenile delinquency by setting minimum and maximum ages of persons that come under the purview of the juvenile courts. As mentioned in Chapter 1, in most states the age range is legally set somewhere between the ages of 7 to 18 with some states setting upper limits at 16, 17, or even 21. But age also becomes an extralegal factor in police discretion as to how youths are treated even if they fit the delimitations established by law. Research shows that below the age of 10, few juveniles are detained or referred to court unless they have committed very serious offenses (Goldman, 1963). Moreover, in some states (Texas, for example), even though children are considered capable of *mens rea* at age 7, their cases will not be heard in a juvenile court before they reach the age of 10. Rather, criminal offenses involving youths under the age of 10 are handled by special family courts, and juveniles are more likely to be determined as "in need of supervision" and made wards of the court for their protection than they are to be adjudicated delinquent and remanded to the juvenile justice system.

Data indicate that one reason for the more lenient treatment of younger juveniles is that their offenses tend to be less serious. But research indicates that over the age of 10, juveniles tend to be handled more harshly by the police with each additional year of age, with those at the upper ages of the juvenile range being most likely to be arrested, detained, and petitioned to juvenile court regardless of the nature of the offense (Goldman, 1963; McEachern and Bauzer, 1967; Terry, 1967).

Understandably, age is a factor in police sometimes handling older youths in exactly the same manner as adults. In the heat of the action, police cannot take the time to check identification to determine a suspect's age. Thus, when youths at the upper age limits of juvenile status are apprehended by the police, especially if they are large and mature in appearance, it may not be until they are being processed at the station that it is discovered that they are under the age of adulthood and must be treated as juveniles.

SEX For many years, it has been assumed that a **chivalry factor** exists in police work *whereby females are treated more leniently by the police than are their male counterparts.* Indeed, research confirms that sex is an important extralegal variable that influences police discretion, but in contrast to conventional wisdom regarding the favoritism experienced by females, studies suggest that there may be somewhat of a "boomerang effect" regarding police treatment of females. That is to say, girls are considered to be less "suspicious" by the police and are less likely to be stopped and questioned unless they have been seen committing a delinquent act. In fact, while a group of teenage boys on the street almost always captures an officer's attention and may lead to a police encounter for "routine questioning," a group of teenage girls is more likely to be considered potential "victims" rather than potential perpetrators of crime. However, when juvenile girls are suspected of delinquency, and especially if they are seen as violating stereotypical or "traditional" gender roles, evidence suggests that they may be treated more harshly by police than males and may, in fact, be more likely than boys to be taken to the station for official processing and referral to court for relatively minor offenses (Armstrong, 1977; Chesney-Lind, 1977; 1988; Chesney-Lind and Pasko, 2004; Chesney-Lind and Shelden, 2004; Steffensmeier and Steffensmeier, 1980; Terry, 1967).

RACE AND ETHNICITY As was discussed in Chapter 3, racial and ethnic minorities are overrepresented in the official data on juvenile delinquency. While official data suggest that the explanation for this phenomenon is that minority youths commit more serious crimes than do whites, studies suggest that there is more to it than that. Researchers who have participated in "ride along" programs with the police have observed that members of racial and ethnic minorities, especially those who appear to be "tough guys" or to be affiliated with gangs, are more likely than whites to be stopped, interrogated, handled roughly, and placed under arrest (e.g., Black and Reiss, 1970; Meehan and Ponder, 2002; Piliavin and Briar, 1964).

Other studies confirm that regardless of the seriousness of offense, racial and ethnic minorities, especially African Americans and Hispanics are more likely to be confronted by the police, and to be arrested, detained, and referred to juvenile court (Dannefer and Schutt, 1982; Fagan, et al., 1987a,b; Goldman, 1963; Huizinga and Elliott, 1987; Lundman, 1996a; Smith and Visher, 1981).

African American and Latino youths' perceptions of police and the criminal justice system are more negative than those of their white counterparts (Hagan, et al., 2005). While arrests of racial and ethnic minorities are disproportionately higher than for whites, research is mixed on the influence of race and **racial profiling**—*using race or ethnicity as the sole criteria for initiating police contact*—in policing juveniles (Lawrence, 2007; Whitehead and Lab, 2006). At least one ride-along study showed that while police verbally expressed more suspicion about minority youths, the suspicion did not influence officers' decisions to initiate contact, stop, or question them

(Alpert, et al., 2005). Evidence suggests, however, that some African American parents teach their children (especially sons) to practice their own form of racial profiling, telling them to assume that all white police officers are racist, and if stopped, to expect the worst, to cooperate fully, and not to give any officer an excuse to arrest or use physical force (White, 2001).

Robert Sampson (1986) pointed out that the extralegal variables of race and social class may be important enough in determining police actions that they contribute to one of the legal factors (prior offenses) that shape police discretion. He noted that because police are more suspicious of minority youths they stop them more often and make a record of the encounter. Thus, when these youths are stopped again, they are already "known" to the police and may be dealt with more harshly the second time because of these "prior contacts" with police.

Ferdinand and Luchterhand (1970) suggested that the differential treatment of minority youths by white police officers may not simply be a matter of racism. They suggested that because the officers and youths come from such disparate social and cultural backgrounds that there is a basic lack of empathy and understanding for minority values and norms. Their research suggests that socioeconomic status may be a more important variable in determining the nature of police–juvenile encounters than is race and ethnicity.

SOCIOECONOMIC STATUS One of the most important influences on a person's attitudes, values, and behavior in a capitalistic society is socioeconomic status (SES). Social class also significantly affects how individuals are viewed and treated by others. Therefore, it is not surprising that SES is an influential factor in police discretion. With few exceptions, the majority of research on youths' SES and their treatment by police indicate that juveniles from lower socioeconomic strata are more likely to come into contact with police than are members of the middle and upper classes. Furthermore, studies suggest that the police are more likely to officially process and refer lower-class juveniles to court than they are youths from higher socioeconomic backgrounds (Cicourel, 1968; Lattimore, et al., 1995; Lundman, 1996a; Sampson, 1986; Terry, 1967; Thornberry, 1973).

Sampson (1986:884) concluded that, "Apparently, the influence of SES on police contacts with juveniles is contextual in nature, and stems from an ecological bias with regard to police control, as opposed to a single individual-level bias against the poor." In other words, juveniles who live in lower SES neighborhoods which have been identified by police as "high crime areas" are more likely to come into contact with police who patrol these areas more heavily, and hence experience a greater likelihood of being detained, arrested, and petitioned to juvenile court, than youths who live in so-called low-crime areas that are not patrolled as frequently. Some police officers indicate that they believe that parents do not play as strong a supervisory role among lower-class families as they do in the middle and upper social classes, and therefore, the police must make a more overt show of social control in lower SES neighborhoods to prevent and control delinquency (Cicourel, 1968).

APPEARANCE, ATTITUDE, AND DEMEANOR OF THE JUVENILE The appearance, attitude, and demeanor of the juvenile when confronted by the police emerge as important variables in influencing police discretion (Dantzker, 2003; Lundman, 1996a,b). Piliavin and

Briar (1964) found that demeanor was the most important factor in determining how police handle apprehended juveniles. Similarly, Morash (1984) found that juveniles who most closely fit the common image of delinquents held by police were most likely to be arrested. Neatly dressed, cooperative, and well-mannered youths are rarely viewed with suspicion, and if they come into contact with police are likely to be released with an informal warning. On the other hand, if a youth fails the "attitude test," by failing to show the proper deference or by appearing to be antagonistic, he or she is more likely to be arrested (Cicourel, 1968; Hohenstein, 1969; Winslow, 1973). Smith and Visher (1981:172) concluded that regardless of other legal and extralegal factors, "failure to display deference toward an officer significantly increases the probability of arrest."

Black and Reiss (1970) discovered an interesting finding regarding the demeanor of youths and their likelihood of arrest. Their study confirmed that disrespectful youths were indeed more likely to be arrested than were respectful youths. They also discovered, however, that juveniles at the other end of the continuum (those who were unusually respectful to the officers) also had a greater likelihood of arrest. Apparently, officers become suspicious of teenagers who "lay it on too thick" and seem "overly respectful" during interaction. Thus, a youth's demeanor plays an important role in the discretionary decisions exercised by officers, and those juveniles who stray too far from officers' expectations in either direction suffer harsher treatment than those who conform to the "nice kid" stereotype (Birzer and Roberson, 2007; Black and Reiss, 1970; Dantzker, 2003; Lundman, 1996a,b; Lundman, et al., 1978; Piliavin and Briar, 1964).

WILLINGNESS OF PARENTS TO COOPERATE When parents can be contacted by the police and show an active interest in their children and a willingness to cooperate with the police, the likelihood is much greater (especially in the case of minor offenses) that a juvenile will be warned and released to parental custody (Dantzker, 2003). Goldman (1963) found that approximately 90 percent of the police officers he interviewed felt that if the parents were available and willing to cooperate with the police, and if in the officer's view the home situation was considered to be "satisfactory," then the officer's preference was to handle the youth informally unless he or she had committed a serious offense. Goldman's findings were supported by the 1967 and 1992 *Task Force Reports on Juvenile Delinquency and Youth Crime,* which reported that family situation along with the attitude and conduct of a youth's parents were important criteria affecting police decisions on disposition of juvenile cases.

CHARACTERISTICS OF THE POLICE OFFICER In addition to the legal and extralegal factors that influence police discretion in handling juveniles, a variable that sometimes goes overlooked is the impact that personal and social characteristics of police officers may have on shaping their interactions with youths. The same sociological characteristics of youths that influence police discretion (i.e., age, sex, race, ethnicity, and socioeconomic status) may also be important for the police officer. For example, while no study has specifically shown that the age of a police officer affects his or her decisions about handling juveniles, research has shown that the length of service and amount of experience officers have may affect their decision-making processes (Sullivan and Siegel, 1972). In general, the longer police officers have been on the force and the more experience they have in handling juveniles, the more cynical, dissatisfied, and disgusted they become with the juvenile justice system (Dantzker,

2003). Other studies have suggested that whether the racial, ethnic, and socioeconomic characteristics between the officers and the juvenile offenders were fairly similar or drastically different also affected police discretion. Officers, like other human beings, relate best to other people who have similar social and cultural backgrounds to them (Ferdinand and Luchterhand, 1970; Wilson, 1968).

Just as a juvenile's attitude and demeanor may affect interaction with police, so too might the attitude, demeanor, and personality of the officer affect the interaction with the juvenile. Some police officers assume a parental attitude toward juveniles and prefer to handle situations informally whenever possible, while others view their role strictly in terms of law enforcement, and prefer to handle even minor offenses in a formal matter. Moreover, while some police officers have an ability to *de-escalate* the intensity or potential for violence in a juvenile encounter by remaining calm and having a calming and reassuring effect on the offender, others may *escalate* the situation through their voice, mannerisms, and demeanor.

Both legal and extralegal factors influence police discretion in handling juveniles and adults. With adults, however, police departments have more clear-cut guidelines regarding what officers should and should not do in certain situations. More importantly, when handling adults, the U.S. Constitution outlines certain elements of **due process,** or *basic legal rights that must be granted to an individual before he or she can be deprived of life, liberty, or property.* Because they were intended to protect adult citizens accused of crimes, unfortunately, the due process procedures are less clear-cut for handling juveniles.

POLICE AND DUE PROCESS

As a result of the popularity of movies and television series about the police, virtually everybody is familiar with the landmark U.S. Supreme Court case of *Miranda* v. *Arizona* and its mandate for police procedures. In fact, the results of the case have had such profound impact on arrest procedures that it has created a new verb in police language—to **Mirandize** a suspect—which means *to advise the suspect of his or her rights.* In the *Miranda* decision, the court ruled that at the time of arrest, suspects must be informed by the police that: "They have the right to remain silent; if they choose to waive that right, anything they say can and will be used against them in a court of law; they have the right to have an attorney present, and if they are unable to afford one, counsel will be appointed for them" (*Miranda* v. *Arizona*, 384 U.S. 436, 1966).

The *Miranda* decision was handed down in an effort to reinforce constitutional rights guaranteed in the Fifth (right against self-incrimination), Sixth (right to counsel), and the Fourteenth Amendments (right to due process). The U.S. Court of Appeals for the Ninth Circuit and the U.S. Supreme Court have ruled that failure to fully "Mirandize" a suspect may constitute a violation of civil rights and that both the department and the arresting officer may be held liable to the suspect for damages (Ronzio, 1993).

These constitutional rights and the *Miranda* ruling, however, apply to adults, where a clear adversary relationship exists between the state and its citizens who are accused of crimes. What about juveniles? According to the *parens patriae* doctrine upon which juvenile courts and juvenile statutes were created, the state intervenes *on behalf* of juveniles for their protection—not *against* them for punishment. Therefore, it was not made clear by the U.S. Supreme Court whether juveniles should be accorded the same rights to due process by the police and courts as adults.

In its 1964 *In re Gault* decision, the Supreme Court implied that it intended for police officers and the courts to provide some of the same due process rights to juveniles that are granted to adults. However, as we discuss in more detail in Chapter 14, Juvenile Courts, in many instances, the police and the courts deprive juveniles of some of the basic rights guaranteed to adults who are accused of committing crimes.

Krisberg and Austin (1978:80) indicated, "because the rights of due process and restrictions on evidence are not rigidly adhered to in juvenile courts, police can take advantage of the situation and use search, seizure, and interrogation procedures that would clearly be illegal if used with adult offenders." One of the problems with due process for juveniles is that technically, in most states juveniles are *detained* rather than *arrested* by the police. Although the difference is largely a matter of semantics, it allows the police to circumvent court rulings and department policies regarding due process during and after the arrest of suspects.

In an effort to protect the due process rights of juveniles taken into custody by police, the National Advisory Commission on Criminal Justice Standards and Goals (1973:764) recommended the following:

1. Police should warn juveniles of their right to counsel and the right to remain silent during questioning.
2. Upon apprehension of a minor, police should notify the parents.
3. Any statements made to police or court officers not in the presence of parents or counsel should be inadmissible in court.
4. Juveniles should not be fingerprinted, photographed, or otherwise put through the usual adult booking process.
5. Juvenile records should be maintained physically separate from adult case records.

These are only guidelines, however, and not mandatory requirements, so local, county, and state police still may exercise a great deal of discretionary power in handling juveniles (Davis, 1971; 1983). Nevertheless, court rulings, these guidelines, and general public sentiment that juvenile law violators should be treated more like adults have led many police departments to develop procedural policies governing interaction with juveniles that afford the youths most, if not all, of the due process rights afforded adults.

A major issue regarding the due process rights of juveniles is under what circumstances a juvenile can waive these rights. Two important Supreme Court decisions address this issue. In the case of *West* v. *United States* (1968), the court ruled that a nine-point analysis should be considered to determine if a juvenile's waiver of rights has validity:

1. The juvenile's age and maturity level.
2. The youth's educational level.
3. If the juvenile has knowledge of the substance of the charge(s) and understands his or her rights to remain silent and to have an attorney present.
4. Whether the accused has been allowed to contact parents, guardian, attorney, or some other interested adult.

5. Whether the interrogation occurred before or after being petitioned to juvenile court, or the filing of an indictment.
6. The methods police and/or the district attorney used for interrogation.
7. The length and duration of interrogations.
8. Whether the accused had ever refused to give voluntary statements on prior occasions.
9. Whether the accused had ever repudiated voluntary statements after interrogation.

In a later case, *Fare* v. *Michael C.* (1979) the court extended these criteria to include the *"totality of circumstances,"* insisting that before juveniles can legally waive their rights, "all the relevant circumstances" surrounding the case must be taken into account.

Despite these court rulings, however, and a host of police department policies regarding the due process rights of juveniles, the application of these rights varies greatly from state to state. A review of case and state laws regarding due process rights of juveniles indicates that state practices vary widely, and that police discretion is still one of the most important determinants of how juveniles will be initially handled when they come in contact with the juvenile justice system (Caeti, 1993).

POLICE, COMMUNITY POLICING, AND DELINQUENCY PREVENTION

We have discussed the "crime prevention" role assumed by many police officers when handling juveniles, but in most large communities, police departments are also involved in delinquency prevention programs (Stevens, 2003). Many of these programs are linked to a renewed interest in **community policing,** which *emphasizes cooperative efforts between the police and other members of the community.*

The *Teens on Patrol* (TOP) program in Rochester, New York, is an example of a successful police–community program aimed at preventing juvenile delinquency. In this program, over one hundred youths are hired during the summer to patrol city swimming pools, parks, and recreational areas, and to report any suspicious or law-violating behavior to the police. These "junior" officers do not make arrests, but they are officially recognized as city employees and carry police radios that put them in direct contact with uniformed officers. Moreover, it is believed that their mere presence and high visibility discourages teenage crime in those areas (Lipson, 1982). In Tulsa, Oklahoma, juveniles who are first-time nonviolent offenders are placed in the Youth Intervention Program in which they ride along with police officers for an average of 150 hours. The program is considered quite successful as the youths tend to view the officers as positive role models (Woodbury, 1991).

A number of other proactive strategies designed to enhance police–juvenile relations and to deter delinquency have been developed across the country. In Reno, Nevada, for example, a *Community Action Team (CAT)* was organized for linking police officers to the community in dealing with community problems and preventing crime and delinquency. Several programs were developed by CAT. *COPS + KIDS* program sponsors a picnic each year for over 2,500 underprivileged youths and their parents. Also, the Reno Police Department participates in the Police Athletic League (*PAL*) program where police officers coach youth boxing and wrestling teams, as well as accompany "at-risk" youths on hiking, backpacking, and camping expeditions. The *NAGs* (Neighborhood Advisory Groups) program in Reno is a cooperative arrangement between police and neighborhood groups that discusses allocation of police resources and crime prevention steps for the community while *GREAT* (Gang Resistance Education And Training) attempts to desensationalize gang membership and educate youngsters about the negative aspects of gang violence in order to deter gang recruitment of new members (Weston, 1993).

In the summer of 1992, the Spokane, Washington, Police Department developed an innovative community policing project called *COPY* (Community Opportunities Program for Youth). Primarily aimed at local youths who were at risk of abusing alcohol or illegal drugs and of joining delinquent gangs, the program involved weekly meetings with police officers, juveniles, and parents in nonthreatening surroundings. Officers chatted informally with the youths in the program and emphasized the positive aspects of law-abiding behavior, staying in school, and developing a conventional work ethic. A follow-up study at the end of the summer that utilized observations, focus group interviews, and survey research indicated very positive outcomes for youths, parents, and the officers who participated in the program (Thurman et al., 1993).

Recognizing that police officers on the beat have firsthand knowledge of the community and its youth, the Westminster, California Police Department initiated the Strategic Home Intervention and Early Leadership Development (SHIELD)

How can police officers playing basketball with youths as part of a community policing program help prevent crime and delinquency?

Program in 1996. Through this program, police identify youths at risk of involvement in violent behavior, gang activities, or drug and alcohol abuse and work with the community, schools, and social service agencies to redirect these youths into nondelinquent activities (Wyrick, 2000b).

Not all police efforts at preventing delinquency have been viewed with unanimously positive community support, however. Research shows that despite widespread support for the idea of community policing, crime control remains the central focus of most police departments (Zhao and Thurman, 1997). In fact, some police programs aimed at delinquency prevention are quite controversial (see Box 13.2). Police programs that "target" specific teenagers for constant surveillance and single them out for differential law enforcement practices have become quite controversial and raise a number of civil rights issues.

The San Antonio police have implemented an innovative but controversial program designed to reduce violent crime by targeting youths known to own or possess firearms. Dubbed WRAT (pronounced "rat"), this program of Weapons Recovery and Tracking appears to be effective in identifying youths who own or possess firearms, and in its first year of operation the program recovered over 250 firearms from youths; and while there is no empirical evidence of direct cause and effect, during that same period, homicides committed by youths dropped by over 40 percent (David, 1997).

Despite some of the controversies, police departments across the country are renewing their efforts to develop community policing and delinquency prevention programs in an effort to work more closely with other community agencies and individuals to stem the tide of rising violence that is plaguing most major cities and a number of suburban and even rural areas. Since the police represent the front lines of delinquency control and prevention, they are an essential part of a juvenile's first official encounter with the juvenile justice system. Thus, along with the office of the district attorney, they help determine whether youths will find themselves in another significant public arena—the juvenile court.

Summary

The streets constitute a social arena where juveniles, especially teenagers, spend a great deal of their time and carry out a wide variety of social activities. During these activities, youths encounter a number of adults who may initiate the process of defining them as delinquent. The front line of the juvenile justice system in the streets is comprised of the police who encounter juveniles in an array of social situations ranging from "routine" traffic stops and informal interactions to life-threatening criminal activities.

Although young children tend to hold positive attitudes toward the police, teenagers and the police often develop more strained attitudes toward one another that may border on a sense of "mutual hostility." Police often feel trapped in a "damned if you do; damned if you don't" situation when policing juveniles, while teenagers often believe that the police enjoy harassing them and their friends and generally overreact to "harmless fun."

When policing juveniles, officers vacillate between a strict *law enforcement* and a more flexible *crime prevention role.* Either way, the police may employ a great deal of discretion in handling juveniles. This discretion is influenced by both legal and extralegal factors that help determine how police officers handle juvenile offenders.

Police discretion coupled with the disparity among states' statutory provisions and interpretations of case law raise a number of issues regarding the *due process* rights to which juveniles are entitled. In some jurisdictions, police department policies dictate that juveniles be afforded all of the basic civil rights and due process procedures that are guaranteed to adults. In others, however, the police may employ vastly different policing techniques with youths that violate many of the basic due process procedures used in handling adults.

Most police departments are now developing and using *proactive* strategies of community policing to help prevent and control delinquency rather than merely *reacting* to youth crime. These strategies include a host of creative and innovative programs to involve police officers with children, adolescents, young adults, and other community members with the goal of developing better police–juvenile and police–community relations. While most of these programs are met with widespread acceptance and community support, a few, such as those that target specific juveniles for intensive police surveillance, are quite controversial and raise some legal and constitutional issues.

In final analysis, the police play a significant role in the *filtering process* that determines the youthful behaviors that can and will be tolerated as well as those that will not. They become the pivotal players in determining who will officially enter the juvenile justice system, be petitioned to juvenile court, and officially become identified as juvenile delinquents.

Concept Integration: Questions and Topics for Study and Discussion

1. How can the concept of "social arena" be applied to the streets? What type of confrontations and "struggles for survival" may take place between juveniles and the police as they interact on the streets?
2. Describe the difference in expectations between the *law enforcement* and *crime prevention* roles fulfilled by the police. How might these differential expectations result in *role strain* and even *role conflict* for police officers?
3. List some of the legal factors that affect police discretion. In your view, which of these factors are most important? Should any of these factors not be considered in handling juveniles?
4. List some of the extralegal factors that affect police discretion. Should any or all of these factors influence police decisions in handling juvenile offenders? If so, which ones? If not, is it possible for police officers *not* to be influenced by these social characteristics?
5. Define *due process.* Should the police afford juveniles the same basic rights of due process that are guaranteed to adults? If so, how should police procedures be changed to insure that juveniles are not denied due process? If not, why not?
6. What innovative community policing strategies have been developed in your community or surrounding communities to enhance police–juvenile relations and prevent delinquency? As a class project, develop a program that police could implement to help prevent delinquency in your local area.

Chapter 14

Juvenile Courts

READING OBJECTIVES

Reading this chapter will help you achieve the following objectives:

1. Understand the concept of due process as expressed in the United States Constitution and Bill of Rights.
2. Explain the motives and ideology of the Child Savers together with their positive and negative impacts upon the juvenile justice process.
3. Understand the historical development of the juvenile court.
4. Provide an overview of the implications of the *Gault* decision and other major decisions by the United States Supreme Court and their impact upon the legal processing of cases involving juveniles.
5. Describe and explain the procedures of the contemporary juvenile court.
6. Identify some of the major criticisms and limitations of the contemporary juvenile court.

INTRODUCTION

In Chapter 10 we introduced the concept of **arena** and illustrated how the schools serve as a social arena in which juveniles strive for social acceptance, a sense of social identity, and a measure of success in an adult-dominated society. In Chapter 13, we further explored this struggle for identity and the confrontations encountered by juveniles in the social arena of the streets. The juvenile court also fits our concept of public arena in much the same way as the schools and the streets. Although it conducts private hearings, the juvenile court symbolically represents society's public disapproval of a youth's behavior and the official response to delinquency by the juvenile justice system.

The United States was founded on the principles and ideals of democracy that all people are created equal under the law and entitled to certain inalienable human and civil rights. So dynamic and compelling was this "American dream" that the nation's founders revolted and separated from England. A later generation suffered a bloody civil war in order to extend these rights to an enslaved minority.

These fundamental rights were codified in the U.S. Constitution and the Bill of Rights. For example, the Fourth, Fifth, Sixth, Eighth, and Fourteenth Amendments to the Constitution combine to guarantee **due process of law**, *which are procedures designed to safeguard the rights of persons accused of crimes.*

The Fourth Amendment prohibits unwarranted and unreasonable arrest; the Fifth protects against self-incrimination; the Sixth guarantees the right to counsel and a jury trial, as well as the right to be informed of specific charges and the right to confront witnesses; the Eighth Amendment prohibits excessive bail and fines and cruel and unusual punishment; while the Fourteenth ensures that no state will be allowed to deprive any citizen of right to life, liberty, or property without due process of law.

In light of these basic legal rights, it is one of the greatest paradoxes that American children and youths were denied many of their constitutional rights in the juvenile justice system until the late 1960s, and in some cases are still denied them today. In order to fully understand the evolving legal status and adjudication process of young people in this country, we first need to explore the historical background out of which the contemporary juvenile court developed.

HISTORICAL BACKGROUND OF THE JUVENILE COURT

Much of U.S. law is based on British common law which exempted children under the age of 7 from legal responsibility for misconduct because they were considered incapable of **mens rea**, which means *"evil intent" or "guilty mind" and refers to one's ability to understand right from wrong, to understand the consequences of one's actions, and then willfully commit a wrongful act.* At age 7 and older, children were considered capable of *mens rea* and were held responsible for their actions in the same ways as adults.

The *chancery courts* arose in England in the 15th century. Part of the reason for their development was to deal with children's problems. The chancery courts required parents to provide support, supervision, and care for their children. The king of England was established as **parens patriae**—*"the father of his country"—which made the king the "ultimate parent" and gave him the right to care for the children of the state if their parents would not or could not do so.* Although the chancery courts were established to deal with problems such as neglect and abuse rather than behavior problems on the part of youths, their existence set an important legal precedent that would have dramatic impact on juvenile courts some four centuries later. The concept of parens patriae established the principle that the state could intervene on behalf of a child even if this involved taking the child from the parents.

Much of 18th- and 19th-century criminology, both in theory and in practice, was structured on the traditional assumption that punishment is the best and most appropriate deterrent of crime. Thus, in the absence of definitive laws and a specialized court system for the legal processing of children, juvenile offenders often were treated and tried as adult criminals. As recently as the latter part of the 19th century, children were tried in criminal courts in both England and the United States; they were detained in the same jails, tried in the same courts, sent to the same correctional facilities, and sometimes even executed (Reid, 2008; Sanders, 1970). While the nature of the offense and the age of the offender generally determined the kind and degree of punishment to be exacted, there were enough cases of children who were executed by society to underscore the prevailing notion that people would avoid behavior they have identified with evil and pain.

Prior to the establishment of the juvenile court, at least three developments occurred during the 19th century which altered the way youthful offenders were treated:

1. In 1825, in New York City, the **House of Refuge** was established. This provided separate correctional facilities for children (usually between the ages of 7 and 14) after they had been convicted in criminal court.
2. In 1841, the city of Boston first tried **probation**, or supervised release, a method of treating juveniles outside of a correctional institution, but still under the supervision of the criminal court.
3. In 1869, the state of Massachusetts officially established probation with supervision for juvenile law violators. (Haskell and Yablonsky, 1978:26)

These developments were linked to the changing attitudes toward childhood and the creation of the concept of adolescence. They represented a desire to hold young law violators accountable for their actions, but also reflected a movement toward handling juvenile offenders differently from adult criminals. Similar trends occurred in other countries (see Box 14.1).

BOX 14.1

CROSS-CULTURAL FOCUS: Development of the Juvenile Court in Canada

As in the United States, the development of a separate juvenile justice system in Canada was linked with the Child Savers Movement. In 1857, two legislative acts were passed to provide special trial procedures and separate institutions for Canadian juveniles. One was an act which called for a more speedy trial for youthful offenders in order to avoid the problems they experienced during long terms of imprisonment prior to going to trial. The other piece of legislation established separate prisons for juveniles. Later, in 1874, Ontario passed an act establishing industrial schools as residential institutions intended to rehabilitate young offenders with less-severe punishment than that inflicted at earlier reformatories.

The Children's Aid Society was formed in Canada in 1891, with an express goal of having a probation officer assigned to each child brought before the court in an effort to protect the child and see that the court acted in his or her best interests. Although the first juvenile court in the world is considered to have been established in Chicago in 1899, records indicate that in 1892 the Toronto police had established a special "children's court" to hear cases involving youthful offenders and in 1893, Canada passed a comprehensive Children's Protection Act which called for special and separate hearings for juveniles.

Nevertheless, it was not until 1908 (nine years after the passage of the Juvenile Court Act which established the first juvenile court in the United States) that Canada passed the Juvenile Delinquents Act establishing the first officially recognized juvenile courts in that country. The new juvenile courts were given exclusive jurisdiction over juvenile cases and emphasized treatment and prevention over punishment. Most youths who appeared before the Canadian juvenile courts were placed on supervised probation, with the court's main objective being rehabilitation of youthful offenders so that they would not become adult criminals. Thus, there are striking parallels between the development of juvenile courts in Canada and in the United States. Today, Canadian and American juvenile courts are very similar in structure, style, and function.

Why do Americans insist that the first juvenile court in the world was established in the United States? Why do you think there are so many striking similarities between American and Canadian juvenile courts?

Sources

Kelso, J. J. 1908. Children's court. *Canadian Law Times and Review* 26:163–166.

Hagan, J., and Leon, J. 1977. Rediscovering delinquency: Social history, political ideology and the sociology of law. *American Sociological Review* 42 (August):587–598.

Varma, K. N. 2007. Parental involvement in youth court. *Canadian Journal of Criminology and Criminal Justice* 49 (April):231–260.

THE CHILD SAVERS MOVEMENT

Steps to provide specialized correctional treatment to children and youths were initiated by a group of influential social reformers in the late 19th century. The *Child Savers,* as they were called, were convinced that urban slum life exerted a corrupting influence on idle youths. "However," the Child Savers insisted, "because of their tender age, delinquent youth[s] could be reclaimed from a criminal life if proper steps were taken" (Platt, 1969:45). They were instrumental in shifting focus away from the criminal nature of delinquency to what was generally considered to be a more humanistic approach built around the medical model and the rehabilitative ideal.

The medical model used by the Child Savers diagnosed nonconforming behavior with such analogous terms as "disease," "illness," and "contagion." In other words, within the **medical model** *crime was viewed as a kind of social pathology, and young people manifested the antisocial behavioral symptoms of criminality as a result of being exposed to it in their environment.* The older the criminal, the more chronic the "sickness," and chances of recovery were considered to be less than those for a young person.

The **rehabilitative ideal** *emphasized the temporary and reversible nature of adolescent crime, if remedial measures were strenuously applied at an early age.* Support for the Child Savers' ideology was forthcoming from the noted penologist Enoch Wines who wrote in 1880: "These delinquent children are born to it; brought up for it; and they must be saved" (cited in Platt, 1969:45).

The Child Savers had their greatest impact in changing the reformatory system. The **reformatory** was well established throughout the United States during the middle of the 19th century as *a special form of institutionalized discipline for teenagers and young adults.* However, the reformatory was recognized as little more than a school for a later career in crime since youngsters were often indiscriminately thrown together with toughened adult criminals and there was little opportunity for education or resocialization that might prepare a young person for a more constructive life (Platt, 1969:46–54).

By the end of the 19th century, the Child Savers had exerted enough political pressure to have laws passed that restructured the reformatory system. According to Platt (1969:54) the reformatory plan developed by the Child Savers included the following principles:

1. Young offenders must be segregated from the corrupting influences of adult criminals.
2. "Delinquents" should be removed from their environment and imprisoned for their own good and protection. Reformatories should be guarded sanctuaries, combining love and guidance with firmness and restraint.
3. "Delinquents" should be assigned to reformatories without trial and with minimal legal requirements. Due process is not required because reformatories are intended to reform and not to punish.
4. Sentences should be indeterminate, so that inmates are encouraged to cooperate in their own reform and recalcitrant "delinquents" are not allowed to resume their criminal careers. . . .

In summary, the reformers in the Child Savers' Movement equated juvenile independence with delinquency and sought to exercise extensive and rigid control over most youthful activities. Moreover, they shifted the responsibility for addressing social problems from the private to the public arena—a development that made "child saving" society's responsibility and led to the development of juvenile courts (Block and Hale, 1991). While the principles that guided the restructuring of the reformatory system and the development of special courts for handling delinquent youths were motivated by idealistic and humanistic values, their arbitrary implementation denied multitudes of young people their basic constitutional right to due process.

THE JUVENILE COURT

The mounting pressure for a judicial system that incorporated specialized processing of juvenile delinquents culminated in 1899 when the Illinois legislature passed the *Juvenile Court Act,* creating the first statewide court especially for children. Today there is a juvenile court in every American jurisdiction, with about 2,800 courts hearing juvenile cases. **Juvenile courts** are *judicial tribunals that deal in special ways with the cases of young people.*[1] The juvenile court is not a criminal court; it is a statutory court whose powers and limitations are defined by the laws of the state in which it exists

Most state statutes regarding juvenile courts do not necessarily create a *separate, independent* juvenile court. Consequently, the role of juvenile judge is only a part-time assignment for many judges (Cox, et al., 2008). Martin Haskell and Lewis Yablonsky (1978:27) reported that in 40 states juveniles were handled in courts whose primary purpose was some other function (either family or criminal courts). In those states a judge who sits on another court (usually criminal) sets aside a day to hear juvenile cases. On that day, the court becomes a juvenile court and follows the procedures that are prescribed for juvenile courts in that state. This practice is still common today.

To distinguish the proceedings of the juvenile court from those of the criminal court where adults are brought to trial, a new vocabulary emerged (see Table 14.1). Rather than a criminal complaint, a juvenile court "petition" is issued ordering the accused offender to appear in court. Similarly, arraignments have come to be called "initial hearings," and convictions have been renamed "findings of involvements." Finally, sentences have been replaced by the more informal and less threatening term "disposition" (Coffey, 1974:37).

Should juveniles be afforded all the rights of due process in juvenile court? If so, why? If not, why not?

[1] This figure is based on estimates from several sources. It is extremely difficult to determine precisely how many juvenile courts exist, since juvenile cases are sometimes handled in separate courts: sometimes in municipal, county, or district courts, and sometimes in family and/or divorce courts.

TABLE 14.1 Terminology used in Juvenile Versus Adult Courts[1]

Juvenile	Adult
Custody	Arrest
Detention	Jail
Petition	Indictment
Hearing (Private)	Trial (Public)
• Intake	• Arraignment and Plea
• Adjudication[2]	• Trial
• Disposition	• Sentencing
Dismissal	Acquittal
Detention (or Placement)	Incarceration
Probation	Probation
Aftercare	Parole

Are the differences in terms used in adult and juvenile courts merely a matter of semantics? Or, do they reflect philosophical and practical differences in how the courts operate?

[1] Terminology in juvenile courts varies among states. This table uses some of the most common language of the juvenile courts.

[2] Where adults are either convicted (found guilty) or acquitted (not guilty), juveniles may be adjudicated INS (in need of supervision), miscreant (guilty of committing what would be a misdemeanor if committed by an adult), or delinquent (guilty of committing what would be a felony if committed by an adult).

The establishment of juvenile courts in 1899 did *not* mean that children were granted the constitutional right to due process. On the contrary, the Child Savers' well-intentioned but discriminatory philosophy and practices became institutionalized in the juvenile court system:

> The goals were to investigate, diagnose, and prescribe treatment, not to adjudicate guilt or fix blame. The individual's background was more important than the facts of a given incident; specific conduct relevant more as symptomatic of a need for the court to bring its helping powers to bear than as prerequisite to exercise of jurisdiction. Lawyers were unnecessary—adversary tactics were out of place, for the mutual aim of all was not to contest or object but to determine the treatment plan best for the child. (Winslow, 1973:134)

In 1920, the U.S. Children's Bureau recommended the following as essential characteristics of the juvenile court:

1. separate hearings,
2. informal procedures,
3. regular probation services,
4. separate detention,
5. special court and probation records, and
6. provision for mental and physical examinations (cited in Belden, 1920:7–10).

While the Children's Bureau had no authority to make policy or enforce its guidelines, its suggestions for the operation of juvenile courts had tremendous influence on juvenile court proceedings. Juvenile hearings were almost always private, usually involving only the juvenile, his or her parents, the judge, and a social worker. Juries were not used, as the issue of innocence or guilt was much less the focus of the hearing than was the question "Why is this juvenile present in court?" There was the assumption that the youth needed help or he or she would not be there, and the judge's primary responsibility was to decide how best to handle the situation. The proceedings were conducted informally with very little attention to the ritualistic legal traditions that dominated adult criminal court proceedings. The judge generally addressed the juvenile by first name and asked a number of questions of the juvenile and his or her parents; the strict rules regarding testimony and evidence in criminal cases were not always applied. Thus, the juvenile hearing in the early juvenile court often resembled an informal conference more than a formal trial.

The traditionally informal and nonlegalistic nature of the juvenile court has changed a great deal in recent years. Today, more juveniles and their families secure legal counsel and more attorneys are involved in juvenile court proceedings. Several significant U.S. Supreme Court cases have impacted upon the legal rights extended to juveniles who appear before the juvenile court. One of the results has been that hearings have taken on a more formal atmosphere, and judges tend to handle them similarly to criminal proceedings. And, as we shall see in Chapter 15, today, juvenile courts are more likely to remand violent offenders to adult criminal courts than ever before.

JUVENILE COURTS AND DUE PROCESS

Juvenile courts were established for the protection of children, so due process was not included. When a youth was petitioned to a juvenile court, the court philosophically and legally was acting on behalf of the youth. Therefore, the adversary relationship which exists in criminal courts (*State of Nebraska* v. *John Doe*) was considered to be absent from the juvenile court. For that reason, the rigid ritual, rules of evidence, and other formal procedures of the criminal court were not established as part of the juvenile court. Consequently, basic constitutional rights (especially those of due process) were not accorded to juveniles in their hearings.

In 1954, in the *Holmes* case, the U.S. Supreme Court ruled that since juvenile courts were not criminal courts, the constitutional rights guaranteed to persons accused of crimes did not apply to juveniles (*In re Holmes,* 1954). Holmes was an 18-year-old boy who was arrested while riding in a stolen car. As a result of his juvenile court disposition, he was sent to a state training school. Holmes's lawyer appealed the case on the basis that Holmes had not been represented by counsel; had not been properly informed of the charges against him; had not been advised of his rights (especially the right not to testify against himself); that much of the testimony against Holmes should have been deemed inadmissible; and that Holmes had not actually committed an illegal act. In response to the appeal, the Supreme Court reaffirmed the position that an adversary relationship does not exist in juvenile court. Chief Justice Horace Stern asserted that the court was not trying to punish a criminal but rather to salvage a boy who might become one (*In re Holmes,* 1954). In other words, due process was not necessary since the court was attempting to help and reform rather than punish the youth.

Due process, even in a limited form, was not to become a part of juvenile court procedure until 1967, and then it developed through some rather interesting events.

In June of 1964, Gerald Gault, along with another boy, was taken into custody in Gila County, Arizona, for allegedly making obscene phone calls to a neighbor woman. Both of Gault's parents were away from home and were not notified of his detention. On the following day, Gault was petitioned to the juvenile court (although his parents did not see the petition). Gault's mother attended the hearing. The judge informally questioned Gault about the phone calls. The disposition of the case resulted in Gault being adjudicated delinquent and committed to the Arizona State Industrial School for the remainder of his minority (six years). The same charge against an adult would have resulted in a fine of $5 to $50, or imprisonment for not more than two months (Neigher, 1967). The case was appealed based on the issues that Gault had not been advised of his rights (especially against self-incrimination) and was not allowed to deny the charges or cross-examine the only witness against him (Neigher, 1967). The final appeal went before the U.S. Supreme Court, and in what is viewed as a landmark decision in juvenile justice, the Supreme Court in 1967, under Chief Justice Earl Warren, handed down the *Gault* decision (*In re Gault*, 1967), which resulted in

1. Right to notice of charges against the juvenile.
2. Right to counsel.
3. Right to face and cross-examine witnesses.
4. Right to refuse to answer self-incriminating questions.
5. Right to a transcript of the proceedings.
6. Right to appeal.

While the *Gault* decision was a major development in officially providing a measure of due process in juvenile hearings, care must be taken not to overestimate the impact of the case. The decision did *not* provide to juveniles all the constitutional rights afforded adult criminal suspects. A limitation of the decision is that because of the wording, it is not clear whether the rights outlined therein must be accorded the juvenile or whether those rights can be waived by the juvenile's parents. In many cases that might be a moot point, but in cases where the parents originate a petition against their own child, the difference could be extremely important. Regardless, the *Gault* decision had tremendous impact on the juvenile justice system. More juveniles began seeking counsel, being represented in their hearing, and appealing their cases (Coxe, 1967). Perhaps the most significant impact of the *Gault* decision is the recognition by the U.S. Supreme Court that even in juvenile cases an adversary relationship exists, and in order to protect the best interests of the juvenile, at least limited due process must prevail.

Several other important U.S. Supreme Court decisions have impacted upon the issue of due process in the juvenile justice system. For instance, in 1966, the famous *Miranda* decision was issued which ruled that when adults are arrested, they must be informed of their right to remain silent, that any statements made by them can be used against them in court, that they have the right to legal counsel, and that if they cannot afford legal counsel, the court will appoint them an attorney (*Miranda* v. *Arizona*, 1966). The *Gault* decision implied that these rights also must be afforded a juvenile when taken in custody, although it did not expressly state this. In subsequent U.S. Supreme Court decisions, the Court has contended that juveniles are entitled to the rights against self-incrimination outlined in the *Miranda* decision. There is some question, however, whether juveniles can waive those rights without their parents or attorney being present.

Another important U.S. Supreme Court decision was that of *Kent* v. *United States* in 1966. Morris A. Kent was a 14-year-old boy who had been arrested in 1959 for several housebreakings and attempted purse snatchings. Kent appeared before the juvenile court in the District of Columbia and was placed on probation. Two years later, while investigating a housebreaking, robbery, and rape case, police found fingerprints at the scene that matched those of Morris Kent. Kent (then 16 years old) was taken into custody and interrogated over a period of two days, during which he admitted his involvement in the crime under investigation and offered information about several other similar offenses he had committed. No record exists to establish when Kent's mother was notified that he was in custody, but after four days of his detention, she secured an attorney's services. The attorney filed several motions with the juvenile court including one asking for psychiatric and psychological examination of Kent. After approximately one week of detention of Kent, the juvenile judge waived jurisdiction (because he was 16, the juvenile court had exclusive jurisdiction in the case) and recommended that he be held over for trial in the District Court of the District of Columbia. No hearing was held in juvenile court, and there was no response to any of the motions filed by Kent's attorney (including a request that the juvenile court not waive its jurisdiction). Further, the juvenile judge issued no statement of reasons for waiving jurisdiction.

A grand jury was convened and indicted Kent on three charges of housebreaking, three counts of robbery, and two counts of rape. Despite protests by Kent's attorney that Kent was mentally incompetent to stand trial, a trial was held. Interestingly, Kent was found not guilty by reason of insanity on the two rape charges but was found guilty on the charges of housebreaking and robbery. He was sentenced to serve 5 to 15 years on each count, or a total of 30 to 90 years. The case was appealed to the U.S. Court of Appeals on the grounds that Kent was unlawfully detained and interrogated and was deprived of counsel, and his parents were not notified. Kent's attorney contended that young Kent had been deprived of the basic constitutional rights that would have been granted an adult facing the same charges, yet Kent was tried as an adult in criminal court. The appellate court upheld the conviction, and the case eventually came before the U.S. Supreme Court. The Supreme Court ruled that in order for a juvenile court to waive its exclusive jurisdiction, a hearing must be held (*Kent* v. *United States*, 1966). In its opinion, the Court stated, "We do not mean by this to indicate that the hearing must conform with all of the requirements of a criminal trial, or even of the usual administrative hearing; but we do hold that the hearing must measure up to essentials of due process and fair treatment" (cited in Cox, et al., 2008:273). Justice Fortas expressed some of the problems associated with the juvenile court, lamenting, "There is evidence, in fact, that there may be grounds for concern that the child receives the worst of both worlds: that he gets neither the protections accorded to adults nor the solicitous care and regenerative treatment postulated for children" (Cox, et al., 2008:270).

At least four other Supreme Court rulings had significant impact upon due process in juvenile courts: *In re Winship* (1970), *McKiever* v. *Pennsylvania* (1971), *Breed* v. *Jones* (1975), and *Schall* v. *Martin* (1984). Two of these cases extended the rights of due process in juvenile court (*In re Winship*, 1970; *Breed* v. *Jones*, 1975), and two of them denied specific elements of due process for juveniles (*McKiever* v. *Pennsylvania*, 1971; *Schall* v. *Martin*, 1984). *In re Winship* (1970) addressed the question whether "proof beyond a reasonable doubt" is required during the adjudication stage of a juvenile court hearing when the youth is charged with an act that would be a crime if committed by an adult (cited in Cox, et al., 2008). The case involved a 12-year-old boy who allegedly broke into a locker and stole $112 from a woman's purse. While the judge was convinced that Winship had committed the act, he acknowledged that there was no proof beyond a reasonable doubt. Winship was adjudicated delinquent and ordered to be placed in a state training school for a period of 18 months subject to yearly extensions until he reached the age of majority (potentially for 6 years). When his case was brought before the U.S. Supreme Court, the Court ruled that proof beyond a reasonable doubt was necessary in a juvenile court hearing where a crime had been committed. The Court concluded, "civil labels and good intentions do not themselves obviate the need for criminal due process safeguards in juvenile courts" (Cox, et al., 2008:277). Further due process rights were guaranteed to juveniles when the Supreme Court ruled that juveniles, like adults, were protected against **double jeopardy,** or *being tried twice for the same offense* (*Breed* v. *Jones*, 1975). In that case, the court ruled that a youth cannot be tried in a criminal court for the same offense for which he or she has been tried as a delinquent in juvenile court.

The Supreme Court sent mixed signals regarding its commitment to extending the rights of due process to the juvenile court. In the case of *McKiever* v. *Pennsylvania* (1971), the court ruled that juveniles were not guaranteed the right to a trial by jury. Approximately three-fourths of the states follow that ruling and do not provide jury trials for juveniles (Mahoney, 1985:553). Later, in the case of *Schall* v. *Martin* (1984), the Court held that youths could be held without bail if they were being held for their own protection or the protection of society. In these two cases the court reflected a shift back toward the rehabilitative and protective philosophy of the earlier juvenile court. Consequently, there is some ambiguity as to what rights are guaranteed juveniles when they are petitioned to juvenile court. It appears that in some areas, the extent of due process granted juveniles must be determined on a case-by-case basis. However, based upon the legal precedence set in the aforementioned juvenile cases, in most states, juveniles are advised of their legal rights when detained, parents are notified as soon as possible, and juveniles are allowed legal counsel during all phases of the justice process.

JUVENILE COURT PROCEDURES

While juvenile court policies and procedures vary across and within states, juvenile courts are characterized by three main operational procedures: *intake, adjudication,* and *disposition.*

Intake

The intake procedure begins when the juvenile court receives a referral on a particular youth. In most states, **referral** *means that the juvenile's name has been given to the court.* Referrals can come from a variety of sources including police, parents, schools, and others. Typically, the largest number of referrals comes from the police (see Table 14.2).

Upon receiving the referral, one of the officers of the court (usually a probation officer) is assigned to investigate the case to determine how the case best can be handled. A decision must be made on whether to hold or release the juvenile while the case is being investigated. The nature of the referral is the main criterion at that point. When possible, juveniles being referred for minor offenses are released into the custody of

TABLE 14.2 Juvenile Court Referrals by Source

Source of Referral	Percent
Law enforcement	81.0
Parents, relatives	3.5
School	2.9
Probation officer	2.5
Social agency	1.2
Other courts	2.4
Other	6.5
Total	100.0

Who might be some of the "other" sources for juvenile court referrals?

Source: Adapted from *Juvenile Court Statistics—2000.* Pittsburgh: National Center for Juvenile Justice, U.S. Department of Justice, 2004.

their parents. If the intake officer views it as appropriate, an intake interview with the youth and the youth's parents or legal guardian may be requested. More serious offenders, or those who for some reason cannot or should not be released to parents, are usually detained. The district attorney has primary responsibility for this decision. Ideally, the probation officer conducts a thorough investigation into the youth's social background by interviewing teachers, neighbors, and others who might provide insight into the situation. The probation officer then may recommend that the case be dismissed entirely, be referred to some other agency, or may move that a petition be filed with the juvenile court for a hearing. A **petition** is *an official statement that contains the important facts of the case,* such as the action that prompted the petition, along with relevant information about the juvenile and the youth's parents or guardians.

During the intake procedure in some states, the judge also has the option of declaring the juvenile to be an "adult" and ordering that the case be referred to an adult criminal court. In recent years, harsher attitudes toward juvenile law violators have resulted in increased numbers of youths being remanded to adult criminal courts. In 1988, over 4,000 youths were sent to state prisons after being prosecuted and convicted as adults (*Christian Science Monitor,* 1988), and in 1997 the U.S. House of Representatives passed a bill that provided financial incentives for states to remand to adult courts juveniles who are 15 years of age and older and had committed serious felonies (Reibstein, 1997).

There is some argument as to whether a youth is more likely to be certified as an adult based upon the seriousness of the offense and age (Fagan, et al., 1987a) or upon extralegal factors such as the race, ethnicity, and family situation of the offender (Leiber and Mack, 2003; Osbun and Rode, 1984; Singer, 1993). Males are overwhelmingly more likely than females to be waived to adult courts, and blacks are more likely than whites (Puzzanchera, et al., 2004). As pointed out earlier, as a result of *Kent* v. *United States* (1966), a hearing must be held and justification given for waiving jurisdiction by the juvenile court. Some states have revised their juvenile codes to provide for automatic waiver of juvenile court jurisdiction. For example, in some states a juvenile over the age of 16 who commits an act that would be considered a felony if committed by an adult, is automatically certified as an adult, and handled by adult criminal court. In those states, for a juvenile to be handled in juvenile court instead of the adult criminal court, a **reverse certification** hearing must be held to *declare the youth a juvenile.*

The length of time for intake procedures varies. The court attempts to work as expeditiously as possible while taking the necessary time to evaluate a youth's background and social circumstances. According to established juvenile justice standards, the intake process should not exceed 30 days (Miller, et al. 1985:242).

Adjudication

If a petition is filed and the youth has a hearing, the adjudication process takes place. **Adjudication** refers to *making a judgment or ruling.* This phase of the juvenile court proceeding is analogous to the trial phase of adult judicial proceedings. The judge (usually with assistance from a probation officer and the district attorney) must decide whether to dismiss charges or adjudicate the juvenile as *neglected, dependent,* or *delinquent.* During this stage evidence will be heard, and the judge will attempt to determine if the reason for which the juvenile was petitioned is valid, and if so, what should be done about it. If the child is adjudicated as neglected or dependent, the court identifies the youth as **INS** (in need of supervision). Youths sent to the court as a result of having been neglected, abused, wayward, truant, or runaways are most likely to be adjudicated INS.

A **delinquent** adjudication means that *the juvenile has committed a wrongful act for which the judge feels the youth must be held accountable.* Juveniles who have committed acts which would be a crime if committed by an adult are most likely to be adjudicated delinquent. Figure 14.1 shows the types of cases typically handled by juvenile courts.

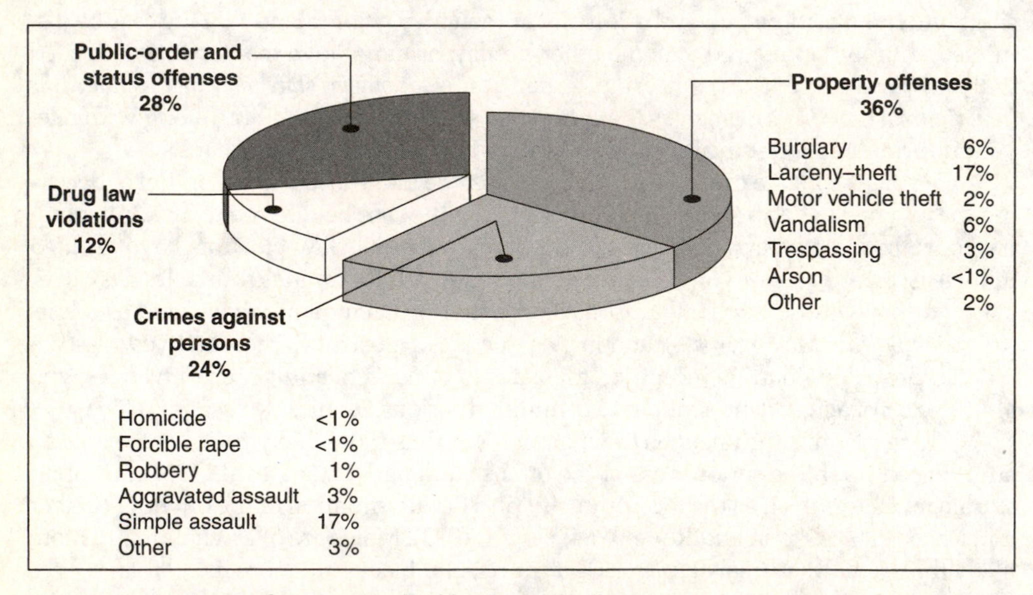

FIGURE 14.1 Types of Cases Handled by Juvenile Courts.

Are you surprised by the types of cases handled by juvenile courts? Is this what the media would lead you to believe?

How do the data in Figure 14.1 comport with the image you have of juvenile delinquency from the televisions, newspapers, and the Internet?

Source: Adapted from Juvenile Court Statistics *2003–2004.* (Pittsburgh, PA: National Center for Juvenile Justice, 2007). Note: Totals may not add up to 100 percent because of rounding.

The adjudication hearing for a juvenile accused of committing a criminal act is likely to take on many of the characteristics of an adult criminal trial. Attorneys are likely to be used, and in a few states, juveniles are even granted the right to a trial by jury. There are some notable distinctions, however, most prominent of which is that the juvenile hearing remains closed to the public, whereas adult criminal trials are open. There has been increased pressure to open juvenile hearings to public scrutiny, particularly in light of events which have resulted in allowing media coverage (including cameras in the courtrooms) of adult trials (Day, 1984). The protective philosophy of the juvenile court has been reemphasized, however, as juvenile courts steadfastly have refused to hold open hearings for fear of public stigmatization of the youths involved. Louis Day (1984) contended that the increased public interest in juvenile delinquency will heighten the demand for public access to juvenile court hearings and records, and ultimately will force the Supreme Court to determine two issues: (1) whether juvenile proceedings are criminal cases, subject to the same constitutional requirements as adult cases and (2) the degree of access the media and public should have to juvenile hearings. So far, no such ruling has been forthcoming.

During the adjudication phase, children brought before the court may have their parents, guardian, and/or legal counsel present. While established as an informal hearing, the adjudication phase has become increasingly formalized and legalistic. More juveniles and their parents are seeking legal advice and securing counsel for juvenile cases. The juvenile's right against self-incrimination is acknowledged, and juveniles are allowed to present a defense to the charges filed against them.

What role do juvenile probation officers play during the intake, adjudication, and disposition stages of juvenile court?

As one Supreme Court Justice noted, "This court believes that although the juvenile court was initially created as a social experiment, it has not ceased to be part of the justice system" (Miller, et al., 1985:554).

Disposition

Disposition is *the stage of the hearing most analogous to sentencing in a criminal court.* Occurring after adjudication, it is the process by which the judge must decide the best way to handle the juvenile's case. The judge must attempt to do what is best for the child while also protecting the community and preserving the integrity of the law. At least in philosophy, the disposition is supposed to be oriented toward treatment that will benefit the youth, rather than toward punishment.

During disposition, the judge has several alternatives from which to choose. The district attorney plays an important part in making recommendations to the judge, but the judge has extensive discretionary power in determining the disposition of the case. The judge can choose to dismiss the case and release the juvenile to parents or guardians. Estimates vary, but roughly 50 percent of all juvenile cases are dismissed. If the juvenile is adjudicated as INS, the judge can declare the youth a "ward of the court" and order placement in foster care. Because of the insufficient number of adequate foster homes, however, this disposition may be ruled less often than others. If the juvenile's problem is thought to be a result of some type of emotional disturbance, the judge probably will order a psychiatric report and the youth may be sent to a residential treatment center.

If the youth is adjudicated delinquent, the judge has three basic alternatives. The one most widely used is to place the juvenile on formal probation. While on probation, the juvenile must adhere to a specific set of guidelines and meet periodically with an assigned probation officer. If probation is deemed inappropriate, the judge can send the juvenile to a minimum security correctional institution. If the offense is of a serious nature, or the juvenile has appeared before the court several times, the judge may decide to send the offender to a maximum security correctional facility for youths. These institutions often are called "state training schools" and to a large extent operate as prisons for offenders under the age of majority.

Several factors influence the outcome of the dispositional phase of juvenile hearings. As already mentioned, one factor is the extent and variety of alternatives available to the judge. As Mahoney (1985:555) pointed out, "a problem related to plea negotiating for juveniles is that in many juvenile courts there is essentially a small range of disposition alternatives."

Variables such as seriousness of the offense, prior record, age, race, and sex of the offender all enter into the discretionary decision of the juvenile court judge (Chesney-Lind and Pasko, 2004; Leiber and Mack, 2003; Minor, et al., 1997). Just as the police are influenced by a variety of extralegal factors such as race, age, and sex of the offender in deciding how to handle juveniles on the street, so are the courts. For example, William Arnold (1971), Terry Thornberry (1973), Robert Perry (1985), Jeffrey Fagan, et al. (1987a), and Edmund McGarrell (1993) all found that blacks and youths from lower socioeconomic backgrounds typically received harsher dispositions in juvenile court. Similarly, while it has been acknowledged that paternalistic attitudes of police and court officials may lead to lower arrest rates and fewer petitions to juvenile court for females, Meda Chesney-Lind (1977) found that once detained and petitioned to court, females are likely to be treated more harshly than their male counterparts regardless of seriousness of the offense (Chesney-Lind and Pasko, 2004).

Other variables related to dispositional decisions include the extent of demonstrated parental interest in the child and the case (Aurand, 1998; O'Quin, et al., 1985), known membership in a juvenile gang (Zatz, 1985), and prior dispositions (Thornberry and Christenson, 1984). Through a longitudinal study, Thornberry and Christenson (1984) found that the single most important determinant of the type and severity of disposition levied against a particular youth was the type and severity of previous dispositions. They found that rather than dispositions becoming increasingly severe with each repeat offense by an individual, the same disposition was very likely to be imposed over and over again. Joseph Sanborn (1996) concluded that it is almost impossible to determine precisely the impact of any specific factors on dispositional outcomes.

Several states provide juvenile judges with another dispositional alternative: **blended sentencing** *where a serious or violent juvenile offender is adjudicated delinquent in a juvenile court or waived to adult court and found guilty of a felony and given both a juvenile court disposition and an adult sentence.* The adult sentence is "suspended" and the juvenile court disposition is implemented. If the juvenile fulfills the disposition then the adult sentence is dismissed. If he or she fails to fulfill the terms of the disposition, the adult sentence (which might include incarceration in adult correctional facility) is imposed.

THE ROLE OF ATTORNEYS IN JUVENILE COURT

The role of attorneys in juvenile court is not as clear-cut as it is in adult criminal court. It has been only since the *Gault* decision of 1967 that attorneys have been introduced into the juvenile court proceeding; since then, they have played an increasingly important role in the contemporary juvenile court.

The District Attorney

Each state is divided into judicial districts, and a public election is held in each district to elect a prosecuting attorney to represent the state in criminal cases within the district. Thus, when the police or a citizen signs a petition alleging misconduct by a child or young person, the office of the district attorney comes in contact with the youngster. Before this petition is filed with the court and a hearing is scheduled, the district attorney may investigate the case and exercise one of three basic options:

1. Refuse to prosecute for lack of evidence and release the child.
2. Defer prosecution and place the child on informal probation. In many such cases the district attorney may make an arrangement with the child's parents not to prosecute if they will keep the child under close supervision.
3. Expedite the filing of the petition and prosecute the child in the juvenile court for the alleged offense.

Former juvenile judge Ted Rubin (1980) concluded that as a result of the *Gault* decision (which provides the right to counsel for juveniles), prosecuting attorneys have taken a much more active role in the juvenile court, especially during the intake phase. We can view the district attorney as the law-enforcing officer in the median position between the police officer and the juvenile court judge. Here, the **filtering process** (see Figure 14.2) is continued, as many cases are treated informally and not

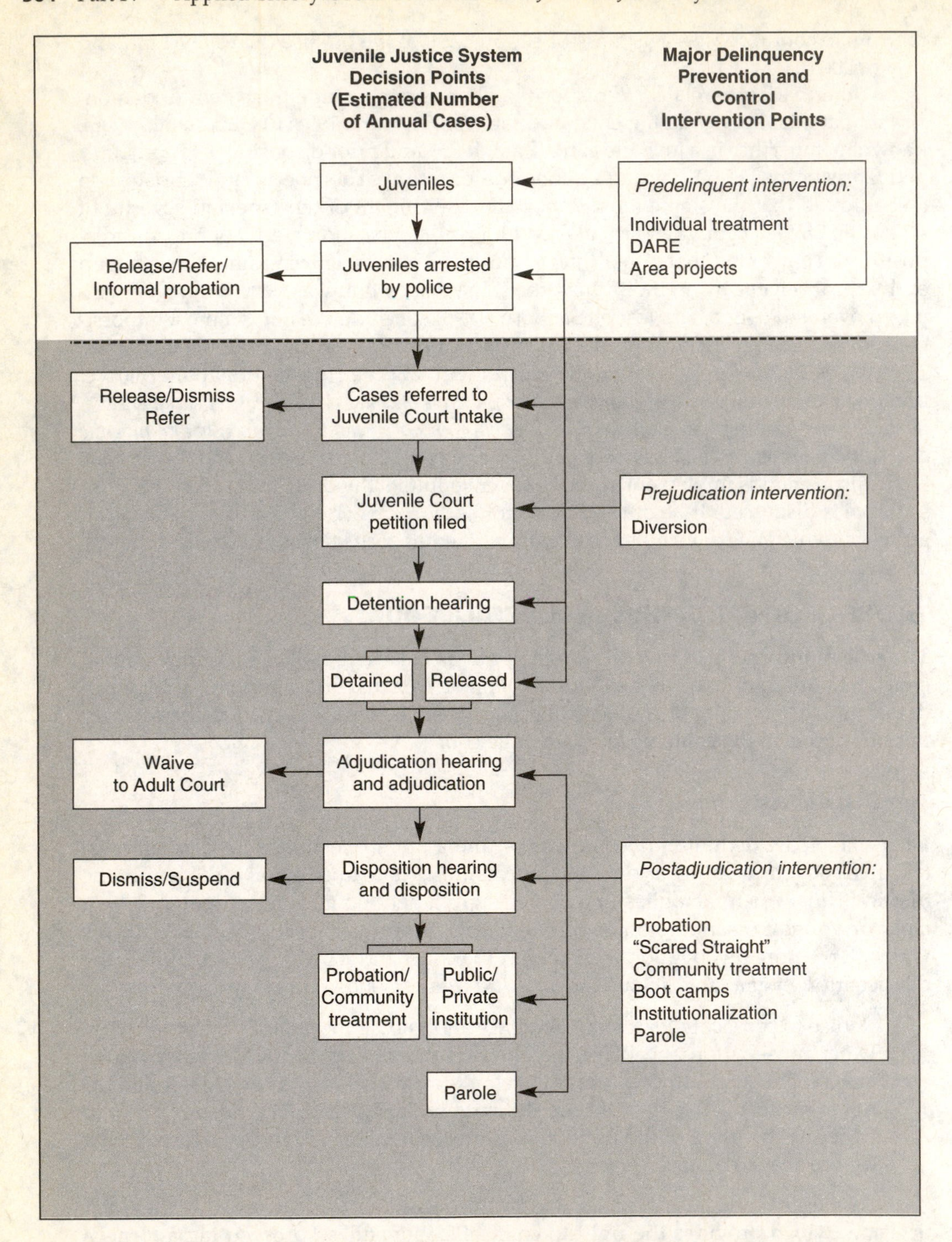

FIGURE 14.2 Filtering Process in Juvenile Justice System: The Courts.
How does this diagram relate to the Filtering Process by police in Chapter 13?

Source: Adapted from Caseflow Diagram, Office of Juvenile Justice and Delinquency Prevention, http://ojjdp.ncjrs.org/facts/casejpg.html.

sent on to court. In this way, many young people avoid an official record of delinquency and the state avoids much expensive litigation. If the petition is formally filed with the court, the court procedures described in the previous section officially begin.

The district attorney can be involved in all three stages of the juvenile court proceedings. This officer may make recommendations to the judge regarding whether the case should be handled in juvenile court or transferred to adult criminal court. Along with a court services officer, the district attorney also advises the judge on adjudication and dispositional alternatives.

The Defense Attorney

The role of the defense attorney in juvenile court is both ambiguous and controversial (see Box 14.2). Since due process has been introduced into the juvenile justice system, more juveniles and their parents are seeking legal representation when appearing in juvenile court. The attorney for the juvenile performs many of the same functions as a defense attorney in criminal court. However, because of the less formal atmosphere of the juvenile court, and the more relaxed rules on testimony and evidence, the youth's attorney may not be able to protect the youth in some of the same ways a criminal lawyer can defend an adult in criminal court. While a juvenile may plead the Fifth Amendment (right not to testify against oneself), this behavior may be more likely to antagonize the judge than to help the juvenile's case. Similarly, Anne Mahoney (1985:556) discovered that in states where juveniles were entitled to jury trials, it was quite possible that such a request might produce negative results for the youth because the court could penalize those youths who asked for jury trials. While the criminal judge's decision hinges upon the legal and technical ramifications of the case, it must be remembered that the juvenile court judge's decision rests primarily upon what the judge considers best for the juvenile. Thus, even though an attorney may provide counsel which legally protects the youth, it may in fact not favorably alter the adjudication and disposition decisions (Burrus and Kempf-Leonard, 2002).

CRITICISMS OF THE JUVENILE COURT

Since 1899, when the first juvenile court was established, it has undergone a great deal of scrutiny and criticism from different sectors in society. One of the most prevalent criticisms has been that the juvenile courts are "too easy" on juveniles and have a tendency to coddle and protect what are basically just young criminals. As a juvenile officer in the Los Angeles Police Department put it, "Some of these hoodlums are back on the street before I finish the paper work!" (Carter, 1976:124).

From its inception, the juvenile court has been viewed almost as a parent, charged with protecting those who are sent to it. The juvenile court was founded upon the philosophies of protection and rehabilitation. In a society where people are reading about teenaged rapists, murderers, and muggers, many citizens question the legitimacy of "protecting" juvenile offenders. A rather bizarre case that brought public attention to this issue occurred in 2000 when police charged 39-year-old Michael Skakel (a member of the Kennedy family) with the murder of his neighbor whom he allegedly bludgeoned to death 24 years earlier when he was only 15 years of age. Initial proceedings took place in a juvenile court due to his age at the time of the murder. This placed a

BOX 14.2

CONTROVERSIAL ISSUE: The Use of Attorneys in the Juvenile Court

The *Gault* decision of 1967 by the U.S. Supreme Court brought major changes into the juvenile court process. Lauded as a landmark decision, one of its important effects upon juvenile justice was the determination that juveniles and/or their parents have the right to legal counsel when petitioned to the juvenile court. Since that ruling, many juveniles and their parents have opted to have legal counsel present for their hearings before the juvenile court.

While the role of attorneys in adult criminal court is well established, it remains somewhat ambiguous and controversial in juvenile court hearings. The role of the district attorney in the prosecution of juvenile delinquency has become very similar to that in a criminal case. Since the *Gault* decision, prosecutors have taken a much more active role in juvenile court procedures. In fact, Rubin (1980) contended that the intake process of the court is dominated by the prosecutor.

The defense attorney, on the other hand, has a less clear-cut role in the juvenile court. The Institute of Judicial Administration and the American Bar Association (IJA/ABA) suggested in their *Juvenile Justice Standards Project* (1977) that there are three roles that the attorney can fulfill in the juvenile court: (1) officer of the court, (2) guardian, and (3) advocate. In the first role, the attorney becomes an aide to the juvenile judge in attempting to help the judge determine what is best for the youth, This role seems most appropriate in cases of neglect, abuse, and other situations in which the juvenile appears before the court more as a "victim" than as an "offender." The guardian role involves a situation in which the attorney takes control of all of the juvenile's interests in the hearing, and, to be effective, requires that the juvenile and the juvenile's parents passively follow all advice given by the attorney. This role seems most appropriate when the juvenile is very young, mentally incompetent, or not accompanied by parents or legal guardian when appearing before the court. The advocate role is the traditional role assumed by attorneys when representing a client in adult criminal court. In this role, the attorney attempts to represent the client's best legal interests, and defends the juvenile against the charges outlined in the court petition. It is the third role which is most likely to be adopted by attorneys secured to represent juveniles who have committed offenses that would be a crime if committed by an adult.

The role assumed by the attorney in juvenile court may be controlled to some degree by the type of juvenile court in which he or she appears, and may be limited by the type of juvenile judge presiding over the hearing. In the due process type of court discussed in this chapter, the attorney probably will have every opportunity to assume the advocate role on behalf of the juvenile. On the other hand, in the traditional court, where the judge assumes almost total control of the hearing, and in which the due process rights of the juvenile are severely limited, the attorney may be restricted in choice of role in the proceeding.

The impact of increased involvement of attorneys in the juvenile court is unclear. It is generally agreed that their presence in the juvenile court has increased the formality of court proceedings and made judges more aware of the due process rights of the juvenile, However, research on attorneys' influence on the actual adjudication and disposition rulings by juvenile courts indicates that the presence of attorneys has made very little difference (e.g., Burrus, et al., 2002; Sosin and Sarri, 1976). In a collection of research articles, Sarri and Hasenfeld (1976) found that attorneys' impact upon the juvenile court is minimal, and that virtually all others involved in the court procedures exert more influence over the outcome of the hearing (e.g., judge, social workers, court officers, parents, and juvenile).

It has been argued that attorney involvement in juvenile courts has had a more significant impact upon their proceedings than is readily discernible from the types of research that have been conducted (Naffine and Wundersitz, 1991). In other words, although adjudication rates and types of disposition do not appear to have been significantly affected, perhaps more subtle changes have occurred owing to attorney representation in juvenile court. While the juvenile court hearing is technically informal, and the judge enjoys wide latitude in terms of discretion, no doubt the presence of legal counsel on behalf of a youth indicates a recognition that the juvenile court is still a legal proceeding and that regardless of the subjective nature of adjudication and dispositional decisions, the rights of the juvenile will be preserved to the fullest extent possible. While the juvenile court was established to act in the best interests of the juveniles brought before it, representation by legal counsel may underscore that effort.

Based upon your reading of this chapter and this box, what do you think the role of attorneys should be in the juvenile court? Should every juvenile be represented by legal counsel? If so, why? If not, why not? In your opinion, has the impact of attorneys on the juvenile court primarily been positive? or negative?

Sources

Burrus, G. W. Jr. and Kempf-Leonard, K. 2002. The questionable advantage of defense counsel in juvenile courts. *Justice Quarterly* 19:37–68.

Feld, B. C. 1999. *Bad kids: Race and the transformation of juvenile court.* New York: Oxford University Press.

Naffine, N., and Wundersitz, J. 1991. Lawyers in the children's court: An Australian perspective. *Crime and Delinquency* 37 (July):374–392.

Rubin, H. T. 1980. The emerging prosecutor dominance of the juvenile court intake process. *Crime and Delinquency* 26 (July):299–318.

Sarri, R., and Hasenfeld, Y. (Eds.). 1976. *Brought to justice? Juveniles, the courts and the law.* Ann Arbor: University of Michigan, National Assessment of Juvenile Corrections.

Sosin, M., and Sarri, R. 1976. Due process—reality or myth? In R. Sarri and Y. Hasenfeld (Eds.). *Brought to justice? Juveniles, the courts, and the law.* Ann Arbor: University of Michigan, pp. 176–206.

number of legal roadblocks in the case before the district attorney could eventually get the case remanded to adult criminal court (AP, Stamford, CT, 2001; Lavoie, 2000).

Many critics of the court are shocked by its lenient dispositions and believe its philosophy should not be applied to youths who commit serious criminal offenses. Police often feel helpless in attempting to control the problem, knowing that many of their efforts at law enforcement will be negated by benevolent, well-meaning, or politically sensitive juvenile judges. Victims of juvenile offenders are often reluctant to file complaints or press charges because previous experience has shown that very little will be done to the juveniles; and often they are back on the streets the very same day, seeking revenge. In some states, the most severe penalty for a juvenile is to be adjudicated "delinquent" and institutionalized for a brief period of time. For example, a case in New York that received much media attention focused on a 15-year-old boy who committed a premeditated and particularly vicious murder. He was sent to a juvenile institution for 18 months (AP, New York, 1978). On the basis of such cases, some members of society perceive the juvenile court as more helpless and impotent than benevolent and protecting.

Conversely, another criticism of the juvenile court has been that it is "too hard" on juveniles and tends to overreact to relatively minor offenses. Because a major goal of the juvenile court is to prevent juvenile offenders from becoming adult criminals, there may be a tendency on the part of some juvenile judges to treat relatively minor offenses very seriously in an effort to impress upon the juvenile that any further law violation will not be tolerated. As noted in the *Gault* case, the punishment for an

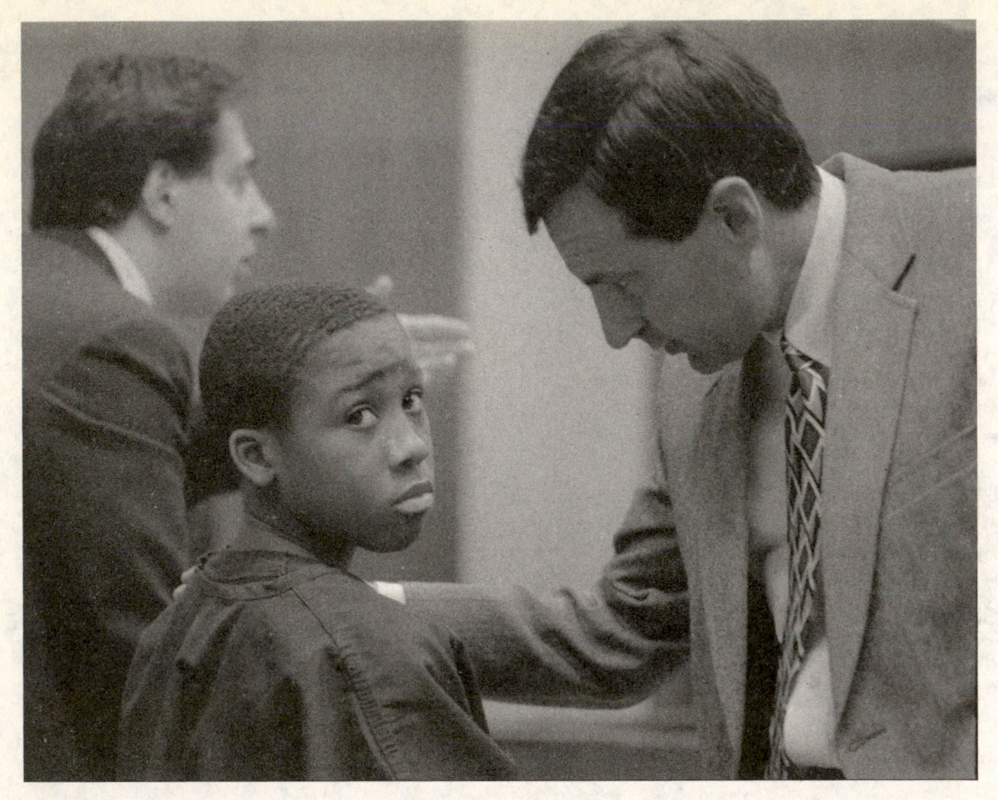

This 11-year-old was charged with first degree murder when he shot an 18-year-old stranger outside a convenience store. Should his case be handled in juvenile court or remanded to adult court? What are the issues with each option?

adult who made an obscene phone call would have been a minor fine or brief incarceration. Instead, Gault was ordered institutionalized for a period of six years! This type of disposition seems extreme in proportion to the severity of the alleged offense. In some cases, much of what might be viewed as merely "adolescent mischief" is treated as if it were a major crime in order to "teach the youth a lesson." Unfortunately, the lesson taught may not be the one desired. When petty offenses are treated as major ones, at least in the mind of the juvenile, the difference between the two may become blurred. For example, in a state where murder and truancy might both result in 18 months of institutionalization, the vastly significant difference between the two acts becomes symbolically reduced. Several researchers have linked the widespread procedure of indeterminate sentencing (no specified length of sentence) by juvenile courts to terms of incarceration for juveniles often being longer than those for adults who commit the same offense (e.g., ACLU, 1978; Lightholder, 1978; Sleeth, 1978). Consequently, the question of discrimination against juveniles arises as a legal issue to be addressed. Recent trends in juvenile justice indicate that this issue may be dissipated, as juvenile courts appear to be focusing their attention much more on the smaller number of serious juvenile offenders as opposed to the nonserious status offenders who have traditionally monopolized juvenile court dockets (Regnery, 1986). Nevertheless, the punishment ideology appears to dominate today's juvenile court (Bazemore and Umbreit, 1995). Many states have rewritten their juvenile codes to change the purpose of juvenile courts from *prevention, diversion,* and *treatment,* to *community protection, offender accountability, crime reduction, deterrence,* and *punishment* (Griffin, et al., 2005).

The absence of total due process continues as another point of criticism of the juvenile court. As a result of the Supreme Court decisions discussed earlier in this chapter, and the increased utilization of legal counsel in juvenile hearings, this criticism has been reduced somewhat. Much of the concern now focuses upon preserving the rights of youths charged with status offenses. Since these youths have not violated criminal laws and are more likely to be adjudicated "in need of supervision" as opposed to "delinquent," their hearings are often much more informal. Consequently, the legal rights of these juveniles may not be protected as much as if they had been arrested for a criminal act. For example, Jan Costello and Nancy Worthington (1981) expressed concern that many states were circumventing the Juvenile Justice and Prevention Act, which prohibits the incarceration of status offenders.

Perhaps the most persistent criticism leveled at the juvenile court has been that its jurisdiction is too broad. As former judge of the Denver Juvenile Court Ted Rubin (1976:66) expressed:

> This court is a far more complex instrument than outsiders imagine. It is law, and it is social work; it is control and it is help; it is the good parent, and, also, the stern parent; it is both formal and informal. It is concerned not only with the delinquent, but also with the battered child, the runaway, and many others. . . . The juvenile court has been all things to all people.

The criticism is that the juvenile court has tried to be too many different things to too many different people. In broadening its jurisdiction to attempt to cover virtually all of the problems that involve juveniles, the court may have inadvertently diluted its ability to successfully handle any of them. Barry Feld (1993:403) laments that "the juvenile court has been transformed from an informal, welfare agency into a scaled-down, second-class criminal court . . . that diverts status offenders, waives serious offenders to adult courts, punishes delinquent offenders, and provides more formal procedures." This "jack-of-all trades, master of none" image has plagued the contemporary juvenile court. Feld (1999, 2003) also points out that juvenile courts have much broader discretion than adult criminal courts, a fact that may lead to age, race, and gender bias in court decisions.

Francis Allen (1976:417) discussed several of the problems involved in juvenile justice, and pointed out that many of the court's "difficulties arise from an insufficient conception of the court's role and the court's capabilities." Rubin (1979) further discussed some of the problems encountered by the juvenile court in attempting to handle too broad a range of cases. He contended that there is a definite need for a juvenile court, but it should not be expected to handle all types of cases. For example, he suggested that neglected and abused children should probably be handled by divorce and family courts.

THE MULTIFACETED JUVENILE COURT

One of the difficulties faced by juvenile courts resides in the fact that there is no such thing as *the* juvenile court. Rather, juvenile courts vary from state to state in their size, nature, jurisdiction, and procedures. In short, there are a variety of juvenile courts. Throughout this chapter we have compared and contrasted juvenile courts to adult criminal courts. In the process, we have discovered that while there are notable similarities between the two, there remain distinctive differences.

It has been suggested that contemporary juvenile courts no longer resemble the earlier chancery court out of which they developed, but are also unlike adult criminal courts. In an attempt to analyze the juvenile court as a "people-processing organization," Hasenfeld and Cheung (1985) pointed to the multidimensional personality of juvenile courts. They indicated that juvenile courts are faced with a "dual and contradictory mandate" of projecting a "social service orientation," while responding to the more legalistic orientation of preserving "law and order" (Hasenfeld and Cheung, 1985:806). In an effort to explain how the court attempts to fulfill this dual mandate, Hasenfeld and Cheung (1985: 819–820) created the following typology of juvenile courts based upon the proportion of cases handled judicially (formally brought before a judge), and the rate of commitment (proportion of juveniles committed to juvenile institutions):

1. ***Interventionist Court:*** characterized by a high proportion of its cases being handled judicially, and by a high commitment rate; this is the traditional juvenile court that emerged from the child-saving movement.
2. ***Paternalistic Court:*** characterized by a low proportion of cases handled judicially and a high commitment rate; this is the most commonly found juvenile court which tries to combine social rehabilitation with community protection.
3. ***Ritualistic Court:*** characterized by a high proportion of its cases being handled judicially and a low rate of commitment; this court exercises its formal judicial authority, but feels less pressure to protect the community.
4. ***Minimalistic Court:*** characterized by both a low proportion of cases handled judicially and a low commitment rate; this court represents an attempt to legally reform juvenile courts by elevating their legal status and removing the judge from the political arena.

David Aday (1986) created a simpler typology of juvenile courts based on important variations in court structure and procedure. He identified two different types of juvenile courts: the **traditional court** and the **due process court**. According to Aday (1986:111), the two courts were distinguishable by the following characteristics:

Traditional Court

1. ***Low task differentiation:*** decisions about cases are made by court staff; the prosecutor does not participate in decisions to file formal petitions;
2. ***Centralized authority:*** the judge administers probation and other court services;
3. ***Low discretion for court services staff:*** probation staff cannot assign juveniles to informal probation;

4. ***Status offender jurisdiction:*** the court routinely handles cases alleging status offenses;
5. ***Low formalization:*** adjudication and disposition hearings are not bifurcated.

Due Process Court

1. ***High task differentiation:*** court services staff participate separately in decisions; the prosecutor participates in decisions to file formal complaints;
2. ***Decentralized authority:*** the judge does not administer probation or other court services; these services are administered within the State Department of Social Services;
3. ***High discretion for court services staff:*** probation staff assign juveniles to informal probation; the court does not handle such cases;
4. ***Status offender jurisdiction:*** the court routinely handles cases alleging status offenses;
5. ***Low formalization:*** there is no requirement to bifurcate adjudication and dispositional hearings.

In the *traditional court* the role of the judge is to enact the philosophy of *parens patriae;* consequently, the roles of attorneys, staff, parents, and others in the court are minimized. The traditional court attempts to perpetuate a social service orientation. According to Aday (1986:115), "particularistic characteristics of juveniles and/or offenses influence decisions" and "attorney use represents token compliance with due-process requirements and has no effect on decision making." On the other hand, the *due process court* is dominated by legal factors (especially nature of offenses) in its decision making, and attorneys play a prominent role in determining the outcome of cases (Aday, 1986). In the two types of courts studied by Aday, some interesting data emerged regarding rates of detention, probation, and commitment. We have constructed Table 14.3 to illustrate his findings, which still apply to juvenile courts today.

As can be seen in Table 14.3, the traditional court was more likely to detain juveniles before their hearing, but once juveniles appeared before the judge, the largest percentage were likely to be placed on formal probation. The due process court detained far fewer juveniles, electing to simply warn and release almost three-fourths (73 percent) of those with whom it came in contact. The traditional court and due

TABLE 14.3 Dispositions in Traditional and Due Process Courts

	Traditional Court (percentage)	Due Process Court (percentage)
Detained juveniles	50.0	16.1
Unofficially warn and release	24.3	73.0
Placed on probation	63.6	20.2
Committed	12.1	6.9

Would you predict that juvenile courts of the future will tend to be more traditional or more due process oriented?

Source: Created from data in D. P. Aday, Jr. Court structure, defense attorney use, and juvenile court decisions. *Sociological Quarterly* 27(1), 1986:112.

process court differed in severity of dispositions, with almost twice the proportion of juveniles appearing before the traditional court being committed to a juvenile institution as compared to those from the due process court.

THE FUTURE OF THE JUVENILE COURT

Given the historical development of the juvenile court and the many criticisms directed toward it, the future of the juvenile court is unclear. Conservatives, moderates, liberals, and radicals have different views on what the future should hold for the juvenile court, but almost all agree that some changes must and will occur. One of the dilemmas faced by the juvenile court is how to combine the rehabilitative philosophy of *parens patriae* upon which it was founded with contemporary retributive trends that insist the court must punish serious juvenile offenders. Many believe that the juvenile court must adopt an alternative model of *restorative justice* that sanctions serious criminal behavior while also attempting to return the juvenile to society as a productive citizen (Bazemore and Umbreit, 1995). While there is much disagreement over how to reform the juvenile court, there is some consensus that at least five changes are in order:

1. Limit its jurisdiction
2. Operate under the provisions of due process
3. Be administered by competent judges
4. Have adequate court personnel
5. Have adequate availability of alternatives for disposition

It is much easier to list these items than it is to implement them, but all of these changes are feasible. In Chapter 17 of this book we explore these and other possibilities for reforming the juvenile justice system.

Summary

The juvenile court is a relatively young institution in the United States, established in Chicago in 1899. Yet, the historical and legal traditions of the court are much older and can be traced to the chancery courts of 15th-century England. During its short history in this country, the juvenile court has extended its jurisdiction and has had dramatic influence on the lives of those with whom it has come in contact.

The establishment of the American juvenile court roughly corresponded to changing attitudes about childhood and represented a major development in separating youthful offenders from hardened criminals. With its protective philosophy, and overall goal of deterring troubled youths from becoming adult criminals, the juvenile court has made numerous contributions in the handling of juveniles. Perhaps one of its most significant contributions has been its symbolic representation of the notion that the state is genuinely concerned about its youths. It has been there to intervene on the behalf of abused, neglected, and misdirected youths.

Despite its laudable philosophy and numerous accomplishments, the juvenile court also has been the target of widespread criticism from a variety of sources. Too lenient, too harsh, too broad in its scope, too narrow in its power, the juvenile court in the view of many has become an ineffective mockery of what it was meant to be. Partly in response to some of these criticisms, and partly as a result of Supreme Court intervention, the juvenile court has undergone numerous changes since it first came into operation. Probably one of the most prominent changes has been in its shift toward a more formal legalistic approach to juvenile criminal offenses. The introduction of elements of due process and increased involvement of attorneys has altered its once informal omnipotent procedures.

In Chapters 15, 16, and 17 we address the inherently social nature of juvenile justice and the issue of modifying the social structure in an effort to mobilize the total community toward delinquency prevention, treatment, and control.

Concept Integration: Questions and Topics for Study and Discussion

1. Explain due process and discuss how its introduction into the juvenile court has influenced the philosophy and operation of the court.
2. List some of the positive and negative influences the Child Savers Movement exerted on the juvenile justice process.
3. Describe the historical development of the juvenile court.
4. Describe and explain the procedures of the contemporary juvenile court. In what ways are they different from those of the adult criminal court?
5. Identify some of the limitations and major criticisms of the juvenile court. What changes might be made in the juvenile court to overcome the limitations and address the criticisms?

Chapter 15

Juvenile Corrections

READING OBJECTIVES

Reading this chapter will help you achieve the following objectives:

1. Understand the sociological concept of social control and explain how it relates to deterrence theory and juvenile delinquency.
2. Distinguish between voluntary, informal, and formal methods of social control.
3. Define the concepts of juvenile probation, restitution, detention, incarceration, and aftercare.
4. Distinguish between different types of juvenile facilities such as detention facilities, training schools, and group homes.
5. Understand the process by and extent to which juveniles are remanded to adult criminal courts and placed in adult jails and prisons.
6. Summarize the use of capital punishment for juveniles who have been convicted of capital offenses in adult criminal courts.
7. Identify some of the more prominent community corrections programs designed to deinstitutionalize youths and divert them from the juvenile justice system.

INTRODUCTION

We have emphasized the social nature of juvenile delinquency throughout this book. Just as we looked to human society and culture in defining delinquency and for providing insight into causal explanations, we now turn to those same sources for controlling juvenile delinquency.

This chapter focuses upon controlling juvenile delinquency, *not* eliminating it. Most social problems are never fully eliminated. Despite multimillion-dollar programs and armies of professionals committed to the eradication of problems such as crime, suicide, mental illness, and juvenile delinquency, the problems persist. Ironically, some of our most strenuous efforts to eliminate a social problem may, in fact, only help perpetuate it, and in some cases, create other problems. For example, as we will discuss in Chapter 16, some of our efforts to prevent delinquency have led to a preoccupation with identifying and treating "predelinquents." This attempt at identifying delinquents before they have committed delinquent acts involves identifying dubious "symptoms" in early childhood. As the labeling perspective indicates, identifying and then treating a child as a "predelinquent" may, in fact, later create the very phenomenon that one is trying to prevent.

This should not discourage us from seeking programs aimed at controlling social problems such as delinquency, but should caution us against anticipating the discovery of some panacea leading to utopian solutions. A pragmatic objective is to develop realistic social mechanisms for reducing and controlling delinquency. By **social control** we mean *those aspects of society and culture, which are designed to reduce the incidence of juvenile delinquency and to minimize its negative impact upon members of society.*

Every society establishes norms to regulate human behavior and provides guidelines for social interaction. Similarly, societies have established numerous ways of dealing with those individuals who violate the norms (folkways, mores, and laws) of their society. These *methods of enforcing norms* are referred to as **sanctions**, and can be either positive or negative. When people conform to normative expectations they receive positive sanctions in the form of respect, honors, awards, and social acceptance. When they violate norms their behavior is negatively sanctioned, or punished, in an attempt to control their behavior. These methods of social control can be divided into three general categories: voluntary, informal, and formal, and are linked to the idea of deterrence. First, we will briefly look at deterrence theory, and then we will turn to specific areas of social control.

SOCIAL CONTROL AND DETERRENCE THEORY

At the heart of all social control is a fundamental belief in **Deterrence Theory**—*that deviance will be discouraged (deterred) if social sanctions for nonconformity are perceived to be certain, swift, and severe* (Gibbs, 1975; Schneider, 1990). Recall from Chapter 8, that like some of its predecessors, deterrence theory assumes that juveniles are rational, logical beings who prefer to be rewarded for their conformity rather than be punished for their deviance. Thus, the theory contends that if youths know that meaningful social sanctions will be forthcoming, they are less likely to commit delinquent acts.

Ideally, the goal of society is to sanction juvenile delinquency in such a way as to incorporate elements of both specific and general deterrence (see Chapter 8). This is difficult, however, as some people may be more affected by one type of deterrence than another, and some youths learn only from personal experience (specific deterrence), while others can learn from the experiences of others, which is the key to general deterrence (Matsueda, et al., 2006; Paternoster and Piquero, 1995). Chapter 16 discusses a variety of treatment and prevention programs aimed at deterring juvenile delinquency. Box 15.1 deals with the controversial caning of an American teenager in Singapore, a punishment used in that culture in an effort to deter vandalism and other property crimes.

VOLUNTARY SOCIAL CONTROL

The most fundamental and effective method of social control is **voluntary control**, which most members of society *impose upon themselves.* Voluntary social control is dependent upon effective socialization so that societal members *internalize* the shared values and norms of their society. The socialization process involves not only teaching social norms to societal members, but also causing individuals to believe in the moral and ethical validity of those norms. Thus, the teaching of social **values**, *attitudes about the rightness and wrongness of acts,* is just as important as teaching people the appropriateness of acts, if not more important. For example, most of us refrain from committing forcible rape, murder, or armed robbery not only because such acts violate formal norms and are defined as criminal, but also because we believe it is wrong to commit such actions against our fellow human beings. We obey many of our criminal laws not because we fear the consequences of violating them, but because most of us believe in the validity of such laws and would never consider violating them. On the other hand, in the aftermath of natural disasters such as floods, earthquakes, hurricanes, and tornadoes, we often see how quickly the restraints learned through socialization can be overcome as the police and National Guard must be called upon to keep some people from looting the remains of the damaged property of their fellow citizens.

Some sociological theories of juvenile delinquency claim that inadequate or unsuccessful socialization leads to delinquency. For example, the social learning

BOX 15.1

CROSS-CULTURAL FOCUS: The Caning of an American Youth in Singapore: Justice or Abuse?

Reports of an American teenager spraying paint on some parked cars is not considered shocking in an era when nightly news reports are filled with incidents of armed robbery, aggravated assault, forcible rape, and murders committed by youths under the age of 18. While such acts of vandalism would not be ignored, they quite likely would warrant a small fine, perhaps some financial restitution to the victims, and six months to a year on probation—if they were committed in the United States. Michael Fay, an 18-year-old from Kettering, Ohio, however, did not receive such a light sentence from the courts in Singapore. In a city where chewing gum is a fineable offense, vandalism of automobiles is taken quite seriously, and Michael Fay was sentenced to four months in prison, a $2,220 fine, and six lashes with a rattan cane on his bare buttocks for his participation in the offense.

Fay's sentence sparked an international debate between East and West over human rights issues and fueled an age-old argument in the United States over whether the American juvenile and criminal justice systems are too lenient and should more closely model some of their harsher counterparts in other parts of the world. At one point, President Clinton intervened on Fay's behalf, and while unsuccessful in his request that the young man be spared the caning and released to return to the United States, the Singapore government did decide to reduce the flogging from six lashes to four.

Many Americans disagreed with the president's appeal for leniency for Michael Fay and insisted that America's juvenile and criminal justice systems could learn a valuable lesson from Singapore's. Almost 40 percent of Americans in a *Newsweek* poll indicated that they approved of the punishment (Elliott, 1994). They cited Singapore's low crime rates as evidence that their "get tough" approaches to crime and delinquency are more successful than those practiced in the United States. On the other hand, critics of the Singapore criminal justice system argued that Americans would be ill-advised to turn their back on the U.S. Bill of Rights and copy the harsh example of Singapore. Fay's parents contended that Michael's confession was coerced from him, and there were allegations that other American teens involved in the incident were beaten by the police during interrogation while some Singapore youths who may also have been involved were set free.

What do you think? Should teenagers or adult criminals be subjected to corporal punishment? Would caning or other types of corporal punishment act as a specific deterrent to delinquency? Would they serve as a general deterrent? Would incorporating corporal punishment into American corrections represent an innovative approach to deterring crime and delinquency, or a giant step backwards?

Sources

Elliott, M. 1994. Crime and punishment, the caning debate: Should the U.S. be more like Singapore? *Newsweek*, April 18:18–22.

National Review. 1994. Singapore blues. May 16:79.

Newsweek. 1994. I tried to ignore the pain, Interview: Michael Fay on his caning in Singapore. July 4:36.

Newsweek. 1994. Singapore: After the caning, "Mike's in pain." May 16:41.

theories contend that delinquency, as well as conformity, must be learned through socialization. Hence, the major agents of socialization—family, religion, school, peers, and mass media—all play an important role in helping a juvenile internalize society's norms.

Walter Reckless (1961) emphasized social control as being the primary, distinguishing element between those who commit and those who refrain from committing delinquent acts. The first layer of insulation against delinquency in Reckless' Control Theory is that of *inner containment*. This inner containment is primarily a result of effective socialization. When juveniles internalize society's values and norms as their own, they are much less likely to violate those values and norms. This element of voluntary social control relies upon the individual's set of values to act as a sufficient barrier to committing delinquent acts. What many of us refer to as conscience is in fact the manifestation of voluntary social control.

Another aspect of voluntary social control developed through effective socialization is the process whereby individuals acknowledge their membership in society and simultaneously recognize society as being part of them. Often referred to as a *social bond* (Hirschi, 1969), this acknowledgment promotes the conformity to social norms, and helps prevent involvement in delinquent acts. Because voluntary control is dependent upon the socialization process, the role of the family cannot be overemphasized. Primary responsibility for teaching appropriate values and behaviors rests with the family. The family's choice of neighborhood, schools, and church attendance all impact the socialization process. Perhaps most important are the role models provided in a family by parents and older siblings.

In a society where there are infinitely more potential deviants than there are formal agents of social control, the importance of voluntary social control cannot be overestimated. If juveniles are going to conform to society's rules most of the time it is more dependent upon their willingness to do so, than upon the ability of adults to prevent them from committing delinquent acts. Through effective socialization and developing a sense of attachment to society, most juveniles refrain from committing serious delinquent acts.

INFORMAL SOCIAL CONTROL

When the internalization of social norms is insufficient for an individual to maintain behavioral control, it may be necessary for the social group to implement a second line of defense against deviance: **informal social control** mechanisms, *which include such tactics as gossip, ridicule, humor, ostracism, and peer pressure.* Despite their informality, the impact of these methods of social constraints should not be underestimated. They are especially powerful when exercised by groups characterized by close, informal, face-to-face, interdependent relationships. Hence, the family, peer groups, and members of the immediate neighborhood or other primary social groups can act as important agents of social control in discouraging nonconforming behavior.

Ferdinand Toennies ([1887] 1961) developed a theoretical continuum in an attempt to better understand the nature of social interaction and network of social relationships within different types of social structures. At one end of the continuum was the gemeinschaft type of community. The **gemeinschaft** community *is characterized by a smaller population, less complex division of labor, and is dominated by primary face-to-face social interaction.* In this type of community, informal mechanisms dominate social control strategies because they are so effective in this type of social structure.

While much of contemporary U.S. society has moved away from the gemeinschaft end of the continuum, there are many smaller communities and even sections of larger cities that resemble this type of social organization. For example, in rural America, informal social control mechanisms are still utilized more than formal types of social control. When a juvenile commits a delinquent act such as getting drunk over the weekend and driving a car through somebody's front yard, it is likely that the entire community will know about it by Monday morning. Rather than placing the juvenile under formal arrest and levying a fine, the local sheriff may simply pay a visit to the juvenile's parents. The parents might pay for the damage through some type of informal agreement with the injured party and promise the sheriff not to let such an incident happen again. Not only will the parents play a key role in attempting to control the juvenile's behavior through some type of disciplinary action, but the entire community probably will become involved in the social control process. Through whispering, finger-pointing, looks of disgust, and various degrees of ostracism, the community can express its lack of tolerance for the delinquent act and issue a warning that similar acts should not be committed in the future. San Antonio, Texas, has had some success with a program in which students convicted of vandalism are placed on probation and have a sign put in their front yards that reads "Graffiti Offender on Probation Lives Here." The police and court officials contend that the resulting shame and informal sanctions from the neighborhood are more effective than anything the police or courts could do to try to prevent further acts of vandalism (AP, San Antonio, 1999).

Ostracism, *the experience of being expelled from a social group*, may serve as one of the most powerful and effective informal social control mechanisms available to a community or social group. Human beings are social by nature, and the inability to interact with others can be extremely punitive. Through real or threatened ostracism, a juvenile's peer group can exert extreme pressure upon individual members to conform to the group's expectations for behavior.

On the negative side, if the group is encouraging delinquency, an otherwise conforming youngster may feel compelled to break the law in order to gain acceptance by friends. Social learning theories, especially differential association, point out the significance of the peer group in influencing a juvenile into delinquent or nondelinquent activities.

On the positive side, if the peer group demands conformity to the law, the juvenile whose inner containment is not strong enough to prevent delinquency may be sufficiently constrained by the group. This *outer containment*, as Reckless (1961) called it, serves as another layer of insulation against delinquency for those who have not sufficiently internalized the norms. As Farrell and Swigert (1982) indicated, rejection from the group may serve as a significant deterrent for the deviant.

Some of the informal strategies for dealing with less-serious juvenile offenders have included trying to involve them in what are considered to be positive activities with more desirable peers and role models. Problem juveniles often are encouraged to join baseball and soccer teams, Boy Scouts, YMCA, and other youth organizations in the hope that these juveniles will be less inclined to become involved in delinquency. In the past, as juvenile boys in trouble approached the age of 18, they often were encouraged to join the military service. It was thought that the discipline, rigor, and positive aspects of military life would prevent young men from further law-violating behavior.

FORMAL SOCIAL CONTROL

In large, complex, urban societies with heterogeneous populations that prevail in much of the United States, social relations are likely to be secondary as opposed to primary in nature. This represents the other end of Toennies' ([1887] 1961) theoretical continuum, the **gesellschaft** society *characterized by a larger population, a complex division of labor, secondary relationships, and formal social control.* In these social circumstances citizens, legislators, police, and court officials respond more formally to law violations by juveniles. Occasional drinking, fighting, minor vandalism, and various forms of mischief might be tolerated in a small rural community, but the same behavior in larger towns and cities is perceived as juvenile crime and a threat to the social order. Therefore, delinquency evokes outcries for public protection and dictates that formal methods of social control be brought into action.

Schools, police, and courts as agents of social control were discussed in previous chapters. In school, juveniles experience both informal and formal sanctions for their deviant behavior. All the informal social control mechanisms discussed in the previous section can be imposed by other students, teachers, and administrators. However, the school staff and administrators also can implement more formal social control procedures. Varying degrees of formal punishment, suspension, and expulsion are ways in which school officials can negatively sanction a student's undesirable behavior. In addition, school officials can petition a student to juvenile court, and initiate formal delinquency proceedings against a youth for serious offenses.

The police also can utilize both informal and formal techniques of control. When police officers issue warnings, or question juveniles and then release them, they are exercising informal social control over the youths' behavior. When neighbors see a teenager delivered home in a squad car, many of the informal social control mechanisms such as gossip and ridicule are initiated. Because they are employed as formal agents of social control, however, police are most associated with the formal sanctions at their disposal. As noted in Chapter 13, police can arrest, detain, create an official record, and petition a juvenile to court for law-violating behavior. Thus, the police emerge as one of the most significant elements of formal social control of juvenile delinquency.

The juvenile court was discussed in Chapter 14, and the formal dispositional alternatives available to it were cited. Once a juvenile appears before the juvenile court, even if released outright, a formal control mechanism has been implemented. Despite its attempt to conduct informal hearings, the court represents an official governmental institution and, hence, is by its very nature a formal agent of social control.

Juvenile Probation

One of the most widely used methods of formal social control for juveniles in the United States is probation (see Figure 15.1). Juvenile probation officers usually are involved in the juvenile court's intake procedure, and can be influential in making recommendations to the juvenile judge. Probation also is one of the dispositional alternatives to incarceration for juveniles. **Probation** is *a form of supervised release in which a juvenile adjudicated as delinquent is allowed to remain free from institutionalization, but must adhere to a strict set of guidelines imposed by the court.* Additionally, the youth is required to report to a probation officer on a regular schedule. Probation is thought to have been used first by John Augustus in Boston in 1841 (Culbertson and Ellsworth, 1985). Augustus bailed out

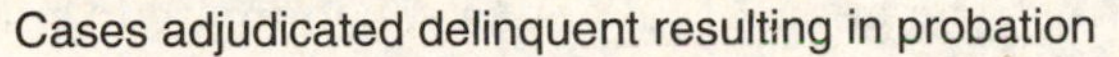

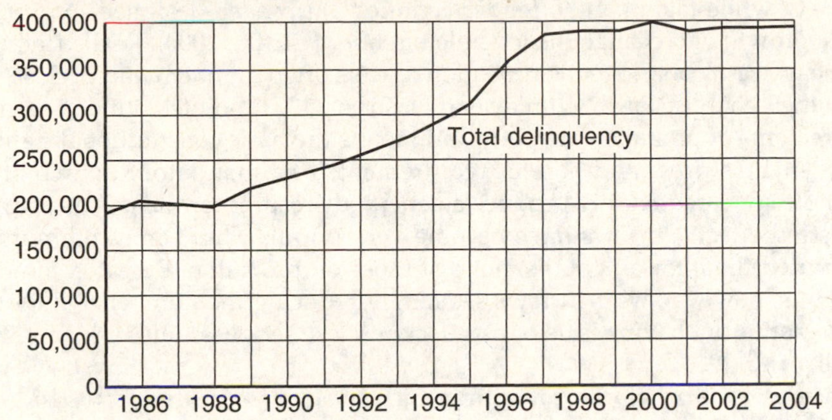

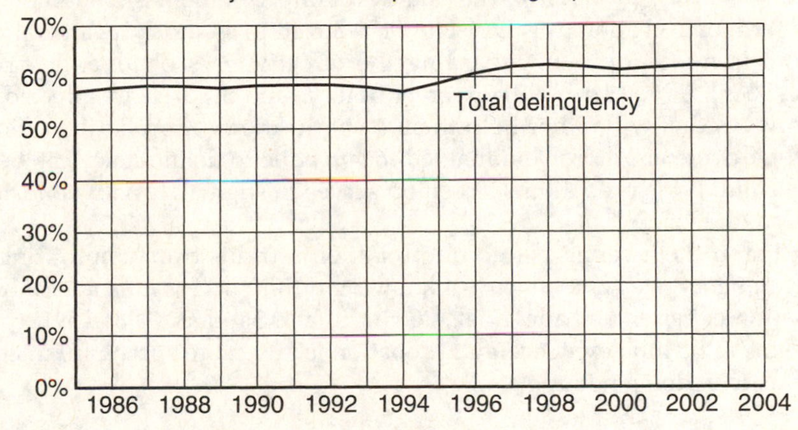

FIGURE 15.1 Juvenile Delinquency and Probation.
Why is probation the most often used disposition by Juvenile Courts?

Source: Puzzanchera, C. L., A. L. Stahl, T. A. Finnegan, N. Tierney, and H. N. Snyder, 2004. *Juvenile court statistics 2000.* Pittsburgh: National Center for Juvenile Justice, pp. 48–49.

offenders and "in addition to providing them with emotional support, he made efforts to find his probationers jobs" (Culbertson and Ellsworth, 1985:127). When a juvenile lacks the necessary degree of voluntary self-control and does not respond to informal societal pressures to conform, probation can be used to implement formal restraints. Theoretically, probation is assumed to provide outer containment (or external restraint and control) for a juvenile while helping to resocialize the youth to a new set of values which it is hoped will provide sufficient inner containment (or self-control). Thus, probation rules serve not only to prohibit law violations and establish curfews and other restrictions upon behavior, but they also often include guidelines such as requiring school attendance beyond the compulsory attendance age, church attendance, charity work, and enforced savings (Imlay and Flasheen, 1971).

Ideally, probation combines both the punitive and rehabilitative aspects of juvenile corrections by negatively sanctioning a juvenile's delinquent behavior and reinforcing dominant social norms. The goals of juvenile probation are to protect public safety while taking an "offender-centered" approach designed to promote individual growth and change the juvenile offender (Griffin, 2000). Realistically, because of heavy caseloads, juvenile probation officers often cannot maintain close contacts with their charges. Further, Imlay and Flasheen (1971) pointed out that many of the requirements of probation are petty and violate the basic constitutional rights of juveniles (such as dress and haircut requirements and mandatory church attendance), and may paradoxically produce a general disrespect for the law as opposed to the desired effect. Curfews have become very popular and some communities have instituted them for all youths, not just those on probation. Research indicates mixed results, however, with curfews seemingly reducing the number of minor offenses by youths, but having little or no effect on more serious crimes (Adams, 2003; McDowell, et al., 2000).

Some states utilize **shock probation**, which *involves a short prison stay designed to shock the youth and to impress upon him or her the seriousness of the problem and potential consequences of further delinquency.* The "shock" of imprisonment is then followed by a specified term of probation (this is also often referred to as **shock incarceration**).

There is mixed opinion regarding the effectiveness of juvenile probation (Krisberg, 2005). As Sanders (1981:258) reported: "Some children are affected by probation in ways that will either help them or harm them. A probation officer who helps a child overcome a problem that led the juvenile to delinquency can be said to 'cure' the child. If the probation disposition serves to stigmatize a juvenile, it can be said to harm the youth."

Further, if the juvenile placed on probation refrains from committing subsequent delinquency, we have no way of knowing if this success is *because of* or *despite* the probation experience (Lane, et al., 2005). In fact, Sanders (1981:259) contended "there seems to be little evidence that probation is any more successful in changing delinquents than doing nothing at all."

Restitution and "Restorative Justice"

Most of the public criticism leveled at juvenile probation has centered on the perception that it is too lenient and allows juvenile offenders to escape punishment and accountability for their criminal actions. Gennaro Vito (1985), however, contended that probation, especially if linked with some form of victim restitution, *is* punitive and can be an effective way of diverting juveniles from incarceration while holding them accountable for their law-violating behavior. **Restitution** *requires the offender to compensate the victim (either the actual victim or the state) either in monetary payments or in labor for losses related to the offense.* It is used most often in property offenses such as burglary, larceny–theft, and vandalism in which an actual dollar figure can be placed upon the victim's losses. Calvin Remington (1982) positively evaluated the Ventura Restitution Project, which attempts to make juvenile offenders understand the ramifications of their delinquent behavior and make them take responsibility for their actions, as being a viable social control mechanism. Robert Evans and Gary Koederitz (1983) summarized that restitution coupled with probation is a promising, logical, and effective means of achieving the dual goals of deterrence and punishment for law-violating juveniles. A major study sponsored by the National Center for Juvenile Justice showed that recidivism rates for robbery, assault, burglary, and auto theft were lower for juveniles who were ordered to pay restitution to their victims (Butts and Snyder, 1992).

Victim restitution, when coupled with involvement of community correctional programs, represents a new **restorative justice model** of juvenile justice *which focuses on accountability, restitution, and community involvement in the corrections process.* This model combines punitive and treatment approaches and attempts to "restore" justice to those most affected—the offender, the victim(s), and the community (Bazemore and Day, 1996; McEvoy and Mika, 2007; McGarrell, 2001; Vito, et al., 1998).

Juvenile Placement

A prominent form of formal social control of juvenile delinquents is **placement**, *which involves putting a juvenile in a residential facility or incarcerating them in an institution.* As a result of increased violence and probation violations, large numbers of youths are placed in residential and institutional facilities each year. Due to antiquated methods of data collection, it is very difficult to know precisely how many youths are being held in juvenile institutions at any given time, but as the United States entered the 21st century, there were over 3,000 juvenile facilities, most of which were facing serious problems of overcrowding (Batts and Adams, 2001; OJJDP, 2002). There are several types of institutions whose primary purpose is the incarceration of juvenile offenders. In order to simplify categorization of these institutions, James Carey and Patrick McAnany (1984:291) divided them into three basic types: detention facilities, training schools, and group homes.

DETENTION FACILITIES **Detention facilities** *serve as places to detain, or hold, juveniles who are awaiting a hearing in juvenile court.* Communities provide various types of detention facilities for youths. In cities with large numbers of juvenile offenders, there usually are distinct facilities which separate them from adult offenders. "Juvenile halls," as these centers often are called, usually are located near the juvenile court, and might even be operated in conjunction with the court, thereby housing juvenile probation and parole officers and other juvenile court personnel. In smaller communities, where delinquency is less prevalent, juveniles are more likely to be detained in adult jails.

Juvenile detention facilities vary among states and among cities within states. Although in 1980, and again in 2002, Congress passed an amendment to the Juvenile Justice and Delinquency Prevention Act of 1974 calling for the removal of all juveniles from adult jails, in some cases, the juvenile detention center is simply a jail cell. It seems logical that juvenile detention would be reserved for the more serious offenders, and in many instances that may be the case. However, we should be reminded that the police often make the decision as to whether to detain a youth, and a variety of factors beyond the seriousness of offense are taken into consideration.

TRAINING SCHOOLS Juvenile **training schools** are *long-term facilities for housing juveniles and serve a function analogous to adult prisons.* Virtually every state has at least one of these facilities (sometimes one for boys and one for girls). They may operate under various names such as "state industrial schools" or "reformatories" but share the common characteristic of being a place where juvenile courts can send youthful offenders for an extended period of time. In some states, these facilities are even called "juvenile prisons," which reflects a trend toward including punishment as part of juvenile correction philosophy (Housewright, 2000). As in adult prisons, security is a prominent concern, and custody is of primary importance. However, in keeping with the general philosophy of the juvenile court, there is usually an attempt to integrate treatment and rehabilitation into the custody procedures.

These long-term incarceration facilities conform to Erving Goffman's (1961:xiii) concept of a **total institution**—"*a place of residence and work where a large number of like-situated individuals, cut off from the wider society for an appreciable period of time, together lead an enclosed, formally administered round of life.*" In other words, juveniles eat, sleep, work, go to school, and play within the confines of the institution. Goffman (1961) discussed the social worlds that are constructed in total institutions in which all spheres of one's life take place within the confines of one social setting, and pointed out that there is often a subterranean social world constructed by the inmates that may run counter to the official social structure of the institution.

The corrections literature is replete with studies analyzing the advantages and problems, successes and failures associated with this type of incarceration. Sanders (1981) pointed out that regardless of the treatment or rehabilitation efforts introduced into long-term incarceration facilities for juveniles, the staffs of these types of institutions tend to be increasingly concerned with basic custodial control. As in adult prisons, intimidation, stabbings, fights, and rapes are part of institutional life in many of these facilities (*Christian Science Monitor*, 1988; Schwartz, 1989; Hubner, 2005).

Michael Sherraden and Susan Downs (1984) conducted an empirical historical study of the institutionalization of juvenile delinquents from 1820 to 1970 and pointed out that institutionalization rates were highest during the second half of the 19th century and again during the 1960s. The resurgence in the institutionalization of juveniles refocused public attention on many of the problems associated with incarcerating juveniles.

Zvi Eisikovits and Michael Baizerman (1982) interviewed 43 violent youthful offenders in one Midwestern state who had been incarcerated in either maximum-security youth facilities or adult prisons. In assessing how these youngsters "did time," they found that youths in both types of institutions lost sight of getting out and instead learned to adapt to the institutional life imposed upon them. The youths learned quickly that violence was the norm in the institution and that treatment language and jargon could be used to manipulate correctional officials into shortening their sentences. In short, the researchers concluded that the young offenders learned to be "con artists" who did not benefit from the institutionalization but merely adapted to it. Many officials who deal with delinquency contend that the state training schools are a costly failure (costing anywhere from $20,000 to $45,000 per youth per year) where young law violators are warehoused and hardened into a "lifetime of lawlessness and . . . become permanent and costly liabilities of society" (Ryan, 1980:21).

An overview of institutional effectiveness over the decades from 1970 to 2000 shows mixed results. While some programs were moderately effective in reducing recidivism rates, others were miserable failures, and many seemed to show little difference than if the juvenile had been placed on probation (Hubner, 2005; Whitehead and Lab, 2006).

GROUP HOMES The third category of juvenile institutions revolves around the group home concept. These facilities can include halfway houses, drug and alcohol rehabilitation homes, and various types of youth shelters. Juveniles can be placed there either by the courts or by parents who feel that a change in home environment will benefit the juvenile. **Group homes** *usually resemble a dormitory type of living facility with juveniles being supervised during parts of the day and at night, while being allowed limited participation in the larger community either to attend school or work at part-time jobs.* Box 15.2 examines the controversy over institutionalization versus community treatment in group homes.

One of the forerunners of this type of juvenile institution was the so-called Provo Experiment begun in 1956 in Provo, Utah (Empey and Rabow, 1961). This program involved a group home setting and allowed a limited number of juveniles to live together under staff supervision while working and attending school in the larger community. The program was considered highly successful and has been copied in other parts of the country. Other community-based treatment programs for juveniles have been developed as an alternative to incarceration. These treatment programs are discussed in Chapter 16, which deals with various treatment strategies and prevention efforts for juvenile delinquency.

PRIVATE FACILITIES There also are a number of privately operated juvenile institutions across the United States. Initially, as many state facilities became overcrowded, and state revenues declined, it was believed that private institutions offered superior alternatives to those of the states. David Schicor and Clemens Bartollas (1990) found, however, that many private juvenile facilities suffered from some of the same problems as state-run institutions. Complicating the problems further, they noted, was that the desire to make profits in the private sector sometimes leads to a higher resident-to-staff ratio and inadequate professional services. Schicor and Bartollas (1990) summarized that there should be a nationwide effort to evaluate private facilities; a thorough examination of their fiscal policies, and a mechanism for supervision and control of private facilities to see that they at least meet minimum state standards.

Juvenile Aftercare

Another method of formal social control is aftercare. Aftercare for juveniles is the equivalent of parole for adults. In fact, in some states, the term "juvenile parole" is still used. **Aftercare** refers to *release of a juvenile who has been incarcerated in some type of institutional setting under the supervision of an officer of the court for a prescribed period of time.* In most states the officer of the court involved is a juvenile probation/parole officer who also may have been actively involved in the initial intake process for the youth (see Chapter 14). Upon release, the juvenile meets with an aftercare supervisor and agrees to a specific set of restrictions. These conditions vary according to various classification schemes used to determine the "risk level" of the youth, but, regardless of classification, are similar to those of probation (Maupin, 1993). They usually include requirements such as school attendance, curfew, notification of whereabouts, and often a list of specific individuals with whom the juvenile is forbidden to associate. Violation of any of the terms may result in the juvenile being returned to a custodial facility. Pragmatically, juvenile aftercare and probation are virtually identical, with the distinction being that probation is used *instead of* incarceration, while parole or aftercare is used *after* incarceration. Both are forms of conditional release under the supervision of an officer of the court.

BOX 15.2

CONTROVERSIAL ISSUE: Institutionalization versus Community Treatment

Fear of crime and harsher attitudes toward youthful law violators have resulted in thousands of juveniles being convicted in adult criminal courts and incarcerated in state prisons. Serious and chronic offenders who are not remanded to adult criminal courts are increasingly being placed in juvenile institutions which approximate prison conditions. These facilities are plagued by fights, stabbings, intimidation, rape, gangs, and other forms of violence.

In 1972, in a bold and controversial move, Massachusetts closed all of its state training schools for juveniles and sought alternatives to incarceration for its delinquents. Numerous other states followed Massachusetts' lead, either closing all of their juvenile institutions or significantly reducing their populations by choosing community treatment alternatives for delinquent youths. A popular alternative is placement in a group home located in the community. California, for example, has one of the largest networks of group homes in the nation. Whether group homes are more effective in the treatment and prevention of delinquency than the more traditional and punitive method of incarceration is hotly debated.

While the problems of youths in training schools and prisons have been widely discussed, the alternative of community treatment is not without its problems. For one thing, neighborhood residents often oppose group homes on the basis that they create safety risks and decrease property values. Further, when group homes are established, they often suffer from high turnover in staff and poor monitoring of the homes and the juveniles. Some counties find that they become the dumping grounds for out-of-county delinquents from larger urban areas that do not have adequate facilities to house their own clients.

Juvenile judges, police officers, youth workers, social workers, and politicians often find themselves in a dilemma over how to handle the rising numbers of juvenile offenders. Adult prisons are overcrowded, and even many ardent "get tough" advocates are reluctant to place youths in them. On the other hand, with little community support and few resources for community treatment, the alternatives sometimes are reduced to "lock 'em up" or "turn 'em loose"—neither of which provides a satisfactory solution to the problem. Exacerbating the problem is the lack of systematic evaluation of both institutionalization and community treatment programs to determine their effectiveness (*Law Enforcement News,* 1997).

Based on your reading of this and previous chapters, what do you think? What are the arguments for and against institutionalization and community treatment? Which is most likely to reintegrate a delinquent youth back into society? Can you cite some facts to back up your opinion?

Sources

"Do you get what you pay for? With CJ efforts, not necessarily." *Law Enforcement News* 23 (May 15) 1997:1, 18.

"Kids' prisons that don't reform," *Christian Science Monitor,* September 29, 1988:B2–B8.

Lawrence, R. 2008. Reexamining community corrections models. In Lawrence R. and Hemmens, C. (Eds.). *Juvenile justice: A text/reader*, pp. 424–435. Los Angeles: Sage.

Schillinger, Kurt and Sullivan, C. "Treating kids in the community works in theory, but not always in practice." *Christian Science Monitor,* September 29, 1988:B2–B8.

In an effort to make juvenile aftercare more effective, the Office of Juvenile Justice and Delinquency Prevention launched an Intensive Aftercare Program (IAP) based on four factors: (1) prerelease and preparatory planning during incarceration, (2) structured transition that requires participation of aftercare staff, (3) long-term reintegrative activities, and (4) working with offenders and targeted support systems (e.g., family, schools, and community agencies) (Altschuler and Armstrong, 1996). Today, there is more interest than ever in effectively reintegrating juvenile offenders back into the community under supervised release and intensive aftercare (Altschuler, et al., 1999), but studies reveal that aftercare has not been very effective (Wiebush et al., 2005).

One of the problems with this form of social control is that the large numbers of juveniles on probation and parole at any one time create extremely high caseloads for the court officers. Consequently, it is often difficult for probation and aftercare officers to meet regularly with all their charges, and some juveniles may be able to violate some of the conditions for their release without it coming to the attention of their supervisors. As a mechanism of formal social control, when supervised release becomes unsupervised, its effectiveness is significantly reduced.

Waiver: Remanding Juveniles to Adult Courts

Increased rates of violence committed by young offenders, frustration with the juvenile justice system, and increasing public sentiment that we must "get tough" on crime and criminals have led to a popular movement to certify juveniles who commit serious violent crimes as adults and to remand them to adult criminal courts for trial (see Figure 15.2). Four criteria are generally considered in waiving a case: age, seriousness of the offense, preponderance of evidence, and amenability of treatment. Research conducted by the National Center for Juvenile Justice found that two

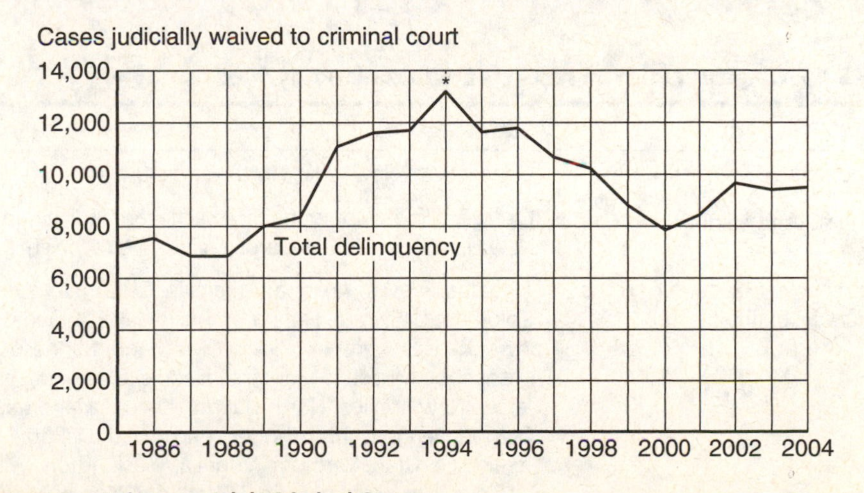

FIGURE 15.2 Waivers to Adult Criminal Courts

*The number of cases judicially waived to criminal court peaked in 1994 at 12,100 cases.

Source: A. L. Stahl, Puzzanchera C., Livsey, S., Sladley, A., T.A. Finnegan, N. Tierney, and H.N. Snyder, 2007. *Juvenile court statistics 2004.* Pittsburgh: National Center for Juvenile Justice, p. 38.

criteria tend to figure prominently, however, in remanding juveniles to adult courts: the extent of a juvenile's court history and the seriousness of the offense (Snyder, et al., 2000; Stahl, et al., 2007).

In 1997, the U.S. House of Representatives gave its stamp of approval to the process of certifying serious violent juvenile offenders over the age of 15 as adults by offering $1.5 billion in incentive grants to state juvenile justice systems that incorporated such a provision in their juvenile codes (Reibstein, 1997). Under the house bill, adult trials for juveniles as young as 14 would be routine for violent federal crimes. Many states already have statutes that call for automatically certifying violent offenders over a certain age (16 and above) as adults, and as we mentioned in Chapter 14, in those states a *reverse certification* hearing must be held to retain jurisdiction over the case in juvenile court (see Table 15.1). In those states where automatic adult certification does not occur, there is some debate over whether juvenile judges should make the decision to certify juveniles as adults and remand them to adult criminal court, or whether that discretion should reside with the district attorney's office, since he or she is an elected official and is charged with prosecuting violent crimes.

The movement to remand juveniles to adult courts is motivated by a "get tough" approach in the hopes that they will receive longer and harsher sentences, but research reveals that while the sentences may be longer than those meted out by juvenile courts, actual time spent in custodial facilities by youths sentenced in adult courts usually does not exceed what they would have received from a juvenile court (Fritsch, et al., 1996). Also, there is mounting evidence that whether in juvenile or adult courts, judges are cognizant of the fact that they are dealing with a juvenile and tend to mete out what they consider age-appropriate sentences (Kupchik, 2007).

In New York State, Judge Michael Corriero handles about 160 cases per year involving 13-, 14-, and 15-year-olds charged with armed robberies, aggravated assaults, rapes, and murders. Although he can issue up to life sentences for crimes such as murder, Corriero tries to be "firm, but fair," and he sends almost 60 percent of the

TABLE 15.1 Age at Which all suspects are Automatically Tried as Adults

Age	States
16 and above (3 states)	Connecticut, New York, North Carolina
17 and above (9 states)	Georgia, Illinois, Louisiana, Massachusetts, Michigan, New Hampshire, South Carolina, Texas, Wisconsin
18 and above (38 states plus the District of Columbia)	Alabama, Alaska, Arizona, Arkansas, California, Colorado, Delaware, Florida, Hawaii, Idaho, Indiana, Iowa, Kansas, Kentucky, Maine, Maryland, Minnesota, Mississippi, Missouri, Montana, Nebraska, Nevada, New Jersey, New Mexico, North Dakota, Ohio, Oklahoma, Oregon, Pennsylvania, Rhode Island, South Dakota, Tennessee, Utah, Vermont, Virginia, Washington, West Virginia, Wyoming, plus the District of Columbia

Should there be an age cutoff at which juveniles should automatically be tried as adults? If so, what should that age be? What are the benefits of "automatic certification"? What are the drawbacks?

Source: Office of Juvenile Justice and Delinquency Prevention. Pittsburgh, PA, 2006.

young offenders who appear before him for counseling. If they stay out of trouble and are not rearrested within a year, he sentences them to five years' probation (Reibstein, 1997).

Although Corriero's approach may not satisfy the "get tough" advocates, it may reflect a sensible approach to the growing problem of violent juvenile crime. While research on the effects of trying juveniles as adults is sparse, a systematic study was conducted on over 2,700 juveniles who were remanded to adult criminal courts in Florida compared with a matched sample of delinquents who were retained in the juvenile courts. This study found that by every measure and definition of recidivism employed, reoffending rates were greater among those who were transferred to adult courts than those who were retained in the juvenile system (Bishop, et al., 1996). Moreover, research conducted by the MacArthur Foundation indicates that juveniles do not understand the complexities of the adult criminal court system (AP, Washington, 2003b).

If more juveniles are being certified as adults and remanded to stand trial in adult criminal courts, it follows that more young offenders are also being sentenced to adult jails and prisons. This phenomenon is placing even greater burdens on already crowded local jails and state prison systems whose success in handling adult corrections is questionable.

Juveniles in Adult Jails and Prisons

Between 1990 and 2007 the nation's jail population went over 770,000 (see Table 15.2). During that same period, the number of juveniles held in adult jails increased from 2,301 to 6,837. Despite the fact that Congress passed a law in 1980 calling for the removal of all juveniles from adult jails, various state statutes and judicial practices allow juveniles to be incarcerated in adult jails.

In 2002, Congress passed the Juvenile Justice Delinquency Prevention Act, which became effective on October 1, 2003. The goals of the act were to assist state and local governments in preventing and controlling juvenile delinquency and to improve the juvenile justice system. The act called for:

- Deinstitutionalization of status offenders;
- Sight and sound separation of juvenile and adult offenders;
- Removal of juveniles from adults jails and lockups; and
- Elimination of the disproportionate representation of minorities in the juvenile justice system.

Despite the requirements of the JJDP Act of 2002, as Table 15.2 illustrates, at the end of 2007, almost 7,000 juveniles were still being held in adult jails.

In addition to the number of juveniles being held in local adult jails, states are now sending more violent offenders under the age of 18 to minimum-, medium-, and maximum-security adult prisons. Problems associated with placing young offenders in adult jails and prisons have been well documented (e.g., Carmichael, 2006; Flaherty, 1990; McGee, 1971; Soler, 1998), and all too frequently incidents of assaults, forcible rapes, and murders occur when juveniles are housed in adult facilities with older inmates.

As states increasingly certify juveniles as adults, district attorneys, judges, and correctional officials must grapple with the reality that sentencing youths to adult

John Lee Malvo (aka Lee Boyd Malvo), 17, confessed to being the "trigger man" in at least two of the 20 shootings, including 13 deaths, perpetrated by the so-called Washington Snipers in 2002. Should he be tried as an adult? If so, why? If not, why not?

© Mark Wilson/Getty Images/Liaison

prisons can be tantamount to ordering their execution. Consequently, many states are rethinking the harshness of their sentencing laws, attempting to keep juveniles out of adult court and adult correctional facilities (AP, *Dallas Morning News*, 2007).

CAPITAL PUNISHMENT FOR JUVENILES AND *ROPER* V. *SIMMONS*

The ultimate form of social control is capital punishment. The execution of criminal offenders is one of the most controversial elements of the American criminal justice system, and that controversy is compounded when it involves the execution of juveniles or of adults who committed their capital offenses while still under the age of majority.

The United States has executed a total of 286 juveniles. The first sufficiently documented juvenile execution occurred in Roxbury, Massachusetts, in 1642 when 16-year-old Thomas Graunger was executed for committing bestiality (Streib, 1987:55).

In 1972, the U.S. Supreme Court ruled in the case of *Furman* v. *Georgia* that capital punishment was discriminatory and constituted "cruel and unusual punishment," which is prohibited by the Eighth Amendment to the Constitution. The Court ordered its discontinuance, and inmates on death row awaiting execution had their sentences commuted to life imprisonment. However, in 1976, the Supreme Court ruled that

TABLE 15.2 Demographic Trends in Jail Populations

Jail Populations by Age and Gender, 1990–2007	Year	Number of Jail Inmates (One-Day Count)		
		Adult Males	Adult Females	Juveniles
	1990	365,821	37,198	2,301
	1991	384,628	39,501	2,350
	1992	401,106	40,674	2,804
	1993	411,500	44,100	4,300
	1994	431,300	48,500	6,700
	1995	448,000	51,300	7,800
	1996	454,700	55,700	8,100
	1997	498,678	59,296	9,105
	1998	520,581	63,791	8,090
	1999	528,998	67,487	9,458
	2000	543,120	70,414	7,615
	2001	551,007	72,621	7,613
	2002	581,411	76,817	7,248
	2003	602,781	81,650	6,869
	2004	619,908	86,999	7,083
	2005	646,807	93,963	6,759
	2006	661,329	98,577	6,104
	2007	673,697	100,047	6,837

Can you discern some interesting patterns in these figures? If federal law prohibits it how can you explain almost 7,000 juveniles being held in adult jails?

Source: Bureau of Justice Statistics Correctional Surveys (The Annual Survey of Jails and Census of Jail Inmates) as presented in Correctional Populations in the United States, 1997, and Prison and Jail Inmates at Midyear series, 1998–2006, and Jail Inmates at Midyear 2007. Bureau of Justice Statistics http://www.ojp.usdoj.gov/bjs/.

three states (Florida, Texas, and Georgia) had rewritten their capital punishment statutes in such a way as to conform to the Constitution. Several states wrote new capital punishment statutes in compliance with the Supreme Court's guidelines, and in some states, these new statutes included the right to execute juveniles who committed capital offenses. In fact, among the 36 states that reenacted the death penalty, nine set no minimum age for execution (Arizona, Delaware, Florida, Maryland, Oklahoma, South Carolina, South Dakota, Washington, and Wyoming) (Seligson, 1986:5). Twenty-seven states enacted capital punishment statutes that specified a minimum age at the time the crime was committed, and several of those set the minimum age below the age of majority. Since that time additional states added execution to their arsenal of punishments and eight states specified no minimum age.

The constitutionality of executing juveniles was legally challenged numerous times, but the Supreme Court never clearly resolved the issue until 2005. The Supreme Court agreed to decide the issue of constitutionality in the 1982 case of *Eddings* v. *Oklahoma.* However, in a 5 to 4 vote, the court avoided deciding the constitutionality issue and simply sent the case back for resentencing, urging the lower court to consider age as a mitigating factor (Streib, 1987). In 1989, in the case of *Stanford* v. *Kentucky*, the

U.S. Supreme Court ruled that executing juveniles was not unconstitutional. Again in 2003, an Oklahoma case involving a 17-year-old on death row challenged the constitutionality of executing juveniles but resulted in a 5 to 4 decision by the U.S. Supreme Court, this time overturning a stay of execution from an appellate court.

Seventeen-year-old Christopher Simmons was sentenced to death in Missouri in 1993 for breaking into a house, tying up a woman, and driving her to a state park where he and another youth threw her off a bridge to her death. A series of appeals in state courts were rejected, but Simmons's execution was stayed by the Missouri Supreme Court until the U.S. Supreme Court ruled on the constitutionality of executing the mentally ill in the *Atkins* v. *Virginia* case in 2002. After that case, in which the Court ruled that execution of the mentally ill violated the Eighth Amendment's prohibition against cruel and unusual punishment, the Missouri Supreme Court agreed to hear the Simmons case. This time, the Missouri court ruled that executing juveniles was contrary to public opinion and that since the U.S. Supreme Court had ruled that executing the mentally ill constituted cruel and unusual punishment, the majority of Americans would probably see executing juveniles in the same light. In 2005, the Simmons case reached the U.S. Supreme Court in the form of *Roper* v. *Simmons* (Roper was the name of a state correctional official) when Missouri's department of corrections appealed the previous ruling. In a landmark 5–4 opinion, the U.S. Supreme Court ruled that "the standards of decency have evolved so that executing minors is considered cruel and unusual punishment" prohibited by the Eighth Amendment. All those awaiting execution on death rows in the United States who had committed their offenses while under the age of 18 had their sentences commuted to life in prison. Among those was one John Lee Malvo, the "Washington sniper" who had shot 22 innocent motorists, 13 of whom died.

Despite "get tough" attitudes toward crime and youthful offenders, many states and local communities have devised some innovative correctional programs for wayward juveniles. The aims of many of these programs include deinstitutionalization, community corrections, and diversion from the juvenile justice system.

DEINSTITUTIONALIZATION, COMMUNITY CORRECTIONS, AND DIVERSION

The juvenile court was founded upon the philosophy of protection and rehabilitation, and its foremost goal has been preventing juvenile offenders from becoming adult criminals. Despite widespread criticism, research indicates that there still is much public support for juvenile rehabilitation efforts (Moon, et al., 2000). Consequently, over the years, juvenile corrections has experienced a noticeable trend toward deinstitutionalization, community corrections, and the diversion of youths from the formal juvenile justice system.

Deinstitutionalization simply means *avoiding the placement of juveniles in correctional institutions.* The Juvenile justice and Delinquency Prevention Act of 1974 called for the development of a series of deinstitutionalization programs for status offenders. Deinstitutionalization is most likely to be pursued for nonserious juvenile offenders.

Jerome Stumphauzer (1986:5) summarized the need for deinstitutionalization of juveniles by evaluating the imprisonment of youths in the following manner: "A worse social learning program could not be designed: remove the youth from the very society to which he must learn to adapt, expose him to hundreds of criminal peer models and to criminal behaviors he hasn't learned (yet), and use punishment as the only learning principle to change behavior!"

As an alternative to institutionalization and traditional institutional methods, Stumphauzer (1986:9–11) suggested using social teaming techniques as follows:

1. ***Institutional programming.*** If institutionalized, use token economies, positive rewards for conforming behavior, humane approaches to negatively sanction nonconforming behavior, and positive role modeling along with positive reinforcement.
2. ***Behavioral family contracting.*** Teaching and positively reinforcing nondelinquent behavior in the family setting.
3. ***Social skills training.*** Teaching the skills of problem solving and relating to authority figures.
4. ***Probation contracting.*** Written agreements between juvenile probation officers and juveniles on probation regarding acceptable and unacceptable behaviors and the attendant rewards and punishments for each.
5. ***School programming.*** Using social learning techniques in the school to emphasize rewards for nondelinquent behavior, rather than focusing all attention on punishing rule-violating behavior.
6. ***Clinical behavior therapy.*** Training youths in techniques of self-control, anger control, and dealing with stress.
7. ***Employment skills training.*** Providing youths with necessary job skills, and the skills necessary for finding, applying for, and interviewing for employment.
8. ***Group treatment homes.*** Group homes using "teaching parents" as models, doing chores with emphasis upon positive reinforcement.
9. ***Community change and prevention.*** Instead of waiting for delinquency to occur and then making arrests, using positive reinforcement and social learning techniques in parks, recreation centers, housing projects, and so on, to acknowledge, reward, and encourage conforming behavior.

William Sheridan (1967) estimated that approximately 30 percent of all inmates in juvenile correctional institutions were there for committing **status offenses**—*acts that would not have been illegal if they had been committed by adults* (such as truancy and running away). He contended that placing these offenders in institutions pinned the "delinquent label" upon them and exposed them to the influence of more sophisticated delinquent peers, increasing the likelihood that they would continue their delinquency upon release. Richard Rettig (1980) argued that juvenile detention facilities were overpopulated with youths who did not belong in institutions. He contended that institutionalization has a place in juvenile corrections, and could provide a positive experience, if it is reserved for those youths who really need to be confined (those who pose a serious threat to the community). This philosophy is underscored by several researchers who contend that secure confinement of juveniles in institutions should be an option of last resort reserved for only the most serious violent offenders (Austin, et al., 2005). Today, based on the Juvenile Justice and Delinquency Prevention Act of 2004, no status offenders are supposed to be placed in institutions.

House Arrest

House arrest, *a program in which youths are confined to their homes and closely supervised by their parents with routine unannounced visits or phone calls from a probation officer*, has become a popular alternative to institutionalization. Specific house arrest programs vary, but most require the youths to attend school, observe a strict curfew, notify their parents (and sometimes the probation officer) of their whereabouts at all times, abstain from drugs and alcohol, and avoid places or companions who might encourage them to get into trouble (Ball, et al., 1990). Some of these programs require that the youths wear electronic bracelets, necklaces, or anklets that can be monitored 24 hours a day, and sound an alarm if the detainee strays too far from a certain location or fails to report in at a certain time. The Wayne County Juvenile Court in Detroit developed and evaluated three in-home intensive supervision programs as alternatives to juvenile institutional commitment. When evaluated, the in-home programs were as effective as commitment, but cost only about one-third as much. Both self-reported and official recidivism rates indicated virtually no difference two years later for those committed and those going through the in-home programs (Barton and Butts, 1990). Other research also suggests that, although not a panacea, intensive supervision of juveniles (even those who committed felonies) is an effective alternative to incarceration (Greenwood and Rand, 1993; Wiebush, 1993).

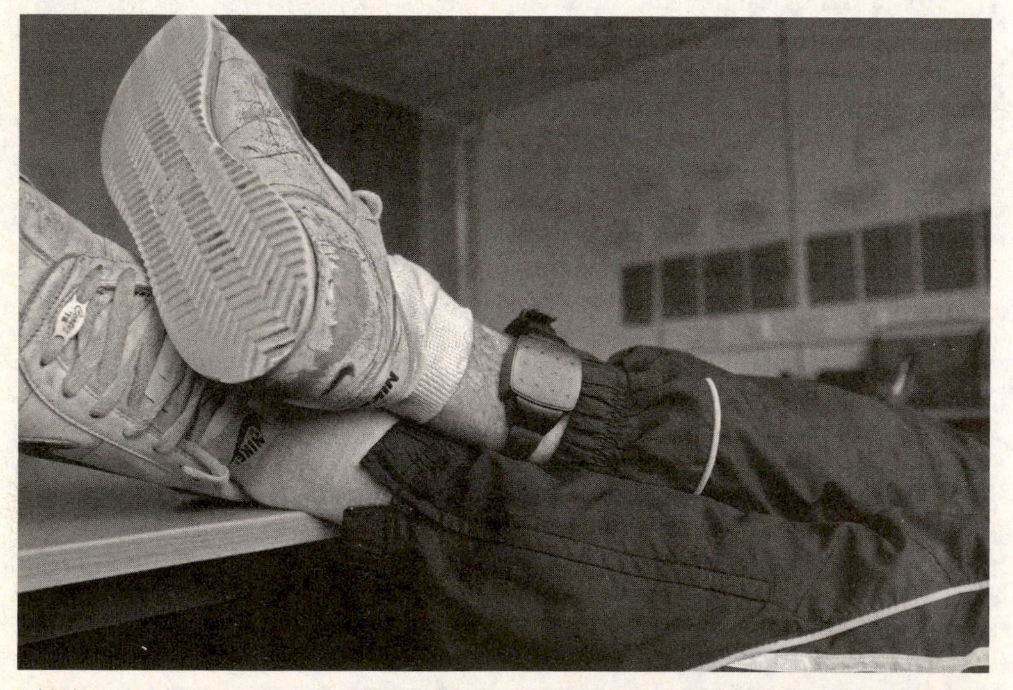

Ankle bracelets help monitor juvenile offenders as an alternative to institutionalization. Do you believe such devices are effective means for helping to curb delinquency? What other options do you think might be just as, or even more effective?

Diversion refers to *an attempt to divert, or channel out, youthful offenders from the juvenile justice system.* Like deinstitutionalization, diversion is intended for status and nonserious property offenders. Richard Lundman (1993) argues that diversion should be the standard response for juveniles who have committed status offenses and nonviolent crimes. There is some disagreement over the term "diversion." Dean Rojek (1982:316) pointed out that to some it means "simply the process of turning offenders away from the traditional juvenile justice system," while for others, it "connotes not only a turning away but also a referral to a community alternative." As a result, diversion and deinstitutionalization often are interrelated in community efforts to deal with less-serious juvenile offenders.

Youth Service Bureaus

The President's Commission on Law Enforcement and Administration of Justice (1967) suggested the creation of youth service bureaus to work with juvenile offenders in local communities. These bureaus were designed to work with nonserious juvenile offenders, but, depending upon the particular community, provide a wide range of service to youthful law violators. The establishment of youth service bureaus launched the move toward diverting youths, especially status offenders and other nonserious delinquents, from the juvenile court (Sherwood, 1972).

With the money and support provided by federal and state governments during the 1960s and 1970s for social programs aimed toward reducing poverty, crime, delinquency, and other social problems, youth service bureaus gained widespread acceptance. Bureaus were established in virtually every community of any size, and programs were developed to aid juveniles in matters related to family, school, and the law. Although the 1980s brought severe cuts to numerous social agencies and programs, youth service bureaus continue to exist in many communities, working closely with law enforcement, juvenile courts, schools, and other social agencies.

One of the criticisms leveled at the youth service bureaus, and at similar diversionary programs is that, while well-intended, they may involve youths in the juvenile justice system who have committed very minor noncriminal offenses, which might be less problematic if ignored. Frederick Howlett (1973) criticized the youth service bureau as being another manifestation of the "child-saving movement." He suggested that rather than involving such minor offenders in the youth service bureau, communities should redefine their concept of deviance, especially in regard to the types of behaviors they will and will not tolerate on the part of juveniles. We explore this issue in more detail in Chapter 17, Rethinking the Delinquency Problem.

Scared Straight!

Diversion can take many directions. One of the best-known diversionary programs is the *Scared Straight!* program begun by inmates serving life sentences at Rahway State Prison in New Jersey. Roughly based on Deterrence Theory, utilizing the concepts behind shock probation and shock incarceration, this program briefly exposes juveniles to some of the harsh realities of life in a maximum-security prison. Small groups of juvenile offenders are taken to Rahway to spend a day inside the institution. The youths are shown the brutal side of prison life, highlighted by a session during which inmates serving life sentences for crimes such as murder, rape, multiple assaults, and other violent offenses, shout at and harass the juveniles through racial epithets, threats, and innuendos about homosexual rape. While there is no actual physical contact between inmates and the youths, the threat of physical violence is ever-present. The program gained national attention when actor Peter Falk hosted an award-winning television documentary on the subject. The program boasted impressive statistics regarding its success rate (90 to 95 percent) in deterring participants from involvement in later delinquency.

John Heeren and David Schicor (1984) analyzed the program and suggested that the documentary was perhaps more successful than the actual program. John Finckenauer (1982) concurred and seriously questioned the alleged success rate of the Scared Straight! program. He conducted a study on youths who had completed the program at Rahway and compared them to a control group of teenagers who had committed similar offenses but who did not participate in the program. His findings indicated that the control group actually fared better in the first six months following their initial offenses (in terms of not committing subsequent offenses) than did the group who were exposed to Scared Straight! Finckenauer (1982:4) concluded that the Scared Straight! program, much like other delinquency prevention programs, is illustrative of what he calls the "panacea phenomenon"—the "continuing search for a cure-all." This attempt to remedy a very complex social problem by means of a simplistic solution is not new, and as Finckenauer (1982:4) summarized, "The highway of delinquency prevention history is paved with punctured panaceas." Lundman (1993) agreed, and he called for the permanent abandonment of all efforts to "scare" juveniles out of delinquency, contending that these programs lead to *more* not *less* delinquency.

Nevertheless, the documentary appealed to public perception that crime was increasing at an alarming rate, but here was an innovative program that was playing a small part in alleviating it. Following the documentary, several states began steps to implement similar programs. While the Rahway program may not have been the cure-all hoped for by many, and its success rate was not the 90 to 95 percent claimed, to many people it seemed like a valid attempt to turn delinquent teenagers' lives around; and after all, perhaps doing something—anything—was better than doing nothing.

In 1992, Norwegian prison officials decided to copy the Scared Straight! program at Ullersmo with the expressed goal "to scare youngsters off a path of crime" (Finckenauer and Gavin, 1999:147). Two years later, an Oslo television station aired a controversial documentary very similar to the television program that had been so popular in the United States. The Norwegian public responded far differently, however, than did the American viewers. The Norwegian public was outraged by the barbarism of the program, and newspapers criticized it with comparisons to medieval torture, the Nazi regime, and even the Gestapo. Meanwhile, Norwegian criminologists pointed out that the program was ethically questionable, violated traditional Norwegian values, and had little or no deterrent effects on the youths submitted to it. An evaluation of the Ullersmo project discovered that although the youths who participated in it indicated that they were scared by the inmates while inside the prison, almost all of them said that it had no impact on their behavior once they left. Perhaps the most discouraging of the evaluators' findings were that several of the girls who participated in the program became infatuated with one or more of the prisoners and some of the boys came away viewing the inmates as heroes or positive role models (Finckenauer and Gavin, 1999). Norwegian officials terminated the project shortly thereafter.

Petrosino and his associates (2002) concluded from their research that programs like Scared Straight! are likely to do more harm than good, and it would be better to do nothing than expose youths to such a progam.

Despite empirical evidence that the Scared Straight! program has little or no deterrence effect on American youths who participate in it, it continues to appeal to the American public and the media who seem frustrated that nothing else seems to work, and, as critics note, because it appeals so strongly to the "myth of deterrence by aversion" (Finckenauer and Gavin, 1999:217).

In 2006, yet another version of Scared Straight! was implemented by the Manatee, Florida, Sheriff's Department for youths whose parents deemed them "out of control" (Blue, 2006).

S.H.A.P.E.U.P.

Inmates serving life sentences at the Colorado State Penitentiary learned of the highly publicized and critically acclaimed Scared Straight! program developed at Rahway, and decided to create a similar, but distinctively different, program for at-risk juveniles in Colorado. Their program is designed to bring delinquents to a maximum-security prison in order to Show How A Prison Experience Undermines People (S.H.A.P.E.U.P.). Unlike the Scared Straight! program, inmates involved in S.H.A.P.E.U.P. neither use abusive language nor shout threats at the juveniles who participate in the program. Rather than trying to scare the youths, their goal is to educate them to the realities of prison life. Over the course of a day, the juveniles are given a thorough tour of the maximum-security facility including the orientation area, isolation cells, death row, and the ominous gas chamber. Inmates serving life terms candidly and calmly discuss a typical day in prison focusing on the boredom, monotony, deprivation, dehumanization, and violence in vivid but nonsensational terms. A deputy warden shows the youths contraband, including the deadly weapons, that have been taken from inmates during routine searches along with photos of young inmates who have been murdered or committed suicide within the prison walls. At the end of the day an inmate serving life encourages the youths to think about what they saw and whether they want such an institutionalized existence to be part of their futures.

A week later, the juveniles return to the prison with their parents. Both the youths and their parents tour the prison and then meet as a group with the inmates to discuss life in prison. The youths are asked to recall all of the fun and meaningful things they have done during the past week—where they went, people they saw, school events, parties, and so on—and then are reminded that the inmates have spent 24 hours a day each day of that same week in the prison, doing the same things with the same people.

S.H.A.P.E.U.P. seems to have tremendous impact on the youths who participate in it, and unlike Scared Straight! it involves the parents in the process. Also, the follow-up visit apparently reinforces the stark realities presented in the initial prison tour. While it is sometimes difficult to track youths who have participated in the program, data indicate that their recidivism rates are much lower than those who have committed similar offenses but not participated in the program. Moreover, inmates who participate in the program seem to benefit from the program as well, turning idle prison time into a meaningful experience for them and the young people they meet.

VisionQuest

VisionQuest is a Tucson-based private program designed to rehabilitate "hard-core juvenile delinquents through positive experiences and physical challenges in the wilderness" (www.vq.com, 2008). VisionQuest maintains wilderness camps in Arizona, Delaware, Florida, Maryland, New Jersey and Pennsylvania. The program utilizes a practice involving a *rite of passage* similar to that used by the Crow and Cheyenne Indians. Juveniles in the program are expected to complete three "quests," which include working with wild horses and stubborn mules, a six-month wagon train experience, and an eight-week program of training wild mustangs. The program is structured to teach juveniles a strong sense of responsibility and a pragmatic understanding of the need to abide by social norms. After completing their quests, the youths experience a ritual ceremony signifying their accomplishments and marking their entrance into adulthood. One researcher who studied the program indicated that the youths were not merely "playing cowboys and Indians," but were "struggling to cope with real and difficult circumstances without the protection or cocoon of traditional institutional programs" (Gavzer, 1986:10). In addition to the wilderness experiences, the program includes daily schoolwork, the earning of a weekly allowance, counseling sessions, and immediate accountability to adult supervisors for behavior. Approximately 15 states send juvenile offenders to VisionQuest at a cost estimated to be approximately half that of traditional institutionalization. The program is considered to be relatively successful.

Juvenile Boot Camps

Juvenile boot camps simultaneously reflect the deinstitutionalization and "get tough" movements in juvenile corrections while also implementing elements of shock incarceration and probation. These programs usually involve relatively short stays (30 to 90 days, but sometimes up to six months) in a military-style boot camp. Juveniles usually wear uniforms, sleep in tents or barracks, and rise early in the morning to run, do calisthenics, and perform a variety of military drills and hard labor chores. Drill-sergeant-like supervisors bark orders at the young offenders as they try to shock them into realizing the consequences of their delinquency while instilling discipline in them so that they will refrain from repeating their offenses.

While these boot camps capture a great deal of media attention and satisfy the public's need to get tough on young offenders, and for the short term require youths to be accountable for their actions, their long-term effectiveness is doubtful (Cullen, et al., 2005; MacKenzie and Armstrong, 2004; Mackenzie and Souryal, 1991; Page, 1999). Arizona, one of the first states to implement boot camps, scrapped the program after seven years, deciding that the $1.5 million per year program was a dismal failure. Data indicated that only 22.6 percent of those admitted to Arizona's boot camps successfully completed the program and that the recidivism rate was no better than for those who had been placed on probation, placed in traditional institutions, or sent to jail. Arizona's Director of the State Department of Corrections concluded that while the boot camps were great for public relations and were politically popular, they were not good public policy. As one critic of the program concluded,

Why do military-style boot camps receive so much public and political support despite research that shows they are ineffective in reforming delinquents and preventing future crime and delinquency on the part of participants?

© The Image Works

"Officials found out that you don't correct problems by . . . getting in their faces and calling them scum . . . marching and making [delinquents] eat bad food isn't going to help a kid with a drug problem" (Schwartz, 1996:49A). As Arizona was scrapping its juvenile boot camps, several other states announced plans to copy it. Barry Krisberg (2005:78) noted, most juvenile boot camps are never evaluated, and those that are evaluated have been shown to be ineffective, but they appeal to the public and allow politicians "to talk with macho bravado without being held accountable for the poor results of these programs." This is what Cullen and his associates (2005) called "common sense corrections"—those programs that people seem to think will work, despite all evidence to the contrary.

Other Diversion Programs

A variety of other diversionary programs have been developed and implemented throughout the United States. [no paragraph] Despite differences in specific aspects of diversionary programs, they all share some common goals. Most important for these programs is to divert juveniles from official adjudication procedures in an effort to avoid the stigma associated with being labeled a juvenile delinquent. Moreover, these programs are designed to ease the caseloads of overcrowded juvenile courts and overworked correctional officials so that their efforts can be focused on more serious chronic juvenile offenders.

EVALUATION OF DEINSTITUTIONALIZATION, COMMUNITY CORRECTIONS, AND DIVERSION

Several studies have been conducted in an attempt to evaluate various deinstitutional, community, and diversionary programs across the country, and have resulted in mixed findings. The Office of Juvenile Justice and Delinquency Prevention (2005) reported that community-based facilities were more effective than traditional institutions for violent juvenile offenders. Mark Pogrebin and his associates (1984) reported moderate success in the Colorado diversionary programs they evaluated, as did Robert Regoli and coworkers (1985), although they pointed out that using recidivism rates is not always a valid measure of success. William Selke (1982), on the other hand, assessed the Youth Services Bureau in Michigan as being unsuccessful, and suffering from insufficient staffing.

Elizabeth Wilderman (1984) evaluated Colorado's diversionary program as reducing recidivism somewhat, but pointed out that it negatively labeled some juveniles simply on the basis of participation in it, whose offenses were so minor that they would have been better handled if ignored. This same theme has dominated the critical assessments of many juvenile diversionary programs. For example, Bruce Bullington and his associates (1978) argued that the interest in diversion and community corrections is faddish and that one of the major problems of these programs is that while they were developed to divert juveniles from the juvenile justice system, they involve juveniles in correctional programs who previously would have been ignored by the formal system. Hence, rather than bringing *fewer* youths into the system, diversion actually brings in *more* (Frazier and Lee, 1992). Rojek (1982:321) registered the same criticism when he pointed out: "In theory, diversion is perceived to be a process of deflecting offenders away from the traditional juvenile justice system. However, there is strong evidence that this deflection may result in another form of encapsulation."

Even the argument of reduced costs has come under scrutiny. Rojek (1982: 318–320), for example, indicated that while diversion and community corrections were being touted as more humane and cost efficient, their tendency to "widen the net" and identify more juveniles as delinquent represents a substantial investment of resources toward controlling "questionable acts of deviance." Anne Mahoney (1981) also pointed to the "net-widening" aspects of deinstitutionalization, community corrections, and diversion and raised concerns about increased costs to the families of delinquents who were brought into treatment programs. In a position paper, the National Advisory Committee for Juvenile Justice and Delinquency Prevention (1984) expressed similar concern when it noted that the wording of the Juvenile Justice Act of 1974 has caused federal money to be diverted to handling noncriminal acts of delinquency. The committee recommended that a new federal policy be developed focusing on serious juvenile delinquency. Charles Logan and Sharla Rausch (1985) concluded that efforts at diversion and deinstitutionalization are pointless unless they are accompanied by a movement toward decriminalization of status offenses.

Finally, constitutional, legal, and ethical issues have been raised regarding community corrections and diversionary programs. Bullington and associates (1978) argued against the widespread development of diversionary programs because they viewed them as violating the civil liberties that were assured by the *Gault* decision. They viewed the biggest problem of diversion as involving disposition without adjudication. Bortner, Sutherland, and Winn (1985) found that there was differential treatment of blacks by the courts, with black females being more likely to be institutionalized for status offenses, while whites were more likely to be diverted and deinstitutionalized. Karen Lucken (1997) warned that as private agencies become more involved in community correctional programs that much of the discretion in the handling of juveniles is being turned over to businesspeople seeking to make a profit as opposed to juvenile justice personnel whose primary concern is supposed to be the youth in trouble. Cullen and his colleagues (2005) remind us that innovative correctional programs do not necessarily work just because common sense tells us that they should, and we hope that they do.

Summary

In this chapter we have pointed out that every society attempts to encourage conformity to its norms and to control deviant behavior. The three general categories of social control involve *voluntary, informal,* and *formal* mechanisms. Voluntary social control relies upon successful socialization and the internalization of social norms and values. An individual's self-concept, personality, and overall socialization experience help determine the extent to which he or she will voluntarily refrain from committing delinquency. The development of a *social bond* or positive attachment to society seems to create a stronger likelihood of conformity among juveniles.

If a juvenile's internal voluntary control is not strong enough to prohibit law violation, a variety of informal social control mechanisms can be implemented by society. Gossip, ridicule, humor, ostracism, and peer pressure all can help control a juvenile's behavior. The nature of the offense as well as the type of society or community in which the juvenile resides help influence the type of informal social control that may be utilized and its probable effectiveness.

The third type of societal defense against delinquency is formal social control. The schools, police, courts, and various social agencies all play an important role in implementing formal social control measures against juveniles. Formal techniques of social control, such as juvenile probation, incarceration in juvenile institutions, and various community programs are utilized in an attempt to prevent and control delinquency. In serious cases, juveniles may be remanded to adult courts and sent to adult jails or prisons. Capital punishment existed as the ultimate form of social control for youths up until the *Roper* v. *Simmons* case in 2005 when the U.S. Supreme Court declared it a violation of the Eighth Amendment against cruel and unusual punishment to execute juveniles.

All forms of social control are aimed at the goal of *deterrence* in the hopes of reducing juvenile delinquency by applying negative sanctions to youths who violate society's norms. According to Deterrence Theory, if these sanctions are certain, swift, severe, and made known to others, they will not only reduce the likelihood that the specific individual who was punished will repeat his or her delinquency, but also will act as a general deterrent, discouraging others from committing delinquency.

Juvenile delinquency, like other forms of social deviance, is not likely to be eliminated. However, members of society must attempt to alleviate the problems associated with it by minimizing its negative consequences.

Concept Integration: Questions and Topics for Study and Discussion

1. Explain what is meant by the term *social control* and how this concept differs from the attempt to eliminate delinquency.
2. Explain what is meant by *voluntary social control*. How is voluntary social control achieved? In what ways can voluntary control of delinquency be made more effective?
3. List and describe several techniques of informal social control that can be utilized against delinquency. In what type of community or society is informal social control likely to be most effective?
4. Give several examples of formal social control of juvenile delinquents. How do these methods differ from voluntary and informal techniques of social control? In your opinion, is formal control *more* or *less* effective than voluntary and informal social control? Why?
5. The case of *Rover* v. *Simmons* (2005) abolished the death penalty for offenders who committed their crimes while juveniles. In your opinion, should capital punishment be meted out to juvenile offenders? Why? Why not?
6. Identify some of the contemporary programs of deinstitutionalization, community corrections, and diversion. What are the strengths of these approaches to delinquency? What are some of their weaknesses?

Part V

APPLIED THEORY: STRATEGIES FOR DEALING WITH JUVENILE DELINQUENCY

INTRODUCTION: Treatment and Prevention in a Social Context

In this book we are studying the social problem of juvenile delinquency from a sociological perspective. In this concluding section, we examine the social processes involved in attempting to reduce, treat, and prevent juvenile delinquency.

Sociologists seldom assume that any form of crime or juvenile delinquency can be totally eliminated. As indicated in Part One, norm violation occurs in every society, and, in fact, deviance can be both functional and dysfunctional in its consequences. Strategies for treating and preventing delinquency, therefore, must be developed, practiced, and evaluated in a social context.

Chapter 16 deals with specific treatment and prevention strategies for juvenile delinquency. Treatment and prevention programs are necessarily linked to theories about what causes delinquency. The chapter begins with a discussion of the treatment **ideology**—*a set of ideas or beliefs on which some established practice is based*—and outlines some of the most prevalent treatment strategies used in dealing with juvenile delinquents. The prevention ideology is summarized and some of the more prominent delinquency prevention programs that have been used in this country are discussed.

Chapter 17 concludes the book with suggestions for applying sociological theories to rethinking the problem of juvenile delinquency. It reiterates the social nature of delinquency, and makes some specific recommendations for meaningful social change in the way that we view juvenile delinquency and its associated problems. Specific suggestions are made for reducing the marginal status of adolescence, decriminalizing status offenses, standardizing juvenile codes, revising juvenile courts, and modifying juvenile corrections. The chapter, and hence, the book conclude with a proposal for **redefining** juvenile delinquency.

We do not consider Part Five or Chapter 17 as the end. Rather, we hope that the information and discussion presented in Chapters 16 and 17 stimulate your thinking and elicit your participation in the societal quest to better understand and control juvenile delinquency.

Chapter 16

Treatment and Prevention Strategies

READING OBJECTIVES

Reading this chapter will help you achieve the following objectives:

1. Understand the treatment ideology in juvenile corrections.
2. Understand the prevention ideology in juvenile corrections.
3. Summarize some of the major juvenile treatment programs in the United States.
4. Summarize some of the major delinquency prevention programs in the United States.
5. Develop a sociological perspective on the treatment and prevention of juvenile delinquency.

INTRODUCTION

Chapter 15 discussed social control as it involves societal intervention into an individual's life in an attempt to regulate social behavior. When a person's behavior is regarded as deviant, and the decision is made to formally or informally intervene, there are three overriding ideological approaches that society may take: *punishment, treatment,* and/or *prevention.* Chapter 15 focused on the punishment ideology, illustrating how societal members inflict social reprimands ranging from gossip and ridicule to imprisonment and death upon those who have violated social norms. Chapter 15 ended, however, by discussing the movement toward deinstitutionalization, community corrections, and diversion, in efforts to keep juveniles out of the criminal justice system. Some of these programs attempted various strategies to prevent recurrences of delinquency and bring us to the subject of Chapter 16.

In this chapter, we focus on the treatment and prevention approaches to the social control of delinquency. From the outset, it should be noted that these three ideological approaches are not mutually exclusive. While proponents of one often view themselves as fundamentally at odds with the ideas of the others, there are marked similarities in the three approaches. All of them represent the attempts of society to regulate the behavior of its members. While these ideologies differ in their specific approaches to dealing with the problem of delinquency, more often than not, delinquency programs integrate aspects of all three (punishment, treatment, and prevention) to some extent.

The treatment and prevention ideologies are particularly compatible. While treatment programs are **reactive** in nature in that they are *implemented after a juvenile has been adjudicated delinquent,* they attempt not only to treat the juvenile delinquent, but also to prevent any future involvement in delinquent behavior. Prevention is a **proactive strategy,** based on the assumption that if the underlying causes of delinquency can be identified and eliminated *before the delinquency occurs,* delinquent behavior can be prevented.

TREATMENT IDEOLOGY AND DELINQUENCY TREATMENT PROGRAMS

The **treatment ideology** *follows the rehabilitative philosophy of the juvenile court.* Treatment programs usually are based upon the assumption that delinquent behavior is a manifestation or symptom of some other deeper problem. The treatment ideology applies the medical model to delinquency. Delinquency is viewed as analogous to disease, and treatment programs typically take on medical and clinical characteristics. Consequently, *symptoms* of delinquency are observed, in order to make a proper *diagnosis,* so that the appropriate *treatment* strategy can be pursued.

The treatment ideology takes an individualistic approach to delinquency, viewing delinquents as being socially and psychologically maladjusted or disturbed. Treatment programs attempt to readjust or remove what is disturbing the juvenile so that the youth can overcome the source of trouble, and go on to lead a normal life. Psychiatry and psychology dominate many of the current treatment strategies in juvenile delinquency, and increasingly, the medical-model analogy is taken literally in some of these programs, especially those aimed at alcohol and drug abuse (see Box 16.1).

Treatment programs can be undertaken either in conjunction with or apart from an institutional setting. Thus, just as treatment philosophies are compatible with the prevention ideology, they need not be at odds with the concept of punishment. Many juvenile institutions, particularly state training schools and reformatories, incorporate treatment strategies into the process of rehabilitation. While utilizing confinement in an institution as a means of social control and punishment, various treatment strategies are often used to attempt to reform the juvenile and prevent any further delinquent or criminal activity. James Robison and Gerald Smith (1971) pointed out that what has often been viewed as punishment versus treatment ideologies in corrections is not accurate, as these are not opposites. The two approaches are not mutually exclusive but can be used in conjunction with each other. Robison and Smith contended that it was more accurate to view the choice not as being between treatment and punishment, but between one type of treatment or punishment alternative and another.

A variety of strategies and techniques have been used in the treatment of juvenile delinquents. While it would be impossible (and pointless) to discuss them all, we describe briefly some of the specific and representative types of treatment programs.

BOX 16.1

CONTROVERSIAL ISSUE: Applying the Medical Model in the Treatment of Delinquency

One of the most alarming trends in juvenile delinquency over the past decades has been the increased use of alcohol and other drugs by teenagers. In the past, these problems were usually addressed by parents, school officials, social workers, youth agencies, and juvenile court officials. More recently, health-care professionals have become the primary providers of treatment and rehabilitation for youths with alcohol and drug abuse problems.

The health-care industry has become particularly skilled at promoting the medical model of alcohol, drug abuse, and related forms of delinquency, such as truancy, running away, and teen suicide. In sophisticated magazine, newspaper, and television advertisements, both private and public health-care facilities promise beleaguered parents that they can cure everything from failing grades to depression, but focus most heavily on their ability to treat and cure teenagers' alcohol and drug addictions.

The treatment of drug abuse and alcoholism among U.S. teens has grown into a multimillion-dollar industry with virtually every major health-care facility in the nation offering some type of treatment program aimed directly at teenagers. Most of these programs are expensive, with parents or insurance companies paying between $200 and $2000 per day for treatment.

(*Continued*)

The major controversy over these alcohol and drug-abuse treatment programs centers on whether or not they work. There has been no systematic longitudinal research on the effectiveness of these programs, but preliminary studies suggest that they are no more effective than earlier less-expensive methods. One independent study indicates that 80 percent of the adolescents who complete such programs return to drug or alcohol use within a year (Hollandsworth, 1990). Another showed that while these programs often are successful during the short term, even with adequate aftercare, they do not seem to be effective over the long term (Sealock et al., 1997). Research indicates that many of these programs use simplistic and punitive behavior modification techniques that have been used for decades in juvenile state training schools. As one researcher put it, "Hospitals are rapidly becoming the new jails for middle-class and upper-middle-class kids" (Schwartz, 1989: 143). Critics charge that although drug and alcohol treatment programs occur in hospitals or hospital-like facilities and are supervised by doctors, very little medicine or science is actually involved. Most medical facilities are anxious to jump on the juvenile psychiatric treatment bandwagon, however, because drug and alcohol abuse programs help fill empty hospital beds, and with laws preventing the incarceration of juvenile status offenders, these programs offer alternatives for parents and juvenile court officials who do not know where else to turn.

From a sociological perspective, these programs fail to recognize the inadequacy of the medical model in explaining juvenile delinquency, even in the areas of alcohol and drug abuse, which indeed have physiological and biological consequences. There is general consensus among prominent researchers that drug and alcohol abuse among teenagers is better viewed as a result of problems in interpersonal and social relationships and hence not likely to be successfully treated in a program based on the medical model. Brief intervention strategies involving families and friends have been shown to be more effective than hospitalization and medical treatment (Monti, et al., 2005). Most importantly, medical treatments for socially oriented problems should not be used by parents or juvenile authorities merely as substitutes for harsher criminal sanctions.

Why do you think the medical model of delinquency and treatment has become so popular and powerful in the United States? From a sociological perspective, what are some of the major weaknesses of this medical model, both in explaining and in treating delinquency?

Sources

Hollandsworth, Skip. 1990. Can kids on drugs be saved? *Texas Monthly* 18 (June):107–111, 153–162.

Monti, P. M., Colby, S. M., and O'Leary, T. A. 2005. *Adolescents, alcohol, and substance abuse: Reaching teens through brief interventions.* New York: Guilford Press.

Schwartz, Ira M. 1989. Being abused at better prices. Chapter 7, in *(In) justice for juveniles: Rethinking the best interests of the child.* pp. 131–148. Lexington, MA: Lexington Books.

Sealock, M. D., Gottfredson, D. C., and Gallagher, C. A. 1997. *Journal of Research in Crime and Delinquency* 34 (May):210–236.

Behavior Modification

Behavior modification is based upon principles derived from research in experimental psychology, and is associated with the work of prominent psychologist, B. F Skinner (1938, 1971). As the term implies, **behavior modification** is *a treatment technique that attempts to modify or change an individual's behavior.* Behavior modification operates on the principle that the consequences of an individual's actions play an important part in determining future actions. If an individual receives gratification, or *positive reinforcement,* from a particular act, the same or similar acts are likely to be repeated in the future. On the other hand, if an individual views the consequences of an act as undesirable, or experiences *negative reinforcement* from a particular behavior, that act or similar acts are unlikely to be repeated in the future.

Behavior modification is compatible with the *social learning theories* of delinquency and has been used in many juvenile correctional facilities and other applied settings (Kazdin, 2008). In a facility wherein the daily behavior of juveniles can be readily observed and evaluated, the principles of behavior modification have been used to reward approved actions while punishing (or at least *not* rewarding) undesirable behavior. Different methods can be and have been used to provide the positive and negative reinforcement viewed as essential to behavior modification (Martin and Pear, 2006).

For example, juvenile institutions often operate on a "level system" or utilize a merit– demerit approach to encourage incarcerated youths to obey rules and demonstrate acceptable behavior. Level classifications are developed with different behavioral expectations required to move from one level to the next. As juveniles earn merits or otherwise meet the requirements to move up to the next higher level, they are rewarded with more privileges, and higher status within the institution. For example, an institution that establishes five levels may set five curfew or "lights out" times for the various levels. Those who are on the lowest level might have to be in their rooms with lights out by 9:00 p.m., while those on the next highest level would be allowed to stay up until 9:30; whereas those on the highest level might not be required to be in their rooms until 11:00 p.m. Other rewards and privileges, such as time away from the institution to attend a movie, increased visitation privileges, or increased recreation time, can be utilized to motivate the youths to improve their behavior and perhaps earn their release, or at least make their stay in the facility more palatable. Conversely, failure to meet behavioral expectations would lead to demerits or being moved to a lower-level classification, with the loss of certain privileges.

It is difficult to compare and evaluate the effectiveness of behavior modification in the treatment of delinquents, as different techniques of behavior modification are utilized in a wide range of environments. Elery Phillips and his associates (1971) found the token economy system to be effective in dealing with adolescents, and Robert Rutherford (1975) reported case studies in which the use of behavioral agreements between supervising adults and juveniles was effective in modifying behavior in the home, the school, the community, and the institution. Token economies are utilized in many institutional settings, and can reinforce (either positively or negatively) behavior through the use of tokens, coins, chits (institutional coupons), or some other tangible object which has monetary value within the institution. Behavioral contracts can be utilized in any setting in which those in authority clearly delineate the rules and the appropriate behaviors expected from the youths for receiving certain desired rewards (e.g., good grades, merits, money). Douglas Kivet and Carol Warren (2002) conducted ethnographic research at a group home for boys that used behavior modification as its primary treatment technique, and found that staff often escalated or de-escalated juveniles' offending behaviors with eye contact and through interaction with the youths.

Some problems arise in the use of behavior modification with juveniles. One is that in order to be effective, almost constant monitoring and evaluation of behavior are required. If periods of time elapse when a juvenile's behavior goes unnoticed, unrewarded or unpunished, the principles of behavior modification are violated, and its effectiveness diminished. Another problem is that of determining appropriate positive and negative reinforcements for particular youths and specific behaviors. What is viewed as a reward by some may be viewed with ambivalence or even negatively by others. Thus, appropriate punishment for one youth may only encourage the undesired behavior on the part of another.

Another potential problem related to behavior modification resides in the use of punishment as negative reinforcement. While proponents of the treatment technique view it as humane, its implementation could take on cruel and inhumane proportions. For example, various forms of child abuse might be rationalized by the abusive parent as being appropriate punishment for undesirable behavior. Likewise, with available technology in drugs and equipment, the potential rewards and punishments for behavior are almost unlimited.

Finally, one of the problems with behavior modification involves the extent to which the desired behavioral changes continue once the environment is changed and the anticipated positive and negative reinforcements are not immediately forthcoming. The corrections literature is replete with examples of how the "ideal inmate" does not necessarily become the "ideal citizen" after release. It is difficult yet possible to constantly monitor a juvenile's behavior while institutionalized, but it is virtually impossible in the larger society outside. In society, seldom are all behaviors accompanied by a rigid structure that gives immediate rewards and punishments. Complicating the situation further is that in the larger social world, the juvenile has a variety of reference groups from which the potential rewards and punishments can come. As was discussed in Chapters 9 and 11, the family often must compete with the peer group in reinforcing the values and behavior of youths.

Reality Therapy and Choice Theory

Reality Therapy is associated with the work of William Glasser (1965; 2001), and is a *treatment strategy that focuses upon the individual understanding the consequences of one's actions and accepting responsibility for them.* Unlike most psychotherapeutic techniques that dwell upon a person's past in order to understand the causes of present behavioral problems, reality therapy is based on **Choice Theory,** which *focuses upon the present and the choices that people make and the consequences of those choices.* Glasser contended that concentrating upon individuals' past experiences was useless in effectively resolving present problems, and potentially could provide excuses and rationalizations that would exempt them from taking responsibility for their own actions.

As a technique for dealing with juvenile delinquents, reality therapy is much less concerned with *why* the juvenile committed the delinquent act, as with *what* can be done to ensure that the youth does not commit the same or similar acts in the future. In fact, why the act was committed is treated as irrelevant. Regardless of what problems the youth may have encountered in childhood—broken home, child abuse, inadequate socialization, poor environment, or other negative circumstances—the *reality* of the situation is that the youth has committed an act (made a choice) resulting in trouble with the law, and now must accept responsibility for that action (consequences of the choice). You may remember from Chapter 6 that Sykes and Matza (1957) contended that delinquent youths usually realize that they have violated society's norms, and experience a sense of guilt over having done so. However, they rationalize their actions through techniques of neutralization, one of which is *denial of responsibility.* Reality therapy directly attacks that neutralization technique, insisting that juveniles acknowledge that they are responsible for their behavior (Edgette, 2006).

Reality therapy has been used widely with juveniles in both institutional and parole or probation settings. Glasser's research indicated that if the therapist develops an intimate relationship with the youth, gains the youth's trust, and genuinely cares about changing the individual's behavior, it can be very successful. Phillip Cole and Joseph Hafsten (1978) found that when reality therapy techniques were used during juvenile probation, they were effective in changing behavior. One of the elements of Cole and Hafsten's probation program included victim restitution. They believed that some form of restitution symbolically represented the juvenile's acknowledgment of responsibility for the offense. The Ventura Restitution Project specifically aims to make juvenile offenders understand the ramifications of their delinquent behavior by making it clear that they have direct responsibility for their actions (Remington, 1982). While it does not involve the intense individual approach that reality therapy demands, the project is based upon the primary assumptions of reality therapy—that individuals must accept responsibility for and the consequences of their actions.

Another program encompassing the reality therapy approach is TOUGHLOVE. Described as a "self-help program for parents, youths, and communities," TOUGHLOVE literature points out that the program deals in *behavior, not in emotions.* The program is one of crisis intervention to provide support groups for those whose lives are directly affected by the negative effects of delinquency. Avoiding the assignment of blame, the program emphasizes the need for responsible action on the part of all to alleviate the problem.

The California Youth Authority also uses a reality therapy–based program called Lifeskills. The program works with chronic juvenile offenders and has shown moderate success in teaching basic life skills such as getting up on time, going to school or work, and taking responsibility for one's actions (Josi and Sechrest, 1999).

Group and Individual Counseling and Therapy

Many group and individual counseling techniques have been followed in treating juvenile delinquents, both inside and outside institutional settings. Reality therapy is one example of these counseling techniques. It would be impossible to delineate all of the counseling strategies that have been employed, but because juveniles place so much emphasis on peers, group therapy strategies are very popular in working with delinquents (Christner, 2007). Sometimes, even the simple process of intervening and playing the role of mediator to resolve conflicts between two or more youths can effectively avoid confrontations that could possibly escalate into serious problems or even violent crimes (OJJDP, 2000). Psychiatrists, psychologists, social workers, probation and parole officers, and virtually everybody else who has worked with delinquent youths have engaged in some aspect of individual and group counseling in an attempt to resolve the problems associated with delinquency. Effective therapy relies on reliable mental health assessments for juveniles, something that research shows has been questionable at best (Wasserman et al., 2004).

The Wilderness Therapy Expedition in Oregon is known as the "last chance" for many teenagers who have been in trouble with their families, schools, and the

Group counseling is a popular treatment technique with juvenile offenders? What sociological theories help explain why it might be successful? Why does it not work for all troubled youths?

Mary Kate Denny/PhotoEdit

law (*ABC Primetime*, 2002). The program involves 21 days of silent hiking through the wilderness and mountains carrying 65-pound backpacks. Known as the trek, the hike is both physically and emotionally demanding. Daytime temperatures often reach over 100 degrees Fahrenheit, and nighttime temperatures hover in the low 50s to mid-40s. Participants are required to hike in total silence, but each evening when camp is set up, there is a group therapy session during which the youths are encouraged to talk about the day's events, their families, their feelings, and anything they believe can help them straighten out their lives. Some participants receive one-on-one counseling after the group sessions. The end of the trek involves 72 hours of solo isolation in the mountains for the youths to reflect on their problems and what they have learned during the wilderness experience. In some cases, the trek can be extended or even repeated. Most youths who have participated in the program indicate that it was a very meaningful experience, and their parents often say that their children were "totally changed" as a result (*ABC Primetime*, 2002).

The common elements shared by almost all programs that utilize counseling as part of their treatment strategy is that they view delinquency from an individualistic perspective. Even group counseling techniques operate on the premise that the group can help the individual overcome a particular situation, and resolve the problems that caused the delinquent behavior. With few exceptions, counseling techniques, whether conducted individually or in a group context, are dominated by the psychogenic approach to delinquency and ignore the sociological context in which juvenile delinquency occurs.

PREVENTION IDEOLOGY AND DELINQUENCY PREVENTION PROGRAMS

The **prevention ideology** is *based on the assumption that the best way to deal with the problem of juvenile delinquency is to intervene early and prevent it.* Thus, whether the cause of delinquency is viewed as social, psychological, or physiological–biological, the preventive strategy attempts to identify the causal factors, and to intervene and alter those factors before delinquent behavior occurs.

Delinquency prevention strategies have been dominated by the psychiatric perspective. Michael Hakeem (1957–1958) pointed out that even some sociologists working in criminology and corrections have tended to adopt the psychiatric approach to delinquency, viewing the problem of delinquent behavior as being rooted in the individual psyche. That is not to say that sociology has not played a role in delinquency prevention. In a later section of this chapter we illustrate how the sociological perspective has been incorporated successfully into some delinquency treatment and prevention programs.

Many delinquency prevention programs, however, view delinquency as abnormal, and, like the treatment strategies just discussed, perceive delinquency from the medical model analogy. Delinquency is viewed as an individual anomaly, and as such, early diagnosis, identification, and intervention are considered important for effective prevention.

Early Identification

At the heart of the concept of delinquency prevention is the need to identify as early as possible the behaviors of children that are considered to be "warning signs" of impending delinquency. Prevention strategies assume that there are characteristics of "predelinquency" which, if caught soon enough, may be altered in time to prevent actual delinquency. In a pamphlet entitled "What Parents Should Know About Juvenile Delinquency and Juvenile Justice," Waln Brown (1983:12) provided a checklist for parents of what he considered to be a "partial list of delinquent acts and inappropriate childhood behaviors" for which parents should be on the alert, including behaviors ranging from being moody to actual law violations (see Table 16.1).

A longer and even more exhaustive list of "predelinquency" symptoms was developed by a delinquency prevention project sponsored by the U.S. Children's Bureau in St. Paul, Minnesota. That list comprised all sorts of childhood behavior, including bashfulness, crying, daydreaming, nailbiting, silliness, thumbsucking, and bedwetting (cited in Hakeem, 1957–1958). Hyperactivity has also been identified as a "predelinquency" symptom, and Dan Hurley (1985) indicated that early detection and intervention could significantly reduce the likelihood of "high-risk" children becoming criminals.

Predelinquents and Early Intervention

The search for symptoms of "predelinquency" underscores the psychiatric assumption that delinquency is a form of individual pathology that, like a disease, must be diagnosed early and treated before it consumes the person beyond hope of "cure." The important second phase in the prevention ideology is to intervene in the individual's

Table 16.1 Partial List of Delinquent Acts and Inappropriate Childhood Behaviors

- Alcohol use
- Bad temper
- Cheating
- Complaints by neighbors
- Cruelty to people or animals
- Destructive
- Discipline problems in school
- Discourteous
- Disobedient
- Drug use
- Fighting
- Hanging out at places that have a bad reputation
- Inconsiderate
- Irresponsible
- Lack of friends
- Law violations
- Losses or gains of large sums of money
- Lying
- Moody
- Poor school grades
- Running away from home
- Regularly misses family meals
- Secretive
- Sexual misconduct
- Smoking
- Stays out late
- Stealing
- Swearing
- Threatens family members
- Truancy
- Verbally abusive

What strikes you about this list of "inappropriate" behaviors? Do you think they are valid indicators of future delinquency? How would labeling theorists view this list?

Source: Waln K. Brown, *What parents should know about juvenile delinquency and juvenile justice,* The William Gladden Foundation, 1983. Reprinted with permission.

life so as to alter a purported predisposition toward delinquency. This raises the question as to what type of intervention is most appropriate. No real consensus has arisen about this dilemma. Any and all of the treatment strategies discussed earlier in this chapter have been proposed and tried, along with numerous other methods to prevent the juvenile from continuing on a path toward delinquency. Behavior modification is particularly popular as a method of early intervention in hopes of preventing unruly and defiant children from growing into delinquent teens (Bernstein, 2006).

In at least one type of situation—youthful arson—early identification and intervention apparently have been successful. Clifford Karchmer (1984) found five juvenile firesetter counseling programs, in San Francisco, Dallas, Los Angeles, Mesa (Arizona), and Prince Georges County (Maryland), in which firefighting personnel offered in-house counseling for young arsonists. A critical factor in the success of these programs apparently rests in the ability to diagnose potential juvenile firesetters as early as possible and begin intensive counseling as soon as possible.

Like the treatment strategies discussed earlier in this chapter, the prevention ideology and most prevention programs fail to put delinquency into its social context. Delinquency is viewed as an individual matter, and attempts to prevent it are primarily aimed at intervening into a person's life in order to alter future behavior. While morally uplifting, most of these preventive programs are sociologically bankrupt. As Liazos (1974) pointed out, virtually all programs based upon these assumptions have failed miserably.

Jackson Toby (1965) discussed the problems of early identification and intensive treatment of delinquency in regard to some of the problems related to accurate prediction, type of treatment, and its efficacy. He analyzed the Cambridge–Somerville Youth Study and the New York City Youth Board Prediction Study. One of the studies

(Cambridge–Somerville) employed the *extrapolation technique* of delinquency prediction, in which youths who had exhibited antisocial behavior are identified and treated. The other (New York City Youth Board) followed the *circumstantial vulnerability approach,* which is based more heavily upon sociological research and identifies those youths whose family and neighborhood characteristics have been linked with delinquency. The problem, according to Toby, was that both studies overpredicted delinquency, and he pointed out that the stigmatization of being identified as predelinquent may exceed or at least offset any benefits that might be derived from treatment. He summarized, "Early identification and intensive treatment, though probably not as erroneous as the flat-world theory, is more a slogan or a rallying cry than a realistic assessment of the difficulties that delinquency control programs must overcome" (Toby, 1965:160).

Another problem that arises with delinquency prevention is the legal and moral issues that accompany intervention into a person's life *before* the commission of an illegal act. The U.S. judicial system and juvenile corrections are based upon intervening *after* a wrongful act has been committed and state intervention because of presumed future law violation is unconstitutional and illegal.

SOCIOLOGICAL APPROACHES TO DELINQUENCY TREATMENT AND PREVENTION

While most delinquency treatment and prevention programs are dominated by the individualistic approach to delinquency, sociologists also are concerned with delinquents and reducing the likelihood of their further involvement in delinquent behavior. More comprehensive programs are based on juvenile needs assessment that includes but is not limited to psychological problems, physical problems, sexual abuse, violence, family problems and deviance, educational deficits, and problems related to peer associations (Towberman, 1992). There have been numerous sociological contributions to delinquency treatment and prevention, and sociologists continue to search for new and innovative methods toward this end.

Rather than approaching the problem as being one of individual anomaly or pathology, the sociological approach takes into account the influence of society on the individual. Consequently, sociologically oriented programs that have attempted to "treat" delinquents and prevent (or at least reduce) further delinquency have approached delinquency as socially created and defined, and influenced by the social and cultural environment. In this section we briefly examine some of the classic programs that have approached the handling of delinquents from a sociological perspective. Then, we describe some of the more recent attempts to apply a sociological perspective to the problem of delinquency treatment and prevention.

The Chicago Area Project

One of the first and most notable attempts to apply sociological principles to the treatment and prevention of juvenile delinquency was the Chicago Area Project. The Project began in the 1930s and was developed out of the theoretical framework of Shaw and McKay (see Chapter 6) and what later became known as the Chicago School of Thought regarding delinquency.

BOX 16.2

CROSS-CULTURAL FOCUS: Delinquency Prevention in Japan

In response to a major wave of juvenile delinquency following World War II, Japanese officials created two juvenile guidance centers to spearhead their delinquency-prevention efforts. By the mid-1980s, there were 660 juvenile guidance centers with approximately 70,000 citizens working as guidance volunteers in Japan. Most of these guidance centers operate under the auspices of the Child Welfare Law, but nine of them are managed by municipal police departments as part of the juvenile justice system. Located in a wide variety of communities, the primary purpose of these centers is to identify juveniles who commit minor violations and to intervene and supervise them in an effort to prevent them from becoming serious offenders.

Japanese culture places tremendous emphasis on the family, and it still is considered the most important social institution in preventing juvenile delinquency. The family in Japan, however, is undergoing numerous changes, as are all social institutions, some of which contribute to increased delinquency (Foljanty-Jost, 2004). These centers represent an organized effort for the community to supplement and reinforce family supervision of youngsters through the cooperation of citizen volunteers and the police. Many volunteers organize patrols looking for juveniles involved in smoking, loitering, curfew violations, shoplifting, and other relatively minor offenses. When detected, these youths are identified as "predelinquents" and their names are turned over to the police. Rather than being officially processed through the juvenile justice system, however, these youths are assigned to one of the centers for guidance and supervision.

Evaluations of the effectiveness of these guidance centers are mixed. Some argue that many youths caught in the early stages of delinquency may be diverted from lives of serious crime by this early identification and intervention. Others argue that identifying these youths as "predelinquents" and reporting their names to the police apply a negative label which may lead to a self-fulfilling prophecy and produce a "net-widening" effect, eventually bringing more youths into the juvenile justice system. In Japan, as in the United States, the impact of delinquency prevention efforts is difficult to assess, and society runs a risk of inadvertently increasing the very activity it is trying to prevent.

What cultural differences between Japan and the United States affect how the two countries approach delinquency treatment and prevention? As U.S. influence permeates Japanese culture, do you suspect that their approaches to delinquency will become more similar or dissimilar?

Sources

Foljanty-Jost, Gesine (Ed.), 2004. *Juvenile delinquency in Japan: Reconsidering the crises*. Boston: Brill.

Yokoyama, Minoru. 1989. Net-widening of the juvenile justice system in Japan. *Criminal Justice Review* 14 (Spring):43–53.

Shaw and McKay (1942) identified several Chicago neighborhoods in which crime and delinquency were extraordinarily high (as were other forms of social deviance). They contended that any program attempting to reduce delinquency in those areas would have to be developed in the communities themselves, utilizing human and institutional resources from within the neighborhoods, with only minimal guidance (and necessary funding) coming from external agencies (Shaw and McKay, 1942).

It was obvious that informal social control mechanisms were not working in the high delinquency neighborhoods in Chicago. Shaw and McKay believed, however, that some of those areas, such as the Russell Square neighborhood, known as "the Bush," had sufficient territorial and ethnic identity to effectively utilize local social institutions and some of the authority figures in the neighborhood to reduce and help prevent delinquency (Schlossman and Sedlak, 1983).

The Chicago Area Project was distinctively sociological in its approach. Rather than focusing upon individual delinquents, it focused upon the revitalization of meaningful social networks within the community. One of its first accomplishments was to establish organized recreational facilities for youths in the high delinquency areas. While recreation was not viewed as a resolution for delinquency, the formation of athletic teams and leagues required cooperative group efforts among juveniles and adults in the neighborhoods. In the Russell Square area, there were approximately 15 well-established gangs (Schlossman and Sedlak, 1983). Street workers were called upon to make contacts with the gangs and help structure recreational activities in an effort to reduce involvement in delinquent activities. The workers were successful in organizing intramural basketball and baseball leagues and involving gang members in organized recreation. Soloman Kobrin (1959) assessed the general accomplishment of the Chicago Area Project as a success.

Shaw and McKay presented reports on official delinquency rates ten years after the implementation of the Chicago Area Project that indicated substantial declines in official delinquency in the neighborhoods participating in the program. However, the success of the Chicago Area Project was not equal in all neighborhoods. As Steven Schlossman and Michael Sedlak (1983) pointed out, the key to success of the project was the involvement of indigenous leaders. Naturally, the same types of leaders and their abilities would not exist in all neighborhoods.

Kobrin's (1959) 25-year assessment of the Chicago Area Project was favorable. While delinquency was not totally eradicated in the targeted neighborhoods of Chicago, it was apparently substantially reduced. Schlossman and Sedlak (1983) also viewed the project as generally successful, especially the work in the Russell Square area. The project, however, was not without criticism. Some residents of the community questioned whether workers in the project were too tolerant of delinquents. Because the street workers were willing to work with persistently and seriously delinquent youths, some critics charged that they were indirectly encouraging delinquency. Further, some of the private agencies in the area apparently resented the use of indigenous leaders and what they considered the rejection of their expertise (Schlossman and Sedlak, 1983). Nevertheless, the project stimulated the sociological imagination of scholars around the country, and other cities implemented similar programs in their own communities.

The Mid-City Project

The Mid-City Project was developed in Boston in the early 1950s. The project operated between 1954 and 1957 in lower-class slum neighborhoods and focused on executing "action programs directed at three of the societal units seen to figure importantly in the genesis and perpetuation of delinquent behavior—the community, the family, and the gang" (Miller, 1962:168).

The Mid-City Project used street workers to establish close ties with juvenile gangs in Boston. They helped the gangs establish organized recreational activities, club meetings, dances, fundraising dinners, and other acceptable social activities. They also helped gang members with problems related to employment, school, and obtaining legal counsel.

Though based on the same sociological assumptions that underlay the Chicago Area Project, the Mid-City Project differed in some important ways. For one thing, the Chicago Area Project was envisioned and implemented as a long-term program designed to rehabilitate the community from within. The Mid-City Project, on the other hand, was designed as a three-year program with three distinctive phases, developed and overseen from outside the community. Another important distinction was that the Mid-City Project relied heavily on psychiatric counseling techniques. Phase Two (Phase One was the Contact and Relationship Establishment phase, and Phase Three was the Termination Phase) involved the use of behavior modification, individual psychotherapy, and regular psychiatric counseling (Miller, 1962). Thus, while sociologically inspired, like many other treatment and prevention strategies, the Mid-City Project was dominated by the psychogenic model.

Sociologist Walter B. Miller evaluated the Mid-City Project. His final assessment of the program was mixed. Miller (1962) viewed much of the work of the street workers with gangs as successful; however, when he posed the important evaluation question, "Was there a significant measurable inhibition of law-violating or morally disapproved behavior as a consequence of Project efforts?" his answer, with minor qualifications, was no. The project was not deemed a total failure, however, as some improvement was measured in school performance of participants, and the project played an important part in establishing and strengthening social organizations and institutions within the community, whose efforts at delinquency reduction might not be readily measurable over the short term, but might have some long-term impact.

Mobilization for Youth

Mobilization for Youth was begun in the early 1960s on the Lower East Side of Manhattan, and represented an attempt to apply Richard Cloward and Lloyd Ohlin's (1961) Theory of Differential Opportunity structures in urban slum areas (see Chapter 6) to delinquency prevention in the community. The primary focus of the project was to organize the residents of the Lower East Side into social networks which would open channels of access to legitimate opportunities for achieving success in school, business, government, and other social institutions and agencies (Mobilization for Youth, 1961).

Unfortunately, the Mobilization for Youth project met with a great deal of resistance in the community, and fell far short of its ambitious expectations. Nevertheless, the project applied sociological theory directly to a social problem, and even in its failure, gave credence to the sociological perspective that the nature of the problem of delinquency goes beyond the individual juveniles who commit deviant acts, and that consequently, any meaningful program to control or reduce delinquency must also reach beyond those individuals.

Minnesota Youth Advocate Program/Urban League

The Minnesota Youth Advocate Program was a school-based program begun in 1971 designed to help youths who had been in correctional institutions readjust to school and the community. The program had four specific objectives: increased school persistence, improved school performance, reduced recidivism, and reduced reinstitutionalization (Higgins, 1978). This program represented the sociological perspective in attempting to effectively reintegrate formerly institutionalized youths back into the social institutions and networks of the community. It required readjustment, not only on the part of the juvenile offender, but also on the part of the school, the family, and the community.

Paul Higgins (1978) evaluated the program on its effectiveness in achieving its four specific goals. When he compared participants in the program with a control group of juveniles who had been released from institutions but not exposed to the program, he found no significant differences between the two groups on any of the four objectives.

The Minnesota Youth Advocate Program gave way to the Minneapolis Urban League, which sponsors a Youth Advocacy program. The program targets youths of color who are "at risk" for committing criminal behavior and tries to increase school attendance and performance in order to reduce juvenile delinquency. In 2005, approximately 100 youths participated in the program with a modicum of success (Minneapolis Urban League, 2006).

Neighborhood Youth Corps and Job Training

Neighborhood Youth Corps programs were developed during the 1960s and implemented in major cities throughout the United States. The thrust of the Neighborhood Youth Corps was to provide vocational training and better work opportunities for disadvantaged and delinquent youths. Like the Mobilization for Youth program, the Neighborhood Youth Corps sought to provide delinquent youths access to legitimate avenues of opportunity.

Gerald Robin (1969) studied the programs of the Neighborhood Youth Corps in Cincinnati and Detroit. He compared stratified random samples of participants in the programs with control group subjects who had applied to the program but were not accepted. In both cities, Robin found that participation in the Neighborhood Youth Corps program was unrelated to delinquency prevention or reduction. He concluded that the assumption that providing better occupational opportunities for youths in order to reduce delinquency has more theoretical than practical value. B. Dalia Johnson and Richard Goldberg's (1982) evaluation of a Massachusetts vocational rehabilitation program came to much the same conclusion.

Neighborhood Youth Corps still exists today in numerous communities, but over the past three decades, the Neighborhood Youth Corps has given way to a number of neighborhood centers and programs whose aims are to prevent and reduce delinquency. Project CRAFT (Community Restitution and Apprenticeship Focused Training) offers job training, paid apprenticeships, and job placement for youths in several states. Its goal is to not only provide employment skills and opportunities, but to also help develop important personal and social skills (Hamilton and McKinney, 1999). Research has shown that chronic exposure to poverty, drugs, and violence leads to hopelessness, despair, distrust—and delinquency. Thus, successful intervention strategies for neighborhood youth centers and job training programs should include: street outreach and referral, needs and interest assessments, supportive personal relationships with adults, positive role models, peer group discussions, family interventions, neighborhood projects, education and job training, clear-cut program objectives, close attention to job placement, and long-term follow-up (Frey, 1999; Greene, 1993).

The Highfields Project

Not all sociologically oriented treatment and prevention programs involved such ambitious attempts at mobilizing and focusing community resources as the aforementioned programs. One of the classic small group treatment programs in a sociological framework was the Highfields Project begun in New Jersey in 1950.

The Highfields Project took boys who had been placed on probation by the court and assigned them to a facility where they lived, worked, and played in supervised small social groups. The Highfields Project stressed guided group experiences and the strengthening of conformity to social expectations of the group. The boys were allowed to go to town, attend movies, visit the drugstore soda fountain, go skating, and participate in other social activities, but they returned to the facility by a specified hour. The project was limited to 16- and 17-year-olds who were beyond the age of compulsory school attendance. The facility did not provide formal education but stressed vocational development and focused upon providing work for the boys for which they were paid. The expectation was that after experiencing the short-term treatment program, the boys would be much less likely to participate in further delinquency upon their return to their communities.

H. Ashley Weeks (1958) evaluated the Highfields Project by comparing the success rate of boys who went through the program to that of boys who had committed similar offenses but who were sent to Annandale Farms, the New Jersey State Reformatory for males. Weeks addressed three basic research questions:

1. Did delinquents who participated in the program show lower recidivism rates than boys in other kinds of programs?
2. Did delinquents in the program change their attitudes, values, and beliefs about their families, the law, and their perspectives on life?
3. Did delinquents in the program change their basic personalities or the behavior through which they demonstrated their personalities?

In answer to the first question, recidivism rates were lower for the Highfields participants, but not dramatically. The answer to the second and third questions was no (Weeks, 1958). Still, the project was viewed as having been effective with a large number of the boys.

The Provo Experiment

The Provo Experiment was begun in 1956 in Provo, Utah. It was based on the Subcultural and Differential Association Theories of delinquency (see Chapters 6 and 7). The Provo Experiment insisted that delinquency is acquired from social groups and the only way to treat it is in a group context.

Habitual juvenile offenders between the ages of 15 and 17 were assigned to the Provo Experiment utilizing the Pinehills Center for many of its activities. Boys lived at home but participated in various group programs at the center during the day. The program was based on the assumption that when boys are around other boys, peer pressure becomes the primary motivation for behavior. The Provo Experiment attempted to capitalize upon that peer influence by putting the boys into social situations in which pressure from within the group would lead to conformity to social norms. The experiment attempted to make conventional and delinquent alternatives clear to the participants; lead delinquents to question the value and utility of delinquent activities; and help conventional alternatives appear more positive to the boys (Empey and Rabow, 1961).

There was no specified length of stay in the program. Emphasis was placed on developing good working habits and seeking to find meaningful employment for the boys in the community. Overall, Empey and Rabow (1961) viewed the Provo Experiment as successful. They suggested that changing the boys' attitudes and values toward work, while they experienced group encouragement and support for conformity to conventional norms, helped reintegrate them into the community in a way that was likely to reduce further involvement in delinquency.

The Millcreek Youth Correctional Facility

The Millcreek Youth Correctional Facility for serious offenders, located in Ogden, Utah, emphasizes social responsibility in its rehabilitation efforts. The maximum-security facility houses approximately 60 of the most dangerous and violent juvenile offenders in Utah (NBC News, 1987). Although monitored by closed-circuit television, kept behind locked doors, and surrounded by a high fence, the youths are encouraged to contribute to the social group and environment to which they belong and are rewarded for doing so. Group counseling, intense social interaction with positive role models (workers and counselors in the facility), and positive reinforcement seem to make dramatic changes in the youths' behavior after release. When Barry Krisberg studied the Millcreek program, he found that released youths had fewer arrests, and, if arrested, had committed less-serious offenses (NBC News, 1987).

The Paint Creek Youth Center

The Paint Creek Youth Center in Bainbridge, Ohio, is an example of a cooperative effort funded by state, federal, and private sources that serves up to 34 males convicted of first- or second-degree felonies. It focuses on developing occupational, independent living, and social skills while providing drug and alcohol counseling, and teaching problem-solving techniques, values clarification, victim awareness, anger management, personal hygiene, and human sexuality (OJJDP, 1988). A follow-up study on former residents of the Paint Creek facility showed disappointing results, however, with self-report delinquency data indicating virtually no difference between boys who had been through the program and those who had not (Greenwood and Rand, 1993). The famous Boys Town established by Father Edward Flanagan in Nebraska in 1917, however, reportedly still enjoys moderate success carrying out a similar agenda (Santoli, 1992).

Project New Pride

Project New Pride began in Denver, Colorado, in 1973 and has since been copied across the United States. The project's goal is to reintegrate hard-core juvenile offenders between the ages of 14 and 17 back into the community so they can become productive family members, students, and workers. Each juvenile who participates in the year-long project is intensively involved in alternative schooling, counseling, and job training for a six-month period and then slowly reintegrated into the community over the following six months, during which they are expected to attend school and work at a job.

Project New Pride also offers counseling to the families of the juveniles who participate in the program. Like other community correctional programs, the success rate of Project New Pride is difficult to determine, but it is considered to be a cost-effective approach to juvenile corrections, usually costing approximately one-fifth the expense of housing a juvenile offender in an institution (Project New Pride, 1985). Because of its perceived success, Project New Pride has been replicated in several states and still operates today.

Mentoring Programs

An innovative approach to delinquency prevention that has been around for quite some time, but increased in popularity during the 1990s, is mentoring. There are numerous mentoring programs across the United States. While they vary in their specific approaches, all share the common element of targeting "at risk" children—those from single-parent and low-income families, and providing them with positive adult role models (mentors). **Mentoring programs** typically *use adult volunteers who commit a certain amount of time each week (2–6 hours) to work one-on-one with a youngster to encourage academic, personal, social, athletic, and artistic development in an effort to prevent delinquency.* These programs are cost-effective, and have been shown to improve school attendance and performance, reduce antisocial behavior (e.g., smoking, alcohol, and drug abuse), and otherwise discourage and decrease involvement in delinquent activities (Grossman and Garry, 1997; Probst, 2006).

Big Brothers/Big Sisters is one of the oldest and best-known mentoring programs and served as a model for the federal JUvenile Mentoring Program (JUMP) created in

Mentoring programs for elementary and middle school students have been shown to be effective in delinquency prevention. What sociological theories might help explain the success of these types of programs?

1992 and administered by the Office of Juvenile Justice and Delinquency Prevention (OJJDP). Congress authorized $19 million to fund JUMP, and in 1994–95 OJJDP created 41 mentoring programs that in their first year served over 2,000 at-risk youths in 25 states. Volunteer mentors include police officers, firefighters, school teachers, senior citizens, and business people. A two-year evaluation of the program indicated that mentored youths were less likely than members of a matched control group to skip school, use drugs or alcohol, get in fights, or be involved in vandalism or other delinquent acts. Moreover, the mentored youths reported improved relationships with their parents and peers (Grossman and Garry, 1997).

An innovative program called Discovery, developed in Massachusetts, matches juvenile delinquents with college students who serve as counselors, confidants, and positive role models for the youths. The college students, who have completed a set of prescribed courses in criminal justice, receive college credit for their participation. They meet with the delinquents one-on-one in two-hour sessions between four and ten times during a semester. They also hold group meetings with the delinquents and discuss school, hobbies, dating, relationships, crime, jobs, and other matters of mutual interest. A survey of participants showed that out of approximately 200 juveniles and 200 college students who have participated in the program, all of the college students and over 95 percent of the delinquents expressed satisfaction with it (Greenberg, 1990). The juveniles reported that they had been positively influenced by their college role models, and as a result of the program had begun to think more positively about their futures.

Mentoring programs reflect cooperative efforts among juveniles, parents, and adult volunteers to help disadvantaged youths in an effort to prevent juvenile delinquency. Other programs reflect similar efforts and combine schools, churches, and other agencies in an effort to mobilize entire communities for delinquency prevention.

Other Programs

Bruce Berg (1984) described a program for juveniles tried in an eastern correctional facility which followed social scientific theory in delinquency prevention. This program included the clinical sociological technique of **sociodrama**, *a method involving role playing, intergroup relations, and collective ideologies*. This program, run by inmates, was judged highly successful because of its flexibility, cost-effectiveness, and positive impact upon the participants.

David Farrington (1985) explored the issue of delinquency prevention in the 1980s, and concluded that attempting to change basic social institutions (such as family, schools, and church), along with focusing on individuals, is a worthwhile effort. Similarly, Thomas Gullotta and Gerald Adams (1982) indicated that delinquency prevention must integrate theory and practice. They cited education, competency promotion, community organization, and natural caregiving as being the four important tools in delinquency prevention. A project in Louisiana designed to facilitate reentry into the community by adjudicated delinquents incorporated many of those elements into its program (Behre, et al., 1982). San Diego developed a system wide strategy to reduce delinquency which involved cooperation among social services, criminal justice agencies, and other community organizations. It involved consistent, early intervention for even minor offenses with the implementation of graduated sanctions based on offense history and the nature of the offense. A two-year assessment of the program indicated that it was successful in reducing juvenile crime (Pennell,et al., 1990).

Increasingly, the family is recognized as an important component in the treatment and prevention of delinquency (Wasserman, et al., 2000).

Since there is a long-established link between child maltreatment and delinquency, increasing emphasis has been placed on the role of Child Protective Services in preventing delinquency (Wiebush, Freitag, and Baird, 2001). Social welfare agencies are encouraged to intervene early in child maltreatment cases, conduct thorough risk assessments, and, where possible, provide parenting training and other support services to the family. When it is determined that the child must be removed from the family, emphasis is placed on finding good foster homes with nurturing familial environments that will help to prevent delinquency and other adolescent problems.

While there is a lack of consensus as how best to attempt to prevent delinquency, a common trend in juvenile justice has been toward the deinstitutionalization of juveniles and diversion from the juvenile justice system. Consequently, communities and their various agencies are viewed as playing an important role in delinquency prevention.

MOBILIZING THE COMMUNITY TO PREVENT DELINQUENCY

Various forms of community involvement have arisen to combat delinquency and street crimes. Most forms of community involvement are encouraged as long as they stop short of **vigilantism**—*people taking the law into their own hands.* Law enforcement officials publicly view vigilantism negatively while occasionally unofficially sanctioning it in its milder forms. The reaction of the general public is harder to assess, but at least in some cases, groups and individuals have been applauded for their actions against alleged criminals and delinquents.

Crimestoppers and Hotlines

Crimestoppers, Crime Hotlines, and various other programs encourage citizens to call a particular phone number and provide anonymous tips about various crimes in the area. If the information leads to the arrest and/or conviction of persons involved in a particular crime, some type of monetary reward usually is offered. These programs have become popular, and most large communities, and many small ones, sponsor such a program. Local newspapers and radio stations often participate in advertising the program and helping to fund the rewards, and local television stations often provide "reenactments" of crimes while urging viewers to call the "hotline" if they have any information relating to the crimes.

These programs are somewhat similar to the Neighborhood Watch programs discussed in the next section, except that they do not involve citizens becoming actively involved in crime prevention, or being involved in neighborhood patrols. Rather, the programs rely upon *private citizens informing upon one another.* Hence, we have coined the term **pseudovigilantism** to describe this phenomenon. Vigilantism involves citizens taking the law into their own hands because they feel the state to be unable or unwilling to enforce the law. Crimestoppers, on the other hand, involves private citizens aiding the state in its law enforcement efforts. This is also the intent of the Neighborhood Watch programs; hence they operate from the same philosophical stance. Yet, the Neighborhood Watch programs demand actual community involvement in the law enforcement process, and in some cases, some citizens become far too involved to suit the police. The "hotline" programs involve the sharing of information. A 1986 study of the success of the Crimestoppers and similar programs indicated that community participation in these types of programs is minimal. Two groups seem most likely to participate: the business community and the criminals themselves who may provide information about crimes committed by their associates (Rosenbaum, Lurigio, and Lavrakas, 1986:3). Nevertheless Rosenbaum and colleagues (1986) found that Crimestoppers was a very cost-effective method of social control in that the anonymous tips leading to the solution of previously unsolved crimes (usually property offenses) generally led to the recovery of goods which far exceeded the cost of the monetary awards for the information.

Neighborhood Watch and Youth Crime Watch

Neighborhood Watch programs have been developed in almost every community. These programs are approved by the police and involve citizens joining together to reduce crime in their neighborhoods. These programs are aimed at reducing burglary, vandalism, and other property offenses, many of which involve juvenile offenders. Representatives from the police department usually meet with interested members of the neighborhood and conduct a brief training session on how to reduce property crimes by better protecting their homes with various locks and alarms, and more importantly, how to be more observant. Residents are encouraged to watch each other's homes and to call the police if they notice any unusual or suspicious behavior in the neighborhood. Signs are posted in the neighborhood declaring that it participates in the watch program and that the police will be called. In some cases, however, local communities have formed neighborhood patrols armed with walkie-talkies or cell phones, and occasionally guns, who sometimes attempt to apprehend suspected offenders and make citizens' arrests.

Youth Crime Watch is a specialized version of Neighborhood Crime Watch that was organized when adults realized that youth volunteers often knew far more about what was going on in neighborhoods than did the adults. Youth Crime Watch focuses on good citizenship and involves more than simply watching for criminal activities in neighborhoods. Youth Crime Watch programs receive funding from a national nonprofit organization to: provide drug and crime prevention education, establish youth patrols, create mentoring programs, provide conflict resolution training, establish community networks and partnerships, and send youths to the annual National Youth Crime Prevention Conference (Jones, 1999).

Guardian Angels

One of the better-known examples of **neovigilantism**—*private citizens taking on the role of law enforcers*—is the Guardian Angels. Founded in New York City in 1979 by Curtis Sliwa, this group of young adults and teenagers operates as self-appointed organized patrols of the streets, alleys, and subways of many larger cities. What began as a group with just 13 members by 1982 had over 2,000 members in 41 cities (*Time*, 1982:21). In 1987, the Guardian Angels claimed to have a membership of "over 5,000 in 67 American, Canadian, and Mexican cities," and today, the International Alliance of Guardian Angels has chapters in virtually every major city throughout the United States, Canada, Mexico, and the European continent. They have their own Website and even have a special chapter known as "Cyber Angels" that promote safety over the Internet.

Outfitted in their distinctive red berets, the Angels go out on patrol to reduce many of the street crimes in which juveniles are likely to participate. Members of the Guardian Angels contend they are merely exercising their rights as private citizens and acting within the law as civilian extensions of the police force.

Many law enforcement officials view the Guardian Angels in a different light, seeing them as vigilantes who hamper official law enforcement and could be potentially dangerous. When speaking on college campuses or his radio program, Sliwa vehemently denies that the Guardian Angels are vigilantes, preferring to refer to them as simply "concerned citizens." However, in their own literature they describe their efforts in their "war against drugs" in the following way: "Increasingly, we are being called upon by frustrated residents and small-business owners to assist them in reclaiming their streets from the drug dealers. We have mounted major anti-drug and crackdowns on crack campaigns in Los Angeles, West Palm Beach, Florida and 42nd Street/Times Square in New York."

In the same pamphlet, they estimated that their patrols had made over 800 citizens' arrests and that their presence had deterred countless other crimes. Thus, their actions clearly fit the definition of vigilantism. Where the Guardian Angels differ from most other forms of vigilantism and neovigilantism is that while they patrol, apprehend, and arrest, they do not routinely mete out punishment to their captives. Instead, they detain the alleged offenders until legal authorities arrive to take them into custody.

S.H.O.D.I.

A controversial program in Ventura, California, Colorado Springs, Colorado, and Jacksonville, Florida, is called S.H.O.D.I. (Serious Habitual Offender Drug Involved). Consistent with the assumptions of Control Theory (i.e., if an individual's inner containment is not strong enough to prevent deviance, societal measures of outer containment must be imposed), S.H.O.D.I. concentrates on monitoring the behavior of known juvenile offenders. Using computers, law enforcement personnel study arrest records to pinpoint the serious and habitual juvenile offenders in a particular area. Once identified, their names are placed on a list that is circulated to all law enforcement officers. If stopped, even for the most minor violation, these youths are arrested and taken to the police station. Social workers called "trackers" are assigned to these youths to monitor their behavior 24 hours a day if necessary. The trackers check to ensure that the youths are not violating curfew, skipping school, using drugs or alcohol, or committing any other infractions. While some of the youths' attorneys complain that the program amounts to little more than police harassment and unfair labeling of their clients, law enforcement officials are convinced that it is an effective way to reduce juvenile delinquent activities (Kline, 1993; *NBC News*, 1987).

Gang Intervention and Prevention Programs

Increased gang activities spawned numerous delinquency prevention programs. Along with the increased efforts of law enforcement personnel to thwart the illegal drug trafficking and increased violence among juvenile gangs, other groups formed to help rid their neighborhoods of gangs and their activities. One such group called "Mothers Against Gangs" was organized to focus increased media attention on the problem of teenaged gangs and their victims, in much the same way that MADD (Mothers Against Drunk Driving) did with the problem of drunk driving.

Other communities have decided that uniting mothers against gangs may be an important first step, but is not enough. Orange County, California, has developed a community-wide antigang program that includes monthly meetings of law enforcement officials, school counselors, parents, and gang counselors in an effort to provide night and weekend activities for teenagers as an alternative to becoming involved in gangs. Costa Mesa converted a former junior high school into a teen center and also utilizes YMCA, school, and church facilities to provide meaningful activities for teens (Ramirez, 1994). New York City offers similar programs and includes conflict resolution as part of its program encouraging teenagers to sign contracts that they will not resort to violence when they have disagreements with their peers (Minton, 1995). And Fort Worth, Texas, initiated a controversial program in which the city hired six known gang leaders to work with the police department as gang counselors, prepared to intervene and negotiate peace between rival gangs, discourage recruitment of new members, and dissuade violence (Douglas and Martin, 1994; Floyd, 1994).

Community-based gang intervention programs are highly controversial, and very little research has been conducted to evaluate their effectiveness. One program, however, has been systematically evaluated, and apparently has been effective in reducing gang membership and violence. *Neutral Zone,* a program developed in Mountlake Terrace, Washington, and replicated in several other Washington communities, offers already gang-affiliated and potential gang members attractive and safe recreational and social activities as alternatives to running with their gangs on Friday and Saturday nights. Data collected from direct observation, interviews, and official crime statistics indicate that the program has been successful in reducing gang activities and other delinquency (Thurman, et al., 1996).

Research indicates three major facts: (1) gang formation is not limited to urban underclass areas, (2) gang members come from a variety of backgrounds and are not limited to males, the poor, minorities, or children of single-parent families, and (3) once juveniles join a gang, they usually become involved in criminal activities. Consequently, efforts to prevent gang involvement must be aimed at the entire youth population and must involve all the major social institutions, including family, school, church, social agencies, and law enforcement (Esbensen, 2000; Huff, 2002).

EVALUATION OF DELINQUENCY TREATMENT AND PREVENTION STRATEGIES

In this chapter, we summarized evaluative studies of delinquency treatment and prevention strategies where they are available. One of the frustrating aspects of delinquency prevention and treatment, however, is the lack of systematic research on both the short-term and long-term effects of most programs (*Law Enforcement News,* 1997; Krisberg, 2005). Moreover, when research on the effectiveness of treatment and prevention programs is conducted, the results are often mixed (Zimring, 2006). If we review the research that has been conducted, however, some general trends and patterns can be discerned.

Research indicates that the medical model that dominates many of the delinquency treatment programs—especially those related to alcohol and drug abuse—is inadequate because it focuses on the individual and symptoms rather than causes of problems,

Why are dispositional alternatives such as performing community service sometimes more effective than harsher measures such as incarceration?

ignoring the larger social context in which the delinquency occurs. Many of the sociologically based prevention programs, however, have met with moderate success. In general those programs that have focused on involving entire communities and the important institutions within which juveniles interact on a daily basis—family, school, church, neighborhood, and so on,—have met with the most success (Lipsey, 1999; Whitehead and Lab, 2006). Moreover, the most successful strategies have been those where parents, businesses, social agencies, school officials, and law enforcement agencies have combined efforts to reduce, control, and prevent delinquency. Still, in the end, when two very important questions are posed—"Do treatment and prevention strategies work?" and "Do you get what you pay for?"—unfortunately the most accurate answer is: "Not necessarily" (*Law Enforcement News*, 1997). This prompts us to urge a dramatic "rethinking" of the delinquency problem in the next and final chapter of the book.

Summary

This chapter examined the treatment and prevention ideologies in juvenile corrections and described some specific treatment and prevention strategies used for juvenile delinquents. Clearly, traditional delinquency treatment and prevention programs have been dominated by the medical model and psychiatric approach. Hakeem (1957–1958) indicated that the psychiatric approach focuses upon predelinquency, its causes, symptoms, and cures, and that while the psychiatric approach carries great prestige, its lofty status is not deserved. He charged that it is based on very little empirical verification and that the labeling of children as predelinquent is arbitrary and sometimes even whimsical. He urged that sociologists should turn to their own concepts and theories to develop programs for the treatment and prevention of delinquency. Likewise, the sociologist and criminologist Donald Cressey (1955) lamented that when dealing with corrections, even sociologists often have ignored sociological theories and reform techniques. He insisted that delinquents are products of social interaction and any attempt to reform them must focus upon social groups and group processes.

We then reviewed some of the treatment and prevention programs which have incorporated sociological theory into their strategies. Some of the classic delinquency programs were discussed and the evaluations of their relative strengths and weaknesses presented.

Recent trends in preventing and treating delinquents have turned toward community involvement. Evaluations of these various programs have produced mixed conclusions.

While it is important for society to develop new and innovative approaches to dealing with delinquents and delinquency, it is equally important that its members not get caught up in what Finckenauer (1982) called the "panacea phenomenon." As he pointed out, the search for a "cure-all" persists because of two rather naive and simplistic ideas: "doism" and "newism." "Doism" is the ". . . . belief that it is better to do something than nothing," and "newism" is the "appeal of approaches or programs because they are new" (Finckenauer, 1982:27).

From the sociological perspective, it is unrealistic to assume that society can eliminate a problem such as juvenile delinquency. Rather, social control, treatment, and prevention programs should be aimed at reducing the number of deviant acts, and, more importantly, at reducing their negative social impact. Many of the programs described in this chapter have shown evidence of success, while others have been much less effective. Delinquency is such a complex phenomenon that any attempt to control, treat, or prevent it must take its complexity into account. As Hurley (1985:68) indicated, "There is no field of knowledge that does not apply to delinquency, barring perhaps Plate Tectonics." Similarly, Sheldon Rose and Jeffrey Edleson (1987:xiii) argued for the "multi-method approach" to dealing with delinquency which "draws upon problem-solving techniques, the modeling sequence, and an operant, cognitive change, relaxation, socio-recreational, small-group, relational, and extra-group methods of intervention."

In keeping with the theme of this book, it is our contention that juvenile delinquency is inherently social in nature and that any meaningful attempts to deal with it will have to approach it within the social context in which it occurs. In Chapter 17 we explore a sociological approach to rethinking the problem of juvenile delinquency.

Concept Integration: Questions and Topics for Study and Discussion

1. Explain the treatment ideology in juvenile corrections. What are some of its strengths? What are some of its weaknesses?
2. Explain the prevention ideology in juvenile corrections. What are some of its strengths? What are some of its weaknesses? How can this ideology be implemented from a sociological perspective?
3. Summarize some of the major treatment programs for juvenile delinquents in the United States. What are the major weaknesses of these programs? How might they be improved to overcome those weaknesses?
4. Summarize some of the major prevention programs for juvenile delinquents in the United States. What are the major weaknesses of these programs? How might they be improved to overcome those weaknesses?
5. How has the sociological perspective been applied to delinquency treatment and prevention programs? Devise a hypothetical plan utilizing sociological concepts for your own community which could treat and prevent delinquency.

Chapter 17

Rethinking the Delinquency Problem

READING OBJECTIVES

Reading this chapter will help you achieve the following objectives:

1. Briefly review the social nature of juvenile delinquency and the social processes involved in defining, treating, controlling, and preventing this social problem.
2. Summarize some of the major recommendations that have been made for rethinking the problem of juvenile delinquency.
3. Reexamine various social values, norms, laws, institutions, policies, and issues associated with juvenile delinquency.
4. Explore some imaginative and innovative ways of creating meaningful social change to help alleviate some of the social conditions which contribute to juvenile delinquency.
5. Explore the redefinition of juvenile delinquency.

INTRODUCTION

In this final chapter, we underscore the social nature of juvenile delinquency and present suggestions and recommendations to help alleviate the problem. Many of these suggestions come from leading professionals in the fields of law, criminology, social work, and the social and behavioral sciences and some are uniquely ours. Some of the recommendations have been attempted and implemented, and others have been routinely ignored.

We have reached the point where most textbooks on juvenile delinquency come to a conclusion. The ending is often highlighted by a nebulous summation—something to the effect of "now that we have defined, explored, and examined the nature of the problem, further research is needed in order to provide a more thorough understanding. . . ." As Haskell and Yablonsky (1978:543) noted: "Sociologists are reluctant to make recommendations for changes in the law, . . . the criminal justice system, or in correctional policies. The prevailing attitude . . . is that sociologists should maintain scientific objectivity in their studies, report the results of their research, and leave the conclusions to be drawn by others."

Perhaps it is the nature of our traditional scientific training that makes many sociologists reluctant to make suggestions for intervention strategies. Or perhaps it stems from the fact that sociologists are essentially theoreticians and not practitioners. From a pragmatic standpoint, it may be that it is much easier to discern and describe the nature of a problem than it is to suggest ways of dealing with it. Whatever the case, one of the most frustrating experiences for students of sociology has been the tendency for sociologists to eagerly participate in the exploration, discussion, and critique of social issues, only to retreat from any meaningful attempt to resolve them. Our own backgrounds and experiences tempt us to do the same thing. However, we agree with the assertion that "sociologists with years of experience in the field of delinquency should freely present their opinions and recommendations, even though many of their assertions are not based on firm empirical evidence" (Haskell and Yablonsky, 1978:544). For it is also an intrinsic part of our established perspective to exercise a *sociological imagination* (Mills, 1959) in which we apply knowledge and expertise in creative and innovative problem-solving ways.

We should first acknowledge that not everybody believes that meaningful social changes are necessary in order to handle juvenile delinquency. There are those who believe that all that is needed to curb delinquency is stricter rules, better law enforcement, and harsher punishments. This "get tough on crime/delinquency" attitude surfaces from time to time, as the social and cultural pendulum swings from the more liberal to the more conservative to the reactionary. We suggest, however, that any meaningful approach to the social problem of delinquency must go beyond the mere "tightening" of social control on youths. Rather, large-scale changes in cultural attitudes, values, and beliefs, along with changes in social institutions and practices, are necessary if the challenge of dealing with juvenile delinquency is to be met. We challenge the reader to approach this chapter with an open mind and to explore the possibilities for social change presented herein.

THE SOCIAL NATURE OF JUVENILE DELINQUENCY

Adolescence is a social product that reflects the dominant attitudes, values, and beliefs of American culture. Largely as a result of urbanization and industrialization, Americans created the concept of adolescence and its accompanying normative expectations in an effort to differentiate and regulate the social status, role, and legal treatment of people in this category from adult members of society. One of the results was the prolongation of the period of transition from childhood to adulthood. Another was the creation of a new form of social deviance—juvenile delinquency.

Prolonging the transition from childhood to adulthood in urban industrial America has been functional in many ways. For example, it has extended the time spent on formal education, delayed entry into the work force, delayed marriage (which in turn has had positive effects on reducing birthrates), and extended the period of time available for anticipatory socialization into future adult roles. On the other hand, it also has had some negative consequences. One of these is the *marginality* experienced by individuals who have biologically and physiologically matured into young adulthood, while socially and legally being denied access to meaningful adult roles.

Paul Goodman (1962), in *Growing Up Absurd,* laid the philosophical foundation for understanding the unique problems experienced by U.S. youths. He pointed out that a youth subculture forms, in part, in response to the difficulty of growing up in a society that forces adult values upon juveniles who are not allowed to fully participate in the social system. As Frank Musgrove (1965) pointed out, the creation of adolescence, and the fact that youths experience social "limbo," denies them the opportunity to acquire the basic skills, knowledge, and other attributes required in adult life. The marginal status between child and adult, contributes to adolescent deviance and a vast amount of misunderstanding and negative stereotypes toward American youths (Males, 1996, 1999; Marvel, 2002).

How to react to the social deviance of youths has been problematic for American society. Floundering among the divergent philosophies of protecting, treating, rehabilitating, and punishing juveniles for their misbehavior, policies and programs have been developed that have attempted to do one or another, or all simultaneously. While there have been numerous individual successes, overall the result has been over a century of indecisive and ineffective efforts toward alleviating the problem of juvenile delinquency.

In an effort to stem juvenile delinquency and prevent adult crime, some argue that America's adolescents not only have been *marginalized*, but also *demonized*, and efforts have been made to control and criminalize almost all adolescent behavior (Males, 1996, 1999; Marvel, 2002). Media stereotypes have further exacerbated the problem by creating and perpetuating negative stereotypes of teenagers, leading to widespread fear of America's youth (Dotter, 2002; Marvel, 2002; Yanich, 2005). Mike Males (1996) points out that there is even a new word for this demonization, **ephebiphobia**—*the fear of youths.*

A major element of the problem has stemmed from the inability or reluctance on the part of many to recognize and understand the social dimensions of juvenile delinquency. Often viewed apart from its social context, delinquency has been approached as a discrete problem to be studied, analyzed, and treated. The consequence has been disjointed efforts at control and prevention aimed at specific individuals, or, in some cases, when viewed more sociologically, at families, neighborhoods, gangs, and communities. The vast majority of these efforts, however, have ignored the broader societal context of juvenile delinquency.

In harmony with this idea of changing the social milieu in order to reduce crime, delinquency, and other forms of deviant behavior, criminologists, sociologists, and behavioral scientists welcomed the urban renewal projects of the 1960s and 1970s. These projects cleared massive slum areas to make way for new apartment complexes and expanding central business districts. Endorsement of the projects was based upon the inaccurate hypothesis that slums have little or no social organization, and the premature conclusion that the lack of strong local social organization was responsible for the high incidence of crime and delinquency in such areas. It was assumed that environmental manipulation such as razing old tenements and clearing out urban blight would strike at a fundamental cause of juvenile delinquency and other social problems.

Unfortunately, the sociological lessons learned from classic studies such as William F. Whyte's *Street Corner Society* (1943) and Elliot Leibow's *Tally's Corner* (1967) were ignored. These works indicated that while social organization in urban slums was different from that experienced by middle-class society, it was far from nonexistent. The traditional urban renewal projects that ruptured social networks and the sense of community exemplify the failure to comprehend or incorporate the social dynamics of a neighborhood in dealing with social problems such as juvenile delinquency.

In a 1967 Presidential Task Force Report, Virginia Burns and Leonard Stern (1967) pointed out the multifaceted nature of juvenile delinquency, and warned that the problem cannot be resolved through small or simple programs. Rather, they suggested a comprehensive effort to change the social system that produces conditions and strains conducive to the development of juvenile delinquency and other forms of youthful misconduct. An assessment of the impact of the Task Force Report 25 years later indicated that little progress had been made, and that many of the suggestions for social reform in that report had been ignored (Conley, 1994).

We agree with Burns and Stern's assessment that a problem as complex as delinquency cannot be resolved through Band-Aid types of programs that treat symptoms rather than basic causes. In fact, we contend that if the social problem of juvenile delinquency is to be realistically approached, nothing short of major social and cultural change is necessary. This change must go beyond projects or programs aimed at individual delinquents, their families, and neighborhoods.

The Office of Juvenile Justice and Delinquency Prevention (1979) acknowledged the significance of social reform in dealing with delinquency. It rejected delinquency prevention programs based upon delinquents' proposed biological differences, personality differences, or learning disabilities. It also rejected all programs based upon early identification and intervention that used criteria such as personality tests, socioeconomic status, broken or intact homes, or the criminal histories of parents. The accompanying risks of labeling and self-fulfilling prophecy were viewed as far outweighing any potential benefits of those programs. The Office of Juvenile Justice and Delinquency Prevention insisted that the programs with the most likelihood of producing long-lasting benefits were those that focus upon organizational change, especially those that utilize the school as one of the critical institutions for implementing social change.

From a sociological perspective, juvenile delinquency is inherently social in nature. From the cultural values that undergird the social norms defining delinquency, to the peers, parents, teachers, police, juvenile courts, correctional institutions, and media that react, reinforce, and respond to it, the social dimensions are ever present. Consequently, if society is to deal effectively with the problem of juvenile delinquency, its members must evaluate the problem in its broadest and most fundamental social context. This necessitates the total *rethinking of the problem of delinquency*—its definition, its social causes, social context, and its social consequences. In our view, this process of rethinking the problem necessitates eliminating or at least reducing the social and legal marginality experienced by juveniles. It also should include standardizing juvenile codes (or eliminating them altogether), decriminalizing status offenses, revising juvenile courts, and modifying juvenile corrections. Further, such an effort must include strengthening the family institution, changing the educational system to provide improved socialization, and totally redefining the concept of juvenile delinquency.

ELIMINATING THE MARGINAL STATUS OF JUVENILES

The marginal status of youths and the ambiguous normative expectations associated with their social positions may weaken their social bonds with larger society. As social control theorists point out, the weaker the social bond the stronger the likelihood of norm violation. It has been argued that one of the most significant steps toward delinquency reduction would be to provide youths with more meaningful roles and enhanced status in society. For example, Haskell and Yablonsky (1978:546) indicated that society should "remove blocks to adult status," especially in regard to the legal and illegal discrimination in employment faced by youths. Roy Lotz and associates (1985:353) pointed out the importance of integrating youths into activities and decision making in the larger society: "Quite simply, many youths do not feel that they belong to, or make any difference to, the communities where they live. And persons who behave irresponsibly may do so, in part, because they have few opportunities to be responsible."

This position is confounded by the phenomenon of rapid social change in today's society. It is no longer easy to predict what the future will be as technology further impacts upon society, culture, and lifestyle, so it is difficult for today's youths to foresee their future places in society.

Nevertheless, there are at least two ways society could reduce or eliminate the marginal status of adolescence and the resulting alienation and norm violation of today's youths. First would be to establish meaningful rites of passage into adulthood near the onset of puberty. Second is to accompany those rites of passage with innovative and appropriate social expectations and opportunities to participate in important decision-making social roles.

Rites of Passage

Throughout the life course, individuals move through a series of age-related phases or stages of development. The **life course** refers to *the successive role and status changes that each person occupies in society as a consequence of growing older.* Arnold Van Gennep ([1908] 1960) was one of the first to conceive of life as a series of passages or transitions from one stage to another and from one biological phase and social status to another. These transitions are both biological and social, for while physical aging may be perceived as a biological–physiological process, how a person is viewed and treated at any particular age is based on sociocultural definitions. The life course is graphically illustrated in Figure 17.1.

You will note in Figure 17.1 that the upper horizontal line depicts the life course as the individual develops through the biological stages of childhood, adulthood, and old age. Each of these three stages is set apart and delimited by the physiological events of birth, puberty, menopause (medical science indicates that males may also experience a form of menopause), and death.

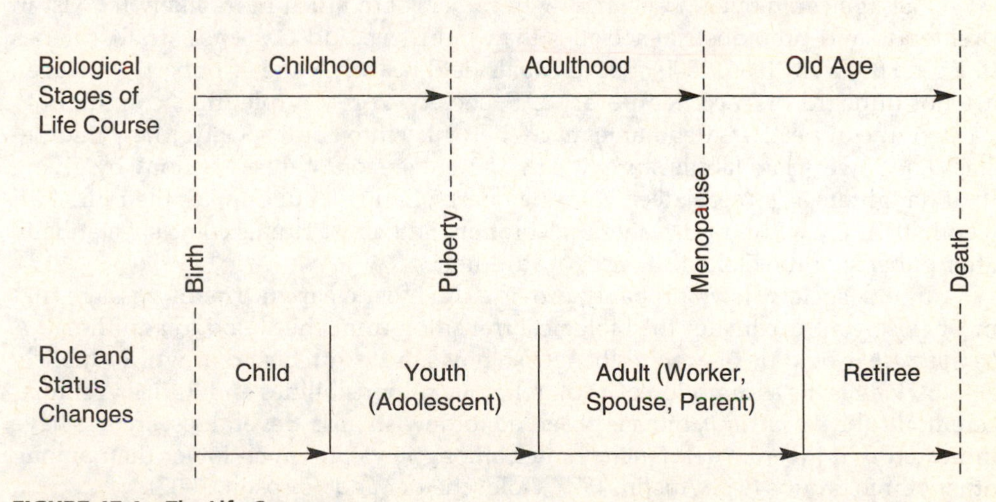

FIGURE 17.1 The Life Course.

Can you go back and look at Life Course and Maturation theories in Chapter 8 and see how they relate to this figure?

Source: Based on Arnold Van Gennep. *The Rites of Passage* (translated by Monika B. Vizedom and Gabriel L. Caffee). Chicago: University of Chicago Press, 1960 [1908].

In many small and preliterate societies these natural events parallel the simple sequence of social roles and statuses that are imputed to people during their lifetimes. For example, in American Samoa, puberty is a time of family and community celebration and ceremony as children leave childhood behind and take on the rights and responsibilities of adulthood (Mead, 1928). Later, as an individual's physical strength and reproductive powers decrease, public acknowledgment and ceremony again implement the transition from adult worker to an honored social role associated with advanced age. Van Gennep ([1908] 1960) called these ceremonies linking age changes and other biological phenomena with changes in social status "rites of passage." Wendall Oswalt (1986:106) defined a **rite of passage** as *"ceremonial recognition of a major change in social status, one that will alter permanently a person's relationship with members of the greater community."*

In contemporary U.S. society, we practice several ceremonies that serve as symbolic passage rituals. For example, christening and baptismal ceremonies, high school graduation exercises, college commencements, wedding ceremonies, retirement parties, and funerals all serve to ritualize and formalize the transition from one life stage and social status to another. Many of these ritual events, however, have little or no relationship to the biological stages of the life course. Again referring to Figure 17.1, the lower horizontal line represents the sequence of different roles and status positions that most persons experience in contemporary American society. In contrast to the societies referred to earlier, in which the transition from childhood to adulthood is easy and natural, there is a rather uneven "fit" between many of the biological stages and the different social roles and status positions one is expected to occupy. Especially problematic is the artificial social stage of *adolescence* which cuts across the two naturally occurring biological life stages of childhood and young adulthood.

Passage ceremonies associated with puberty are much more likely to exist in preliterate and preindustrial societies than industrial and post-industrial societies like ours (Oswalt, 1986, 2005). Social rituals held near the time of puberty, however, are not unheard of in contemporary U.S. society. For example, the "coming out" party of the upper-class debutante marks her entry into adult society. Many middle-class and lower-class families provide their own version of this ceremony by giving their daughters a "sweet sixteen" birthday party; Latina families mark their girls' fifteenth birthday with a quinceañera celebration. Still, these rituals come substantially after puberty or the biological onset of adulthood.

In our society, Jews probably provide the most clear-cut rite of passage that most closely approximates the biological transition from childhood to adulthood. A *bar mitzvah* is held on or around the Jewish boy's thirteenth birthday, which publicly acknowledges his assumption of adult religious responsibilities and duties. A similar ceremony, the *bat mitzvah,* often is observed for Jewish girls. Several researchers have indicated that juvenile delinquency rates among Jews are much lower than among other ethnic groups (e.g., Austin, 1977; Goldscheider and Simpson, 2007).

Bret Stephenson (2007), a counselor for at-risk adolescents, points out that for tens of thousands of years, cultures have raised boys who made the transition to manhood without the need for juvenile courts, youth detention centers, residential treatment facilities, and military-style boot camps. These cultures did not, and many today do not, experience vandalism, teen violence, and other forms of delinquency,

Could American society develop a secular rite of passage that might be as effective in reducing marginality and easing the transition from childhood to adulthood as the Bar Mitzvah and Bat Mitzvah ceremonies are for Jews?

© Corbis RF

because they provide a smooth transition from boyhood to manhood through meaningful rites of passage. Stephenson contends that the United States could do the same thing for American youths.

Why not develop and encourage meaningful social rituals to symbolize the rite of passage from childhood to adulthood that roughly coincide with the onset of puberty for all American youths? Surely such rituals and experiences are possible for an imaginative and creative society such as ours. Because of the pluralistic nature of American society, different racial, ethnic, religious, and social class groups could devise their own ceremonies that would be meaningful to them. For example, since many Jews already observe such a practice, there would be no need for them to change their ceremony. For other groups, the rite of passage need not have a religious connotation. A secular ceremony focusing upon rights and duties of adult citizenship or some similar topic would suffice. The significance would reside in the symbolic aspects of the ceremony which would signify to all that the young person participating in it was leaving childhood and entering adulthood. In order for such a ceremony to be successful, it would have to be institutionalized and internalized by everyone as being one of the most important rituals in our society. This ceremony could become a time of familial and community celebration and a time of fulfillment and achievement for youths. We have clear-cut rites of passage to ease and announce the transition between other stages of the life course, for example, weddings, graduation exercises, and funerals. However, our culture includes no such standard or widely recognized device for moving our maturing children into adulthood. Why not?

Meaningful Social Participation

A Presidential Task Force Report on delinquency prevention, emphasized that there is a strong need to involve young people in a much more meaningful and responsible way in the affairs of society that affect them (Burns and Stern, 1967; Conley, 1994). The Juvenile Justice Standards Project (1977:2) also insisted that juveniles "should have the right to decide on actions affecting their lives and freedom, unless found incapable of making reasoned decisions." Adolescence is perceived by many as a time of irresponsibility, confusion, and financial dependency, yet many older teenagers are eager to assume the responsibility of young adulthood.

The Youth Development and Delinquency Prevention Administration (1972: 28–30) addressed the problem of lack of meaningful social roles on the part of adolescents and suggested the following principles:

1. Delinquent behavior in the young has as its most general cause the exclusion of the young from socially acceptable, responsible, and therefore personally gratifying roles.
2. Roles are made available to the young by the institutions in which they participate.
3. With respect to the problem of delinquency, the critical matter in institutional role allocation is the acquisition of roles that impart a legitimate identity to the individual.
4. Since roles are a product of institutional design and procedure, and since obstruction to a favorable course of youth development arises from failure to provide roles creating legitimate identity, a rational strategy of delinquency reduction and control must address the task of institutional change.
5. Among the institutions significant in the lives of young persons during the period of maximum vulnerability to delinquency and/or withdrawal, the school is of central importance.
6. The process through which illegitimate identities are formed and a commitment to delinquent activity arises among adolescents is best understood by contrast with the formation and maintenance of legitimate identity by adults.
7. The tie of the young person to the school as his "institutional home" is maintained and reinforced by (a) the direct rewards of approval for valued academic and social performance; and (b) the indirect rewards of a credible promise of a desirable occupational future.

There is no reason, other than cultural tradition, why juveniles cannot occupy more meaningful social roles that more thoroughly integrate them into larger society. For example, in Ramona, California, a group of youngsters formed Kidco, a successful corporation headed by a 12-year-old boy. The company, staffed by children between 9 and 14 years of age, developed a secret formula for exterminating gophers. Unfortunately, their thriving business was shut down and criminal sanctions were threatened by the state government, because they did not have a license to do extermination work—a license for which applicants must be at least 18 years of age! The corporate head of Kidco, Dickie Cessna, summarized their dilemma: "We do not think it is fair . . . because we are just some little kids who want to do a good job killing gophers and selling manure instead of being out with a gang getting in dutch [trouble]. Still we seem to be in trouble all the time thanks to some dumb laws" (*The Daily Tidings,* 1977:3).

If a meaningful rite of passage is developed that signifies the movement into adult status, why not accompany that movement with the rights, responsibilities, and duties associated with adulthood? Mentoring programs such as those discussed in Chapter 16 could be developed to link youths with positive role models who could help them learn to fulfill social responsibilities and enhance their self-esteem. Young adults could serve on juries (especially in cases involving other young adults). Where communities have experimented with teen courts, the results have been quite positive, reducing overcrowded juvenile courts' loads and providing teenagers with opportunities to learn and use adult values and life skills (Godwin, 1996, Breen, 2006). The National Youth Network, established in 1997, is an example of how young people between ages 14 and 21 have demonstrated that they can team up to help prevent and solve youth problems if given a chance (Gruber, 1998). Youths in this program unite with each other and adults to distribute information, advocate youth involvement in positive community activities, and promote policies and programs that prevent crime and delinquency. Youths also should be allowed to compete for jobs for which their physical strength, educational background and training qualify them, and to serve on school, community, state, and even national commissions, boards, and committees under the direction of older encouraging adults. It makes sense to allow students to serve on local school boards. Some examples of meaningful participation on the part of youths are described in Box 17.1.

In 1971, the Twenty-sixth Amendment was added to the U.S. Constitution changing federal voting laws to allow 18-year-olds to vote. This change came about in response to the complaint that young men aged 18 and over were being drafted to serve in military combat in Vietnam but were not allowed to participate in the political process. Lowering the voting age to 18 was opposed by some, but was considered to be a step in the right direction by most. Perhaps it was not a large-enough step. Should the voting age be lowered even further? In some states, the legal age of criminal majority is as low as 16 years. In many states, juvenile courts can relinquish jurisdiction of juveniles below that age to adult courts where they are held accountable for their criminal actions, especially in the case of serious felonies such as homicide. There are inmates in adult prisons for criminal offenses they committed while only 15 or 16 years old. In those cases, the individuals were considered legally responsible for their actions and held accountable in the same way as adults. In less dramatic fashion, most states issue driver's licenses to 16-year-olds (and some states offer permits or licenses to 14- and 15-year-olds), and hold them accountable for obeying traffic laws in the same manner as adults. We know that juveniles aged 14, 15, and 16 are physically capable of performing many adult functions. Their exclusion from meaningful adult roles usually is based on what is perceived as their emotional and psychological immaturity rather than their lack of physical abilities. Perhaps this so-called *emotional and psychological immaturity* is nothing more than **social retardation**. People in this age group are caught in the social paradox in which they are physically capable (and in some cases even physically superior) of performing roles occupied by their parents and other adults; yet, they are socially and legally prohibited from fulfilling that potentiality. Why? At least, we could eliminate the stereotype that all youths are disqualified and treat full societal participation as an individual matter. American society has moved in that direction at the other end of the life course by eliminating mandatory retirement at age 65.

BOX 17.1

CROSS-CULTURAL FOCUS: Meaningful Social Participation for Youths

- In Great Britain a conference on Youth Participation is held each year in which teenagers meet with leaders in education, business, and industry to discuss and develop programs which empower British youth and provide them meaningful opportunities to demonstrate their leadership abilities. There is an established need for children and young people to be leading and influencing action that impacts upon them as individuals and society as a whole (http://www.participationworks.org.uk/).
- In Germany, a Youth Participation Resource Centre was established to coordinate nationwide efforts to get young people involved in community service, conferences, and leadership positions where they networked and worked side by side with community leaders in planning and implementing social programs—especially those that affect youths (http://www.eryica-eurodesk eyca.net/2006Compendium/25.pdf).
- In Japan, teenagers are used to help develop and promote a number of HIV/STD prevention programs because research indicates that such programs are far more likely to be successful than those devised and implemented solely by adults. Youths design programs that are more appealing and more persuasive to their peers (Yoshida, et al., 2004).
- In Odessa, Texas, Teen Court was developed to hear cases of defendants between the ages of 10 and 16 charged with traffic violations and misdemeanors such as public intoxication, shoplifting, running away, vandalism, and disorderly conduct. Six teenage jurors make a recommendation for sentencing to a retired district judge who presides over the court. If the youth successfully completes the sentence, all charges are dismissed and no criminal record is maintained.
- In Lockesburg, Arkansas, a 13-year-old was elected to serve on the City Park Committee. His membership was not an honorary position. Rather, he served as a full-fledged active member. During the summer months he devoted a great deal of time to working at the park. During the school year, he attended all meetings of the committee and worked weekends on park responsibilities.

What do all theseexamples share in common? They all represent social situations in which teenagers have been treated as responsible citizens. Each refers to actual cases in which individuals legally considered minors—"adolescents" or "juveniles"—have been judged to be mature enough to be held accountable for their actions in the same manner as adults.

These items indicate that treating teenagers as adults is not totally unheard of in American society. Doubtless, there are numerous other specific examples which could be included here. However, that is not the norm. Typically, people under the age of majority are not granted the rights or the responsibilities commonly associated with adulthood.

Without question, treating teenagers as adults has mixed consequences. If society believes in trial by a jury of one's peers, teenagers should sit on juries. If society believes in policing its neighborhoods, teenagers may be recruited for the job. And, if society believes that it is just to execute its murderers, teenagers may be executed.

On the other hand, if society insists on treating teenagers as something other than adults, it can resign itself to innumerable social problems, not the least of which is juvenile delinquency. The choices are difficult, but they eventually must be made.

Using your sociological imagination, can you think of other meaningful ways in which teenagers could take on adult responsibilities and fulfill meaningful statuses and roles in American society?

How and why does meaningful social participation help prevent juvenile delinquency?
© James Marshall/The Image Works

Good judgment, social responsibility, and commitment to meaningful social roles do not magically occur when a person reaches a particular chronological age. Rather, individuals must learn them through effective socialization and the observation of exemplary role models. In addition, we learn to participate in meaningful social roles through actual experience in occupying them. Within the family, church, and school, juveniles must be provided greater access to full participation in social decision-making processes. Conformity to social norms would be more likely if juveniles participated in the norm-creating and norm-interpreting processes. As Schur (1973:167–168) commented, "There is some evidence that the most potent deterrent to delinquency lies in bonds of attachment to conventional society." Attachment to conventional society would be enhanced if juveniles were more realistically and meaningfully allowed to participate in it.

STANDARDIZATION OR ELIMINATION OF JUVENILE CODES

Juvenile law is statutory law. That means that each state legislature establishes the juvenile code for its state through the passing of statutes. It is possible that 50 different states may have 50 different juvenile codes. This is also true for criminal codes which are created through the statutory process; however, steps have been taken to standardize criminal codes across the United States. For example, the FBI, which compiles official crime data for all 50 states, the District of Columbia, and Puerto Rico in its annual *Uniform Crime Reports*, sets forth standard definitions for criminal offenses (see Chapter 3). While state legislatures enact their own criminal statutes, most simply reiterate the definitions for specific criminal offenses set forth by the FBI. Consequently the definitions of murder, forcible rape, aggravated assault, robbery, burglary, larceny–theft, auto theft, and arson are remarkably similar from state to state. While states may vary in what they classify as **misdemeanors**—*less-serious crimes usually punishable by fine and/or imprisonment for less than a year,* as opposed to **felonies**—*more-serious crimes punishable by fine and/or imprisonment for more than a year,* the fact that all of these acts are classified as *criminal* to some degree standardizes the legal codes.

Much of the dilemma in defining delinquency stems from the lack of standardization of juvenile codes. One way to resolve this problem would be to standardize juvenile codes across the country by establishing uniform minimum and maximum ages for the jurisdiction of the juvenile court, perhaps ages 7 to 16. Sixteen might be the logical age cutoff between juvenile and adult, since, as Regnery (1985:1) noted, 16-year-old boys commit crimes at a higher rate than any other single age group, and "these are criminals who happen to be young, not children who happen to commit crimes." The remaining question would be whether there should be any circumstances under which an individual under the maximum age of jurisdiction should be remanded to the adult criminal court. If juvenile courts and juvenile corrections were significantly changed, this might not be as significant an issue as it is today. We discuss some possible revisions later in this chapter.

Once the age of jurisdiction is uniformly established, juvenile delinquency should be more clearly defined. Steven Cox and colleagues (2008:12) pointed out: "A basic difficulty with legal definitions of delinquency is that they differ from time to time and from place to place, an act that is delinquent at one time and in one place may not be delinquent at another time or in another place."

Most of the problems related to inconsistency in juvenile codes are associated with the age of jurisdiction of the juvenile court and that part of the definition which concludes that delinquency is *any act adjudicated as delinquent by a juvenile court.* One way to clarify the definition would be to limit the extent of delinquency to those acts which would be criminal if committed by adults. Thus, juvenile courts would deal only with criminal behavior committed by juveniles. This would eliminate the time, energy, and effort currently focused upon juveniles who commit status offenses.

Another possible option for solving the problem of unstandardized juvenile codes would be to eliminate them altogether. If a meaningful rite of passage from childhood to adulthood were established that eliminated the marginal status of adolescence, it might be sufficient to simply treat those who have been granted adult status as *adults.* This would mean that those considered children would be relieved of legal responsibility for law-violating behavior (this legal responsibility could be transferred to their parents), and those considered adults would be held legally responsible for their actions. As Albanese (1993:14) pointed out:

> The underlying issue here is that the age of majority is arbitrary. There is no magic that occurs at age eighteen that makes one a responsible adult. In fact, we all know some young people who are mature and responsible at age fifteen, and those that are still trying at age twenty-one. . . .

> An alternative is to abolish the age of majority. . . . Instead all crime suspects, regardless of age, would be tried at a fact-finding hearing where some combination of punishment and/or treatment would be determined by a judge after a complete investigation of the suspect's background. This punishment and/or treatment would be administered regardless of age. It would hopefully be gauged to the type of offense, offender's needs, maturity, skill level, and the safety of the community.

This type of change would require dramatic alteration of present cultural and social attitudes, values, and beliefs.

DECRIMINALIZATION OF STATUS OFFENSES

If the decision is made that states should retain separate juvenile codes, those codes should be as precise as adult criminal statutes. Schur (1973:169) recommended that "juvenile statutes should spell out just what kinds of behavior are legally proscribed, and should set explicit penalties for such violations (with perhaps some limited range of alternatives available to sentencing judges)." One way to do that would be to eliminate all status offenses. This does *not* mean that norms regulating adolescent behavior would be eliminated. Instead, these norms would be informal in nature, and their violation would be dealt with *socially,* rather than *legally.* Parents, school officials, clergy, and social workers would enforce these norms and impose sanctions, rather than the police, court officials, and correctional officers. This would limit juvenile delinquency to *only* those acts that would be criminal if committed by adults. The widespread adoption of youth curfews, adolescent loitering laws, and *zero-tolerance* policies have done the exact opposite. More and more adolescent behaviors that are legal for adults have been made illegal for juveniles (Marvel, 2002).

A very small number of youths account for an unusually large proportion of all serious juvenile crime. Longitudinal studies of large birth cohorts over a period of time have found that the assumption that most offenders progress through a delinquent career pattern from less-serious to more-serious offenses is questionable (e.g., Moffitt, 1993; Wolfgang, et al., 1972). Rather, a small number of persistent *chronic* juvenile offenders tend to continue a career of crime into adulthood, committing more-serious offenses as they get older (Wolfgang et al., 1987). Steven Lab (1984) found that the vast majority of his subjects were involved in victimless crimes and status offenses, such as truants, runaways, beer drinkers, and curfew violators, and that over two-thirds (67 percent) ceased their delinquency before the fourth offense, regardless of whether or not they were apprehended and legally processed. Presently, those juveniles must be handled by the same court which handles abused, neglected, and dependent children, as well as muggers, robbers, rapists, and murderers. In an attempt to be "all things to all people," the juvenile court has been criticized as a failure.

The decriminalization of status offenses would reduce the caseload of juvenile courts. This would allow court personnel, judges, social workers, police, and others who work with juveniles to concentrate their efforts on serious juvenile offenders.

There appears to be widespread support for the decriminalization of status offenses. The Juvenile Justice Standards Project (1977) recommended that all status offenses be removed from juvenile court jurisdiction. Charles Logan and Sharla Rausch

(1985) concluded that deinstitutionalization of status offenders is pointless unless it is accompanied by decriminalization of status offenses. Some states have indeed decriminalized status offenses. In those states, the behaviors are no longer considered law violations, and juveniles who engage in those behaviors are referred to child protective services or family courts as opposed to law enforcement and juvenile court personnel. This is not to say that the behaviors categorized as status offenses are not problematic, nor that they should be ignored. Rather, the point is that they need not be treated as *legal* problems. Truancy is a school problem. Running away is a family problem. Many of the status offenses represent social problems that violate adult values about what is appropriate behavior for youngsters. If the prohibited behaviors are considered harmful or problematic, there is no reason why they cannot be handled by appropriate social agencies, family courts, departments of public welfare, and institutions outside the criminal justice system. Families, schools, churches, and social agencies in the community that have relinquished responsibility for youth to the legal system could reassert their significance in the socialization process.

REVISION OF THE JUVENILE COURT

The juvenile court has received widespread criticism from a variety of sources. These criticisms have ranged from assertions that the court is too lenient to claims that it is too harsh; from concerns about its devastating impact on youngsters who come before it, to the shocking realization that to many juveniles it is little more than a joke. Regardless of one's philosophical perspective, it appears almost unanimous that the juvenile justice system, most notably the juvenile court, is in serious need of revision.

Just as juvenile delinquency is part and product of the society that has created it, so is the juvenile court. Any attempt to revise the juvenile court must consider the social milieu in which it operates. As Krisberg and Austin (1978:569) noted: "To state the obvious—the juvenile justice system operates within society. Its efforts and consequences are circumscribed and guided by the social arrangements of that particular historical, material, and cultural context which is society."

In Chapter 14, we suggested the future juvenile court should include limited jurisdiction, full implementation of due process, competent professional judges in every court, adequate and trained court personnel, and wider availability of a variety of dispositional alternatives. Here, we briefly expand on those recommendations.

Limited Jurisdiction

In our view, the juvenile court should not attempt to be all things to all people. By spreading itself so thinly, the court is proving itself woefully inadequate much of the time. The jurisdiction of the juvenile court should be limited to persons under the age of majority who have committed acts that violate criminal laws and bring adults before a criminal court.

Much of what is brought to the attention of the juvenile court could be handled better through other courts, nonlegal channels, other agencies, or, even be ignored. Child abuse and neglect are serious problems and cannot be ignored. But should the same court that handles youthful murderers, rapists, robbers, and burglars attempt to deal with these? We think not. We contend that abused, neglected, and dependent children classified as in need of supervision should be handled in family courts rather than juvenile courts. This would accentuate the fact that these juveniles are *victims* and *not offenders*. Likewise, while status offenses such as truancy, smoking, and drinking may need attention, it is not necessary to deal with them in the same way (or in the same court) as serious criminal offenses.

It should be noted, however, that despite the arguments for the elimination of status offenses from juvenile court jurisdiction, there still are people who believe they should be retained as a function of the juvenile court. These arguments focus on the lack of alternatives for handling such problems, and the belief that families, schools, and other social agencies need the official support of the legal system to deal with the types of problems identified as status offenses (Myren, 1988). While acknowledging that the behaviors associated with status offenses are problematic, we believe that streamlining the juvenile court's jurisdiction is necessary. Consequently, we contend that status offenses should be removed from the juvenile courts, and problems associated with those behaviors be addressed by other social agencies and institutions such as the family, school, church, welfare departments, counseling services, and others. These revisions would substantially limit the jurisdiction of the juvenile court, reduce its caseload, and allow it to focus its attention on dealing with youthful criminal offenders.

In order to facilitate these changes in the juvenile courts, a number of juvenile statutes, criminal statutes, social attitudes, and values would have to be significantly revised. Two very important changes that would help streamline the juvenile court would involve the standardization of juvenile laws within each state and across the nation, and developing a standard age limit that legally distinguishes juveniles from adults in all 50 states.

Due Process

Once the juvenile court is limited to dealing with criminal law violations, the full constitutional and legal rights of all who appear before it must be ensured (Krisberg and Austin, 1993; Krisberg, 2005). Limited due process has made its way into the juvenile court through important U.S. Supreme Court decisions, and an increasing number of juveniles are represented by attorneys when they appear before the court. Currently, however, the juvenile court is not a criminal court in which a clear-cut adversarial relationship exists between the state and the accused. Consequently, all the rights guaranteed to an adult criminal offender are not granted to a juvenile who may have committed the same offense. This should be changed.

If the court's jurisdiction were limited as we have suggested, only juveniles who have allegedly committed criminal acts would appear before the court, and a judicial adversary relationship would exist. The youth would be charged with violating a criminal statute. Though the case would be handled in a special court designed for such a purpose, all the basic rights of due process accorded the suspected adult criminal should also be available to the youthful offender. The right to know the charges, have counsel present during questioning and at the hearing, and the presumption of innocence until proven otherwise should be necessary components of the revised juvenile court. The rights to not testify against oneself, trial by jury, and open access to records also should be included. The right to appeal decisions should exist. The specific details of implementation would have to be worked out in each state (e.g., would the jury consist of adults; or of the literal peers of the accused—other juveniles?), but the complete application of due process should be an intrinsic part of the court proceeding.

Professional Judges and Court Personnel

The role of the juvenile judge is critical, and, if the juvenile court is to be successful, this role must be filled by the most competent people available. Yet, in most states, juvenile judges are either elected by the people or appointed by governmental officials. This is not to imply that they are incompetent, but that the criteria for selection have less to do with legal and professional training than with political activity and party loyalty. Steven Cox and colleagues (2008) lamented that while many juvenile judges have the best interests of juveniles at heart, far too many show unfamiliarity with juvenile codes.

The judge in a juvenile court should at least have a degree in law, be a member of the bar, be knowledgeable about juvenile statutes, and have some experience in legal proceedings. Further, some training in or at least familiarity with the areas of early childhood development, sociology, and adolescent psychology would be beneficial.

In addition to the judge, other well-trained court personnel and consultants should be available in order to carry out the mission of the juvenile court (i.e., protect the juvenile while also protecting society). The specific types of professionals might vary in different courts, but should include social workers, psychologists, and paralegal professionals who would be responsible for background checks, social investigations, and prehearing screening. Regardless of the specific make-up of the court personnel, the judge should have all the necessary professionals to call upon in order to best decide a case. This would require total community support in addition to the hiring of persons for that specific purpose.

Dispositional Alternatives

The availability of wider dispositional alternatives also would necessitate large-scale community support. Often juvenile judges have no choices other than the extremes of incarceration in a maximum-security institution, or outright release. Other alternatives should be available such as placement in foster homes, treatment centers, community youth projects, youth shelters, and hospitals. In most states, these options exist in theory, but in some states, not in practice. The lack of availability of qualified foster parents, lack of proper diagnostic and treatment centers, and the insufficient funding common in most states have limited the dispositional alternatives available to the juvenile judge. Most communities could be offering many more placements than are now being offered.

In Chapter 16 we described some of the treatment and prevention programs that have been developed and tried in various parts of the country. It is imperative that those programs which have been successful be supported, and it is important for sociologists, criminologists, social workers, juvenile justice officials, and community leaders to develop creative and innovative programs so that juvenile judges have a wide variety of dispositional alternatives.

Other Revisions

In 1977, a special conference on Juvenile Justice Standards convened in Washington, DC. Members of that conference concluded their meetings with the following recommendations for revising juvenile courts:

1. Status offenses should be removed from juvenile court jurisdiction.
2. Visibility and accountability of decision making should replace unrestrained discretion and closed proceedings.
3. Juveniles should have the right to decide on actions affecting their lives and freedom, unless found incapable of making reasoned decisions.
4. Role of parents in juvenile proceedings should be redefined, especially when there is potential conflict between the interests of the juvenile and the parents.
5. Limitation should be imposed on detention, treatment, or other intervention prior to adjudication and disposition.
6. Strict criteria should be established for waiver of juvenile court jurisdiction to regulate transfer of juveniles to adult criminal court. (Juvenile Justice Standards Project, 1977:2)

Ira Schwartz (1989) proposed an agenda for juvenile court revision which concluded that the *parens patriae* model of the juvenile court should be discarded. He indicated that delinquency proceedings should be opened to the public and the media so that they are subjected to the same scrutiny and accountability as criminal courts. Overall, Schwartz emphasized that the structure and quality of juvenile courts needed serious improvement, and that the number one priority of the courts should be dispensing justice.

Numerous scholars have made similar recommendations in an attempt to salvage the juvenile justice system and allow it to regain (or gain for the first time, its most severe critics might contend) its credibility. Others contend that the juvenile court and the juvenile justice system that it represents should not be changed, but abolished altogether (see Box 17.2). Hirschi and Gottfredson (1993), for example, argue that separating offenders on the basis of age is arbitrary and that one justice system for all would be better than two. Interestingly, however, they argue that of the two existing systems, the juvenile model is superior to the adult courts (Hirschi and Gottfredson, 1993).

MODIFICATION OF JUVENILE CORRECTIONS

Regardless of whether the juvenile court is kept as is, substantially revised, or eliminated altogether, there remains a need to dramatically modify juvenile corrections. Two necessary changes in juvenile corrections would begin with the disposition (or sentencing) phase of the correctional process. It has been suggested that juvenile sentencing should be *determinate* in nature, and *proportionate* to the seriousness of the offense (Juvenile Justice Standards Project, 1977; Mahler, 1977).

Determinate sentencing refers to *a disposition that specifies a definite period of time for the individual to be incarcerated, on probation, or otherwise supervised by the state.* In other words, rather than placing a juvenile under the auspices of an institution or court officer for an indefinite period of time, the length of sentence would be clearly delineated

BOX 17.2

CONTROVERSIAL ISSUE: Should Juvenile Courts Be Abolished?

Frustration over the juvenile court's inability to effectively handle serious juvenile offenders has prompted many of its critics to call for its abolition. Francis McCarthy (1977) contended that the legal concept of delinquency began to die with the Gault decision of 1967, and indicated that subsequent attempts to reformulate the legal concept of delinquency have failed. He concluded that delinquency jurisdiction should be removed from the juvenile court and be reverted to the criminal courts where the highly valued interests of society as well as the rights of juveniles can be protected more fully. Prominent criminologist Ernest van den Haag underscored that notion when he asserted:

> I would abolish tomorrow all juvenile courts because they have been a terrible failure. I believe that anyone over thirteen should be dealt with in the adult court. (Cited in Bartollas, 2003:86)

Others added their voices to those calling for abolition of the juvenile court in contending that the rights of juveniles and social justice would be better served if youthful offenders were processed through adult criminal courts (e.g., Feld, 1993; 1997; 1999). Acknowledging that most juvenile offenses are misdemeanors in nature, many urge that even in cases for nonserious offenses it is important that the basic legal principles of criminal court be followed. Most of the calls for abolition of separate juvenile courts are accompanied by a push for decriminalization of status offenses and standardization of legal statutes governing juveniles' behavior. Since all cases brought against juveniles would then involve acts that would be crimes if committed by adults, the criminal court is viewed as the appropriate legal vehicle for their disposition. Many of the advocates for abolition believe that while juveniles should be tried in adult courts, it is still important to separate youthful offenders from adult criminals in correctional settings. Very few advocate incarcerating juveniles in adult prisons, although public opinion polls show that a majority of Americans favor youthful felons being treated as adults (Schwartz et al., 1993). Rather than promoting a "get tough on juvenile crime" philosophy, the juvenile court abolition movement represents more of a movement to guarantee legal due process for juveniles accused of crimes.

Others contend that the move to abolish juvenile courts is misguided, and that while the implementation of juvenile justice has been flawed, the philosophy behind it is not. Diane Dwyer and Roger McNally (1987), for example, insist that the *parens patriae* roots of the juvenile court were a response to important necessary legal reforms, and that to dismantle the juvenile court system would be a grave mistake. They argue that transferring youths to criminal courts would not solve any problems other than to express a lack of confidence in the present concept of juvenile justice. In their view, the abolition of juvenile courts would only lead to more problems as misdirected juveniles would be thrust into an already overburdened and equally ineffective adult criminal justice system. Instead of dismantling juvenile courts, they call for a reaffirmation of the basic protective and rehabilitative philosophy of the court and significant reforms to aid in its fulfillment of its original mission of preventing juvenile delinquents from becoming adult criminals.

Former juvenile court judge, H. Ted Rubin, a vocal critic of juvenile courts, echoed the sentiments of those in favor of reform over abolition. Despite its many flaws and shortcomings, Rubin (1979) believes that a separate system of juvenile justice should be retained. He calls for a major overhaul of juvenile courts which would include the elimination of status offenses, prohibition of the right of waiver of counsel, more accountability for juvenile court personnel (especially judges), and emphasis on due process and judicial fairness in handling juvenile cases.

The debate over whether juvenile courts should be retained or abolished continues. It calls attention to one important area of common consensus regarding juvenile courts, however, and that is the agreement that they are not functioning effectively at present.

Based on your reading of this chapter and the entire book, what do you think? Should juvenile courts be abolished? What would be the advantages? What would be the disadvantages? If not abolished, what significant changes should be made?

Sources

Schmalleger, F. and Bartollas, C. 2008. *Juvenile delinquency*. Boston: Allyn and Bacon.

Dwyer, Diane C., and McNally, Roger B. 1987. Juvenile justice: Reform, retain, and reaffirm. *Federal Probation* 51 (September):47–51.

Feld, Barry C. 1993. Juvenile (in)justice and the criminal court alternative. *Crime and Delinquency* 39 (October):403–424.

Feld, Barry C. 1997. Abolish the juvenile court: Youthfulness, criminal responsibility, and sentencing policy. *Journal of Criminal Law and Criminology* 88:68–136.

Feld, Barry C. 1999. *Bad kids: Race and the transformation of the juvenile court*. New York: Oxford University Press.

McCarthy, Francis B. 1977. Should juvenile delinquency be abolished? *Crime and Delinquency* 23 (April):196–203.

Rubin, H. Ted. 1979. Retain the juvenile court? *Crime and Delinquency* 25 (July):281–298.

Schwartz, Ira M., Guo Shenyang, and John J. Kerbs. 1993. The impact of demographic variables on public opinion regarding juvenile justice: Implications for public policy. *Crime and Delinquency* 39 (January):5–28.

(e.g., 1 year, 2 years, or until the age of majority). This would eliminate the unreasonable power and unlimited discretion of probation officers, institution supervisors, and others who determine how long a juvenile is to remain under court supervision.

Proportionate sentencing means that *the severity of dispositions should be equivalent to the seriousness of the offense committed.* A major problem with juvenile corrections has stemmed from the inappropriateness and inconsistencies of sentences imposed upon juvenile offenders. One reads with horror of a 16-year-old juvenile being sent to a detention facility for a period of 18 months for committing homicide, while another youth aged 13 is remanded to an institution for the remainder of his minority (five years) for shoplifting. Remember, the case that stimulated the landmark *Gault* decision involved a young boy who allegedly made an obscene phone call and was sent to a detention facility for the remainder of his minority (six years), whereas an adult would have received a maximum punishment of a $50 fine and/or 60 days in jail for the same offense. Mahler (1977) pointed out that in most states, juvenile dispositions are indeterminate and *not* related to the seriousness of the offense. He contended that juveniles should know where they are going, why they are going there, and for how long. Further, he suggested that a case assessment bureau should be established to assess the gravity of the offense committed, and to prevent courts from imposing sanctions that are inordinately lenient or harsh.

If juvenile court dispositions are to be effective, there must be a wide range of dispositional alternatives available. For juveniles who have committed serious criminal offenses, some type of maximum-security correctional facility is necessary (Lundman, 1993). The message must be sent out to youthful hoodlums who terrorize innocent citizens that they cannot hide behind their juvenile status. Cox and associates (2008) suggested that those juveniles who commit predatory offenses may have to be institutionalized for the good of society. However, they warned that the "out-of-sight, out-of-mind" attitude should be eliminated through the use of programs designed to increase community contact as soon as possible.

In addition to maximum-security facilities, there should be medium- and minimum-security institutions for less-serious offenders. These centers also could be used to help ease the transition of even the most serious offenders back into the community prior to their release. Those incarcerated in the maximum-security facility could be transferred to a medium-security institution after a period of time, and if they successfully adapt to the increased freedom and responsibility there, they could eventually be transferred to a minimum-security facility before being completely released. Thus, the offender would gradually experience increased freedom and responsibility while still under supervision. Assignment to these facilities should not be made on a random basis or convenience, but on the seriousness of offense, prior offense record, age, and other pertinent factors. This plan would necessitate major changes in existing juvenile institutions, and the creation of many new facilities. In addition to institutions, a number of smaller community treatment programs need to be implemented. Neighborhood and community correctional approaches should be applied to less-serious offenses and community treatment programs such as halfway houses, work furlough, probation, and closely supervised parole need to be expanded. This has been attempted in many areas, but economic policies often limit the amount of federal and state funds available to finance such programs.

Schwartz (1989) suggested that juvenile institutions should be closed entirely. He lamented that juvenile correctional facilities are primarily custodial in nature, promote future criminal careers, experience high recidivism rates, and have no place in an enlightened juvenile justice system.

Closing juvenile correctional institutions indeed represents a workable approach to the problem, especially if the decision were made to eliminate separate juvenile codes and to abolish the juvenile court. Under such a plan, juveniles who are institutionalized for status offenses would be handled outside the legal system by other social agencies. Those who committed criminal acts would be handled by the adult criminal court system. If convicted of a crime, they would be sentenced as adults. This does not mean that they should be placed in adult jails and prisons as they presently exist. It might be that society would establish age-graded correctional institutions and separate criminal offenders on the basis of age. For example, separate correctional institutions could be created for offenders ranging from 16 to 25 years of age, while other facilities could house those between the ages of 26 and 45. Still another institution could be designed to house offenders aged 46 and older.

Another possible approach to the corrections dilemma might be to segregate offenders by types of offense, and to separate first-time offenders from recidivists. This would address problems faced today in both juvenile and adult corrections, in that relatively nonserious first-time offenders now often must be housed in the same facilities (and sometimes even in the same cells) with hardened repeat offenders. Most 16-year-old nonviolent offenders share more in common with the 36-year-old property criminal than with the 16-year-old robber, rapist, or murderer. Type of offense and prior criminal record might be more logical criteria for institutional segregation than mere chronological age.

A final suggestion related to juvenile corrections would be to minimize the stigma associated with adjudication and disposition. Along with being determinate and proportionate, sentences should also be *finite*. In other words, once a juvenile (or adult) is released from a correctional facility, or some other disposition (e.g., probation), the individual's "debt to society" should be erased. Haskell and Yablonsky (1978:557) recommended "amnesty upon completion of sentence" pointing out that once juveniles (and adults) have completed their restitution, it should be over. They suggested that arrest and sentencing records should not be publicly available, thus avoiding the stigma that denies equal access to schools, jobs, and other social activities.

Many researchers recommend more community-based delinquency correctional and prevention programs; however, not all communities have equal resources to provide adequate programs. Krisberg and Austin (1978:574) pointed out that the separation of delinquency prevention from basic human needs creates a false distinction, and insisted, "Reducing crime, improving the quality of education, promoting mental health, and supporting family life are several sides to a common, if complex, human service enterprise." Acknowledging the social nature of delinquency, they pointed out that delinquency research indicates that we should encourage the full healthy development of all youths, stating:

> Local centers . . . could offer educational and counseling programs in . . . health, nutrition, mental health, welfare, parent-effectiveness, and employment. Staffed by community people and professionals, neighborhood-based service centers could provide a vehicle for community organization efforts such as public forums on delinquency and related problems. (Krisberg and Austin, 1978:575)

STRENGTHENING THE FAMILY

Over the past two decades, perhaps no social institution has been paid more political "lip service" and yet more ignored than the family. We learned in Chapters 6 and 9 that a strong social bond with the family is one of the most effective insulators against delinquent behavior. Also, in Chapter 9, we explored some ways in which the family can be involved in delinquency prevention. In this chapter we emphasize that in addition to the many social, legal, and judicial changes we have suggested, the process of rethinking the problem of delinquency must also involve strategies for strengthening the family.

When we suggest strengthening the family, we are not referring to the hollow political rhetoric of promoting "traditional family values." This popular phrase often serves as a thinly veiled slur toward everything from dual-career couples, to same-sex couples, to single-parent, and even poor families, and it urges a return to some mythical idyllic family of the past as portrayed by the media in *Leave It to Beaver* and *Father Knows Best.* Such nostalgia may be comforting, but is hardly practical or desirable. Rather, we suggest that meaningful social changes must be made to accommodate and reinforce the importance of the entire spectrum of families as they exist in today's real world—dual career, single-parent, same-sex, blended, stepfamilies, and others. These changes should include but not be limited to:

- adequate and affordable day care for working couples with children and for single parents;
- paid maternity and paternity leave;

- family leave days for parents of both sexes for children's illnesses, parent–teacher conferences, school functions, sporting events, and so on;
- adequate and affordable health care and health insurance for all families;
- equitable pay for women;
- access to affordable education, job training, and vocational counseling for all;
- educational, counseling, legal, and support services for families that suffer domestic violence;
- support services for families in which a juvenile has broken the law;
- social, moral, financial, and legal accountability of parents for the whereabouts and activities of their minor children.

The family is the primary agent of socialization and the first line of societal defense against juvenile delinquency. If we are serious in our efforts to reduce and prevent delinquent activities, our efforts must begin with strengthening the family. Some states now hold parents of delinquent children accountable for the actions of their minor children (e.g., truancy, property damage, etc.), but few if any provide social, financial, or legal resources to families to deal with these troubled youths. If we are to meaningfully rethink the problem of delinquency, we must provide the resources necessary for families to successfully raise children, and then hold them accountable to do so. This involves rethinking all aspects of society and creating a cooperative effort among all social institutions. In that light, we turn to education.

CHANGING THE EDUCATIONAL SYSTEM

Earlier in this chapter we emphasized the importance of providing meaningful social roles for juveniles that give them greater decision-making power, especially in areas which affect their lives. With the possible exception of the family, no social institution more directly influences the lives of young Americans than the educational system. As Richard Lawrence (2007:301) noted, "true delinquency prevention efforts must begin in the family, the schools, and the community." In our opinion, if meaningful social change is to come about in an effort to reduce the problems associated with juvenile delinquency, the schools will need to play a very significant role.

In Chapter 10, we explored the social arena of the school and its relationship to juvenile delinquency and delinquency prevention. At the end of that chapter, we suggested how the schools might take a more active role in delinquency prevention. Those suggestions included, less emphasis on identifying and labeling "predelinquents"; reeducating and resocializing parents, teachers, and students to the problems associated with the success–failure philosophy of the schools; a wider range of tolerance of nonserious rule violations by students; and reducing some of the bureaucratization of the educational process.

Again, we must recognize the social context in which the schools exist and operate. Substantive changes in the educational process must be accompanied by widespread changes in the attitudes, values, and norms surrounding it. Since the Industrial Revolution, schools have tended to be modeled after the factory. Students entering the system are viewed as "raw materials" to be shaped, formed, and molded into "finished products" upon graduation. The factory model revolutionized education, but not all of its results have been positive. The blue-ribbon panel of experts

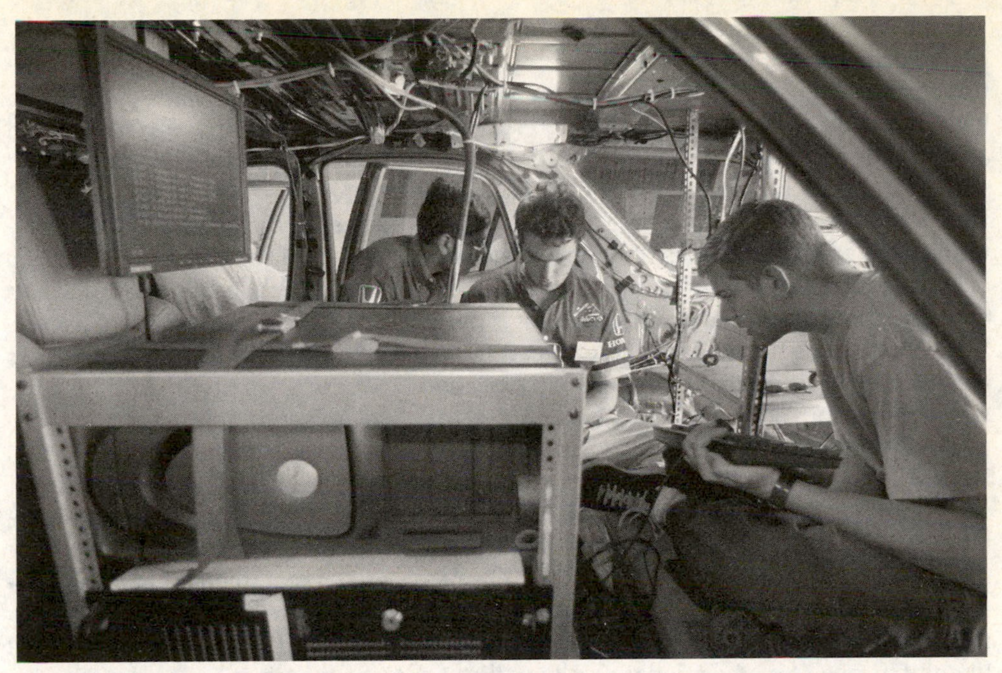

How might providing more high-tech and vocational opportunities in middle and high schools help prevent delinquency?

© Mike Blake/Reuters/CORBIS

who produced the study *A Nation at Risk* (U.S. National Commission on Excellence in Education, 1983) enumerated some of the major problems related to education in America. Even that study, however, did not question the attitudes, values, and norms that provide the foundation for the educational system. Rather, it lamented declining test scores, lack of basic skills, and the failure of the teaching profession to retain the "best and the brightest." While these are significant issues, they do not address the broader scope of the problem. Policies such as "No Child Left Behind" have done far more to promote standardized testing and politicize education than to reform schooling and make education meaningful for youths.

The schools are one of the most important elements in reducing the problems of delinquency, but dramatic changes need to be made in the educational system. For instance, Krisberg and Austin (1978:575) insisted that education must be more broadly defined with an expanded curriculum and a modified idea "about who should be involved in the learning process and where education takes place." They suggested broader community involvement in all aspects of the schools. These and other controversial educational issues must be addressed (Noll, 2009).

In our view, broader community involvement should also include more meaningful participation on the part of juveniles. One of the ways to provide youths with more access to the power structure in education would be to include students on local school boards. This would give them direct input on budget, personnel, and curriculum decisions as well as enhance their identity and status as role models for other youths.

Most colleges and universities allow a degree of student participation in campus government. Students serve on committees, have a student government association, and participate in the evaluation of their professors. These same procedures have not been incorporated at the high school or lower levels. Why not? We are not advocating turning the schools over to the students. Rather, we are suggesting that students should be included in the decision-making process in the school system. J. David Hawkins and Joseph Weis (1980) also viewed the school as one of the potentially most effective sources of delinquency control. They suggested more thorough and broader vocational training, alternative education opportunities, education in civil and criminal law, and more student input into educational programs. We anticipate that more student input might lead to a stronger commitment by students to the common educational endeavor and objective. Such participation would help develop leadership and analytical skills needed for problem solving. Moreover, participation in policymaking and administrative tasks would sensitize students to a broader perspective on many of the problems faced by schools.

Another change to be explored for the public schools is the elimination of compulsory school attendance laws. School attendance is important because a democratic society demands an educated citizenry. Yet many youths feel alienated and experience nothing but frustration and failure in school. When truants are tracked down by police, processed as delinquent, and then forcibly brought back to school, it is not likely that positive educational results will occur. Once a person has undergone the rite of passage denoting the transition into adulthood, the decision to attend school or drop out should rest with that person. If alternative vocational and training programs are made available, the stigma of dropping out of school could be reduced. Those desiring to stay in school and further their formal academic education would not be hampered by having to share limited educational resources with those who do not want to partake of them. Similarly, this should reduce the vandalism and violence in the public schools from those who are "imprisoned" there against their will.

REDEFINING JUVENILE DELINQUENCY

The recommendations made in this chapter amount to nothing short of a total *redefinition* of the concept of juvenile delinquency. In our view, this redefining process is long overdue and essential if society is interested in reducing the problems associated with delinquency. In general, this redefinition must reflect a serious assessment by societal members of what youthful behavior can and cannot be tolerated. Frederick Howlett (1973:492) insisted that "the community clearly must redefine its limits of acceptable behavior." Our current laws prohibit many behaviors that society is willing to tolerate and, in fact, routinely does allow for many. Curfew violation, premarital sexual activities, smoking, truancy, and other status offenses are routinely ignored by some parents, teachers, and law enforcement officials. On the other hand, on occasion, the full force of the justice system may be exercised upon a youth who commits any one of these offenses. Such hypocrisy and random or selective enforcement helps create general disrespect toward the law and the legal process.

Narrowing the definition of delinquency as we have suggested would help reduce the problems of hypocrisy and disrespect. Only those behaviors that are considered beyond toleration by the larger society should be classified as illegal or delinquent.

Schur (1973:154) suggested this approach in his concept of **radical nonintervention,** explaining, "Basically, radical nonintervention implies *policies that accommodate society to the widest possible diversity of behaviors and attitudes, rather than forcing as many individuals as possible to 'adjust' to supposedly common societal standards.*"

The basic principle of radical nonintervention is *"leave the kids alone wherever possible"* [italics in the original] (Schur, 1973:155). At the same time, we suggest that society must seek consensus on some basic nonnegotiable standards of behavior. Those activities that do not seriously threaten the social order would be tolerated; however, those that were deemed beyond the range of tolerance by the larger society would be swiftly and appropriately sanctioned.

We have presented two possible ways in which society can broaden its range of tolerance and reduce some of the problems of juvenile delinquency. One solution is to redefine delinquency so as to standardize juvenile codes and eliminate status offenses. This standardization would include clearly specifying both the minimum and the maximum ages for juvenile court jurisdiction while retaining a sociological perspective on delinquency. Hence, the revised definition of delinquency would be *all acts committed by individuals between the ages of 7 and 16 (or possibly 14 or 15) that would be considered criminal if committed by an adult, place the youth in the delinquent–criminal role, and result in society regarding the juvenile as intolerably deviant.* This new definition alone would resolve some of the problems of delinquency, especially those related to the ambiguity of its meaning. In order for this definition to be effective, however, it would need to be accompanied by some of the widespread modifications and revisions we have suggested in the operation of the juvenile court, and in juvenile corrections. This more concise definition would greatly reduce the quantity of what is considered delinquency, and allow available resources to be redirected in a more effective way toward implementing some of the proposed revisions in the court and correctional system. While the social problem of juvenile delinquency would not be eliminated, it would be significantly reduced. Further, the remaining juvenile delinquency that occurred could be handled more effectively.

A second and perhaps more controversial way to approach the redefinition of juvenile delinquency would be to "define it out of existence." Sociologists view deviance as a natural consequence of the normative system of society. When norms are created, so is deviance. Thus, society cannot hope to eliminate deviance, but must seek methods for controlling it and minimizing its negative impacts upon its members. Consequently, defining juvenile delinquency out of existence will not eliminate the behaviors that currently constitute delinquency. Youngsters would still skip school, run away from home, steal, and even rape and murder. However, while redefining delinquency would not eliminate those behaviors, it would change our reactions to them. Truancy and running away from home would not be illegal acts. Consequently, they would be ignored by the criminal justice system—not ignored by society—but ignored by the legal system. Stealing, raping, and killing, on the other hand, would be crimes—not delinquent acts, but *crimes*—and society would react with justified indignation.

This second alternative would require the most dramatic social changes. Undoubtedly, society would not want to invoke full legal sanctions upon children just because they had reached the age of 7. Instead, children aged 7 would be considered just that—*children.* Children would not be held legally accountable for their actions until they had gone through a formal rite of passage initiating them into adulthood. While this initiation is often associated with the onset of puberty in many societies, it could be adjusted to fit society's agreed-upon age. The rite of passage could be conducted at the age of 14, 15, or 16. From that point on, the individual would be accorded full adult status in society with all the normative expectations associated with adulthood—*rights* as well as *responsibilities.* Thus, any criminal violations would be handled through criminal courts.

There is ample research evidence to suggest that the midteens would be a logical point for legally differentiating between children and adults. For example, Glassner, and colleagues (1983) found that many youths sharply reduced their involvement in illegal activities after age 16. When asked, respondents indicated that they believed that there was a much greater probability of their being adjudicated as an adult and going to prison if arrested after age 16. These findings indicated that being held legally accountable for their actions as adults had a specific deterrent effect on the subjects. Similarly, numerous studies suggest that many juveniles apparently "grow out" of their delinquency somewhere in their midteens and official data indicate that both property and violent offenders tend to peak at about ages 16 and 17 (*FBI Uniform Crime Reports,* 2008).

This **spontaneous remission** or *"aging out" phenomenon whereby juveniles at some point reach a level of maturity where they spontaneously reduce, and eventually even eliminate their involvement in law-violating behavior* may be partially explained by at least three well-known theories discussed in earlier chapters. *Maturation theory* contends that juveniles may "grow out" of their delinquency. *Life cycle theory* contends that as youths progress through the life cycle and assume more conventional roles such as spouse, employee, and others, their values, attitudes, and beliefs are directed toward conformity and away from law violation. *Neutralization theory* can also help explain this process as it contends that delinquents internalize the dominant social norms and are, for the most part, committed to them but through a variety of circumstances may "drift" into delinquency if they can rationalize or "neutralize" their deviance (Sykes and Matza, 1957; 1961). As a youth ages and becomes more mature, he or she is likely to become more committed to conventional norms, making it more difficult to rationalize deviant behavior (Thompson, 1994).

That being the case, perhaps lowering the age of legal accountability to 14 would achieve the same purpose. Youths would know that at age 14 they would socially and legally become adults. This might provide the same type of deterrent effect. In harmony with this idea, we know that young people in our society are reaching puberty at a younger age each generation. Therefore, rite of passage into adult social status would tend to approximate the biological onset of adulthood.

We concur with Stumphauzer's (1986) point that it is important to recognize and reinforce nondelinquency. Unfortunately, most of our attention is focused on punishing delinquents, not on rewarding nondelinquents. More public recognition of conforming and desired behavior by youths could positively reinforce law abiding behavior.

We do not presume to know which direction society should take on this matter. Nor do we presume that these two possible directions in redefining delinquency are the only alternatives. We do believe, however, that it is essential that there be a careful and innovative rethinking of the delinquency problem by our entire society.

This would entail vigorous new directions in research and theory construction to develop theories that can be *applied* by public policymakers and practitioners. More attention must be focused upon social conformity as offering fresh insights into deviant and delinquent behavior. Most researchers and theorists have focused upon the more sensational and interesting deviants, almost to the exclusion of the vast majority of youngsters not involved in serious offenses.

Another dimension to our call for new research and theory emphasizes the need for genuine interdisciplinary studies. Sociologists cannot ignore the accumulating insights from other disciplines. Likewise, other disciplines must not ignore the important contributions of sociology toward explaining and controlling juvenile delinquency.

Summary

The best way to summarize this chapter is to present a list of suggestions and/or recommendations for possible changes that would alter the way Americans view young people, juvenile misconduct, and youthful crime. The goals of these changes would be to more effectively deal with the social problem of juvenile delinquency, and to reduce and/or eliminate its negative impact upon society. Toward those ends, we suggest the following:

1. Delinquency is a social product and therefore must be viewed in its broadest sociological context. This requires societal members to seriously examine the values, attitudes, beliefs, and norms that surround the concept of juvenile delinquency.
2. Reduce or eliminate the marginal status of adolescence. This most effectively could be accomplished by establishing a meaningful rite of passage from childhood to adulthood that roughly coincides with or shortly follows the onset of puberty.
3. Provide meaningful social roles for individuals who have completed the rite of passage into adulthood. Eliminate barriers to reasonable employment based solely on age, and allow full participation in meaningful social roles and decision-making processes.
4. Standardize (or possibly eliminate) juvenile codes. If separate juvenile codes are maintained, there should be a uniform minimum and maximum age of juvenile court jurisdiction across the United States. Similarly, the definition of delinquency should be standardized, simplified, and clarified.
5. Decriminalize status offenses. Legal codes should narrow the concept of delinquency to include only those actions which would be crimes if committed by adults.
6. Revise (or possibly eliminate) the juvenile court system. If separate juvenile courts are maintained, they must be staffed with a wide variety of highly trained specialists. At the very least, all juveniles should be guaranteed the same access to full due process of law as are adults.
7. Modify juvenile corrections. Incorporate determinate and proportionate sentencing into the disposition phase of juvenile justice. Segregate first-time offenders from repeat offenders and nonviolent offenders from violent offenders. Create minimum-, medium-, and maximum-security institutions with emphasis upon community participation in the correctional process, and successful reintegration

into the community as the ultimate goal.

8. Remove the stigma attached to having gone through the juvenile and/or criminal justice system. Punishment for law violations should be finite. Once sanctions have been exercised, societal response to the deviance should end and the youth should be allowed and encouraged to resume his or her life.
9. Strengthen the family by making a wide range of changes that provide social, financial, and legal support for the adequate raising of children, and then hold parents accountable for the whereabouts and activities of their minor children.
10. Change the educational system. Deemphasize the process of identifying "problem children" and "predelinquents." Eliminate the success-failure philosophy which dominates education. Recognize the importance of vocational and technical education as well as traditional academic pursuits, and remove the stigma currently associated with many of those nonacademic programs. Eliminate the "factory model" philosophy of education. Create stronger ties between the community and the schools, and allow students to participate in the decision-making processes in their schools.
11. Redefine juvenile delinquency. Either (a) standardize, clarify, and narrow the definition of delinquency to include only those acts that society clearly cannot and should not tolerate from youths, or (b) eliminate the concept of juvenile delinquency altogether by lowering the age of legal responsibility so that parents would be held legally responsible for law violations of children under the cutoff age, and youthful offenders over that age would be legally handled as adult criminals.
12. Apply new sociological and interdisciplinary approaches to research and theoretical explanations of youthful conformity and deviance. And, apply sociological and interdisciplinary theories to public policy and social practice.

The implementation of some or all of these suggestions would alter dramatically the way our society views juvenile delinquency. Many of the negative consequences of delinquency would be diminished, and perhaps some would even be eliminated. However, it would not eliminate youthful misconduct and law-violating behavior. While youthful deviance might be reduced through implementation of our ideas, as long as we have social norms, we will have social deviance. No society can exist without norms. Therefore, deviance is inherently a part of every society. On the other hand, the way in which society chooses to define and react to deviance can be changed. Perhaps it is time that we do just that in regard to juvenile delinquency.

Concept Integration: Questions and Topics for Study and Discussion

1. Why is it important to view juvenile delinquency within a social context? What dominant values, attitudes, beliefs, and norms surround the concept of delinquency? What social changes would have to occur for society's concept of juvenile delinquency to be significantly altered?
2. Should separate juvenile codes be retained? If not, why not? If so, should they be standardized? Should they be reinforced? Why? Why not? What revisions would you recommend?
3. Do you favor the elimination of status offenses? Why? Why not?

4. Should a separate juvenile court be retained? If not, why not? If so, what modifications should be made in the present juvenile justice system? How might the juvenile court be modified to more effectively deal with the problem of delinquency?
5. What changes would you recommend in the present educational system in an effort to reduce the alienation of youths and lessen or prevent youthful misconduct and law violation?
6. Do you favor redefining the concept of juvenile delinquency? Or legally eliminating the concept altogether? If redefined, what should be the new definition? If eliminated, how would you handle the problems that now constitute delinquency?
7. What rites of passage presently function in American society to ease the transition from childhood to adulthood? Can you think of any new ones that might make this transition easier and possibly alleviate some of the problems faced by today's youths?

GLOSSARY

A Priori A definition of the situation based on earlier pragmatic reasoning and decision.

Achieved Status A status position and level of prestige earned through personal effort that is usually based on educational level, occupation, and income.

Act Conduct or behavior that violates a norm and is legally classified as juvenile delinquency.

Actor The one who acts; the juvenile whose role performance is identified as delinquent.

Adjudication The judgment stage of the juvenile court hearing. Essentially, a juvenile can be adjudicated delinquent, in need of supervision, or neglected, or the case can be dismissed.

Adolescence An artificial stage of the life course in U.S. society between childhood and adulthood in which youths are automatically consigned. Adolescents generally have marginal social status and identity, uncertain roles, and little power or meaningful participation in society.

Adolescent Identity Crisis The role confusion common among U.S. youth as they make the transition from childhood to adulthood.

Aftercare Juvenile parole. Supervised release of a juvenile who must adhere to a set of court-imposed guidelines and periodically report to an officer of the court. Used *after* institutionalization.

Age–Crime Curve The tendency for crime to be committed during an offender's youth that would decline as his or her age advances.

Aggravated Assault One of the FBI Crime Index offenses. An unlawful attack upon another for the purpose of inflicting bodily injury.

Anomie A concept originally developed by Durkheim suggesting a condition of normative confusion or "normlessness" in a society, group, or some persons. The concept (as a general theory of deviance) was expanded by Robert Merton, who said that anomic individuals, frustrated in achieving culturally approved success goals, may turn to illegitimate means of achievement.

Arena A public place where individuals or groups are pitted against each other in struggles to determine dominance and often survival.

Arena Behavior A struggle for status and territory.

Argot Specialized slang or jargon of a particular subculture that promotes group unity and provides a sense of boundary maintenance.

Arson One of the FBI Crime Index offenses. Any willful or malicious burning or attempt to burn a dwelling house, public building, motor vehicle, aircraft, or personal property of another.

Ascribed Status A status position or level of prestige assigned (usually at birth) to an individual on the basis of certain social criteria such as race, sex, and parents' social status.

Atavism A concept developed by Cesare Lombroso of the positive school of criminology. He argued that there is a "born criminal" whose body structure and antisocial behavior reflect an underlying atavism—an earlier, more primitive stage of human evolution.

Audience The members of the social group or society that reacts to the actor and the act and determines if juvenile delinquency has been committed.

Bar Mitzvah A social and religious ceremony that functions as a rite of passage to mark the transition of the 13-year-old Jewish male from childhood to adulthood.

Bat Mitzvah A social and religious ceremony that functions as a rite of passage to mark the transition of the 13-year-old Jewish female from childhood to adulthood.

Behavior Modification Treatment strategy that uses positive reinforcement to encourage desired behavior and negative reinforcement to dissuade undesired behavior.

Birth Order Order of one's birth relative to siblings, that is, first-born, middle, baby.

Blended Sentencing A serious or violent juvenile offender is adjudicated delinquent in a juvenile court or waived to adult court and found guilty of a felony and given both a juvenile court disposition and an adult sentence.

***Breed* v. *Jones*, 1975** U.S. Supreme Court case, which ruled that the double jeopardy doctrine (cannot be tried twice for the same offense) applied to juveniles.

Broken Home Refers to family where one of the parents is not present in the home on a permanent basis.

Broken Windows Policing Police focus on crime and delinquency prevention by reducing criminal opportunities and social disorder.

Bureaucracy A structured organization characterized by a hierarchy of authority; an elaborate system of rules and regulations; where people are treated as "cases" rather than individuals; and where a clear-cut career pattern exists for those working within the bureaucracy.

Burglary One of the FBI Crime Index offenses. The unlawful entry into a structure to commit a felony or theft.

Chicago Area Project Delinquency prevention program developed in Chicago by University of Chicago sociologists, which was based upon an ecological approach to juvenile delinquency. "High delinquency" areas were targeted for programs run by local residents to help deter and prevent juvenile delinquency.

Child Savers Group of concerned clergymen, social workers, and other social reformers during the nineteenth century who embraced the "rehabilitative ideal" for juvenile offenders. Their view that delinquents were products of heredity and brutal urban environments used the "medical model" approach to juvenile delinquency.

Chivalry Factor Initially, females tend to be treated more leniently by police than are their male counterparts.

Choice Theory Focuses upon the present and the choices that people make and the consequences of those choices.

Clique A small group within the youth subculture.

Collective Behavior behavior motivated and influenced by an individual's membership in or identification with a social group.

Collective Efficacy, a group's shared belief in its ability to successfully complete tasks and its extent of social cohesion and trust.

Community Policing Policing that emphasizes cooperative efforts between the police and other members of the community.

Composite Delinquent Profile Based on official sources of delinquency data, it is possible to develop a composite picture of the "typical" delinquent as male, urban, lower class, from a broken home, and so on. However, the composite profile produced by these "correlates of delinquency" may be more stereotypical than typical.

Compulsive Masculinity Exaggerated masculinity, or overemphasis of "manly" traits; believed by some to be caused by the absence of the father from the home.

Concentric Zone Theory A model suggested by Ernest Burgess to depict the concentric pattern of specialized urban land usages and population groupings as they were spatially distributed and organized around the central core of Chicago. Zone II, comprising slums occupied by transitory, impoverished immigrant groups, was considered by Burgess to be especially conducive to crime and other social problems.

Conduct Disorder A term used by the American Psychiatric Association to describe the behavior of adolescents who manifest a repetitive pattern of actions that violate the rights of others and major conduct norms.

Conflict-Oriented Gang In the absence of both legitimate and illegitimate role models, these youths practice predatory violence and intragang warfare.

Conformity Behavior that is in harmony with the dominant normative standards of a social group to which one belongs; normative behavior.

Constitutional Typology A classification scheme of body types that often identifies certain traits of character and personality as corresponding with each body type. A mid-twentieth century version of biological determinism.

Containment Theory A social control theory contributed by Walter Reckless that conceptualizes a double line of defense protecting society against delinquency and other forms of deviance from important norms.

Correlates of Delinquency The statistical correlation or association of certain demographic and social characteristics and factors with delinquent behavior. The data and data-gathering methodologies that support such correlations have been the subjects of extensive debate among scholars.

Counterculture A subculture that rejects the overall attitudes, values, beliefs, and norms of the larger culture and replaces them with an alternative normative system, which conflicts with the larger culture.

Crime-Oriented Gang A youth gang with adult criminal models and committed to such activities as theft, fraud, and extortion.

Crime Prevention Role of Police Police acting as social workers helping juveniles stay out of situations that may lead to delinquency.

Criminal or Delinquent Subculture A subculture that manifests such extreme and negative nonconformity to the normative system of the larger society that its members are generally viewed as antisocial. Its members violate laws as a result of membership in the subculture.

Cross-Cultural A concept incorporated in the content and format of this book to facilitate comparisons of the laws, etiology, treatment strategies, and other dimensions of the national experience with juvenile delinquency in selected countries with those prevalent in the United States.

Cultural Relativity The principle that behavior must be evaluated for conformity or deviance within the cultural context of the specific social group in which the questionable behavior occurred.

Cultural Transmission Theories A group of delinquency theories that share the underlying assumption that the twentieth-century industrialization and urbanization of the United States generated an urban mosaic of ethnic, religious, political, and social-class subcultures, each promulgating and endorsing its own standards of conduct.

Culture The shared and learned beliefs, values, attitudes, traditions, normative expectations, and other forms of knowledge that are passed on from one generation to the next within a society.

Culture Conflict A concept well stated by Thorsten Sellin, who pointed to the abrasive contact between the diverse values, norms, and practices of subgroups within a heterogeneous population, or such culture conflicts between various ethnic minorities, with the dominant culture of the larger society being the seedbed of much crime and delinquency.

Dark Figure of Crime and Delinquency The large amount of violent, property, and status offenses that go unreported to the police and the public.

Decriminalization of Status Offenses A reform of the Juvenile Justice System that would remove truancy, running away, and other so-called juvenile status offenses from the codified state and local laws and from the jurisdiction of juvenile courts.

Defense Attorney Represents the juvenile in juvenile court.

Definition of the Situation, when people define a situation as real, it becomes real in its consequences.

Deinstitutionalization Avoiding the placement of juveniles into correctional institutions.

Delinquency and Drift A variation of Control Theory developed by David Matza, who argues that some ordinarily conforming youths are occasionally unleashed from constraining norms and thus are temporarily free to "drift" into delinquent behavior.

Delinquency and Opportunity An expansion of Merton's Anomie Theory of Deviance applied to juvenile delinquency by Richard Cloward and Lloyd Ohlin. They contend that many lower-class youth not only have differential opportunities for success through legitimate means, but also differential opportunities for achievement through illegitimate means. The kind of illegal opportunities available in a given area, according to Cloward and Ohlin, will determine the kind of gang activity that will emerge: crime-oriented, conflict-oriented, or retreatist or drug-oriented.

Delinquent (adjudication) a juvenile has committed a wrongful act for which the judge feels the youth must be held accountable.

Delinquent Acts as Symptoms A fundamental premise of the psychogenic approach to explaining and treating delinquency is that such misbehaviors are overt manifestations of hidden stress or maladjustment.

Delinquent Gang A group of associating youths with identifiable leaders, organization, and territory, whose lifestyle includes a propensity to engage in collective illegal conduct.

Detention Facilities Places used to detain or hold juveniles who are awaiting a hearing in juvenile court.

Determinate Sentencing A court disposition which specifies a definite period of time for an individual offender to be incarcerated, on probation, or otherwise supervised by the state.

Deterrence Theory A contemporary offshoot of the Classical School of Criminological Thought which takes the position that stern and prompt punishment will successfully discourage many juvenile and adult offenders from repeating their illegal conduct.

Developmental Career The theoretical view of the longitudinal process that results in the fully developed deviant career. This model suggests that there is a developmental history behind the deviant and his or her behavior that involves gradual change in values, attitude, and conduct over time.

Deviant Behavior Conduct that is perceived by society as violating established and widely respected normative expectations for behavior.

Deviant Subculture Any subgroup that deviates markedly from the generally accepted values, norms, and behavioral expectations of the dominant culture.

Dietary Deficiencies This line of inquiry regarding delinquency causation suggests that inadequate nutrition or allergic food reactions can lead to biochemical imbalance and subsequently to hyperactivity and misconduct.

Differential Association Theory A Social Learning Theory developed by Edwin Sutherland that presents a logical sequence through which criminal behavior is learned through primary contact with criminal elements present in one's environment.

Differential Identification An expansion of the Theory of Differential Association by Daniel Glaser who emphasized the extent to which the potential offender identifies with criminal or delinquent role models.

Differential Reinforcement A Learning Theory spin-off from Differential Association by Ronald Akers who suggests that juveniles may be discouraged from repeated misbehavior by punishment or negative social response. On the other hand, some juveniles may continue to pursue delinquent activities because they have received some form of positive reinforcement.

Disposition Stage of the juvenile court hearing where the judge decides what to do with the juvenile before the court. Roughly equivalent to the sentencing stage in adult criminal court.

District Attorney Represents the state in juvenile court cases; prosecutes the case.

Diversion Process of using alternatives for juveniles to remove them from the formal juvenile justice system.

Double Failure A concept suggested by Richard Cloward and Lloyd Ohlin (see *Delinquency and Opportunity*) to describe a youth who fails to achieve material success and enhance social status through legitimate *and* illegitimate means.

Due Process Constitutional safeguards designed to protect persons accused of law-violating behavior. These safeguards must be followed before individuals can be deprived of life, liberty, or property.

Due Process Court Juvenile court characterized by high task differentiation, decentralized authority, high discretion for court services staff. This court routinely handles status offenders and has low formalization.

Dyad A social group comprised of two persons.

Dyslexia A brain malfunction whereby visual signs are scrambled, resulting in a learning disability. This malfunction has hypothesized linkage with delinquent behavior.

Ectomorph A body type in William Sheldon's constitutional typology. He described the type as having a lean and fragile build and possessing a sensitive and introspective personality.

Ego One of the three dimensions of the personality theoretically identified by Freud. The ego in Freud's model is that part of the personality or self that serves as the unifying and pragmatic arbitrator between the impulsive and primal id and the socially sensitive and idealistic superego.

Ego Diffusion A concept suggested by Erik Erikson to describe the confusion and inconsistency of ethics, roles, and behavior that characterize many adolescents as they seek self-identity and adult status.

Ego Ideal A personality, character, or image to which a person may aspire or fantasize.

Ego Identity According to Erikson, "A persistent sameness within oneself and a consistent sharing of some essential character with others." This "ego identity" is acquired during the formative adolescent years as the youth matures.

Electroencephalogram A recording of the summated electrical activity of the neurons in the human brain. It has been found that variations in these brain-wave patterns accompany certain forms of brain abnormalities and different levels of alertness. It has been hypothesized that chronic criminals may also have distinctive EEG patterns.

Electroencephalograph An electronic test with medical applications that measures the frequency and pattern of brain waves. The EEG has been administered to a number of deviant personalities and criminals on the premise that their brains emit abnormal frequencies. Fragmentary findings are only tenuous and inconclusive.

Endomorph A body type in William Sheldon's constitutional typology that he described as having a soft, rotund physical build and a self-indulgent, jolly personality.

Ephebiphobia Fear of youths.

Ethnicity The national and cultural background of a particular group.

Etiology The study of the cause(s) of an event, phenomenon, or behavior.

Extended Family Family where more than two generations live under one roof and cooperate in the economic, social, and psychological support of the family.

"Fag Bashing" Derogatory slang used by youths to describe the beating up (aggravated assault) of homosexuals by male juveniles (also called "gay bashing). Often accompanied by robbery.

Family of Orientation Term sociologists use to refer to family of origin.

Family of Origin The family in which a child is socialized; usually consists of parents and children.

FBI Uniform Crime Report Index Often referred to as the "Index Offenses." The first eight crime categories of the *FBI Uniform Crime Reports,* because of their seriousness, frequency of occurrence, and likelihood of being reported to the police are known as Index Offenses. The first four are often grouped together as "Violent Crimes" directed against persons. The second four are also often treated as a subcategory and are known as "Property Crimes," nonviolent crimes directed against property.

FBI Uniform Crime Reports Annual compilations of the numbers and types of crimes committed in the United States. The reports are based on arrest data collected from a nationwide reporting network of law-enforcement agencies and are tabulated by age, race, sex, place of residence, and other traits of those arrested. The system is designed to measure the extent, fluctuation, distribution, and nature of serious crime in the United States.

Felony A more serious crime punishable by fine and/or imprisonment for more than a year.

Female Auxiliary A branch of male gangs comprised of girlfriends, sisters, groupies, and other females who identify with the male gang.

Feminist Theories To study, analyze, and explain social phenomena from a gender-focused perspective.

Filtering Process Process whereby police and juvenile courts use their discretion to informally handle or "filter out" juveniles from the criminal justice system, based upon a variety of subjective criteria.

Folkways Informal agreements or understandings among the members of society about what is considered appropriate and inappropriate behavior.

Forcible Rape One of the FBI Crime Index offenses. The carnal knowledge of a female forcibly and against her will.

Frustration–Aggression Hypothesis Individuals unable to reach desired goals become frustrated, and this frustration is manifested by aggressive behavior.

***Furman* v. *Georgia,* 1972** U.S. Supreme Court case which ruled that capital punishment constituted "cruel and unusual punishment" and violated the Eighth Amendment to the U.S. Constitution.

Gang A group of recurrently associating individuals with identifiable leadership and internal organization, identifying with or claiming control over territory in a community and engaging individually or collectively in violent or other forms of illegal behavior.

Gang Cluster Several age-graded male subgroups plus a female auxiliary that are formally or informally affiliated or allied for some practical and mutual advantage.

Gang Rape A group or multiple rape of a single victim.

Gault Decision A 1967 decision by the U.S. Supreme Court that reversed the lower court adjudication of 15-year-old Gerald Gault on grounds that the youth did not receive his constitutional rights. For the first time, limited due process was formally granted to America's minors.

Gemeinschaft According to Toennies' theoretical continuum, a community characterized by a smaller population, less complex division of labor, and dominated by primary face-to-face interaction and informal social control.

Gender refers to a cultural understanding of what constitutes masculinity and femininity in a society.

General Deterrence, punishment that discourages others from committing similar acts.

General Theory of Deviance A precise and testable statement of the relationship between variables that is broad enough so as to offer causal explanation for a variety of deviant behaviors (e.g., Merton's Theory of Anomie). As yet, no general theory of delinquency has been developed.

Gesellschaft According to Toennies' theoretical continuum, a community characterized by a larger population, a complex division of labor, secondary social relationships, and formal social control.

Graffiti The distinctive language and symbolism of street gangs that is scrawled in public places to identify gang territories and members, and to challenge rivals.

Group Context of Delinquency A major sociological emphasis in the study of delinquency, since the majority of such conduct is committed by social groupings of varying size, purpose, and organization. Thus, the group becomes the unit of analysis.

Group Homes Facilities where juveniles live in a dormitory-type setting under adult supervision. Youths are generally allowed limited participation in the community, going to school or work for part of the day.

Guardian Angels Group of young adults and teenagers who operate as self-appointed "patrols" of the streets, sidewalks, and subways of many American cities, making citizens' arrests of suspected law violators.

Hate Crimes Crimes directed at people because of their race, ethnicity, religion, sexual orientation, or some other physical or cultural characteristic that sets them apart from the perpetrator.

High Delinquency Area Clifford Shaw's and Henry McKay's term for a particular neighborhood or district (ordinarily in a large city) characterized by a very high incidence of juvenile crime and a local subculture that encourages such behavior.

Highfields Project Small group-treatment program designed for boys in a New Jersey correctional facility. Aimed at strengthening conformity within a group under supervision that would later make readjustment to home, school, and community normative expectations easier.

House Arrest A program in which youths are confined to their homes and closely supervised by their parents. Routine unannounced visits or phone calls are made by a probation officer.

House of Refuge Established in 1825, in New York City, to provide separate correctional facilities for children between the ages of 7 and 14 who had been convicted of crimes.

Human Ontogenetics, a new discipline that deals with the development of the human individual as a biopsychosocial unit from conception until death.

Hyperkinesis A frenetic activity and excitement found by some researchers to have unusually high incidence among the delinquent children in their studies. Often referred to as "hyperactivity."

Id That dimension of the human personality represented in Freud's model as a set of primitive, self-centered impulses and demands.

Ideal Type A conceptual model expressed in a pure and exaggerated form. The core characteristics of a community, an individual, or a pattern of human conduct. This "ideal" abstraction, while hypothetical, may serve as a useful reference point for observations of social phenomena in actual reality.

Ideology a set of ideas or beliefs on which some established practice is based.

Index Offenses The eight most serious crimes listed by the FBI in its crime index: murder, aggravated assault, forcible rape, robbery, burglary, larceny–theft, arson, and motor vehicle theft.

Informal Social Control Methods of social constraint applied by societal members that include gossip, ridicule, humor, ostracism, and peer pressure.

Initiation Rituals Some gangs subject new or aspiring members to special ceremonies, hazings, ordeals, or other requirements in order to demonstrate courage, commitment, and worthiness for membership.

Inner Containment The result of successful socialization and internalization of social norms that enables the individual to exercise effective self-control in resisting temptations to deviate.

***In re Gault*, 1967** U.S. Supreme Court case that granted limited rights of due process to juveniles, including: the right to counsel; the right to face and cross-examine witnesses; the right to refuse to answer self-incriminating questions; the right to a transcript of the proceedings; and the right to appeal juvenile court decisions.

***In re Holmes*, 1954** U.S. Supreme Court case that upheld the concept that the basic constitutional rights of due process afforded adult criminal offenders did not apply to the juvenile court, since an adversary relationship did not exist between the state and the juvenile.

***In re Winship*, 1970** U.S. Supreme Court case in which the court ruled that "proof beyond a reasonable doubt" also applied to juvenile cases.

INS (adjudication) In need of supervision.

Instrumental Theory An innovative approach to explaining juvenile delinquency by the radical theorists Herman and Julia Schwendinger. The Schwendingers' main thesis is that the parents' social class is not the most important variable in determining the delinquency potential for adolescents. Rather, they argue, the youth's relative status position among other teenagers is the best predictor of delinquency. Illegal conduct, to the juvenile involved, can be "instrumental," that is, serving as a vehicle for attaining social identity with his or her particular subgroup.

Intact Home Refers to family in which both parents are present in the home on a permanent basis.

Intake Initial stage of juvenile court proceeding. Petition is read, a court services officer is assigned to the case to conduct a social background investigation, and decisions are made regarding waiver, detention, and other matters.

Integrative Theories The contemporary efforts of scholars to synthesize elements of major theories of deviant and delinquent behavior into general theories with enhanced explanatory power.

Intelligence Quotient (IQ) The ratio of a person's mental age to his or her chronological age. Fifty years ago, psychologists popularized the IQ tests on the assumption that they could identify mental defectives and link their "measured mental capacities" with an inclination to delinquent behavior. In recent years the validity and predictive ability of IQ tests have been strongly challenged.

Interventionist Court Handles a high rate of cases judicially and has a high commitment rate.

Joyriding Theft of an automobile simply for the fun of driving it around for a while. Most common form of juvenile auto theft.

Juvenile Any person in American society under the legal age of majority.

Juvenile Code Statutes or laws that are formally codified and applied by a state legislature to those juveniles within state boundaries and jurisdiction.

Juvenile Court Referral A case of law violation involving a juvenile offender who is referred or assigned to a juvenile court for disposition or adjudication.

Juvenile Courts Judicial tribunals established to deal with the special cases of young people (usually between ages 7 and 18).

Juvenile Delinquency (Synthesized Definition) All acts committed by individuals between the ages of 7 and 16 (or possibly 14) that would be considered criminal if committed by an adult; that place the juvenile in the delinquent or criminal role; and that result in society regarding the juvenile as dangerously deviant.

Juvenile Officers Police officers who receive special training in child development, adolescent psychology, sociology, and counseling, in order to better equip themselves to handle the unique problems associated with policing juveniles.

Juvenilization of Poverty It has been projected that, in the near future, one of every five adolescents will live at or below the poverty level. A number of social scientists contend that such impoverishment is related to increasing violence and other social problems among American youths.

***Kent* v. *United States*, 1966** U.S. Supreme Court decision that ruled that before a juvenile court can waive its jurisdiction a hearing must be held.

Labeling Theory A sociological explanation of juvenile delinquency that focuses on the interaction between the actor and the societal audience that evaluates behavior and thereby imputes a social identity or label to the individual.

Larceny–Theft One of the FBI Crime Index offenses. The unlawful taking, carrying, leading, or riding away of property from the possession of another.

Latchkey Children School-aged children of working parent(s) who return home from school to an empty house and are unsupervised for a period of time.

Law Enforcement Role of Police Police concentrating on arresting juveniles who have committed crimes.

Laws Formal norms that are systematically written down in a legal code that defines their violation as criminal behavior and prescribes the method and degree of punishment.

Legal Age of Majority The chronological age at which a person is no longer considered a minor and commences adulthood (age 18 in most states).

Legal Definition of Delinquency Any act that, if committed by an adult, would be a crime. Involves an age boundary between juvenile and adult offenders.

Liberation Hypothesis, Females have not committed as much crime and delinquency as males, in the past because rigid gender roles provided fewer opportunities for them to do so. As gender roles change and more gender equity is achieved, girls and women will have more equal opportunities to violate laws.

Life Course The successive role and status changes that each person occupies in society as a consequence of growing older.

Loco Parentis Parental role toward juveniles.

Looking-Glass Self A term coined by Charles H. Cooley to describe the process through which an individual's self-evaluation and self-identity reflect how he or she perceives and adopts societal evaluations and expectations.

Lower-Class Focal Concerns Six basic values of trouble, toughness, smartness, excitement, fate, and autonomy that Walter Miller felt are intrinsic to the lower class and that, when acted out by lower-class males, place them in nonconforming opposition to dominant middle-class values and behavioral expectations.

Macrosociology (also Macroscopic Sociology) Focuses on large-scale social units such as large groups, organizations, cultures, and societies.

Mala in se Acts that are considered inherently evil, such as murder and rape.

Mala prohibita Acts that are considered evil only because they are prohibited, such as status offenses by minors.

Malevolent Vandalism The vicious and malevolent destruction of property, as opposed to the more common thoughtless vandalism where the primary motive is fun.

Marginal Persons Those immigrants, outsiders, members of racial or ethnic groups, and other persons of "marginal" and uncertain social status who are on the untenable periphery of mainstream society, or whose commitment and identity are fragmented because they are caught between two conflicting cultures and societies. The condition of social marginality.

Mass Media Any form of information outlet designed to communicate a standardized message to large masses of individuals simultaneously (e.g., newspapers, magazines, radio, television, and movies).

Master Status A status that tends to overpower, in most crucial situations, any other characteristics which might run counter to it.

Maturation Effect The theoretical idea, supported by considerable evidence, that young people typically seem to mature or "grow out" of their deviant behavior in time—without stern societal sanctions (see *Spontaneous Remission*).

***McKiever* v. *Pennsylvania,* 1971** U.S. Supreme Court case in which the court ruled that juveniles do not have the right to a trial by jury.

Medical Model Views crime and delinquency as a social pathology analogous to physical or mental illness. Delinquency is viewed like an "illness" with identifiable "symptoms" needing diagnosis and treatment.

Meidung Edict used by the Old Order Amish that invokes the practice of "shunning" those who have violated the dictates of their religion.

Mens Rea The concept of "evil mind" or criminal intent. Refers to one's ability to understand right from wrong and to understand the consequences of one's actions. In criminal law, a youth must be at least 7 years old to be considered capable of mens rea.

Mentoring Programs Uses adult volunteers who commit a certain amount of time each week to work one-on-one with a youngster to encourage academic, personal, social, athletic, and artistic developments in an effort to prevent delinquency.

Mesomorph A somatotype (body build) in William Sheldon's constitutional typology that he described as muscular and strong and as having an impulsive and energetic personality that predisposes this individual, more than other types, to delinquent behavior.

Microsociology (also Microscopic Sociology) Studies small social units such as individuals and small groups and their interaction.

Mid-City Project Delinquency prevention program in Boston directed at the community, families, and gangs. Based upon the assumption that the roots of delinquency were to be found in the social environment.

Middle-Class Gangs A number of studies indicate that delinquent youth gangs are not exclusively a lower-class phenomenon. While locale, purpose, organization, style and type of misconduct, and societal perception and response may vary significantly from their better-known, lower-class counterpart, the existence and danger of middle-class gangs is well documented.

Minimalistic Court Handles a low proportion of its cases judicially with a low commitment rate.

Minnesota Youth Advocate Program School-based delinquency prevention program in Minnesota that attempted to help institutionalized juvenile delinquents more successfully readjust to school and community upon their release.

***Miranda* v. *Arizona*, 1966** U.S. Supreme Court decision which ruled that adults must be informed of their constitutional rights at the time of arrest in order for any of their testimony to be used as evidence in court.

Mirandize To advise a suspect of his or her legal rights based on the U.S. Supreme Court case of *Miranda* v. *Arizona*.

Misdemeanor A less-serious crime usually punishable by fine and/or imprisonment for less than a year.

Mobilization for Youth Delinquency prevention program developed in Manhattan based on Cloward's and Ohlin's Theory of Differential Opportunities in slum areas of major cities. Attempted to open up legitimate opportunity structures through school, businesses, government, and other social institutions and agencies.

Modes of Individual Adaptive Behavior A typology developed by Robert Merton of five possible responses of individuals to the anomic juxtaposition of culturally approved goals and the institutionalized means of achievement:

I. ***Conformity:*** One who accepts both traditional goals and approved means.
II. ***Innovation:*** One who accepts traditional, cultural success goals but whose sense of anomic frustration leads to innovative, illegal means of reaching those goals.
III. ***Ritualism:*** This person realizes that the idealized, cultural goals are unreachable but continues to strive in the socially expected ways.
IV. ***Retreatism:*** This person, in response to anomie-generating circumstances, abandons both the culturally approved success goals and the institutionalized means of hard work for attaining those objectives.
V. ***Rebellion:*** This malcontent, disillusioned with traditional goals and means, substitutes new objectives and new methods for achievement.

Moral Development Theories Explanatory constructs, principally conceived by Jean Piaget and Lawrence Kohlberg, that depict human cognitive and moral development occurring on a typology of successive stages. An etiological extension of these theories has suggested that criminals and delinquents seem to function at lower, more sensory and selfish levels of moral development.

Mores The more important, formal, and seriously enforced norms of a society. Mores are generally perceived as vital to the cohesion and survival of society.

Motor Vehicle Theft One of the FBI Crime Index offenses. The theft or attempted theft of a motor vehicle.

Mules Individuals who transport narcotics or other illegal substances for drug dealers.

Murder and Nonnegligent Manslaughter One of the FBI Crime Index offenses. The willful killing of one human being by another.

National Juvenile Court Statistical Reporting System Program The National Center for Juvenile Justice and Delinquency Prevention in the U.S. Department of Justice collects data from a nationwide network of participating juvenile courts and publishes annual summaries of juvenile court caseloads. The data are tabulated by age, race, sex, and type of offense or need of the children and youths appearing before the courts.

Near Group A theoretical contribution by Lewis Yablonsky who maintained that most delinquent gangs are midway on a group–mob continuum and are structurally neither groups nor mobs. He described the gang as a "near group" in organization, membership, quality of leadership, and other traits.

Neighborhood Watch Citizen groups in neighborhoods who watch for criminal or delinquent activities and report any suspicious individuals to the police.

Neighborhood Youth Corps Delinquency prevention and treatment program designed to provide vocational training and better work opportunities for disadvantaged and delinquent youths.

Neoclassical Position A modified version of the classical theorists that recognized that not all persons were equally rational and personally responsible for their behavior.

Neovigilantism Renewed wave of vigilantism—private citizens taking on the role of law enforcers.

Neurological Abnormality A mental impairment induced by disease or injury that has been linked by psychiatric research with some forms of aberrant and even occasional antisocial behavior.

Normative (see *Conformity*)

Norms The rules, standards, laws, customs, and beliefs that regulate human behavior and social interaction for a society or social group.

Nuclear Family Family where two generations or less live under one roof and cooperate in the economic, social, and psychological support of the family.

Ostracism The experience of being expelled from a social group.

Outer Containment The formal laws and law enforcement agencies—external to the individual—that restrain most members of society from serious norm violation.

Parens Patriae The legal concept from British Common Law that established the King (or the state) as the "ultimate parent"; provides legal basis for the state to intervene on behalf of children.

Paternalistic Court Handles a low rate of cases judicially but has a high commitment rate.

Personality The unique organization of relatively stable psychological traits possessed by an individual, as revealed by one's interaction with others in his or her environment.

Personality Trait A distinguishing feature, quality, or disposition of mind or character.

Petition Official statement filed by police, parents, school officials, or some other adult which contains the important facts relevant to why the juvenile should appear before the juvenile court.

Pharming Parties Parties at which teens take prescription pain relievers, antidepressants, diet pills, and other prescription drugs to get high instead of drinking alcohol.

Phrenology An early nineteenth-century notion of Joseph Gall who speculated that traits of personality and character and concomitant behavioral proclivities are housed in separate portions of the brain and can be revealed by the scientific study of the bumps and irregularities of the skull.

PLACE Program developed at Syracuse University where youthful first-time offenders attend a 90-minute class session in which they are involved in role playing, mock trials, and discussions on the juvenile justice system and causes of delinquency.

Placement Putting a juvenile in a residential facility or incarcerating him or her in an institution.

Play Group The natural and spontaneous neighborhood play group of urban youngsters was first identified by Frederick Thrasher as the informal and innocuous beginning of the evolution of the predatory, antisocial street gang.

Police Discretion The wide latitude police officers have in deciding how to handle juvenile offenders.

Positive School of Criminology A late nineteenth-century view of criminal behavior based on biological determinism. Lombroso and others believed that predatory, antisocial behavior is genetically programmed in some individuals who, as physical manifestations of an earlier phase of our evolutionary past, are irresistibly attracted to crime.

Posttraumatic Stress Disorder Negative psychological and social repercussions from emotional or physical assault or abuse.

Power Control Theory An explanation of delinquency that views differing levels of male and female involvement in delinquency as a function of social-class position and parental authority manifested in the youth's family.

Predelinquency An early, preliminary stage of personality development that, according to some psychologists and psychiatrists, precedes full development of the delinquent personality and identity.

Predelinquent Based on the "medical model," a youth who exhibits "symptoms" is thought to be associated with juvenile delinquency.

Prescriptive Norms Rules or laws that "prescribe" certain kinds of behavior as appropriate or desirable; societal "thou shalts."

Prevention Ideology Based on the "medical model" approach to delinquency, this strategy attempts to identify "symptoms" of delinquency and "treat" them in order to prevent the delinquency before it occurs.

Primary Deviation An initial, impulsive, or experimental act of deviance (or perhaps several such acts) in which the individual does not internalize a permanent nonconforming role and self-concept.

Primary Group a relatively small intimate group characterized by face-to-face interaction.

Proactive Strategies Programs designed to identify and eliminate delinquency before it occurs.

Probation First established in Boston in 1841, a form of supervised release whereby a juvenile delinquent is allowed to remain free but must adhere to a strict set of guidelines imposed by the court. The juvenile must also periodically report to an officer of the court. Used *instead* of institutionalization.

Profit Motive An economic rationale for gang activities focused on the pursuit of financial gain, as in the marketing of illegal drugs and car thefts.

Projective Test Psychogenic test designed to elicit the unconscious feelings and "projections" of patients by exposing them to unstructured and unidentifiable stimuli.

Property Crimes Crimes committed against property: burglary, larceny–theft, arson, and motor vehicle theft.

Proportionate Sentencing A judicial concept and principle meaning that the severity of dispositions should be roughly equivalent to the seriousness of the offense committed.

Proscriptive Norms Rules or laws that "prohibit" certain kinds of behavior as inappropriate or undesirable; societal "thou shalt nots."

Provo Experiment Delinquency rehabilitation and treatment strategy based on theory of differential association. Used in a facility for habitual delinquent offenders in Provo, Utah.

"Pseudovigilantism" Term coined by the authors to refer to activities such as "crimestoppers," crime "hotlines," and other programs in which individuals do not actually enforce the laws but anonymously call law-enforcement officials with tips regarding criminal or delinquent activities. If these tips lead to arrests, the citizens usually receive some type of monetary reward.

Psychiatry A medical specialty concerned with the diagnosis, treatment, and prevention of disordered or "abnormal" behavior.

Psychoanalysis Various techniques developed and implemented by psychologists and psychiatrists for probing and examining the unconscious forces, motives, and problems behind human behavior.

Psychogenic Approach An eclectic and generic term denoting the common ground shared by psychology and psychiatry as they seek to understand and explain human behavior in general and delinquency in particular.

Psychology A behavioral science that investigates and associates mental processes with behavior.

Psychopath (Sociopath) A severely "flawed personality" in that the individual has not internalized some major values and norms of society. Thus, the psychopath does not differentiate right from wrong in the typical way and feels little guilt over misdeeds or compassion for his or her victims.

Psychopathology Some internal neurological disorder or deeply hidden personality disturbance.

Push factors Are such variables as mental conflict, anxiety, alienation, and frustration.

Pull factors Are such variables as membership in a street gang or participation in a criminal subculture.

Racial Group One of several human groupings that are classified according to observable physical differences, such as skin color, facial features, and hair texture.

Racial Profiling Using race or ethnicity as the sole criteria for initiating police contact.

Radical Nonintervention Policies that accommodate society to the widest possible diversity of behaviors and attitudes rather than forcing as many individuals as possible to "adjust" to supposedly common societal standards—leave the kids alone wherever possible.

Radical Theory A body of sociological etiology that accounts for adult crime and juvenile delinquency as a precipitate of conflict between social classes as their vested interests and values clash, and as law enforcement is differentially applied to the social classes.

Rational Choice Theory An explanation of criminal and delinquent behavior built on the assumption that individuals logically weigh the potential benefits and costs before embarking on deviant and antisocial conduct.

Reactive Strategies Programs designed to intervene and treat a youth after delinquency has occurred.

Reactive Subculture A set of post–World War II theories that shared the view of lower-class youth gangs as being a hostile, subcultural response to middle-class cultural values and goals that have been imposed on all of society.

Reactive Subculture Responses Several sociological theorists (e.g., Cloward and Ohlin, and Cohen) have described lower-class street gangs as viable subcultures with distinctive values, norms, and behavioral practices. These theorists often explained delinquent gang behavior as an alienated reaction to the dominant culture of the middle class. Albert Cohen, for example, saw three possible responses of lower-class boys as they recognize and seek to cope with their disadvantages:

1. *College-Boy Response:* Youths in this category seek upward social-class mobility.
2. *Corner-Boy Response:* This type withdraws into a disenchanted, alienated subculture of lower-class youths.
3. *Delinquent-Boy Response:* The banding together of delinquent youths in a gang whose behavior reflects values that are antithetical to the middle class.

Reality Therapy Treatment strategy that attempts to make the offender take responsibility for his or her actions. Based on the writings of William Glasser.

Reference Group a group with which an individual has a strong sense of identification regardless of his or her actual membership in the group.

Referral Process whereby a juvenile's name is given to the juvenile court.

Reformatory A correctional facility designed to discipline and rehabilitate rather than punish juvenile offenders.

Rehabilitative Ideal Emphasizes the temporary and reversible nature of delinquency if remedial measures are applied early enough.

Reintegrative Shaming Judges require juveniles to publicly acknowledge their wrongdoing and perhaps perform a somewhat degrading or humiliating public service to account for their deviance.

Reliability A fundamental research and methodological objective. A measure can be assumed to have reliability when it yields the same data or results upon replication of the measuring or data-gathering procedure by other investigators.

Restitution The offender is required to compensate the victim(s) for losses related to the offense.

Restorative Justice Model Focuses on accountability, restitution, and community involvement in the corrections process.

Retreatist-Oriented Gang This juvenile group, in the face of their double failure at achieving success in legitimate avenues of success and in attaining proficiency in traditional criminal activities, symbolically retreats into drug abuse and illicit sexual activities.

Reverse Certification In some states, a youth who is over the age of 16 and has committed what would be a felony for an adult will automatically stand trial as an adult unless he or she is "reverse certified" to be treated as a juvenile.

Rite of Passage Symbolic ritual marking the transition from one social role and status to another; one that permanently alters a person's relationship with members of the greater community.

Ritualistic Court Handles a high proportion of cases judicially with a low rate of commitment.

Robbery One of the FBI Crime Index offenses. The taking or attempting to take anything of value from the care, custody, or control of a person or persons by force or threat of force or violence and/or by putting the victim in fear.

Role The behavioral performance expected of a person who holds a certain status in the social group or society.

Role Conflict The fulfillment of one role necessitates the violation of another.

Role Definition of Delinquency Behavior by an individual who sustains a consistent pattern of delinquency over a long period of time and whose life and identity are organized around such deviant behavior.

Role engulfment Becoming caught up in fulfilling the particular role expectations that accompany a master status to the exclusion of the many other statuses and roles a person may occupy.

Role Modeling The learning of social roles from observation, imitation, and the identification with those who occupy those roles.

Role Strain The set of expectations accompanying one role (i.e., law enforcement officer) may be at odds with fulfilling the expectations of another role (i.e., a concerned adult acting on behalf of a child in trouble).

Rorschach Ink-Blot Test One of the projective tests designed to elicit deep, often camouflaged feelings, motives, and needs. The ink-blot test is comprised of a series of nondescript, ink-drop patterns that, since they portray nothing known or prelearned for which there is a predetermined response, are assumed to draw from the subject those hidden, sublimated emotions and drives.

Runaways Juveniles who voluntarily leave their homes.

Sanctions Methods by which norms are enforced. Can be either informal or formal; positive or negative.

Scared Straight! Program begun by inmates at Rahway State Prison in which juvenile offenders spend part of a day at Rahway being shown the more brutal side of life inside a maximum-security prison.

***Schall* v. *Martin*, 1984** U.S. Supreme Court case that ruled youths could be held without bail if they were being held for their own protection or the protection of society.

Screening Device The schools act to "screen out" members of society based upon educational credentials (e.g., diplomas, degrees, etc.), as well as willingness to conform to and internalize dominant attitudes, values, beliefs, and norms.

Secondary Deviation An emergent, repetitive pattern of deviant behavior as an individual's self-concept is altered and the deviant role is assumed.

Secondary Groups, somewhat larger groups characterized by more formal interaction which are usually organized for a specific purpose.

Self-Fulfilling Prophecy Defining a situation or person in a certain way and then acting as if the definition is real may in fact cause the situation or person to become the way they are defined. In schools, labels are applied to students, and they are treated as if the labels are meaningful; consequently students may fulfill the role expectations associated with the label.

Self-Report Study The survey of a part of a population regarding their participation in illegal activity. If the subjects are randomly selected, findings may be generalized to a larger population. If responses are made anonymously this approach is useful in measuring undetected and unreported delinquency.

Sex is based on biological and physical differences between males and females.

Shock Incarceration A short prison stay designed to shock the youth and to impress upon him or her the seriousness of the problem and potential consequences of further delinquency (see *Shock Probation*).

Shock Probation A short prison stay designed to shock the youth and to impress upon him or her the seriousness of the problem and potential consequences of further delinquency (see *Shock Incarceration*).

SHODI (Serious Habitual Offenders Drug Involved) A program used in California, Colorado, and Florida, which uses the computer to identify serious habitual juvenile offenders. When confronted by the police for even the most minor offense, they are immediately arrested and officially processed. The program attempts to maintain awareness of the whereabouts of all known serious habitual offenders.

Short-Term Hedonism A practical and simple conclusion by some students of delinquency phenomena that much juvenile misbehavior is little more than spontaneous adventuring in pursuit of immediate pleasure.

Single-Parent Family A family in which only one parent is present on a permanent basis.

Situational Prostitutes Prostitutes who enter the profession temporarily due to specific social circumstances.

Social Bond Extent to which a youth feels an "attachment" to basic social institutions like the family and school. Believed by Hirschi and others to increase conformity to the conventional norms of society.

Social Bond Theory A social control theory put forward by Travis Hirschi who depicted the juvenile delinquent as lacking sufficient "social bond" to the basic values and expected behaviors of society. He detailed four elements of social bonding that must be effectively activated in early childhood in order to elicit conformity: attachment, commitment, involvement, and belief.

Social Capital A reservoir of resilience in some individuals that enables them to resist the allure of potentially damaging associates and activities. Social capital is acquired initially through nurturing, intergenerational relationship within one's family of origin.

Social Class Social position (status) based upon occupation, education, and income.

Social Conflict The viewpoint of Marx, Dahrendorf, and other "conflict theorists" that the origin of many prevailing social norms can be traced to the unscrupulous efforts of the capitalist class to control and exploit the less-powerful working classes.

Social Consensus The viewpoint of Weber, Durkheim, and other theorists that the source of our dominant social norms has deep cultural roots as the members of society, from generation to generation, organize themselves to meet certain basic survival prerequisites. Over time, traditional ways of fulfilling these societal needs become institutionalized.

Social Contract The voluntary abdication of a measure of personal autonomy and submission to group norms in exchange for enhanced security supplied by a dominant power structure and hierarchy over the social collectivity.

Social Control Those aspects of society and culture that are designed to reduce the incidence of juvenile delinquency and to minimize its negative impact upon the members of society.

Social Control Theories In contrast to other groups of sociological theories, social control theories approach the etiology of delinquency by asking "What causes conformity?" The underlying assumption is that youthful behavior cannot and should not be superficially dichotomized into "delinquent" and "nondelinquent."

Social Disability A concept suggested by James Short and Fred Strodtbeck to describe the lack of interpersonal skills, social assurance, knowledge of the job market, and sophistication in relations with girls that characterize most delinquent gang members.

Social Imperative The intrinsic and compelling need of all social creatures, including humans, to interact with and relate to others of the same species.

Social Interaction The dynamic process of communication and the relationships between humans that are necessary for the physical and emotional health, development, and survival of individuals and groups.

Social Interdependence The symbiotic network of relationships and mutual aid that characterizes successfully functioning and enduring human societies and communities.

Socialization The process whereby individuals learn and internalize the attitudes, values, and behaviors appropriate to persons functioning as members of a society or social group. This shared knowledge or culture content of a social group or society is transmitted to successive generations.

Social Learning Theories A group of sociological theories founded on the assumption that deviant and delinquent behavior can be explained as the product of socialization.

Social Network A fundamental sociological concept used to summarize and explain the interconnected, formal, and informal array of relationships among individual members of society. It follows that human behavior can hardly be conceived of in isolation—without social causes or impacts traceable to others.

Social Organization The generally recognized and accepted pattern or structure of instrumental leadership and behavior utilized by a social group in achieving its objectives.

Social Problem An objective, observable, and verifiable condition within a society that common consensus agrees is a threatening problem, requiring concerted remedial action and about which it is felt that something can be done.

Social Retardation Emotional and psychological immaturity resulting from not allowing youths to assume responsibility for things they are physically capable.

Social Role A set of behavioral expectations that accompany a particular status.

Social Status An individual's prestige position in relation to others in the social group or society.

Social Strain Theories The theoretical explanations of deviance and delinquency grouped together in this category share the underlying assumption that nonconforming behavior arises out of social circumstances in which individuals or groups experience normative confusion or disruption. This normative confusion has a special application to ethnic or social-class minorities under pressure from dominant groups or classes.

Social Structure Hypotheses The popularized premises underlying many programs and policies designed to alleviate social problems. For example, many concluded that poverty is caused by structural features of capitalism. Following this reasoning, it is society that must change, not individuals. Applications to crime and delinquency have been made by several radical theorists.

Societal Response Definition of Delinquency The members of the juvenile's social group or society comprise an "audience" that must perceive and judge the behavior in question as delinquent.

Society The general term for people living in social interdependence in a particular geographic area who socially interact and share a common culture.

Sociobiology A newly developing area of inquiry and study that maintains that social behavior of all species is a product of evolutionary history and genetics. This involves temperament, personality traits, and physical characteristics as each member of a social species unconsciously musters all its resources to protect the gene pool and insure propagation and species survival. While the implications of such hypotheses for deviant and delinquent behavior are numerous and profound, there has been little empirical support thus far.

Sociolegal Definition of Delinquency Those actions that are illegal for juveniles, that place the juvenile in the delinquent role, and that result in society regarding the juvenile as delinquent.

Sociological Imagination The application of sociological knowledge and expertise in creative and innovative problem-solving ways.

Sociological Perspective The observation, analysis, and explanation of human behavior and social phenomena, including juvenile delinquency, that rest upon a careful consideration of the social context or environment in which the behavior or phenomenon occurs.

Sociology The systematic and scientific study of human behavior, social groups, and society.

Sociodrama A method involving role playing, intergroup relations, and collective ideologies.

Sociopath (psychopath) A severely "flawed personality" in that the individual has not internalized some major values and norms of society. Thus, the psychopath does not differentiate right from wrong in the typical way and feels little guilt over misdeeds or compassion for his or her victims.

Solitary Delinquent A significant minority of all juvenile offenses are committed by individuals acting alone. This does not negate their direct and indirect relationships with numerous others who are affected by the illegal behavior.

Specific Deterrence Punishments that discourage an individual from committing similar acts in the future.

Spontaneous Remission The "aging out" phenomenon whereby juveniles at some point reach a level of maturity where they spontaneously reduce, and eventually even eliminate, their involvement in law-violating behavior (see *Maturation Effect*).

Spotter Member of automobile theft ring who "spots" or locates automobiles for theft.

Status The prestige position of a person in relation to other persons in the social group or society.

Status Offenses Acts considered illegal for juveniles because of their minority status. These acts are not against the law if committed by adults (e.g., smoking, drinking or possessing alcohol, truancy, or running away from home).

Street Corner Society A book by William Whyte that takes its title from the informal but highly viable form of social organization in slum neighborhoods.

Street Kids Juveniles who have left home (either voluntarily or involuntarily) for life on the streets and sidewalks of cities.

Street People Bag ladies, chronically unemployed, vagrants, and others among the homeless who inhabit the streets and sidewalks of cities.

Subculture A smaller group within a culture that shares most of the elements of the larger culture, but has some unique attitudes, values, beliefs, and norms that distinguish it from the larger culture.

Subterranean Value System A point made by Gresham Sykes and David Matza in maintaining that delinquents often justify their misdeeds as only transient since they actually subscribe to temporarily "subterranean" adult values of propriety.

"Subway Vigilante" Bernhard Goetz, the individual who shot four youths who allegedly attempted to rob him on a New York subway.

Superego An antithetical or opposite force in the personality that restrains the impulsive id. One of the three personality components in Freud's model.

Swarm An overwhelming and intimidating group of gang members who suddenly invade commercial stores and private homes to loot and assault vulnerable occupants.

Tagging The person becomes the thing he is described as being.

Techniques of Neutralization According to Gresham Sykes and David Matza, many juveniles are able to reduce or neutralize the negative impacts of delinquent behavior such as feelings of personal guilt by extending a set of psychological defense mechanisms. These justifications for deviance are denial of responsibility; denial of injury; denial of the victim; condemnation of the condemners; and appeal to higher loyalties.

Theory A general statement that accurately relates cause-and-effect variables in order to explain events or behavior.

Throwaways Juveniles who are driven from their homes by their parents or untenable living conditions.

Total Institution Term used by Erving Goffman to describe a place where individuals live, work, recreate, and socially interact in an environment isolated from larger society over a long period of time.

TOUGHLOVE Program for parents of "troubled youths." Over 1,500 chapters nationwide where parents meet and provide mutual support as they work out strategies for confronting and dealing with their teenaged children in order to reduce and eliminate their delinquent behavior.

Tracking Educational strategy where students are grouped according to intelligence as measured by standardized tests, academic performance, and other criteria.

Traditional Court Juvenile court characterized by low task differentiation, centralized authority, low discretion for court services staff, routine handling of status offenders, and low formalization.

Training Schools Long-term facilities for housing juvenile offenders (comparable to adult prisons).

Transactional Analysis Treatment strategy which views delinquency as a result of an underdeveloped ego-state. Treatment attempts to move offender to an "I'm OK, you're OK" life position.

Treatment Ideology Follows the rehabilitative ideal of the juvenile court; tends to view delinquency as a result of an individual pathology.

Triad A group of three persons engaged in social interaction.

Truancy "Skipping school"—missing school without the knowledge or consent of parents or guardians—a status offense.

Turf The geographical area or neighborhood dominated by an urban street gang in the struggle with other groups for identity, status, and territory.

Typology A classification system that organizes a diversity of information or objects into predetermined and orderly categories.

Unconscious A subterranean mental reservoir of unfulfilled needs, desires, and feelings accumulated throughout life and not ordinarily available to conscious thought.

Validity A fundamental research and methodological objective. A research operation or statistical measure has validity when it in fact measures whatever it is designed or intended to measure. A finding or conclusion is said to be valid if it accurately reflects factual evidence.

Values Beliefs and ideas that are held in high esteem by a particular group; includes attitudes about what is right and wrong.

Victimization Survey Data-collecting efforts that focus on the victims and their recollections of the crime, circumstances, and the offenders.

Vigilante An unauthorized individual who attempts to enforce the law and administer punishment to law violators.

Vigilantism people taking the law into their own hands.

Violent crimes Crimes that are directed against a person: murder, aggravated assault, forcible rape, and robbery.

VisionQuest Rehabilitation program for hard-core juvenile delinquents who are put through a series of physical challenges in the wilderness. These experiences act as a "rite of passage," geared toward building a more positive self-concept and more mature outlook on life.

Vocational Prostitutes Prostitutes who enter the profession as a career.

Voluntary Control Self-imposed social constraint.

Waiver Decision made by a juvenile judge during the intake procedure to declare a juvenile an "adult" and remand him or her to adult criminal court.

Wilding Slang term created to describe the activities of bands of bored youths on the street who prowl, assault, rob, and rape for "something to do."

Working Mother The mother is employed outside the home.

XYY Hypothesis A chromosomal abnormality that has been tentatively linked to criminal aggression in some mates. However, research on imprisoned criminals with an extra gene carrying chromosome Y has had methodological shortcomings, and findings are very inconsistent.

Youth Service Bureaus Established in local communities to divert youthful offenders from the juvenile justice system.

Youth Subculture The unique attitudes, values, beliefs, and behavioral practices that distinguish a subculture, loosely comprised of all youths ranging in age from early adolescence through the late teens and early twenties.

Zero Tolerance School policies that prohibit the possession, use, sale, or supply of any type of weapon, alcohol, or illegal drug on school premises or at any school-related functions.

REFERENCES

Aaronson, D. E., C. T. Deines, and M. Musheno. 1984. *Public policy and police discretion*. New York: Clark Boardman.

ABC Primetime. 2002. *Whatever it takes: A child's last chance*, May 23.

Abrahamsen, D. 1960. *The psychology of crime*. New York: Columbia University Press.

ACLU. 1978. "*Children's Rights* v. Adult Free Speech: Can They Be Reconciled? *Children's Rights Report* 2 (9) (May):8–11.

Acock, A. C., and D. H. Demo. 1999. Dimensions of family conflict and their influence on child and adolescent adjustment. *Sociological Inquiry* 69 (Fall):641–58.

Adams, G. R., T. Gullotta, and M. A. Clancy. 1985. Homeless adolescents: A descriptive study of similarities and differences between runaways and throwaways. *Adolescence* 20 (Fall):715–24.

Adams, K. 2003. The effectiveness of juvenile curfews at crime prevention. *Annals of the American Academy of Political and Social Science* 587:136–39.

Adams, M. S., J. D. Johnson, and T. D. Evans. 1998. Racial differences in informal labeling effects. *Deviant Behavior* 19:157–71.

Aday, D. P., Jr. 1986. Court structure, defense attorney use, and juvenile court decisions. *Sociological Quarterly* 27 (1):107–19.

Addington, L. A., S. A. Ruddy, A. K. Miller, J. F. DeVoe, and K. A. Chandler. 2002. *Are America's schools safe? Students speak out: 1999 school clinic supplement*. Washington, DC: U.S. Department of Education.

Adler, F. 1975. *Sisters in crime*. New York: McGraw Hill.

Adler, J. 2006. Freud in our midst. *Newsweek* 142 (13) (March 27):43–49.

Adler, P. A., and P. A. Adler. 2002. Teen scenes: Ethnographies of adolescent cultures. *Journal of Contemporary Ethnography* 31 (October):652–60.

Agnew, R. 1984. Goal achievement and delinquency. *Sociology and Social Research* 68 (July):435–51.

———. 1992. Foundation for a general strain theory of crime and delinquency. *Criminology* 30:47–87.

———. 1995. Testing the leading crime theories: An alternative strategy focusing on motivational processes. *Journal of Research in Crime and Delinquency* 32 (November):363–98.

———. 2001. Building on the foundation of general strain theory: Specifying the types of strain most likely to lead to crime and delinquency. *Journal of Research in Crime and Delinquency* 38:319–61.

———. 2005. *Why do criminals offend?* Los Angeles, CA: Roxbury.

Agnew, R., and D. M. Peterson. 1989. Leisure and delinquency. *Social Problems* 36 (October):332–50.

Agnew, R., T. Brezina, J. P. Wright, and F. T. Cullen. 2002. Strain, personality traits, and delinquency: Extending general strain theory. *Criminology* 40 (1):43–74.

Ahmed, E., and V. Braithwaite. 2004. 'What, me ashamed?' Shame management and school bullying. *Journal of Research in Crime and Delinquency* 41 (August):269–84.

Aichorn, A. 1969. *Delinquency and child guidance*. New York: International Universities Press.

Akers, R. L. 1985. *Deviant behavior: A social learning approach*. 3rd ed. Belmont, CA: Wadsworth.

Akers, R. L., M. D. Krohn, L. Lanza-Kaduce, and M. J. Radosevich. 1979. Social learning and deviant behavior: A specific test of a general theory. *American Sociological Review* 44 (August):635–55.

Albanese, J. S. 1993. *Dealing with delinquency: The future of juvenile justice*. 2nd ed. Chicago: Nelson-Hall Publishers.

Alexander, K. L., D. R. Entwisle, and C. S. Horsey. 1997. From first grade forward: Early foundations of high school dropout. *Sociology of Education* 70 (April): 87–107.

Ali, L., and J. Scelfo. 2002. Choosing virginity. *Newsweek* (December 9):61–66.

Allen, F. A. 1976. The juvenile court and the limits of juvenile justice. In *Juvenile delinquency* 3rd ed., ed. R. Giallombardo, 411–19. New York: Wiley.

Alpert, G. P., J. M. MacDonald, and R. G. Dunham. 2005. Police suspicion and discretionary decision making during citizen stops. *Criminology* 43:407–34.

Alter, J., and P. *Wingert. 1995.* The return of shame. *Newsweek* February 6):20–26

Altschuler, D. M., and T. L. Armstrong. 1996. Aftercare not afterthought: Testing the TAP model. *Juvenile Justice* 3 (December):15–28.

Altschuler, D. M., T. L. Armstrong, and D. L. MacKenzie. 1999. Reintegration, supervised release, and intensive aftercare. *Juvenile Justice Bulletin*. Philadelphia: Office of Juvenile Justice and Delinquency Prevention.

Alwin, D. F., and A. Thornton. 1984. Family origins and the schooling process: Early versus late influence of parental characteristics. *American Sociological Review* 49 (December):784–802.

Ambert, A. M. 1999. The effect of male delinquency on mothers and fathers: A heuristic study. *Sociological Inquiry* 69 (Fall):621–40.

American Psychiatric Association. 2000. *Diagnostic and statistical manual of mental disorders DSM-IV-TR.* 4th ed. Arlington, VA: American Psychiatric Publishing/Jaypee.

Amir, M. 1971. *Patterns in forcible rape.* Chicago: University of Chicago Press.

Anderson, E. 1994. The code of the streets. *Atlantic Monthly*, May:81–94.

Anderson, K. S. 2008. Teen school tangled in fight over hairdo. *Dallas Morning News* (January 31):1B.

Annual Report on School Safety. 1998. Washington, DC: U.S. Department of Education, U.S. Department of Justice.

AP Anchorage. 2006. Six held in plot at school. *Dallas Morning News* (April 24):5A.

AP Austin. 2008. Abstinence tab highest in U.S. *Dallas Morning News* (July 14):3A.

AP Chicago. 1997. They're really not ignoring you. *Dallas Morning News* (September 10):4A.

AP Chicago. 2003. Teen drinking figures lowered. *Dallas Morning News* (February 26):5A.

AP *Dallas Morning News*. 2007. States rethinking harshness of juvenile sentencing laws. (December 2):11A.

AP Hempstead, TX. 1993. Ouster of 4 pregnant cheerleaders prompts sexism complaints from Hempstead parents. *Dallas Morning News* (October 3):27A.

AP Houston. 1993. Judge offers to snip time for a snip of hair. *Manteca Bulletin* (November 29):A3.

AP New York. 1978. Cold blooded killer is given 18-month sentence. *Tulsa Daily World* (June 30).

AP New York. 2002. Prescription drug use among kids growing fastest, study says. *Dallas Morning News* (September 19):2A.

AP Red Lion, PA. 2003. Teen kills principal, self at junior high. *Dallas Morning News* (April 25):8A.

AP Riverton, KS. 2006. Sheriff: 5 Teens' school rampage foiled. *Dallas Morning News* (April 21):14A.

AP San Antonio. 1999. Yard signs shame vandals straight. *Dallas Morning News* (September 28):17A.

AP Stamford, CT. 2001. Skakel will be tried as adult. *Dallas Morning News* (February 1):4A.

AP Tallahassee, FL. 1991. Bill allows Florida teachers to stun their unruly students. *Sunday Oklahoman* (January 20):A11.

AP Washington. 1996. Sex rate among teenage girls down for 1st time in 25 years, study finds. *Dallas Morning News* (May 7):10A.

———. 1998a. Use of drugs among teens increases, survey finds. *Dallas Morning News* (August 22):6A.

———. 1998b. Smoking sharply rises among college students, study finds. *Dallas Morning News* (November 18):11A.

———. 1999. Two-thirds of Americans say police would curb violence. *Ashland Daily Tidings* (August 27):1.

———. 1999a. Fewer teens using illegal drugs, government says. *Dallas Morning News* (August 19):3A.

———. 1999b. *Dallas Morning News* (June 19):5A.

———. 2002. Study: Teen girls who are close to mom delay sex. *Dallas Morning News* (September 5):5A.

———. 2003a. Teacher morale, unruly students are concerns, study shows. *Dallas Morning News* (April 24):9A.

———. 2003b. Study: Teens often fail to grasp adult court system. *Dallas Morning News* (March 3):3A.

———. 2003c. Study: Teens give parents thumbs up. *Dallas Morning News* (August 6):6A.

———. 2005a. Fewer teens smoke, but more take pills. *Dallas Morning News* (December 20):8A.

———. 2005b. Oral sex common among older teens. *Dallas Morning News* (September l6):11A.

———. 2005c. School crime rate levels off. *Dallas Morning News* (November 21):5A.

AP Webbers Falls, OK. 1997. Oklahoma officials investigate slaying of teen over lighter. *Dallas Morning News* (February 21):17A.

Ardrey, R. 1966. *The territorial imperative.* New York: Atheneum.

Armstrong, G. 1977. Females under the law—"Protected" but unequal. *Crime and Delinquency* 23 (April): 108–20.

Arnett, J. J. 2007. *Adolescence and Emerging Adulthood: A Cultural Approach.* 3rd ed. Upper Saddle River, NJ: Prentice-Hall.

Arnold, D. O., ed. 1970. *The sociology of subcultures.* Berkeley: The Glendessary Press.

Arnold, W. R. 1971. Race and ethnicity relative to other factors in juvenile court dispositions. *American Journal of Sociology* 77 (2):211–27.

Arnold, W. R., and T. M. Brungardt. 1983. *Juvenile misconduct and delinquency.* Boston: Houghton Mifflin.

Arum, R., and I. R. Beattie. 1999. High school experience and the risk of adult incarceration. *Criminology* 37 (August):515–30.

Ashland Daily Tidings. 2000. Teen saves child from creek. (January 11):B1.

Astone, N. M., and S. S. McLanahan. 1991. Family structure, parental practices and high school completion. *American Sociological Review* 56 (June):309–20.

Atkinson, M., and K. Young. 2008. Flesh journeys: The radical body modification of neoprimitives. In *Extreme deviance*, ed. E. Goode and D. A. Vail, 15–26. LA: Pine Forge.

Aurand, A. 1998. Troubled teens course through overburdened justice system. *Ashland Daily Tidings* (May 28):3.

Austin, J., K. D. Johnson, and R. Weitzer. 2005. *Alternatives to the secure detention and confinement of juvenile offenders*. Pittsburgh, PA: OJJDP.

Austin, R. 1977. Religion and crime control. Paper presented at the Conference of American Society of Criminology, Atlanta, GA.

Bachman, R., and R. Peralta. 2002. The relationship between drinking and violence in an adolescent population: Does gender matter? *Deviant Behavior* 23 (January–February):1–19.

Baker, M. L., J. N. Sigmon, and M. E. Nugent. 2001. Truancy reduction: Keeping students in school. *Juvenile Justice Bulletin* (September 2001). Washington, DC: U.S. Department of Justice, Office of Juvenile Justice and Delinquency Prevention.

Ball, R. A., R. Huff, and J. R. Lilly. 1990. House arrest and juvenile justice. In *Juvenile delinquency: A justice perspective*, ed. R. A. Weisheit and R. G. Culbertson, 168–72. Prospect Heights, IL: Wave land Press.

Bandura, A., and R. A. Walters. 1959. *Adolescent aggression*. New York: The Ronald Press.

———. 1963. *Social learning and personality development*. New York: Holt, Rinehart, and Winston.

Barash, D. P. 1982. *Sociobiology and behavior*. 2nd ed. New York: Elsevier.

Barnes, G. M., M. P. Farrell, and A. Cairns. 1986. Parental socialization factors and adolescent drinking behaviors. *Journal of Marriage and the Family* 48 (February):27–36.

Bartol, C. R., and A. M. Bartol. 1989. *Juvenile delinquency: A systems approach*. Upper Saddle River, NJ: Prentice Hall.

Barton, W. H., and J. A. Butts. 1990. Viable options: Intensive supervision for juvenile delinquents. *Crime and Delinquency* 36 (April):238–56.

Bayh, B. 1975. Our nation's schools—A report card: "A" in school violence and vandalism. In *Preliminary Report of the Subcommittee to Investigate Juvenile Delinquency*. Washington, DC: U.S. Government Printing Office.

Bazemore, G., and M. Umbreit. 1995. Rethinking the sanctioning function in juvenile court: Retributive or restorative response to youth crime. *Crime and Delinquency* 41 (July):296–316.

Bazemore, G., and S. E. Day. 1996. Restoring the balance: Juvenile and community justice. *Juvenile Justice* 3 (December):3–5.

Beasley, C. 1999. *What is feminism? An introduction to feminist theory*. Thousand Oaks, CA: Sage.

Becker, H. 1952. The career of the Chicago public school teacher. *American Journal of Sociology* 57 (March):470–77.

———. 1973. *Outsiders: Studies in the sociology of deviance*. Revised ed. New York: Free Press.

Begley, S. 2007. Are the kids alright? *Newsweek* (September 26):52.

Behre, C., D. Edwards, and C. Femming. 1982. Assessment of the effectiveness of a juvenile transitional center for facilitating re-entry. *Journal of Offender Counseling, Services, and Rehabilitation* 6 (Spring):61–72.

Belden, E. 1920. *Courts in the US hearing children's cases*. U.S. Bureau Publication No. 65. Washington, DC: U.S. Government Printing Office.

Bell, R. R. 1966. Parent-child conflict in sexual values. *Journal of Social Issues* 22 (2):34–44.

———. 1983. *Marriage and family interaction*. 6th ed. Homewood, IL: Dorsey Press.

Belsie, L. 2000. Home alone: Ranks of latchkey kids approach 7 million. *Christian Science Monitor*, October 31.

Benda, B. B. 1997. An examination of a reciprocal relationship between religiosity and different forms of delinquency within a theoretical model. *Journal of Research in Crime* 34 (May):163–86.

Bennett, A., and K. Kahn-Harris., eds. 2004. *After subculture: Critical studies in contemporary youth culture*. New York: Palgrave McMillan.

Berg, B. L. 1984. Inmates as clinical sociologists: The use of sociodrama in a nontraditional delinquency prevention program. *Journal of Offender Therapy and Comparative Criminology* 28 (September):117–24.

Berger, B. M. 1963. On the youthfulness of youth cultures. *Social Research* 30 (Autumn):319–42.

Berger, P. 1963. *An invitation to sociology*. Garden City, NY: Doubleday.

Berger, P., and B. Berger. 1975. *Sociology: A biographical approach*. 2nd ed. New York: Basic Books.

Bergmann, R. 1987. Purdy: Few bullies in Manteca. *Manteca Bulletin* (June 9):A8.

Bernard, T. J. 1990. Angry aggression among the truly disadvantaged. *Criminology* 28 (February):73–96.

Bernstein, J. 2006. *10 days to a less defiant child*. New York: Marlowe and Company.

Beschner, G., and A. S. Friedman., eds. 1986. *Teen drug use*. Lexington, MA: Lexington Books.

Best, J. A. 2006. *Fast cars, cool rides: The accelerating world of youth and their cars*. New York: NYU Press.

Beuhring, T. 2006. Early-onset delinquency: Steps on the path to prison and school dropout. University of Minnesota, Institute on Community Integration Teleconference, February 23, 2006.

Bilchik, S. 1999a. *1996 national youth gang survey*. Washington, DC: U.S. Government Printing Office, U.S. Department of Justice, Office of Juvenile Justice and Delinquency Prevention.

———. July, 1999b. *Report to congress on juvenile violence research*. Washington, DC: U.S. Government Printing Office, Office of Juvenile Justice and Delinquency Prevention.

———. August, 1999c. *OJJDP research: Making a difference for juveniles*. Washington, DC: U.S. Government

Printing Office, U.S. Department of Justice, Office of Juvenile Justice and Delinquency Prevention.

———. 1999d. Family disruption and delinquency. *Juvenile Justice Bulletin* (September, 1999).

Bing, L. 1989. *Harper's Magazine* (March):51–59.

———. 1991. *Do or die*. New York: Harper Collins.

Birenbaum, A., and E. Sagarin. 1976. *Norms and human behavior*. New York: Praeger.

Birzer, M. L., and C. Roberson. 2007. *Policing today and tomorrow*. Upper Saddle River, NJ: Prentice-Hall.

Bishop, D. M., C. E. Frazier, L. Lanza-Kaduce, and L. Winner. 1996. The transfer of juveniles to criminal court: Does it make a difference? *Crime and Delinquency* 42 (April):171–91.

Black, D. J., and A. J. Reiss, Jr. 1970. Police control of juveniles. *American Sociological Review* 35 (February):63–77.

Blerer, L. M. 1980. The meaning of birth order: First born, last born. *Parents* (March):52–55.

Bloch, A. M. 1978. Combat neurosis in inner-city schools. *American Journal of Psychiatry* 135 (October):1189–92.

Block, H., and A. Niederhoffer. 1958. *The gang: A study in adolescent behavior*. New York: Philosophical Library.

Block, K. J., and D. C. Hale. 1991. Turf wars in progressive era juvenile justice: The relationship of private and public child care agencies. *Crime and Delinquency* 37 (April):225–41.

Blue, R. 2006. Out-of-control juveniles get scared straight. *HeraldToday.com*, May 4. http://www.braden.com.

Blum, R. 1987. Contemporary threats to adolescent health in the United States. *Journal of the American Medical Association* 257 (June):3390–95.

Blumstein, A., J. Cohen, J. Roth, and C. A. Visher. 1986. *Criminal careers and "career criminals"*. Washington, DC: National Academy Press.

Bohm, R. M. 1986. Crime, criminal and crime control policy myths. *Justice Quarterly* 3 (June):193–214.

Booth, A., and D. W. Osgood. 1993. The influence of testosterone on deviance in adulthood; Assessing and explaining the relationship. *Criminology* 31 (February):93–102.

Bordua, D. J. 1962. Some comments on theories of group delinquency. *Sociological Inquiry* 32 (Spring):245–60.

Bordua, D. J. 1967. Recent trends: Deviant behavior and social control. *Annals of the Academy of Political and Social Science* 369 (January):149–63.

Bortner, M. A., M. L. Sunderland, and R. Winn. 1985. Race and the impact of juvenile deinstitutionalization. *Crime and Delinquency* 31 (January):35–46.

Bouma, D. H. 1969. *Kids and cops*. Grand Rapids, MI: William E. Erdman.

Bowker, L. H., and M. W. Klein. 1969. On deviance. *Annals of the Academy of Political and Social Science* 312:121–23.

———. 1983. The etiology of female juvenile delinquency and gang membership: A test of psychological and social structural explanations. *Adolescence* 18 (72) (Winter):739–51.

Braithwaite, J. 1989. *Crime, shame, and reintegration*. UK: University of Cambridge.

Brandon, K. 2002. When does spanking a child become abuse? *Dallas Morning News* (September 29):10A.

Braun, C. 1976. Teacher expectations: Sociopsychological dynamics. *Review of Educational Research* 46 (Spring):185–213.

Breen, K. 2006. Peer pressure delivers justice in teen court. *Dallas Morning News* (February 5):1B, 15B.

Brezina, T. 1996. Adapting to strain. *Criminology* 34:39–60.

Brezina, T., and A. R. Piquero. 2007. Moral beliefs, isolation from peers, and abstention from delinquency. *Deviant Behavior* 28 (September–October):433–65.

Bridges, A. 2006. Study: Body art going mainstream. *Dallas Morning News* (June 11):12A.

Brindis, C. 1986. The nation's changing demographic profile: Implications for the family life educator. *Family Life Educator* 5 (Fall):4–9.

Broder, P. K., G. W. Peters, and J. Zimmerman. 1978. *The relationship between self-reported juvenile delinquency and learning disabilities: A preliminary look at the data*. Omaha, NE: Creighton University Institute for Business, Law, and Social Research.

Broder, P. K., N. Dunivant, E. C. Smith, and L. P. Sutton. 1981. Further observations on the link between learning disabilities and juvenile delinquency. *Journal of Educational Psychology* 73 (December):838–50.

Brown, V. K. 1983. *What parents should know about juvenile delinquency and juvenile justice*. York, PA: William Gladden Foundation.

Brownfield, D. 1990. Adolescent male status and delinquent behavior. *Sociological Spectrum* 10 (April–June):227–48.

Brownfield, D., and A. M. Sorenson. 1994. Sibship size and sibling delinquency. *Deviant Behavior* 15 (January–March):45–61.

Browning, C. R., T. Leventhal, and J. Brooks-Gunn. 2005. Sexual initiation in early adolescence: Nexus of parental and community control. *American Sociological Review* 5 (October):758–78.

Browning, Deborah., ed. 2007. *Adolescent identity: A Collection of Readings*. Analytic Press.

Browning, K., D. Huizinga, R. Loeber, and T. P. Thornberry. 1999. *Causes and correlates of delinquency program. OIJDP fact sheet* (April). Washington, DC: U.S. Department of Justice, Office of Juvenile Justice and Delinquency Prevention.

Brunner, R. 1974. Focal points of juvenile crime: Typology and conditions. *Juvenile crime and resocialization*. Congress Report, Stuttgart, W. Germany, New York: Springer Verlag.

Bullington, B., J. Sprowis, D. Katkin, and M. Phillips. 1978. A critique of diversionary juvenile justice. *Crime and Delinquency* 7 (January):59–71.

Bumpass, L. 1984. Some characteristics of children's second families. *American Journal of Sociology* 90 (November):608–23.

Burgess, E. W. 1925. The growth of the city. In *The city*, ed. R. E. Park, E. W. Burgess and R. D. McKenzie, 47–62. Chicago: University of Chicago Press.

Burgess, E. W., and R. L. Akers. 1966. A differential association reinforcement theory of criminal behavior. *Social Problems* 14 (Fall):128–47.

Burkett, S. R., and W. White. 1974. Hellfire and delinquency: Another look. *Journal for the Scientific Study of Religion* 13:455–62.

Burns, V., and L. Stern. 1967. The prevention of juvenile delinquency. In *Task Force Report: Juvenile Delinquency and Youth Crime*, 361–64. President's Commission on Law Enforcement and Administration. Washington, DC: U.S. Government Printing Office, Appendix S.

Burrus, G. W., Jr., and K. Kempf-Leonard. 2002. The questionable advantage of defense counsel in juvenile courts. *Justice Quarterly* 19:37–68.

Bursik, R. J. 1984. Urban dynamics and ecological studies of delinquency. *Social Forces* 63 (December):393–13.

Burt, C. 1925. *The young delinquent*. New York: Appleton.

Bush, K. R., G. W. Peterson, J. A. Cobas, and A. J. Supple. 2002. Adolescent's perceptions of parental behaviors as predictions of adolescent self-esteem in mainland China. *Sociological Inquiry*:503–26.

Butterfield, F. 2002. Study: Teen tobacco, drug, and alcohol use falls. *Dallas Morning News* (December 17):1A.

Butts, J. A., and H. N. Snyder. 1992. *Restitution and juvenile recidivism*. Washington, DC: OJJDP Update on Research, U.S. Department of Justice.

Bynum, J. E. 1996. The California street gangs: motivations and methods. *Research Report*. October 1, 1996.

Caeti, T. J. 1993. Juvenile right to counsel: A case and statute analysis. Paper presented at the Southwest Criminal Justice Educators meeting in Dallas, TX. October 8, 1993.

Calhoun, A. W. 1960. *A social history of the American family: Colonial period*, vol. 1. New York: Barnes and Noble.

Calhoun, T. C., and G. Weaver. 1996. Rational decision-making among male street prostitutes. *Deviant Behavior* 17 (April/June):209–27.

Campbell, A. 1991. *The girls in the gang*. 2nd ed. New York: Basil Blackwell.

Cantelon, S., and D. LeBoeuf. 1997. Keeping young people in school: Community programs that work. *Juvenile justice bulletin* (June). Washington, DC: U.S. Department of Justice, Office of Juvenile Justice and Delinquency Prevention.

Canter, R. J. 1982a. Family correlates of male and female delinquency. *Criminology* 20 (August):149–67.

———. 1982b. Sex differentials in self-reported delinquency. *Criminology* 20 (November): 373–93.

Capaldi, D. M., and G. R. Patterson. 1996. Can violent offenders be distinguished from frequent offenders: Prediction from childhood to adolescence. *Journal of Research in Crime and Delinquency* 33 (May):206–31.

Caplan, P. J. 1981. *Barriers between women*. New York: Spectrum.

Capuzzi, D., and D. R. Gross, eds. 2007. *Youth at risk: A prevention resource for counselors, teachers, and parents*. Washington, DC: American Counseling Association.

Carey, J. T., and P. D. McAnany. 1984. *Introduction to juvenile delinquency: Youth and the law*. Upper Saddle River, NJ: Prentice Hall.

Carmichael, F. 2006. Teen transferred to state prison. *NewsJournal.com*, May 12. http://www.pensacolanewsjournal.com.

Carr, P. J., and G. Alfiera. 2006. Juvenile delinquency and gender. In *Rethinking gender, crime and justice (Feminist readings)*, ed. C. M. Renzetti, L. Goodstein and S. L. Miller, 76–92. Los Angeles: Roxbury Publishing Company.

Carter, R. M. 1976. The police view of the justice system. In *The juvenile justice system*, ed. M. W. Klein, 121–32. Beverly Hills, CA: Sage.

Cashion, B. G. 1982. Female-headed families: Effects on children and clinical implications. *Journal of Marital and Family Therapy* 8 (April):77–85.

Cass, E. 1993. Attorney general affirms importance of family. *Dallas Morning News* (March 21):4A.

Cavan, R. S. 1961. The concepts of tolerance and contraculture as applied to delinquency. *Sociological Quarterly* 2 (Fall):243–58.

Cavan, R. S., and T. N. Ferdinand. 1981. *Juvenile delinquency*. 4th ed. New York: Harper & Row.

CBS News Report. 1986. September 11.

Cernkovich, S. A., and P. C. Giordano. 1987. Family relationships and delinquency. *Criminology* 25: 295–321.

Chambliss, W. J. 1973a. *Functional and conflict theories of crime*. New York: MSS Modular Publications.

———. 1973b. The saints and the roughnecks. *Society* 11:24–31.

———. 1974. The state, the law, and the definition of behavior as criminal or delinquent. In *Handbook of criminology*, ed. Daniel Glaser, 7-43. Chicago: Rand McNally.

Chance, P. 1984. Save our schools: Love a vandal. *Psychology Today* 18 (May):17–18.

Chapman, C. 1976. *America's runaways*. New York: William Morrow.

Chesney-Lind, M. 1977. Judicial paternalism and the female status offender. *Crime and Delinquency* 23 (April):121–30.

———. 1988. Girls in jail. *Crime and Delinquency* 34:150–68.

———. 2004. Girls and vilence: Is the gender gap closing? *VAWnet*, August, http://www.vawnet.org/domesticviolence/research/vawanetdocs/ar_girlsviolence.pdf

Chesney-Lind, M., and R. G. Shelden. 2004. *Girls: Delinquency and juvenile justice*. 3rd ed. Belmont, CA: Brooks/Cole.

Chesney-Lind, M., and L. Pasko. 2004. *The female offender: Girls, women, and crime*. 2nd ed. Thousand Oaks, CA: Sage.

Chin, K. L., J. Fagan, and R. J. Kell. 1992. Patterns of Chinese gang extortion. *Justice Quarterly* 9 (4) (December):625–46.

Christian Science Monitor. 1988. Kid prisons that don't reform: Hope for rehabilitation outside the prison walls. (September 29):B2–B8.

Christner, R. 2007. *Handbook of cognitive-behavior group therapy with children and adolescents*. New York: Routledge.

Cicourel, A. V. 1968. *The social organization of juvenile justice*. New York: Wiley.

Clasen, D. R., and B. Brown. 1985. The multidimensionality of peer pressure in adolescence. *Journal of Youth and Adolescence* 14 (December):451–68.

Cleckley, H. M. 1988. *The mask of sanity*. 5th ed. St. Louis: C. V. Mosby Co.

Clinard, M. B., and R. F. Meier. 2008. *Sociology of deviant behavior*. 13th ed. KY: Wadsworth Cengage.

Cloward, R. A., and L. E. Ohlin. 1960. *Delinquency and opportunity*. New York: Free Press.

CNN. 1993. *Headline News*, November 30.

Coffey, A. R. 1974. *Juvenile justice as a system: Law enforcement to rehabilitation*. Upper Saddle River, NJ: Prentice Hall.

Cohen, A. K. 1955. *Delinquent boys: The culture of the gang*. New York: Free Press.

———. 1966. *Deviance and control*. Upper Saddle River, NJ: Prentice Hall.

Cohen, A. K., and J. F. Short, Jr. 1958. Research in delinquent subcultures. *Journal of Social Issues* 14 (3):20–36.

Cohen, A., and J. Short. 1971. Crime and juvenile delinquency. In *Contemporary social problems*. 3rd ed., ed. R. K. Merton and R. Nisbet, 89–146. New York: Harcourt, Brace, Jovanovich.

Cohen, L., and J. Kluegel. 1978. Determinants of juvenile court dispositions: Ascriptive and achieved factors in two metropolitan courts. *American Sociological Review* 43:162–76.

Coker, V. L. 1993. Personal dress often a type of identification for adolescents. *Greenville Herald Banner* (December 7):A14.

Cole, A. 1993. Diversity revisited. *Modern Maturity* (August–September):10, 12.

Cole, P. Z., and J. W. Hafsten. 1978. Probation supervision revisited: Responsibility training. *Journal of Juvenile and Family Courts* 29 (February):53–58.

Cole, S. 1980. *The sociological method: An introduction to the science of sociology*. 3rd ed. Chicago: Rand McNally.

Coleman, J. S. 1960. The adolescent subculture and academic achievement. *American Journal of Sociology* 65 (January):337–47.

———. 1988. Social capital in the creation of human capital. *American Journal of Sociology* 94 Suppl.:S95–S120.

Collins, R. 1971. Functional and conflict theories of educational stratification. *American Sociological Review* 36 (December):1002–19.

Colvin, M., and J. Pauly. 1983. A critique of criminology: Toward an integrated structural-marxist theory of delinquency production. *American Journal of Sociology* 89 (November):513–45.

Conley, D. 2005. *The pecking order: A bold new look at how family and society determine who we become*. New York: Vintage Press.

Conley, J. A., ed. 1994. *The 1967 President's Crime Commission Report: Its impact 25 years later*. Cincinnati, OH: Anderson.

Conrad, P. 1975. The discovery of hyperkinesis: Notes on the medicalization of deviant behavior. *Social Problems* 23 (2) (April):12–22.

Cooley, C. H. [1902] 1964. *Human nature and the social order*. New York: Schocken Books.

Copes, H. 2003. Societal attachments, offending frequency, and techniques of neutralization. *Deviant Behavior: An Interdisciplinary Journal* 24 (March–April):107–27.

Corliss, R. 1986. Well, hello Mollyl. *Time* 127 (May 26):66–71.

Cornish, D. B., and R. V. Clarke., eds. 1986. *The reasoning criminal*. New York: Springer-Verlag.

Coser, L. 1956. *The functions of social conflict*. New York: Free Press.

Cosner, T. L., and G. L. Larson. 1980. Social fabric theory and the youth culture. *Adolescence* 15 (Spring):99–104.

Costello, B. J. 2000. Techniques of neutralization and self-esteem. *Deviant Behavior: An Interdisciplinary Journal* 2 (1): 307–29.

Costello, J. C., and N. Worthington. 1981. Incarcerating status offenders: Attempts to circumvent the juvenile justice delinquency prevention act. *Harvard Civil Rights—Civil Liberties Law Review* 16 (Summer): 41–81.

Cox, S. M., and J. M. Allen, R. D. Hanser, and J. J. Conrad. 2008. *Juvenile justice: A guide to theory, policy, and practice*. 6th ed. New York: Sage.

Coxe, S. 1967. Lawyers in juvenile court. *Crime and Delinquency* 13 (October):488–93.

Crenson, M. 2001. The teen brain. *Medford Mail Tribune* (January 4):IB.

Cressey, D. R. 1955. Changing criminals: The application of the theory of differential association. *American Journal of Sociology* 61 (September):116–20.

Criminal Victimizations in the United States, 2006. 2008. Rockville, MD: U.S. Department of Justice, Office of Justice Programs; Bureau of Justice Standards.

Culbertson, R. G., and T. Ellsworth. 1985. Treatment innovations in probation and parole. In *Probation, parole, and community corrections: A reader*, ed. L. F. Travis, III, 127–47. Prospect Heights, IL: Waveland Press.

Cullen, F. T., K. R. Blevins, J. S. Trager, and P. Gendreau. 2005. The rise and fall of boot camps: A case study in common sense corrections. *Journal of Offender Rehabilitation* 40:53–70.

Curry, G. D., and S. H. Decker. 2003. *Confronting gangs: Crime and community*. 2nd ed. Los Angeles: Roxbury Publishing Company.

Dahrendorf, R. 1959. *Class and class conflict in industrial society*. Palo Alto, CA: Stanford University Press.

Daily O'Collegian. 1993. Oklahoma State University, Stillwater. (January 12):3.

Daily Tidings. 1977. Kid corporation is in trouble again. Ashland, OR, (November 3):3.

Dallas Morning News. 1993. White gangs organizing, officers say. (October 10):2A.

———. 2003. Many crimes never reported. (March 10):3A.

Daly, K., and M. Chesney-Lind. 1984. Feminism and criminology. *Justice Quarterly* 5:497–538.

Damasio, A. 1999. Brain injury and antisocial behavior. *Nature Neuroscience* 2 (November):1032–1037.

Dannefer, D., and R. K. Schutt. 1982. Race and juvenile justice processing in court and police agencies. *American Journal of Sociology* 87:1113–32.

Dantzker, M. L. 2003. *Understanding today's police*. 3rd ed. Upper Saddle River, NJ: Prentice Hall.

Darling, C. A., and J. K. Davidson. 1986. Coitally active university students: Sexual behaviors, concerns, and challenges. *Adolescence* 21 (Summer):403–19.

Datesman, S., and F. R. Scarpitti. 1975. Female delinquency and broken homes. *Criminology* 13 (May):35–56.

David, W. 1997. The San Antonio youth firearms violence initiative. *Telemasp Bulletin* 3 (February):1–7.

Davis, J. R. 1978. Neighborhood nonsense: The street war. *Terrorists—Youth, biker and prison violence*. San Diego, CA: Grossmont Press.

Davis, K. 1948. Extreme isolation of a child. *American Journal of Sociology* 45:554–65. *Human Society*. New York: Macmillan.

Davis, P. W. 2003. The changing meanings of spanking. In *Social Problems: Constructionist Readings*, ed. J. Best and D. R. Loseke, 6–12. NY: Aldine deGruyter.

Davis, S. M. 1971. Justice for the juvenile: The decision to arrest and due process. *Duke Law Journal*:913–20.

———. 1983. *Rights of juveniles: The juvenile justice system*. 2nd ed. New York: Clark Boardman.

Day, L. A. 1984. Media access to juvenile courts. *Journalism Quarterly* 61 (Winter):751–56.

De Venanzi, A. 2007. Social representations and the labeling of non-compliant youths: The case of Victorian and Edwardian hooligans. *Deviant Behavior* 29 (April): 193–224.

Dealey, S. 2006. America's most vicious gang. *Netscape: Home and Real Estate*. (And from *Reader's Digest*, 2005). (January 28):1–3.

Delamont, S. 2003. *Feminist Sociology*. Thousand Oaks, CA: Pine Forge Press.

Delaney, T. 2006. *American street gangs*. Upper Saddle River, NJ: Pearson/Prentice Hall.

Dembo, R., L. Williams, W. Wothke, and J. Schmeidler. 1992. Examining a structural model of the relationships among alcohol use, marijuana/hashish use, their effects, and emotional and psychological problems over *time* in a cohort of high-risk youths. *Deviant Behavior* 13 (April–June):195–215.

DeMello, M. 2000. *Bodies of inscription: A cultural history of the modern tattoo community*. Durham, NC: Duke University Press.

Demuth, S., and S. L. Brown. 2004. Family structure, family processes, and adolescent delinquency: The significance of parental absence versus parental gender. *Journal of Research in Crime and Delinquency* 41 (February):58–81.

Dentler, R., and K. Erikson. 1959. The functions of deviance in groups. *Social Problems* 7 (Fall):98–107.

Diegmueller, K. 1987. The forgotten juveniles: Crimeless criminals. *Parade* (September 3):14–15.

DiLorenzo, T. J. 1997. Pizza driver safety transcends civil rights. *USA Today* (June 25):13A.

Dinitz, S. and W. Reckless. 1972. *Delinquency prevention*. Columbus, OH: Ohio State University.

Dollard, J., N. Miller, L. Doob, O. H. Mowizer, and R. R. Sears. 1939. *Frustration and aggression*. New Haven, CT: Yale University Press.

Donovan, D. 1990. Meet the world's toughest girls! *Weekly World News* (April 17):33.

Dotter, D. 2002. Creating deviance: Scenarios of stigmatization in postmodern media culture. *Deviant Behavior* 23 (September– October):419–48.

Douglas, J. W. B. 1960. Premature children at primary schools. *British Medical Journal* 1:1008–1013.

Douglas, J., Jr., and R. S. Martin. 1994. Some who have felt gang wrath favor hiring plan. *Fort Worth Star Telegram* (May 15):1, 17.

Doup, L. 2006. "Pharming parties" part of the teen scene. *Dallas Morning News* (May 25):Family Section, 6.

Downey, M. 1993. *The Mort Downey Show*. TV Channel 27, Ft. Worth, TX. September 24.

Dugdale, R. 1910. *The Jukes*. New York: Putnam.

Durkheim, E. 1938. *The rules of sociological method*. Trans. Sarah A. Solovay and John H. Mueller and ed. George E. G. Catlin. New York: Free Press of Glencoe.

———. [1893] 1947. *Division of labor in society*. Trans. George Simpson. New York: Free Press.

———. [1895] 1950. *The rules of sociological method*. Glencoe, IL: Free Press.

———. [1897] 1951. *Suicide: A study in sociology*. Trans. J. A. Spaulding and G. Simpson. New York: Free Press.

———. [1906] 1956. *Sociology and education*. Trans. S. D. Fox. New York: Free Press.

Edgette, J. S. 2006. *Adolescent therapy that really works*. New York: W. W Norton.

Egley, A., and A. Major. 2004. *Highlights of the 2002 National Gang Survey*. Washington, DC: U.S. Government Printing Office, Office of Juvenile Justice and Delinquency Prevention.

Egley, A., and C. E. O'Donnell. 2008. Highlights of the 2006 National Youth Gang Survey. *OJJDP Fact Sheet* (July). Washington, DC: U.S. Government Printing Office.

Eisikovits, Z., and M. Baizerman. 1982. "Doin' time": Violent youth in a juvenile facility and in an adult prison. *Journal of Offender Counseling, Services and Rehabilitation* 6 (Spring):5–20.

Eith, C. A. 2005. *Delinquency, schools, and the social bond*. NY: LFB Scholarly publishing.

Eitzen, D. S., and M. B. Zinn. 1997. *Social problems*. 7th ed. Boston: Allyn and Bacon.

Elkin, F., and G. Handel. 1978. *The child and society: The process of socialization*. 3rd ed. New York: Random House.

Elkind, D. 1991. The child: Yesterday, today, and tomorrow. In *Human development* 19th ed., ed. L. Fenson and I. Fenson, 136–41. Guilford, CT: Dushkin Publishing Co.

Ellis, L. 1987. Religiosity and criminality from the perspective of arousal theory. *Journal of Research in Crime and Delinquency* 24 (3) (August):215–32.

Elliott, D. S. 1966. Delinquency, school attendance and dropout. *Social Problems* 13 (Winter):307–14.

Elliott, D. S., and D. Huizinga. 1985. *Explaining delinquency and drug use*. Beverly Hills, CA: Sage.

Elliott, D. S., and B. J. Morse. 1989. Delinquency and drug use as risk factors in teenage sexual activity. *Youth and Society* 21 (September):32–60.

Elliott, D. S., and H. Voss. 1974. *Delinquency and dropout*. Lexington, MA: Lexington Press.

Elliott, D. S., W. J. Wilson, D. Huizinga, R. J. Sampson, A. Elliott, and B. Rankin. 1996. The effects of neighborhood disadvantage on adolescent development. *Journal of Research in Crime and Delinquency* 33 (November):389–426.

Empey, L. T., and M. L. Erickson. 1966. Hidden delinquency and social status. *Social Forces* 44 (June):546–54.

Empey, L. T., and J. Rabow. 1961. The Provo experiment in delinquency rehabilitation. *American Sociological Review* 26 (October):679–95.

Empey, L. T., and M. C. Stafford. 1999. *American delinquency: Its meaning and construction*. 4th ed. Belmont, CA: Wadsworth.

England, R. W., Jr. 1967. A theory of middle class juvenile delinquency. In *Middle class juvenile delinquency*, ed. E. W. Vaz, 242–51. New York: Harper and Row.

Epstein, R. 2007. Why high school must go: An interview with Leon Botstein. *Phi Delta Kappan* (May):659–63.

Erikson, E. 1956. The problem of identity. *Journal of the American Psychiatric Association* 4 (1) (January):56–121.

———. 1968. *Identity: Youth and crisis*. New York: Norton.

Erikson, K. 1964. Notes on the sociology of deviance. In *The other side*, ed. H. Becker, 9–22. New York: Free Press.

Erickson, M. L., and L. T. Empey. 1963. Court records, undetected delinquency and decision-making. *Journal of Criminal Law, Criminology and Police Science* 54 (4) (December):456–69.

Erickson, M., and G. Jensen. 1977. Delinquency is still group behavior: Toward revitalizing the group premise in the sociology of deviance. *Journal of Criminal Law and Criminology* 68 (2) (June):262–63.

Erlanger, H. S. 1979. Estrangement, machismo, and gang violence. *Social Science Quarterly* 60 (September): 235–48.

Esbensen, F. A. 2000. Preventing adolescent gang involvement. *Juvenile Justice Bulletin* (September):1–11.

Estrabrook, A. 1916. *The Jokes in 1915*. Washington, DC: The Carnegie Institute of Washington.

Evans, R. C., and G. D. Koederitz. 1983. The requirement of restitution for juvenile offenders: An alternative disposition. *Journal of Offender Counseling, Services and Rehabilitation* 7 (Spring–Summer):1–20.

Evans, T. D., F. T. Cullen, V. S. Burton, R. G. Dunaway, G. L. Payne, and S. R. Kethineni. 1996. Religion, social bonds, and delinquency. *Deviant Behavior: An Interdisciplinary Journal* 17:43–70.

Eysenck, H. J. 1979. *Crime and personality*. 2nd ed. London: Routledge and Kegan Paul.

———. 1980. The biosocial model of man and the unification of psychology. In *Models of man*, ed.

A. J. Chapman and D. M. Jones,9-62. Leicester: British Psychological Society.

Fagan, J., and E. Pabon. 1990. Contributions of delinquency and substance use to school dropout among inner-city youths. *Youth and Society* 21 (March):306–54.

Fagan, J., M. Forst, and T. S. Vivona. 1987a. Racial determinants of the judicial transfer decision: Prosecuting violent youth in criminal court. *Crime and Delinquency* 33 (April):259–86.

Fagan, J., E. Slaughter, and E. Hartstone. 1987b. Blind justice? The impact of race on the juvenile justice process. *Crime and Delinquency* 33 (April):224–58.

Family Violence Fund. 2006. *Domestic violence is a serious, widespread social problem in America: The facts.* http://www.endabuse.org.

Farkas, G., D. Sheehan, R. P. Grobe, and Y. Shuan. 1990. Cultural resources and school success: Gender, ethnicity, and poverty groups within an urban school district. *American Sociological Review* 55 (February):127–42.

Farley, M. 2004. *Prostitution, trafficking, and trauma tic stress.* New York: Haworth.

Farnsworth, M., and M. J. Leiber. 1989. Strain theory revisited: Economic goals, educational means, and delinquency. *American Sociological Review* 54 (April):263–74.

Farnworth, M. 1984. Family structure, family attributes, and delinquency in a sample of low- income, minority males and females. *Journal of Youth and Adolescence* 13 (August):349–64.

Farnworth, M., L. Schweinhart, and J. R. BerruetaClement. 1985. Preschool intervention, school success and delinquency in a high-risk sample of youth. *American Educational Research Journal* 22 (Fall):445–64.

Farrell, R. A., and V. L. Swigert. 1982. *Deviance and social control.* Glenview, IL: Scott, Foresman.

Farrington, D. P. 1985. Delinquency prevention in the 1980s. *Journal of Adolescence* 8 (March):3–16.

———. 1989. Early predictors of adolescent aggression and adult violence. *Violence and Victims* 4:79–100.

Fass, P. S. 1977. *The damned and the beautiful: American youth in the 1920s.* New York: Oxford University Press.

FBI. 2008. *Crime in the United States: Uniform crime reports—2007.* Washington, DC: U.S. Government Printing Office.

Feld, B. C. 1993. Juvenile (in) justice and the criminal court alternative. *Crime and Delinquency* 39 (October):403–24.

———. 1999. *Bad kids: Race and the transformation of juvenile court.* New York: Oxford University Press.

Feldman, M. P. 1978. *Criminal behavior: A psychological analysis.* New York: John Wiley.

Felson, M. 1986. Linking criminal choices, routine activities, informal control, and criminal outcomes. In *The reasoning criminal*, ed. D. B. Cornish and R. V. Clarke, 119–28. New York: Springer-Verlag.

Ferdinand, T. N., and E. G. Luchterhand. 1970. Inner-city youth, the police, the juvenile court, and justice. *Social Problems* 17 (Spring):510–27.

Ferrero, G. L. 1911. *Criminal man according to the classification of Cesare Lombroso.* New York: Putnam.

Fields, S. 1993. Time to end teens' new, vicious edge. *Insight* (September 13):28–30.

Figgis, J. N. 1922. *The divine right of kings.* London: Smith.

Figueira-McDonough, J. 1984. *British Journal of Criminology* 24 (October):325–42.

———. 1993. Residence, dropping out, and delinquency rates. *Deviant Behavior* 14 (April–June):109–32.

Finckenauer, J. O. 1982. *Scared straight! And the panacea phenomenon.* Upper Saddle River, NJ: Prentice Hall.

Finckenauer, J. O., and P. W. Gavin. 1999. *Scared Straight: The panacea phenomenon revisited.* Prospect Heights, IL: Waveland Press.

Finkelhor, D., and R. Ormrod. 2001. Homicides of children and youth. *Juvenile Justice Bulletin* (October). Pittsburgh, PA: U.S. Department of Justice, Office of Juvenile Justice and Delinquency Prevention.

Fischer, D. G. 1983. Parental supervision and delinquency. *Perceptual Motor Skills So* (April):635–40.

Fishbein, D. H. 1990. Biological perspectives in criminology. *Criminology* 28 (1):27–72.

Flaherty, M. C. 1990. An assessment of the national incidence of juvenile suicide in adult jails, lockups, and juvenile detention centers. In *Juvenile delinquency: A justice perspective* 2nd ed., ed. R. A. Weisheit and R. G. Culbertson, 173–82. Prospect Heights, IL: Waveland Press.

Flowers, R. B. 2001. *Runaway kids and teenage prostitution.* Westport, CT: Praeger.

Floyd, J. 1994. FW blasted for plan to pay gang leaders. *Dallas Morning News* (May 12):1A, 15A.

Forsyth, C. J., and B. D. Foster. 1993. Trends in female criminality 1943–91. *Free Inquiry in Creative Sociology* 21 (November):135–39.

Foster, J., S. Dinitz, and W. T. Reckless. 1972. Perceptions of stigma following public intervention for delinquent behavior. *Social Problems* 20:202–09.

Fox, R. G. 1971. The XYY offender: A modern myth? *Journal of Criminal Law, Criminology and Police Science* 62 (1):59-73.

Frankfurter, D. 2006. *Evil Incarnate: Rumors of Demonic Conspiracy and Satanic Abuse in History.* Princeton, NJ: Princeton University Press.

Frazier, C. E., and S. R. Lee. 1992. Reducing juvenile detention rates or expanding the official control nets: An evaluation of legislative reform effort. *Crime and Delinquency* 38 (April):204–18.

Freud, S. 1961. The ego and the id. *The complete psychological works of Sigmund Freud*, vol. 19, 12–68. London: Hogarth.

———. 1963. *An outline of psychoanalysis*. Trans. James Strachey. New York: Norton.

Frey, H. E. 1999. Employment and training for court-involved youth: An overview. *OJJDP Fact Sheet* 102 (April):1–2.

Friedenberg, E. Z. 1959. *The vanishing adolescent*. New York: Dell.

———. 1963. *Coming of age in America*. New York: Random House.

———. 1971. The high school as a focus of student unrest. *Annals of American Academy of Political and Social Science* 395 (May):117–26.

Friend, T. 1994. Violence-prone men may be both born and made. *USA Today* (December 14):5D.

Fritsch, E. J., T. J. Cacti, and C. Hemmens. 1996. Spare the needle but not the punishment: The incarceration of waived youth in Texas prisons. *Crime and Delinquency* 42 (October):593–609.

Fuller, R., and R. Myers. 1941. Some aspects of a theory of social problems. *American Sociological Review* 6 (February):24–32.

Furman vs. *Georgia*. 1972. 408 U.S. 238, 371, 1972.

Gaines, L. K., and V. E. Kappeler. 2008. *Policing America*. 6th ed. Cincinnati: Andersen, Lexis/Nexis.

Gamoran, A. 1992. The variable effects of high school tracking. *American Sociological Review* 57 (December):812–28.

Ganiere, D. M., and R. D. Enright. 1989. Exploring three approaches to identity development. *Journal of Youth and Adolescence* 18:283–95.

Gardner, L., and D. J. Shoemaker. 1989. Social bonding and delinquency: A comparative analysis. *Sociological Quarterly* 30 (3):481–500.

Garry, E. M. 1996. Truancy: First step to a lifetime of problems. *Juvenile Justice Bulletin* (October). Washington, DC: U.S. Department of Justice, Office of Juvenile Justice and Delinquency Prevention.

Gavzer, B. 1986. Must kids be bad? *Parade* (March 9):8, 10.

Gelles, R., and M. A. Straus. 1979. Violence in the American family. *Journal of Social Issues* 35 (Spring): 15–19.

Gelman, D. 1990. A much riskier passage. *Newsweek* (Special Edition) (Summer/Fall):10–16.

Getzels, J. W. 1977. Why some children do poorly in school. In *Crucial issues in education* 6th ed., ed. H. Ehiers, 73–76. New York: Holt, Rinehart and Winston.

Geyelin, M. 1992. Study to focus on what leads youths to crime. *Wall Street Journal* (June 5):B1, B6.

Gibbons, D. 1976. *Delinquent behavior*. 2nd ed. Upper Saddle River, NJ: Prentice Hall.

Gibbons, D. 1990. From the editor's desk: A call for some "outrageous" proposals for crime control in the 1990s. *Crime and Delinquency* 36 (2) (April):197–203.

Gibbs, J. P. 1966. Conceptions of deviant behavior: The old and the new. *Pacific Sociological Review* 9 (Spring):9–14.

———. 1975. *Crime, punishment, and deterrence*. New York: Elsevier.

Gil, D. 1970. *Violence against children*. Cambridge, MA: Harvard University Press.

Gilfus, M. E. 1992. From victims to survivors to offenders: Women's routes of entry into street crime. *Women and Criminal Justice* 4:63–89.

Giordano, P. C. 1976. The sense of injustice: An analysis of juveniles' reactions to the justice system. *Criminology* 14 (May):105–106.

Giordano, P. C., S. A. Cernkovich, and J. L. Rudolph. 2002. Gender, crime, and dissidence: Toward a theory of cognitive transformation. *American Journal of Sociology* 107 (4) (January):990–1064.

Glaser, D. 1956. Criminality theories and behavioral images. *American Journal of Sociology* 61 (March):433–44.

Glasser, W. 1965. *Reality therapy*. New York: Harper & Row.

———. 1978. Disorder in our schools: Causes and remedies. *Phi Delta Kappan* 59 (January):331–33.

———. 2001. *Counseling with choice therapy*. NY: Harper paperbacks.

Glassner, B. 1982. Labeling theory. In *The sociology of deviance*, ed. M. M. Rosenberg, R. A. Stebbins and A. Turowetz, 71–89. New York: St. Martin's Press.

Glassner, B., and J. Loughlin. 1987. *Drugs in adolescent worlds: Burnouts to straights*. New York: St. Martin's Press.

Glassner, B., M. Ksander, B. Berg, and B. D. Johnson. 1983. A note on the deterrent effect of juvenile vs. adult jurisdiction. *Social Problems* 31 (December):219–21.

Glueck, S., and E. Glueck. 1950. *Unraveling juvenile delinquency*. Cambridge, MA: Harvard University Press.

———. 1968. *Delinquents and nondelinquents in perspective*. Cambridge, MA: Harvard University Press.

Goddard, H. 1920. *Efficiency and levels of intelligence*. Princeton, NJ: Princeton University Press.

———. 1927. *The Kallikak family: A study in the heredity of feeble-mindedness*. New York: Macmillan.

Godwin, T. M. 1996. A guide for implementing teen court programs. *Qffice of Juvenile Justice and Delinquency Prevention, Fact Sheet #45* (August). Washington, DC: U.S. Department of Justice.

Goffman, E. 1961. *Asylums*. Garden City, NY: Doubleday.

———. 1965. *Behavior in public places*. New York: Free Press.

———. 1967. *Where the action is*. Garden City, NY: Doubleday and Company.

Goffman, E. 1971. *The presentation of self in everyday life*. London: Penguin University Books.

———. 1986. *Stigma: Notes on the management of spoiled identity*. Reissued ed. Upper Saddle River, NJ: Prentice Hall.

Goldman, N. 1963. *The differential selection of juvenile offenders for court appearance*. New York: National Council on Crime and Delinquency.

Goldscheider, C., and J. E. Simpson. 2007. Religious affiliation and juvenile delinquency. *Sociological Inquiry* 37 (January):297–310.

Gonzales, A. R., R. B. Schofield, and G. R. Schmitt. 2005. Co-offending and patterns of juvenile crime. *Report from National Institute of Justice* (NCJ 210360) (December). Washington, DC: U.S. Department of Justice.

Goode, E. 1990. Symposium: Phenomenology and structure in the study of crime and deviance. *Contemporary Sociology* 19 (1):5–12.

———. 2003. Psychiatric drug use up sharply for kids. *Dallas Morning News* (January 14):1A, 12A.

———. 2007. *Deviant behavior*. 8th ed. Upper Saddle River, NJ: Prentice Hall.

Goodman, P. 1962. *Growing up absurd: Problems of youth in the organized society*. New York: Random House.

Goring, C. [1913] 1972. *TheEnglish convict: A statistical study*. Montclair, NJ: Patterson Smith.

Gotlieb, D., J. Reeves, and 'N. D. Tenhouten. 1966. *The emergence of youth societies: A cross-cultural approach*. New York: Free Press.

Gottfredson, G. D., D. C. Gottfredson, and E. R. Czeh. 2000. *National study of delinquency prevention in schools*. Ellicott City, MD: Gottfredson Associates, Inc.

Gottfredson, M. R., and T. Hirschi. 1990. *A general theory of crime*. Stanford, CA: Stanford University Press.

Gove, W. R., and R. D. Crutchfield. 1982. The family and juvenile delinquency. *Sociological Quarterly* 23 (Summer):301–19.

Gracey, H. L. 1977. Learning the student role: Kindergarten as academic boot camp. In *Readings in introductory sociology* 3rd ed., ed. D. H. Wrong and H. L. Gracey, 215–26. New York: Macmillan.

Green, A. 1972. *Sociology*. New York: McGraw-Hill.

Greenberg, D. F. 1977. Delinquency and the age structure of society. *Contemporary Crises* 1 (April):189–224.

Greenberg, N. 1990. How college students can help delinquents. *Journal of Criminal Justice* 18 (1):55–63.

Greene, M. B. 1993. Chronic exposure to violence and poverty: Interventions that work for youth. *Crime and Delinquency* 39 (January):106–24.

Greenspan, R. 2003. The kids are alright with spending. *The ClickZ Network*, September 16, http://www.clickz.com/shoPage.html?page=3077581

Greenwood, P. W. 1992. Substance abuse problems among high-risk youth and potential interventions. *Crime and Delinquency* 38 (October):444–58.

Greenwood, P. W., and S. T. Rand. 1993. Evaluation of the paint creek youth center: A residential program for serious delinquents. *Criminology* 31 (May):263–79.

Greer, C. 1993. How safe is your child's school? *Parade Magazine* (November 7):8.

Griffin, L. 1999. Growing pains. *Dallas Morning News* (April 18):1A.

Griffin, P. 2000. Rethinking juvenile probation: The desktop guide to good juvenile probation practice revisited. *NCJJ in Focus* 2 (September):1–8.

Griffin, P., L. Szymanski, and M. King. 2003. *Juvenile Justice Administration*. St. Paul, MN: West.

———. 2005. National overviews. *State Juvenile Justice Profiles*. Pittsburgh, PA: National Center for Juvenile Justice.

Grossman, J. B., and E. M. Garry. 1997. Mentoring—A proven delinquency prevention strategy. *Juvenile Justice Bulletin* (April). Washington, DC: U.S. Department of Justice, Office of Juvenile Justice and Delinquency Prevention.

Groth, A., and H. J. Birnbaum. 1979. *Men who rape: The psychology of the offender*. New York: Plenum.

Gruber, P. 1998. The national youth network. *Youth in Action* 1 (March):1–2.

Gubrium, J. F., and J. A. Holstein. 2006. *Couples, kids, and family life*. New York: Oxford University Press.

Gullotta, T. P. 1979. Leaving home—Family relationships of the runaway child. *Social Casework* 60 (February): 111–14.

Gullotta, T. P., and G. R. Adams. 1982. Minimizing juvenile delinquency: Implications for prevention programs. *Journal of Early Adolescence* 2 (Summer): 105–17.

Guo, G., M. E. Roettger, and T. Cai. 2008. The integration of genetic propensities into social-control models of delinquency and violence among male youths. *American Sociological Review* 73 (August):543–68.

Hagan, J. A., R. Gihis, and J. Simpson. 1985. The class structure' of gender and delinquency: Toward a power-control theory of common delinquent behavior. *American Journal of Sociology* 90:1151–78.

Hagan, J. A., C. Shedd, and M. R. Payne. 2005. Race, ethnicity, and youth perceptions of criminal justice. *American Sociological Review* 70 (June): 381–407.

Hagedorn, J. M. 1998. *People and folks*. Chicago: Lakeview Press.

Hakeem, M. 1957–1958. A critique of the psychiatric approach to the prevention of juvenile delinquency. *Social Problems* 5:194–206.

Halleck, S. 1971. *Psychiatry and the dilemmas of crime*. Berkeley: University of California Press.

Halvorsen, R., and D. Hawley. 1973. *From gangs to God*. Washington, DC: Review and Herald Publishing.

Hamilton, R., and K. McKinney. 1999. Job Training for Juveniles: Project CRAFT. *OJJDP Fact Sheet* 116 (August):1–2.

Hamner, T. J., and P. H. Turner. 1985. *Parenting in contemporary society*. Upper Saddle Ridge, NJ: Prentice Hall.

Hamparian, D. M., R. Schuster, S. Dinitz, and J. P. Conrad. 1978. *The violent few: A study of dangerous juvenile offenders*, 54–55 and 133–35. Lexington, MA: Lexington Books.

Han, W. S. 1969. Two conflicting themes: Common values versus class differential values. *American Sociological Review* 34 (October):679–90.

Hardman, D. G. 1969. Small town gangs. *Journal of Criminal Law, Criminology and Police Science* 60 (2) (June):173–81.

Hardy R. E., and J. C. Cull. 1973. *Climbing ghetto walls*. Springfield, IL: Charles C Thomas.

Hartl, E. M., E. P. Monelly, and R. D. Elderkin. 1981. *Measuring Delinquency*. Beverly Hills, CA: Sage.

———. 1982. *Physique and delinquent behavior*. New York: Academic Press.

Hasenfeld, Y., and P. P. L. Cheung. 1985. The juvenile court as a people-processing organization: A political economy perspective. *American Journal of Sociology* 90 (January):801–24.

Haskell, M., and L. Yablonsky. 1978. *Juvenile Delinquency*. 2nd ed. Chicago: Rand McNally.

Hastad, D. N., J. O. Segrave, R. Pangrazi, and G. Peterson. 1984. Youth sport participation and deviant behavior. *Sociology of Sport Journal* 1 (December):366–73.

Haviland, W. A., H. E. Prins, D. Walrath, and B. McBride. 2008. *Anthropology*. 12th ed. Belmont, CA: Thomson.

Hawkins, J. D., and D. M. Lishner. 1987. Schooling and delinquency. In *Handbook on crime and delinquency prevention*, ed. Elmer H. Johnson, 179–221. Westport, CT: Greenwood Press.

Hawkins, J. D., and J. G. Weis. 1980. *The social developmental model: An integrated approach to delinquency prevention*. Seattle: Center for Law and Justice, University of Washington.

Hawkins, J. D., T. L. Herrenkohi, D. P. Farrington, R. E. Catalano, T. W. Harschi, and L. Cothern. 2000. Predictors of youth violence. *Juvenile Justice Bulletin* (April). Washington, DC: U.S. Department of Justice, Office of Juvenile Justice and Delinquency Prevention.

Hayes, H. D. 1997. Using integrated theory to explain the movement into juvenile delinquency. *Deviant Behavior* 18:161–484.

Healy, W., and A. J. Bronner. 1926. *Delinquents and criminals—Their making and unmaking*. New York: Macmillan.

———. 1957. *New light on delinquency and its treatment*. New Haven, CT: Yale University Press.

Heimer, K. 1997. Socioeconomic status, subcultural definitions, and violent delinquency. *Social Forces* 75 (March):799–833.

Henggeler, S. 1989. *Delinquency in adolescence*. Newbury Park, CT: Sage.

Hereen, J., and D. Schicor. 1984. Mass media and delinquency prevention: The case of "Scared Straight!" *Deviant Behavior* 5 (1–4):375–86.

Herndon, L. 1993. Bullies can make a kid's life miserable—but don't despair. *The Oregonian* (August 26):A1.

Hernon, P. 1980. Two researchers startled by findings on criminals. News Service, *World Tribune* (February 3): 18-A.

Hersch, P. 1988. Coming of age on city streets. *Psychology Today* 22 (January):28–37.

Higgins, P. S. 1978. Evaluation and case study of a school-based delinquency prevention program. *Evaluation Quarterly* 2 (May):215–35.

Hill, C. R., and F. P. Stafford. 1979. Parental care of children. *Journal of Human Resources* 15 (Spring): 219–39.

Hill, K. G., C. Lui, and J. D. Hawkins. 2001. Early precursors of gang membership: A study of Seattle youth. *Juvenile Justice Bulletin* (December). Washington, DC: U.S. Department of Justice.

Hindelang, M. J. 1973. Causes of delinquency: A partial replication and extension. *Social Problems* 20 (Spring):471–87.

———. 1976. With a little help from their friends. *British Journal of Criminology* 11 (April):109–25.

Hindelang, M. J., T. Hirschi, and J. G. Weis. 1979. Correlates of delinquency: The illusion of discrepancy between self-report and official measures. *American Sociological Review* 44 (December):995–1014.

Hirschi, T. 1969. *Causes of delinquency*. Berkeley: University of California Press.

———. 1983. Families and crime. *Current* 254 (July–August):14–19.

Hirschi, T., and M. R. Gottfredson. 1983. Age and the explanation of crime. *American Journal of Sociology* 89:552–84.

———. 1993. Rethinking the juvenile justice system. *Crime and Delinquency* 39 (April):262–71.

Hirschi, T., and M. J. Hindelang. 1977. Intelligence and delinquency: A Revisionist review. *American Sociological Review* 42:571–86.

Hobbes, T. 1914. *Leviathan (Everyman's Library Edition)*. London: J. M. Dent.

Hochschild, A. 1997. *The time bind: When work becomes home and home becomes work*. New York: Holt Metropolitan Books.

Hoffman, J. P., and S. S. Su. 1997. The conditional effects of stress on delinquency and drug use: A strain theory assessment of sex differences. *Journal of Research in Crime and Delinquency* 34 (February):46–78.

Hogan, D. P., and E. M. Kitagawa. 1985. The impact of social status, family structure, and neighborhood on the fertility of black adolescents. *American Journal of Sociology* 90 (January):825–55.

Hohenstein, W. F. 1969. Factors influencing the police disposition of juvenile offenders. In *Delinquency; Selected studies*, ed. T. Sellin and M. E. Wolfgang, 138–49. New York: Wiley.

Hoobler, R. L. 1973. San Diego, CA: Secondary schools' task force. *Police Chief* 40:28–30.

Horowitz, T. 2003. School vandalism: Individual and social context. *Adolescence* 38 (Spring):131-139

Housewright, E. 2000. Hard time for kids. *Dallas Morning News* (January 4):1A, 6A.

Housewright, E. 2001, Teen abstinence pledges have impact, study says. *Dallas Morning News* (January 4):4A.

Howell, J. C. 1998. Youth gangs: An overview. *Juvenile Justice Bulletin*. Washington, DC: U.S. Department of Justice, Office of Juvenile Justice and Delinquency Prevention.

Howell, J. C., and J. P. Lynch. 2000. Youth gangs in schools. *Juvenile Justice Bulletin*. Washington, DC: U.S. Department of Justice.

Howlett, F. W. 1973. Is the Youth Service Bureau all it's cracked up to be? *Crime and Delinquency* 91 (October):485–92.

Hubner, J. 2005. *Last Chance in Texas: The redemption of criminal youth*. New York: Random House.

Hug, R. 2006. *Beyond subculture: Youth and pop in a multi-ethnic world*. New York: Routledge.

Hughes, E. C. 1945. Dilemmas and contradictions of status. *American Journal of Sociology* 50 (March):353–59.

Huizinga, D., and D. S. Elliott. 1987. Juvenile offenders: Prevalence, offender incidence, and arrest rates by race. *Crime and Delinquency* 33 (April):206–23.

Hulbert, A. 2003. *Raising America: Experts, parents, and a century of advice about children*. New York: Knopf.

Hurley, D. 1985. Arresting delinquency. *Psychology Today* (March):63–68.

———. 1994. They said it couldn't happen here. *Family Circle* (April 26):75–84.

Hurn, C. J. 1978. *The limits and possibilities of schooling*. Boston: Allyn and Bacon.

Imlay, C. H., and C. R. Flasheen. 1971. See what condition your conditions are in. *Federal Probation* 35 (June):3–11.

Inciardi, J. A. 1978. *Reflections on crime: An introduction to criminology and criminal justice*. New York: Holt, Rinehart and Winston.

Inciardi, J. A. 1986. *The war on drugs: Heroin, cocaine, crime, and public policy*. Palo Alto, CA: Mayfield.

———. 2004. *The American drug scene: An anthology*. New York: Roxbury.

Ingersoll, S. 1999. Investing in youth for a safer future. *OJJDD Fact Sheet* 98 (April):1–2.

Inkster, N. D. 1992. The essence of community policing. *Police Chief* 59 (March):28–31.

Ireland, T. O, C. A. Smith, and T. P. Thornberry. 2002. Developmental issues in the impact of child maltreatment on later delinquency and drug use. *Criminology* 40 (2):359–400.

Irwin, J., and D. Cressey. 1962. Thieves, convicts, and the inmate culture. *Social Problems*, 10 (Fall,):142–155, Irwin, K. 2001. Legitimating the first tattoo: Moral passage through formal interaction. *Symbolic Interaction* 24 (1):49–74.

———. 2002. Saints and sinners: Elite tattoo collectors and tattooists as positive and negative deviants. *Sociological Spectrum* 23:27–37.

Isralowitz, R. E. 1981. Youth service caseworkers: Social and legal factors affecting their recommendations to place youths in secure care facilities. *Children and Youth Services Review* 3 (3):233–46.

Jackson, R. L. 2001. Escalating gang woes found worst in California. *San Francisco Chronicle* (May 30): A-3.

Jacobs, J. 1961. *The death and life of great American cities*. New York: Vintage Books.

Jaffe, J., J. Segal, S. Hutman, and S. Barston. 2008. *Blending families: A guide for stepparents*. http://www.helpguide.org/mental/blended_families_stepfamilies.htm

James, J. 1978. *Entrance into juvenile prostitution: Progress report, June 1978*. Washington, DC: National Institute of Mental Health.

———. 1982. *Entrance into juvenile prostitution*. Washington, DC: National Institute of Mental Health.

Jarjoura, G. R. 1993. Does dropping out of school enhance delinquent involvement? Results from a large-scale national probability sample. *Criminology* 31 (May):149–60.

———. 1996. The conditional effect of social class on the dropout-delinquency relationship. *Journal of Research in Crime and Delinquency* 33 (May):232–55.

Jencks, C., M. Smith, H. Acland, M. J. Bane, D. Cohen, H. Gintis, B. Heyns, and S. Michelson. 1972. *Inequality: A reassessment of the effect of family and schooling in America*. New York: Basic Books.

Jennings, W, R. Kilkenny, and L. Kohlberg. 1983. Moral development theory and practice for youth. In *Personality theory, moral development, and criminal behavior*, ed. W. Laufer and J. Day, 281-355. Lexington MA: DC Heath.

Jensen, C. 1972. Parents, peers and delinquent action: A test of differential association perspective. *American Journal of Sociology* 78 (November):562–75.

Jensen, G. F. 1981. *Sociology of delinquency: Current issues*. London: Sage.

Jesness, C. F. 1987. Early identification of delinquent-prone children: An overview. In *Prevention of delinquent behavior*, ed. J. D. Burchard and S. N. Burchard, 140–158. Newbury Park, CA: Sage.

Johnson, B. D., and R. T. Goldberg. 1982. Vocational and social rehabilitation of delinquents: A study of experimentals and controls. *Journal of Offender Counseling Services and Rehabilitation* 6 (Spring):43–60.

Johnson, D. 1998. School hallways increasingly divided into haves—haves-nots. *Dallas Morning News* (October 18):14A.

Johnson, G., T. Bird, and J. W. Little. 1979. *Delinquency prevention: Theories and strategies*. Washington, DC: U.S. Department of Justice.

Johnson, J. N., and K. M. Thomas. 2002. Their first time: At home at night. *Dallas Adorning News* (September 26):1A.

Johnson, M. C., and G. A. Kercher. 2007. ADHD, strain, and criminal behavior: A test of general strain theory. *Deviant Behavior* 28 (March–April):131–52.

Johnson, M. G. 1993. Schools' disclosure of crime information varies. *Ft. Worth Star Telegram* (September 12):A1.

Johnson, M. K., and Glen H. Elder. 2002. Educational pathways and work value trajectories. *Sociological Perspectives* 45 (Summer):113–38.

Johnson, R. E., A. C. Marcos, and S. J. Bahr. 2006 The role of peers in the complex etiology of adolescent drug use. ***Criminology*** 25 (2) (March 7):323–340. Published online. © 2009 American Society of Criminology

Johnstone, J. W. C. 1978. Juvenile delinquency and the family: A contextual interpretation. *Youth and Society* 9 (March):299–313.

Jones, C. L., and C. S. Bell-Bolek. 1986. Kids and drugs: Why, when and what can we do about it? *Children Today* 15 (May–June):5–10.

Jones, V. M. 1999. Youth Crime Watch of America. *Youth in Action* 2 (January):1–2.

Josi, D. A., and D. K. Sechrest. 1999. A pragmatic approach to parole aftercare: Evaluation of a community reintegration program for high-risk youthful offenders. *Justice Quarterly* 16:51–80.

Juby, H., and D. P. Harrington. 2001. Disentangling the link between disrupted families and delinquency. *British Journal of Criminology* 41 (1):22-40.

Junger, M., and I. H. Marshall. 1997. The interethnic generalizability of social control theory: An empirical test. *Journal of Research in Crime and Delinquency* 34 (February):79–112.

Juvenile Justice Standards Project. 1977. *Juvenile justice standards* (October 30–November 3). Washington, DC: National Conference on the Proposed IJA/ABA Juvenile Justice Standards.

Kaiser, C. 1988. *1968 in America*. New York: Weidenfeld and Nicolson.

Kandel, D. B. 1985. On processes of peer influence in adolescent drug use: A developmental perspective. *Advances in Alcohol and Substance Abuse* 4 (Spring–Summer):139–63.

Kantrowitz, B. 1997. Off to a good start: Why the first three years are so crucial to a child's development. *Newsweek*, March 1.

Kaplan, D. A., D. L. Goflzalez, and L. Wilson. 1990. Will the cameras be rolling? *Newsweek* (June 18):52.

Karchmer, C. L. 1984. Young arsonists. *Society* 22 (November/December):78–83.

Katz, J. 1996. *Seductions of crime: Moral and sensual attractions of doing evil*. 3rd ed. New York: Basic Books.

Kaufman, J. G., and C. S. Widom. 1999. Childhood victimization, running away, and delinquency. *Journal of research in crime and delinquency* 36 (November):347–70.

Kauzlarich, D. 2009. *Introduction to criminology*. 9th ed. Rowman and Littlefield.

Kazdin, A. E. 2008. *Behavior modification in applied settings*. Prospect Hts, IL: Waveland.

Keilitz, I., A. Zaremba, and P. K. Broder. 1979. The link between learning disabilities and juvenile delinquency: Some issues and answers. *Learning Disability Quarterly* 2 (Spring):2–11.

Keiser, R. 1969. *The vice lords*. New York: Holt, Rinehart and Winston.

Kelly, D. H. 1977. Labeling and the consequences of wearing a delinquent label in a school setting. *Education* 97 (Summer):371–80.

———. 1982. *Creating school failure, youth crime, and deviance*. Los Angeles: Trident Shop.

Kennedy, L. W., and S. W. Baron. 1993. Routine activities and a subculture of violence: A study of violence on the Street. *Journal of Research in Crime and Delinquency* 30 (1) (February):88–112.

Kenny J. S. 2002. Victims of crime and labeling theory: A parallel process? *Deviant Behavior: An Interdisciplinary Journal* 23 (May–June):235–65.

Kerley, K., X. Xu, and B Sirisunyaluck. 2008. Self-control, intimate partner abuse, and intimate partner victimization: Testing the general theory of crime in Thailand. *Deviant Behavior* 29 (August-September):503–533.

Kersten, J. 1993. Street youths, Bosozaku and Yakuza: Subculture formation and societal reactions in Japan. *Crime and Delinquency* 39 (July):277–95.

Kidwell, J. S. 1981. Number of siblings, sibling spacing, sex, and birth order: Their effects on perceived parent-adolescent relationships. *Journal of Marriage and the Family* 43 (May):315–32.

Kim, T. E., and S. G. Gato. 2000. Peer delinquency and parental social support as predictors of Asian American delinquency. *Deviant Behavior* 21:331–47.

Kim, W. 2000. Should you stay together for the kids? *Time* 156 (3) (September 25):75–82.

Kimbrough, J. 1986. School-based strategies for delinquency prevention. In *Intervention strategies for chronic juvenile offenders*, ed. P. W. Greenwood, 193–206. New York: Greenwood Press.

Kitsuse, J. I. 1972. Deviance, deviant behavior, and deviants: Some conceptual problems. In An *introduction to deviance: Readings in the process of making deviants*, ed. Williams J. Pilstead, 233–43. Chicago: Markham.

Kitsuse, J., and D. Dietrick. 1959. Delinquent boys: A critique. *American Sociological Review* 24 (April):208–15.

Kivett, D. D., and C. A. B. Warren. 2002. Social control in a group home for delinquent boys. *Journal of Contemporary Ethnography* 31 (February):3–32.

Klein, H. 1990. Adolescence, youth, and young adulthood: Rethinking current conceptualizations of life stage. *Youth and Society* 21 (June):446–71.

Klein, M. 1964. Internal structures and age distributions in four delinquent Negro gangs. Paper presented at the annual meeting of the California State Psychological Association, Los Angeles. Youth Studies Center, University of Southern California (mimeo).

———. 1987. Watch out for the last variable. In *The causes of crime: New Biological approaches*, ed. S. A. Mednick, T. E. Moffitt and S. A. Stack25-41 New York: Cambridge University Press.

———. 1971. *Street gangs and street workers*. Upper Saddle River, NJ: Prentice Hall.

———. 1995. *The American Street Gang*. NewYork: Oxford University Press.

Klein, M., and Crawford, L. 1968. Groups, gangs, and cohesiveness. In *Gang delinquency and delinquent subcultures*, ed. J. F. Short, 256–72. New York: Harper & Row.

Kletschka, H. D. 1966. Violent behavior associated with brain tumors. *Minnesota Medicine* 49:1835–55.

Kline, E. M. 1993. Colorado Springs SHO/DI: Working smarter with juvenile offenders. *Police Chief* 60 (April):32–37.

Klinteberg, B. A., T. Anderson, D. Magnusson, and H. Stattin. 1993. Hyperactive behavior in childhood as related to subsequent alcohol problems and violent offending: A longitudinal study of male subjects. *Personality and Individual Differences* 15:381–88.

Kobayashi, E., S. Sharp, and H. G. Grasmick. 2008. Gender and deviance: A comparison of college students in Japan and the United States. *Deviant Behavior* 29 (July):413–439.

Kobetz, R. W., and B. B. Bosarge. 1973. *Juvenile justice administration*. Gaithersburg, MD: International Association of Chiefs of Police, Inc.

Kobrin, J. P., and Peluso, E. 1968. Criteria of status among street gangs. In *Gang delinquency and delinquent subcultures*, ed. J. F. Short, 178–208. New York: Harper & Row.

Kobrin, S. 1959. The Chicago Area Project—25 year assessment. *Annals of the American Academy of Political and Social Science* 322 (March):20–29.

Kohlberg, L. 1981. *The psychology of moral development: The nature and validity of moral stages*. New York: Harper & Row.

Kornblum, W., and J. Julian. 2008. *Social problems*. 13th ed. Upper Saddle River, NJ: Prentice Hall.

Kosut, M. 2006. Mad artists and tattooed perverts: Deviant discourse and the social construction of cultural categories. *Deviant Behavior* 27 (January–February):73–95.

Kozol, J. 1967. *Death at an early age*. New York: Bantam Books.

———. 1991. *Savage inequalities: Children in America's schools*. New York: Crown.

———. 2006. *The shame of the nation: The restoration of Apartheid schooling in America*. New York: Crown.

Kraska, P. B. 1989. The sophistication of Hans Jurgen Eysenck: An analysis and critique of contemporary biological criminology. *Criminal Justice Research Bulletin* 4:1–6.

Kratcoski, P. C. 1982. Child abuse and violence against the family. *Child Welfare* 61 (September–October): 435–44.

Krisberg, B. *1974* Gang youth and hustling: The psychology of survival. *Issues in Criminology* 9(1) (Spring): 115–131.

Krisberg, B., and J. Austin. 1978. *The Children of Ishmael: Critical Perspectives on Juvenile Justice*. Palo Alto, CA: Mayfield.

———. 2005. *Juvenile justice: Redeeming our children*. Thousand Oaks, CA: Sage.

Krohn, M. D., and J. L. Massey. 1980. Social control and delinquent behavior: An examination of the elements of social bond. *Sociological Quarterly* 21 (Autumn): 529–43.

Kropotkin, P. 1914. *Mutual aid: A factor in evolution*. Boston: Extending Horizons Books.

Kuhlen, R. G. 1952. *The psychology of adolescent development*. New York: Harper and brothers.

Kulik, J. A., K. B. Stein, and T. R. Sarbin. 1968. Dimensions and patterns of adolescent antisocial behavior. *Journal of Consulting and Clinical Psychology* 32 (August): 375–82.

Kupchik, A. 2007. Judging juveniles: Prosecuting adolescents in adult and juvenile courts. NY: NYU press.

LA Times. 2007. Anti-spanking idea hits nerve. *Los Angeles Times* (January 20):2A.

Lab, S. P. 1984. Patterns in juvenile misbehavior. *Crime and Delinquency* 30 (April):293–308.

Lane, B. A. 1980. The relationship of learning disabilities to juvenile delinquency: Current status. *Journal of Learning Disabilities* 13 (October):425–34.

Lane, J., S. Turner, T. Fain, and A. Sehgal. 2005. Evaluating an experimental intensive juvenile probation program: Supervision and official outcomes. *Crime and Delinquency* 51 (January):26–52.

Lanza-Kaduce, L., R. L. Akers, M. D. Krohn, and M. Radosevich. 1982. Conceptualization and analytical models in testing social learning theory. *American Sociological Review* 47 (February):169–73.

Larzelere, R. E., and C. R. Patterson. 1990. Parental management: Mediator of the effect of socioeconomic status on early delinquency. *Criminology* 28 (May):301–24.

Lasswell, M., and T. E. Lasswell. 1991. *Marriage and the family*. 3rd ed. Belmont, CA: Wordsworth.

Lastrucci, C. L. 1967. *The scientific approach*. Cambridge, MA: Schenkman.

Lattimore, P. K., C. A. Visher, and R. L. Linster. 1995. Predicting rearrest for violence among serious youthful offenders. *Journal of Research in Crime and Delinquency* 32 (February):54–83.

Lauritsen, J. L. 1993. Sibling resemblance in juvenile delinquency: Findings from the national youth survey. *Criminology* 31 (August):387–401.

Lavoie, D. 2000. Treating 39-year-old slaying suspect as juvenile creates legal maze. *Dallas Morning News* (January 21):7A.

Law Enforcement News. 1997. Do you get what you pay for? WCJ efforts, not necessarily. 23 (May):1, 18.

Lawrence, F. C., G. E. Tasker, C. T. Daly, A. L. Orhill, and P. H. Wozniak. 1986. Adolescents' time spent viewing television. *Adolescence* 21 (Summer):431–36.

Lawrence, R. 2007. *School crime and juvenile justice*. 2nd ed. New York: Oxford University Press.

———. 2008. Reexamining community corrections models. In *Juvenile justice: A text/reader*, ed. R. Lawrence and C. Hemmens, 424–35. Los Angeles: Sage.

Leiber, M. I., and K. Y. Mack. 2003. The individual and joint effects of race, gender, and family status on juvenile justice decision-making. *Journal of Crime and Delinquency* 40 (February):34–70.

Leiber, M. J., and J. M. Stairs. 1999. Race, contexts, and the use of intake diversion. *Journal of Research in Crime and Delinquency* 36 (February):56–86.

Lemann, N. 1986. The origins of the underclass. *AtlanticMonthly* (June):31–68.

Lemert, E. 1951. *Social pathology*. New York: McGraw-Hill.

———. 1967. Deviance, social problems, and control. Englewood Cliffs, NJ: Prentice-Hall.

Lerman, P. 1967. Gangs, networks, and subcultural delinquency. *American Journal of Sociology* 63:63–71.

Lesko, N. 2000. *Act your age: A cultural construction of adolescence*. New York: Routledge Falmer.

Levin, J., and J. McDevitt. 1993. *Hate crimes: The rising tide of bigotry and bloodshed*. New York: Plenum Press.

Levinson, A. 1998. Clean-living movement turns ugly. *Mail Tribune*, Medford, OR. (January 4):3A.

Li, J. H., and R. A. Wojtkiewicz. 1992. A new look at the effects of family structure on status attainment. *Social Science Quarterly* 73 (September):581–95.

Liazos, A. 1974. Class oppression: The function of juvenile justice. *Insurgent Sociologist* 5:2–24.

Liberman, A. 2007. *Adolescents, neighborhoods, and violence: Recent findings from the project on human development in Chicago neighborhoods*. Washington, DC: National Institute of Justice.

Liebow, E. 1967. *Tally's corner: A study of Negro street-corner men*. Boston: Little, Brown.

Lightholder, S. O. 1978. Stay no longer—California juvenile court sentencing practices. *Pepperdine Law Review* 5 (3):769–94.

Linden, R. 1978. Myths of middle class delinquency: A test of the generalizability of social control theory. *Youth and Society* 9 (June):404–32.

Lipschutz, M. R. 1977. Runaways in history. *Crime and Delinquency* 23 (July):321–32.

Lipsey, M. W. 1999. Can intervention rehabilitate serious delinquents? *Annals of the American Academy of Political and Social Science* 564:142–66.

Lipson, K. 1982. Cops and TOPS: A program for police and teens that works. *Police Chief* 49:45–46.

Liska, A. E., and M. D. Reed. 1985. Ties to conventional institutions and delinquency: Estimating reciprocal effects. *American Sociological Review* 50 (August):547–60.

Lloyd, R. 1976. *For money or love: Boy prostitution in America*. New York: Vanguard.

Loeber, R., and T. Dishion. 1983. Early predictors of male delinquency: A Review. *Psychological Bulletin* 94:68–99.

Loeber, R., and D. F. Hay. 1996. Key issues in the development of aggression and violence from childhood to early adulthood. *Annual Review of Psychology* 48:371–410.

Logan, C. H., and S. P. Rausch. 1985. Why deinstitutionalizing status offenders is pointless. *Crime and Delinquency* 31 (October):501–17.

Lombroso, C. 1895. *The female offender*. London: Fisher Unwin.

———. 1911. *Crime, its causes and remedies*. Trans. H. P. Horton. Boston: Little, Brown.

Londer, R. 1987. Can bad air make bad things happen? *Parade Magazine* (August 9):6–7.

Lonsdale, D., and R. J. Shamberger. 1980. Red cell transketolase as an indicator of nutritional deficiency. *American Journal of Clinical Nutrition* 33 (February): 205–11.

Lopoo, L. M. 2007. While the cat's away, do the mice play? Maternal employment and the after-school activities of adolescents. *Social Science Quarterly* 88 (December):1357–73.

Lotz, R., E. D. Poole, and R. M. Regoli. 1985. *Juvenile delinquency and juvenile justice*. New York: Random House.

Lowney, K. 1995. Satanism as oppositional youth subculture. *Journal of Contemporary Ethnography* 23 (January):453–84.

Lucken, K. 1997. Privatizing discretion: "Rehabilitation" treatment in community corrections. *Crime and Delinquency* 43 (July):243–59.

Lundman, R. J. 1993. *Prevention and control of juvenile delinquency*. 2nd ed. New York: Oxford University Press.

———. 1996a. Demeanor and arrest: Additional evidence from previously unpublished data. *Journal of Research in Crime and Delinquency* 33 (August):306–23.

———. 1996b. Extralegal variables and arrest. *Journal of Research in Crime and Delinquency* 33 (August):349–53.

———. 2001. *Prevention and control of juvenile delinquency*. 3rd ed. New York: Oxford University Press.

Lundman, R. L., R. E. Sykes, and J. P. Clark. 1978. Police control of juveniles: A replication. *Journal of Research in Crime and Delinquency* 15 (January):74–91.

Lynxwiler, J., and D. Gay. 2000. Moral boundaries and deviant music: Public attitudes toward heavy metal and rap. *Deviant Behavior* 21 (January–February):63–85.

Lyons, A. L. 1988. *Satan wants you: The cult of devil worship in America*. New York: Mysterious Press.

Mackenzie, D. L., and G. S. Armstrong, eds. 2004. *Correctional Boot Camps*. Thousand Oaks, CA: Sage.

Mackenzie, D. L., and C. C. Souryal. 1991. Boot camp survey. *Corrections Today* (October):90–96.

Mahler, J. M. 1977. *Rational approach to the reality of juvenile crime in America*. Rockville, MD: National Institute of Justice.

Mahoney, A. R. 1981. Family participation for juvenile offenders in deinstitutionalization programs. *Journal of Social Issues* 37 (Summer):133–44.

———. 1985. Jury trial for juveniles: Right or ritual? *Justice Quarterly* 2 (December):553–65.

Major, A. K., A. Egley, J. C. Howell, B. Mendenhall, and T. Armstrong. 2004. Youth gangs in Indian country. *Juvenile Justice Bulletin* (March). Washington, DC: U.S. Department of Justice, OJJDP.

Males, M. 1996. *The scapegoat generation: America's war on adolescents*. New York: Common Courage Press.

———. 1999. *Framing youth: Ten myths about the next generation*. New York: Common Courage Press.

Manley, D. 1979. Status offenders—Helping them cope. *Sunday Oklahoman* (June 17):23

Mann, R., D. Hannah, M. Cohn, P. Annin, and T. Gegax. 1995. Turning in the badges of rebellion. *Newsweek* (February, 6):46.

Marowitz, W. A. 1991. *Bias crime: The law enforcement response*. Chicago: Office of International Criminal Justice.

Martin, G. L., and J. Pear. 2006. *Behavior modification: What it is and how to do it*. 8th ed. Englewood Cliffs, NJ: Prentice Hall.

Marvel, B. 2002. Boxed in, no longer kids, not yet adults: Teens struggle for rights in a wary society. *Dallas Morning News* (December 15):1F, 14F, 16F.

Marx, K. [1867] 1967. *Capital*, ed. Friedrich Engels. New York: International Publishers.

Marx, K., and F. Engels. [1848] 1964. *The communist manifesto*. Trans. Samuel Moore and ed. Joseph Katz. New York: Washington Square Press.

Matsueda, R. L., D. A. Kreager, and D. Huizinga. 2006. Deterring delinquents: A rational choice model of theft and violence. *American Sociological Review* 71 (February):95–122.

Matthews, F. 1983. Diet to help you beat the blues. *National Examiner* (July 26):31.

Matza, D. 1964. *Delinquency and drift*. New York: John Wiley.

———. 1969. *Becoming deviant*. Upper Saddle River, NJ: Prentice Hall.

Matza, D., and C. M. Sykes. 1961. Juvenile delinquency and subterranean values. *American Sociological Review* 26:712–19.

Maupin, J. R. 1993. Risk classification systems and the provision of juvenile aftercare. *Crime and Delinquency* 39 (January):90–105.

Mayer, G. R., T. Butterworth, M. Nafpaktitis, and B. Sulzer-Azaroff. 1983. Preventing school vandalism and improving discipline: A three year study. *Journal of Applied Behavior Analysis* 16 (Winter):355–69.

Mayo Clinic Staff. 2007. Bullying: Help your child handle a school bully. *Mental Health*, April, http://www.mayoclinic.com/health/bullying/MH00126

Mazerolle, P. 1998. Gender, general strain, and delinquency. *Justice Quarterly* 15:65–91.

McAlexander, J. H., and J. W. Schonten, 1989. Hairstyle changes as transition markers. *Sociology & Social Research* 74 (October):58–62.

McCaghy, C. H., T. A. Capron, J. D. Jamieson, and S. H. Carey. 2006. *Deviant behavior: Crime, conflict, and interest groups*. 7th ed. Boston: Allyn & Bacon.

McCall, W. 1999. Born to be bad? Why kids commit crimes. *Ashland Daily Tidings*, Ashland, OR, May 28:1.

McCamey, W. P., G. L. Scaramella, and S. M. Cox. 2003. *Contemporary Municipal Policing*. Boston: Allyn and Bacon.

McCarthy, F. B. 1977. Should juvenile delinquency be abolished? *Crime and Delinquency* 23 (April):196–203.

McClearn, G. E. 1969. Biological bases of social behavior with specific reference to violent behavior. In *Crimes of violence*, vol. 13, ed. D. Mulvihill, M. Tumin and L. Curtis, 1003. Staff Report to the National Commission on Causes and Prevention of Violence. Washington, DC: U.S. Government Printing Office.

McCord, W., J. McCord, and I. Zola. 1959. *Origins of crime*. New York: Columbia University Press.

McDermott, J. 1983. Crime in the school and in the community: Offenders, victims, and fearful youths. *Crime and Delinquency* 29 (April):270–82.

McDermott, M. J., and M. J. Hindelang. 1987. *Juvenile criminal behavior in the United States: Its trends and patterns*. National Institute for Juvenile Justice and Delinquency Prevention, LEAA, U.S. Department of Justice. Washington, DC: U.S. Government Printing Office.

McDowell, D., C. Loflin, and B. Wiersema. 2000. The impact of youth curfew laws on juvenile crime rates. *Crime and Delinquency* 46 (January):76–91.

McEachern, A. W., and R. Bauzer. 1967. Factors related to dispositions in juvenile police contacts. In *Juvenile gangs in context; Theory, research and action*, ed. M. W. Kline, 148–60. Upper Saddle River, NJ: Prentice Hall.

McEvoy, K., and H. Mika. 2007. *Restorative justice: Theory practice, and critique*. Thousand Oaks, CA: Sage.

McGarrell, E. F. 1993. Trends in racial disproportionality in juvenile court processing: 1985–1989. *Crime and Delinquency* 39 (January):29–48.

———. 2001. Restorative justice conferences as an early response to young offenders. *Juvenile Justice Bulletin* (August), Rockville, MD: Office of Juvenile Justice and Delinquency Prevention.

McGee, R. A. 1971. Our sick jails. *Federal Probation* 35 (March):3–8.

McGee, Z. T. 1992. Social class differences in parental and peer influence on adolescent drug use. *Deviant Behavior* 13 (October–December):349–72.

McGloin, J. M., and T. C. Pratt. 2003. Cognitive ability and delinquent behavior among inner-city youth. A life-course analysis of main, mediating, and interaction effects. *International Journal of Offender Therapy and Comparative Criminology* 47 (3):253–71.

McKee, J. B. 1974. *Introduction to sociology*. 2nd ed. New York: Holt Rinehart and Winston.

McNeal, R. B. 1997. High school dropouts: A closer examination of school effects. *Social Science Quarterly* 78 (March):209–22.

McShane, L. 2005. U.S. Teens are using prescription drugs to get high. *Dallas Morning News* (April 22):17A.

Mead, M. 1928. *Growing up in Samoa*. New York: LW. Morrow.

Medford Mail-Tribune. 1996. Close-range shootings replace drive-bys in L. A. (August 4):8B.

Medford Tribune (Oregon Newspaper). 1999. Congressional vote allows posting of Ten Commandments in schools. (June 6):A1.

Meehan, P. J., and M. C. Ponder. 2002. Race and place: The ecology of racial profiling African American motorists. *Justice Quarterly* 18:399–430.

Meese, E. III. 1993. Community policing and the police officer. *Perspectives on Policing*. Boston: National Institute of Justice, U.S. Department of Justice.

Menard, S. 1995. A developmental test of Mertonian anomie theory. *Journal of Research in Crime and Delinquency* 32 (May):136–74.

Menard, S., and B. J. Morse. 1984. A structuralist critique of the IQ-delinquency hypothesis: Theory and evidence. *American Journal of Sociology* 89 (May):1347–78.

Menifield, C. E., W. H. Rose, J. Homa, and A. B. Cunningham. 2001. The media's portrayal of urban and rural school violence: A preliminary analysis. *Deviant Behavior* 22 (September–October):447–64.

Mennel, R. M. 1982. Attitudes and policies toward delinquency in the United States. *Crime and Justice* 4:191–224.

Merton, R. 1957. Social structure and anomie. *American Sociological Review* 3 (October):672–82.

———. 1968. *Social theory and social structure*. enlarged ed. New York: Free Press.

Michalowski, R. J. 1985. *Order, law, and crime*. New York: Random House.

Milich, R., and W. Pelham. 1986. Effects of sugar ingestion on the classroom and playground behavior of attention deficit disordered boys. *Journal of Counseling and Clinical Psychology* 54:714–18.

Miller, E. 1978. We just put them in the cage so they won't get away. *Dallas Morning News* (July 2):1.

Miller, F. W., R. O. Dawson, G. E. Dix, and R. I. Parnas. 1985. *The juvenile justice process*. 3rd ed. Mineola, NY: University Casebook Series, Foundation Press.

Miller, J. 2001. *One of the guys: Girls, gangs, and gender*. New York: Oxford University Press.

———. 2002. The girls in the gang: What we've learned from two decades of research. In *Gangs in America*, ed. C. R. Huff, 175–97. Thousand Oaks, CA: Sage.

———. 2006. Global prostitution, sex tourism, and trafficking. In *Rethinking gender, crime, and justice: Feminist readings*, ed. C. Renzetti and L. Goodstein, 139–54. Los Angeles: Roxbury.

Miller, J. M., and J. P. Rush, eds. 1996. *Gangs: A criminal justice approach*. Cincinatti: Anderson.

Miller, W. B. 1958. Lower class culture as a generating milieu of gang delinquency. *Journal of Social Issues* 14 (3):5–19.

———. 1962. The impact of a "total community" delinquency control project. *Social Problems* 10 (Fall):168–91.

———. 1966. Violent crimes in city gangs. *Annals of the Academy of Political and Social Science* 64 (March): 97–112.

———. 1975. *Violence by youth gangs and youth groups as a crime problem in major American cities*. Washington, DC: U.S. Government Printing Office.

Mills, C. W. 1959. *The sociological imagination*. New York: Oxford University Press.

Minneapolis Urban League. 2006. *Youth Advocacy Program*. http://www.mul.org/youthachievement.cfm

Minor, K. I., D. J. Hartmann, and S. Terry. 1997. Predictors of juvenile court actions and recidivism. *Crime and Delinquency* 43 (July):328–44.

Minton, L. 1995. Tough teens talk about a program that works. *Parade* (January 8):4.

Mitchell, J. C. 1979. Networks, algorithms, and analysis. In *Perspectives on social network research*, ed. P. W. Holland and S. Leinhardt,. New York: Academic Press.

Mitchell, L. 1972. Criminal beginnings in elementary schools. *Ashland Daily Tidings*, Ashland, OR, (November 6):2.

Mobilization for Youth. 1961. *A proposal for the prevention and control of delinquency by expanding opportunities*. New York: Mobilization for Youth, Inc.

Moffitt, L. D., and M. Stouthamer-Loeber. 1993. Explaining the relation between IQ and delinquency; Class, race, test motivate, school failure, or self-control? *Journal of Abnormal Psychology* 102 (May):187–96.

Moffitt, T. 1993. Adolescent-limited and life-course-persistent antisocial behavior. *Psychological Review* 100:674–701.

———. 2003. Pathways in the life course to crime. In *Criminological Theory: Past to Present*, ed. T. Cullen and R. Agnew, 452–57. LA: Roxbury.

Monahan, Y. P. 1957. Family status and the delinquent child: A reappraisal and some new findings. *Social Forces* (March):250–58.

Monk-Turner, E. 1989. Effects of high school delinquency on educational attainment and adult occupational status. *Sociological Perspective* 32 (Fall):413–18.

Monti, P. M., S. M. Colby, and T. A. O'Leary. 2005. *Adolescents, alcohol, and substance abuse: Reaching teens through brief interventions*. Guilford Press.

Moon, M. M., J. L. Sundt, F. T. Cullen, and J. P. Wright. 2000. Is child saving dead? Public support for juvenile rehabilitation. *Crime and Delinquency* 46 (January):38–60.

Moore, J., and J. Hagedorn. 2006. Female gangs: A focus on research. In *The modern gang reader* 3rd ed., ed. A. Egley, C. L. Maxson, J. Miller and M. W. Klein, 192–205. Los Angeles: Roxbury Publishing Company.

Moore, J. P., and C. P. Terrett. 1999. Highlights of the 1997 national youth gang survey. *OJJDP Fact Sheet No.* 97. (March, 1999). Washington, DC: U.S. Department of Justice, Office of Juvenile Justice and Delinquency Prevention.

Moore, J. W. 1985. Isolation and stigmatization in the development of an underclass—The case of Chicano gangs in East Los Angeles. *Social Problems* 33 (1) (October):1–12.

Moore, R. 2005. Alternative to what? Subcultural capital and the commercialization of a music scene. *Deviant Behavior* 26 (May–June):229–52.

Morash, M. 1984. Establishment of a juvenile police record: The influence of individual and peer group characteristics. *Criminology* 22 (February):97–111.

Morgan, O. J. 1982. Runaways—Jurisdiction, dynamics, and treatment. *Journal of Marital and Family Therapy* 8 (January):121–27.

Morris, M. 1989. From the culture of poverty to the underclass: An analysis of a shift in public language. *American Sociologist* 20 (Summer):123–33.

Musgrove, F. 1965. *Youth and the social order*. Bloomington: Indiana University Press.

Muuss, R. E. 1996. *Theories of adolescence*. 6th ed. New York: McGraw-Hill.

Myerhoff, H., and B. Myerhoff. 1964. Field observations of middle-class gangs. *Social Forces* 42 (March):328–36.

Myers, S. 2002. *Police encounters with juvenile suspects: Explaining the use of authority and provision of support*. Washington, DC: National Institute of Justice.

Myren, R. A. 1988. *Law and justice: An introduction*. Belmont, CA: Wadsworth.

Narramore, C. M. 1966. *Encyclopedia of psychological problems*. Grand Rapids, MI: Zondervan Publishing House.

National Advisory Commission on Criminal Justice Standards and Goals. 1973. *Corrections*. Washington, DC: U.S. Government Printing Office.

———. 1984. Serious juvenile crime: A redirected federal effort. National Advisory Committee for Juvenile Justice and Delinquency Prevention. Washington, DC: U.S. Government Printing Office (March). OJJDP.

———. 2002. *Juvenile residential facility census*. http://www.ncjrs.org/html/ojjdp/nrs.bulletin/nrs 2002

National Association of School Psychologists. 2003. Effective discipline. *Dallas Mornings News* (June 1):3B.

National Crime Prevention Council. 2007. *Juvenile Court Statistics Revealed*. www.ncpc. typepad.com/prevention.

National Institute of Justice. 1990. Massive study will trace developmental factors that cause or prevent criminality. *NIJ Reports* 220 (May–June):2–3.

NBC *Dateline*. 1993. Television report, September 30.

NBC News. 1987. Crime, punishment, and kids. *NBC News Special*, July 26.

NBC Nightly News. 1997. Police make daytime sweeps of urban shopping malls, May 17.

NBC Television News Report. 1994. Sacramento, CA, January 15.

Needham, N. R. 1986. Big bucks in little hands. *NEA Todays* (November):16–17.

Needle, J., and W. V. Stapleton. 1983. *Report of the National Juvenile Justice Assessment Centers, Police Handling of Youth Gangs*. Washington, DC: U.S. Department of Justice, Office of Juvenile Justice and Delinquency Prevention.

Neigher, A. 1967. The Gault decision: Due process and the juvenile courts. *Federal Probation* 31 (December):8–18.

Neill, S. B. 1978. Violence and vandalism: Dimensions and correctives. *Phi Delta Kappan* 59 (January):302–07.

Nettler, G. 1984. *Explaining crime*. 3rd ed. New York: McGraw-Hill Book Co.

Neubauer, C. 2007. *Daycare and children*. National Institute of Health.

Newman, G. 1978. *The punishment response*. Philadelphia: JB Lippincott.

New York Times News Service. 1996. Day care found not to harm infant's trust. *Dallas Morning News* (April 21):4A.

———. 1999. Fewer teens find drugs "cool," study says. *Dallas Morning News* (November 22):7A.

———. 2003a. Drug testing may not deter students. *Dallas Morning News* (May 17):16A.

———. 2003b. Study: 1 in 5 have sex before age 15. *Dallas Morning News* (May 20):6A.

———. 2004. Teens practicing sexual restraint. *Dallas Morning News* (March 7):11A.

Newman, F., and P. J. Caplan. 1981. Juvenile female prostitution as a gender constant response to early deprivation. *International Journal of Women's Studies* 5 (2):128–37.

Nightline Gang Report. 2005. American Broadcasting Company. August 4, 2005.

NIJ. 2004. *Toward safe and orderly schools—The National Study of Delinquency Prevention in Schools* (November). Washington, DC: National Institute of Justice.

Nofziger, S., and K. Don. 2005. "Violent Lives: A Lifestyle Model linking Exposure toViolence to Juvenile Violent Offending." *Journal of Research in Crime and Delinquency* 42 (1):3–26.

Noll, J. W., ed. 2009. *Clashing views on controversial educational issues*. 15th ed. Dubuque IA: McGraw-Hill/Dushkin.

Nye, E. I. 1958. *Family relationships and delinquent behavior*. New York: Wiley.

———. 1974. Emerging and declining family roles. *Journal of Marriage and the Family* 36 (May):238–45.

O'Brien, S. 1983. *Child pornography*. Dubuque, IA: Kendall-Hunt.

O'Quin, K., C. C. Vogler, and T. S. Weinberg. 1985. Parental interest, juvenile misbehavior and disposition recommendations. Paper presented at the 1985 meeting of the Society for the Study of Social Problems.

OJJDP. 1979. *Delinquency prevention: Theories and strategies*. Washington, DC: Law Enforcement Assistance Administration, U.S. Department of Justice.

———. 1988. A private-sector corrections program for juveniles: Paint Creek Youth Center. Pittsburgh, PA: Office of Juvenile Justice and Delinquency Prevention, U.S. Department of Justice.

———. 2000. *Youth in Action. Want to Resolve a Dispute: Try Mediation*. Washington, DC: U.S. Department of Justice.

———. 2002. *Juvenile residential facility census*. http:www.ncjrs.org/html/ojjdpnrs/bulletin/nrs_2002

———. 2005. *Planning community-based facilities for violent juvenile offenders as part of a system of graduated sanctions*. http://www.ojjdp.ncjrs.org.

———. 2008. *Truancy prevention*. Pittsburg, PA: Office of Juvenile Justice and Delinquency Prevention, www.ojjdp.ncjrs.org/truancy

Okaty, G. J. 1991. Kids at school/Kids at risk. *Police Chief* 58 (May):39–41.

Orcutt, J. D. 1983. *Analyzing deviance*. Homewood, IL: Dorsey Press.

———. 1987. Differential association and marijuana use: A closer look at Sutherland (with a little help from Becker). *Criminology* 25 (2):341–58.

Osbun, L. A., and P. A. Rode. 1984. Prosecuting juveniles as adults: The quest for "objective" decisions. *Criminology* 22 (May):187–202.

Osgood, D. W, L. D. Johnston, P. M. O'Malley, and J. C. Bachman. 1988. The generality of deviance in late adolescence and early adulthood. *American Sociological Review* 53 (February):81–93.

Oswalt, W. H. 1986. *Life cycles and lifeways: An introduction to cultural anthropology*. Palo Alto, CA: Mayfield.

———. 2005. *This land was theirs: A study of Native North Americans*. New York: Oxford University Press.

Pagani, L., B. Boulerice, K. Vitaro, and R. E. Trembley. 1999. Effects of poverty on academic failure and delinquency in boys: A change and process model approach. *Journal of Child Psychology and Psychiatry* 40 (November):1209–19.

Page, C. 1999. Juvenile boot camps don't live up to hype. *Dallas Morning News* (December 11):33A.

Parade. 1987a. Readers respond on capital punishment. *Parade* (January 25):10.

———. 1987b. Tough for teenagers. (March 22):15.

Park, R. E. 1928. Human migration and the marginal man. *American Journal of Sociology* 33 (May):881–893.

———. 1936. Human ecology. *American Journal of Sociology* 42 (July):1–15.

Park, R. E., F. Burgess, and R. D. McKenzie. 1924. *The city*. Chicago: University of Chicago Press.

Parker, D. 2003. Art in the name of God. *Dallas Morning News* (January 10):25A.

Parsons, T. 1942. Age and sex in the social structure of the United States. *American Sociological Review* 7 (October):604–16.

———. 1947. Certain primary sources and patterns of aggression in the social structure of the western world. *Psychiatry* 10 (May):167–81.

Patchin, J. W. 2006. *The family context of childhood delinquency (Criminal Justice Recent Scholarship)*. El Paso, TX: LFB publishing.

Paternoster, R., and A. Piquero. 1995. Reconceptualizing deterrence: An empirical test of personal and vicarious experiences. *Journal of Research in Crime and Delinquency* 32 (August):251–86.

Patterson, K. 2002. Dad's drinking pattern holds clues about kids. *Dallas Morning News* (December 30):2C.

———. 2003a. Higher lead levels found in delinquent youth. *Dallas Morning News* (January 13):2C.

———. 2003b. Violent lyrics can fuel aggression, study shows. *Dallas Morning News* (May 12):2E.

Payne, A. A., and S. Salotti. 2007. A comparative analysis of social learning and social control theories in the prediction of college crime. *Deviant Behavior* 28 (November–December):553–73.

Pearson, G. 1984. The original Hooligans. *A supplement to History Today* (May):83.

Pearson, G. H. J. 1958. *Adolescence and the conflict of generations*. New York: W. W. Norton.

Pennell, S., C. Curtis, and D. C. Scheck. 1990. Controlling juvenile delinquency: An evaluation of an interagency strategy. *Crime and Delinquency* 36 (April):257–75.

Perez, D. M., W. G. Jennings, and A. R. Grover. 2008. Specifying general strain theory: An ethnically relevant approach. *Deviant Behavior* 29 (August–September):544–78.

Perry, B. 2001. *In the name of hate: Understanding hate crimes*. New York: Routledge.

Perry, R. L. 1985. Differential dispositions of black and white juveniles: A critical assessment of methodology. *Western Journal of Black Studies* 9 (Winter):189–97.

Petrosino, A., C. Turpin-Petrosino, J. Buehler. 2002. "Scared Straight" and other juvenile awareness programs for preventing juvenile delinquency. *Cochrane Database of Systematic Reviews* (2). Art. No.: CD002796. DOI: 10.1002/14651858.CD002796.

Phillips, E. L., E. Phillips, D. Fixsen, and M. Wolf. 1971. Achievement place: Modification of the behaviors of predelinquent boys within a token economy. *Journal of Applied Behavior Analysis* 4 (Spring):45–59.

Piaget, J. 1948. *The moral judgment of the child*. Glencoe, IL: Free Press.

Piliavin, I., and S. Briar. 1964. Police encounters with juveniles. *American Journal of Sociology* 70 (September): 206–14.

Pincus, J. H. 1979. Mental problems found in delinquents. *Tulsa World* (April 30):10.

Pink, W. T. 1984. Schools, youth and justice. *Crime and Delinquency* 30 (July):439–61.

Platt, A. M. 1969. *The child savers*. Chicago: University of Chicago Press.

———. 1977. *The child savers: The invention of delinquency*. 2nd ed. Chicago: University of Chicago Press.

Plotnick, R. D. 1992. The effects of attitudes on teenage premarital pregnancy and its resolution. *American Sociological Review* 57 (December):800–8.

Plunkett, S. W., and C. S. Henry. 1999. Adolescent perceptions of interparental conflict, stressors, and coping as predictors of adolescent family life satisfaction. *Sociology Inquiry* 69 (Fall):599–620.

Poe-Yamagata, E., and J. A. Butts. 1996. *Female offenders in the juvenile justice system*. Pittsburgh, PA: U.S. Department of Justice, Office of Juvenile Justice and Delinquency Prevention, National Center for Juvenile Justice.

Pogrebin, M. R., B. D. Poole, and R. M. Regoli. 1984. Constructing and implementing a model juvenile diversion program. *Youth and Society* 15 (March):305–24.

Polk, K. 1975. Schools and the delinquency experience. *Criminal Justice and Behavior* 2 (December):315–38.

———. 1984. The new marginal youth. *Crime and Delinquency* 30 (July):462–80.

Polk, K., and W. B. Schafer, eds. 1972. *School and delinquency*. Upper Saddle River, NJ: Prentice Hall.

Pollack, O. 1950. *The criminality of women*. Philadelphia: University of Pennsylvania press.

Pollock, V., S. A. Mednick, and W. F. Gabrielli, Jr. 1983. Crime causation: Biological theories. In *Encyclopedia of Crime and Justice*, vol. 1, ed. Sanford H. Kadish, 7-42. New York: Free Press.

Poremba, C. D. 1975. Learning disabilities, youth and delinquency: Programs for intervention. In *Progress in learning disabilities*, vol. 3, ed. H. R. Myklebust, 123–49. New York: Grune and Stratton.

Porter, E. 2006. Women in workplace—Trend is reversing. *San Francisco Chronicle* (March 2):A2.

Portune, R. 1971. *Changing adolescent attitudes toward police*. Cincinnati: Anderson.

Pratt, T. C., M. G. Turner, and A. R. Piquero. 2004. Parental socialization and community context: A longitudinal of the structural sources of low self control. *Journal of Research in Crime and Delinquency* 41 (August):219–43.

President's Commission on Law Enforcement and Administration of Justice. 1967. *Juvenile delinquency and youth crime*. Washington, DC: U.S. Government Printing Office.

Preston, S. H., and J. MacDonald. 1979. The incidence of divorce within cohorts of American marriages contracted since the Civil War. *Demography* 16:1–25.

Probst, K. 2006. *Mentoring for meaningful results*. Minneapolis: Search Institute.

Project New Pride. 1985. *Project New Pride*. Washington, DC: U.S. Government Printing Office.

Puzzanchera, C. L., A. L. Stahl, T. A. Finnegan, N. J. Tierney, and H. N. Snyder. 2004. *Juvenile Court Statistics 2000*. Pittsburgh, PA: National Center for Juvenile Justice.

Puzzanchera, C. M. 2000a. Delinquency cases waived to criminal court, 1988–1997. *OJJDP Fact Sheet (February, 2000 #02)*. Washington, DC: U.S. Department of Justice.

———. 2000b. Self-reported delinquency by 12-year-olds, 1997. *OJJDP Fact Sheet (February, 2000 #03)*. Washington, DC: U.S. Department of Justice.

Quinney, R. 1970. *The social reality of crime*. Boston: Little, Brown & Co.

———. 1974. *Critique of legal order: Crime control in capitalist society*. Boston: Little, Brown and Company.

———. 1975. *Criminology: An analysis and critique of crime in America*. Boston: Little, Brown.

———. 1980. *Class, state, and crime*. 2nd ed. New York: Longman.

Rabin, A. I. 1961. Psychopathic personalities. In *Legal and criminal psychology*, ed. H. Toch, 389-393. Hinsdale, IL: Holt, Rinehart and Winston.

Ragavan, C., and M. Guttman. 2004. Terror in the streets. *US News and World Report* (December 13):21–24.

Ramirez, D., Jr. 1994. Orange County suburb gives teens alternative to gangs. *Fort Worth Star Telegram* (March 6):A8.

Ramos, P. 1989. When he was shot, I thought it could have been me. *Hartford Courant* (June 4): D1, D4.

Rankin, J. H. 1983. The family context of delinquency. *Social Problems* 30 (April):466–79.

Recer, Paul. 1999. Study: No lasting harm for working mom's kids. *Dallas Morning News* (March 1):1A.

Reckless, W. 1961. A new theory of delinquency and crime. *Federal Probation* 25 (December):42–46.

Reckless, W., S. Dinitz, and E. Murray. 1956. Self concept as an insulator against delinquency. *American Sociological Review* 21 (December):744–46.

Reed, B., S. Knickelbine, and M. Knickelbine. 1983. *Food, teens, and behavior*. Manitowoc, WI: Natural Press.

Regnery, A. S. 1985. Getting away with murder: Why the juvenile justice system needs an overhaul. *Policy Review* 34 (Fall):1–4.

Regnery, A. S. 1986. A federal perspective on juvenile justice reform. *Crime and Delinquency* 32 (January):39–51.

Regoli, R. M., and E. D. Poole. 1979. Assessing drift among institutionalized delinquents. *Journal of the American Criminal Justice Association* 42 (Winter/Spring):47–55.

Regoli, R. M., and J. D. Hewitt. 2003. *Delinquency in society: A child-centered approach*. New York: McGraw-Hill.

Regoli, R. M., B. Wilderman, and M. Pogrebin. 1985. Using an alternative evaluation measure for assessing juvenile diversion programs. *Children and Youth Services Review* 7 (1):21–38.

Rehm, L. 1983. Psychology. *Academic American Encyclopedia*, vol. 15, 593–98. Danbury, CT: Grolier, Inc.

Reibstein, L. 1997. Kids in the dock. *Newsweek* (May 26):70.

Reid, K. 2002. *Truancy: Short and long-term solutions*. New York: Routledge Falmer.

Reid, S. T. 2008. *Crime and criminology*. 12th ed. New York: Oxford University Press.

Reige, M. G. 1972. Parental affection and juvenile delinquency in girls. *British Journal of Criminology* 12 (January):55–73.

Reiss, A. J., Jr. 1961. The social integration of queers and peers. *Social Problems* 9 (Fall):102–20.

Reiss, A. J., Jr., and A. L. Rhodes. 1964. An empirical test of differential association theory. *Journal of Research in Crime and Delinquency* 1 (January):5–18.

Remington, C. 1982. Restitution can work for serious offenders. *Change: A Juvenile Justice Quarterly* 5 (2): 9–10.

Rettig, R. P. 1980. Considering the use and usefulness of juvenile detention: Operationalizing social theory. *Adolescence* 15 (Summer):443–59.

Reuters (News Service). 1990. A kiss is Just a kiss—but watch out. *Dallas Morning News* (April 22):2-F.

Richards, L. 1988. The appearance of youth subculture: A theoretical perspective on deviance. *Clothing and Textiles Research Journal* 6 (Spring):56–64.

Richards, P., R. A. Berk, and B. Forster. 1979. *Crime as play: Delinquency in middle-class suburbs*. Cambridge, MA: Ballinger.

Rimland, B., and G. E. Larson. 1981. Nutritional and ecological approaches to the reduction of criminality, delinquency, and violence. *Journal of Applied Nutrition* 33 (2):39-52.

Ritzer, G. 1986. *Social problems*. 2nd ed. New York: Random House.

Roberts, A. R. 1981. *Runaways and non-runaways in an American suburb—An exploratory study of adolescent and parent coping*. New York: John Jay Press.

Robin, G. D. 1969. Anti-poverty programs and delinquency. *Journal of Criminal Law, Criminology, and Police Science* 60 (Fall):323–31.

Robins, L. N. 1975. Alcoholism and labelling theory. In *The labelling of deviance*, ed. W. R. Gove, 21–33. Beverly Hills: Sage.

———. 1978. Aetiological implications in studies of childhood histories relating to antisocial personality. In *Psychopathic behavior: Approaches to research*, ed. R. D. Hare, and O. Schalling, 252–72. New York: John Wiley.

Robison, J., and G. Smith. 1971. The effectiveness of correctional programs. *Crime and Delinquency* 17 (January):67–80.

Rogers, D. 1977. *The psychology of adolescence*. 3rd ed. Upper Saddle River, NJ: Prentice-Hall.

———. 1985. *Adolescence and youth*. 5th ed. Upper Saddle River, NJ: Prentice Hall.

Rojek, D. C. 1982. Juvenile diversion: A study of community cooptation. In *Readings in Juvenile Delinquency*, ed. D. C. Rojeck and C. P Jensen, 316–22. Lexington, MA: D.C. Heath.

Roncek, D. W, and D. Faggiani. 1985. High schools and crime: A replication. *Sociological Quarterly* 26 (Winter):491–505.

Roncek, D. W., and A. LoBosco. 1983. The effect of high schools on crime in their neighborhood. *Social Science Quarterly* (September):598–613.

Ronzio, J. A. 1993. Upping the ante on Miranda. *Police Chief* 60 (May):10–13.

Rose, S. D., and J. L. Edleson. 1987. *Working with children and adolescents in groups*. San Francisco: Jossey-Bass.

Rosen, L. 1985. Family and delinquency: Structure or function? *Criminology* 23:553–73.

Rosen, L., and K. Neilson. 1982. Broken homes. In *Contemporary criminology*, ed. L. D. Savitz and N. Johnson, 126–35. New York: Wiley.

Rosenbaum, D. P., A. J. Lurigio, and P. J. Lavrakas. 1986. *Crimestoppers—A national evaluation*. Washington, DC: National Institute of Justice.

Rosenberg, M. M., R. A. Stebbins, and A. Turowetz, eds. 1982. *The sociology of deviance*. New York: St. Martin's Press.

Ross, E. 2003. Study: Single-parent kids pay later. *Dallas Morning News* (January 24):1A.

Roszak, T. 1969. *The making of a counterculture: Reflections on the technocratic society and its youthful opposition*. Garden City, NY: Doubleday.

Roth, M. 1968. Cerebral disease and mental disorders of old age as causes of antisocial behavior. In *The mentally abnormal offender*, ed. Rueck and Porter, 35–38. Boston: Little Brown.

Roy-Stevens, C. 2004. Overcoming barriers to school reentry. *OJJDP Fact Sheet* (October). Washington, DC: U.S. Deparetment of Justice.

Rubin, H. T. 1976. *The courts: Fulcrum of the justice system*. Pacific Palisades, CA: Goodyear. 1977. The juvenile court's search for identity and responsibility. *Crime and Delinquency* 23 (January):1–13.

———. 1979. Retain the juvenile court? *Crime and Delinquency* (July):281–98.

———. 1980. The emerging prosecutor dominance of the juvenile court intake process. *Crime and Delinquency* 26 (July):299–318.

Ruefle, W., and K. M. Reynolds. 1995. Curfews and delinquency in major American cities. *Crime and Delinquency* 41 (July):347–63.

Rutherford, R. B., Jr. 1975. Establishing behavioral contracts with delinquent adolescents. *Federal Probation* 39 (March):28–32.

Rutter, M. 1980. *Changing youth in a changing society: Patterns of adolescent development and disorder*. Cambidge, MA: Harvard University Press.

Ryan, B. 1980. Should delinquents be locked up? *Parade* (October 12):21, 23.

Salzman, L. 1980. *Treatment of the obsessive personality*. New York: Jason Aronson, Inc.

Samenow, S. E. 1984. *Inside the criminal mind*. New York: Times Books.

SAMHSA. 2008. National Survey on Drug Use and Health, September, 2007. *Dallas Morning News* (February 4):5A.

Sampson, R. J. 1986. Effects of socioeconomic context on official reaction to juvenile delinquency. *American Sociological Review* 51 (December):876–85.

Sampson, R. J., and J. H. Laub. 1993. *Crime in the making*. Cambridge: Harvard University Press.

———. 1994. Urban poverty and the family context of delinquency: A new look at structure and process in a classic study. *Child Development* 65 (April):523–40.

Sampson, R. J., J. D. Morenoff, and F. Earls. 1999. Beyond social capital: Spatial dynamics of collective efficacy for children. *American Sociological Review* 64:633–60.

Sampson, R. J., S. W. Raiudenbush, and E. Felton. 2003. Collective efficacy and crime. In *Criminological Theory: Past to Present* 3rd ed., ed. F. T. Cullen and R. Agnew, 119–23. LA: Roxbury.

San Francisco Examiner. 1999. Teen runs toward responsibility: Aids Columbine victim. (October 29):A9.

Sanborn, J. B., Jr. 1996. Factors perceived to affect delinquent dispositions in juvenile court: Putting the sentencing decision into context. *Crime and Delinquency* 42 (January):99–113.

Sanders, W. B. 1970. *Juvenile offenders for a thousand years*. Chapel Hill: University of North Carolina Press.

———. 1981. *Juvenile delinquency: Causes, patterns, and reactions*. New York: Halt, Rinehart and Winston.

———. 1994. *Gang bangers and drive-bys: Grounded culture and juvenile gang violence*. New York: Aldine De Gruyter.

Sandhu, H. 1977. *Juvenile delinquency: Causes, control, and prevention*. New York: McGraw-Hill.

Santoli, A. 1992. Why boys town still works. *Parade* (February 9):20–21.

Sarnecki, J. 1982. *Criminality and peer relations: Study of juvenile delinquency in a Swedish community*. Stockholm, Sweden: Brottsforebyggande Radet.

———. 1983. *Criminal juvenile gangs*. Stockholm, Sweden: Brottsforebyggande Radet.

Satir, V. 1972. *Peoplemaking*. Palo Alto, CA: Science and Behavior Books.

Sato, I. 1987. *Play theory of delinquency: Toward a general theory of "action."* From a draft of concluding chapter of a doctoral dissertation submitted to University of Chicago.

Satterfield, J. H. 1978. The hyperactive child syndrome: A precursor of adult psychopathy? In *Psychopathic behavior: Approaches to research*, ed. R. D. Hare and O. Schalling, 329–46. New York: John Wiley.

Savelli, L. 2005. *Gangs across America and their symbols*. Looseleaf Law publications.

Savitz, L. D., M. Lallix, and L. Rosen. 1978. *Fear of school-based crimes and rational responses. From Theoretical perspectives on poverty and school crimes*, vol. 2. New York: National Council on Crime and Delinquency.

Scarpitti, F., E. Murray, S. Dinitz, and W. C. Reckless. 1960. The "good" boy in a high delinquency area: Four years later. *American Sociological Review* 25 (August):555–58.

Scelfo, J. 2007. Spanking smackdown. *Newsweek* (February 5):16.

Schaefer, R. T. 2009. *Race and Ethnicity in the United States*. 5th ed. Upper Saddle River, NJ: Prentice-Hall.

Schafer, W. E., and K. Polk. 1976. Delinquency and the schools. In *Task force report: Juvenile delinquency and youth crime*, 228–34. The President's Commission on Law Enforcement and the Administration of Justice. Washington, DC: U.S. Government Printing Office.

Schauss, A., C. Simonsen, and J. Bland. 1979. Critical analysis of the diets of chronic juvenile offenders, Part 1. *Journal of Orthomolecular Psychiatry* 8 (3):149–57.

Schicor, D. 1983. Socialization: The political aspects of a delinquency explanation. *Socialization Spectrum* 3 (January–March):85–100.

Schicor, D., and C. Bartollas. 1990. Private and public juvenile placements: Is there a difference? *Crime and Delinquency* 36 (April):286–99.

Schlossman, S. L. 1977. *Love and the American delinquent*. Chicago: University of Chicago Press.

Schlossman, S., and M. Sedlak. 1983. The Chicago area project revisited. *Crime and Delinquency* 29 (July):398–462.

Schmid, R. E. 2007. Eldest boys have highest IQ, study finds. *Dallas Morning News* (June 22):5A.

Schneider, A. L. 1990. Deterrence and juvenile crime. New York: Springer-Verlag.

Schoenthaler, S., and W. Doraz. 1983. Type of offenses which can be reduced in an institutional setting using nutritional intervention. *International Journal of Biosocial Research* 4:74–84. And item, Diet and crime. *International Journal of Biosocial Research* 4:29–39.

Schulte, B. 1997. Spanking kids may make them worse. *Dallas Morning News* (August 15):1A, 18A.

Schur, E. M. 1969. *Our criminal society*. Upper Saddle River, NJ: Prentice Hall.

———. 1973. *Radical non-intervention: Rethinking the delinquency problem*. Upper Saddle River, NJ: Prentice Hall.

———. 1984. *Labeling Women Deviant*. New York: Random House.

Schwartz, D. 1996. Getting the boat: Arizona dropping camps far youth offenders. *Dallas Morning News* (August 11):47A, 49A.

Schwartz, G., and D. Merten. 1967. The language of adolescents: An anthropological approach to the youth culture. *American Journal of Sociology* 72 (March):453–68.

Schwartz, I. M. 1989. *(In)justice for juveniles: Rethinking the best interests of the child*. Lexington, MA: Lexington Books.

Schwartz, J. 1990. Stalking the youth market. *Newsweek* (Special Edition) (Summer/Fall):34–36.

Schwendinger, H., and J. J. Schwendinger. 1985. *Adolescent subcultures and delinquency*. New York: Praeger.

Sebald, H. 1997. *Adolescence: A social psychological analysis*. 4th ed. Upper Saddle River, NJ: Prentice-Hall.

Segrave, J. O., and D. N. Hastad. 1984. Interscholastic athletic participation and delinquent behavior: An empirical assessment of relevant variables. *Sociology of Sport Journal* 1 (June):117–37.

———. 1985. Evaluating three models of delinquency causation for males and females: Strain theory, subculture theory, and control theory. *Sociological Focus* 18 (January):1–17.

Seligson, T. 1986. Are they too young to die? *Parade* (October 19):4–7.

Selke,W. L. 1982. Diversion and crime prevention: A time-series analysis. *Criminology* 20 (November):395–406.

Sellin, T. 1938. *Culture conflict and crime*. New York: Social Science Research Council.

Senate Subcommittee on Juvenile Justice. 1983. *Gang violence and control*. Hearings before the subcommittee on juvenile justice of the Committee on the judiciary. United States Senate, Ninety-Eighth Congress, First Session on Gang Violence and Control in the Los Angeles and San Francisco Areas with a View to What Might Be Done by the Federal Government (Westwood, CA, February 7, and San Francisco, February 9).

Seward, R. R. 1978. *The American family: A democratic history*. Beverly Hills, CA: Sage.

Shah, S. A., and L. H. Roth. 1974. Biological and psychophysiological factors in criminality. In *Handbook of criminology*, ed. D. Glaser, 120. Chicago: Rand McNally.

Shakespeare, W. 1623. *As You Like It* (Act II. Sc. vii, 1. 139).

Shaw, C. R., and H. D. McKay. 1931. *Social factors in juvenile delinquency: Report on the causes of crime*, vol. 2. Washington, DC: National Commission on Law Observance and Enforcement.

———. 1969. *Juvenile delinquency in urban areas*. Rev. ed. Chicago: University of Chicago Press.

Sheldon, W., E. M. Hartl, and P. McDermott. 1949. *Varieties of delinquent youth*. New York: Harper & Row.

Sheridan, W. H. 1967. Juveniles who commit noncriminal acts: Why treat in a correctional system? *Federal Probation* 31 (March):26–30.

Sherman, E. 1986. Teenage sex: A special report. *Ladies Home Journal* 103 (October):138, 199, 202–06.

Sherman, L. W., and R. A. Berk. 1984. The specific deterrent effects of arrest for domestic assault. *American Sociological Review* 49:261–72.

Sherman, L. W., and D. A. Smith, J. D. Schmidt, and D. P. Rogan. 1992. Crime, punishment, and stake in conformity: Legal and informal control of domestic violence. *American Sociological Review* 57:680–90.

Sherraden, M. W., and S. W. Downs. 1984. Institutions and juvenile delinquency in historical perspective. *Children and Youth Services Review* 6 (3):155–72.

Sherwood, N. 1972. *The Youth Service Bureau: A key to delinquency prevention*. Paramus, NJ: National Council on Crime and Delinquency.

Shoemaker, D. J. 2005. *Theories of delinquency: An examination of explanations of delinquent behavior*. 5th ed. New York: Oxford University Press.

Short, J. F., Jr. 1957. Differential association and delinquency. *Social Problems* 4 (January):233–39.

———. 1960. Differential association as a hypothesis: Problems of empirical testing. *Social Problems* 8 (Summer):14–25.

———. 1968. *Gang delinquency and delinquent subculture*. New York: Harper & Row.

———. 1987. Exploring integration of the theoretical levels of explanation: Notes on juvenile delinquency. In *Theoretical integration in the study of deviance and crime: Problems and prospects*, 00–00. Albany, NY: Unpublished proceedings of the Albany Conference, May 7–8.

———. 1987. *Delinquency and society*. Upper Saddle River, NJ: Prentice Hall.

———. 1990. Exploring integration of the theoretical levels of explanation: Notes on juvenile delinquency. In *Delinquency and society*, 243-259. Upper Saddle River, NJ: Prentice Hall.

———. 1998. The level of explanation problem revisited—the American Society of Criminology (1997 Presidential Address). *Criminology* 36 (February):3–36.

Short, J. F., Jr., and F. L. Strodtbeck. 1965. *Group process and gang delinquency*. Chicago: University of Chicago Press.

Short, J. F, Jr., R. A. Tennyson, and K. I. Howard. 1963. Behavior dimensions of gang delinquency. *American Sociological Review* 28 (June):411–28.

Siegel, L. J. 2009. *Criminology*. 10th ed. Belmont, CA: Wadsworth Cengage.

Silverman, E. J., and S. Dinitz. 1974. Compulsive masculinity and delinquency: An empirical investigation. *Criminology* 11 (February):498–515.

Simons, R. L., J. F. Robertson, and W. R. Downs. 1989. The nature of the association between parental rejection and delinquent behavior. *Journal of Youth & Adolescence* 18 (June):297–310.

Simons, R. L., L. G. Simons, and L. E. Wallace. 2004. *Families, delinquency, and crime*. Los Angeles: Roxbury.

Singer, M. 2006. *The face of social suffering*. Long Grove, IL: Waveland Press.

Singer, S. I. 1993. The automatic waiver of juveniles and substantive justice. *Crime and Delinquency* 39 (April):253–61.

Skagit Valley Herald. (Sedro Woolley, WA). 1997. Children charged in poisoning plot. (February 5):A2.

Skinner, B. F. 1938. *The behavior of organisms*. New York: Appleton-Century-Crofts.

———. 1971. *Beyond freedom and dignity*. New York: Knopf.

Skolnick, J. 1966. *Justice without trial*. New York: Wiley.

Sleeth, V. 1978. Child is a child, except when he's not—California's new approach to disposition of youthful offenders. *California Western Law Review* 14 (1):124–52.

Smallenger, F., and C. Bartollas. 2008. *Juvenile delinquency*. Boston: Allyn and Bacon.

Smith, D. A., and C. A. Visher. 1981. Street-level justice: Situational determinants of police arrest decisions. *Social Problems* 29 (December):167–77.

Smith, E. A. 1962. *American youth culture*. Glencoe, IL: Free Press.

Smith, K. 2000. Who's minding the kids? Child care arrangements. *Current population reports*. U.S. Bureau of the Census.

Smith, P. M. 1955. Broken homes and juvenile delinquency. *Sociology and Social Research* 39 (May–June):307–11.

Snyder, H. N., T. A. Finnegan, E. H. Nimick, M. H. Sickmund, D. P. Sullivan, and N. J. Tierney. 1989. *Juvenile Court Statistics, 1985* (April). Pittsburgh, PA: U.S. Department of Justice, Office of Juvenile Justice and Delinquency Prevention, National Center for Juvenile Justice.

Snyder, H. N., and M. Sickmund. 2006. *Juvenile offenders and victims: 2006 national report*. Washington, DC: U.S. Government Printing Office, Department of Justice, Office of Juvenile Justice and Delinquency Prevention.

Snyder, H. N., M. Sickmund, and E. Poe-Yamagata. 2000. *Juvenile transfers to criminal court in the 1990s: Lessons learned from four studies*. Washington, DC: OJJDP, U.S. Department of Justice.

Soler, M. 1998. Prosecuting children as adults. *Dallas Morning News* (April 15):1J.

Spergel, I. 1964. *Racketville, slum town, haulberg: An exploratory study of delinquent subcultures*. Chicago: University of Chicago Press.

Spergel, I. A., and G. D. Curry. 1988. Socialization to gangs: School—community gang prevention and control study. *Research Report*. School of Social Service Administration, University of Chicago.

Stagliano, P. A., and I. A. Hyman. 1983. State department of education activities to reduce school violence and vandalism. *Phi Delta Kappan* 65 (September):67–68.

Stahl, A. L., C. Puzzanchera, S. Livsey, A. Sladky, T. A. Finnegan, N. Tierney, and H. N. Snyder. 2007. *Juvenile Court Statistics 2003–2004*. Pittsburgh, PA: National Center for Juvenile Justice.

Stanford University. 1994. *Press release: School tracking harms millions, sociologist finds*. Stanford, CA: Stanford University, 3-21-94.

Stark, E. 1986. Young, innocent and pregnant. *Psychology Today* 20 (October):28–35.

Statistical Abstract of the United States. 1990. Washington, DC: U.S. Government Printing Office.

Stattin, H., and D. Magnusson. 1989. The role of early aggressive behavior in the frequency, seriousness, and types of later crime. *Journal of Consulting and Clinical Psychology* 57:710–18.

Steffensmeier, D. J., and R. Steffensmeier. 1980. Trends in female delinquency: An examination of arrest, juvenile court, self-report, and field data. *Criminology* 18 (1) (May):62–85.

Stein, R. 2008. Study finds oral sex not common for teen virgins. *Dallas Morning News* (May 20):4A.

Steinmetz, S. K., and M. A. Straus. 1973. The family as cradle of violence. *Society* 10 (September–October):50–56.

Stephenson, B. 2007. *From boys to men: Spiritual rites of passage in an indulgent age*. South Paris, ME: Park Street Press.

Stevens, D. J. 2003. *Applied community policing in the 21st century*. Boston: Allyn and Bacon.

Stockard, J. 1997. *Sociology: Discovering society*. Belmont, CA: Wadsworth.

Stockton Record (California). 1997. Gang member urinates in court. (April 4):A-4.

Stonequist, E. H. 1937. *The marginal man*. New York: Charles Scribners Sons.

Straus, M. A., R. Gelles, and S. Steinmetz. 1980. *Behind closed doors: Violence in the American family*. Garden City, NY: Doubleday.

Streib, V. L. 1987. *Death penalty for juveniles*. Bloomington: Indiana State University Press.

Strickland, D. E. 1982. Social learning and deviant behavior: A comment and critique. *American Sociological Review* 47 (February):162–67.

Strong, B., C. DeVault, and T. F. Cohen. 2007. *The marriage and family experience: Relationships in a Changing Society*. 10th ed. Wadsworth.

Stumphauzer, J. S. 1986. *Helping delinquents change: A treatment manual of social learning approaches*. New York: Haworth Press.

Sullivan, D. C., and L. J. Siegel. 1972. How police use information to make a decision: An application of decision games. *Crime and Delinquency* 18:253–62.

Sullivan, N. 2001. *Tattooed bodies: Subjectivity, textuality, ethics, and pleasure*. New York: Praeger. *Adolescence: A social-psychological analysis*. Upper Saddle River, NJ: Prentice Hall.

Sulloway, F. J. 1998. *Born to rebel: Birth order, family dynamics, and creative lives*. New York: Vintage Press.

Sumner,W. G. [1906] 1959.*Folkways*. Boston: Ginn and Company, Sutherland.

E. H. 1939. *Principles of criminology*. Philadelphia: J. B. Lippincott.

Sutherland, E. H., and D. R. Cressey. 1943. *Principles of Criminology*. Philadelphia: J.B. Lippincott.

———. 1961. *White collar crime*. New York: Holt, Rinehart and Winston.

———. 1978. *Criminology*. 10th ed. Philadelphia: J. B. Lippincott.

Sykes, G. M. 1980. *The future of crime*. Washington, DC: Alcohol, Drug Abuse, and Mental Health Administration, National Institute of Mental Health.

Sykes, G. M., and D. Matza. 1957. Techniques of neutralization: A theory of delinquency. *American Sociological Review* 22 (December):664–70.

Tannenbaum, D. J. 1977. Personality and criminality: A summary and implications of the literature. *Journal of Criminal Justice* 5:225–35.

Tannenbaum, F. 1938. *Crime and Community*.Boston: Ginn and Company.

Terry, R. M. 1967. Discrimination in the handling of juvenile offenders by social control agencies. *Journal of Research in Crime and Delinquency* 4:218–30.

Thio, A. 2006. *Deviant behavior*. 8th ed. Boston: Allyn and Bacon.

Thomas, E. 1986. America's crusade: What is behind the latest war on drugs. *Time* 128 (September 15):60–68.

Thomas, G., A. Reifman, G. M. Barnes, and M. P. Farrell. 2000. Delayed onset of drunkenness as a protective factor for adolescent alcohol misuse and sexual risk taking: A longitudinal study. *Deviant Behavior* 21 (March–April):181–210.

Thomas, W. I. 1931. *The unadjusted girl*. Revised ed. Boston: Little, Brown and Co.

Thomas, W. I., and F. Znaniecki. 1927. *The Polish peasant in Europe and America*. New York: Knopf.

Thompson, W. E. 1994. Spontaneous remission. In *Encyclopedia of criminology*, 1303. New York: Macmillan.

Thompson, W. E., and R. A. Dodder. 1986. Containment theory and juvenile delinquency: A reevaluation through factor analysis. *Adolescence* 21 (Summer): 365–76.

Thompson, W. E., and J. V. Hickey. 2008. *Society in Focus: An Introduction to Sociology*. 6th ed. New York: Allyn & Bacon.

Thompson, W. E., J. Mitchell, and R. A. Dodder. 1983. An empirical test of Hirschi's control theory of delinquency. *Deviant Behavior* 5:11–22.

Thomson, B., and E. R. Fielder. 1975. Gangs: A response to the urban world. In *Gang delinquency*, ed. D. S. Cartwright, B. Thomson and H. Schwartz, 149–50. Monterey, CA: Brooks/Cole.

Thornberry, T. P. 1973. Race, socioeconomic status, and sentencing in the juvenile justice system. *Journal of Criminal Law and Criminology* 64 (March):90–98.

Thornberry, T. P. 1987. Toward an interactional theory of delinquency. *Criminology* 25:863–91.

Thornberry, T. P., and J. H. Burch. 1997. Gang members and delinquent behavior. *Bulletin*. Washington, DC: U.S. Government Printing Office, U.S. Department of Justice, Office of Juvenile Justice and Delinquency Prevention.

Thornberry, T. P., and R. L. Christenson. 1979. Sentencing disparities in the juvenile justice system. *Journal of Criminal Law and Criminology* 70 (Summer):164–171.

Thornberry, T. P., and R. L. Christenson. 1984. Juvenile justice decision-making as a longitudinal process. *Social Forces* 63 (December): 433–44.

Thornberry, T. P., M. Moore, and R. L. Christenson. 1985. The effects of dropping out of high school on subsequent criminal behavior. *Criminology* 23 (1):3–18.

Thornton, A. 1985. Changing attitudes toward separation and divorces: Causes and consequences. *American Journal of Sociology* 90 (January):856–72.

Thornton, W. F., Jr., and L. Voigt. 1992. *Delinquency and justice*. 3rd ed. New York: McGraw-Hill, Inc.

Thrasher, F. M. 1927. *The gang*. Chicago: University of Chicago Press.

———. 1936. *The gang*. 2nd ed. Chicago: University of Chicago Press.

Thurman, Q. C., A. L. Giacomazzi, and P. Bogen. 1993. Research note: cops, kids, and community policing—an assessment of a community policing demonstration project. *Crime and Delinquency* 39 (October):554–64.

Thurman, Q. C., A. L. Giacomazzi, M. D. Reisig, and D. G. Mueller. 1996. Community-based gang prevention and intervention: An evaluation of the neutral zone. *Crime and Delinquency* 42 (April):279–95.

Time. 1977. The youth crime plague. 110, 2 (July 11, 1977):18–28.

———. 1982. Guardian Angels' growing pains. (January):21.

———. 1986. Growing pains at 40. *Time* 127 (May 19): 22–41.

———. 1995. (February 6):46.

Tittle, C. R. 1974. Prisons and rehabilitation: The inevitability of disaster. *Social Problems* 21 (3):385–95.

———. 1995. *Control balance: Toward a general theory of deviance*. Boulder, CO: Westview.

Toby, J. 1965. An evaluation of early identification and intensive treatment programs for predelinquents. *Social Problems* 13 (Fall):160–75.

Toennies, F. [1887] 1961. Gemeinschaft and gesellschaft. In *Theories of Society* 3rd ed., vol. 1, ed. T. Parsons et al., 19–201. Glencoe, IL: Free Press.

Toman, W. 1970. Birth order rules all. *Psychology Today* (December):45–49, 68–69.

Toplin, R. B. 1975. *Unchallenged violence: An American ordeal*. Westport, CT: Greenhaven Press.

Towberman, D. B. 1992. National survey of juvenile needs assessment. *Crime and Delinquency* 38 (April):230–38.

Treas, J. 2002. How cohorts, education, and ideology shaped a new sexual revolution on attitudes toward nonmarital sex, 1972–1998. *Sociological Perspectives* 45 (Fall):267–83.

Tressel, P. 1993. Manteca teen shot following "staring" match at Taco Bell. *Manteca Bulletin* (July 11):A-1.

Triplett, R., and G. R. Jarjoura. 1997. Specifying the gender—class relationship: Exploring the effects of educational expectations. *Sociological Perspectives* 40 (2):287–316.

Truckenmiller, J. L. 1982. Predicting vandalism in a general youth sample via the HEW youth development model's community program impact scales, age, and sex. Paper presented at the 90th Annual Convention of the American Psychological Association, Washington, DC, August 23–27, 1982.

Trump, K. S. 1998. *Practical school security: Basic guidelines for safe and seare schools*. Thousand Oaks, CA: Corwin Press/Sage Publications.

Tulsa World. 1990. Mugging to finance night of dancing led to slaying. (September 7):A9.

Turk, A. T. 1969. *Criminality and the legal order*. Chicago: Rand McNally.

Tyler Morning Telegraph. 2008. March 2.

U.S.Bureau of the Census. 2008. *Population estimates*. http://www.census.gov/population/www/projections/2008projections.html

U.S. Bureau of the Census. 2008. *Statistical Abstract of the United States*. 128th ed. Washington, DC: U.S. Government Printing Office.

U.S. Department of Education. 2005. *Indicators of school crime and safety*. Washington, DC: U.S. Department of Education.

U.S. Department of Justice. 1974a. *First Annual Report of the National Institute of Law Enforcement and Criminal Justice*. LEAA. Washington, DC: U.S. Government Printing Office.

———. 1974b. *Standards and goals for juvenile justice*. Washington, DC: U.S. Government Printing Office.

U.S. Department of Justice. 1993. LEMAS Reports—1990. Pp. 33–71 in R. G. Dunham and G.P. Alpert, eds. *Critical issues in policing: Contemporary readings*. 2nd ed. Prospect Hts. IL: Waveland.

U.S. Department of Justice. 1999a. *Highlights of findings from the Rochester youth development study*. Washington,

D.C.: Office of Juvenile Justice and Delinquency Prevention.

———. 1999b. *Highlights of findings from the Pittsburgh youth study*. Washington, D.C.: Office of Juvenile Justice and Delinquency Prevention.

U.S. Department of State. 2000. Statement by the President in the year 2000 annual report on school safety. Washington DC: U.S. Department of State.

U.S. National Commission on Excellence in Education. 1983. *A nation at risk*. Washington, DC: U.S. Government Printing Office.

U.S. Senate Subcommittee on Delinquency. 1977. *Challenge for the third century: Education in a violent environment*. Washington, DC: U.S. Government Printing Office.

Vail, D. A. 1999. Tattoos are like potato chips . . . you can't have just one: The process of becoming and being a collector. *Deviant Behavior* 20 (July–September):253–73.

Van den Haag, E. 1975. *Punishing criminals: Concerning a very old and painful question*. New York: Basic Books.

Van Gennep, A. [1908] 1960. *The rights of passage*. Trans. M. B. Vizedom and G. L. Caffee. Chicago: University of Chicago Press.

Vander Ven, T. 2003. *Working mothers and juvenile delinquency*. New York: LFB Scholarly Publishing.

VanderZanden, J. 1986. *Core sociology*. New York: Alfred A. Knopf.

———. 1990. *The social experience: An introduction to sociology*. 2nd ed. New York: McGraw-Hill.

Varma, K. N. 2007. Parental involvement in youth court. *Canadian Journal of Criminology and Criminal Justice* 49 (April):231–60.

Vaz, E. W., ed. 1967. *Middle-class juvenile delinquency*. New York: Harper & Row.

Vedantam, S. 2001. Kid care, behavior linked in study. *Dallas Morning News* (April 19):1A.

Victor, J. S. 2004. Sluts and wiggers: A study of the effects of derogatory labeling. *Deviant Behavior* 15:63–85.

Vigil, J. D. 1997. *Learning from gangs: The Mexican-American experience*. (EDO-RC-97-1, February, 1997). Charleston, WV: ERIC/CRESS Clearinghouse on Rural Education and Small Schools.

Vito, G. F. 1985. Probation as punishment: New directions and suggestions. In *Probation, parole, and community corrections: A reader* 3rd ed., ed. L. F. Travis, 73–9. Prospect Heights, IL: Waveland Press.

Vito, G. F., R. Tewksbury, and D. G. Wilson. 1998. *The juvenile justice system: Concepts and issues*. Prospect Heights, IL: Waveland Press.

Vognar, C. 1998. The rhyme and reason behind hiphop's mainstream success. *Dallas Morning News* (September 6): J1–J5.

Vowell, P. R., and F. M. Howell. 1998. Modeling delinquent behavior: Social disorganization, perceived blocked opportunity, and social control. *Deviant Behavior: An Interdisciplinary Journal* 19 (October–December):361–95.

Vowell, P. R., and D. C. May. 2000. Another look at classic strain theory: Poverty status, perceived blocked opportunity, and gang membership as predictors of adolescent violent behavior. *Sociological Inquiry* 30 (1) (Winter):42–60.

Waldo, G., and S. Dinitz. 1967. Personality attributes of the criminal: An analysis of research studies: 1950–1965. *Journal of Research in Crime and Delinquency* 4:185–201.

Walker, S. 1983. *The police in America*. New York: McGraw-Hill.

Walters, G. D., and T. N. White. 1989. Heredity and crime: bad genes or bad research? *Criminology* 27 (August):455–79.

Ward, D. A., and C. R. Tittle. 1993. Deterrence or labeling: The effects of informal sanctions. *Deviant Behavior: An Interdisciplinary Journal* 14:43–64.

Warr, M. 1993. Age, peers, and delinquency. *Criminology* 31 (February):17–25.

Washington Post. 1997. Day care doesn't hurt kid's learning, study says. *Dallas Morning News* April 4:1A, 19A.

Washington Post. 2002. Spanking causes more problems than it cures. *Dallas Morning News* June 26:4A.

Wasserman, G. A., L. S. Miller, and L. Cothern. 2000. Prevention of serious and violent juvenile offending. *Juvenile Justice Bulletin*, OJJDP (April):1–12.

Wasserman, G. A., S. J. Ko, and L. S. McReynolds. 2004. Assessing the mental health status of youth in juvenile justice settings. *Juvenile Justice Bulletin*, OJJDP (August):1–7.

Watts, W. D., and L. S. Wright. 1990. The relationship of alcohol, tobacco, marijuana, and other illegal drug use to delinquency among Mexican-American, black, and white adolescent males. *Adolescence* 97 (Spring):171–81.

Weber, M. [1922] 1968. Bureaucracy. In *Economy and society: An outline of interpretive sociology* 3 Vols., ed. G. Roth and C. Wittich, Trans. E. Fischoff et al., 956–1005. New York: Bedminster Press.

Weber, M. [1925] 1947. *The theory of social and economic organization*. Trans. A. M. Henderson and T. Parsons. New York: Free Press.

Weeks, H. A. 1958. *Youthful offenders at Highfields*. Ann Arbor: University of Michigan Press.

Weeks, J. R. 2008. *Population: An introduction to concepts and issues*. 10th ed. Florence, KY: Cengage.

Wein, B. 1970. *The runaway generation*. New York: David McKay Co.

Weis, J. G. 1980. *Jurisdiction and the elusive status offender: A comparison of involvement in delinquent behavior and status offenses*. Washington, DC: U.S. Government Printing Office.

Weisberg, D. K. 1985. *Children of the night: A study of adolescent prostitution*. Lexington, MA: Lexington Books.

Wells, L. E., and J. H. Rankin. 1995. Juvenile victimization: Convergent validation of alternative measurements. *Journal of Research in Crime and Delinquency* 32 (August):287–307.

Wells, M., and H. Sandhu. 1986. The juvenile runaway: A historical perspective. *Free Inquiry in Creative Sociology* 14 (November):143–47.

Werthman, C. 1976. The function of social definitions in the development of the gang boy's career. In *Juvenile delinquency* 3rd ed., ed. R. Giallombardo, 327–47. New York: Wiley.

Werthman, C., and I. Piliavin. 1967. Gang members and the police. In *The police*, ed. D. J. Bordua, 56-98. New York: Wiley.

Weston, J. 1993. Community policing: An approach to youth gangs in a medium-sized city. *Police Chief* 60 (August):80–84.

WHC. 2008. *Teen pregnancy*, http://www.womenshealthchannel.com/teenpregnancy/index.shtml

Wheeler, M. 1993. *Lies, damn lies, and statistics. The manipulation of public opinion in America*. New York: Laurel Edition, Dell.

Whitbeck, L. B., and R. L. Simons. 1990. Life on the streets: The victimization of runaway and homeless adolescents. Paper presented at the Midwest Sociological Society meeting April 11–14, 1990, Chicago, IL.

White, J. E. 2001. We're all racial profilers: Sure, cops see Black youths as suspect, so do blacks. *Time* 157 (April 23):45.

White, J. L. 1992. *The troubled adolescent*. Boston: Allyn & Bacon.

White, R., and J. Wyn. 2008. *Youth and Society*. 2nd ed. NY: Oxford University Press.

White, R. W. 1981. *The abnormal personality*. 5th ed. New York: The Ronald Press.

Whitehead, J. T., and S. P. Lab. 2006. *Juvenile justice: An introduction*. 5th ed. Albany, NY: Lexis Nexis, Anderson.

Whittemore, H. 1992. Dads who shaped up a school. *Parade Magazine* (September 27):20–22.

Whyte, W. F. [1943] 1993. *Street corner society*. 4th ed. Chicago: University of Chicago Press.

Wiatrowski, M. D., D. B. Griswold, and M. K. Roberts. 1981. Social control theory and delinquency. *American Sociological Review* 46 (October):525–41.

Wiebush, R. G. 1993. Juvenile intensive supervision: The impact on felony offenders diverted from institutional placement. *Crime and Delinquency* 39 (January):68–89.

Wiebush, R. C., R. Freitag, and C. Baird. 2001. Preventing delinquency through improved child protective services. *Juvenile Justice Bulletin*, OJJDP (July):1–19.

Wiebush, R. G., D. Wagner, B. McNulty, Y. Wang, and T. N. Lee. 2005. *Implementation and outcome evaluation of the intensive aftercare program, final report*. Washington, DC: Office of Juvenile Justice and Delinquency Prevention.

Wilderman, E. 1984. Juvenile diversion: From politics to policy. *New England Journal of Human Services* 4 (Summer):19–23.

Wilkinson, K. 1974. The broken family and juvenile delinquency: Scientific explanation or ideology? *Social Problems* 21 (June):726–39.

Williams, F. P., and M. D. McShane. 2004. *Criminological theory*. 4th ed. Upper Saddle River, NJ: Prentice Hall.

Williams, H., and P. V. Murphy. 1990. The evolving strategy of police: A minority view. *Perspectives on policing*. Boston: National Institute of Justice, U.S. Department of Justice.

Williams, J. H. 1994. Understanding substance use, delinquency involvement, and juvenile justice system involvement among African-American and European-American adolescents. Unpublished diss., University of Washington, Seattle.

Williams, T. 2001. Report challenges school rules. *Dallas Morning News* (February 24):1A, 25A.

Willing, R. 2000. When children kill, who takes the blame? *USA Today* (March 3):3A.

Wilson, B. 2006. *Fight, flight, or chill: Subcultures, youth, and rave into the twenty-first century*. Montreal: McGill-Queen's University Press.

Wilson, E. O. 1978. *Sociobiology: The new synthesis*. Cambridge, MA: Harvard University Press.

Wilson, J. Q. 1968. *Varieties of police behavior*. Cambridge, MA: Harvard University Press.

———. 1997. *The moral sense*. New York: Free Press.

Wilson, J. Q., and R. J. Herrnstein. 1985. *Crime and human nature*. New York: Simon & Schuster.

Windle, M. 1989. Substance use and abuse among adolescent runaways: A four-year follow-up study. *Journal of Youth & Adolescence* 18 (August):331–44.

Winfree, L. T., and C. T. Griffiths. 1977. Adolescents' attitudes toward the police: A survey of high school students. In *Juvenile delinquency: Little brother grows up*, ed. T. N. Ferdinand, 78–99. Beverly Hills, CA: Sage.

Winfree, L. T., Jr., T. V. Backstrom, and G. L. Mays. 1994. Social learning theory, self-reported delinquency, and youth gangs: A new twist on a general theory of crime and delinquency. *Youth and Society* 26 (December):147–77.

Wingert, P., and B. Kantrowitz. 2002. Young and depressed. *Newsweek* (October 7):52–60.

Winslow, R. H., ed. 1973. *Juvenile delinquency in a free society*. 2nd ed. Encino, CA: Dickenson.

Wire Reports. 2007a. Drug use by teens drops. *Dallas Morning News* (December 12):8A.

———. 2007b. Teen birth rate rises after 15 years. *Dallas Morning News* (December 6):15A.

Wolfgang, M. E., R. M. Figlio, and T. Sellin. 1972. *Delinquency in a birth cohort*. Chicago: University of Chicago Press.

Wolfgang, M. E., T. P. Thornberry, and R. M. Figlio. 1987. *From boy to man, from delinquency to crime*. Chicago: University of Chicago Press.

Woodbury, R. 1991. Putting the brakes on crime. *Time* (September 2):65.

Woodward, K. L. 1998. The new holy war. *Newsweek* (June 1):26–28.

Wright, J. P., F. T. Cullen, and N. Williams. 1997. Working while in school and delinquent involvement: Implications for social policy. *Crime & Delinquency* 43 (April):203–21.

Wyrick, P. A. 2000a. Vietnamese youth gang involvement. *OJJDP Fact Sheet #1* (February 2000). Washington, DC: U.S. Department of Justice.

———. 2000b. Law enforcement referral of at risk youth: The SHIELD program. *Juvenile Justice Bulletin* (November).

Yablonsky, L. 1959. The delinquent gang as a near group. *Social Problems* 7 (2) (Fall):108–17.

Yablonsky, L., and M. R. Haskell. 1988. *Juvenile delinquency*. 4th ed. New York: Harper and Row.

Yabroff, J. 2008. The myths of teen sex. *Newsweek* (June 9):55.

Yanich, D. 2005. Kids, crime and local television news. *Crime and Delinquency* 51 (January): 103–32.

Yinger, J. M. 1960. Contraculture and subculture. *American Sociological Review* 25 (October):625–35.

———. 1982. *Countercultures: The promise and the peril of a world turned upside down*. New York: Free Press.

Yochelson, S., and S. E. Samenow. 1977. *The criminal personality*, vol.1(1976) and vol.11(1977). New York: Jason Aronson Co.

Yoshida, T., T. Watanabe, N. Mizushima, M. Tarui. 2004. Effectiveness of youth participation in the process of developing HIV/STI prevention program for youth in Japan. *International Conference on AIDS* (15th: 2004 July 11–16: 15:abstract no. C11410 Bangkok, Thailand).

Youth Development and Delinquency Prevention Administration. 1972. *Delinquency prevention through youth development*. Youth Development and Delinquency Prevention Administration Pub. no. (SRS) 73–260 13. Washington, DC: U.S. Government Printing Office (May):28–30..

Zastrow, C. 1992. *Social problems: Issues and solutions*. 3rd ed. Chicago: Nelson-Hall.

Zatz, M. S. 1985. Los Cholos: Legal processing of Chicano gang members. *Social Problems* 33 (October): 13–30.

Zellner, W. W. 1995. *Countercultures: A sociological analysis*. New York: St. Martin's Press.

Zeman, N. 1990. New rules of courtship. *Newsweek* (Special Edition) (Summer/Fall):24–27.

Zhang, L., W. F. Wieczorek, and J. W. Welte. 1997. The impact of age of onset of substance use on delinquency. *Journal of Research in Crime and Delinquency* 34 (May):253–68.

Zhang, L., and S. Zhang. 2004. Reintegrative shaming and predatory delinquency. *Journal of Research in Crime and Delinquency*, 41 (4):433–53.

Zhao, J., and Q. C. Thurman. 1997. Community policing: Where are we now? *Crime and Delinquency* 43 (July):345–57.

Zieman, G. L., and G. P. Benson. 1980. School perceptions of truant adolescent boys. *Behavioral Disorders, Programs, Trends and Concerns of Children with Behavioral Problems* 5 (August):212–22.

Zimring, F. E. 2006. *Changing lives. Delinquency prevention as crime control policy*. Chicago: University of Chicago Press.

Zingraff, M. T., J. Leiter, K. A. Myers, and M. C. Johnsen. 1993. Child maltreatment and youthful problem behavior. *Criminology* 31 (May):173–88.

NAME INDEX

SUBJECT INDEX